Philosophical Foundations of Education

Seventh Edition

HOWARD A. OZMON

SAMUEL M. CRAVER

Virginia Commonwealth University

Merrill
Prentice Hall

Upper Saddle River, New Jersey
Columbus, Ohio

Library of Congress Cataloging-in-Publication Data

Ozmon, Howard.
    Philosophical foundations of education / Howard A. Ozmon, Samuel M. Craver.—7th ed.
      p. cm.
    Includes bibliographical references (p.) and index.
    ISBN 0-13-042399-8
    1. Education—Philosophy—History. 2. Education—Aims and objectives. 3. Education—Study and teaching.
I. Craver, Samuel M. II. Title.
    LB14.7 .096 2003
    370'.1—dc21   2002020181

Vice President and Publisher: Jeffery W. Johnston
Executive Editor: Debra A. Stollenwerk
Assistant Editor: Daniel J. Parker
Editorial Assistant: Mary Morrill
Production Editor: Mary Harlan
Production Coordination: Sharon Anderson, BookMasters, Inc.
Design Coordinator: Diane C. Lorenzo
Cover Design: Jason Moore
Cover Art: Artville/Bobbi Tull
Text Design and Illustrations: BookMasters, Inc.
Production Manager: Pamela D. Bennett
Director of Marketing: Ann Castel Davis
Marketing Manager: Krista Groshong
Marketing Coordinator: Tyra Cooper

This book was set in Times by BookMasters, Inc. It was printed and bound by R.R. Donnelley & Sons Company. The cover was printed by Phoenix Color Corp.

Pearson Education Ltd.
Pearson Education Australia Pty. Limited
Pearson Education Singapore Pte. Ltd.
Pearson Education North Asia Ltd.
Pearson Education Canada, Ltd.
Pearson Educación de Mexico, S.A. de C.V.
Pearson Education—Japan
Pearson Education Malaysia Pte. Ltd.
Pearson Education, *Upper Saddle River, New Jersey*

10 9 8 7 6 5 4 3 2 1
ISBN: 0-13-042399-8

Preface

The purpose of this volume is to show how philosophical ideas about education developed over time, with due regard to historical influences and settings, and with an emphasis on how these ideas continue to have relevance for education and life. This book was conceived as an introductory text in the philosophy of education, but it leads students from simple to complex philosophical ideas. Many variables needed to be considered in selecting ideas, philosophers, and an organizational format, and the guiding rule for the book has been to select those influences that we believe have had the most relevance for education. Each chapter examines a general philosophy, such as realism, and shows its applications in aims, curriculum, methods, and teaching. An assessment of each philosophy also is provided, including how other scholars have viewed it.

Some ideas included here are more than 2,000 years old, but they often appear in the panoply of ideas that continue to influence people because old and new ideas are useful tools for evaluating the world. Idealism, though not a particularly influential philosophy today, might be a useful counterpoint by which to compare and evaluate today's materialist culture. Marxism and existentialism, though declining in popularity, still might be useful paradigms for examining a person's individual life and his or her relationship with other persons in the larger society.

The philosophies of education presented here are essentially arranged in chronological order, which helps the student see how ideas evolved. We have tried to avoid unnecessary philosophical and educational jargon, but one needs to know a terminology to talk about ideas in a philosophical fashion. Technical expression is kept to a minimum, however. With regard to format, we realize that not all philosophers agree with a "systems" or "schools" approach and that this issue has serious pros and cons. We do believe that for beginning students, often those who might be encountering philosophy for the first time, the benefits of this organizational approach outweigh the disadvantages because it provides a useful way of synthesizing ideas.

The study of philosophy of education should help sharpen students' ideas about education and give them ways to think about education in a broad sense. The study of philosophy not only assists students in developing necessary analytical skills and encourages critical perspectives but also provides useful perspectives on the importance of education. It is impossible to include in a volume of this size every philosopher or every leading philosophical idea that has had some educational importance, but we hope that the material presented will stimulate students to explore further the philosophical foundations of education and to cultivate ideas about education and life.

Organization of the Book

By presenting several philosophical positions and showing how philosophy developed in an organized and orderly fashion, we hope the reader will be better able to grasp the essential elements and basic principles of each philosophy and to see how they have influenced educational theory and practice.

However, the organization of the book by schools of thought is not meant to foster slavish emulation of any one school, combination of schools, or even a school approach. The usefulness of this approach lies in showing the following:

- How past philosophy developed.
- How it has been organized.
- How it has been used to help devise educational policies and practices.

After all, the major role of philosophy in education is not to formulate some grand scheme but to help develop the educator's thinking capacities.

The creative genius of individuals, combined with particular cultural developments, produced philosophies of education. Individual philosophers seldom set out simply to construct a system, and many of them reject being identified with any school of thought. The cutting edge of philosophy is not a system, but free and wide-ranging thought grappling with human problems. Perhaps the test of any era of human history is not whether it built a system to bind together irreconcilable conflicts but how it enabled the resolution of those conflicts. Each era, however, also must write its own "philosophy" or consensus anew.

New Features of the Seventh Edition

- General editing and updating of each chapter
- Revisions in idealism, Eastern philosophy, pragmatism, and postmodernism
- Updating of selected readings and bibliographic material
- Online Research activities using the Companion Website
- Useful Web sites and Internet links

Chapter Organization

Each chapter provides a discussion of a specific philosophy and

- Its historical development.
- Its current status.
- Its influence on education.

- A critique of its leading ideas.
- Online Research activities.
- Readings by major philosophers and theorists (primary source materials).

Taken together, these chapters provide a chronological development of philosophy of education. In addition, each chapter is followed by an annotated listing of selected readings by philosophers who have been identified with that philosophy or who offer important criticisms and insights about it. The selections have been chosen carefully to illustrate leading themes in each chapter. They also have been selected to furnish students with additional primary source materials of sufficient length and depth to provide some firsthand acquaintance with leading works in the field. These selections are meant to give insight without overwhelming students and to whet their appetite to do further reading in philosophy of education from the philosophers themselves.

INSTRUCTOR'S MANUAL

The instructor's manual for this textbook contains chapter overviews, projects, identifications (words from each chapter that students are asked to identify), discussion and essay questions, as well as multiple choice questions. This manual can be obtained by contacting your Prentice Hall sales representative or by calling Prentice Hall's Faculty Field Services at 800-526-0485.

ACKNOWLEDGMENTS

We wish to thank the many students and colleagues too numerous to name who, over the years, have given invaluable advice and helpful criticism.

In addition, we appreciate the input from the following reviewers: Patricia Elmore, Jacksonville State University; Richard Farber, The College of New Jersey; Rebekah Kelleher, Wittenberg University; and Ann K. Nauman, Southeastern Louisiana University.

We also thank all those who have reviewed past editions and whose suggestions have helped improve each edition.

Howard A. Ozmon
Samuel M. Craver

Discover the Companion Website

The Prentice Hall Companion Website: A Virtual Learning Environment

Technology is a constantly growing and changing aspect of our field that is creating a need for content and resources. To address this emerging need, Prentice Hall has developed an online learning environment for students and professors alike—Companion Websites—to support our textbooks.

In creating a Companion Website, our goal is to build on and enhance what the textbook already offers. For this reason, the content for each user-friendly website is organized by topic and provides the professor and student with a variety of meaningful resources. Common features of a Companion Website include:

For the Professor—

Every Companion Website integrates **Syllabus Manager™**, an online syllabus creation and management utility.

- **Syllabus Manager™** provides you, the instructor, with an easy, step-by-step process to create and revise syllabi, with direct links into Companion Website and other online content without having to learn HTML.
- Students may logon to your syllabus during any study session. All they need to know is the web address for the Companion Website and the password you've assigned to your syllabus.
- After you have created a syllabus using **Syllabus Manager™,** students may enter the syllabus for their course section from any point in the Companion Website.
- Clicking on a date, the student is shown the list of activities for the assignment. The activities for each assignment are linked directly to actual content, saving time for students.
- Adding assignments consists of clicking on the desired due date, then filling in the details of the assignment—name of the assignment, instructions, and whether it is a one-time or repeating assignment.
- In addition, links to other activities can be created easily. If the activity is online, a URL can be entered in the space provided, and it will be linked automatically in the final syllabus.
- Your completed syllabus is hosted on our servers, allowing the convenient updates from any computer on the Internet. Changes you make to your syllabus are immediately available to your students at their next logon.

For the Student—

- **Topic Overviews**—outline key concepts in topic areas.
- **Web Links**—a wide range of websites provide useful and current information related to each topic area.
- **Readings**—suggested readings for further study of certain aspects of the topic areas.
- **Resources**—a list of links to more general resources within each topic area.
- **Organizations**—lists of links to organizations pertinent to certain topic areas.
- **Electronic Bluebook, Message Board, and Chat**—these features are available to users, and the opening page of the website will elaborate on their use

To take advantage of these and other resources, please visit the *Philosophical Foundations of Education*, Seventh Edition, Companion Website at

www.prenhall.com/ozmon

Contents

3 *Eastern Philosophy, Religion, and Education*   *91*

4 *Pragmatism and Education*   *127*

5 *Reconstructionism and Education*   *167*

6 *Behaviorism and Education*   *200*

7 *Existentialism, Phenomenology, and Education*   *234*

8 *Analytic Philosophy and Education*   *269*

Introduction

It could be said that philosophy of education began when people first became conscious of education as a distinct human activity. Preliterate societies did not have the long-range goals and complex social systems of modern times, and they did not have the analytic tools of modern philosophers, but even preliterate education involved a philosophical attitude about life. Humanity had a philosophy of education long before the formal study of philosophy began and before people understood what that study could mean in educational development.

In earlier times, education was primarily for survival. Children were taught the skills necessary for living. Gradually, however, people came to use education for a variety of purposes. Today, education still can be used for survival, but it is also for better use of leisure time and refinements in social and cultural life. As the practice of education has developed, so also have theories about education; however, it has become easy to overlook the connection between philosophical theory and educational practice and to deal with practice apart from theory. Today's dilemma might be because people seem to be more involved with the practical aspects of education than with the development and analysis of educational theory and its connection with practice. Better theory and better practical methods are needed, as well as a concerted effort to join the two intelligently. Thinking about education without considering the practical world means that philosophers of education become web spinners of thought engaged in mere academic exercises. Conversely, tinkering with educational methods without serious thinking results in practices that have little substance or meaning.

THE NEED FOR PHILOSOPHY OF EDUCATION

The philosophical study of education seems imperative today because this is a critical era of transition. Change always has occurred, but seldom at the current accelerated rate that has created what Alvin Toffler calls "future shock." At a time when humans may be entering a new age, a postmodern era, it is easy for people either to embrace more and more change with little thought of eventual consequences or to

1

resist change and keep old values despite the consequences. Educational philosophers, regardless of their particular theory, suggest that solutions to problems can be achieved best through critical and reflective thought about the relationship between unsettling changes and enduring ideas.

It might be said that philosophy of education is merely the application of philosophical ideas to educational problems; however, the practice of education can lead to a refinement of philosophical ideas. This is not to say that philosophy of education is not a discipline of its own, but that it draws heavily on the work of philosophers, old and new, and also seeks to implement some of their ideas in the practice of education. Educational philosophy is a way not only of looking at ideas but also of learning how to use ideas in better ways. No intelligent philosophy of education is involved when educators do things simply because they were done in the past. A philosophy of education becomes significant only when educators recognize the need to think clearly about what they are doing, and to see what they are doing in the larger context of individual and social development.

Many major philosophers have written about education, probably because education is such an integral part of life that it is difficult to think about not having it. Humans are tool-making beings, but they are also education-making beings because education always has been closely connected with the development of civilization. Thinking about life in general often has been related to thinking about education in particular, and education has been viewed as a way of improving life. This is as true today as it ever has been.

The study of philosophy does not guarantee that people will be better thinkers or educators, but it does provide valuable perspectives to help people think more clearly. The word *philosophy* literally means "love of wisdom"—a dedicated inquiry into ideas, traditions, innovations, and ways of thinking. Philosophers have been acute observers of human events and have articulated their observations in ways that might be instructive. Educators can be helped by a careful study of philosophical ideas, and they can gain insight from philosophy to help them better understand educational problems. Educators can choose to disregard the philosophical approach to problems, but in doing so they ignore a vital and important body of thought.

BRANCHES OF PHILOSOPHY

In essence, philosophy of education is the application of the fundamental principles of philosophy to the theory and practice of education, and the problems and issues of education in turn help inform philosophical thought. Many great philosophers have written about education, such as Plato, Aristotle, Aquinas, Locke, Rousseau, Kant, Herbart, Spencer, Nietzsche, Dewey, and Russell. Even those who did not write about education directly, such as Sartre and Marx, still provided views about nature and society that had great impact on education. Sartre's views about individuality, for example, greatly influenced the educational views of the 1960s and 1970s, and they still have influence today in many educational circles. Marx was one who, though not writing educational treatises *per se*, provided ideas that greatly shaped educational practices in the former Soviet Union and in many other places, as well.

The traditional view of philosophy is that it is composed of four major branches: metaphysics, epistemology, logic, and axiology.

- *Metaphysics* is the branch of philosophy that deals with ultimate reality. It asks questions such as the following. "What is real?" "What is the meaning of change?" "Does the universe have design and purpose?" "Are children born evil or good?" "Do humans have free will?"
- *Epistemology* studies the methods, structure, and validity of knowledge. "Where does knowledge come from?" "What is true?" "How much does the knower contribute to the knowing process?" "Is truth permanent or changing?"
- *Logic* deals with the rules and techniques of reasoning. It considers the validity of ideas. "What can people say without contradicting themselves?" "How do people make their arguments clear?" "How do people make their thoughts orderly and reasonable?"
- *Axiology* looks at judgments, rightness or wrongness, goodness, and principles of conduct. "What should people do?" "What are desirable values?" It also deals with aesthetics, which relates to the human concept of beauty. "How do people make judgments about what they see, touch, and hear?" "What is beautiful?"

These divisions of philosophy relate directly to education. For example, in terms of metaphysics, education needs to be concerned with various views of reality and their limitations. Educators need to realize that the curriculum is a statement of prevailing views on reality and that what is emphasized in education reflects existing notions about the nature and purpose of the universe. Students also should be encouraged to shape their own intelligent views of what is real, rather than uncritically accept the views handed down to them.

Epistemology should be of concern to educators because it deals with the origins of knowledge and what it is, how it is transmitted, and how people learn it. Views about learning and what one should know directly relate to this branch of philosophy. Logic as a philosophical discipline helps students communicate and think clearly. Many philosophers, such as Aristotle, believe that logic is the foundation of all philosophical thinking. The study of axiology deals with rightness and wrongness and helps frame a consistent set of values to live by. It encourages people to examine what is beautiful, as well as to develop a concern for the environment.

In this book, many problems and issues are considered. One technique that is used is to push problems back to their metaphysical, epistemological, logical, and axiological underpinnings. For example, one might ask the question "What should be in the curriculum?" but in order to answer this question, it is also important to consider the nature of the learner. In considering the questions "What should one learn, and what is the value of learning?" it is also important to consider how the curriculum should be organized and on what rationale it is based. Thus, one encounters questions of a metaphysical, epistemological, axiological, and logical nature. To answer some of these questions, one could turn for guidance to philosophers who have studied and written about these problems. This does not ignore that science also might provide clarity or answers to these questions, but often the questions asked do not lend themselves to scientific measurement; they require answers based more on reasoning than on scientific analysis or experiment. In some instances, the best answers can be found in the writings of idealists, depending on time, place, and circumstance. In other instances, one might believe that existentialists provide better answers. Regardless of what direction one chooses, it is obvious that one should know and bring to bear on educational problems the best ideas available, including the ideas of educational philosophers from any time or place.

One role of philosophy in any era has been to examine critically the intellectual disputes of the day and to suggest alternative ways of thinking. Another role has been to develop sensitivity to the logic and language used in constructing solutions to problems, whether in education or in other endeavors. It is possible to trace the history of ideas by tracing the development of philosophical thought, and the history of philosophy reflects some of humanity's best thinking, our collective human wisdom, so to speak. To think philosophically is to reflect on who we are, what we are doing, why we are doing it, and how we justify our efforts.

Education is involved with the world of ideas and the world of practical activity; good ideas can lead to good practices, and good practices can lead to good ideas. To act intelligently in the educational process, the educator needs the things that philosophy can provide—an understanding of thinking processes and the nature of ideas, the language people use, criticisms of cultural and social traditions, and perspectives on how these could have practical impact. For educators, philosophy should be a professional tool and a way of improving the quality and enjoyment of life as it helps one gain a wider and deeper perspective on human existence and the surrounding world.

Despite the depth of thought it provides, philosophy does not appeal to everyone, in part because it provides no clear-cut answers to every pressing problem. Philosophy does provide some clear answers, but philosophers also disagree on many issues, and it is often from disagreements that the search for new ideas is invigorated. Some people would like to avoid disagreement and have clear-cut answers, but they overlook an important understanding about the development of ideas: If no disagreement had occurred about ideas, purposes, and ways of doing things, if no dissatisfaction were voiced with "the way things are," then human progress would have been curtailed significantly. Disagreement often has brought about change for the better, and it could continue to do so.

Many differences in educational viewpoints have arisen because of changes in society that require changes in viewpoints and behaviors. It would be gratifying if social and educational change resulted from people reflectively examining issues and clarifying alternatives. In the past, great social and cultural changes were thought to be largely beyond human control. Those who tried to study the changes and make recommendations to meet the challenges sometimes had limited influence over the direction that events would take. Perhaps great historical changes could have been managed better if sufficient thought and foresight had been applied, but in their absence, change ran its own capricious course. Gradually, some observers came to understand that education could help people better meet the challenges of change. Important parts of Plato's philosophical work were devoted to this end in ancient

Greece, and John Dewey attempted to use philosophy in similar ways in the twentieth century in the United States.

As people sought to develop more control over social forces through education, however, they were faced with the problem of which controls were best and what directions the controls should take. This dilemma led to questions of whether social control through education did more harm than good. For example, today people can be controlled through behavioral conditioning in education, but whether such control is good is subject to much debate. Philosophy offers an avenue to examine such issues, the values involved, and the basic assumptions behind the contending arguments that might have implications for human life, freedom, and education.

Some people, however, come to philosophy looking for the answers to highly debatable issues, and when they fail to find them, they reject philosophy, complaining that it is ambivalent and difficult to understand. Some question the value of studying philosophy at all, saying that it has no relevance for practical life. However, many problems that philosophers have pondered—the relationship of individual freedom to social responsibility, the nature of a good society, the purposes of education, and the meanings of terms and concepts—are as relevant today as ever.

Practically everything done in education reflects some point of view that may not be readily apparent to the student, the parent, or even the educator. Perhaps a viewpoint itself is unclear or is a loose collection of ideas all lumped together without much logic or coherence, or perhaps it might be kept purposefully vague for hidden reasons related to special interests, a power elite, or cultural dominance. Such cases need to be clarified and sorted out, but because many educators lack the understandings and skills that promote such clarification, they continue to drift in a sea of rhetorical slogans and patchwork panaceas. Attempts to solve educational problems often result in a chaotic jumble of programs, superficial bickering among ideological camps, and sloganeering. "Practical" educators assume that philosophical theory should be thrown out so people can get on with the "real" tasks at hand. The problem with this practical outlook is that its advocates approach educational problems with the same old attitudes and remedies. They assume that they can read the face of the real world, an intelligible universe unencumbered by ivory-tower intellectual schemes, without realizing that such a view is itself based on metaphysical assumptions.

It seems that educators, like everyone else, are caught up in their own humanity. No certainty exists with regard to all facets of life in any known approach to education because *the* perfect approach has not yet been invented. People are left with the necessity to think about what they do, and to attempt to reason out and justify their actions so that they are coherent, meaningful, and directed toward desirable educational ends.

Some critics maintain that no logical connections can be made between philosophical thought and the practical world of education; that is, philosophical reflection has no necessary logical connection with what ought to be done in a practical educational context. This might be true, logically speaking, but it has not kept philosophers and educators from attempting to make such connections. No logical connection may exist between, for example, Plato's view of the good society and his construction of educational means to achieve that view. However, many people have made such connections between philosophy and education, whether logical or otherwise, and educational programs have been developed and instituted, drawing heavily on Plato and other philosophers in the process. This can be seen in recommendations concerning the aims and purposes of education, curriculum content, teaching methods, and many other areas of educational endeavor. Although Plato lived more than 2,000 years ago, what he and his contemporaries said and thought about life and education still influences people—even if they are unaware of it. Part of the task of the student of education, then, is to become familiar with traditional philosophical ideas about education and to understand the impact they have had and continue to have on people's thinking, for better or for worse.

Certain ideas and recommendations about education have a great deal of influence today, particularly in shaping public attitudes about returning to the basics and moral values. Philosophers often have recommended certain basics and values that figure in educational recommendations, and philosophical traditions and recommendations are part of the working ideas and traditions of contemporary society. Many people assume these things to be true and obvious without questioning their origins. Thus, they might accept blindly many educational recommendations without knowing whether they are justified in light of current conditions. The student who seeks to become an educator needs to be informed about educational ideas and traditions in order to sift through rhetoric and argument and to reach a more intelligent understanding of the contemporary world.

THEORY AND PRACTICE IN EDUCATION

Some philosophers of education make little distinction between philosophy of education and educational theory. In 1942, John S. Brubacher wrote that "several theories or philosophies" could be used as guides to solutions of educational problems. In this view, philosophy of education is a discipline "peculiarly competent to tell what should be done both now and later on." It has much to offer in the way of theory even though philosophers might disagree about what theory or theories to carry out. In Brubacher's view, the need for philosophy becomes most apparent when the educator, parent, or learner confronts questions about the proper aims and means of education.

In trying to select content or choose a method then, one must decide what one's goal is and what aims or objectives are actually being proposed in the process. The development of educational aims is complicated, however, and gives rise to numerous philosophical questions: Do *true* aims exist? Does the nature of life and the universe itself demand certain aims? Can people know what the proper aims of education are? Do aims flow only from the practical life that human beings face in the everyday world, from the highest universal values, or from a combination of the practical and the universal?

In deciding what the aims should be, one also is confronted with determining what kinds of curricula and techniques will be most suitable for achieving those aims.

Many new questions must be confronted then—philosophical questions concerning the nature of knowledge, learning, teaching, and so on. Brubacher believed that few educators could pursue such questions or give adequate responses about why schools should be operated in particular ways. He maintained that the study of philosophy of education would help educators build more adequate theoretical bases and hence more adequate education.

By 1955, Brubacher was attempting to get educators to focus their attention on pressing problems and to use philosophical theory to deal with them. He identified six widespread concerns about education that philosophy of education could address: (1) anxiety that education is adrift; (2) concern that educational aims are vague, conflicting, and not conducive to loyalty; (3) beliefs that standards have been seriously relaxed; (4) uncertainty about the role of education in a democratic society; (5) concern that schools give students too much freedom and do not foster respect for authority and control; and (6) fears that schools have become too secular and neglect religion. These problems sound familiar because they are perhaps as significant today as they were when Brubacher first wrote about them. His point that philosophy of education could help solve them might not be accepted on a much wider scale today than it was in 1955, but his insistence that such pressing issues could not be treated satisfactorily without an understanding of one's philosophical assumptions about education and culture still seems valid.

Brubacher, of course, did not originate the notion that philosophy and educational theory are connected. This connection has a long tradition, but perhaps Dewey made the most thoroughgoing link between the two in *Democracy and Education* in 1916. According to Dewey, the theory of education is a set of generalizations and abstractions about education. Most people probably think that abstraction is useless in practical matters, but Dewey maintained that it could serve a useful purpose as "an indispensable trait in the reflective direction of activity." In this sense, theoretical abstractions (or generalized meanings) have a connection with actual, practical affairs. Things are generalized so that they have broader application, and a theory of education contains generalizations that are applicable to many situations. Theory becomes abstract in the remote sense when it ignores practical application; in the useful sense, however, abstraction broadens meanings to include any person or situation in like circumstances.

For example, Dewey observed that people might know many things that they cannot express. Such knowledge remains merely personal and cannot be shared unless it is abstracted or, put another way, expressed in some public language; then, it can be shared and critically analyzed for improvement. In other words, for people to share thoughts and experiences, they must consider the experience of others and put their ideas in language that they can understand. Not only must experience be shared, it also must be taken back into practice for testing. In this way, practice expands theory and directs it toward new possibilities.

Almost everyone has had at least some experience with this because everyone has shared some kind of experiences with others. People might ask friends or acquaintances how they accomplished something, or they could tell them how they did it and recommend their way to them. Experienced teachers do this often. They exchange ideas and methods that they have found fruitful in achieving certain educational goals. In this sense, they are theorizing or building theory even though the theory might not be sophisticated. One person tries another's approach and afterward discusses it. Experienced teachers find ways to redefine goals and to vary, expand, or redirect their approaches for future use; hence, practical approaches and goals are generalized or abstracted. These approaches and goals are tested and found successful, or they are altered, improved, or discarded.

In this way, theory and practice can build upon each other. Look, for example, at Charles Darwin's theory of the origin of species. Others previously had enunciated most of the central ideas of his theory. Even his investigations of flora and fauna during the famous voyage of the *Beagle*, though contributing to biological discoveries, did not add much to the theory itself. Of major theoretical significance was how Darwin connected many different observations into a coherent, comprehensive system that explained natural phenomena in useful ways. Thus, the world gained a renowned theory that has been influential in contemporary life.

In the sophisticated meaning of the term *theory*, the role of philosophy becomes crucial. In Dewey's view, philosophy deals with aims, ideas, and processes in a certain totality, generality, or ultimateness. It involves an attempt to comprehend varied details of life and the world and to organize them into an inclusive whole. It also involves a philosophical attitude, indicated by endeavors to achieve unified, consistent, and comprehensive outlooks on human experience. This is often what is meant by "love of wisdom." Complete certainty of knowledge is always lacking, and terms such as *totality* and *ultimateness* refer more to a consistency of attitude than to any final certainty of knowledge. Philosophy, then, is connected with thinking about and seeking what is possible, not arriving at complete knowledge. It does not furnish solutions so much as it defines difficulties and suggests intellectual methods for dealing with solutions or clarifying them.

The philosophical demand for a total attitude, Dewey held, arises from the need to integrate activities among the conflicting interests of life. It is an effort to develop a comprehensive point of view with which to resolve conflicts and to restore some consistency in life. In this sense, philosophy aims at reconciliation. This is shown in philosophers' efforts to attack the puzzles of life and to bring clarity to confused situations. Such efforts also might include the struggles of individuals to bring clarity to their own lives, but philosophy at its most comprehensive level seeks to deal with discrepancies and puzzles that affect the larger community. For example, Plato's search for enduring values was influenced by the political and social upheavals of his time. René Descartes's attempt to find indubitable truth was a result of the widespread doubt caused by scientific thought. Francis Bacon's view that scientific method provided useful knowledge was a direct challenge to traditional theological explanations of natural phenomena. Jean-Paul Sartre's analysis of human consciousness was an effort to understand individual significance in a modern world of indifference. Gilbert Ryle's concept of the mind challenged older views of the mind as a "ghost in the machine."

The need to connect philosophy with societal issues becomes clearer when one considers education because education is one of those human activities that concerns the whole community. To Dewey, education offers a vantage point "from which to penetrate to the human, as distinct from the technical, significance of philosophic discussion." When philosophy is viewed from the standpoint of education, the life situations that it studies are never far from view. As Dewey stated in *Democracy and Education*, "If we are willing to conceive education as the process of forming fundamental dispositions, intellectual and emotional, toward nature and our fellow men, philosophy may even be defined as *the general theory of education.*"

In the basic points thus far discussed, certain elements stand out. First is the assertion that philosophy can enable people to build more adequate educational theory. This assertion is based on several points, one of which is philosophy's role in clarifying aims and methods and critically analyzing cultural assumptions about education. Second and more central, however, is the role of philosophy in providing overall perspective. This role is illustrated by the philosophical attitude of "thinking about what is possible"; this effort is largely dominated by concern for integration and continuity. In this sense, philosophy can be considered educational theory in the most general sense.

Educational theory may also include more than philosophy, however, because it uses relevant contributions from many fields. Theory serves as a guide to organize thought about education and helps provide order and clarity to the process. Theory serves as a directive to educational practice by helping educators clarify and organize educational practice reflectively. Central to philosophical and theoretical discourse on education are (1) the necessity for reflection and (2) the organization of ideas for eventual practical activity.

A common assumption many people make is that *good* theory should be directly applicable to practical life—that it can be plugged into actual situations and yield direct results. If the theory does not work, then it is *bad* theory. This assumption might be the reason many people show disdain for theory and call it impractical, for few if any educational theories can be applied directly to practical conditions in the sense that one applies aspirin to a headache. Those who attempt such applications of theory seldom fail to be disappointed.

Why this is so relates to the characteristics of theory and practice. The point has been made that theory and practice must be connected and that each can inform and expand the other. To affirm a connection, however, is far from saying that a direct or one-to-one relationship exists between theory and practice. When Dewey said that philosophy is the general theory of education, he also said, "It is an idea of what is possible, not a record of accomplished fact. Hence, it is hypothetical, like all thinking." In *Contemporary Theories of Education*, Richard Pratte characterized educational theory as a directive for practice, but he also noted that "a theory is an instrument, a guide to thought, not necessarily a guide to direct practice."

Yet, theory serves a practical function in many ways, and if the "plug-in" approach usually is doomed to failure, it is often not so much the fault of any given theory as it is its application. One practical feature of theory is its *general* nature. It contains ideas and propositions that allow for comparison, contrast, readjustment, and criticism from a variety of sources because they are stated in a public sense and are not limited to the subjective thoughts of private individuals.

Theoretical discourse invites argument and counterargument; otherwise, it ceases to be theoretical and passes into dogma or accepted fact. Theory also aids in providing us with a more comprehensive perspective. It helps us evaluate or place in perspective what we are doing or could be doing. It helps us locate ourselves in relation to an overall or larger perspective. In addition, theory invites an attitude of seeking out possibilities, an attitude that constantly seeks a new or better way. Finally, theory aids in defining difficulties, clarifying confusions in thought and language, and sorting out and organizing plans for action. It provides a rationale and gives direction to practical activity.

Practice, in contrast, provides raw materials and a testing ground for theory. The value of a theory might well reside in what difference it makes in the practical world. William James was fond of quoting the biblical passage "By their fruits shall ye know them"; the character of consequences or outcomes helps determine the validity of any theory. For James, if a theory does not help one communicate better, criticize assumptions and actions, gain perspective, seek out new possibilities, and order and direct practice, then it had better be let go or revised in new directions because it has lost its connection with practice, and fruitful interchange has ceased.

These, then, are some practical aspects of theory. A prescription of detailed classroom activities, however, is seldom one of the practical applications of theory. The reasons for this are obvious enough if one examines the characteristics of theory. A major characteristic is that theory suggests possibilities; however, this does not mean that any theory could foresee all the possible practical situations confronting an educator in the fluid world of ongoing activity. Conditions change, people come and go, and even individual persons change and develop, so it is virtually impossible to establish preexisting rubrics that always will be applicable. The *suggestion of possibilities* aids people in organizing their thinking about educational activity, but it does not dictate the activity.

What does theory accomplish? It helps people organize specific practices or practical activities with a sense of direction, purpose, and coherence. It gives order and organization to administration, curriculum, and daily plans, and it aids us in constructing specific teaching and learning objectives and accompanying methods and techniques. This is the practical connection of educational theory to educational practice; in this sense, educational theory can be applied to educational practice.

THE QUEST IN PHILOSOPHY OF EDUCATION

An era of transition from an old order to a new one seems to be occurring. Some observers say that people are suffering so much from the impact of rapid development in many fields that they are stumbling blindly from "future shock," unable to deal with their problems. Others say that we are leaving the modern era and entering a postmodern era, a time of experimentation when old values are being altered in various aspects of life, including education. Perhaps every era faces similar difficulties of transition. Currently, the level of confusion seems to be considerable; as far as we can tell, no synthesis or coalescence has been achieved. It often seems that disillusionment is the rule, rather than the exception, and it has led some social theorists (such as Robert Bellah) to call for a renewal of communal life.

The postmodern attitude definitely has shaken philosophical complacency. In Europe, for example, Jacques Derrida and Michel Foucault have criticized established philosophical and cultural assumptions forcefully. Critical philosophers, such as Jurgen Habermas, have sought to go beyond modernist views and to understand the bases of human community in new ways. In the United States, Richard Rorty has criticized old ways of thinking and has attempted to develop a new perspective that could be called *postmodern neopragmatism.* Such developments, which often start on the unorthodox fringes, have a way of dislodging what once seemed to be secure philosophical modes of thought. Perhaps the only thing one can be sure about is that changing times demand new ways of thinking.

Thus, uncertainty seems to be a fact of life, and old ideas are being challenged. Perhaps the philosophical task, despite contemporary movements that challenge old verities and promise new certainties, is still a search for wisdom. This appears to be an inclusive search requiring many voices. From Plato on, attempts have been made to see humanity's development in some understandable, coherent, and orderly fashion. Descartes believed that he was beginning anew to construct an orderly way of thinking that would be incontestable. This same attitude of seeking certainty in thinking is found in Kant, Hegel, Marx, and some contemporary philosophers. More recently, the feeling for such philosophical certainty either has vanished or been seriously modified. Dewey talked about facts and true propositions but couched them in the rhetoric of "warranted assertions." Richard Rorty recommends a "conversation of culture" that includes many philosophical voices that can be admired or critiqued. Some observers say that this is a postmodernist era when everything is subject to flux and change and old absolutes are deposed by new uncertainties.

The current mood in philosophy of education is generally toward understanding issues in specific contexts, rather than a return to the idea that the individual, society, and education can be understood in an overriding system of thought. There is an acute reluctance to explain actions and events in terms of great and overriding systems. Thus, philosophical thinking in education has moved into a new arena. However, if philosophers no longer seek to provide general explanations and descriptions of the overriding scheme of things, a reasonable query is Who will? According to Harry S. Broudy, many people will continue to identify philosophy with the search for wisdom and will look to philosophy of education for more than "logical purity and wholesome skepticism." They are not and do not want educators and educational institutions to be neutral about their children's futures.

This expectation for philosophical guidance in education might be unwarranted, as recent developments in philosophy of education seem to declare, but as Broudy put it, "if the philosophy of education ignores or merely makes fun of this need, it will be satisfied by nonphilosophical sources." Broudy emphasized certain things that educators have a right to expect from philosophy of education, including attention to the problems of education in general and schooling in particular, clarification of educational concepts and issues, and rational discourse and freedom of inquiry. One direction that educational discourse has been taking is represented by

Stanley Aronowitz and Henry Giroux, who advocate a radical reappraisal and change in today's approaches to education.

Despite the uncertainties in contemporary philosophy of education, it is still evident that the philosophical task is one of constant probing and inquiry. Participation in the questioning and challenging attitude of philosophy is what this book's authors hope to encourage. This inquisitive restlessness makes philosophy an enduring human enterprise—one that is never completed but is always in the making. The search for wisdom might simply be an intensive search for better ways of thinking about human predicaments, and this search involves education no less than other human concerns. Philosophy, when undertaken in this vein, is not a separate and exclusive search but part of human life and education.

DEVELOPING A PHILOSOPHICAL PERSPECTIVE ON EDUCATION

Educators need to see that philosophy of education can make a difference in their outlook or activity. They should use philosophical ideas and thought patterns in ways that can lead to more consciously directed activity. This does not mean an uncritical acceptance of every philosophical idea or recommendation; rather, it means a responsible examination of existing societal and educational conditions in light of philosophical analysis and criticism.

Some philosophers of education have suggested a responsible eclecticism in building a personal philosophy of education. In suggesting this approach, they point out that no two people are at the same level in their intellectual and psychological development. Furthermore, perhaps no single educational philosophy is suitable at any particular moment because philosophies have their ebb and flow and their value depends on particular needs of the times. This might mean striking out in new philosophical directions, but it may also include a critical examination of a variety of philosophical viewpoints for the insights they provide. It also might mean going to philosophy outside one's own cultural traditions. Eastern philosophy, for example, provides contrasts to Western philosophical traditions and offers alternative vantage points from which to view education. Indeed, the current philosophical temperament calls for the inclusion of different and divergent ways of thinking. The danger of eclecticism is that it could result in an unexamined smorgasbord of ideas filled with contradictions and conflicts.

Developing a philosophical perspective on education is not easy. It is necessary, however, if a person wants to become a more effective professional educator. A sound philosophical perspective helps one see the interaction among students, curriculum, administration, and goals, and in this sense philosophy becomes practical. Of equal importance is the educator's need for a philosophical perspective to give depth and breadth to personal and professional endeavors.

The study of philosophy of education can be an exciting and challenging venture that allows people to encounter some of the great and enduring ideas of human thought. It enables educators to understand what has gone on in the past in education and to develop the kinds of perspectives and intellectual tools that will help them deal with the educational problems of today and the years ahead.

SELECTED READINGS

www.utm.edu/research/iep/ (accessed March 26, 2002). A useful and general encyclopedia of philosophy. Students may access biographical backgrounds, analyses of leading philosophers' works, and adaptations of philosophers' works from public domain sources.

Idealism and Education

Idealism is perhaps the oldest systematic philosophy in Western culture, dating back at least as early as Plato in ancient Greece. Of course, philosophy and philosophers existed before Plato, but Plato developed one of the most historically influential philosophies of education. From ancient times until the modern era, idealism was a dominant philosophical influence. In terms of American philosophical thought, idealism had a major impact on educational ideology in the nineteenth century, heavily influenced by German idealism. Although idealism has waned as a philosophical force, it is still alive in certain areas such as contemporary religious studies and certain aspects of moral philosophy.

Generally, idealists believe that ideas are the only true reality. It is not that all idealists reject matter (the material world); rather, they hold that the material world is characterized by change, instability, and uncertainty, whereas some ideas are enduring. Thus, *idea-ism* might be a more correct descriptive term for this philosophy. We must guard against oversimplification, however, and attempt to get at a fuller and more wide-ranging understanding of this complex philosophy.

To achieve an adequate understanding of idealism, it is necessary to examine the works of selected outstanding philosophers usually associated with this philosophy. No two philosophers ever agree on every point, so to understand idealism or any other school of thought properly, it is wise to examine the various approaches of individual philosophers. This will be accomplished by an exploration of three areas: Platonic idealism, religious idealism, and modern idealism and its characteristics.

DEVELOPMENT OF IDEALISM

One leading thinker of ancient Greece was Socrates (469–399 B.C.), who challenged the material concerns of his contemporaries. Socrates went about Athens questioning its citizens, particularly the Sophists, about their "unexamined" way of life. Socrates saw himself as a kind of gadfly who prodded people into thinking. He was later brought to trial in Athens and was executed for his beliefs. Although Socrates' ideas were only transmitted orally through a dialectical question-and-answer approach, Plato wrote them down and illustrated both the Socratic method and Socrates' thinking.

It has been debated often whether or not Plato added to these dialogues because he wrote about them many years after they occurred. The general view is that Plato added a great deal and put the dialogues in a literary form that has had enduring value. Because the ideas of Socrates and Plato are considered almost indistinguishable today, scholars generally refer to these writings as Platonic philosophy.

Platonic Idealism

Plato (427–347 B.C.)

Plato was a Greek philosopher who started as a disciple of Socrates and remained an ardent admirer of him throughout his life. Plato is largely known for his writings in which Socrates is the protagonist in a series of dialogues dealing with almost every conceivable topic. Two of his most famous works are *The Republic* and *Laws*. After Socrates' death, Plato opened his own school, the Academy, where students and professors engaged in a dialectical approach to problems.

According to Plato, people should concern themselves primarily with the search for truth. Because truth is perfect and eternal, it cannot be found in the world of matter, which is imperfect and constantly changing. Mathematics demonstrates that eternal truths are possible. Such concepts as $2 + 2 = 4$ or that all points of a perfect circle are equidistant from the center always have been true (even before people discovered them), are true, and always will be true. Mathematics shows that universal truths with which everyone can agree can be found, but mathematics constitutes only one field of knowledge. Plato believed that we must search for other universal truths in such areas as politics, society, and education; hence, the search for absolute truth should be the quest of the true philosopher.

In *The Republic*, Plato wrote about the separation of the world of ideas from the world of matter. The world of ideas (or forms) has the Good as its highest point—the source of all true knowledge. The world of matter, the ever-changing world of sensory data, is not to be trusted. People need, as much as possible, to free themselves from a concern with matter so that they can advance toward the Good. This can be done by transcending matter through the use of the dialectic (or critical discussion), in which one moves from mere opinion to true knowledge.

The dialectic can be described as follows: All thinking begins with a thesis, or point of view, such as "War is evil." This view can be supported by pointing out that war causes people to be killed, disrupts families, destroys cities, and has adverse moral effects. As long as we encounter only people of similar persuasion, we are not likely to alter our point of view. When we encounter the antithesis (or opposite point of view) that "War is good," however, we are forced to reexamine and defend our position. Arguments advanced to support the notion that war is good might include the belief that war promotes bravery, helps eliminate evil political systems, and produces many technical benefits through war research. Simply put, the dialectic looks at both sides of an issue. If our antagonists are philosophers who are seriously interested in getting to the truth of the problem of whether war is good or evil, then they will engage in a dialogue in which both advancement and retrenchment might occur.

Plato believed that given ample time to argue their positions, the two discussants would come closer to agreement, or synthesis, and therefore closer to truth (which might be that war has good and bad aspects). Those who simply argued to win or who would not maintain a critical perspective could not accomplish this kind of dialectic. For this reason, Plato thought that preparation in the dialectic should involve a lengthy period of education beginning with studies in mathematics. He was particularly critical of inexperienced people who used the dialectic, because he believed that students are not mature enough for training in the dialectic until age 30.

Plato saw the dialectic as a vehicle for moving from a concern with the material world to a concern with the world of ideas. Supposedly, the dialectic crosses the "divided line" between matter and idea. The process begins in the world of matter with the use of the brain, the tongue, gestures, and so forth, but it ends in the world of ideas with the discovery of truth. In the *Allegory of the Cave*, Plato depicted prisoners chained in a world of darkness, seeing only shadows on a far cave wall that they took for reality. Imagine one of these prisoners freed from his chains, advancing up a steep slope and into the sunlight, eventually able to see the sun, realizing it as the true source of heat and light. He would be happy in his true knowledge and wish to contemplate it even more. Yet, when he remembers his friends in the cave and returns to tell them of the real world outside, they will not listen to someone who cannot now compete with them in their knowledge of shadows. If the fortunate one insists on freeing the prisoners, they might even kill him.

The meaning of the allegory is this: We ourselves are living in a cave of shadows and illusions, chained by our ignorance and apathy. When we begin to loosen ourselves from our chains, it is the beginning of our education; the steep ascent represents the dialectic that will carry us from the world of matter to the world of ideas—even to a contemplation of the Good represented by the sun. Note Plato's admonition that the man, now a philosopher who has advanced into the realm of true knowledge, must return to the cave to bring enlightenment to the others. This points to Plato's strong belief not only that philosophizing should be an intellectual affair, but also that the philosopher has a duty to share his learning with others, doing this even in the face of adversity or death.

Plato did not think that people create knowledge, but rather that they discover it. In another interesting myth, he conjectured that the human soul once had true knowledge but lost it by being placed in a material body, which distorted and corrupted that knowledge. Thus, people have the arduous task of trying to remember what they once knew. This "Doctrine of Reminiscence" is illustrated by Socrates, who spoke of himself as a midwife who found humans pregnant with knowledge, but knowledge that had not been born or realized. Through his discussions with people, Socrates sought to aid them in giving birth to ideas that in some cases they never knew they had. In the *Meno*, Plato described Socrates' meeting with a slave boy, and through skillful questioning, Socrates shows that the boy knows the Pythagorean theorem even though he does not know that he knows it.

In *The Republic*, Plato proposed the kind of education that would help bring about a world in which individuals and society are moved as far as they are capable of moving toward the Good. He understood fully that most people do believe in matter as an objective reality, individual differences exist, and injustice and inhumanity are ways of life. He wished to create a world in which outstanding people, such as Socrates, could serve as models and would be rewarded instead of punished. Plato suggested that the state must take an active role in educational concerns and offer a curriculum that leads bright students from concrete data toward abstract thinking.

It is interesting to note that Plato thought that girls and boys should be given an equal opportunity to develop themselves to the fullest, but those who showed little ability for abstractions should go into pursuits that would assist in the practical aspects of running a society. Those who demonstrated proficiency in the dialectic would continue their education and become philosophers in positions of power to lead the state toward the highest Good. Plato believed that until philosophers were the rulers, states would never pursue the highest ideals of truth and justice.

Plato's idea was that the philosopher-king must be not only a thinker but also a doer. He must supervise the affairs of the state, and like the philosopher who made his way out of the cave and yet returned to teach others, he must see that his wisdom pervades every aspect of state life. Needless to say, such a ruler would have no interest in materialism or even in ruling, but he would rule out of a sense of duty and obligation because he is the most fit to rule. Such a ruler could be male or female, and Plato seriously championed the notion that women should occupy equal positions in the state, including the military. Plato's philosopher-king would be not only a person of wisdom but also a good person because he believed that evil stems more from ignorance than from anything else.

Even though his theories about society have never been fully implemented, Plato did attempt to establish such a society under the patronage of Dionysius II of Syracuse but failed when the tyrant finally realized what Plato was doing. The value of Plato's ideas is that they have stimulated thinking about the meaning and purpose of humanity, society, and education and have even entered into modern thought and practice in many subtle ways. Who would not, for example, want the best person to lead our state, assuming we know what best means? Today, we provide an educational system with great state involvement that has much to say about what occupation people eventually will pursue as a result of the education they receive. We also recognize the tremendous influence of social class in education, as in Plato's utopian society, where he separated people into three classes: workers, military personnel, and rulers.

It is widely believed that philosophizing about the arts in Western culture began with Plato. Plato discussed painting, sculpture, architecture, poetry, dance, and music. Although he saw art as imitation (even imitation of imitation) and not true knowledge, Plato strongly believed that art (including literature) needed to be regulated and even censored so that it portrayed things in a more virtuous light. In this way, then, art could become a useful part of the educational process.

Plato influenced almost all philosophers who came after him, whether they supported or rejected his basic ideas. Indeed, there is much merit in the observation by philosopher Alfred North Whitehead that modern philosophy is but a series of foot-notes to Plato.

Religious Idealism

Idealism has exerted considerable influence on religion. For example, Judaism, a pre-cursor of Christianity, included many beliefs that are compatible with idealism. In Ju-daism and Christianity, the idea of one God as pure Spirit and the Universal Good can be readily recognized as compatible with idealism. When Alexander the Great spread Greek culture around the Mediterranean world, there was also a proliferation of Greek schools; consequently, many writers of the New Testament had been at least partially influenced by Greek culture and philosophy. Paul, who wrote a considerable portion of the New Testament, was born Saul of Tarsus; Tarsus was a city heavily in-fluenced by Greek (or Hellenistic) culture and thought. One can find a heavy tinge of idealism in Paul's writings, stemming from both Jewish and Greek traditions. Like-wise, Muhammad and Islamic thought reflect Greek ideas with idealistic implications.

Augustine (354–430 A.D.)

The founders of the Roman Catholic Church were heavily influenced by idealism. Au-gustine was born into, and reared under, the influence of Hellenistic culture. In the *Confessions*, he described his early life of paganism and the debauchery of his youth until his conversion to Christianity in 386. He became a priest in 391, and in 395 was appointed Bishop of Hippo. Augustine connected the philosophy of Platonists and Neoplatonists with Christian beliefs. In *The City of God*, he described the City of God and the City of Man as divisions of the universe parallel to Plato's schemata of the World of Ideas and the World of Matter. Like Plato, Augustine believed that the senses were unreliable and that belief in God rests ultimately on faith. "We must first believe," he wrote, "in order that we may know." In Plato's philosophy, the soul has knowledge that is obscured by being imprisoned in the body. In Augustine's inter-pretation, the soul was blackened by Adam's fall from grace, which resulted in human doubt and uncertainty.

Augustine was much concerned with the concept of evil and believed that be-cause man inherited the sin of Adam, he was engaged in a continuous struggle to re-gain the kind of purity he had before the fall. This idea is akin to Plato's myth about the star: Souls that lived near the Good were exiled to the world of matter to suffer pain and death and must struggle to return to the spiritual existence they once had.

Augustine readily accepted Plato's notion of the "divided line" between ideas and matter, but he referred to the two worlds as the World of God and the World of Man. The World of God is the world of Spirit and the Good; the World of Man is the material world of darkness, sin, ignorance, and suffering. Augustine believed that one should, as much as possible, release oneself from the World of Man and enter into the World of God. Although no one is able to do this in any final sense until after death, he believed that a person could transcend this world by concentration on God through meditation and faith.

Augustine, like Plato, believed that people do not create knowledge: God already has created it, and people can discover it through trying to find God. Because the soul is the closest thing people have to divinity, Augustine believed, we should look within our souls for the true knowledge that exists there. He thus promoted an intuitive approach to education and agreed with Plato that concentration on physical phenomena could lead us astray from the path of true knowledge. Like Plato, Augustine was a strong supporter of the dialectical method of learning: Some written dialogues between Augustine and his illegitimate son Adeodatus use the dialectic to facilitate discovering true ideas about God and humanity.

Augustine's ideas about the nature of the true Christian found more acceptance among those who leaned toward a monastic conception of Christianity. Such monastics believed that the Christian should cut himself off from worldly concerns and meditate. Augustine agreed with Plato in his reservations about the arts. He thought that too much of an interest in earthly things could endanger the soul. He even questioned the use of church music because it might deflect one from concentrating on the real meaning of the Mass.

Augustine patterned his educational philosophy after the Platonic tradition. He believed that worldly knowledge gained through the senses was full of error but that reason could lead toward understanding, and he held that, ultimately, it was necessary to transcend reason through faith. Only through faith, or intuition, can one enter the realm of true ideas.

Augustine believed that the kind of knowledge to be accepted on faith would be determined by the Church. The Church would determine not only unquestioned beliefs (such as the idea of the Trinity) but also the proper kind of education. Augustine did not believe that the right kind of learning was easy. The child, an offspring of Adam, is prone to sin, and his evil nature must be kept under control to develop the good that is deep inside. Studies should concentrate on acceptance of the Church's truths.

One question that Augustine pondered in *De Magistro* was "Can one man teach another?" He believed that one cannot teach another in the traditional sense but can direct the learner with words or other symbols or "signs." Learning must come from within, and all true knowledge ultimately comes from God. Augustine was the greatest of the Christian Platonists, and his stress on the role of the learner's spontaneous and God-directed intelligence had great implications for Christian education for many centuries.

It is not surprising that idealism and religion have been closely intertwined. Christianity, in particular, promotes the idea of God as transcendent and pure Spirit or Idea. In addition to this is the Christian concept that God created the world out of Himself or out of Spirit or Idea. This resembles the Platonic concept that true reality is, after all, basically Idea.

It is not surprising that religious idealism exerted tremendous influence on education and schooling. Early Christians were quick to realize that Christianity would fare better if its adherents were given some kind of systematic teaching. When they established schools, they established them in patterns with which they were familiar. Thus, many Jewish and Greek ideas about the nature of humanity, society, and God went into the Christian schools along with the distinctly Christian ideas. For centuries, the Christian church was the creator and protector of schooling, and the generations educated in those schools were taught the idealist point of view.

The mutuality of idealism and Judeo-Christian religion was brought together in a unity of European culture by the Middle Ages and afterward. This helps explain several characteristics of modern thought. To Plato, ultimate reality is Idea and our bridge to it is the mind. To the Judeo-Christian, ultimate reality is God and our bridge to it is the soul. It seemed a logical step to connect Idea and God on the one hand, and mind and soul on the other. Thus, humanity's contact with ultimate reality is by means of mind and soul (or their congeners: self, consciousness, and subjectivity).

DEVELOPMENT OF MODERN IDEALISM

By the beginning of the modern period in the fifteenth and sixteenth centuries, idealism had come to be largely identified with systematization and subjectivism. This identification was encouraged by the writings of René Descartes, George Berkeley, Immanuel Kant, Georg W. F. Hegel, and Josiah Royce.

René Descartes (1596–1650)

Born in the small town of La Haze, France, René Descartes was educated by the Jesuits, for whom he retained admiration but with whom he developed dissatisfaction because of their doctrinaire teachings. Although his philosophical thinking challenged Catholic doctrine on many points, it seems that he remained sincere in his Catholicism.

It is difficult and misleading to classify such an original thinker as Descartes into one philosophical school. Certainly, much of his philosophy can be characterized as idealism, but he also contributed much to philosophical realism and other thought systems. For current purposes, the significant works of Descartes to be considered are his celebrated *Discourse on Method* and *Meditations on First Philosophy*.

Principally in *Discourse*, Descartes explored his "methodical doubt," whereby he sought to doubt all things, including his own existence. He was searching for ideas that are indubitable; he thought that if he could discover ideas that are "clear and distinct," then he would have a solid foundation upon which to build other true ideas. He found that he could throw all things into doubt except one—that he himself was doubting or thinking. Although he could doubt that he was doubting, Descartes still could not doubt that he was thinking. In this manner, he arrived at the famous Cartesian first principle: *Cogito, ergo sum,* "I think, therefore I am."

The Cartesian *cogito* has stimulated much philosophical thought since Descartes's time. Traces of it can be found in many modern philosophies. The *cogito,* however, supports the tradition of idealism because it reaffirms the centrality of mind in the relation of the human being to the world.

Descartes realized that even though the *cogito* was indubitable, he could not move easily from that stage to other indubitables. Objects outside the *cogito* are grasped by the senses, and the senses are notoriously subject to error. Furthermore, any particular idea or thought depends on other ideas. One cannot think of a triangle, for example, without considering angles, degrees, lines, and so forth. Thus, Descartes encountered the necessity of one idea referring to another. He wanted to arrive at the idea at which further reference stopped. He found it impossible to arrive at any idea—even the indubitable *cogito*—that did not refer to something other than itself, except the idea of Perfect Being. Descartes thought that he had, by arriving at Perfect Being, encountered God, the infinite and timeless Creator, the source of all things.

Thus, Descartes arrived at the two principles on which he based his system: the *cogito* and the Deity. He had the indubitability of human thought in the *cogito* and the foundation for all the objects of thought in the Deity. From these principles, he proceeded to build a philosophy that has, in one way or another, influenced most all philosophy since. That some of these principles are within the tradition of idealism can be readily seen: Finite mind contemplates objects of thought founded in God (in Platonic terms, human mind contemplates the ultimate reality of ideas). For Descartes, the way he arrived at his principles—the method of his analysis—brought new life into philosophy. The Cartesian method was extended into numerous fields of inquiry, including the natural sciences.

George Berkeley (1685–1753)

George Berkeley was born and educated in Ireland and spent most of his professional life as a minister in the Episcopal Church of Ireland. While still a young man, he developed most of his innovative ideas, writing several treatises on philosophy, including *Principles of Human Knowledge.* Berkeley contended that all existence depends on some mind to know it; if no minds exist, then for all intents and purposes nothing exists unless it is perceived by the mind of God. Berkeley was attacking a central tenet of philosophical realism—that a material world exists independent of mind.

According to Isaac Newton, the universe is composed of material bodies moving in space and controlled by mathematical laws, such as the law of gravity. Berkeley held that no one had experienced such matter firsthand and, further, that such a theory is a conception of mind. Berkeley thought that people made a common error in assuming that such objects as trees, houses, and dogs exist where there is no mind to perceive them. Instead, to say that a thing exists means that it is perceived by some mind—*esse est percipi* (to be is to be perceived). To the classic question "Does a tree falling in the middle of a forest make a sound if no one is around to hear it?" Berkeley would answer "no, if we rule out the idea of it being perceived by God." There is no existence without perception, but things might exist in the sense that they are perceived by God.

Berkeley's philosophical views were strongly conditioned by his religious views. He held that immaterial substance (ideas or spirit) has been profaned by science and that science has brought on "the monstrous systems of atheists." What exists or has being is not matter: It is Spirit, Idea, or God. Berkeley's efforts can be viewed as a kind of last-ditch stand against the encroachments of science and scientific realism that holds to the materialistic thesis.

Berkeley refuted matter by showing that matter cannot exist except as a form of mind. We can know things only as we consciously conceive them, and when we think of the universe existing before finite minds can conceive it, we are led to assume the existence of an Omnipresent Mind lasting through all time and eternity. Thus, we might say that although people may not be conscious of the trees falling throughout eternity, God is. Berkeley was a champion of ideal realities and values whose main purpose is to make evident the existence of God and to prove that God is the true cause of all things.

The Scottish-born philosopher David Hume, however, proved to be the greatest antagonist to the ideas of Berkeley. Hume was born in Edinburgh, Scotland, studied law, and later served in France as a member of the English embassy. His writings were not widely received at their inception and, according to his own accounts, "fell deadborn from the press." His major work, *Treatise upon Human Nature*, written when he was only 26, is one of the strongest attacks on idealism ever written. Although Hume began with an acceptance of the Berkeleian principle *esse est percipi,* he concluded that all we can know are our own impressions and ideas, and we have no genuine basis for asserting the reality of either material or spiritual substances. Hume could find nothing to justify a necessary connection or causation. To connect one occurrence with another, Hume pointed out, is merely the habit of expecting one event to follow another on the basis of an indefinite series of such happenings. All we can know is that we have ideas and impressions, one following another in a kind of chaotic heap.

Whereas Berkeley believed that his philosophy had dealt adequately with atheism, Hume believed that no more justification could be found for the existence of a deity than for the existence of matter. Thus, just as Berkeley thought that he had destroyed atheism and materialism, so Hume believed that he also had destroyed the concept of mind and God. Hume recognized that his theories resulted in a kind of skepticism that affected religion and science, but he was unable to reconcile the paradox of a seemingly sensible world with the logic of human thought.

Today, Berkeley's ideas might seem strange, but the concepts he developed have influenced scholars in many fields. His notion of the centrality of the subjective mind and of the existence of anything being dependent on a perceiving mind has helped influence scholars to study further the nature of perception and the objects of thought.

Immanuel Kant (1724–1804)

The German philosopher Immanuel Kant was born in humble conditions, the son of a saddler. Educated in schools of his hometown, Königsberg, he eventually became perhaps the most famous professor the University of Königsberg ever had. Kant generally is recognized as one of the world's great philosophers.

Among other things, Kant's work was a critique of past systems in which he sought to pull off a "Copernican revolution" in the field of philosophy. Two important works that he accomplished in this effort were *Critique of Pure Reason* and *Critique of Practical Reason*, in which he sought to bring order to the divergent and warring philosophical camps of rationalism and empiricism.

Rationalists sought universal truths or ideas by which a coherent system and structure of knowledge could be deduced. They distrusted sense perception because its results are so individualized and erratic. The empiricists, in contrast, held to the immediate perceptions of experience because these are practical and connected with everyday life. They rejected rationalism because it is so abstract and disconnected from the practical.

Kant saw that the skirmishes between these divergent philosophical views were getting nowhere. He accepted the validity and reliability of modern science and believed that the constant bickering between the two positions was doing nothing to further science through the development of a compatible philosophical view of knowledge. Kant's idealism comes from his concentration on human thought processes. The rationalist, he held, thinks analytically, whereas the empiricist thinks synthetically. He worked out a system based on *a posteriori* (synthetic) and *a priori* (analytic) logical judgments that he called *synthetic a priori* judgments.

He thought that he had arrived at a new system whereby we could have valid knowledge of human experience established on the scientific laws of nature. In short, we would have the best of rationalist and empiricist insights gathered together in a unified system. This would give science the underpinnings it needed, because Kant understood that science needed an empirical approach in order to discover universal laws of nature. He also recognized the importance of the human self or mind and its thought processes as a prime organizing agent in accomplishing this system.

Kant had to face the problem of the thinking subject and the object of thought. He rejected Berkeley's position that things are totally dependent on mind because this notion would reject the possibility of scientific law. He also was caught by the problem of how subjective mind could know objective reality. He concluded that nature, or objective reality, is a causal continuum—a world connected in space and time with its own internal order. Subjective mind cannot perceive this order in itself or in totality because when subjective mind is conscious of something, it is not the thing-in-itself *(das Ding an sich)*. Mind is conscious of the experience (the *phenomenon,* the aspect of the thing-in-itself). The thing-in-itself is the *noumenon.* Each experience (phenomenon) of a thing is one small, additional piece of knowledge about the total thing (noumenon). Thus, all we know is the content of experience. When we go beyond this, we have entered into the rationalist argument and into speculation on the ultimate or noumenal reality of things-in-themselves, or we have become engaged in moral and ethical considerations.

Kant explored the moral and ethical realm primarily in *Critique of Practical Reason*. His effort was to arrive at universal postulations concerning what we might call moral ideals, moral imperatives, or moral laws. This aspect of Kant's thinking was not tied to nature, so we might call this his spiritual side.

Many of Kant's efforts were directed toward refuting the skepticism of Hume because Kant wanted to show that real knowledge is possible. His efforts to do this were clouded by the uneasy way he united apparently opposing themes, such as phenomenon and noumenon, the practical and the pure, and subjectivity and objectivity. The two *Critiques* illustrate this conflict because one speaks to the logic of thought and the other to its practical applications. In *Critique of Pure Reason*, the result ends up close to Hume's skepticism because Kant found it impossible to make absolutely universal and necessary judgments about human experience purely on rational and scientific grounds.

In his *Critique of Practical Reason*, he had to switch gears and go to the practical side—the moral and ethical side—where he thought universal judgments could and should be made. Thus, his moral or practical philosophy consists of moral laws that he held to be universally valid—laws that he called "categorical imperatives"—such as "Act always so that you can will the maxim or the determining principle of your action to become a universal law."

This line of thinking permeates Kant's writings on education, a matter he considered of primary moral concern. He held that "the greatest and most difficult problem to which man can devote himself is the problem of education." One categorical imperative that he established in his moral philosophy was to treat each person as an end and never as a mere means. This imperative has greatly influenced subsequent thought about the importance of character development in education. Most of his educational statements are maxims derived from his categorical imperatives. He held that humans are the only beings who need education and that discipline is a primary ingredient of education that leads people to think and seek out "the good." Children should be educated not simply for the present but also for the possibility of an improved future condition, which Kant called the "idea of humanity and the whole destiny of mankind." For the most part, he thought that education should consist of discipline, culture, discretion, and moral training.

The essence of education should not be simply training; however, to Kant, the important thing was enlightenment, or teaching a child to think according to principles as opposed to mere random behavior. This is associated closely to his notion of will. The education of will means living according to the duties flowing from the categorical imperatives. In fact, Kant thought that an important part of a child's education was the performance of duties toward oneself and others.

We can readily see Kant's idealism in his concentration on thought processes and the nature of the relation between mind and its objects on the one hand and universal moral ideals on the other. Even though his attempts to bring about a "Copernican revolution" in philosophy failed, his systematic thought has greatly influenced all subsequent Western philosophy, idealistic and otherwise.

Georg Wilhelm Friedrich Hegel (1770–1831)

Georg Hegel is perhaps the capstone of idealistic philosophy in the modern era. He was born in Stuttgart, Germany, and led a rather normal and uneventful life as a youth, receiving his education until the age of 18 in his native city. He then went to the University of Tübingen and majored in theology, graduating in 1793. He showed no particular promise as a budding philosopher, according to his professors, and for the next several years he worked as a tutor with little economic success. He continued to study, and after he received a small inheritance from his father, his efforts became more successful. For a while, he was a lecturer at the University of Jena and then rector of a secondary school until 1816. He was a professor at the University of

Heidelberg for 2 years and in 1818 became a professor of philosophy at the University of Berlin, remaining there until his death.

Although practically all of his major works were written before he went to Berlin, there he became a prominent and overriding figure in philosophy. One can find elements of his thought in such disparate recent philosophies as Marxism, existentialism, and American pragmatism. In examining Hegel, one must look at three major aspects of his system: logic, nature, and spirit. Three of his important books are *Phenomenology of Mind*, *Logic*, and *Philosophy of Right.*

One striking characteristic of Hegel's philosophy is his logic. He thought he had developed a perfect logical system that corrected the inadequacies of Aristotelian logic. The word *dialectic* best fits Hegel's logic, and it often has been portrayed as a rather mechanical warring between thesis and antithesis, with the result being a synthesis. Yet, his logic was not quite that inflexible because it included many variations and shadings of the triadic categories. Even more to the point, Hegel conceived of thought as a continuum, not as a series of mechanical synthetic unions. It could be said that the continuum is characterized by a moving, constant "synthesizing"—a moving, growing, ever-changing thought process.

Hegel maintained that his logical system, if applied rigorously and accurately, would arrive at Absolute Idea. This is similar to Plato's notion of unchanging ideas. The difference is that Hegel was sensitive to change (even though some of his critics charge that his explanation of change is a failure). Change, development, and movement are all central and necessary in Hegel's logic. Even Absolute Idea is the final stage only as it concerns thought process because Absolute Ideas have an antithesis—Nature.

To Hegel, Nature is the "otherness" of Idea—its opposite. He did not view Idea and Nature as absolutely separate, a dualism at which Descartes arrived, because to Hegel, dualisms are intolerable as any final stage: There must be a final synthesis. In holding this view, Hegel was not denying the ordinary facts, stones, and sticks of everyday life; rather, these are a lower order of reality and not the final synthesis.

The final stage or synthesis of Idea and Nature is Spirit, and this is where the final Absolute is encountered. Absolute Spirit is manifested by the historical development of a people and by the finest works of art, religion, and philosophy. Yet, these manifestations are not Absolute Spirit; they are only its manifestations. Hegel did not think that this final and perfect end had been reached, but he did think that there was a final end toward which humans move, however slowly and tortuously, and however many backslides we might make. In this view, Hegel's idealism is most apparent—the search for final Absolute Spirit.

One major feature of the Hegelian system is movement toward richer, more complex, and more complete syntheses. To Hegel, history showed this movement just as much as logical thought processes did. It is as if the entire universe, in Hegel's view, is moving toward completion and wholeness. Thus, in Hegel's system, if we examine any one thing, then we are always referred to something else connected with it. Such was the case with the development of civilization; that is, history moved in a dialectical, rational process. Those who are familiar with the thought of Karl Marx will note similarities with Hegel because Marx was much indebted to him.

Hegel's thought no longer holds the preeminent position it once held. One reason is that his system led to a glorification of the state at the expense of individuals. It led some of his followers to believe in a mystical, foreordained destiny in the face of which individuals are powerless. In this view, individuals are mere parts or aspects of the greater, more complete, and unified whole—the state.

Hegel has had considerable influence on the philosophy and theory of education. Ivan Soll has attempted to show some of Hegel's contributions to philosophy of education—contributions that must be viewed against the grand manner in which Hegel saw philosophical problems. Hegel seemed to think that to be truly educated, an individual must pass through the various stages of the cultural evolution of humankind. This idea is not as preposterous as it might seem at first glance because he held that individuals benefit from all that has gone before them. This idea can be illustrated by referring to the development of science and technology: To a person who lived 300 years ago, electricity was unknown except as a natural occurrence, such as lightning. Today, practically everyone depends on electric power for everyday use and has a working, practical knowledge of it entirely outside the experience of a person from 300 years ago. A contemporary person can easily learn elementary facts about electricity in a relatively short time; that is, he or she can "pass through" or learn an extremely important phase of our cultural evolution.

Hegel thought that it was possible (if not always probable in every case) for at least some individuals to know everything essential in the history of humanity's collective consciousness. Today, because of the knowledge explosion and the increasing complexity and extent of human knowledge, such an encompassing educational ideal is naive. Yet, Hegel's position retains some credibility because the need to pass on the cultural heritage and to develop an understanding of people's paths to the present still exists. Even to Hegel, the attainment of such a universal and encyclopedic knowledge was an ideal, possible only to elite scholars.

Josiah Royce (1855–1916)

One of the most influential American exponents of Hegelian idealism at the beginning of the twentieth century was Josiah Royce. Royce maintained that the external meaning of a thing depends entirely on its internal meaning—that is, its "embodiment of purpose." He argued that embodiment of purpose is the criterion of "mentality" and that the internal essence of anything is mental. Royce, like most idealists, believed his philosophical views corresponded closely with religious teachings (the Christian religion in his case), and he spent much effort demonstrating their compatibility.

Royce believed that ideas are essentially purposes or plans of action and that the fulfillment of ideas is found when they are put into action. Thus, purposes are incomplete without an external world in which they are realized, and the external world is meaningless unless it is the fulfillment of such purposes. Whose purposes are fulfilled? Royce answered in Hegelian terms that it is the Absolute's purposes. He believed that one of the most important things for a person to develop is a sense of loyalty to moral principles and causes. This implies a spiritual overtone in which one achieves the highest good by becoming a part of the universal design. The influence of this kind of thinking is evident in the educational enterprise in terms of teaching people not only about the purposes of life but also about how they can become active participants in such purposes.

Following Kant and Hegel, interest in idealism continued in several countries. German idealism influenced an important movement in England, seen in the writings of Coleridge, Wordsworth, Carlyle, and Ruskin. The English school of idealism included such philosophers as Thomas Hill Green (whose writings included suggestions for ethical, political, and economic reforms) and Francis Herbert Bradley (who argued strongly against empiricism, utilitarianism, and naturalism).

In the United States (in addition to the work of Royce), transcendentalism (including the writings of Ralph Waldo Emerson) reflected idealist philosophy. William Torrey Harris was another American philosopher and educator involved with idealism; he later became the director of the Concord School of Philosophy, where he was active in an attempt to merge New England transcendentalism with Hegelian idealism.

IDEALISM AS A PHILOSOPHY OF EDUCATION

In general, idealists have shown a great concern for education, and many have written extensively about it. Plato made education the core of his utopian state, *The Republic*. Augustine gave extensive attention to the need for Christians to become aware of the importance of education. Kant and Hegel wrote about education or referred to it a great deal in their writings, and both made their living as teachers. More recently, such idealists as A. Bronson Alcott, William Torrey Harris, Herman Horne, William Hocking, Giovanni Gentile, and J. Donald Butler have tried systematically to apply idealist principles to the theory and practice of education.

Perhaps one of the most notable idealist educators in the nineteenth century was Bronson Alcott. An American transcendentalist whose ideas were a mixture of the philosophies of Plato, Plotinus, Kant, Hegel, Carlyle, and Emerson, he frequently contributed to the transcendentalist periodical *The Dial.* Alcott expounded a kind of absolute idealism with the belief that only the spiritual is real and material things are an illusion of the senses. He was interested in the education of the young and opened a school at the Masonic Temple in Boston in 1834 that became known as the Temple School. Alcott was actively involved in the school, where his daughter Louisa May Alcott, who became a well-known writer, was a student. Unlike many of his contemporaries, he advocated feminism, denounced slavery, and believed in the innate goodness of people. He chose Biblical selections espousing childhood innocence for lessons and used a conversational method of teaching that encouraged children to discuss moral problems openly. He published his *Conversations with Children on the Gospels* as a way to introduce children to sacred literature. Alcott put great weight on the intuitive knowledge of children and believed that the most important goal in education was character building. Later in life, he was appointed superintendent of schools in Concord, Massachusetts.

His assistant at the Temple School was Elizabeth P. Peabody, who opened in Boston in 1860 one of the first kindergartens in America based strongly on the ideas of Alcott and Friedrich Froebel. Another educator greatly influenced by Alcott was

William Torrey Harris, who was U.S. Commissioner of Education from 1889 to 1906. Harris credited Alcott with turning his philosophical beliefs toward idealistic channels.

Aims of Education

Idealists generally agree that education should not only stress development of the mind but also encourage students to focus on all things of lasting value. Along with Plato, they believe that the aim of education should be directed toward the search for true ideas. Another important idealist aim is character development because the search for truth demands personal discipline and steadfast character. This aim is prevalent in the writings of Kant, Harris, Horne, Gentile, and others. What they want in society is not just the literate, knowledgeable person, but the *good* person.

Search for Truth

One major emphasis of idealist philosophy is the search for truth. Plato thought that truth cannot be found in the world of matter because such a world is impermanent and ever changing. At the Academy, students were encouraged to reach out toward the conceptual world of ideas, rather than the perceptual world of sense data. According to idealists, the material world is not a real world anyway but analogous to the shadows and illusions with which the prisoners in the cave contented themselves. Plato believed that one must break away from the chains of ignorance. Such a person would then be on the road to enlightenment and might become a philosopher. In Plato's view, philosophical wisdom, or the conception of true ideas, is the highest aim of education and one toward which all people should strive.

Idealists always have stressed the importance of mind over matter. Some idealists, such as Berkeley, reject the idea that matter exists by itself, whereas others, like Augustine, take the position that matter might exist in a generally detrimental way. Platonic idealists maintain that a proper education will include examining such areas as art and science, which should lead the student to the more speculative and abstract subjects of mathematics and philosophy. In any event, idealists place less stress on the study of physical and concrete areas than on the nonphysical and the abstract. The important thing for the idealist is to arrive at truth, and truth cannot be ever shifting.

Some idealists, although not adhering strictly to the Platonic idea that truth is eternal and perfect, do believe that truth is substantial and relatively permanent. Thus, for such idealists there might be many truths, even conflicting ones, but they are truths of a more lasting nature; consequently, many idealists favor studies in religion and the classics—two areas that contain enduring ideas.

Augustine, a Neoplatonist, agreed with Plato that the highest aim is a *search* for the truth, but he believed even more strongly than Plato that truth has overwhelming spiritual implications. According to Augustine, the search for truth is a search for God, and a true education leads one to God. Because God is pure idea, God can be reached only through contemplation of ideas; therefore, a true education is concerned with ideas rather than matter.

Other idealists have maintained that there might be levels of truth. Kant, for example, maintained the truths of pure reason and practical reason. Hegel thought that truth is in development, moving from the simple to richer and more complex ideas. Many religions claim that their ideas are true even though they are in conflict with each other. This is why many idealists believe it is not truth *per se* that is important, but the search for truth. Even Socrates seemed to imply this position by stating that all ideas are open to challenge; a literal translation of the term *philosopher* is not simply a discoverer of truth but a lover of it—by implication, a seeker of truth.

Some modern educators who share many things with idealist philosophy have compiled lists of Great Books that contain points of view as disparate as the Bible, Marx's *Das Kapital*, Augustine's *Confessions*, and Voltaire's *Candide.* The idea behind using such books is not that any or all of them contain the final truth, but rather that they contain some of the best and most lasting ideas conceived by humanity. Even though the books are different, many of the selections complement each other. Most noticeable, however (even with the books on science), is that they extol thinking and ideas rather than mere sense data, and concentrate on great concerns rather than on mere particulars. One book often found on such lists is Herman Melville's *Moby Dick.* Readers would go awry if they found the book to be only a sea story or believed that it concentrated only on such things as the kinds of ships used or the numbers of whales caught. *Moby Dick* is a work containing great ideas about justice, evil, and courage—ideas that one needs to ponder. The aim is not to see this or any other book as a literal rendering of events but as something that provides insight into ourselves and the universe. The value of any major work in art or science lies in its carrying us to a higher point in our thinking. We should use literature and art as vehicles for moving us not only into the world of ideas but also into the realm of great ideas—ideas that are of substantial value to us in understanding truth.

Idealists conceive of people as thinking beings who have minds capable of seeking truth through reasoning and of obtaining truth by revelation. They see people as beings who breathe, eat, and sleep, but above all as thinking beings whose thoughts can range from the ridiculous to the sublime. For example, Plato believed that the lowest kind of thinking should be called mere opinion. On this level, people's ideas are not well thought out and are usually contradictory. People can aspire to wisdom, meaning they can improve the way they think and the quality of their ideas. They can obtain ideas that are of substantial value and endurance, if not perfect and eternal. People can come closer to this ideal by using the thinking of others or with the assistance of others' writings. The important point is to direct our thinking toward more universal concepts than those employed in the perfunctory matters of day-to-day living. Reading the daily newspaper, for example, might be useful for learning what is happening in the world, but the newspaper does not generally assist us in understanding *why* something is happening. This understanding demands not only thought on our part but also the ability to relate the thinking of others to a critical understanding of the problem. Some have contended that the Bible, *Moby Dick*, and *The Republic* do not speak to our current concerns about pollution, weapons of mass destruction, and racial bigotry. The idealist would reply that although individuals might not find specific answers to every particular problem in such works, they can find issues dealt with in a general way that is more conducive to an understanding of specific problems and their solutions. The Bible, for example, deals with the problems of war and bigotry, and *Das Kapital* speaks at length about many economic problems that are still significant. Our failure to deal adequately with our current problems is not from a lack of facts but from failure to use the facts in relations to great and encompassing ideas.

Self-Realization

The idealist emphasis on the mental and spiritual qualities of human beings has led many idealist philosophers to concentrate on the concept of individuals and their place in education. This flavor of idealism gives it a subjectivist orientation as opposed to its more objective aspects. The subjectivist side is held by many to be one of idealism's more redeeming features, especially in regard to education.

J. Donald Butler, a twentieth-century educator, held that the concern for the individual is one primary characteristic that makes idealism still viable for modern people. His analysis of the problem, in *Idealism in Education*, indicates that self lies at the center of idealist metaphysics and (we may conclude) at the center of idealist education. Accordingly, he finds that the self is the prime reality of individual experience; that ultimate reality can be conceived as a self; and that it might be one self, a community of selves, or a Universal Self; hence, education becomes primarily concerned with self-realization. Butler quotes Gentile in saying that self-realization is the ultimate aim of education.

Such a theme has its roots deeply embedded in the idealist tradition. Descartes placed the thinking self at the base of his metaphysical schema and his methodological search with his famous *cogito:* "I think, therefore I am." Some scholars date modern subjectivism from this development. Such thinkers as Berkeley further developed the notion of subjective reality, which led to solipsism on the one hand and skepticism on the other. Berkeley's notion that things do not even exist unless perceived by the subjective individual mind, or the mind of God, gave impetus to the subjectivist trend of idealist educational thought. Because thinking and knowing are central in educational concerns, it is little wonder that idealism has exerted so much influence on educational views about individual mind and self.

Even though subjectivism is a major wing of idealism, we must not forget another equally powerful idealist notion—the relationship of the part to the whole or the symbiotic relationship of the self to society. Plato could not even conceive of the individual apart from a specific place and role in society. This same theme, though enunciated differently, can be seen in Augustine's view of the connection of finite human to infinite God. In the modern era, this theme was perhaps most fully developed by Hegel. He held that the individual must be related to the whole because only in the setting of the total relationship can the real significance of a single individual be found. This led Hegel to assert that individuals find their true meaning in serving the state, a statement that is close to Plato's idea. Hegel would even go so far as to say that one must relate oneself to the totality of existence, the cosmos, in order to gain true understanding of oneself.

The impact of these ideas on education is readily apparent in the writings of Horne, Gentile, and Harris, all of whom have influenced modern education. Horne, an American idealist in the early twentieth century, maintained that education is an account of people finding themselves as an integral part of a universe of mind. The learner is a finite personality growing into the likeness of an infinite ideal. Because of the learner's immaturity, the teacher's role is to guide the learner along the correct paths toward the infinite. This calls for the teacher to be a well-informed person and one who has the knowledge and personal qualities necessary to accomplish this feat. The education of willpower becomes central here because it is easy for the learner to be lured away from the desired path by the siren calls of corruption and untruth, a problem often discussed by Augustine and other religious thinkers. For Horne, education should encourage the "will to perfection" for the student and is an activity whereby one shapes oneself into the likeness of God—a task that requires eternal life for its fulfillment.

Gentile, an Italian idealist, thought that the individual is not only a part of a community of minds but also connected with the mind of God; hence, all education is religious education. He maintained that one primary function of education is to open the soul to God. Harris, an American educator and idealist philosopher, proposed that education should lead people to what he called "a third level of enlightenment." This involves the individual becoming aware of the spiritual nature of all things, including union with God and personal immortality. The influence of Hegel's thought is prominent in Harris's educational philosophy, particularly where he recommends taking the student up through insight into the personal nature of the Absolute. For Harris, human development and education are a series of dialectical experiences.

Many believe that the humanistic psychology of Abraham H. Maslow reflects an idealistic philosophical position because of its emphasis on self-realization. Maslow was an American psychologist who, in the beginning, was influenced by Freudian and behaviorist beliefs. He broke from these beliefs and emphasized freedom and humanity's capacity for self-actualization. Maslow believed that human nature consists of a hierarchy of needs that are genetic in origin. The most basic needs are for air, water, shelter, sleep, and sex. Next are safety and security. As people become more secure, they seek love and belongingness, self-esteem, and esteem from others. Above these needs is a need for truth, order, justice, and beauty. Healthy individuals, according to Maslow, seek to move up the ladder of needs to achieve their full potential.

Although self-realization is a central aim of idealist education, this does not mean that the self is realized in isolation. Idealists believe that the individual self is only a part and can have meaning only in a larger context.

Character Development

Many idealists are concerned with moral character as an outgrowth of thinking and thoughtful actions. The movement toward wisdom itself, the idealist would argue, results from a moral conviction. Augustine thought of God as the highest wisdom and the movement toward wisdom (or God) as the highest moral principle. This concept probably is expressed best by Hegel, who described the dialectic as a movement going from the simple to the complex in terms of Spirit trying to understand itself. Hegel believed that the individual can know God, and he argued against theologians who said that God is unknowable. Humans achieve their fullest stature when they understand the movement toward wisdom and fully participate in it, according to Hegel.

One of the more prominent advocates of character development as a proper aim of education was Kant. He made reason, not God, the source of moral law; consequently, the only thing morally valuable is a good will. People who have a good will know what their duty is and conscientiously seek to do that duty. Kant promoted what he called a "categorical imperative;" that is, one should never act in any manner other than how one would have all other people act. The proper function of education, then, is to educate people to know and do their duty in ways that respect the categorical imperative. This is character education, and idealists generally agree, as Butler has pointed out, that any education worthy of the name is character education. The education of character includes not only a sense of duty but also the development of willpower and loyalty.

Horne emphasized the education of the will. By this, he meant that students should be educated to resist temptations and to apply themselves to useful tasks. The education of the will involves effort because, Horne believed, education is directly proportional to the effort expended. Whereas some educators maintain that children should follow only their interests, Horne held that the development of willpower enables a child to do things that might not be particularly interesting but are extremely valuable. Even though a person might not be highly intelligent, Horne maintained, effort would enable the person to achieve far beyond the point to which mere interest would have taken him or her.

Such idealists as Gentile, who supported the Fascist regime of Benito Mussolini, emphasized the development of loyalty as an important aspect of character education. Along with Hegel, Gentile thought that the destiny of the individual is tied to the destiny of the state and that, consequently, it is necessary for the individual to have a strong sense of loyalty to the state. Proper character education would thus develop the attribute of loyalty because an individual without loyalty would be incomplete. When the teacher acts according to the interests of the state, the true interests of the student are being met. By the same token, a student's proper role is to abide by the authority of the teacher.

Methods of Education

Most idealists who look at our schools today are dismayed at what they find. They see students regimented into studying facts, later becoming specialists of some kind, and using those specialties with little humane concern for their fellow human beings. Modern students seem like robots surveying bits and scraps of everything, thereby obtaining an "education" with little depth, operating on the basis of rules rather than on inner conviction.

Idealists lean toward studies that provide depth, and they would strongly suggest a modification of the view that things should be studied simply because they are new or meet material needs. Idealists find that much of the great literature of the past has more pertinence to contemporary problems than what is considered new and relevant. Almost any contemporary problem, idealists would argue, has its roots in the past. Such problems as the relation of the individual to society have been debated extensively by great philosophers and thinkers. To ignore what great minds have to say in these areas is to ignore the most relevant writings about them.

Idealists do not favor specialized learning as much as learning that is holistic. They ask us to see the whole rather than a disjointed collection of parts. The holistic approach leads to a more liberal attitude toward learning. Although such subjects as the natural sciences are useful, they are of maximum value only when they help us see the whole picture.

Plato believed that the best method of learning was the dialectic. Through this critical method of thinking, he believed, the individual could see things *en toto*. *The Republic*, which is essentially the fruit of dialectical thinking, attempted to integrate a wide range of learning into a meaningful whole. Plato believed that we can develop our ideas in ways that achieve syntheses and universal concepts. This method can be learned, but it requires a critical attitude, a background in mathematics, and extended study. The dialectic is a winnowing-out process in which ideas are put into battle against each other, with the more substantial ideas enduring the fray.

Although this method is not often used in schools today, the dialectic was widely used as an educational technique throughout the Middle Ages. Ideas were to be placed in the arena of battle; only if they emerged victorious would there be some reason for believing in them. Churchmen, such as Peter Abelard, used the dialectic in vindicating the truths of Christian doctrine. Abelard's famous *Sic et Non* was a way of looking at both sides of the question and allowing the truth to emerge.

In addition to dialectical method, some idealists maintain that truth also is received through intuition and revelation. Augustine practiced the dialectic, but he also put great stress on the intuitive approach to knowledge. His argument was that God, the Inner Light of human beings, could speak to us if we made ourselves receptive. Augustine believed that we should reject materialistic concerns as much as possible so that we can attune ourselves with God. One still finds this approach used in monasteries or in contemplative religious orders.

Even outside strictly religious schools, most idealists advocate a conceptual method that includes both the dialectic and the intuitive approach to learning. Plato held that one does not learn as much from nature as from dialogues with other people. Augustine believed that although one may be blind and deaf, incapable of any perception through the senses, one still can learn all the important truths and reach God.

Many modern idealists champion the idea of learning through the dialectic or contemplation, but these methods are not as widely applied as they once were. Today, some idealists lean more toward the study of ideas through the use of classical works or writings and art that express great ideas. Idealists do believe, however, that any study of great books should be undertaken with experienced leadership and with an emphasis on the comprehension of ideas rather than on the mere memorization and classification of information. They would insist on a seminar type of instruction with opportunity for ample dialogue between teacher and student. Furthermore, idealists attracted to such an approach would emphasize those ideas that have perennial value—that is, ideas that have withstood the test of time across the centuries.

Although one might easily see how this idealist approach can be applied to college-level education, it might not be so apparent how it could be used in elementary and secondary schools. One must be clear on the purpose of learning. The idealist is not concerned primarily with turning out graduates with specific technical skills but with giving students a broad understanding of the world in which they live. The curriculum revolves around broad concepts rather than specific skills. In elementary and preschool education, students are encouraged to develop habits of understanding, patience, tolerance, and hard work that will assist them later when they undertake more substantial studies. This is not to say that students cannot learn some important ideas at any age, but the earliest years of education prepare the student by developing the skills to undertake more in-depth work later.

The idealist emphasizes the importance of the teacher. The teacher should not only understand the various stages of learning but also maintain constant concern about the ultimate purposes of learning. Some idealists stress the importance of emulation in learning because they believe that the teacher should be the kind of person we want our children to become. Idealists have used Socrates as a prototype of learning and as a model for emulation.

Butler maintains that modern idealist educators like to think of themselves as creators of methods rather than as mere imitators. They prefer alternative ways of approaching learning, but they still like to see at least an informal dialectic in operation. In questioning and discussion sessions during which the dialectic operates, the teacher should help students see alternatives they might otherwise have missed. Although the dialectical process can be informal, it should not become a mere pooling of the ignorance of immature students; the teacher should participate to maintain the integrity of the process.

The lecture method still has a place in the idealist's methodology, but lecture is viewed more as a means of stimulating thought than as merely a conveyance of information. In fact, some idealist teachers discourage note taking so students will concentrate on the basic ideas. To the idealist, the chief purpose of a lecture is to help students comprehend ideas. Idealists also use such methods as projects, supplemental activities, library research, and artwork. Such diverse activities however, grow out of the topic of study at hand. This illustrates the idealists' desire to show the unity of knowledge and their dislike for random and isolated activity.

One cardinal objective of idealism and idealistic education is the ancient Greek directive to "know thyself." Self-realization is, as noted previously, an important aim of education; hence, idealists stress the importance of self-directed activity in education. In essence, they believe that a true education occurs only within the individual self. Although teachers cannot get inside students' minds, they can provide materials and activities that influence learning. The response of the learner to these materials and activities constitutes education. The sources of this action are personal and private because, to the idealist, all education is self-education. Teachers must recognize that they cannot always be present when learning occurs and should attempt to stimulate students so that learning continues even when the teacher is not present. The project method is one concrete example of self-directed activity. The idealist insists only that the nature of any such activity be on a high plane of thought.

Curriculum

Although not underemphasizing the development of a curriculum, idealists stress that the most important factor in education at any level is to teach students to think. The psychologist Jean Piaget and others have shown that it is reasonable to expect students to demonstrate some critical regard for the material they are exposed to at various stages of development, even with nursery tales that are read to them.

Idealists generally agree, however, that many educational materials used by students are inadequate. Although the materials might help teach such skills as reading, idealists do not understand why such skills cannot be taught in ways that also develop conceptual ability. One might argue that the McGuffey readers, widely used in schools in the late nineteenth and early twentieth centuries, taught the student something in addition to reading. They fostered ideas about parental relationships, God, morality, and patriotism. A counterargument might be that these are the wrong kinds of concepts, but are the more recent sterile readers used in schools an improvement?

Although most idealists claim that they are opposed to the use of reading material for indoctrination, they do not see why reading material cannot, while it is helping a student learn to read, encourage thinking about ideas involving humaneness, truth, and fair play. Although few books and materials for children express such ideas, idealists still believe that the teacher should encourage a consideration of ideas in the classroom. A teacher should help students explore curriculum materials for ideas about the purposes of life, family, the nature of peer pressures, and the problems of growing up.

With older students, one can use materials that are more appropriate to their age. *Treasure Island*, *The Adventures of Tom Sawyer*, and *Peter Pan* are well written and lend themselves admirably to a discussion of ideas. For high school students, even more idea-engendering material is available: *The Iliad*; *Hamlet*; *Twice-Told Tales*; and *Wind, Sand, and Stars*. Because these materials are already used in some classrooms, one might wonder what is so special about the way idealists would use them. Idealists charge that teachers are not always equipped to use such materials for the ideas contained in them. Such books could become, in the eyes of teachers and students, another hurdle to get over—another benchmark or list of books to be read.

Idealists believe that ideas can change lives. Christianity was once merely an idea, and so was Marxism, but such ideas have transformed whole societies. Idealists think that humans can become more noble and rational by developing the ability to think. They have encouraged the use of the classics for humanizing learning experiences. Whatever factors are involved in humanity's evolutionary past, the idealist holds that the most important part of one's being is one's mind. It is to be nourished and developed. It can accumulate facts, but it also can conceptualize and create.

Idealists charge that schools neglect this important consideration of mind. They add that even when the classics are taught, students often are required to memorize dates and names without due attention to the creative aspects of the mind. Creativity will be encouraged when students are immersed in the creative thinking of others and when they are stimulated to think reflectively. This can come about only in an environment that promotes the use of the mind.

Although some idealist educators stress classical studies, this does not mean that such studies are all they emphasize. Indeed, some idealists recommend studies that are distinctly modern. For example, Harris developed a curriculum centered around five studies: mathematics and physics, biology, literature and art, grammar, and history. Horne suggested seven major studies: physics, biology, psychology, mathematics, grammar, literature, and history. Harris and Horne believed that these areas are important enough to be considered on every curriculum level and broad enough to contain even elective studies.

The sciences are represented heavily in both of these recommendations. This indicates that such idealists as Harris and Horne did not disregard the development of new knowledge. Neither Harris nor Horne saw any incompatibility between studies in the liberal arts and the natural sciences. In fact, they maintained that a more complete understanding of the universe necessitates studies in both the arts and the sciences.

Role of the Teacher

Idealists have given considerable attention not only to the search for truth but also to the persons involved in it. The teacher whom idealists favor is philosophically oriented, can assist students in choosing important material, and infuses them with a desire to improve their thinking in the deepest possible way. Perhaps the best way to understand this is by looking at Socrates as a prototype of the teacher the idealists would like to have. Socrates spent much time analyzing and discussing ideas with others, and he was deeply committed to action based on reflection. The idealist-oriented teacher would seek to have these Socratic characteristics and would encourage students to better their thinking and their lives on the basis of such thinking. Idealists are, in general, greatly concerned with character development, which they believe should be one of the foremost goals of a good education.

Idealist philosophy is also concerned with the student as one who has enormous potential for moral and cognitive growth. The idealist tends to see the individual as a person whose moral values need to be considered and developed by the school. Although the idealist might not always be willing to give "evil" an objective existence, it is present in the sense that students may choose things that are harmful. Therefore, idealists maintain, the school has an obligation to present students with ideal models for development, and they would agree with Plato that religious ideas should be presented in ways students can use for guidance.

From the idealist's perspective, the teacher is in a unique and important position. The teacher's duty is to encourage students to ask questions and to provide a suitable environment for learning. The teacher exercises judgment about the kinds of materials that are most important and encourages diligent study of material that is of more ultimate worth. In this view, teaching is a high moral calling, and teachers should serve as exemplary models—persons after whom students can pattern their lives.

The idealist position has ramifications for the way we look at the individual. Rather than seeing people simply as biological organisms in nature, idealists see them as the possessors of an "inner light," a mind or soul. For religious idealists, the student is important as a creation of God and carries within some of the godliness that the school should seek to develop. Most idealists, whether religious or not, have a deep feeling about the individual's inner powers (such as intuition), which must be accounted for in any true education. Too much of what passes for education deals with filling a person with something rather than bringing out what is there—the truths that already exist. As discussed earlier, Plato spoke of the Doctrine of Reminiscence, whereby the soul regains the true knowledge it lost by being placed in the "prison house" of the body. The dialectic is the tool for regaining this lost wisdom.

Augustine thought that truth is inherent in the soul of the individual. Education is the process of bringing these truths to the surface; because many of these truths are directly related to God, education is the process of salvation. Education can be conceived as consisting not only of the dialectic but also of the technique of meditation to bring out truths already possessed by the soul. This outlook on education was characteristic of medieval monastic education, in which salvation was to be achieved not by direct action but by meditation. Even today, many religious institutions practice such an approach as a part of students' formal training. Some church schools still set aside a portion of time for students to meditate on ultimate meanings.

CRITIQUE OF IDEALISM IN EDUCATION

Idealism often is considered a conservative philosophy of education because much of its thrust is to preserve the cultural traditions. This is borne out by an examination of idealists' concern for perennial and ultimate truths and their notion that education is largely a matter of passing on the cultural heritage. Many adherents point to the strengths of idealism, such as the following:

- The high cognitive level of education that idealists promote.
- Their concern for safeguarding and promoting cultural learning.
- Their great concern for morality and character development.
- Their view of the teacher as a revered person central to the educational process.
- Their stress on the importance of self-realization.
- Their stress on the human and personal side of life.
- Their comprehensive, systematic, and holistic approach.

Historically, the influence of idealism on education has been so strong that even today it is hard to find schools that do not in some way reflect idealist principles. Although idealism's influence has suffered in recent decades, no other philosophy has affected education for so long. Beginning with Plato in the fourth century B.C., through scholasticism in the Middle Ages, to Kant and Hegel, and up to the twenty-first century, idealism has been a dominant force.

Several factors have contributed to a weakening of idealism in contemporary affairs: Industrialization and technological advances have taken their toll, developments in science have brought about fundamental challenges to idealistic principles, the renewed vigor of realism and naturalistic philosophies has put more emphasis on the material as opposed to ideal aspects of life, and the contemporary emphasis on newness as opposed to cultural heritage and lasting values has eroded the idealist position.

Many idealists counter that certain ideas contained in traditional writings, some written more than 2,000 years ago, are as relevant today as ever. They maintain, with Ecclesiastes, that "There is nothing new under the sun" because many problems that we face today are problems that philosophers and others faced long ago. Plato, for example, dealt extensively with the problems of government, society, individuality, and language.

Opponents of idealism have long searched for ways to get around what to them is the conservative nature of idealism. In effect, they object primarily to its fundamental premises. For example, the idealist notion of a finished and absolute universe waiting to be discovered has hindered progress in science and the creation of new ideas and processes. If one accepts the concept of absolute ideas, it is not possible to go beyond those ideas without questioning or doubting their absoluteness. This was one chief problem that modern science had in gaining acceptance, for science is premised on tentativeness and hypotheses rather than on stability and axioms. Indeed, modern science is characterized by physicist Werner Heisenberg's indeterminacy principle, which holds that one cannot accurately measure simultaneously the position and the momentum of a subatomic particle; that is, the act of measuring one property will alter the other. In addition, Albert Einstein's theory of relativity has been used to challenge the idealist assertion of a fixed universe.

Still another cause of the weakening of idealism is the historical decline of the influence of traditional religion in contemporary affairs. Because idealism has been linked intimately with traditional religion, the weakening of the one has led to the weakening of the other. Indications are, however, that the decline in religion might be changing. Although the influence of traditional organized religion has decreased, interest has increased in mysticism, Eastern religious thought, and various forms of meditation that take new directions from the more traditional religious views. In addition, a resurgence of evangelical Christianity in recent years has placed considerable emphasis on education of the young. These developments usually have idealistic underpinnings, especially in their views on the proper aims and content of schooling.

From the standpoint of education, several issues need further scrutiny. The idealist influence on education has been immense, but that influence might not always have been beneficial. Although idealist education has emphasized the cognitive side of humankind, it has tended toward intellectualism to the detriment of the affective and physical sides. It also has often ignored the many people who find its cognitive emphasis narrow and pedantic. This has led to the charge that idealism leans toward intellectual elitism.

The problem of elitism goes deep into idealism's roots. Plato advocated an intellectual elite of philosopher-kings. Augustine argued for the superiority of the monastic life over the secular because of the higher quality of mind and intelligence to be found there: Monks were a select group set aside for special treatment. Idealists have tended to view formal education not for the masses, but for a chosen few who could understand and appreciate it properly; consequently, they have concentrated on education for the upper classes of society, particularly for those going into leadership positions in government or the church. This factor often has led formal education to be viewed as a luxury, available only to the privileged few. To the extent that idealist regimes have tried to extend at least some formal schooling to the public, the view has been that vocational and technical studies are sufficient for the masses, whereas liberal studies are suitable only for the elite. Although not all idealists have thought this way, the tendency toward elitism generally has been recognized.

John Paul Strain stated that one has to go back several years in the journals on education to find an article on idealism. One might think that this conspicuous absence indicates that idealism is no longer a viable philosophy of education; yet, the reverse is true, Strain stated. When people refer to idealism as a philosophy of education, they generally mean Hegelian idealism, which was dominant in the nineteenth century and influenced such thinkers as Dewey and Horne. Although it is difficult today to find philosophers of education who are true idealists, idealism does exist in the thought patterns of American education. It focuses on heritage and culture, reading and writing, and intelligence and morality. We also might add to this list such things as respect for parental authority, law and order, discipline, and patriotism. Strain says that the thought pattern of idealism also encourages progress, strong institutions, self-control, discipline, and the importance of education.

Strain's views might reflect why many philosophers of education have not wished to be identified with idealism—with its religious character on the one hand and its subservience to political authority on the other. Hegel believed that the best form of government was a constitutional monarchy, and Strain favors a similar approach to government today. Strain is correct when he says that idealism still flourishes as a historical pattern of thought that exerts a powerful, often subtle influence on our thinking.

Hegel's influence also runs counter to political subservience and has lent itself to educational philosophies of liberation. According to Carlos Torres, Hegelian philosophy had a major impact on the thought of Paulo Freire, a Brazilian philosopher of education in the late twentieth century. Although phenomenology, existentialism, Christian personalism, and humanist Marxism heavily influenced Freire, Hegel's philosophy was a key element in Freire's political thought, especially as developed in his best-known work, *Pedagogy of the Oppressed.* Freire used Hegelian dialectics to analyze the relationships between self-consciousness and social consciousness, and how such dialectical tensions figure in domination, fear, and cultural transformation.

However, Freire went beyond Hegel's logical structures to a synthesis that is political and transformative. For Freire, education involves the act of knowing, but it is not merely transmitting facts and it is not necessarily carried out in classrooms. Traditional concepts of education should be secondary to the kind of education that is based on shared experience and critical reflection. The crucial element of education is not wrapped up in the Hegelian dialectic as logical argumentation, but in going beyond the logical structures of reason to actual practice (or *praxis*) in the experienced world. Thus, education must move beyond idealism to emancipation and liberation in the world of actual experience.

According to Torres, the foundation of Freire's philosophical and educational methodology lies in heightened conscious awareness and socially transformative action. Like Hegel, Freire believed education is an act of theoretical and practical reason, but it also should have political consequences leading to liberation from domination oppression of the masses, and oppressions related to class, race, and gender.

Despite its generalist approach to studies, idealism is sometimes susceptible to the charge of shortsightedness with regard to the affective and physical aspects of human nature. If we include in our definition of *affective* not only the aesthetic but also the emotional and personal-social side of life, then such a charge gains credence. An idealist curriculum can be overly bookish, and although attending to books is not bad in itself, if we fail to recognize students' emotional and social needs, then we are not attending to the complete person. Idealists claim to be holistic and universal, yet when their cognitive and bookish approach becomes extreme, they seem to fail to take their own advice about holism. For example, it is one thing to learn about human nature from reading enduring scholarly treatises on the subject, but it is another to engage purposefully in social relationships with fellow human beings in the everyday world. Reading extensively about "goodness" does not make someone good. Consequently, idealist knowledge is often only armchair knowledge rather than the insight that comes from interaction with other people.

In recent years, the idealist curriculum has come increasingly under attack for lacking relevance. Idealists have offered some compelling defenses, but an element of truth in the charge will not go away. To the extent that some idealists concentrate only on works of the past, the charge gains credibility. Certainly, the great writings of the past might provide insights, and we should study them, but this does not mean that we should ignore contemporary ideas and writings.

One claim made by idealists is that they give more attention to the development of character than do advocates of other philosophies. This is probably true, but it also raises serious questions as to why idealists are so concerned with character development and what kind of character they want to develop. Often, what purports to be character development in idealist philosophy is conformity and subservience on the part of the learner. Harris, for example, said that the first rule to be taught to students is order; students should be taught to conform to general standards and to repress everything that interferes with the function of the school. More explicitly, students should have their lessons ready on time, rise at the tap of the bell, and learn habits of silence and cleanliness. One might well question whether this is character development or training for docility.

This kind of character training might assist in educational and social stability, but it is often at the expense of creativity and self-direction. The kind of character training that idealists promote also might make students gullible—willing to accept ready-made ideas without serious examination. Many of the so-called great ideas, for example, rest on premises or assumptions that are questionable and, in the final analysis, might be socially harmful. Gentile and Royce, for example, spent much time dealing with the concept of loyalty as central to the development of character. Although loyalty might be socially useful in some cases, it also may be harmful when it encourages the learner to submerge all questioning and intellectual independence with regard to concepts involving church, state, or school.

Some idealists, such as Butler, emphasize the self-realization aspect of character education; yet, such self-realization often is seen as a derivative of a Universal Self. Hence, even under a softer idealist approach, the Individual Self is subsumed under a larger and more important concern—that is, the Universal Self or God. This line of reasoning can be traced back to Hegel, who saw the individual person achieving meaning by serving the state.

Another aspect of idealist philosophy that deserves attention is the contention that the primary function of philosophy is to search for and disseminate truths. One finds this view elaborated by Plato, who believed that truth is perfect and eternal. Even today, idealists point out that the search for wisdom is a search for truth—an ongoing pursuit that each new generation of students must undertake, although the final answers might always be the same. This viewpoint leads to a type of staticism; the assumption is that we have the truth already at hand. The danger in this belief is that it discourages a search for new ideas and develops dogmatism and a false sense of security. Although idealists maintain that modern individuals are too relative and tentative in their thinking, the absoluteness of many idealists might be a more serious weakness.

Although this attitude characterizes some idealists, others have a more pluralistic conception of truth, maintaining that there might be many truths rather than one, not only for the sake of new knowledge but also for the intellectual stimulation provided. Like all other philosophies, idealism has many shades and meanings, and it would be grossly unfair to lump all idealists together. Each thinker describes or reinterprets ideas in light of his or her experiences, and thus no two are the same. Idealists do, however, share certain views in such areas as character development and the importance of education.

PLATO

THE REPUBLIC

The Republic *often has been considered one of the greatest expressions of idealist philosophy and Plato's most thorough statement on education. Writing in the fourth century* B.C., *Plato described his utopian view of human society. It was not unusual for him to depict central ideas in allegorical format. In this selection, he shows Socrates attempting to explain how achieving higher levels of thought (thinking philosophically) is akin to prisoners escaping from their shadowy prison in a cave. Plato demonstrates the painful difficulty of the ascent toward wisdom and its potentially dangerous consequences. Many scholars believe that the story parallels Socrates' own life and death.*

And now, I said, let me show in a figure how far our nature is enlightened or unenlightened:—Behold! human beings living in an underground den, which has a mouth open towards the light and reaching all along the den; here they have been from their childhood, and have their legs and necks chained so that they can not move, and can only see before them, being prevented by the chains from turning round their heads. Above and behind them a fire is blazing at a distance, and between the fire and the prisoners there is a raised way; and you will see, if you look, a low wall built along the way, like the screen which marionette players have in front of them, over which they show the puppets.

I see.

And do you see, I said, men passing along the wall carrying all sorts of vessels, and statues and figures of animals made of wood and stone and various materials, which appear over the wall? Some of them are talking, others silent.

You have shown me a strange image, and they are strange prisoners.

Like ourselves, I replied; and they see only their own shadows, or the shadows of one another, which the fire throws on the opposite wall of the cave?

True, he said; how could they see anything but the shadows if they were never allowed to move their heads?

And of the objects which are being carried in like manner they would only see the shadows?

Yes, he said.

And if they were able to converse with one another, would they not suppose that they were naming what was actually before them?

Very true.

And suppose further that the prison had an echo which came from the other side, would they not be sure to fancy when one of the passers-by spoke that the voice which they heard came from the passing shadow?

No question, he replied.

To them, I said, the truth would be literally nothing but the shadows of the images.

That is certain.

And now look again, and see what will naturally follow if the prisoners are released and disabused of their error. At first, when any of them is liberated and compelled suddenly to stand up and turn his neck round and walk and look towards the light, he will suffer sharp pains; the glare will distress him, and he will be unable to see the realities of which in his former state he had seen the shadows; and then conceive some one saying to him, that what he saw before was an illusion, but that now, when he is approaching nearer to being and his eye is turned towards more real existence, he has a clearer vision,—what will be his reply? And you may further imagine that his instructor is pointing to the objects as they pass and requiring him to name them,—will he not be perplexed? Will he not fancy that the shadows which he formerly saw are truer than the objects which are now shown to him?

Far truer.

And if he is compelled to look straight at the light, will he not have a pain in his eyes which will make him turn away to take refuge in the objects of vision which he can see, and which he will conceive to be in reality clearer than the things which are now being shown to him?

True, he said.

And suppose once more, that he is reluctantly dragged up a steep and rugged ascent, and held fast until he is forced into the presence of the sun himself, is he not likely to be pained and irritated? When he approaches the light his eyes will be dazzled, and he will not be able to see anything at all of what are now called realities.

Not all in a moment, he said.

He will require to grow accustomed to the sight of the upper world. And first he will see the shadows best, next the reflections of men and other objects in the water, and then the objects themselves; then he will gaze upon the light of the moon and the stars and the spangled heaven; and he will see the sky and the stars by night better than the sun or the light of the sun by day?

Certainly.

Last of all he will be able to see the sun, and not mere reflections of him in the water, but he will see him in his own proper place, and not in another; and he will contemplate him as he is.

Certainly.

He will then proceed to argue that this is he who gives the season and the years, and is the guardian of all that is in the visible world, and in a certain way the cause of all things which he and his fellows have been accustomed to behold?

Clearly, he said, he would first see the sun and then reason about him.

And when he remembered his old habitation, and the wisdom of the den and his fellow-prisoners, do you not suppose that he would felicitate himself on the change, and pity them?

Certainly, he would.

And if they were in the habit of conferring honors among themselves on those who were quickest to observe the passing shadows and to remark which of them went before, and which followed after, and which were together; and who were therefore best able to draw conclusions as to the future, do you think that he would care for such honors and glories, or envy the possessors of them? Would he not say with Homer,

"Better to be the poor servant of a poor master," and to endure anything, rather than think as they do and live after their manner?

Yes, he said, I think that he would rather suffer anything than entertain these false notions and live in this miserable manner.

Imagine once more, I said, such a one coming suddenly out of the sun to be replaced in his old situation; would he not be certain to have his eyes full of darkness?

To be sure, he said.

And if there were a contest, and he had to compete in measuring the shadows with the prisoners who had never moved out of the den, while his sight was still weak, and before his eyes had become steady (and the time which would be needed to acquire this new habit of sight might be very considerable), would he not be ridiculous? Men would say of him that up he went and down he came without his eyes; and that it was better not even to think of ascending; and if any one tried to loose another and lead him up to the light, let them only catch the offender, and they would put him to death.

No question, he said.

This entire allegory, I said, you may now append, dear Glaucon, to the previous argument; the prison-house is the world of sight, the light of the fire is the sun, and you will not misapprehend me if you interpret the journey upwards to be the ascent of the soul into the intellectual world according to my poor belief, which, at your desire, I have expressed—whether rightly or wrongly God knows. But, whether true or false, my opinion is that in the world of knowledge the idea of good appears last of all, and is seen only with an effort; and, when seen, is also inferred to be the universal author of all things beautiful and right, parent of light and of the lord of light in this visible world, and the immediate source of reason and truth in the intellectual; and that this is the power upon which he who would act rationally either in public or private life must have his eye fixed.

I agree, he said, as far as I am able to understand you.

Moreover, I said, you must not wonder that those who attain to this beatific vision are unwilling to descend to human affairs; for their souls are ever hastening into the upper world where they desire to dwell; which desire of theirs is very natural, if our allegory may be trusted.

Yes, very natural.

And is there anything surprising in one who passes from divine contemplations to the evil state of man, misbehaving himself in a ridiculous manner; if, while his eyes are blinking and before he has become accustomed to the surrounding darkness, he is compelled to fight in courts of law, or in other places, about the images or the shadows of images of justice, and is endeavoring to meet the conceptions of those who have never yet seen absolute justice?

Anything but surprising, he replied.

Any one who has common sense will remember that the bewilderments of the eyes are of two kinds, and arise from two causes, either from coming out of the light or from going into the light, which is true of the mind's eye, quite as much as of the bodily eye; and he who remembers this when he sees any one whose vision is perplexed and weak, will not be too ready to laugh; he will first ask whether that soul of man has come out of the brighter life, and is unable to see because unaccustomed to the dark, or having turned from darkness to the day is dazzled by excess of light. And he will count the one happy in his condition and state of being, and he will pity the other; or, if he have a mind to laugh at the soul which comes from below into the light, there will be more reason in this than in the laugh which greets him who returns from above out of the light into the den.

That, he said, is a very just distinction.

But then, if I am right, certain professors of education must be wrong when they say that they can put a knowledge into the soul which was not there before, like sight into blind eyes.

They undoubtedly say this, he replied.

Whereas, our argument shows that the power and capacity of learning exists in the soul already; and that just as the eye was unable to turn from darkness to light without the whole body, so too the instrument of knowledge can only by the movement of the whole soul be turned from the world of becoming into that of being, and learn by degrees to endure the sight of being, and of the brightest and best of being, or in other words, of the good.

Source: Plato, *The Republic*, translated by B. Jowett. New York: Dolphin Books, 1960, pp. 205–208.

KANT

EDUCATION

Kant believed that education is "the greatest and most difficult problem to which man can devote himself." In the following selection, he shows how education can be used to shape human character through maxims, or enduring principles for human activity. Although written in the eighteenth century, this essay shows a decidedly contemporary concern for child development and learning through activities. Kant stressed character development and a commitment to duty. This concern is illustrated in his descriptions of various maxims and how they should give certain results.

Moral culture must be based upon "maxims," not upon discipline; the one prevents evil habits, the other trains the mind to think. We must see, then, that the child should accustom himself to act in accordance with "maxims," and not from certain ever-changing springs of action. Through discipline we form certain habits, moreover, the force of which becomes lessened in the course of years. The child should learn to act according to "maxims," the reasonableness of which he is able to see for himself. One can easily see that there is some difficulty in carrying out this principle with young children, and that moral culture demands a great deal of insight on the part of parents and teachers.

Supposing a child tells a lie, for instance, he ought not to be punished, but treated with contempt, and told that he will not be believed in the future, and the like. If you punish a child for being naughty, and reward him for being good, he will do right merely for the sake of the reward; and when he goes out into the world and finds that goodness is not always rewarded, nor wickedness always punished, he will grow into a man who only thinks about how he may get on in the world, and does right or wrong according as he finds either of advantage to himself.

"Maxims" ought to originate in the human being as such. In moral training we should seek early to infuse into children ideas as to what is right and wrong. If we wish to establish morality, we must abolish punishment. Morality is something so sacred and sublime that we must not degrade it by placing it in the same rank as discipline. The first endeavour in moral education is the formation of character. Character consists in readiness to act in accordance with "maxims." At first they are school "maxims," and

later "maxims" of mankind. At first the child obeys rules. "Maxims" are also rules, but subjective rules. They proceed from the understanding of man. No infringement of school discipline must be allowed to go unpunished, although the punishment must always fit the offence.

If we wish to *form the characters* of children, it is of the greatest importance to point out to them a certain plan, and certain rules, in everything; and these must be strictly adhered to. For instance, they must have set times for sleep, for work, and for pleasure; and these times must be neither shortened nor lengthened. With indifferent matters children might be allowed to choose for themselves, but having once made a rule they must always follow it. We must, however, form in children the character of a child, and not the character of a citizen. . . .

Above all things, obedience is an essential feature in the character of a child, especially of a school boy or girl. This obedience is twofold, including absolute obedience to his master's commands, and obedience to what he feels to be a good and reasonable will. Obedience may be the result of compulsion; it is then *absolute:* Or it may arise out of confidence; it is then obedience of the second kind. This *voluntary* obedience is very important, but the former is also very necessary, for it prepares the child for the fulfillment of laws that he will have to obey later, as a citizen, even though he may not like them.

Children, then, must be subject to a certain law of *necessity.* This law, however, must be a general one—a rule which has to be kept constantly in view, especially in schools. The master must not show any predilection or preference for one child above others; for thus the law would cease to be general. As soon as a child sees that the other children are not all placed under the same rules as himself, he will at once become refractory.

One often hears it said that we should put everything before children in such a way that they shall do it from *inclination*. In some cases, it is true, this is all very well, but there is much besides which we must place before them as *duty*. And this will be of great use to them throughout their life. For in the paying of rates and taxes, in the work of the office, and in many other cases, we must be led, not by inclination, but by duty. Even though a child should not be able to see the reason of a duty, it is nevertheless better that certain things should be prescribed to him in this way; for, after all, a child will always be able to see that he has certain duties as a child, while it will be more difficult for him to see that he has certain duties as a human being. Were he able to understand this also— which, however, will only be possible in the course of years—his obedience would be still more perfect.

Every transgression of a command in a child is a want of obedience, and this brings *punishment* with it. Also, should a command be disobeyed through inattention, punishment is still necessary. This punishment is either *physical or moral*. It is *moral* when we do something derogatory to the child's longing to be honoured and loved (a longing which is an aid to moral training); for instance, when we humiliate the child by treating him coldly and distantly. This longing of children should, however, be cultivated as much as possible. Hence this kind of punishment is the best, since it is an aid to moral training—for instance, if a child tells a lie, a look of contempt is punishment enough, and punishment of a most appropriate kind.

Physical punishment consists either in refusing a child's requests or in the infliction of pain. The first is akin to moral punishment, and is of a negative kind. The second form must be used with caution, lest an *indoles servilis* should be the result. It is of no use to give children rewards; this makes them selfish, and gives rise to an *indoles mercenaria*.

Further, obedience is either that of the child or that of the *youth*. Disobedience is always followed by punishment. This is either a really *natural* punishment, which a man brings upon himself by his own behaviour—for instance, when a child gets ill from overeating—and this kind of punishment is the best, since a man is subject to it throughout his life, and not merely during his childhood; or, on the other hand,

the punishment is artificial. By taking into consideration the child's desire to be loved and respected, such punishments may be chosen as will have a lasting effect upon its character. Physical punishments must merely supplement the insufficiency of moral punishment. If moral punishment have no effect at all, and we have at last to resort to physical punishment, we shall find after all that no good character is formed in this way. At the beginning, however, physical restraint may serve to take the place of reflection.

Punishments inflicted with signs of *anger* are useless. Children then look upon the punishment simply as the result of anger, and upon themselves merely as the victims of that anger; and as a general rule punishment must be inflicted on children with great caution, that they may understand that its one aim is their improvement. It is foolish to cause children, when they are punished, to return thanks for the punishment by kissing hands, and only turns the child into a slave. If physical punishment is often repeated, it makes a child stubborn; and if parents punish their children for obstinacy, they often become all the more obstinate. Besides, it is not always the worst men who are obstinate, and they will often yield easily to kind remonstrance.

The obedience of the growing *youth* must be distinguished from the obedience of the *child*. The former consists in submission to rules of duty. To do something for the sake of duty means obeying reason. It is in vain to speak to children of duty. They look upon it in the end as something which if not fulfilled will be followed by the rod. A child may be guided by mere instinct. As he grows up, however, the idea of duty must come in. Also the idea of shame should not be made use of with children, but only with those who have left childhood for youth. For it cannot exist with them till the idea of honour has first taken root.

The second principal feature in the formation of a child's character is *truthfulness*. This is the foundation and very essence of character. A man who tells lies has no character, and if he has any good in him it is merely the result of a certain kind of temperament. Some children have an inclination towards lying, and this frequently for no other reason than that they have a lively imagination. It is the father's business to see that they are broken of this habit, for mothers generally look upon it as a matter of little or no importance, even finding in it a flattering proof of the cleverness and ability of their children. This is the time to make use of the sense of shame, for the child in this case will understand it well. The blush of shame betrays us when we lie, but it is not always a proof of it, for we often blush at the shamelessness of others who accuse us of guilt. On no condition must we punish children to force the truth from them, unless their telling a lie immediately results in some mischief; *then* they may be punished for that mischief. The withdrawal of respect is the only fit punishment for lying.

Punishments may be divided into *negative* and *positive* punishments. The first may be applied to laziness or viciousness; for instance, lying, disobedience. Positive punishment may be applied to acts of spitefulness. But above all things we must take care never to bear children a grudge.

A third feature in the child's character is *sociableness*. He must form friendships with other children, and not be always by himself. Some teachers, it is true, are opposed to these friendships in schools, but this is a great mistake. Children ought to prepare themselves for the sweetest enjoyment of life.

If a teacher allows himself to prefer one child to another, it must be on account of its character, and not for the sake of any talents the child may possess; otherwise jealousy will arise, which is opposed to friendship.

Children ought to be open-hearted and cheerful in their looks as the sun. A joyful heart alone is able to find its happiness in the good. A religion which makes people gloomy is a false religion; for we should serve God with a joyful heart, and not of constraint.

Children should sometimes be released from the narrow constraint of school, otherwise their natural joyousness will soon be quenched. When the child is set free he soon recovers his natural elasticity. Those games in which children, enjoying perfect freedom, are ever trying to outdo one another, will serve this purpose best, and they will soon make their minds bright and cheerful again. . . .

Children should only be taught those things which are suited to their age. Many parents are pleased with the precocity of their offspring; but as a rule, nothing will come of such children. A child should be clever, but only as a child. He should not ape the manners of his elders. For a child to provide himself with moral sentences proper to manhood is to go quite beyond his province and to become merely an imitator. He ought to have merely the understanding of a child, and not seek to display it too early. A precocious child will never become a man of insight and clear understanding. It is just as much out of place for a child to follow all the fashions of the time, to curl his hair, wear ruffles, and even carry a snuffbox. He will thus acquire affected manners not becoming to a child. Polite society is a burden to him, and he entirely lacks a man's heart. For that very reason we must set ourselves early to fight against all signs of vanity in a child; or, rather, we must give him no occasion to become vain. This easily happens by people prattling before children, telling them how beautiful they are, and how well this or that dress becomes them, and promising them some finery or other as a reward. Finery is not suitable for children. They must accept their neat and simple clothes as necessaries merely.

At the same time the parents must not set great store by their own clothes, nor admire themselves; for here, as everywhere, example is all-powerful, and either strengthens or destroys good precepts.

Source: Immanuel Kant, *Education*, translated by Annette Charton. Ann Arbor, MI: University of Michigan Press, 1960, pp. 83–94.

SELECTED READINGS

Butler, J. Donald. *Idealism in Education.* New York: Harper and Row, 1966. A compact and insightful treatment of philosophical idealism in contemporary education. This book is a good starting point for examining idealism in education.

Kant, Immanuel. *Education.* Translated by Annette Charton. Ann Arbor, MI: University of Michigan Press, 1960. A historically influential work that examines education as both a theoretical and a practical endeavor. This book introduces the Kantian influence into many aspects of education from discipline to curriculum.

Plato. *The Republic.* New York: Oxford University Press, 1945. One of the most famous treatises on education ever written. This work has influenced countless people across the centuries. It is a highly speculative and utopian approach to education as the basis of the good society.

Strain, John Paul. Idealism: A Clarification of an Educational Philosophy. *Educational Theory* 25:263–271, 1975. A survey of the contributions of philosophical idealism to education in the twentieth century. Although the author recognizes the declining popularity of the idealist approach to philosophy, he points out that many people still hold an idealist philosophy of education that reveals itself in continuing traditions and practices.

Torres, Carlos Alberto. "Education and the Archaeology of Consciousness: Freire and Hegel." *Educational Theory* 44:429–445, 1994.

www.ed.uiuc.edu/EPS/educational-theory/Contents/44_4_Torres.html (accessed April 5, 2002). An analysis of the continuing influence of the idealist philosopher Georg Hegel. According to Torres, educational philosopher Paulo Freire used Hegel's ideas of the dialectic between individual consciousness and surrounding social conditions to help him better understand individual morality in overcoming oppression, a key ingredient in Freire's theory of critical pedagogy.

www.hegel.org/ (accessed April 5, 2002). Homepage of the Hegel Society of America. This site has "Hegel links throughout the Internet," which students might find informative, including Hegelian influences on philosophy of education.

naks.ucsd.edu/ (accessed April 5, 2002). Homepage of the North American Kant Society. Provides links to relevant texts and electronic sources of Kant and his interpreters.

Companion Website

ONLINE RESEARCH

Utilizing some of the Web sites included in this book, as well as Topics 2, 3, and 4 of the Prentice Hall Foundations Web site found at *www.prenhall.com/ozmon,* answer the following question with a short essay: What is idealism and how has it influenced educational theory and practice? You can write and submit your essay response to your instructor by using the "Electronic Bluebook" section found in any of the topics of the Prentice Hall Foundations Web site.

2

Realism and Education

Like idealism, realism is one of the oldest philosophies in Western culture and dates back at least as early as ancient Greece. Because of its respectable age, realism has had a variety of proponents and interpretations, as diverse as classical and religious realism and scientific, natural, and rational realism. Because of this confusing array of variations, it seems most reasonable to approach this philosophy from common threads interwoven throughout its long history.

Perhaps the most central thread of realism is what can be called the *principle or thesis of independence.* This thesis holds that reality, knowledge, and value exist independently of the human mind. In other words, realism rejects the idealist notion that only ideas are real. The realist asserts, as fact, that the actual sticks, stones, and trees of the universe exist whether or not there is a human mind to perceive them. In one sense, matter is real to the realist; however, this does not mean that all realists are rampant materialists. What is important is that matter is an obvious example of an independent reality. To understand this complex philosophy, one must examine its development from classical times, how it was transformed by the scientific revolution, and what it is today.

CLASSICAL TRADITIONS

Aristotelian Realism

Aristotle (384–322 B.C.)

Plato believed that matter had no lasting reality and that we should concern ourselves with ideas. It was Plato's pupil Aristotle, however, who developed the view that although ideas might be important in themselves, a proper study of matter could lead to better and more distinct ideas. Aristotle studied and taught at Plato's Academy for about 20 years and later opened his own school, the Lyceum. His differences with

Plato were developed gradually, and in many respects, he never got out from under Plato's influence.

According to Aristotle, ideas (or forms) such as the idea of God or the idea of a tree can exist without matter, but no matter can exist without form. Each piece of matter has universal and particular properties. The particular properties of an acorn, for example, are those things that are peculiar to it and that differentiate it from all other acorns. These properties include its size, shape, weight, and color. No two acorns are exactly alike, so one can talk about some particular properties of any acorn as different from those of all other acorns. Each acorn, however, shares the universal property that can be called "acornness" with all other acorns.

Perhaps the difference between particular and universal properties can be understood better by referring to humans at this point. People, too, differ in their particular properties. They have different shapes and sizes, and no two are exactly alike. Yet, all people do share in something universal, and this could be called their "humanness." Both "humanness" and "acornness" are realities, and they exist independently and regardless of any one particular human or acorn. Thus, *forms* (universals, ideas, or essences) are the nonmaterial aspects of each particular material object that relate to all other particular objects of that class.

Nonmaterial though form may be, it is arrived at by examining material objects that exist in and of themselves, independent of us. Aristotle believed that people should be much involved in studying and understanding the reality of all things. Indeed, he agreed with Plato on this position. They differed, however, in that Aristotle thought one could get to form by studying particular material things, and Plato thought form could be reached only through some kind of reasoning, such as the dialectic.

Aristotle argued that the forms of things, the universal properties of objects, remain constant and never change but that particular components do change. The shell of an acorn may disintegrate and an acorn can be destroyed, but the form of all acorns, or acornness, remains. In terms of people again, although individual persons die, humanness remains. Even if all human beings were to die, humanness would remain, just as the concept of circularity would remain even if all existing material circles were destroyed.

In terms of the development of people, it can be seen that as children, individuals have the particular characteristics of children. As they grow, however, their bodies change and they enter the phase of growth called adolescence; later, they become adults. However, humanness remains even though the developmental process of the individual changes several times. Thus, form remains constant although particular matter changes. Aristotle and Plato agreed that form is constant and matter is always changing, but Aristotle believed that form is within particular matter and is even the motivating force of that matter. By the same token, the modern philosopher Henri Bergson spoke about an *élan vital,* or *vital principle,* that each object has and that directs it in terms of fulfilling its purpose. This can be seen in the actual growth process of an acorn fulfilling its purpose in becoming an oak tree. It must take in the proper amount of sun and water, it must set its roots just so deep, and it must receive nourishment in the proper way. Each object, Aristotle thought, has a tiny "soul" that directs it in the right way.

Aristotle was a scientist and a philosopher, and he believed that although science and philosophy can be separated artificially, a relationship exists between them in which the study of one aids in the study of the other. Studying the material aspects of an acorn (its shell, its color, and so forth) should lead to a deeper contemplation of what the acorn is—that is, its essence or form.

Of course, much depends on asking the right questions. There are scientific questions and there are philosophical questions, and they can overlap. If one goes to the seashore and picks up a shell, one could ask many scientific questions about that shell: What is it composed of? How long has it been here? What lived in it? How much does it weigh? Such questions abound, and answering them would tell quite a bit about the shell, but the questions would be asking only about its particular physical aspects.

Other kinds of questions could be asked, too: What is its meaning? Who or what created it? What is its purpose? These kinds of questions are basically philosophical although they can be brought out by scientific investigation. This would support Aristotle's claim that the deeper we go into matter, the more we are led to philosophy.

The most important questions we can ask about things relate to their purposes. Aristotle believed that each thing has a purpose or function. What is the purpose of a fish? If we examine it carefully, we might say that its purpose is to swim. The purpose of a bird is to fly. What, though, is humanity's purpose? Aristotle argued that because humans are the only creatures endowed with the ability to think, their purpose is to use this ability. Thus, we achieve our true purpose when we think, and we go against this end when we do not think or when we do not think intelligently.

According to Aristotle, design and order are present in the universe, for things happen in an orderly way. An acorn becomes an oak tree and not a sycamore. A kitten becomes a cat and not a dog. The universe can be understood by studying it in terms of its purposes. Thus, whatever happens can be explained according to purpose: The acorn follows its destiny, and the kitten follows its destiny. With regard to humans, we already have seen that our purpose is to think, but we admit that we can refuse to think or we can think poorly. We can avoid thinking by not paying attention, by misdirecting our thinking, or by otherwise subverting thinking. Aristotle believed that we can refuse to think and therefore go against the design of the universe and the reason for our creation; hence, humans have free will. When humans go against this purpose, however, they suffer the consequences of erroneous ideas, poor health, and an unhappy life, among other things.

Aristotle believed that the person who follows a true purpose leads a rational life of moderation, avoiding extremes. There are two Aristotelian extremes: the extreme of too little and the extreme of too much. In terms of eating, if one eats too much, one will suffer from obesity, lack of energy, poor health in general, or death. The moderate man or woman—the thinking person—avoids such excesses. For Aristotle, the proper perspective is the Golden Mean, a path between extremes.

Aristotle's concept of the Golden Mean is illustrated by his notion of the soul as an entity to be kept in balance. He spoke of the three aspects of the soul being vegetative, animative, and rational. When humans vegetate, they are following the extreme of too little; when they are angry and hostile, they are following the extreme of too much. When they use reason to keep vegetative and animal aspects in harmony, they are following the path for which they were designed and are fulfilling their purpose. This idea can be related to Plato's concept of the ideal state, in which the good state is one where all of its classes—that is, brass (vegetative), silver (animal), and gold (rational)—are in balance and harmony. Aristotle believed that a good education helps achieve the Golden Mean and thereby promotes the harmony and balance of soul and body.

Balance is central to Aristotle's view. He saw the whole universe in some balanced and orderly fashion. As far as humans are concerned, he did not view body and mind in opposition as Plato did; rather, he viewed body as the means by which data come to us through sense perception. The raw data of sense perception are organized by the reasoning of mind. Universal principles are derived by mind from an examination of the particulars by sense perception and from organizing the resulting observations into rational explanations. Thus, body and mind operate together in a balanced whole with their own internal consistencies.

Aristotle did not separate a particular thing from its universal being. Matter and form are not two different kinds of being, but fundamental aspects of the same thing. Form is in matter; formless matter is a false notion, not a reality. The important thing to see is that all matter is in some stage of actualization. Whereas Plato was primarily interested in the realm of forms or ideas, Aristotle tried to unite the world of matter with the world of forms. An example of this is his view of actuality and potentiality. Actuality is that which is complete and perfect—the form. Potentiality refers to the capability of being actualized or gaining perfection and form. It is the union of form and matter that gives concrete reality to things. In other words, an individual acorn contains form and matter that make up the "real" acorn that we experience.

This relationship between form and matter is illustrated further by Aristotle's conception of the Four Causes:

1. *The Material Cause:* the matter from which something is made.
2. *The Formal Cause:* the design that shapes the material object.
3. *The Efficient Cause:* the agent that produces the object.
4. *The Final Cause:* the direction toward which the object is tending.

In commonsense language, when talking about a house, the material it is made of (the wood, bricks, and nails) is its Material Cause; the sketch or blueprint followed in constructing it is its Formal Cause; the carpenter who builds it is its Efficient Cause; and its Final Cause is that it is a place in which to live, a house.

Matter is in process, moving to some end. In this respect, Aristotle's thought is similar to the modern view of evolution and the notion of an open-ended universe. The difference between Aristotle's view and this modern view is that Aristotle saw this movement headed toward a final end, so for him the universe is only so open ended. The power that holds all creation and process together is the Unmoved Mover (or God), by which Aristotle meant the power or source to which matter points beyond itself, an Ultimate Reality; hence, God is the First Cause, the Final End, the Unmoved Mover, beyond all matter and form. In this respect, Aristotle's philosophy is as esoteric as Plato's. Yet, for Aristotle, God is a logical explanation for the order of the universe—its organizational and operational principle.

Indeed, organization is essential to Aristotle's philosophy. He believed that everything can be organized into a hierarchy. For example, human beings are biologically based and rooted in nature; however, they strive for something beyond themselves. If they are characterized by body, they also are characterized by soul, or a rational aspect, or the capacity to move from within. If body and soul are balanced, they are also organized, and soul is of a higher order than body—more characteristically human than anything else. For Aristotle, human beings are the rational animals, most completely fulfilling their purpose when they think, for thinking is their highest characteristic. So it is, with Aristotle, that everything is capable of being ordered because reality, knowledge, and value exist independent of mind, with their own internal consistency and balance capable of being comprehended by mind.

To search out the structure of independent reality, Aristotle worked on logical processes. Plato used the dialectic to synthesize opposing notions about truth. Aristotle was concerned with truth, too, and he sought access to it through attempting to refine the dialectic. The logical method he developed was the *syllogism,* which is a method for testing the truth of statements. A famous but simplistic version of it goes as follows:

> All men are mortal.
>
> Socrates is a man;
>
> therefore, Socrates is mortal.

The syllogism is composed of a major premise, minor premise, and conclusion. Aristotle used the syllogism to help people think more accurately by ordering statements about reality in a logical, systematic form that corresponds to the facts of the situation under study.

Aristotle's logical method is deductive; that is, it derives its truth from generalizations, such as "All men are mortal." One problem with this method is that if either of the premises is false, the conclusion might be false. A catch comes in determining the truth of the premises: By what method do we test their accuracy? If we continue to use the syllogism, then we also must continue to rely on unproven general premises. Aristotle's logical method runs contrary to his insistence that we can better understand form (general principle) by studying specific material objects.

In this latter instance, Aristotle's thrust is inductive; that is, truth is found by way of specifics, or the process goes from specifics to the general. His syllogism, however, goes from generalizations (All men are mortal) to specific conclusions (Socrates is mortal). As some critics pointed out, the syllogistic approach can lead to many false or untenable positions. Not until the sixteenth century did Francis Bacon devise a different, more inductive approach.

The chief good for Aristotle is happiness; however, happiness depends on a virtuous and well-ordered soul. This can come about only as we develop habits of virtue that are shaped through the proper kind of education. Education necessitates the development of reasoning capacity so that we can make the right kinds of choices. As already indicated, this means the path of moderation. An acceptance and following of such a principle becomes the core of Aristotle's educational proposals. Although Aristotle did not go into specific detail about his educational ideas, he believed that the proper character would be formed by following the Golden Mean. This would result in desirable social development and would assist the state in producing and nurturing good citizens. In *Politics*, Aristotle further developed his view that a reciprocal relationship exists between the properly educated person and the properly educated citizen.

The Aristotelian influence has been immensely important and includes such things as recognizing the need to study nature systematically, using logical processes in examining the external world, deriving general truths through a rigorous study of particulars, organizing things into hierarchies, and emphasizing the rational aspects of human nature.

Religious Realism

Thomas Aquinas (1225–1274)

Thomas Aquinas was born near Naples, Italy, in 1225. His formal education began at age five when he was sent to the Benedictine monastery at Monte Cassino. Later, he studied at the University of Naples, and in 1244, he became a Dominican friar, dedicating his life to obedience, poverty, and intellectual toil. In 1245, Aquinas was sent to the University of Paris, where he studied under Albertus Magnus, a renowned scholar of Aristotelian philosophy. He studied and taught at the University of Paris until 1259, when the Dominicans sent him back to Italy to help organize the curriculum for Dominican schools. He returned to Paris in 1268 and served the remainder of his life as a professor of theology and as an educational leader for the Dominicans. He died on March 7, 1274.

Aquinas first encountered the work of Aristotle while studying in Naples. This began a lifelong passion of attempting to reconcile Aristotelian philosophy with Christian concepts. He accepted Aristotle's realistic view that humanity is a combination of matter and mind, or body and soul. Aristotle taught that a human is a natural being with a natural function but that our highest good comes through thinking. Aquinas connected this with the idea of Christian revelation and maintained that because we are children of God, our best thinking should agree with Christian tenets. He spent much of his intellectual life showing that the word of God as represented by revelation is consistent with the thinking of Aristotle.

Aristotle's ideas had a great impact on Christianity; in many respects, they have tended to encourage the secularization of the church, as opposed to the monasticism engendered by the writings of Augustine. Gradually, the ideas of Aristotle were incorporated into Christianity and provided it with a different philosophical base. Aquinas became the leading authority on Aristotle in the Middle Ages and found no great conflict between the ideas of the pagan philosopher and the ideas of Christian revelation. He argued that because God is pure reason, the universe is reason, and by using our reason, as Aristotle suggested, we could know the truth of things.

Aquinas also emphasized using our senses to obtain knowledge about the world; his proofs of God's existence, for example, depend heavily on sensory observation.

Aquinas believed that God created matter out of nothing and that God is, as Aristotle stated, the Unmoved Mover who gives meaning and purpose to the universe. In his monumental work *Summa Theologica*, Aquinas summed up the arguments dealing with Christianity and used the rational approach suggested by Aristotle in analyzing and dealing with various religious questions. As a matter of fact, many of the supporting arguments in Christian religion are derived from the work of Aquinas regardless of what branch of Christianity is considered. Roman Catholicism considers the philosophy of Thomas Aquinas (*Thomism*) to be its leading philosophy.

Aquinas was first of all a churchman. For him, all truths were eternally in God. Truth was passed from God to humans by divine revelation, but God also had endowed humans with the reasoning ability to seek out truth. Being the churchman that he was, Aquinas would not subordinate revelation to reason, but he did want to give reason a proper place. He viewed theology as the primary concern and philosophy as the "handmaiden of theology." Thus, by recognizing the supremacy of theology, he was able to explore more fully the philosophical development of religious thought.

Aquinas agreed with Aristotle that universals are determined by a study of particulars. He accepted the thesis of independence and "form" as the principal characteristic of all being. He upheld the "principle of immanence" that is akin to Aristotle's view of each existence moving toward perfection in form. Although he agreed that soul is the form of body, he held that soul is not derived from humanity's biological roots; rather, soul is a creation, immortal, and from God. Aquinas epitomized the *Scholasticism* of the Middle Ages, an approach that emphasized the human's eternal soul and salvation. The Scholastics integrated Aristotle's philosophy with the teachings of the church, and Aquinas fulfilled an important role in this task by working out the relationship between reason and faith.

The "Angelic Doctor," as Aquinas sometimes was called, was interested in education, as his work with the Dominicans indicates. In addition to the educational ideas in *Summa Theologica*, he also wrote *De Magistro (On the Teacher)*, which dealt specifically with his philosophy of teaching. For example, he questioned whether one human can teach another directly or whether the role of teaching is God's alone. His view was that only God should be called Teacher in the ultimate sense: If a person teaches, however, then teaching is accomplished (as Augustine pointed out at an earlier time) only by and through symbols. One human mind cannot communicate directly with the mind of another, but it can communicate indirectly.

It often is said that a physician heals the body; in truth, it is nature that heals from the inside, and all the physician can do is apply external treatments and inducements. So it is with teaching: Only God can touch the inside—the soul—directly. All the teacher can do is attempt to motivate and direct the learner through signs, symbols, and the techniques of encouragement. In other words, a teacher can only "point" the learner to knowledge and understanding with signs and symbols. Nevertheless, teaching is a way to serve humankind, and it is part of God's work in this world. Leading the student from ignorance to enlightenment is one of the greatest services one person can give to another.

Aquinas agreed with Augustine that humans are born with original sin and that life is a testing period, but he disagreed with the idea that we can know truth only through faith. Aquinas believed that God is pure reason and that when God created the world, He made it possible for us to acquire true knowledge by studying the world through the use of observation and reason. God gave us reason so that we could know Him better and discern the true purpose and meaning of life. Aquinas believed that faith might be used for things humans cannot yet understand but that ultimately all religious truths can be understood and reaffirmed through reason. He also believed that most things already could be proved through reason, such as God's existence, and that faith was necessary only when reason had reached its limits.

In *Summa Theologica*, Aquinas debated the primary questions that faced Christian thought and used Aristotelian philosophy to provide insight into such questions. Both Augustine and Aquinas helped fuse the Middle Eastern religious beliefs of Judaism and Christianity with Western philosophical traditions derived from Plato and Aristotle.

Central to the thought of Aquinas was the Judeo-Christian belief that each person is born with an immortal soul. Continuing the thought of Platonic idealism as well as Aristotelian realism, he maintained that the soul possesses an inner knowledge that can be brought out to illuminate one's life more completely. The major goal of education, as Aquinas saw it, is the perfection of the human being and the ultimate reunion of the soul with God. To accomplish this, we must develop the capacities to reason and to exercise intelligence.

Here, Aquinas's realism came to the forefront because he held that human reality is not only spiritual or mental but also physical and natural. From the standpoint of the human teacher, the path to the soul lies through the physical senses; education must use this path to accomplish learning. Proper instruction directs the learner to knowledge that leads to true being by progressing from a lower to a higher form. This illustrates Aquinas's Aristotelianism because his view includes a developmental cosmology of progressing from the lower to the higher, or movement toward perfection.

Aquinas's views on education are consistent with his philosophical position. Knowledge can be gained from sense data, and it can lead one to God, provided the learner views it in the proper perspective. In essence, he believed that one should proceed from the study of matter to the study of form. He disagreed with Augustine that we could know God only through faith or some intuitive process; rather, Aquinas maintained that humans could use their reason to reach God through a study of the material world. Thus, he saw no inconsistency between the truths of revelation accepted on faith and the truths arrived at through careful, rational observation and study. Aquinas believed that a proper education is one that fully recognizes the spiritual and material nature of the individual. Because he thought that the spiritual side was the higher and more important, Aquinas was strongly in favor of primary emphasis on the education of the soul.

In the view of Aquinas, the primary agencies of education are the family and the church; the state—or organized society—runs a poor third. The family and the church have an obligation to teach those things that relate to the unchanging principles of moral and divine law. According to Aquinas, the mother is the child's first teacher, and because the child is molded easily, it is the mother's role to set the child's moral tone.

The church stands as the source of knowledge of the divine and should set the grounds for understanding God's law. The state should formulate and enforce laws on education, but it should not abridge the educational primacy of the home and church.

Aristotle and Aquinas held to a dualistic doctrine of reality. This can be seen in Aristotle's view of matter and form and in Aquinas's view of the material and spiritual sides of humankind. This dualism was carried on later in the great conflict between scientific and religious views of reality.

DEVELOPMENT OF MODERN REALISM

One chief problem of classical realism was its failure to develop an adequate method of inductive thinking. Although classicists had developed the thesis that reality, knowledge, and value can be ascertained by studying particulars, they still were caught in an essentially deductive style of thinking. They often had their truths in hand at the start, never really doubting a First Cause or an Unmoved Mover. Modern realism developed out of attempts to correct such errors, and these corrective attempts were at the heart of what today is called the scientific revolution that swept Western culture. Of all the philosophers engaged in this effort, perhaps the two most outstanding realist thinkers were Francis Bacon and John Locke. Both were involved in developing systematic methods of thinking and ways to increase human understanding.

Francis Bacon (1561–1626)

Francis Bacon was not only a philosopher but also a politician in the courts of Elizabeth I and James I. He was not successful in his political efforts (he was removed from office in disgrace), yet his record in philosophical development is much more impressive. Bacon's philosophical task was ambitious, if not pretentious, in scope. He claimed to take all knowledge as his field of investigation. That he nearly accomplished this is testimony to his genius. Perhaps his most famous work is *Novum Organum*, in which he challenged Aristotelian logic.

Bacon attacked the Aristotelians for contributing to the lethargic development of science by their adoption of theological methods of thought. The problem with theology was that it started with dogmatisms and *a priori* assumptions and then deduced conclusions. Bacon charged that science could not proceed this way because science must be concerned with inquiry pure and simple—inquiry not burdened with preconceived notions. Bacon held that science must begin in this fashion and must develop reliable methods of inquiry. By developing a reliable method of inquiry, humans could be freed from dependence on the occurrence of infrequent geniuses and could develop knowledge through the use of effective methods of inquiry. Bacon believed that "knowledge is power" and that through the acquisition of knowledge, we could deal more effectively with the problems and forces that beset us on every side. To accomplish these things, he devised what he called the "inductive method."

Bacon opposed Aristotelian logic primarily because he thought that it yielded many errors, particularly concerning material phenomena. For example, religious thinkers (such as Aquinas and the Scholastics) accepted certain axiomatic beliefs about God—that He exists, is just, is all powerful, and so forth—and then they deduced all sorts of things about the use of God's power, His intervention in human affairs, and so on. Bacon's inductive approach, which suggests beginning with observable instances and then reasoning to general statements or laws, counteracts the Scholastic approach because it demands verification of specific instances before a judgment is made.

After observing instances of water freezing at 32° Fahrenheit, for example, a general law might be stated that water freezes at 32° Fahrenheit. This law is valid, however, only so long as water continues to freeze at that temperature. If, because of a change in atmospheric or terrestrial conditions, water no longer freezes at 32° Fahrenheit, then the law must be changed. People also can alter their beliefs through deduction, but they are less likely to change their beliefs when they begin with supposedly absolute truths than when they begin with neutral data and hypotheses.

A historical example of this involved the dispute between Galileo and the Catholic Church about the position of Earth in the solar system. The Church defended the Ptolemaic theory that Earth is the center of the universe and the other celestial bodies, including the sun, revolve around it. This position was supported by several deductions. To begin with, because God created Earth, it was reasonable to assume that He would place it in the center. Also, because God chose to place humans on Earth, Earth must have had an important place in the plan of creation; this gives added weight to the importance of Earth being centrally located. The story in the Bible about Joshua fighting a difficult battle and asking God to make the sun stand still seemed to give even more support to this position.

Galileo, however, argued for the Copernican theory that the sun and not Earth is the center of the universe because Earth rotates on its axis and revolves about the sun. The position of Nicolaus Copernicus (as set forth in *The Revolutions of the Heavenly Bodies*) was interpreted by the Church as belittling Earth and God's plan, and was incompatible with the veracity of revelation. Galileo's use of a telescope to give empirical proof to the Copernican position increased the wrath of the Church. Reportedly, a priest who had been invited into Galileo's study to look through the telescope for proof claimed that the devil was putting those things there for him to see. Church officials required that Galileo refute his position, yet such scientists as Johann Kepler, Tycho Brahe, and Isaac Newton later substantiated his work in whole or in part.

Because the scientific or inductive approach uncovered many errors in propositions that were taken for granted originally, Bacon urged that people should reexamine all previously accepted knowledge. At the least he believed, we should attempt to rid their minds of various "idols" before which they bow down and that cloud their thinking. Bacon described four such idols:

1. *Idol of the Den:* People believe things because of their own limited experiences. If, for example, a woman had several bad experiences with men with mustaches, she might conclude that all mustached men are bad, a clear case of faulty generalization.
2. *Idol of the Tribe:* People tend to believe things because most people believe them. Numerous studies show that many people change their opinions to match those of the majority.

3. *Idol of the Marketplace:* This idol deals with language because Bacon believed that words often are used in ways that prevent understanding. For instance, such words as *liberal* and *conservative* might have little meaning when applied to people because a person could be liberal on one issue and conservative on another.

4. *Idol of the Theatre:* This is the idol of our religions and philosophies, which might prevent us from seeing the world objectively. Bacon called for a house-keeping of the mind, in which we should break away from the dead ideas of the past and begin again by using the method of induction.

Induction is the logic of arriving at generalizations on the basis of systematic observations of particulars. The general thrust of this view can be found in Aristotle, but Aristotle never developed it into a complete system. According to Bacon, induction involves the collection of data about particulars, but it is not merely a cataloging and enumeration of data. The data must be examined; where contradictions are found, some ideas must be discarded. In addition, facts must be processed or interpreted at the same time. Bacon maintained that if the inductive method were well developed and rigorously applied, it would benefit us to the extent that it would give humans more control over the external world by unlocking the secrets of nature.

John Locke (1632–1704)

Following Bacon's lead, John Locke sought to explain how we develop knowledge. He attempted a rather modest philosophical task: to "clear the ground of some of the rubbish" that hindered people's gaining knowledge. In this respect, he was attempting to rid thought of what Bacon called idols.

Locke was born in England, the son of a country lawyer. He was educated at Westminster School and at Christ Church College at Oxford, where he was later a fellow. His education was classical and scholastic. He later turned on this tradition, attacking its Aristotelian roots and its Scholastic penchant for disputations, which he thought were mere wrangling and ostentation.

Locke's contributions to realism were his investigations into the extent and certainty of human knowledge. He traced the origin of ideas to the object of thought, or whatever the mind entertains. For Locke, there are no such things as innate ideas. At birth, the mind is like a blank sheet of paper, a *tabula rasa,* on which ideas are imprinted. Thus, all knowledge is acquired from sources independent of the mind or as a result of reflection on data from independent sources. In other words, all ideas are derived from experience by way of sensation and reflection.

Locke did not overly concern himself with the nature of mind itself but concentrated on how ideas or knowledge are gained by mind. External objects exist, he argued, and they are characterized by two kinds of qualities: primary qualities (for example, solidity, size, and motion) and secondary qualities (for example, color, taste, smell, sound, and other "sense" qualities). Primary qualities can be called *objective* (adhering or directly connected with the object), and secondary qualities can be called *subjective* (dependent on people experiencing them).

Locke was an empiricist. He respected the concrete and practical but distrusted abstract idealisms; consequently, what we know is what we experience. People experience the qualities of objects, whether these are material or ideational qualities. The data with which the mind operates are *experienced* data, and although they come from without, mind can combine and order experience and can become aware of its operations. Thus, knowledge depends on sensation *and* reflection.

Concerning the nature of the external objective world, Locke had little to say. He basically assumed its existence, and he explained this existence with the *doctrine of substance;* that is, substance or external reality is a necessary support for experience. Thus, he assumed an independent reality but did not try to prove it. His major contribution to philosophy was the development of an acute awareness of experience. Rather than speculation about innate ideas or essences or an independent material reality, his field of investigation was human experience and human knowledge.

Locke's views on education, as expressed in *Some Thoughts Concerning Education*, are not as theoretical as his speculations on epistemology. They are practical ideas about conduct, laziness, rewards and punishments, and other generalities in the educational process. Locke's ideas led to the kind of "gentlemanly" education for which English education is noted. One might argue that despite Locke's philosophical penchant for democracy, his educational ideas lend themselves to an aristocratic elitism.

CONTEMPORARY REALISM

For the most part, contemporary realism has tended to develop most strongly around concerns with science and scientific problems of a philosophical nature. This movement occurred mostly in the twentieth century and has been associated with the development of such new schools of thought as logical positivism and linguistic analysis. Yet, within this development the basic thesis of independence continued.

Two outstanding figures in twentieth-century realism were Alfred North Whitehead and Bertrand Russell. These men had much in common, including the fact that both were English and they collaborated on mathematical writings. Eventually, they both came to teach in some outstanding universities in the United States and were interested in and wrote about education. With all of this in common, they went in different philosophical directions. Whitehead's direction was almost Platonic in his search for universal patterns; Russell went toward mathematical quantification and verification as the basis of philosophical generalization.

In addition to the works of Whitehead and Russell, the philosophy of realism has continued to develop, and two exponents in the late twentieth and early twenty-first centuries are the American philosophers Hilary Putnam and John R. Searle. Putnam, who has a background in mathematics and philosophy, is a professor emeritus of philosophy at Harvard University. Searle is a professor of philosophy at the University of California at Berkeley.

Alfred North Whitehead (1861–1947)

One of the most fruitful things creative philosophers do is bring about reconciliation between contending systems of thought. Aquinas did this when he reconciled Aristotelianism with Christianity. Kant did this in trying to reconcile science and traditional values. Whitehead sought to do this by attempting to reconcile some aspects of idealism with realism, thereby reconstructing the philosophical bases of modern science.

Alfred North Whitehead came to philosophy through mathematics. He coauthored with Russell a work entitled *Principia Mathematica.* He was past age 60 when he turned to philosophy on a full-time basis as a professor of philosophy at Harvard. One of his outstanding philosophical treatises is *Science and the Modern World*, and some of his major statements on education can be found in *The Aims of Education and Other Essays.*

Process is central to Whitehead's philosophy because he held that reality *is* process. A person encounters in this process actual entities or *occasions* (the real "things" or objects), *prehensions* (relational processes between the experiencing person and experienced objects), and *nexus* (extended time sequences in which occasions and prehensions fit together in ongoing existence).

In many respects, Whitehead sought to unite philosophical oppositions, such as subjective perception and objective entities, and he believed that people must recognize both aspects. He rejected a bifurcated reality yet recognized the individuality of a thing in itself and the relational or universal aspects of things. He objected to going too far in one direction to the detriment of the other direction. He rejected the separation of the mental into a realm by itself because mental activity had to be viewed in the context of experience. He preferred realism as a philosophy because he thought it helped people correct the excesses of subjective thought.

It might appear that Whitehead rejected the thesis of independence. This is true to the degree that he did not see objective reality and subjective mind as absolutely separate. They are together in an organized unity or pattern. Yet, at the same time, this organic unity itself can be seen as an active system, an ultimate reality so to speak, that operates according to its own principles in process. Philosophy is simply a search for pattern in the universe. Humans can never grasp pattern in any complete sense although they may get aspects of it. Ultimately, the universe does have rationality to it and is not mere arbitrariness.

We might say that Whitehead was following solidly in the footsteps of Aristotle because it is apparent that pattern in Whitehead's terms is similar to form. He also followed Aristotle in going to particulars to discern pattern, yet he deviated because he held that particulars are events that have to be viewed in terms of an open-ended process. Thus, his events are not inert particulars but are organic to, and moving with, process and according to pattern.

This brings us to a consideration of Whitehead's view of education. To him, the important things to be learned are ideas. In this sense, one can say that he was Platonic. He was adamant in urging that education be concerned with "living ideas," but ideas connected with the experience of learners—ideas that are useful and capable of being articulated. He warned against learning inert ideas simply because it was done in the past. This shows his organic orientation that education should enable people to get into the flow of existence and the process-patterns of reality.

Bertrand Russell (1872–1970)

Bertrand Russell was born in Wales in comfortable economic circumstances. He received his degree in philosophy and mathematics at Cambridge University. One of the first-rate minds of the twentieth century, Russell exerted considerable influence as a writer and a teacher. Some of his books are *Our Knowledge of the External World*, *Religion and Science*, and the famous work he coauthored with Whitehead, *Principia Mathematica* (1910–1913). In the field of education, he wrote *Education and the Social Order* and *Education and the Modern World*, as well as other books. He taught at Cambridge, the University of Chicago, and the University of California in addition to other places.

Russell was a controversial figure. During World War I, he was imprisoned for his pacifist activities. His distaste for Victorian morality, especially his views on sex and marriage, often led him into conflict with others. In the 1960s, he was at the center of the "Ban the Bomb" movement and anti–Vietnam War protests in England and Europe. Russell was a maverick realist in some respects. Where Whitehead concluded that the universe is characterized by pattern, so did Russell, but Russell believed that these patterns can be verified with precision and be analyzed mathematically. There is a need, he held, to merge the logical and mathematical so that pattern can be discerned verbally (or semantically) and mathematically.

Russell held that the role of philosophy is analytic and synthetic; that is, it should be critical in its analytic phase by showing the logical fallacies and errors in past systems, and it should be constructive in its synthetic phase by offering hypotheses about the nature of the universe that science has not yet determined. Russell believed, however, that philosophy should be mainly analytic and that it should base itself on science because only science has any genuine claim to knowledge. From the standpoint of science, one can see Russell's adherence to realism and what has been called the thesis of independence. It was not so much the results of science as the methods that he accepted. By using these methods, he hoped to arrive at valid philosophical constructions—not constructions of large generalization, but rather piecemeal, detailed, verifiable constructions.

One could get two sorts of particular data on independent reality: hard data and soft data. *Hard data* are the facts of the situation—facts that can withstand the scrutiny of reflection and remain intact. *Soft data* are such things as beliefs that can be neither verified nor denied with any degree of certainty. Russell's stated purpose was to base his philosophical constructions as much as possible on the hard and verifiable side (the side of science), but he also recognized the soft side. This, he held, should make us more sensitive to over-generalizing and its accompanying dangers of arriving at false certainties.

By using a cautious or more temperate approach to science, Russell hoped that we could begin to solve such perplexing problems as poverty and ill health. He thought of education as the key to a better world. If people would use existing knowledge and apply tested methods, then through education they could eradicate such problems as poverty and thus transform the world. Russell even speculated that if this were done on a wide scale, the transformation could conceivably be accomplished in just one generation.

For a time, Russell tried to put some of his educational ideas to work at the school he founded called Beacon Hill. However, his radicalism met resistance, and his own driving inquisitiveness soon led him to other causes and reforms. Although his efforts in education at Beacon Hill met with limited success, Russell continued to the end of his life to try to bring about changes through education that he deemed beneficial to humanity.

Hilary Putnam (1926–)

Hilary Putnam has attempted to construct a variant form of realism he calls "internal realism" in *Reason, Truth, and History* in 1981. He has refined it in such later works as *The Many Faces of Realism*, *Realism with a Human Face*, and *Words and Life*. Putnam embraces a view of philosophy along the following lines: In our attempts to understand ourselves and the world, philosophy becomes the education of grown-ups. He also has said that if a philosophy can be put into a nutshell, then it belongs in one. With that admonition in mind, what follows is but a brief overview of some central elements of Putnam's work.

As Putnam sees it in *Realism with a Human Face*, the tradition of realism influenced by the physics of Newton in the seventeenth century saw the universe as a giant machine, a view that gave people a "God's-eye view" of the whole universe. Humans were tiny subsystems in that machine but still capable of engaging the totality in their thought processes, reminiscent of Descartes' *cogito*. Science has continued to affect realism, and in the twentieth century, physicists in the field of quantum mechanics introduced a "cut" between the observer and the universe; that is, the universe is so complex that the human mind is incapable of comprehending the totality in one big picture. We are forced to see the universe as observers dependent on the theoretical apparatuses used to measure the universe in experimental situations; hence, we get a wave picture (as in electromagnetic wave theory), a particle picture (as in atomic theory), and so forth. From this perspective, a God's-eye view of the universe is simply not possible.

When Russell and Whitehead attempted to develop a totalistic symbolic language (a God's-eye view of logic and language) in *Principia Mathematica*, they attempted to generalize about particular languages from the standpoint of an ideal language standing on the outside. It was as if they thought that armed with an ideal language, they could bring order and logical clarity to a bewildering diversity. Despite their brilliant efforts, their project met with failure. According to Putnam, what came out of such failures in modern philosophy is the view that *if* people cannot take a God's-eye view, *then* two important traditional branches of philosophical study are dead: *metaphysics* (theory of ultimate reality) and *epistemology* (theory of knowledge). Among the outgrowths of this perception are a turn toward relativism and deconstruction, and the development of a new movement in philosophy called *post-modernism*. Putnam thinks that these are "anti-realist" views and are neither correct nor the only alternatives.

Putnam himself is critical of metaphysical realism, and he rejects the claims that (1) the world consists of a fixed totality of objects independent of the human mind, (2) there is only one true description of that independent world, and (3) truth involves correspondence of what we say about that world with the way the world really is. In *Representation and Reality*, Putnam summarizes what he calls "internal" realism (or sometimes "pragmatic" realism). He accepts the commonsense view that stars exist and are not created by language (or mind) but can be described by language. Thus, an "objective" reality exists, but it must be understood in the sense of "conceptual relativity." For example, suppose you take a friend into a room furnished with a chair and a table with a lamp, a notebook, and a pen. You ask her, "How many objects are in the room?" She replies, "Five. A chair, a table, a lamp, a notebook, and a pen." You might add, "How about you and me; aren't we also objects in the room?" Your friend would likely agree, but if you took it to other levels, such as asking how many pages are in the notebook or how many molecules are in the lamp and are they also objects in the room, your friend would likely think that you were playing a joke on her. In Putnam's view, people's notions of "object" depend on the circumstances of the situation and what we mean by the word, our "conceptual scheme" so to speak. Thus, conceptual relativity is needed; that is, what is meant by *object* depends on (is relative to) the conceptual scheme with which we approach the "objective" world. According to Putnam, the error of metaphysical realism, particularly scientific realism, has been to assume that a single system of organisms and their physical environment as determined or discovered by science contain all the objects to which anyone could refer. For Putnam, people may invent creative new uses of words so that what is meant by the term *object* is not fixed once and for all as reality.

In *The Many Faces of Realism*, Putnam argues that by conceptual relativity, he does not mean that "anything goes," a vulgar relativism that sinks into solipsism and absolute subjectivity. Putnam maintains that, indeed, some facts in the world are not invented by language or mental representations; rather, when talking about "facts," people need to understand the "conceptual scheme," meaning the language people use to describe them.

Putnam's philosophical journey has led him closer to pragmatism and the ideas of William James and John Dewey, although he still identifies primarily with realism.

John R. Searle (1932–)

John Searle accepts the traditional realist view that an external world exists independent of human consciousness and that the truth of statements about that world is dependent on how well those statements correspond to the external world. Searle's interests have drawn him to explain social reality or how an objective reality of marriage, money, government, sports, cocktail parties, and universities can exist in a world made up entirely of physical particles and fields of force. In *The Construction of Social Reality*, he argues against the modern tendency to interpret all reality claims as nothing more than human creations in which there are no "brute facts" but only constructions of the human mind. Indeed, social reality is created by the conscious and intentional acts of human organisms for their own convenience, but consciousness has a biological and physical base in the nervous system or brain. Searle believes that if people accept the fact of a biologically and physically based consciousness, then they will see no separation between mind and body.

For Searle, reality can be approached from at least two angles: brute facts and social facts. It is brute fact that Mt. McKinley has ice and rock on its upper elevations, but it is social fact that people can write poetry about the beauty of the mountain or pass laws that protect the environment of the mountain. Social reality is anchored in the natural or physical world, but it also has mental or conscious dimensions. For example, money is a brute fact as a printed piece of paper, a coin stamped in metal, or even an electronic blip in a computer memory bank, but it is also a conscious and intentional symbolic representation invented for human convenience as a medium of exchange to buy goods and services. As such, it is a social or "institutional" fact.

Hence, Searle distinguishes between the features of the world that are facts of physics and biology and those that are facts of society and culture. *Brute facts* are independent of social institutions, whereas *social facts* exist only within social institutions or social relationships that are themselves factual. *Social reality* is anchored in the brute factual reality of the physical universe because it is created by biological human organisms that have the capacity to (1) assign functions to brute existences, (2) engage in individual and collective conscious intentionality regarding the status and value of those functions, and (3) develop constitutive rules regarding them. *Intentionality* refers to the capacity of the human mind to represent (or symbolize) for itself the things and conditions of the external world that are other than itself. This makes it possible to have a conscious mental life. For example, humans can shape pieces of wood into functional objects called (in English) "desks" and "chairs." As such, desks and chairs do not exist only as lumps of wood (brute natural objects), but as functional objects intentionally created by humans to serve their needs. We can have thoughts and carry on conversations about their experiences of the world in symbolic form, and they can shape parts of that external world to their own purposes, such as taking natural materials and making them into cooking utensils, tools, computers, and life-saving medications.

As Searle sees it, social objects made from brute nature, such as chairs or paper money, can wear out with use, but social facts, such as institutions, do not wear out in the same sense. Social reality also must be seen as "institutional facts." Each time people use an institution, the use seems to renew it rather than wear it out. For example, people once used the barter system as a means of economic exchange, but money proved to be a more convenient mode of economic life. Far beyond the physical bits of paper or metal that wear out, the social function of money became consciously and intentionally institutionalized by users. The greater convenience of using money renewed and even strengthened the economic institution of money. The same can be said of schools because their significance lies not as physical objects (for example, buildings, campuses), but as social institutions that have a high functional value. The school institution is renewed with use when each use fulfills conscious intentions, and this renews human commitment to the institution.

According to Searle, an essential ingredient of social reality is language because language is how we constitute reality through *symbolization* and *representation*. We can examine the biological world and see that animals such as bees or ants have social life, but human social life is much more complex because humans can use language to represent or symbolize not only the things of the external world, but also the things of internal conscious thought and feeling. Of course, humans can have thoughts without language, but they are rather primitive biological inclinations and cognitions; through language, people constitute institutional facts that make up so much of social reality. *Institutional facts* exist only through linguistic devices that constitute them. A piece of paper, in and of itself, cannot be money unless people believe that it is—that is, unless people constitute it as such through assigning function, status, and operative rules. Language makes this possible, but it brings in no mysterious, otherworldly, "subjective" reality because language and institutions can be studied as objective factual conditions themselves.

REALISM AS A PHILOSOPHY OF EDUCATION

Realism is a complex philosophy because of its many varieties: classical realism, religious realism, scientific realism, and others. This confusion dates back to Aristotle because although his prominence in philosophy was primarily derived from his differences with Platonic philosophy, probably more similarities than differences exist overall between Plato and Aristotle. The primary confusion over realism could be between a religious realism and a secular or scientific realism. Religious realism would show how similar Aristotle's philosophy is to that of Plato and Aquinas; secular realism would relate Aristotle's work more to the development of scientific philosophy through the works of Bacon, Locke, and Russell. Whitehead can be said to incorporate aspects of each in his interpretation of realism.

Aims of Education

Plato, as an idealist, believed that such abstractions as truth, goodness, and beauty could be reached only through a study of ideas, primarily through the use of the dialectic. Aristotle, in contrast, believed that ideas (forms) also are found by studying the world of matter. Plato and Aristotle end up at the same place, but their methods of getting there are different. Plato believed that one acquires knowledge of ideas through contemplation of ideas; Aristotle believed that one could acquire knowledge of ideas or forms through a study of matter. Whereas Plato rejected matter as an object of study or as a real entity, Aristotle used matter as an object of study to reach something further.

For the religious realist, matter is not important in itself unless it leads to something beyond itself. Aristotle recognized that one may look at any object simply as a scientific study, but this would be dealing only with one aspect of matter. A scientist finding a rock in a creek bank may examine it descriptively in terms of size, shape, weight, and so on. Such concerns, however, should also lead to philosophical questions relating to the beginnings and purpose of the rock. This process is illustrated by contemporary scientific efforts to study the moon. Specimens brought back by the astronauts are studied intensively. Many photographs and television compositions have been made on the natural makeup of the moon, but these have not been made simply to catalog its shape, size, and weight; rather, the purpose has been much deeper. Scientists and thinkers of various disciplines are interested in discovering knowledge about the very origins of our universe. This shows that scientific inquiry can lead to the most profound and ultimate kinds of philosophical questions. Thus, one can transcend nature and use it to venture into the realm of ideas.

For the religious realist, the prime reason for the study of nature is to transcend matter. The argument might run thusly: God, who is pure spirit, created the world. He created it out of nothing, but He put himself into the world, giving it order, regularity, and design. By studying the world carefully and by discovering its order and regularity, we can come to know more about God. Religious realists, such as Aquinas, would say that this is our prime purpose: God created the world to provide a vehicle through which people could come to know Him. Thomists maintain that the curriculum should include practical and speculative knowledge. For example, education helps the individual become self-aware so that one can think about one's actions. Through the practical study of ethics, one is led to the higher plain of ultimate reality, or metaphysics. Thomists believe that true education is always in process and never becomes complete; it is a process of the continuing development of the human soul.

Many thinkers (not necessarily philosophical realists) have believed that nature could provide us with something greater than itself. William Wordsworth, Ralph Waldo Emerson, and Henry David Thoreau, all nineteenth-century romanticists, used the theme that nature could be transcended by thought and that individuals could venture into higher realms of thought. Religious realists believe that this kind of transcending should be the principal aim of education.

Secular realists, in contrast, emphasize the sensory material world and its processes and patterns, rather than the transcendent spiritual world to which sensory data might lead. Their approach is basically scientific. The scientific movement beginning with Bacon ushered in an era of thought that stressed not only an understanding of the material world but control of it as well. Aristotle pointed out the order and regularity of the material world; by this same process, scientists came to talk about the laws of nature.

Secular realism stresses an understanding of the material world through the development of methods of rigorous inquiry. Bacon first suggested that people should clear their minds of the idols of generalization, language, and philosophy. Deduction, which was the prevailing method of thought prior to Bacon, was based primarily on rational thought. Reason alone, however, had led to many errors in Aristotle's thinking and to the metaphysical extravagances of the Scholastics. It was reason, no matter how ill concealed, that produced such imaginings as mermaids, devils, centaurs, and the like. For the secular realist, the way out of this dilemma—that is, deciding which ideas are true—is to verify these ideas in the world of experience.

Locke gave great support to Bacon's empiricism by showing that no ideas are innate but that through reflection or reason we can create ideas, such as the idea of a purple cow, that do not exist in the world of experience. The empirical movement that Bacon and Locke encouraged requires that ideas be subject to public verification. This means ideas that cannot be proved through scientific experiment must be considered only as hypotheses.

Secular realists promote a study of science and the scientific method. They believe that people need to know the world in order to use it to ensure their own survival. This idea of survival is an important one. For example, Herbert Spencer, the nineteenth-century British philosopher and social scientist, placed self-preservation as a primary and fundamental aim of education. In other words, the things children most need to know are those things that maintain their existence as individuals, as family members, and as citizens. The secular realist sees human control over nature as a vast improvement from our early beginnings when we were at the mercy of nature. Human misunderstanding of nature, such as the superstitious explanations for typhoons and floods, led to many false beliefs. Today, continued advancement depends on an even greater understanding and control of nature. Technical skill got humans into the ecological mess, but the secular realist would add that it also can get us out of it.

Secular realism maintains that essential ideas and facts can best be learned only by a study of the material world. It places great stress on the study of basic facts for the purpose of survival and for the advancement of technology and science. One could say that technical schools, such as the Massachusetts Institute of Technology, are realist in their approach to education. The former Soviet Union seemed to prefer this approach to education for technical and political purposes. In the United States, support has been strong for a more technical and scientific education since the launching of *Sputnik* in 1957. Many education critics at the time, such as Admiral Hyman Rickover, argued that American education had become too "soft," dealing with "fads and frills," and that education needed to return to basic studies, like mathematics and science.

Realism as an educational philosophy has long been with us in one way or another, but it tends to assert itself most in times of turmoil. It is almost as if people have other educational philosophies when they can afford them, but realism is a necessity. The claim is that people always will have some need for basic factual data and such subjects as reading, writing, and arithmetic.

This desire to return to realism was particularly strong after the Soviets launched their first satellite. Many people believed that the U.S.'s second-place technical position in this respect was in large measure a result of schools not teaching enough basic subject matter, particularly in science and mathematics. Rickover pointed to the dearth of competent scientists in this country as compared with the Soviet Union. He also praised Swiss education for its adherence to basics and believed that the American system should do likewise. He laid much of the blame for our lack of technical know-how and creativity at the door of John Dewey and the progressives, who were promoting an education that Rickover thought was not only superficial but also dangerous in terms of our survival. An even more caustic critic was Max Rafferty, whose book *Suffer Little Children* was extremely popular and who believed that basic subject matter and other staples of American education, such as a concern for religion, patriotism, and capitalism, were being neglected.

A group of educators who were greatly concerned with the decline of basic subject matter in American schools formed an organization called the Council for Basic Education. This organization has fought strenuously to keep and add basic subject matter in schools—not only the three R's (reading, writing, and arithmetic) but also such subjects as science and history. A leading spokesperson for this council at that time, James Koerner, believed that part of the problem lay in the training of teachers, who were given survey courses instead of more basic studies and who came to the classroom intellectually impoverished.

A major problem, according to the realists, is a general cultural malaise caused by a lack of commitment to fundamental values. This is shown in the breakdown of discipline and disregard for basic traditions. Perhaps the best illustration of this is the fact that schools have drifted away from a concentration on the essentials of reading, writing, arithmetic, and character development.

The "open education" movement, which gained attention in the late 1960s and early 1970s, is an example of this drift. Rather than have students study essential but not always exciting subjects, a do-your-own-thing ethic was instituted in which students were encouraged to explore and discover things that interested them personally. This created a problem, many realists charge, because children seldom have clearly identified interests with enough focus to direct their needed educational development. In addition, they do not always know what is best for them or what they need, and this is confirmed by adults who in later life claim that such educational approaches failed to prepare them for the real world. Perhaps the crowning evidence of the failure of "discovery" and "open" approaches, realists argued, was the embarrassing number of high school graduates who were functionally illiterate.

The breakdown of commitment to basic cultural values is not limited to education but is reflected in the larger society. In the 1960s and 1970s, the confusion surrounding the Vietnam War and the U.S. role in it was but one example. Today, democracy depends as much on public debate of issues as ever before, but many realists think that the willingness of organized society to allow young adults to rebel against authority when the country is engaged in international competition continues to reflect the extent of the breakdown and the failure of education to secure allegiance to basic knowledge and values.

Another illustration of the realist charge that schools have long ignored basic values was the Watergate scandal in the early 1970s, in which government officials, including the president, were involved in a cover-up of illegal and unethical political activities. Continuing scandals at the highest levels of government and society show that this problem is still with Americans. Critics point out that the people involved in such scandals all went through American schools, yet the schools apparently failed to instill those character traits and basic values necessary for ethical conduct and leadership.

This failure can be seen not only at the local and national levels but also in international affairs. Many critics point to the erosion of America's political, economic, and military power. Americans have been held hostage at times by weak foreign governments, and the United States has been virtually powerless to act. Probably most frustrating of all are those occasions when American economic power, a much-vaunted strength in the past, is at the mercy of small nations that control energy resources. Many nations have viewed education as a weapon to achieve economic, political, and military power, and critics wonder why Americans do not use this resource now by showing a commitment to education through an expansion of funds and programs, rather than the budgetary restraints that are currently fashionable.

Some realists argue that the talent of our most precious resource—the intellectually gifted—is being squandered. "Watered down" courses and "fads and frills" have limited the development of superior students by bringing them down to the level of the common denominator. Textbooks reflect this in their simplified reading material and content geared to the mythical average student. Instead of pulling students up to their academic capabilities, such practices only pull them down to an accepted average.

Modern exponents of a classical realist outlook have championed an approach called the Great Books of the Western World, an approach also embraced by some idealists. First articulated by such figures as Robert Hutchins and Mortimer Adler, this approach stresses understanding knowledge that has been passed down through the ages. Thus, the curriculum should be organized around those great works that, though some may be centuries old, still present fundamental knowledge about individual and social existence, human institutions, intellectual and moral endeavor, and the natural order. St. John's College at Annapolis has such a program in operation and is a good example of the kind of education that advocates of classical realism would favor. At St. John's, students read the classics, analyze them, and then apply them to better understand current problems. Students also are encouraged to read such modern writers as William Faulkner and Ernest Hemingway and even recent contemporary writers as supplementary readings. The emphasis in classical and modern readings, however, is on universal truths that are germane to people in all times and places.

Following this line of reason, one proposal for educational reform that has elicited much interest since 1982 is *The Paideia Proposal* by Adler on behalf of the members of the Paideia Group. In this proposal, the basic recommendations are (1) that schooling be a one-track system and (2) that it be general, nonspecialized, and nonvocational. Although Adler gave due consideration to skills (such as problem solving) and to subjects (such as mathematics, history, geography, and social studies), he also placed a strong emphasis on ideas found in philosophy, literature, and art. This gives Adler's views an idealistic tint, but he argued that this body of knowledge is an independent reality that students need to know. For Adler, all students should encounter these great ideas, and the best way of teaching them is through the Socratic (*maieutic*) method of questions and answers. Adler's approach to education harkens back to classical Greece and the philosophy of Aristotle.

Adler's proposals, although at first receiving a great deal of attention from the press, have not resulted in major educational reforms so far. Many educators maintain that Adler promotes an elitist conception of education whereby only intelligent students are able to master the material with any real depth. Another criticism has been that this is just another form of a back-to-the-basics movement. In *Paideia Problems and Possibilities*, a sequel to *The Paideia Proposal*, Adler argued that although there are some similarities to a back-to-the-basics movement, one difference is that the Paideia approach emphasizes a discussion approach that generally is not used in teaching the basics. In response to the charge of being elitist, Adler claimed that his approach to learning was designed for all students, not just those who are college bound.

Critics of "basic education" consider its advocates as alarmists crying wolf and say that the basics approach to education looks back to the American schools of a bygone era. These critics assert that basic education is a conservative approach, a realism more interested in facts than in multicultural understanding, creativity, and human relationships. Many educators maintain that facts can be taught in a pleasant atmosphere without the rote-style education associated with realism. Realists respond by saying that this argument is often a cover-up for schools neglecting the hard tasks of education.

In the 1980s, a widely discussed government report, *A Nation at Risk*, was written by the National Commission on Excellence in Education and was issued by Terrel H. Bell, then U.S. Secretary of Education. This report made the following recommendations for all high school students: 4 years of English, 3 years of mathematics, 3 years of science, 3 years of social studies, and $1/2$ year of computer science. For those going to college, 2 years of a foreign language also were recommended. Generally, the report supported more rigorous and measurable standards in schools, a more effective use of the existing school day, and a longer day or a lengthened school year. In addition, the report also recommended higher teaching standards, an aptitude for teaching as well as demonstrated competence by teachers, and a leadership role by principals and superintendents.

Critics pointed out that these proposals contained nothing new and that they seemed to reinforce many of the reforms recommended by conservative or rightist educational organizations. With regard to the report, perhaps the most significant thing was the title of the report itself; that is, the National Commission on Excellence believed that unless its reforms were implemented, Americans faced crucial national risks. Many interpreted the central risk to be one of not matching other countries economically and militarily.

This instigated a series of proposals for educational reforms issued by diverse sources, such as the Twentieth Century Fund's *Making the Grade* and the Education Commission of the States's *Action for Excellence*. Together, all of the varied calls for reform led to changes in American education, primarily in the form of greater accountability, higher graduation standards, and widespread testing. It did not, however, lead to appreciably higher levels of funding or, it should be added, appreciably higher levels of student achievement. Today, the calls continue for similar kinds of educational reform, and every presidential candidate makes education a high priority.

All of this shows a common realist theme: Students should be equipped with objective knowledge of the past and present and assisted in the advancement of knowledge. Realists argue that this can be done only by providing students with basic and essential knowledge, and with a no-nonsense, no-coddling-of-students type of approach.

Although realists share many similar concerns, variations among them exist. They agree that schools should promote the essentials, but they each define *essential* from a different perspective. For instance, Whitehead was almost idealistic in his rec-ommendation that education be concerned primarily with ideas, but he condemned what he referred to as "scraps of information" and "inert ideas" because ideas should be learned in a practical and useful context. What makes his thought realistic is his view that one learns most truly from the material world in which one actually lives. He defended classical and specialized studies if these studies have important applications now. Inertness, he held, is a central hazard in all education; consequently, Whitehead's view of the essentials might be different from what someone else views as necessary because he had a distinct notion of what education should include.

Realists put great emphasis on the practical side of education, and their con-cept of practical includes education for moral and character development. John Locke, Johann F. Herbart, and Herbert Spencer held that the chief aim of education should be moral education. Whitehead was close to this position when he said that "the essence of education is that it be religious." Spencer (in his essay "What Knowl-edge Is of Most Worth?") held that science provides for moral and intellectual edu-cation because the pursuit of science demands integrity, self-sacrifice, and courage. For Locke, good character is superior to intellectual training; however, Locke's views on character education seem to have been directed primarily at the English gentry of his day who were supposed to set examples for the rest of society. Herbart thought that moral education is founded on knowledge, and Spencer agreed with this theory.

Thus, we can see different approaches to a common thrust. Realists agree that education should be based on essential and practical knowledge that exists inde-pendent of the knower, but they vary in their individual approaches to independent reality. Another common thread is that the essentials and practicalities of education lead to something beyond themselves, a view that is distinctly Aristotelian; that is, it proceeds from matter to form, from imperfection to perfection. Realists are Aris-totelian in viewing education as the process of developing rational powers to their fullest so that the good life can be achieved.

Methods of Education

The secular realist maintains that a proper understanding of the world requires an understanding of facts and ways of ordering and classifying knowledge. The estab-lishment of scientific laws, for example, depends on verification of up-to-date factual data. Secular realists believe that schools should teach such fundamental facts about the universe, and a good school program will present material in interesting and en-joyable ways. Not only facts but also the method of arriving at facts must be taught. The realist places enormous emphasis on critical reason aided by observation and experimentation.

Secular realism has had more recent impact on the philosophy of education than has religious realism. It is not surprising, for example, that critics such as Hy-man Rickover and James Bryant Conant were also scientists. The kind of education they promote is primarily technical and leads to specialization. The idea of special-ization, which is so repugnant to the idealist, arose out of the efforts to refine and es-tablish definitive scientific knowledge. Secular realists charge that the generalist is prone to wide flights of fantasy, little of which can be verified. It is important to establish what humans know, and this can be accomplished only by drawing together the efforts of many people, each one working on a small component of knowledge. Realists believe less in the personality of the teacher than in the effectiveness of the teacher to impart useful knowledge about the world, whether through lectures, didactic teaching, or the latest computer technology.

Realists support formal ways of teaching, and although they see such objectives as self-realization as valuable, realists maintain that self-realization best occurs when students are knowledgeable about the external world. Consequently, they must be exposed to facts, and didactic and other direct techniques can be efficient, organized, and orderly ways to accomplish this objective. However, realists insist that whatever the method used, it should be characterized by the integrity that comes from systematic, organized, and dependable knowledge.

Reflect for a moment on our chaotic history and how people have suffered because of an ignorance of facts about such things as a balanced diet, diseases, and the causes of natural disasters—knowledge we take for granted today. Our grasp of knowledge and the enjoyment of a better life have come as a result of a slow but steady accumulation of facts. People could not exist for long without knowledge of at least some basic facts. Realists think that the factual side of learning need not be painful or boring. In fact, they hold that learning should be enjoyable as well as useful. Locke thought that play is a distinct aid to learning (as did Friedrich Froebel, the nineteenth-century founder of the kindergarten). Locke seems to have had a good grasp of child psychology, and he advocated methods that seem modern today. In addition to asserting the usefulness of play, he urged that children should not be vexed by boring lessons, that they should not be pushed beyond their level of readiness (even if this means a year's delay in learning to read), that children should be given positive rewards to encourage further learning, and that the teacher should never force children to achieve beyond their natural inclinations. In many respects, Locke stands as a forerunner of modern educational theory. His recognition that children should not be pushed beyond their ability and readiness sounds current, and his sensitivity to a child's "natural inclinations" has a strong resemblance to the major tenets of modern theories of child growth and development.

Although some realists, such as Locke, developed organized theories about specific educational concerns, such as the nature of childhood or the impact of the environment, others (such as Whitehead) looked into more general patterns in human activity. Whitehead spoke of the "rhythmic" flow of education that can be discerned in three primary stages. First is the *stage of romance* (up to about age 14), in which the child's educational activity should be characterized mainly by discovering broad themes, shaping questions, and devising new experiences. The second stage (from ages 14 to 18) is the *stage of precision*, characterized by the disciplined study of specific and particular knowledge. Stage three, the *stage of generalization* (from age 18 to around 22), focuses on students becoming effective individuals capable of dealing with immediate experiences whereby they apply the principles of knowledge to life.

Despite the attention given to the nature of the child and the flow of experience by realist thinkers like Locke and Whitehead, critics of realism point out that in practice, realism is rigid. They charge that, in fact, realist theory results in such practices as Herbart's five formal steps of learning: preparation, presentation, association, systematization-generalization, and application. Russell Hamm charges that such an approach leads mechanically to reviewing homework, presenting new material, having a question-and-answer period, doing desk work, and receiving new homework assignments. Herbart, for example, also recommended that children be kept occupied as much as possible and that corporal punishment be used when necessary. His recommmendations reflect the realist affinity for precision and order. The desire for order and precision is found in such practices as ringing bells, setting time periods for study, departmentalization, arranging daily lesson plans, course scheduling, increasing specialization in the curriculum, prepackaged curriculum materials, and line-staff forms of administrative organization.

Although realists promote the importance of knowledge about the physical universe, the ends to which religious and secular realists put such knowledge are different. The religious realist believes that knowledge ultimately should lead to things beyond itself, such as God or Truth. One fundamental obligation of the teacher is to help the student know about the world and see the use of this knowledge as a way of reaching ultimate truths. In some parochial schools, for example, students study such areas as geography, history, and science, but these subjects are presented in ways that emphasize religious ideas or morality. The secular realist, however, tends to see knowledge about the physical world primarily in its use-value in improving technology and advancing civilization. Although realists generally teach the same things, they might teach them for different purposes.

Many realists support competency, accountability, and performance-based teaching. They assume that educational growth in terms of competency, performance, and knowledge of the facts can be achieved and is measurable to a considerable extent. Furthermore, although it is difficult to measure a student's growth in such areas as values, ethical considerations, and social relations, realists generally maintain that anything that exists can be measured in some form. The best way to approach and deal with such problems as ethics is through knowledge about the facts of ethics. Perhaps, for example, the best ethics show people how to put themselves in tune with the laws of the universe.

Contemporary realists also emphasize the importance of scientific research and development. The scientific movement in education has occurred primarily since 1900 and has brought about the advancement of knowledge in the psychology and physiology of education and developmental approaches to education. This movement also has been largely responsible for the extensive use of IQ tests, standardized achievement tests, diagnostic tests, and competency tests. Curricula have reflected the impact of science in the appearance of standard work lists, homogeneous grouping of students on the basis of intelligence, and standardized and serialized reading textbooks. The movement also has spawned the application of more precise and empirically based administrative techniques. A more recent development is the growing extent to which computer technology is used in schools. Although some of these developments have met with resistance and counterproposals, this aspect of realism in education also has met with a degree of acceptance by many educators.

Some contemporary critics of American education find the realist faith in scientific technology as a regrettable tendency. Other critics, though they accept the need for science and the usefulness of new technology, quarrel with the underlying realist theory as contributing to the misuse of science and technology, largely because they think that realists are too accepting and uncritical of things labeled scientific or technological. Whatever position one takes on this issue, the existence of such an issue is witness to the vitality that realist ideas still have.

Curriculum

Although realists have different views about what subjects should constitute the curriculum, they agree that studies should be practical and useful. Locke approved of such practical studies as reading, writing, drawing, geography, astronomy, arithmetic, history, ethics, and law—with supplementary studies in dancing, fencing, and riding. Locke emphasized the educational value of physical activity, and he believed that children should spend much time in the open air and should accustom themselves to "heat and cold, shine and rain." He focused his attention on the complete person and included not only intellectual concerns but also diet, exercise, and recreation. He believed that instruction in reading should begin as soon as a child is able to talk and that writing should begin soon afterward. He promoted studies in languages, particularly French and Latin, and also favored gardening and carpentry, as well as the idea of "a grand tour" of Europe with one's tutor, as useful educational experiences.

In perusing Locke's writings, one finds two types of curricula in his system: one for the rich and one for the poor. Locke proposed that all children between ages 3 and 14 whose parents were on relief should be sent to a work school for as long as they resided with their parents. They should earn their way at this school so as not to burden the local government financially. While there, they should have a "belly-full of bread daily" and in cold weather "a little warm water gruel." They were to be taught the manual skills of spinning, knitting, and "some other part of woolen manufacturing" and be given "some sense of religion."

A historical feature of the realist curriculum has been the great attention given to the use of didactic and object studies in education. For example, John Amos Comenius, a theologian and educator in the sixteenth century, was the first to introduce an extensive use of pictures in the educational process. He believed that it was possible for an individual to obtain all knowledge if provided with the proper kind of education. This proper kind of education should be based on a curriculum to perfect one's natural powers by training the senses. He stressed the importance of studying nature, and his curriculum included such subjects as physics, optics, astronomy, geography, and mechanics. In stressing this "pansophic" goal of achieving all knowledge, Comenius believed that schools should be enjoyable places with sympathetic teachers.

This idea of developing the senses in education also was adopted by Jean Jacques Rousseau, Johann Pestalozzi, and Friedrich Froebel, among others. Pestalozzi held that "sense impression of Nature is the only true foundation of human instruction, because it is the only true foundation of human knowledge." All that follows, he believed, is a result of this sense impression. Pestalozzi promoted such skills as spinning and gardening, with such subjects as arithmetic to be correlated with nature by having children apply numbers to objects. Froebel, who studied at the Pestalozzian Institute of Frankfort, also believed in "object studies"; his primary educational methods focused on "gifts," songs, and games. Although Froebel's educational techniques began in the material world with material objects, he saw all things unified in God, who expresses Himself in physical nature and in the human spirit.

Herbart was another realist educator who was strongly influenced by Pestalozzi. Herbart criticized what he characterized as the atomistic curriculum of his day. He believed in a system of "correlation and concentration" whereby each subject would bear on and be integrated with other related subjects. Teaching, he believed, should be multilateral. Geography, economics, and history should be taught so that the student can see relationships that provide the basis for new knowledge. Herbart thought that ideas are kept alive through interest and that one function of education is to see that ideas are retained in the mind through books, lectures, and other teaching devices.

Another educator who promoted interest and the use of objects in the educational process was Maria Montessori. The Montessori method provides all sorts of experiences with blocks, cylinders, and geometric patterns. These objects assist not only in the cognitive development of the child but in physical development, as well.

Although her approach originally was designed for children with mental disabilities, Montessori later expanded it to include all children. She believed that adults can know children by observing them, and she thought that too many educators interfere with children's "spontaneous activity." In *The Secret of Childhood*, she maintained that children have a secret world of their own that educators can learn about if they make the effort. Education means removing barriers from the path a child takes to discover the world and therefore should consist of a prepared environment with materials that children can use and that teach them how to learn. This method is solidly in keeping with the realist educational advocacy of sense perception and object lessons.

When we look at an overview of what realist educators propose for a curriculum, we see that it tends to be mental and physical, emphasizes subject matter about an external objective reality, and is highly organized and systematic in its approach.

Role of the Teacher

One purpose of education from the earliest times has been to teach students the kinds of things that members of society need to know in order to survive. In ancient Egypt, students were expected to know the religious and political demands and how to prepare for an afterlife. In Greece and Rome, young men were taught oratory as a way of improving their stations in life. In the Middle Ages, a few were prepared for the priesthood, and others were taught the code of chivalry. In the early history of North America, for example, Native Americans had elaborate ceremonies through which to educate the young in the ways of the tribe.

Education always has been used as a way of teaching essential things to people. In this respect, it has served a valuable function. The need for knowing these essentials is no less today, argues the realist. In fact, it is probably greater because there are more things to learn than ever before. When people fail to teach a child how to read and write, they doom that child to difficulty in finding a job, in understanding vital information, and in developing socially. It is possible that because of this limitation, the child will become a liability rather than an asset to society. In the same way, when people fail to teach a child the kinds of preparation and skills needed for technological and scientific development, they are not using schools to their fullest capacity.

Realists emphasize the role of the teacher in the educational process. The teacher should present material in a systematic and organized way and should promote the idea that one can use clearly defined criteria in making judgments about art, economics, politics, and science. For example, some realists would assert that a work of art, such as a painting, can be evaluated in terms of objective criteria, such as the kind of brush stroke used, the shading of colors, the balance and quality of the subject matter, and the message conveyed. The same thing applies to the activity of education; one can use certain objective criteria in judging whether particular activities are worthwhile—for example, the type of material presented, how it is organized, whether it suits the psychological makeup of the child, whether the delivery system is suitable, and whether it achieves the desired results.

Although realists argue that education should develop technical skills and turn out specialists and scientists, they are not opposed to education in the humanities. They do find, however, that schools are not teaching the humanities in ways conducive to cognitive development or respect for traditional knowledge and values. This type of issue is hotly debated in education circles today, particularly those in higher education, and it concerns the impact of what might be called postmodern theories of education. Allan Bloom's *The Closing of the American Mind*, Dinesh D'Souza's *Illiberal Education,* and Roger Kimball's *Tenured Radicals* are but three books that have gained attention by attacking what the authors believe is the negative impact of postmodern and multicultural educational theories. In essence, the critics believe that postmodernism is eviscerating liberal education by promoting a mindless relativism and turning schools away from teaching traditional knowledge or the discovery and dissemination of new knowledge.

Some realist philosophers have been drawn into this debate. John Searle sees the postmodernist challenge as striking at the very roots of the Western rationalist tradition that was founded on realism. Searle identifies what he sees as six basic propositions of the Western rationalist–realist tradition that are at stake:

1. Reality exists independently of the human mind.
2. Although our representations of external reality are made through the human invention called language, this does not mean that what we describe is merely subjective.
3. Truth is found in accurate representations of independent reality, and a statement is true if and only if it corresponds to the facts (the correspondence theory of truth).
4. Knowledge is objective and not dependent on subjective attitudes or feelings.

5. Logic and rationality provide the intellectual standards of what it means to be reasonable.
6. These intellectual standards are not "up for grabs," but provide objective criteria for intellectual excellence and achievement.

As Searle sees it, the Western rationalist position always has been subject to criticism, including self-criticism, but what postmodernists are seeking is not criticism in order to establish new standards of rationality, but rather the abandonment of standards of objectivity, truth, and rationality in favor of social and political transformations they find appealing. The humanities are the part of the curriculum that have been most vulnerable. In some such departments, it seems that the emphasis is not on teaching individuals to develop identities with a universal intellectual culture, but rather to define themselves by their race, class, gender, or ethnicity. In place of objective standards of truth, postmodernists embrace multicultural representativeness as the standard for curriculum content and the composition of the faculty. Rather than discussing great works of literature, the talk is about texts; rather than an academic subject as a domain to be studied, multidisciplinary studies are featured; rather than objective studies of various topics, topics become causes to be advanced or condemned. Not every realist philosopher sees the postmodern multicultural challenge as a threat, however. Hilary and Ruth Anna Putnam have found cultural pluralism to be a feature that educators can use to great advantage.

Realist educators such as Harry Broudy would like teachers to take a critical look at what they are doing. It is hoped that when they see the negative effects that trends in contemporary education may be having, they will return to more basic subject matter. Realists complain that they have been equated with such caricatures as Charles Dickens's Mr. Gradgrind and Washington Irving's Ichabod Crane. They say that they are not promoting only memorization and rote learning of facts, nor do they dismiss problem solving, projects, and enjoyable experiences in learning activities. They do, however, believe that such experiences should be fruitful in terms of producing students who have needed knowledge and skills. Further, they would like to see institutions of higher education turn out capable teaching specialists who would serve as models for the future development of students.

CRITIQUE OF REALISM IN EDUCATION

Realism has steadily gained ground in American education. To say that this advance began with *Sputnik* and the accompanying clamor in 1957 and 1958 would not be true, although that event certainly accelerated the movement. Realism received its major thrust from the industrial and technological age that has characterized American society from the late nineteenth century to the present. It is little wonder that schools in the United States would see as their major task the training and preparation of professionals and technicians in a society where professionalism and technical skills are so highly prized. Yet, many critics decry this state of affairs as shortsighted and dehumanizing, pandering primarily to material concerns. Although classical and religious realists still recognize the higher ends of moral and spiritual values, critics charge that scientific realists generally maintain a materialistic conception of human nature that is biased toward social control and social order.

Although the problems of order and control often are laid at the door of secular and scientific realism, evidence suggests that the bias toward order and control goes back to Aristotle and Aquinas. These thinkers tended to see the universe in terms of an independent reality with its own internal and systematic order. Thus, people must adapt and adjust to this reality, and dreams and desires have to be subsumed under its demands. The contemporary outcome of this view is the pressure to adjust to the needs of the corporate industrial state and the demands of an international market economy. In some countries, a realist outlook has been used to support totalitarian regimes, religious systems, and other worldviews that seem to seek overriding, controlling authority.

Dewey tried to counteract what he considered the negative aspects of both realism and idealism by showing that what we know as real is neither totally in the mind nor totally objective and external; rather, he argued that human reality consists of individuality and environment. Instead of adjustment to environmental and social conditions as a one-way movement, Dewey advocated the use of intelligence to transform the world to be more in line with human values. Dewey's detractors have accused him of promoting the "life adjustment" movement in education, but this movement is more characteristic of realism than of Dewey's philosophy.

Perhaps the most vocal critics of realism are those with an existentialist orientation and many postmodernists. They attack realism because it has advocated the idea of a fixed and intelligible universe capable of being perceived objectively by the observing intellect. This view, they charge, has been promoted through the centuries, through the Age of Reason and the Enlightenment, and into the contemporary scene of the technological society. It has deified reason to the detriment of the total human by ignoring passion, emotion, feeling, and irrationality. If we truly want to understand the human being in the world, then we must consider the totality or entirety of the individual, a totality that realism tends to ignore. Realists claim that they do view human beings in their entirety and that their entirety is one of dependence on a universe much larger than themselves. Critics reply that the realist view of the totality of the human being in the world is conditioned by preconceived notions about the universe.

These preconceived notions often lead realists to conclusions about humanity that create difficulties in the field of education. For instance, Whitehead disparages "the dull average student," despite the fact that such average students constitute a majority of the school-age population. Realists seem more concerned with the necessity of students measuring up to the standard curriculum than with seeing them as individuals. Russell believed in the love of knowledge for its own sake despite all of his talk about individuality, subjectivity, and humanistic concerns. He spoke of "excellencies" as the desirable things to achieve in education, a view that probably would meet with little resistance, except the underlying assumption is that achievement of these excellencies has to be measured against external criteria. The net result of views expressed by Whitehead and Russell is that students come to be seen in terms of subservience to a superior entity, such as the curriculum or standards of excellence. This problem is central to the criticism of the purported dehumanizing effects of realism.

This point of contention is illustrated further by the controversy over liberal and vocational education. Although many realists support the need for both, they seem to view liberal education as intensive studies in the arts and sciences for superior students and believe that slower students should be given a narrower technical-vocational training. James Conant, for example, studied the social conditions of inner cities and concluded that the conditions faced by the urban poor, particularly the black poor, are breeding grounds for "social dynamite." Critics point out that although Conant could have devised uplifting, sensitive, and humanitarian reform proposals, he recommended that poor people be given vocational education. Such outlooks all too often result in one kind of education for the "superior" people and another kind of education for everybody else.

Despite the historical insistence of realists on holism, they have for good or bad encouraged a movement in education toward specialization. This might be a corollary of the knowledge explosion everyone is facing, and realists, like others, are caught up in this problem. Their tendency to concentrate on specialized, piecemeal modules of knowledge does little to cure the problem. Comenius advocated a "pansophist" approach in education to enable individuals to use reason to gain all knowledge. Many realists have promoted this idea historically, but their proclivity for the piecemeal approach does not lend itself to holistic and unified conclusions.

Today, the realist ideal of the scientist and technician shows little recognition of the unity of knowledge because scientists often work on one small component of a larger entity without understanding that larger entity or appreciating its implications for humanity. Thus, it is possible for a scientist to work on a project that has antisocial or antihuman implications without being aware of it. The highly trained technician working on expensive space technology at Cape Canaveral might ignore the fact that the expensive gadgetry takes up resources that otherwise could be used to alleviate human misery.

Realism displays a bias in favor of a fact-based approach to knowledge. Although this has its laudable aspects, it is also susceptible to various errors. What was once thought to be indisputable fact in so many cases is now considered to be interesting myth and outright ignorance, such as the Ptolemaic cosmology once supported by religious realism. Even the "laws" of modern physics, which have tremendous research and experimentation behind them, could fall to new ideas in the future.

Confusion also arises over what is meant by the term *fact* because there are "facts of reason" and "facts of empirical research." Aristotle thought it self-evident that objects of different weights fall at different speeds. Not until Galileo was this "fact of reason" overturned by empirical research; he reportedly tested the proposition and found it false. If one keeps these problems in mind, it is understandable that a "factual" approach could lead to closed-mindedness and narrowness. If one already has the truth in hand (whether religious or scientific), then one hardly is motivated to search further. This point of view is antiphilosophical to the extent that it discourages an open mind and the unshackled search for wisdom.

One controversy that has its roots in the realist tradition is the problem of testing. A realist assumption (as expressed by E. L. Thorndike) that anything that exists, exists in some quantity and can be measured, has led to a plethora of standardized tests ranging from the IQ tests for young children to college board and national teachers' examinations. The testing movement has been touted as scientific and fact based, and it has gained an almost uncritical acceptance in some quarters.

The same kind of criticism can be directed toward statistical research studies, such as opinion surveys and other kinds of data sampling. The assumption is that what one finds by statistical research is scientific and factual; this, in turn, leads the researcher to believe that these findings reveal some truth. What can happen is the "pygmalion effect"; that is, the data could influence the way a teacher views the members of the class. The dangers of such a faith in "factual data" have received widespread attention in various professional journals, but it seems that testing is hardly abating and might even be growing more common. It is almost as if educators are caught in the clutches of a blind faith in anything labeled "scientific fact."

It often is claimed that the testing movement is one area where science has had its greatest impact on education. This movement has accelerated in recent years in conjunction with the clamor for accountability, cost-effectiveness, and meeting the demands of international economic competition. Testing has been directed toward finding some way to gauge teacher effectiveness and student performance more efficiently, and many states already require students to pass competency tests before graduation.

Some school systems also make competency tests mandatory for prospective teachers. The National Teachers Examination *(Praxis)* is another kind of test designed to ensure that teachers have a grasp of the fundamentals of the profession before being licensed. Such a trend can provide valuable objective support to those concerned with educational quality, but some critics argue that such tests are culturally biased and are punitive against various social groups. Perhaps in light of the controversies over testing, we should consider the other extreme, presented by the Russian educator Makarenko, who said that whenever he received a file on a student, he threw it into the fire lest it color his objective opinion of that person.

Finally, the realist advocacy of discipline and hard work can be criticized for various internal difficulties. Some religious realists have supported the doctrine of original sin, a view that has led to a belief that the human being is by nature corrupt, lazy, and prone to wrongdoing. Although modern secular realists might reject this view, remnants of it linger in education, for hard work and discipline are considered good for us and the concept that students' heads should be filled with "factual truth" so that they do not come to a bad end lives on.

The "hard work and discipline" syndrome and the emphasis on factual truth have been attacked and disputed vigorously by thinkers from Rousseau to contemporary proponents of experiential learning. These advocates maintain that it makes just as much sense to take an opposite view: People are basically good, energetic, and naturally inquisitive. Education should not be forced on people; rather, it should be made available in a palatable and enjoyable fashion. Both of these positions are extreme and susceptible to the same basic error; that is, they are too sure that human nature can be determined or that it is basically oriented toward good or bad behavior. The point is that realism has been criticized for the weakness of a narrow, restrictive view of human nature and that this view has had a debilitating effect on schooling and educational theory.

Despite its shortcomings, a realist philosophy of education often finds strong support from many educators, parents, business leaders, religious institutions, and grassroots America. The realist approach appears to favor a no-nonsense education that concentrates on things most people consider important. A large percentage of the public believes that lack of discipline is the number one problem found in schools today, and the emphasis on discipline in realist philosophies of education appeals to this sector of the public.

The emphasis on discipline includes not only behavior but also a disciplined approach to subject matter, learning, and life activities. When one seriously examines existing school practices here and abroad, one may find that more schools are following realist educational principles than those of any other single philosophy.

ARISTOTLE

THE POLITICS AND ETHICS OF ARISTOTLE

Aristotle thought that a primary aim of education is to produce a virtuous person. He believed that education should not be limited to the schoolroom but is a function of the state, as well. His approach to wisdom was "practical," using the methods of science as well as philosophy. A major concern was to shape understanding and "correctness of thinking." Aristotle's educational writings have had a significant impact on the development of Western education. His thought has greatly influenced conceptions of education in the humanities and the sciences, and his ideas have found favor with secular and religious thinkers in education.

What constitution in the parent is most advantageous to the offspring is a subject which we will hereafter consider when we speak of the education of children, and we will only make a few general remarks at present. The temperament of an athlete is not suited to the life of a citizen, or to health, or to the procreation of children, any more than the valetudinarian or exhausted constitution, but one which is in a mean between them. A man's constitution should be inured to labor, but not to labor which is excessive or of one sort only, such as is practised by athletes; he should be capable of all the actions of a freeman. These remarks apply equally to both parents.

Women who are with child should be careful of themselves; they should take exercise and have a nourishing diet. The first of these prescriptions the legislator will easily carry into effect by requiring that they shall take a walk daily to some temple, where they can worship the gods who preside over birth. Their minds, however, unlike their bodies, they ought to keep unexercised, for the offspring derive their natures from their mothers as plants do from the earth.

As to the exposure and rearing of children, let there be a law that no deformed child shall live, but where there are too many (for in our State population has a limit), when couples have children in excess, and the state of feeling is averse to the exposure of offspring, let abortion be procured before sense and life have begun; what may or may not be lawfully done in these cases depends on the question of life and sensation.

And now, having determined at what ages men and women are to begin their union, let us also determine how long they shall continue to beget and bear offspring for the State; men who are too old, like men who are too young, produce children who are defective in body and mind; the children of very old men are weakly. The limit, then, should be the age which is the prime of their intelligence, and this in most persons, according to the notion of some poets who measure life by periods of 7 years, is about 50; at 4 or 5 years later, they should cease from having families; and from that time forwards only cohabit with one another for the sake of health, or for some similar reason.

As to adultery, let it be held disgraceful for any man or woman to be unfaithful when they are married, and called husband and wife. If during the time of bearing children anything of the sort occurs, let the guilty person be punished with a loss of privileges in proportion to the offence.

After the children have been born, the manner of rearing them may be supposed to have a great effect on their bodily strength. It would appear from the example of animals, and of those nations who desire to create the military habit, that the food which has most milk in it is best suited to human beings; but the less wine the better, if they would escape diseases. Also all the motions to which children can be subjected at their early age are very useful. But in order to preserve their tender limbs from distortion, some nations have had recourse to mechanical appliances which straighten their bodies. To accustom children to the cold from their earliest years is also an excellent practice, which greatly conduces to health, and hardens them for military service. Hence many barbarians have a custom of plunging their children at birth into a cold stream; others, like the Celts, clothe them in a light wrapper only. For human nature should be early habituated to endure all which by habit it can be made to endure; but the process must be gradual. And children, from their natural warmth, may be easily trained to bear cold. Such care should attend them in the first stage of life.

The next period lasts to the age of 5; during this no demand should be made upon the child for study or labor, lest its growth be impeded; and there should be sufficient motion to prevent the limbs from being inactive. This can be secured, among other ways, by amusement, but the amusement should not be vulgar or tiring or riotous. The directors of education, as they are termed, should be careful what tales or stories the children hear, for the sports of children are designed to prepare the way for the business of later life, and should be for the most part imitations of the occupations which they will hereafter pursue in earnest. Those are wrong who [like Plato] in the *Laws* attempt to check the loud crying and screaming of children, for these contribute towards their growth, and, in a manner, exercise their bodies. Straining the voice has an effect similar to that produced by the retention of the breath in violent exertions. Besides other duties, the directors of education should have an eye to their bringing up, and should take care that they are left as little as possible with slaves. For until they are 7 years old they must live at home; and therefore, even at this early age, all that is mean and low should be banished from their sight and hearing. Indeed, there is nothing which the legislator should be more careful to drive away than indecency of speech; for the light utterance of shameful words is akin to shameful actions. The young especially should never be allowed to repeat or hear anything of the sort. A freeman who is found saying or doing what is forbidden, if he be too young as yet to have the privilege of a place at the public tables, should be disgraced and beaten, and an elder person degraded as his slavish conduct deserves. And since we do not allow improper language, clearly we should also banish pictures or tales which are indecent. Let the rulers take care that there be no image or picture representing unseemly actions, except in the temples of those gods at whose festivals the law permits even ribaldry, and whom the law also permits to be worshipped by persons of mature age on behalf of themselves, their children, and their wives. But the legislator should not allow youth to be hearers of satirical Iambic verses or spectators of comedy until they are of an age to sit at the public tables and to drink strong wine; by that time education will have armed them against the evil influences of such representations.

We have made these remarks in a cursory manner—they are enough for the present occasion; but hereafter we will return to the subject and after a fuller discussion determine whether such liberty should or should not be granted, and in what way granted, if at all. Theodorus, the tragic actor, was quite right in saying that he would not allow any other actor, not even if he were quite second-rate, to enter before himself, because the spectators grew fond of the voices which they first heard. And the same principle of association applies universally to things as well as persons, for we always like best whatever comes first. And therefore youth should be kept strangers to all that is bad, and especially to things which suggest vice or hate. When the 5 years have passed away, during the 2 following years they must look on at the pursuits which they are hereafter to learn. There are two periods of life into which education has to be divided, from 7 to the age of puberty, and onwards to the age of 1 and 20. [The poets] who divide ages by sevens are not always right: We should rather adhere to the divisions actually made by nature; for the deficiencies of nature are what art and education seek to fill up.

Let us then first inquire if any regulations are to be laid down about children, and secondly, whether the care of them should be the concern of the State or of private individuals, which latter is in our own day the common custom, and in the third place, what these regulations should be.

No one will doubt that the legislator should direct his attention above all to the education of youth, or that the neglect of education does harm to States. The citizen should be moulded to suit the form of government under which he lives. For each government has a peculiar character which originally formed and which continues to preserve it. The character of democracy creates democracy, and the character of oligarchy creates oligarchy; and always the better the character, the better the government.

Now for the exercise of any faculty or art a previous training and habituation are required; clearly therefore for the practice of virtue. And since the whole city has one end, it is manifest that education should be one and the same for all, and that it should be public, and not private—not as at present, when everyone looks after his own children separately, and gives them separate instruction of the sort which he thinks best; the training in things which are of common interest should be the same for all. Neither must we suppose that anyone of the citizens belongs to himself, for they all belong to the State, and are each of them a part of the State, and the care of each part is inseparable from the care of the whole. In this particular the Lacedæmonians [Spartans] are to be praised, for they take the greatest pains about their children, and make education the business of the State.

That education should be regulated by law and should be an affair of state is not to be denied, but what should be the character of this public education, and how young persons should be educated, are questions which remain to be considered. For mankind are by no means agreed about the things to be taught, whether we look to virtue or the best life. Neither it is clear whether education is more concerned with intellectual or with moral virtue. The existing practice is perplexing; no one knows on what principle we should proceed—should the useful in life, or should virtue, or should the higher knowledge, be the aim of our training; all three opinions have been entertained. Again, about the means there is no agreement; for different persons, starting with different ideas about the nature of virtue, naturally disagree about the practice of it. There can be no doubt that children should be taught those useful things which are really necessary, but not all things; for occupations are divided into liberal and illiberal; and to young children should be imparted only such kinds of knowledge as will be useful to them without vulgarizing them. And any occupation, art, or science, which makes the body or soul or mind of the freeman less fit for the practice or exercise of virtue, is vulgar; wherefore we call those arts vulgar which tend to deform the body, and likewise all paid employments, for they absorb and degrade the mind. There are also some liberal arts quite proper for a freeman to acquire, but only in a certain degree, and if he attend to them too closely, in order to attain perfection in them, the same evil effects will follow. The object also which a man sets before him makes a great difference; if he does or learns anything for his own sake or for the sake of his friends, or with a view to excellence, the action will not appear illiberal; but if done for the sake of others, the very same action will be thought menial and servile. The received subjects of instruction, as I have already remarked, are partly of a liberal and partly of an illiberal character.

The customary branches of education are in number four; they are—(1) reading and writing, (2) gymnastic exercises, (3) music, to which is sometimes added (4) drawing. Of these, reading and writing and drawing are regarded as useful for the purposes of life in a variety of ways, and gymnastic exercises are thought to infuse courage. Concerning music a doubt may be raised—in our own day most men cultivate it for the sake of pleasure, but originally it was included in education, because nature herself, as has been often said, requires that we should be able, not only to work well, but to use leisure well; for, as I must repeat once and again, the first principle of all action is leisure. Both are required, but leisure is better than occupation; and therefore the question must be asked in good earnest, what ought we to do when at leisure? Clearly we ought not to be amusing ourselves, for then amusement would be the end of life. But if this is inconceivable, and yet amid serious occupations amusement is needed more than at other times (for he who is hard at work has need of relaxation, and amusement gives relaxation, whereas occupation is always accompanied with exertion and effort), at suitable times we should introduce amusements, and they should be our medicines, for the emotion which they create in the soul is a relaxation, and from the pleasure we obtain rest. Leisure of itself gives pleasure and happiness and enjoyment of life, which are experienced, not by the busy man, but by those who have leisure. For he who is occupied has in view some end which he has not attained; but happiness is an end which all men deem to be accompanied with pleasure and not with pain. This pleasure, however, is regarded differently by different persons, and varies according to the habit of individuals; the pleasure of the best man is the best, and springs from the noblest sources. It is clear then that there are branches of learning and education which we must study with a view to the enjoyment of leisure, and these are to be valued for their own sake; whereas those kinds of knowledge which are useful in business are to be deemed necessary, and exist for the sake of other things. And therefore our fathers admitted music into education, not on the ground either of its necessity or utility, for it is not necessary, nor indeed useful in the same manner as reading and writing, which are useful in money-making, in the management of a household, in the acquisition of knowledge and in political life, nor like drawing, useful for a more correct judgment of the works of artists, nor again like gymnastic, which gives health and strength; for neither of these is to be gained from music. There remains, then, the use of music for intellectual enjoyment in leisure; which appears to have been the reason of its introduction, this being one of the ways in which it is thought that a freeman should pass his leisure; as Homer says—

"How good is it to invite men to the pleasant feast,"

and afterwards he speaks of others whom he describes as inviting

"The bard who would delight them all."

And in another place Odysseus says there is no better way of passing life than when "Men's hearts are merry and the banqueters in the hall, sitting in order, hear the voice of the minstrel." It is evident, then, that there is a sort of education in which parents should train their sons, not as being useful or necessary, but because it is liberal or noble. Whether this is of one kind only, or of more than one, and if so, what they are, and how they are to be imparted, must hereafter be determined. Thus much we are now in a position to say that the ancients witness to us; for their opinion may be gathered from the fact that music is one of the received and traditional branches of education. Further, it is clear that children should be instructed in some useful things—for example, in reading and writing—not only for their usefulness, but also because many other sorts of knowledge are required through them. With a like view they may be taught drawing, not to prevent their making mistakes in their own purchases, or in order that they may not be imposed upon in the buying or selling of articles, but rather because it makes them judges of the beauty of the human form. To be always seeking after the useful does not become free and exalted souls. Now it is clear that in education habit must go before reason, and the body before the mind; and therefore boys should be handed over to the trainer, who creates in them the proper habit of body, and to the wrestling-master, who teaches them their exercises.

The happy man will need external prosperity, so far forth as he is man; for human nature is not sufficient of itself for contemplation; but the body must be in health, and it must have food and all other care and attendance. We must not however imagine that the person who is to be happy will want many and great goods, because we say that without external good he can be blessed; for self-sufficiency does not consist in excess, nor does action. But it is possible to perform honourable things without being lord of earth and sea; for a man may be able to act according to virtue with moderate means. We may see this plainly: for private individuals are thought to perform good acts no less than men in power, but even more so. And it is sufficient to have a competence, for the life of that man will be happy, who energizes according to virtue. Solon also perhaps gave a good description of the happy man, when he said, that in his opinion it was he who was moderately supplied with external goods, who had done the most honourable deeds, and lived temperately; for it is possible that men who have moderate possessions should do what they ought. Anaxagoras also seems to have conceived the happy man to be neither rich nor powerful, when he said, that he should not be surprised if he was thought absurd by the multitude; for they judge by externals, having a perception of such things only.

The opinions of wise men, therefore, seem to agree with what has been said; such statements, therefore, carry with them some weight. But we judge of truth, in practical matters, from facts and from life, for on them the decisive point turns; and we ought to try all that has been said by applying it to facts and to life; and if our arguments agree with facts, we may receive them; but if they are at variance, we must consider them as mere words. He also who energizes according to intellect, and pays attention to that, and has it in the best state, is likely to be most beloved by the gods; for if any regard is paid to human affairs by the gods, as it is thought that there is, it is reasonable to suppose that they would take pleasure in what is the best and nearest allied to themselves: but this must be the intellect; and that they would be kind in return to those who love and honor this most, as to persons who pay attention to their friends, and who act rightly and honorably. But that all these qualities especially belong to the wise man, is quite clear; it is probable, therefore, that he is at the same time most dear to the gods, and most happy; so that even in this way the wise man must be the happiest man. . . .

[It] is thought that men become good, some by nature, others by practice, others by teaching. Now it is plain that whatever belongs to nature is not in our own power, but exists by some divine causes in those who are truly fortunate. But reasoning and teaching, it is to be feared, will not avail in every case, but the mind of the hearer must be previously cultivated by habits to feel pleasure and aversion properly, just as the soil must, which nourishes the seed. For he who lives in obedience to passion, would not listen to reasoning which turns him from it; nay, more, he would not understand it. And how is it possible to change the convictions of such a man as this? On the whole, it appears that passion does not submit to reasoning,

but to force. There must, therefore, previously exist a character in some way connected with virtue, loving what is honourable, and hating what is disgraceful. But to meet with right education in the path of virtue from childhood is difficult, unless one is brought up under such laws: For to live temperately and patiently is not pleasant to the majority, and especially to the young. Therefore, education and institutions ought to be regulated by law; for they will not be painful when they have become familiar.

Perhaps it is not sufficient that we should meet with good education and attention when young; but since when we arrive at man-hood we ought also to study and practice what we have learned, we should require laws also for this purpose: In short, we should want laws relating to the whole of life; for the masses are obedient to compulsion rather than to reason, and to punishments rather than to the principle of honour. Therefore, some think that legislators ought to exhort to virtue, and to urge men on by appealing to the principle of honour, since those who are good in their practice will obey when they are led; but to impose chastisements and punishments on those who are disobedient and naturally indisposed to virtue, and to banish altogether the incurable; because he who is good, and lives with regard to the principle of honour, will obey reason; but the bad man desires pleasure, and is corrected by pain, like a beast of burden. Therefore, it is a common saying, that the pains ought to be such as are most opposed to the pleasures which are loved.

Now, then, as has been said, he that is to be a good man must have been educated well, and have been made to form good habits, and thus continue to live under good institutions, and never practise what is bad, either involuntarily or voluntarily; and this is to be done by living in obedience to some intelligent principle, and some right regulation, which has the power of enforcing its decrees. But the paternal authority has no strength, nor compulsory force; nor, in short, the authority of any one man, unless he is a king, or some one of that sort; but the law does possess a compulsory power, since it is reason proceeding from a certain prudence and intelligence; and besides, men hate those individuals who oppose their appetites, even if they do it rightly; but the law is not odious when it prescribes what is good. In the city of Lacedæmon [Sparta] alone, with a few others, the legislator seems to have paid attention to education and institutions; whilst in most states such matters have been neglected, and each lives as he pleases, like the Cyclops,

> Administering the law for his children and wife.

It would therefore be best that the state should pay attention to education, and on right principles, and that

it should have power to enforce it: But if neglected as a public measure, it would seem to be the duty of every individual to contribute to the virtue of his children and friends, or at least to make this his deliberate purpose.

Source: Aristotle, *The Politics,* translated by B. Jowett. New York: Colonial Press, 1899, pp. 192–199; Aristotle, *The Nicomachean Ethics,* translated by R. W. Browne. London: Henry G. Bohn, 1853, pp. 284–288.

LOCKE

SOME THOUGHTS CONCERNING EDUCATION

Locke's educational writings are classics of pedagogy that dominated the eighteenth century and still influence people today. Basing his observations on experience, Locke aimed his educational proposals at producing the well-mannered, well-informed English gentleman. In addition to being a philosopher, Locke was also a physician; and it is not surprising that he included in his writings, in addition to intellectual concerns, the topics of health, exercise, and physical growth and development. He presented a liberal and humane view of education, especially as compared with what existed in his day. Although he advocated democracy, his educational recommendations were aimed primarily at the children of the upper classes. He emphasized individuality, self-discipline, the importance of reasoning with the child, and development of character as well as intellect.

A sound mind in a sound body, is a short, but full description of a happy state in this world; he that has these two, has little more to wish for; and he that wants either of them, will be but little the better for any thing else. Men's happiness, or misery, is most part of their own making. He whose mind directs not wisely, will never take the right way; and he whose body is crazy and feeble, will never be able to advance in it. I confess, there are some men's constitutions of body and mind so vigorous, and well framed by nature, that they need not much assistance from others; but, by the strength of their natural genius, they are, from their cradles, carried towards what is excellent; and, by the privilege of their happy constitutions, are able to do wonders. But examples of this kind are but few; and I think I may say, that, of all the men we meet with, nine parts of ten are what they are, good or evil, use-

ful or not, by their education. It is that which makes the great difference in mankind. The little, or almost insensible, impressions on our tender infancies, have very important and lasting consequences: and there it is, as in the fountains of some rivers, where a gentle application of the hand turns the flexible waters into channels, that make them take quite contrary courses; and by this little direction, given them at first, in the source, they receive different tendencies, and arrive at last at very remote and distant places.

I imagine the minds of children, as easily turned, this or that way, as water itself; and though this be the principal part, and our main care should be about the inside, yet the clay cottage is not to be neglected. I shall therefore begin with the case, and consider first the health of the body, as that which perhaps you may rather expect, from that study I have been thought more peculiarly to have applied myself to; and that also which will be soonest dispatched, as lying, if I guess not amiss, in a very little compass.

How necessary health is to our business and happiness; and how requisite a strong constitution, able to endure hardships and fatigue, is, to one that will make any figure in the world; is too obvious to need any proof. . . .

This being laid down in general, as the course ought to be taken, it is fit we come now to consider the parts of the discipline to be used a little more particularly. I have spoken so much of carrying a strict hand over children, that perhaps I shall be suspected of not considering enough what is due to their tender age and constitutions. But that opinion will vanish, when you have heard me a little farther. For I am very apt to think, that great severity of punishment does but very little good; nay, great harm in education: And I believe it will be found, that, *ceteris paribus,* those children who have been most chastised, seldom make the best men. All that I have hitherto contended for, is, that whatsoever rigour is necessary, it is more to be used, the younger children are; and, having by a due application wrought its effect, it is to be relaxed, and changed into a milder sort of government. . . .

Manners, as they call it, about which children are so often perplexed, and have so many goodly exhortations made them, by their wise maids and governesses, I think, are rather to be learned by example than rules; and then children, if kept out of ill company, will take a pride to behave themselves prettily, after the fashion of others, perceiving themselves esteemed and commended for it. But, if by a little negligence in this part, the boy should not put off his hat, nor make legs very gracefully, a dancing-master will cure that defect, and wipe off all that plainness of nature, which the à-la-mode people call clownishness. And since nothing appears to me to give children so much becoming confidence and behaviour, and so to raise them to the conversation of those above their age, as dancing; I think they should be taught to dance, as soon as they are capable of learning it. For, though this consist only in outward gracefulness of motion, yet, I know not how, it gives children manly thoughts and carriage, more than any thing. But otherwise I would not have little children much tormented about punctilios, or niceties of breeding.

Never trouble yourself about those faults in them, which you know age will cure. . . .

I place virtue as the first and most necessary of those endowments that belong to a man or a gentleman, as absolutely requisite to make him valued and beloved by others, acceptable or tolerable to himself. Without that, I think, he will be happy neither in this nor the other world. . . .

When he can talk, it is time he should begin to learn to read. But as to this, give me leave here to inculcate again what is very apt to be forgotten, viz. that great care is to be taken, that it be never made as a business to him, nor he look on it as a task. We naturally, as I said, even from our cradles, love liberty, and have therefore an aversion to many things, for no other reason, but because they are injoined us. I have always had a fancy, that learning might be made a play and recreation to children; and that they might be brought to desire to be taught, if it were proposed to them as a thing of honour, credit, delight, and recreation, or as a reward for doing something else, and if they were never chid or corrected for the neglect of it. . . .

Thus children may be cozened into a knowledge of the letters; be taught to read, without perceiving it to be any thing but a sport, and play themselves into that which others are whipped for. Children should not have any thing like work, or serious, laid on them; neither their minds nor bodies will bear it. It injures their healths; and their being forced and tied down to their books, in an age at enmity with all such restraint, has, I doubt not, been the reason why a great many have hated books and learning all their lives after: It is like a surfeit, that leaves an aversion behind, not to be removed. . . .

The Lord's prayer, the creed, and ten commandments, it is necessary he should learn perfectly by heart; but, I think, not by reading them himself in his primer, but by somebody's repeating them to him, even before he can read. But learning by heart, and learning to read, should not, I think be mixed, and so one made to clog the other. But his learning to read should be made as little trouble or business to him as might be. . . .

When he can read English well, it will be seasonable to enter him in writing. And here the first thing should be taught him, is to hold his pen right; and this he should be perfect in, before he should be suffered to put it to paper: For not only children, but any body else, that would do any thing well, should never be put upon too much of it at once, or be set to perfect themselves in two parts of an action at the same time, if they can possibly be separated. . . .

As soon as he can speak English, it is time for him to learn some other language: This nobody doubts of, when French is proposed. And the reason is, because people are accustomed to the right way of teaching that language, which is by talking it into children in constant conversation, and not by grammatical rules. The Latin tongue would easily be taught the same way, if his tutor, being constantly with him, would talk nothing else to him, and make him answer still in the same language. But because French is a living language, and to be used more in speaking, that should be first learned, that the yet pliant organs of speech might be accustomed to a due formation of those sounds, and he get the habit of pronouncing French well, which is the harder to be done, the longer it is delayed.

When he can speak and read French well, which in this method is usually in a year or two, he should proceed to Latin, which it is a wonder parents, when they have had the experiment in French, should not think ought to be learned the same way, by talking and reading. Only care is to be taken, whilst he is learning those foreign languages, by speaking and reading nothing else with his tutor, that he do not forget to read English, which may be preserved by his mother, or some body else, hearing him read some chosen parts of the scripture or other English book, every day. . . .

At the same time that he is learning French and Latin, a child, as has been said, may also be entered in arithmetic, geography, chronology, history, and geometry too. For if these be taught him in French or Latin, when he begins once to understand either of these tongues, he will get a knowledge in these sciences, and the language to-boot.

Geography, I think, should be begun with; for the learning of the figure of the globe, the situation and boundaries of the four parts of the world, and that of particular kingdoms and countries, being only an exercise of the eyes and memory, a child with pleasure will learn and retain them: And this is so certain, that I now live in the house with a child, whom his mother has so well instructed this way in geography, that he knew the limits of the four parts of the world, could readily point, being asked, to any country upon the globe, or any county in the map of England; knew all the great rivers, promontories, straits, and bays in the world, and could find the longitude and latitude of any place before he was 6 years old. These things, that he will thus learn by sight, and have by rote in his memory, are not all, I confess, that he is to learn upon the globes. But yet it is a good step and preparation to it, and will make the remainder much easier, when his judgment is grown ripe enough for it: Besides that, it gets so much time now, and by the pleasure of knowing things, leads him on insensibly to the gaining of languages.

When he has the natural parts of the globe well fixed in his memory, it may then be time to begin arithmetic. By the natural parts of the globe, I mean several positions of the parts of the earth and sea, under different names and distinctions of countries; not coming yet to those artificial and imaginary lines, which have been invented, and are only supposed, for the better improvement of that science.

Arithmetic is the easiest, and consequently the first sort of abstract reasoning, which the mind commonly bears, or accustoms itself to: and is of so general use in all parts of life and business, that scarce any thing is to be done without it. This is certain, a man cannot have too much of it, nor too perfectly. . . .

As nothing teaches, so nothing delights, more than history. The first of these recommends it to the study of grown men; the latter makes me think it the fittest for a young lad, who, as soon as he is instructed in chronology, and acquainted with the several epochs in use in this part of the world, and can reduce them to the Julian period, should then have some Latin history put into his hand. The choice should be directed by the easiness of the style; for wherever he begins, chronology will keep it from confusion; and the pleasantness of the subject inviting him to read, the language will insensibly be got, without that terrible vexation and uneasiness which children suffer where they are put into books beyond their capacity, such as are the Roman orators and poets, only to learn the Roman language. When he has by reading mastered the easier, such perhaps as Justin, Eutropius, Quintus Curtius, & c. the next degree to these will give him no great trouble: And thus, by a gradual progress from the plainest and easiest historians, he may at last come to read the most difficult and sublime of the Latin authors, such as are Tully, Virgil, and Horace. . . .

Though the systems of physics, that I have met with, afford little encouragement to look for certainty, or science, in any treatise, which shall pretend to give us a body of natural philosophy from the first principles of bodies in general; yet the incomparable Mr. Newton has shown, how far mathematics, applied to some parts of nature, may, upon principles that matter of fact justify, carry us in the knowledge of some, as I may so call them, particular provinces of the incomprehensible universe. And if others could give us so good and clear an account of other parts of nature, as he has of this our planetary world, and the most considerable phenomena observable in it, in his admirable book *Philosophiæ naturalis principia mathematica*, we might in time hope to be furnished with more true and certain knowledge in several parts of this stupendous machine, than hitherto we could have expected. And though there are very few that have mathematics enough to understand his demonstrations; yet the most accurate mathematicians, who have examined them, allowing them to be such, his book will deserve to be read, and give no small light and pleasure to those, who, willing to understand the motions, properties, and operations of the great masses of matter in this our solar system, will but carefully mind his conclusions, which may be depended on as propositions well proved. . . .

Though I am now come to a conclusion of what obvious remarks have suggested to me concerning education, I would not have it thought, that I look on it as a just treatise on this subject. There are a thousand other things that may need consideration; especially if one should take in the various tempers, different inclinations, and particular defaults, that are to be found in children; and prescribe proper remedies. The variety is so great, that it would require a volume; nor would that reach it. Each man's mind has some peculiarity, as well as his face, that distinguishes him from all others; and there are possibly scarce two children, who can be conducted by exactly the same method. Besides that, I think a prince, a nobleman, and an ordinary gentleman's son, should have different ways of breeding. But having had here only some general views in reference to the main end and aims in education, and those designed for a gentleman's son, who being then very little, I considered only as white paper, or wax, to be moulded and fashioned as one pleases; I have touched little more than those heads, which I judged necessary for the breeding of a young gentleman of his condition in general; and have now published these my occasional thoughts, with this hope, that, though this be far from being a complete treatise on this subject, or such as that every one may find what will just fit his child in it; yet it may give some small light to those, whose concern for their dear little ones makes them so irregularly bold, that they dare venture to consult their own reason, in the education of their children, rather than wholly to rely upon old custom.

Source: John Locke, "Some Thoughts Concerning Education," in *The Works of John Locke*, vol. X. London: W. Otridge and Son et al., 1812, pp. 6–7, 35, 50, 128, 143–144, 147–148, 150, 152, 172–173, 175–176, 186–187, 204–205.

SELECTED READINGS

Broudy, Harry S. *Building a Philosophy of Education.* Upper Saddle River, NJ: Prentice Hall, 1961. Presents a strong case for realism in modern education and an appeal for more fundamental and basic approaches and studies in schools. This book is regarded as one of the better statements of realism in education.

Putnam, Hilary, and Putnam, Ruth Anna. "Education for Democracy." *Educational Theory* 43(4):361–376, Fall, 1993. *www.ed.uiuc.edu/EPS/Educational-Theory/Contents/43_4_Putnam.asp* (accessed April 5, 2002). A review of John Dewey's views on cultural pluralism as an antidote to the anti-realism of much postmodern educational theory. The authors argue that Dewey's ideas might help people better understand and articulate the need for multicultural education today.

Searle, John R. "Rationality and Realism: What Is at Stake?" *Daedalus* 122(4):55–83, Fall, 1993. A defense of leading principles of realism and the Western rationalist tradition in higher education. The author critiques the anti-realism of postmodern educational theories as they have influenced contemporary higher education.

Whitehead, Alfred N. *The Aims of Education and Other Essays.* New York: Free Press, 1957. A collection of wide-ranging essays on education. This volume shows Whitehead's approach to philosophical patterns of thought. It is particularly incisive in its critique of inertness in education and attention to the creative process.

www.greatbooks.org/index.html (accessed April 5, 2002). Site for The Great Books Foundation. Provides information on the Foundation, its programs, and publications.

www.nd.edu/Departments/Maritain/ndjmc.htm (accessed April 5, 2002). Web site of the Jacques Maritain Center. Provides access to the works of Maritain and others on Thomistic and realist philosophy and philosophy of education.

www.paideia.org/ (accessed April 5, 2002). Homesite of the National Paideia Center. This site promotes the educational philosophy of Mortimer Adler. It provides brief explanatory materials but also links to other sites that might support its objectives.

www.c-b-e.org/ (accessed April 5, 2002). Homepage of the Council for Basic Education. The site provides information about the council, its objectives and programs, and links to other sites that could be helpful to users.

Companion
Website

ONLINE RESEARCH

Utilizing some of the Web sites included in this book, as well as Topics 2 and 3 of the Prentice Hall Foundations Web site found at *www.prenhall.com/ozmon*, answer the following question with a short essay: What are some of the specific practices in American education that can be traced to a realistic approach to education? You can write and submit your essay response to your instructor by using the "Electronic Bluebook" section found in any of the topics of the Prentice Hall Foundations Web site.

3

Eastern Philosophy, Religion, and Education

From the beginning, religion has played a role in human endeavors. Evidence from Stone Age paintings made in prehistoric times shows that religious ideas and rituals were used to ensure success in hunting and agriculture. Before philosophy, religion addressed such crucial issues as the creation of the world, the meaning of life, an afterlife, ethical views, and happiness. Religion manifested itself in rituals, festivals, and pilgrimages, as well as manuscripts, paintings, statues, temples, poetry, cathedrals, saints, and scholars. Even through Freud's time, in *Civilization and Its Discontents* and *The Future of an Illusion*, it was argued that religion has many negative aspects, yet it helped make civilization possible.

Eastern ideas are among the oldest of religious beliefs, and these ideas have a long and varied history. Their range not only in terms of years but also in ideas is enormous, and it is a fascinating study in the historical development of human thinking. This fascination increases when one compares and contrasts these ideas with Western thinking.

Eastern philosophy will be considered in four major areas of thought: Indian, Chinese, Japanese, and Middle Eastern. Although each culture has many different philosophical beliefs, common threads also exist. If any one idea is paramount, it is a concentration on the inner rather than the outer life. Eastern philosophy, unlike the West's more empirical philosophy, stresses intuition, inner peace, tranquility, attitudinal development, and mysticism. Eastern beliefs, often because of their early origins, have had a significant historical impact on Western thought, and the influences of Judaism and Christianity, both Middle Eastern in origin, are an obvious case in point. The appeal of Eastern beliefs remains important today, particularly as an antidote to Western philosophical complacency and a concentration on the material aspects of life.

THE DEVELOPMENT OF EASTERN THOUGHT

Most studies of Western philosophy begin with the Greeks. Greek philosophy, as a systematic development of thought, began in the sixth century B.C.with Thales, who was followed later by Pythagoras and Socrates. Yet some evidence supports the view that Platonic philosophy owed much to Indian philosophy, with its emphasis on the illusory quality of matter and other idealist tendencies. At the time when ancient Greek thought began, philosophy already had reached a high stage of development in India and China.

Perhaps Greek philosophy was unique in its emphasis on rationality rather than mysticism and supernaturalism. Western philosophy tended to emphasize logic and materialism; Eastern philosophy stressed the inner rather than the outer world, intuition rather than sense, and mysticism rather than scientific discoveries. This differs from school to school, and Chinese philosophy is, as a whole, much less mystical than Indian philosophy, but overall they begin with the inner world, which then reaches out to the outer world of phenomena.

It is sometimes charged that most Indian and Chinese beliefs are not philosophies but religions. Because of the early beginnings of these ideas, they showed a strong bent toward the spiritual side of nature, and their stories were full of gods and goddesses, much like Greek mythology. However, unlike the Greeks, who tried to separate philosophy from religion, Indian and Chinese religions and philosophies often are intertwined. Religious doctrines are merged with philosophical views about the nature of the world and one's interaction with it.

Most Western philosophers still argue that philosophical and religious studies should be separated, but think how difficult it would be to separate Thomas Aquinas the theologian from Thomas Aquinas the philosopher. It is true that religious thought, rather than philosophy, has tended to rely more on deduction, faith, intuition, and mysticism, but many philosophies, even modern ones, also laud these approaches today. The separation is difficult, particularly when looking so far back. One can hardly expect early civilizations to have a sophisticated or scientific idea about the nature of the universe and humanity's place in it. Perhaps we should not attempt such a strict delineation, but rather ask how these ideas have contributed to a growing understanding of the world and its people—a world that to Eastern philosophers was sometimes hostile but also benevolent and understandable.

FAR EASTERN AND INDIAN THOUGHT

The Far East or Eastern Asia, which includes China, Korea, Japan, and India, comprises an enormous land area with an immense population. Indigenous people have lived in the same geographic area for a long time, and Eastern and Southern Asia are noted for their relatively stable traditions. In these areas, traditions and taboos encourage an attitude skeptical of change that might undermine religious and social mores, but great social diversity still exists between various cultures. In the past, many cultures in the Far East often were better organized, more advanced technologically, and richer than in the West.

Eastern thought has always seemed somewhat mysterious and exotic to Westerners: An abject sense of duty in some cases, an emphasis on a rigid class structure, strong familial ties, and ancestor veneration generally are not found or promoted in Western society. Eastern philosophers are equally repulsed by the West's excessive concern for material goods, social advancement, and changing moral standards. The differences between East and West often seem so great that one may wonder whether any bridge is possible between these viewpoints. Perhaps the great stumbling blocks are a lack of understanding between these two cultures, their enormous historical diversity, and their differences in expectations and motivations.

The West has greatly influenced the East politically and economically; the East, in turn, has enriched the West philosophically and spiritually. Because of the ethnocentrism prevalent in both cultures, not as much serious dialogue has taken place as should have. To understand the Eastern position, one must set aside Western biases and Western aims. When they do, Westerners find much to admire and learn from Eastern philosophy.

Indian Thought

Indian philosophy has a long and complex history. Before Moses, Buddha, or Christ, sages in India were contemplating the meaning of life. In Indian thought almost every shade of belief can be found, ranging from idealism to materialism, monism to pluralism, and asceticism to hedonism. Great emphasis is placed on a search for wisdom in Indian philosophy, but this need not mean a rejection of worldly pleasures. Although it emphasizes speculation, Indian philosophy has a practical character. It began as a way to solve the basic problems of life, as well as to improve life. For example, early people faced mental and physical suffering and sought to understand the reasons for this; speculation about the world helped provide answers about the world around them. Indian philosophers seem to insist that knowledge should be used to improve social and communal life and that people should live according to their ideals. Indian philosophy also has a prevailing sense of universal moral justice, in which individuals are responsible for what they are and what they become.

Hinduism

Philosophy and religion are closely intertwined in Hindu tradition. Their roots reach back 2,500 years to a civilization that flourished in the Indus Valley from 2500 B.C. to 1700 B.C. The cardinal principles of Hinduism are the divinity of the soul, the unity of existence, the oneness of Godhead, and a harmony of religions. Hinduism has no known founder, no prophets, and no definite set of doctrines. It dates back to prehistoric times, and early Hindus worshiped gods that represented powers in nature. Gradually, some came to believe that although divinities are in separate forms, these forms are part of one universal spirit called *Brahman*. Many divinities make up Brahman. The most important are Brahma, creator of the universe; Vishnu, its preserver; and Shiva, its destroyer. Hinduism's growth parallels the growth of the people who settled in India, and it is more a way of life than a dogma. Hinduism generally does not encourage asceticism or a renunciation of the world; consequently, it does not discourage desire but believes that one should be able to control and regulate it. Basically, Hindus believe that humans should not devote their lives to the pursuit of mere worldly success.

The beginnings of Hindu philosophy are found in three basic texts: the *Vedas*, the *Upanishads*, and the *Epics*. These writings appeared from about 1200 B.C. to A.D. 200.

Vedas. *Veda* means "knowledge," and the *Vedas* existed for centuries before they finally were written down. They are the oldest Hindu scriptures. The *Vedas* were a group of hymns, chants, and treatises of a people who called themselves Aryans. Early Vedic religion was a worship of nature with anthropomorphic overtones. To the Vedic Indian, the universe consisted of three entities: earth, atmosphere, and heaven. A flood meant that the rivers were angry; favorable weather meant that the gods were pleased. This polytheistic view of the universe included numerous gods, such as Agni, god of fire; Indra, god of thunder and rain; and Varuna, who controls and regulates the seasons. The first section of the *Vedas* consists of mantras that praise and propitiate the gods. The gods also are supplicated with sacrifices and oblations. There are good spirits, such as the spirit of the dawn; and there are bad ones, such as the demons of drought and darkness. The gods and demons fight continual battles, with the gods generally overpowering the demons. Vedic literature involves a continuing attempt to effect a harmony between people's material needs and their spiritual lives. To the Vedic believer, the following were the fundamental spiritual truths of the *Vedas:*

1. An Ultimate Reality is all pervading and is the final cause of the universe.
2. This Reality is an uncreated, self-luminous, and eternal spirit.
3. Religion, or Dharma, consists of meditating on this Spirit and leading a life of virtue and righteousness.
4. The human soul is divine, with the entire universe a manifestation of the Supreme Spirit.

The Vedic seers believed that humans are spirit and not merely body or mind. As spirit, human beings are divine in essence. Unlike other animals, humans can realize their divinity because God is within them. People cannot see this when lust, anger, or greed motivates them; hence, these evils must be removed and the heart and mind purified. This purification process might take several lifetimes of reincarnation.

Upanishads. Arthur Schopenhauer, a nineteenth-century German philosopher, said that reading the *Upanishads* "has been the consolation of my life, and will be of my death." The *Upanishads*, which means "secret teachings," were built on the *Vedas* but carried Vedic thought to a new dimension. The *Upanishads* were much more lofty and intellectual than the *Vedas*, and the gods receded into the background. No matter how crude, they marked the beginning of real philosophical speculation in India. In the *Upanishads*, sacrifices are looked down on, contemplation rather than worship is extolled, and divine knowledge is the important thing. The message is to merge self (Atman) with the supreme (Brahman), whereby Atman and Brahman come together. Whereas women occupied an inferior role in Vedic literature, in the *Upanishads* they were elevated to equal status with men.

The *Upanishads* promote a monistic conception of the deity. The Brahman is all powerful, all pervading, infinite, eternal, impersonal, and an indescribable Absolute. All creatures find their beginning and their end in Him. The *Upanishads* tell of a life full of miseries continued by transmigration to new lives as a result of one's actions *(karma)*. The *Upanishads* support the quest for a true understanding of the nature of Brahman. Brahman is the supreme reality, just as God is central in Christian thought. It is that on which all depends and is the source of all things: seas, mountains, rivers, plants, and the essences of all things. Because Brahman is in everything that exists, to deny Brahman is to deny one's own being.

Because Brahman is the only absolute reality, one must be absorbed into Brahman to achieve liberation. The best way to accomplish this task is to find a teacher, a knower of Brahman. Instruction, however, is secret and is to be imparted only to qualified students. The student is advised to approach humbly a spiritual teacher *(guru)* who is well versed in Vedic scriptures, as well as in knowledge of Brahman. Such a teacher can then impart knowledge of the imperishable truth. In the Vedic literature, one sees the development of religious thought from polytheism to monotheism. The idea of monotheism is even more pronounced in the *Upanishads*, where "Brahman is everywhere and Brahman alone."

Hinduism also teaches that the soul never dies. When the body dies, the soul is reborn. The soul can be reborn in an animal or a human. The *law of karma* states that every action affects how the soul will be born in the next reincarnation. If a person lives a good life, the soul will be born into a higher state; a person who leads an evil life might return as a snake or a worm. Reincarnation continues until one reaches spiritual perfection, and then the soul enters a new level of existence called *moksha* from which it never returns. According to the Hindu doctrine, animals also have souls, and cows, in particular, are sacred animals.

Another aspect of Hinduism is the development of laws. These laws exercised great weight in Hindu life and established codes that still influence Hindu social life. One of the great lawgivers of Hindu thought was Manu, said to be one of the chief authors of *Laws of Righteous Conduct*, which probably was completed within the first few centuries of the Christian era, as Westerners date history.

Manu placed the Brahmin class at the top of the social hierarchy. *Brahmins* are people of learning, thinkers, priests, teachers, and seekers of Brahman and are expected to lead lives of simplicity and austerity. Beneath the Brahmins are the *Kshatriyas*, people of courage and energy but without the intelligence of Brahmins. Beneath the Kshatriyas are the *Vaisyas*, merchants and professionals who tend to seek wealth and power as ends in themselves. The *Sudras* are laborers and servants. Beneath the Sudras are the *"untouchables"*—people considered not much above the level of lower animals. Although Manu did not believe that caste was necessarily inherited, a hereditary caste system did develop, and the caste system became a rigid part of Hindu society. The Indian constitution in 1950 outlawed the caste system and gave the untouchables full citizenship, but much discrimination still remains an integral part of Indian life.

Manu established three desired stages in a man's life. In the first stage, the student learns training and discipline of mind and body under a guru or teacher who requires no fee. No prescribed course of study or method is set, and learning is determined by the capacity of the student. Learning is to be for its own sake and not for gain. In the second stage (around 25 years of age), a man is expected to marry, and family becomes an important consideration. At this stage, men realize their duty to the sage, the gods, their ancestors, animals, and the poor. In the third stage (around 50 years of age), a man gives up his household to his son and either retires to a forest hermitage or assists the community as a wise counselor or advisor.

Manu also established three desired stages in a woman's life. A female is first subject to her father or brothers, then to her husband, and after her husband's death, to her sons. She must never be independent and must constantly worship her husband as a god even if he is "devoid of good qualities." She always must be cheerful and clever in the management of household affairs. Women may never perform a sacrifice, vow, or fast apart from their husbands. Although Manu's plan has lost its vitality because of modern social and economic changes, it still is considered by many to be the ideal life plan for Hindus.

Epics. In Indian philosophy, the two greatest epics are the *Ramayana* and the *Mahabharata*. The more significant of these is the *Mahabharata*, which contains the *Bhagavad-Gita*, written between 200 B.C. and A.D. 200. The first section of the *Gita* advocates the pursuit of various yogas, the second elaborates pantheistic doctrine, and the third expounds principles of Purusha and Prakriti and other tenets of this philosophy. The *Gita* promotes the idea that the whole world of nature and the universe of name and form are all illusion. The only reality is Spirit, and there should be stern devotion to duty, as well as an emphasis on the functions allotted to each caste at birth. In the *Gita*, God speaks to humans more intimately and in more detail, thus achieving a more personal form.

The *Bhagavad-Gita*, a poem of some 700 verses in 18 chapters, describes a great war that took place before 1000 B.C. between the Kauravas and the Pandavas, who were cousins, for succession to the throne. One great warrior, Arjuna, ponders the consequences of war and the meaning and nature of existence. The questions posed by Arjuna are answered by Krishna (identified with the god Vishnu), who explains to Arjuna why he should fight. Arjuna is told that he must fulfill his *dharma*, the obligations of his life, and that only in this way can salvation be achieved. The deeper concerns of their discussion involve motivation, purpose, and the meaning of any human action. The ideal individual accepts pain and pleasure with equal tranquility. With unshakable resolve, one should no longer be swayed by joy, envy, anxiety, and fear, but become patient, steadfast, and forgiving.

The *Bhagavad-Gita* expresses divine compassion for humanity. Krishna does not stress intellectual qualities as much as he does feelings of devotion and duty. In "the Way," which is the path to wisdom, there is a simplicity in salvation, and God and humanity are not enemies but companions. An important major theme of the *Gita* is that salvation is open to all and that Brahman accepts all.

The notion of yoga is most clearly associated with the *Bhagavad-Gita*, which discusses the sage who, through serenity, ascends into yoga. It is frequently interpreted as a "union with the Absolute," whereby one might "yoke" one's soul with the world-soul. Historically, the most significant form of yoga has been the classical system of Patanjali, founded in the second century A.D. and described in the *Yoga Sutras.* Patanjali did not state a philosophy as much as a method of instruction on how to induce certain psychological states. *Yoga* is a set of mental and physical exercises designed to free the soul from reliance on the body so that the soul can unite with Brahman. The three external steps of yoga are (1) right posture, (2) right breathing, and (3) control of the senses. The body is to be so controlled that it will offer no impediment to the serious practice of meditation. One learns to pay no attention to sounds, sights, skin sensations, or any other distraction. Emotions also are controlled so that concentration can be fixed toward reaching freedom and illumination.

Modern Hinduism

A modern renaissance of Hinduism has been led by such men as Rabindranath Tagore, Sri Aurobindo, Sarvepalli Radhakrishnan, and Mahatma Gandhi. Gandhi was born in Porbandar, Northwest India, where his father was a provincial prime minister. In 1891, he received a degree in law from University College in London. When he returned to India, he gave up his law practice in order to promote social reform. He was prominent in civil disobedience and protests that resulted in independence for India from Great Britain in 1947.

According to Gandhi, religion should be practical. God is not to be realized by meditating in some cave but by living in the world. God is truth, and the best way to seek truth is by practicing nonviolence *(ahimsa)* in word, thought, and deed. People should lead lives of love and service toward others, and religion should mold our social, economic, educational, and political lives. Gandhi was opposed to the traditional concepts of untouchability, enforced widowhood, and child marriage. He advocated equal rights for women, promoted admission to temples and schools for all people, endorsed the kind attitude toward lower animals generally practiced by Hindus, and strongly encouraged manual labor for everyone. He believed that God is not an abstraction, but rather a living presence, "an indefinable mysterious power that pervades everything." Gandhi believed that one cannot know God completely in this life and can, at best, achieve only a partial vision of the Truth, which should encourage in people a tolerant attitude toward the views of others. One should be willing, however, to suffer for one's own convictions without making others suffer. Gandhi realized that absolute nonviolence might not be possible but that one should move in this direction.

One of the biggest controversies with Hinduism today is the subject of caste. Although the concept of "untouchables" or *dalits,* which literally means "broken people," has been outlawed, and even though one of the presidents of modern India was himself from the dalit caste, the tradition lives on. Some Indians say the country needs people to do the undesirable work, and dalits fulfill this role. No subject in India creates a greater division of opinion as the subject of caste, which has been promoted for centuries by religion and philosophy.

For Westerners, the closest visible element of the Hindu tradition probably is the Hare Krishna movement where one sees young people with shaved heads, wearing robes and beating drums. This sect was founded in the United States in 1966 by A. C. Bhaktivedanta Swami Prabhupada. Members lead an ascetic life, abstaining from meat, drugs, and gambling. They also refrain from sexual activity except for the purpose of having children. Many do community work, recruit members, and work at various jobs. A similar group is the Divine Light Mission. Both have centers in North America and throughout the world.

Buddhism

Although Buddhism is identified primarily with China, it began in India. Siddhartha Gotama (563 B.C. to 483 B.C.) was born within the current boundary of Nepal. These dates are somewhat uncertain, as is information about the life and teachings of the *Buddha* ("Enlightened One"), as he was called. The Buddha wrote nothing down, and most writings about him arose a considerable time after his death.

According to tradition, when the Buddha was born, the trees of Lumbini Park burst into bloom. He was born a prince named Gotama, the son of a rich Hindu raja, and was destined for rulership. He was cared for by 32 nurses in three palaces, and his father attempted to shield him from all unpleasantness during his youth. At 19, Gotama was married to a princess, Yasodhara, who bore him a son named Rahula. It would appear that Gotama had a perfect life, but when he was 29, he had several visions. First, he saw a wrinkled and toothless old man bent over a stick, then a diseased man with fever, and after that a corpse wrapped in cloth being carried in procession to the funeral pyre. These experiences caused Gotama to search for serenity in the face of the evils of existence: old age, sickness, and death. In his fourth vision, he met a wandering holy man who convinced him that he should leave his wife and son and seek enlightenment. Such enlightenment would free him from life's sufferings.

Gotama studied under a succession of teachers and took up the role of an ascetic, living, it is said, on one grain of rice a day. One day, he wandered into a village near Gaya and sat under a bo tree until he gained enlightenment, described as a state of great clarity and understanding of the truth about the way things are. Gotama believed that people could find release from suffering in *nirvana,* a state of complete happiness and peace. To achieve nirvana, people had to free themselves from desires for worldly things. His first sermon was called the "Sermon on the Turning of the Wheel of the Law," which dealt with the problem of suffering and how to overcome it. He believed that personal gratification is the root and cause of suffering in the world. In his sermon, he put forth the Four Noble Truths:

1. Life is suffering.
2. The cause of this suffering is desire.
3. Suffering can be eliminated when desire is extinguished.
4. Desire can be eliminated through the eightfold path, consisting of:
   a. *Right understanding*—understanding things as they are and having knowledge of where one is and where one wants to go.
   b. *Right speech*—not telling lies, backbiting, slandering, and engaging in foolish gossip or harsh and abusive language. One must not speak carelessly. If one can't say anything useful, one should keep "noble" silence.
   c. *Right conduct*—avoiding destruction to life and property. One should promote harmonious and peaceful living, adopt an honorable profession, and have no dishonest dealings or illegitimate sexual intercourse.

   d. *Right vocation*—desiring to follow the correct path and to put knowledge into practice.

   e. *Right effort*—directing one's energies toward wholesome states of mind.

   f. *Right mindfulness*—having a vigilant attitude toward desire, anger, hope, and fear.

   g. *Right concentration*—disregarding passionate desires and evil thoughts and developing spiritual awareness.

   h. *Right thought*—maintaining a selfless renunciation and detachment, with thoughts of love and nonviolence.

Buddhism holds with Hinduism that the universe is *samsara*, a stream without end in which the law of karma operates. People must overcome samsara, and the only way to do this is to obtain freedom from the cycle of births and deaths by realizing nirvana. As in Hinduism, the Buddha believed in reincarnation: Good deeds lead to rebirth as a good and wise person; evil deeds lead to rebirth as a poor and sickly person.

The Buddha rejected the notion of ritual and ceremonies, as well as the knowledge and religious authority maintained by the Brahmins. He also objected to mystery, speculation, and the concept of a personal God. He eschewed worship and never prayed although, ironically enough, he was to become a god worshiped through prayer by millions of people. He spent much of his life teaching and directing his disciples to (1) use ordinary discourse and make points gradually, (2) observe a proper sequence of ideas, (3) use words of compassion, (4) avoid irrelevant matters, and (5) avoid caustic remarks against others. He did not believe that one should explain the tenets of Buddhism all at once but should begin with that which is elementary and related to the student's condition. More difficult ideas should be put forth in stages followed by higher teachings.

Before beginning a discussion, the Buddha tried to form an idea of a person's view by posing appropriate questions. He then used similes, parables, fables, and verses. In addition to meticulous attention to his own style of teaching, the Buddha gave studious attention to the conduct and training of his disciples, correcting their weaknesses through patience and advice.

Only with great misgiving did the Buddha later receive women into discipleship. His early teachings encouraged his followers to shun women, even their gaze. Female disciples who became nuns were to keep a certain distance from the master and to remain in a totally submissive role. For those men who were to become Buddhist monks and live a life of poverty, meditation, and study, the Buddha established an order, the Sangha. This order lived under definite rules and regulations known as the Monk's Rules, which constituted an important part of Buddhist scripture. Some 227 rules governed a monk's conduct, including four great prohibitions. An ordained monk could not (1) have sexual intercourse, (2) take what has not been given to him, (3) deprive any creature of life, not even a worm or an ant, and (4) boast of any superhuman perfection. Monks were to meet regularly and examine themselves for any lapse in standards. If a member thought that he was guilty of some infraction, then he was expected to make a public confession of it.

Today, Buddhist monks, noticeable by their brightly colored saffron robes, continue the teachings of Gotama. They argue that suffering occurs when one is not in harmony with the universe. Suffering is the result of a wrong attitude, and the craving for things results in unhappiness. When one follows the "middle path" of avoiding extremes and renounces desire, happiness will ensue.

Although adherents to Hinduism are found mostly in India, Buddhists are found in Myanmar (Burma), Sri Lanka, China, Tibet, Korea, Japan, Cambodia (Kampuchea), and Laos, as well as in India. Buddhism, after flourishing in India for 1,500 years, lost its foothold there and was driven away by Hinduism or was absorbed by it. It has persisted for more than 2,500 years but has undergone profound changes during that time. Many newer schools of thought have developed, some coexisting with older ones, and many writings composed centuries after the Buddha's death have been ascribed to him. In its first phase, Buddhism stressed nonattachment; in its second phase, it stressed concern for humanity and the desire to become Buddha-like; and in the third, it emphasized a sense of harmony with the universe, in which one is under no constraint to change forces within or without. With all its changes, however, it has maintained a recognizable character and continuity.

The great leader of Tibetan Buddhists is the fourteenth Dalai Lama, whose name is Tenzin Gyatso. He is believed to be a reincarnation of the Buddha. When the Chinese army invaded Tibet in 1959, they destroyed monasteries and killed many monks. They forced the Dalai Lama into exile. He went to India and received the Nobel Peace Prize in 1989 for his nonviolent opposition to Chinese rule in Tibet. The Dalai Lama travels widely and presents a message of hope and compassion to the people of the world.

Jainism

The Jain religion is in many ways similar to Hinduism and Buddhism. Jains are followers of the Jinas. The term *Jina* is an appellation given to one who has attained enlightenment. Jainism is similar to Buddhism in that both originated in the same part of India, opposed prevailing orthodox views, rejected the caste system and a personal God, used many identical terms, and gave great importance to the concept of noninjury. Both also rejected Vedic literature and extolled nirvana—release from the birth-death cycle. Unlike Buddhism, however, Jainism is confined mostly to India.

Jains believe that every living thing consists of an eternal soul called the *jiva* and a temporary physical body. The eternal *jiva* is imprisoned in the body as a result of worldly activities. Each *jiva* is reincarnated in many bodies before it is finally freed. After being free, it exists eternally in a state of perfect knowledge and bliss. Jains do not believe in a God but worship 24 spiritual teachers called *Tirthankaras* and use them for guides in their daily lives. Jain monks and nuns devote their lives to meditation and studying the scriptures. The ideal or supreme purpose of Jainism is the realization of the highest or the Absolute perfection of human nature, which in its original purity is free of all kinds of pain or bondage.

Traditional belief is that the development of Jainism was connected primarily with Vardhamana Mahavira. The scion of a princely family, Mahavira was born at Kshatriyakundagrama, a suburb of Vaisali (modern Basarh, Bihar state), near modern Patna. The traditional date of his birth is 599 B.C., but scholars believe that this date is 40 or more years too early because Mahavira appears to have been a younger contemporary of Gotama. When Mahavira was 30, certain gods appeared and urged him to renounce the world. According to legend, he stood beneath a holy asoka tree and renounced all possessions, removed all clothing, and pulled out his hair by hand, indicating an end of concern for the body and a willingness to face pain. He is considered to be the last prophet, and the religion is older than his birth date would suggest.

Mahavira is considered to be the 24th and greatest of the *Tirthankaras*. After his death, his followers included Emperor Chandragupta, founder of India's great empire.

Jains believe that theirs is the oldest religion in the world, even antedating Hinduism. A prophet named Parsvanatha lived 250 years before Mahavira, and a predecessor of Parsvanatha supposedly died 84,000 years before Mahavira's nirvana. Thus, adherents believe that the religion is eternal. After the death of his parents, Mahavira became an ascetic for 12 years and is said to have attained nirvana at Pava around 527 B.C. The oral teachings of Mahavira were later put into written form and consist of the following philosophical and ethical doctrines:

1. The human being is dual in nature, both spiritual and material.
2. One must control the material world by one's spiritual nature.
3. One can separate one's soul from karmic matter by one's own efforts.

Before taking vows, each Jain must give up certain faults. A Jain must not (1) entertain any doubts about the soundness of Jain theory, (2) adopt another faith, (3) question the reality of the fruits of karma, and (4) associate with hypocrites. The vows that the Jain then takes are as follows:

1. To avoid injury to any form of life; not to hurt anyone by word or deed. One should cover one's mouth to prevent injury to the air, and one should avoid stepping on any living thing. One should not scratch for fear of injuring a parasite and should avoid agriculture that may injure animals, such as worms in the soil. One should also avoid the killing of all animals, including fish. Jains have been active in providing hospitals for sick animals and for putting numerous bird feeders in the streets. Jains also believe that people should avoid psychological injury, and if people follow this doctrine, they might achieve peace and fellowship.
2. To speak no untruths; to utter no falsehoods, rash or harsh speech; and to speak no ill of others or give bad advice.
3. To steal nothing and not become a victim of greed or envy.

These vows are to be accepted by all Jains. Those who are to be in the highest order (known as *yatis*) take two additional vows:

4. To practice chastity, either fidelity in marriage or the renouncing of all sexual contact.
5. To renounce all attachments and neither love nor hate any object.

Other vows, primarily for householders, include avoiding unnecessary travel, limiting things in daily use, guarding against evils, keeping specific times for meditation, maintaining special periods of self-denial, serving occasional days as monks, using no alcohol or other drugs, and giving alms in support of yatis. The Jains put such an emphasis on following these vows that despite their great concern for life, they believe that Jains should commit suicide by starvation if they are incapable of following them.

Jains believe that the universe has existed for all eternity, undergoing an infinite number of revolutions produced by the powers of nature without the intervention of any external deity. The world is uncreated and indestructible. They believe that trying to prove God's existence is a hopeless cause, yet they recognize a higher deity *(paramadevata)* as the object of veneration—namely, the *Jina,* the teacher of sacred law, who (being free from all passions and delusions and being omniscient) has reached perfection after annihilating all his karma.

The Jains have a philosophy that rejects systems as absolutes and affirms them only as partial truths. This is known as the doctrine of *syaduada,* or "maybe." No judgment is absolutely true or absolutely false.

Jains promulgate seven propositions about reality:

1. Maybe, reality is.
2. Maybe, reality is not.
3. Maybe, reality is and is not.
4. Maybe, reality is indescribable.
5. Maybe, reality is and is indescribable.
6. Maybe, reality is not and is indescribable.
7. Maybe, reality is, is not, and is indescribable.

During the twelfth and thirteenth centuries, the Jain community experienced great Hindu opposition to their atheistic and anti-Vedic doctrines. Through the centuries, Jainist views have suffered several schisms; the most serious involves the doctrine of absolute nonviolence. Dr. Albert Schweitzer, who was a Christian but who also followed some tenets of Jainism, declared that he killed germs only when they attacked a higher organism (humans), and that he did not go around indiscriminately killing germs. Other questions about killing are raised, such as "If a snake were about to kill me, could I kill the snake?" Although the Jains have firmly entrenched views of tolerance and nonviolence, many have questioned whether these views can succeed in a world where violence seems necessary under certain extreme conditions.

Chinese Thought

As in India, religion has been a powerful force in Chinese thought. Ancient Chinese governments drew heavily on religious thought in framing their governmental decrees, and social and economic life was tied in with religious convictions. Religion, philosophy, government, and social life were all intertwined in an attempt to help humanity achieve harmony with the universe and with life.

Much of Western philosophy emphasizes conflict, such as the conflicts between philosophy and religion, business and labor, and progress and the environment, as well as individual rights and governmental authority. In Chinese philosophy, more emphasis is placed on harmony, and correct thinking and good behavior can help one achieve such harmony. This harmony of government, business, and family could then lead toward a higher synthesis.

Confucianism

Confucius (551 B.C. to 479 B.C.) was born in the state of Lu of a poor and common background. As a youth, he was given responsibility in the house of Baron Chi. He later became a magistrate in the model town of Chung-tu, then a Grand Secretary of Justice, and finally Chief Minister. During his lifetime, he traveled and taught people about government and the ways of a gentleman. After his death, his disciples collected his conversations and sayings and put them together into a book known as the *Analects*. For more than 2000 years, Confucianism was the most important force in Chinese life. It affected education, government, and personal behavior. Confucius was The Ultimate Sage-Teacher, and is remembered for his wise sayings.

At the peak of Confucius's career, approximately 3000 students gathered around him. He taught them philosophy and music, with a particular emphasis on ethics. The word Confucius used to describe the moral order was *li*. Many talked of li, but few lived it. The Confucian ideal of the superior individual is one who lives a life of rightness, virtue, and propriety. Confucius realized that his views were at variance with those of the nobility, who believed that one was a gentleman because of birth. Confucius argued that being a gentleman was a question of conduct and character. His students were the nobility as well as the poor, and Confucius stated that he never refused instruction to anyone.

Confucius believed that humans are social beings. They must interact with society without necessarily surrendering to it, and the moral individual will attempt to change others to conform to the moral path. Confucius even exhorted his followers to criticize a ruler if they found him to be unjust. He was interested in political authority and established Five Constant Virtues that he thought a ruler should follow in governing his people:

1. *Benevolence:* Always think first of what is good for the people.
2. *Righteousness:* Do not do to your subjects what you would not want them to do if you were in their place.
3. *Propriety:* Always behave with courtesy and respect toward your subjects.
4. *Wisdom:* Be guided by knowledge and understanding.
5. *Sincerity:* Be sincere and truthful in all you do.

Confucius believed that people need standards or rules for life, and rules were developed for a wide range of social activities. He also believed that the self should not come before society because people have overriding obligations to parents, ancestors, and society as a whole. What is needed is sincerity in both personal and public conduct. Confucius taught that one's own well-being depends directly on the well-being of others.

Confucius stressed the importance of education, but he believed that building moral character was more important than merely teaching skills or imparting information. This moral approach emphasized practicality, part of which dealt with relationships with one's parents. Sons should obey and defer to their parents and respect the wisdom they gained in their journeys through life. If a man followed these and other correct principles, he could become *chûn-tzu,* the true gentleman, as a result of his moral development. The chûn-tzu was distinguished by faithfulness, diligence, and modesty. He would not serve an evil prince or seek mere personal profit, and he would lay down his life for the good.

Confucius believed that the superior individual develops Five Constant Virtues (as opposed to the Five Constant Virtues for a ruler, listed previously):

1. Right Attitude.
2. Right Procedure.
3. Right Knowledge.
4. Right Moral Courage.
5. Right Persistence.

These virtues, if practiced, would lead to a new society based on the principles of justice and wisdom.

Confucius never intended to start a religion, nor did he emphasize religious practices, God, a savior, sacrifice, or even salvation; instead, he emphasized the here and now and service to humanity. His aim was to educate a person to be a good father, mother, son, daughter, friend, and citizen. Confucius believed that every person should strive for the continual development of self until excellence is achieved.

The first Europeans to encounter the religious traditions of China were Jesuit missionaries. Some of these missionaries felt strongly that there could be a reconciliation of Confucianism with Christianity and referred to Confucius as "The Chinese Aristotle." However, Confucianism was so pervasive in China for so many centuries that up until the twentieth century, prospective civil servants took examinations based upon Confucian canons.

Taoism

Lao-tzu (circa fifth century B.C.) served for some time in the imperial court and saw its corruptive nature. He was aware of Confucian thought but criticized its "self-sufficient air [and] overweening zeal; all that is of no use to your true person." Lao-tzu set down his teachings in a small volume known as *Tao Te Ching.* It has had a great influence in China and has provided guidance in troubled times. Whereas Confucianism greatly emphasizes the fulfillment of external obligations and rules (e.g., If the mat was not straight, the master would not sit), Taoism emphasizes the development of the inner life where one can meet any difficulty. The Taoist ideal is a person who avoids conventional social obligations and leads a simple, spontaneous, and meditative life close to nature. Rather than develop sophistication, one should promote a "return to infancy."

The central concept of Taoism is *Tao,* which means "the Way or Path." It is the way the universe moves—the way of perfection and harmony. It is conformity with nature. Perhaps the most significant quality of the Tao is nonaction, letting things alone, and not forcing one's personal desires into the natural course of events. It is a noncompetitive approach to life. Taoists believe that the best leader is one who rules by letting things alone and using moderation, and that conflict and war represent a basic failure in society because they bring ruin to states and disrespect for life.

In the *Tao Te Ching,* Lao-tzu says, "Man conforms to earth; Earth conforms to Heaven; Heaven conforms to Tao; and Tao conforms to the way of Nature." When things are allowed to take their proper course, perfection and harmony exist in the universe. People were originally happy but suffer now as a result of the changes brought by civilization. The best thing to do, therefore, is to live in tranquil communion with nature. This applies even to death because it is part of the vast cosmic changes whereby all things ebb and flow. Taoism became a kind of mystical philosophy—a nature mysticism—for nature possesses something greater than logic. People need to share in nature's truth and to seek union with the Absolute, the Tao, something that cannot be known or seen or even talked about. To be close to nature, early Taoists led solitary lives in remote parts of China, whereas later sects achieved a sort of compromise between nature and societal life.

Lao-tzu believed that one should not rebel against the fundamental laws of the universe. "Do nothing," *wu wei,* is the famous injunction of Taoists. This does not mean doing nothing at all but doing nothing that is unnatural or not spontaneous. Most importantly, people should not strain or strive after anything but let things come naturally. Many are familiar with the Yin (male) and Yang (female) symbol, which stresses the opposing but harmonious forces in nature. Taoism stresses that one must live in harmony with the external world.

A strong sense of relativism pervades Taoist philosophy. Lao-tzu tells that beauty, the taste of foods, and the location of one's residence fit no absolute standards. Deer eat grass, snakes like centipedes, and owls enjoy mice. With moral problems, too, Taoists believe there is a "thus" and a "not thus," and who is to say which is correct? Things should be allowed to run their course within the all-embracing universe.

Taoism also speaks to political practice. When there is no interference with freedom and no special privilege, then happiness and peace will ensue. Taoists rejected the idea of rulership by divinity or birth, and often engaged in nonresistance against power and militarism. They believe that proper individuals would give up their lives to achieve social justice. Taoists also believe that people can govern themselves, and Taoist writings convey a strong sense of anarchy. They believe that governments tend to impose rules on the people that are inconsistent with the natural flow of life. They oppose war and repressive government and argue that the more laws there are, the more thieves and bandits multiply. Nor does a death penalty work, for the people do not fear death. The best ruler would be the Taoist sage, who governs in the interests of the people as a whole and who is beyond good and evil and above emotion. He might destroy a city and kill its inhabitants with impunity if he thought that this action was in the interest of the totality.

Another major figure in the development of Taoism was Chuang-tzu (399 B.C. to 295 B.C.). In the book *Chuang-tzu*, he advocates transcending the world rather than reforming it. To achieve such emancipation, one should engage in "free and easy wandering," "fasting of the mind," and "forgetting." The Tao, as Chuang-tzu saw it, means a detachment from the self and the world. Both life and death must be accepted as a part of nature. Thus, an individual should face life with great indifference and with humor.

Japanese Thought

The major historical base for Japanese philosophy is to be found in Shinto. This early religion of Japan lives on today but is not as influential as it once was. *Shintoism* encouraged nature worship, which meant the worshiping of trees, mountains, rocks, and waves. Emperor worship and the use of rituals, sorcery, divination, and purification rites also were practiced. By A.D.1000, Japan had 3000 shrines where Shintoists worshiped 3000 deities. The center of Shinto worship is the Sun Goddess, Amaterasu, who is the symbol of the things most sacred in Japanese life.

The Japanese perspective is one of acceptance and enjoyment of life and kinship with nature. Intuition often is prized over intellectualization, and religious views often are interwoven with ideas about nature and family. The feeling for loyalty, purity, and nature is strong. Today, the Japanese are a remarkable people who have used Eastern and Western influences while maintaining much of their cultural and philosophical heritage. They have been successful in fusing Confucian, Buddhist, and Taoist beliefs and practices in ways that incorporate them with a distinctly Japanese perspective. One example is the development of Buddhism, which began in India, flourished in China, and was adapted and transformed to fit a Japanese perspective, becoming Zen Buddhism.

Zen Buddhism

Buddhism probably entered Japan around A.D. 552. It was encouraged as a way of promoting national and political unity. Prince Shotoku Taishi (A.D. 573 to 621 A.D.) was deeply devoted to Buddhism and believed that it would assist in developing social harmony. He encouraged Buddhist priests to lecture in Japan and helped create Buddhist temples. In time, however, the Japanese modified Buddhism considerably, adapting it to Japanese culture and life. Zen Buddhism was founded in China around the sixth century by an Indian monk named Bodhidharma, who was popularly known as *Daruma*. It did not reach Japan until 1191, when several schools of Zen were established, such as the Rinzai and Soto schools.

Zen has no saviors, paradise, faith, or god. It has no books or scriptures, nor does it teach: It only points. It proposes to discipline the mind and to free it. Its advocates emphasize that Zen is neither a philosophy nor a religion in the Western sense: It does not preach a doctrine; it does not proselytize. It promotes the idea that one can explore new paths without giving up one's own religious beliefs or philosophies.

Zen emphasizes dependence on oneself rather than on outside sources for answers and wisdom. It depends more on intuition than on intellectual discovery and holds that logical thinking and verbalization might prevent enlightenment. The insight obtained from any experience cannot be taught or communicated, yet disciplines and techniques can orient one toward enlightenment *(satori)*. The important thing is to develop a "third eye." This third eye helps people see things in addition to what their two eyes show and should be attuned to the things around them.

Enlightenment is not obtained only in isolated meditation but can be achieved at any time—while people work, walk in the fields, or converse with a friend. Even ordinary things in people's daily lives can hide some deep meaning that the third eye uncovers. Daisetz Suzuki said that the question "What is Zen?" is at once easy and difficult to answer. A person lifts a finger and there is Zen. One sits in silence and there is Zen. Everything one does or says is Zen, and everything one does not do or say is Zen. Zen is in, with, and around everything. There is Zen in the garden, and Zen in all people.

Zen emphasizes silent meditation, aiming to awaken the mind in each person. Enlightenment comes through an immediate and intuitive understanding of reality that awakens one's Buddha nature. Zen Buddhists insist that one cannot realize this through intellect, reason, or logic; rather, one must transcend the framework of rational thinking. Even in literature, such as haiku poetry (a poem usually consisting of 17 Japanese syllables), one learns to transcend ordinary ways of thinking:

The still pond, ah!

A frog jumps in

The waters sound.

The primary methods of Zen are *zazen*, *koan*, and *sanzen*. These methods are designed to help one reach *satori*. *Zazen* is seated meditation in which one sits in a lotus position with half-open eyes looking straight ahead in contemplation. A *koan* is a statement or riddle on which Zen students meditate, such as "What was the appearance of your face before your ancestors were born?" The *koan* helps one acquire a radically different perspective on life. *Sanzen* is meditation with consultation. The student might meditate on a *koan* and consult privately with a master. The master helps correct the student's false conceptions and prejudices.

Zen methods also can include some physical violence, such as striking the student with a stick of bamboo to unlock the mind. The master also might shout at students and make them do physical exercises. These methods are encouraged as a way to awaken the student by cutting off the reasoning process and the desire to rationalize the universe. These awakening experiences are for the purpose of making something happen. When they are successful, they trigger an experience of enlightenment.

As Zen flourished and its followers increased, monasteries where Zen ideals could be realized were instituted. Monks stressed the importance of work, an ascetic way of life without possessions or waste, and a life devoted to a realization of all their faculties, where there is no real literary education but rather learning by doing. No definite timetable is set for becoming a Zen master; one lifetime might not be enough. No amount of reading, teaching, or contemplation is enough to become a Zen master. It is something that is the life of wholeness responding to wholeness—an unconditional union with all that is.

The influence of Zen Buddhism has been felt widely in Japanese culture—in its literature, drama, painting, archery, judo, swordsmanship, karate, and the tea ceremony. As they are often practiced, these arts emphasize concentration of the mind and the harmony of people and nature.

MIDDLE EASTERN THOUGHT

The Middle Eastern nations include Egypt, Turkey, Iran, Israel, and the Arab countries. For many centuries, this area has been commercially significant, and the history of the Middle East has been one of great conflict and influence. Many philosophies and religions owe their origins to thought that began in the Middle East, and Middle Eastern thought still stands as a challenge to Western ideas and traditions. Many thinkers have seen the Middle East historically as a meeting ground between the civilizations of the East and the West. The predominant language of the Middle East today is Arabic, and despite the variety of philosophies and religions, the predominant religious view is Islamic.

Today, Judaism and Christianity are seen as important influences within Western cultural traditions. Indeed, when someone speaks of Western religious traditions, the term *Judeo-Christian* often is applied to it. Judaism and Christianity had their origins in Middle Eastern cultural settings, and it can be argued that one cannot fully understand the Old Testament or the New Testament unless one sees them in terms of their Middle Eastern cultural and geographic roots. Judaism and Christianity began in the Middle East but have been subjected to Western influences that have altered them in many ways.

Judaism

Judaism traces its beginnings from Hebraism, beginning with the call of Abraham (circa 1750 B.C.), through Yahwehism and the giving of the Torah to Moses and the people, through Biblical Judaism, and through the Mishnaic and the Talmudic period. The classical age of Judaism began with Moses and extended until the completion of the Talmud many centuries later.

Abraham traveled around the Fertile Crescent area of the Tigris and Euphrates valleys. As a legendary hero, he was said to have come from Mesopotamia into Palestine about 2000 B.C. His mission was to find a new land and a new faith. He believed in one Supreme God who ruled the world and had a special interest in humanity. His grandson, Jacob, who received the name Israel from an angel, took up residence in Egypt with his numerous progeny known as Israelites. Here, they were put into slavery by those who ruled Egypt between 1750 B.C. and 1580 B.C. Under the leadership of Moses, the Israelites escaped from Egypt into the desert, and 40 years later they reached the edge of Canaan. After Moses's death, Joshua led the Hebrews into Canaan, where they established a monarchy under the military leader Saul. Under Kings David and Solomon, this area became the Israelite Empire. Judaism still has many roots in its early development as a religion and philosophy of wandering tribes. It antedates Christianity and Islam and contributed greatly to the development of both.

Central to Judaism is the Hebrew Bible, known as the Old Testament, which tells of the origins and development of the Jewish people. According to the Bible, God (*Yahweh)* gave the Ten Commandments to Moses on Mount Sinai. Jewish scripture also includes the Torah, the Prophets, and Writings. The *Torah* (Sacred Scriptures) consists of five books: Genesis, Exodus, Leviticus, Numbers, and Deuteronomy. In addition to the Sacred Scriptures is the *Talmud*, a collection of customs and laws, which is an extension of the Torah.

Philo of Alexandria, who was a Jewish philosopher, put the basic beliefs of Judaism into five fundamental concepts:

1. Belief in God.
2. Belief that there is only one God.
3. Belief that God created the world but the world is not eternal.
4. Belief that there is only one universe.
5. Belief that God cares for the world and all its creatures.

In earlier conceptions of Judaism, God was viewed anthropomorphically, with physical attributes the same as humans' and with such similar feelings as hate, jealousy, love, and vindictiveness. In later conceptions, God becomes more idealized, incorporeal, and mystical. He is "I am who am." This God is not only a spiritual entity but also omniscient, omnipotent, and eternal. God is a just God, who metes out justice to people for the character of their lives. There is also a belief in the coming of a Redeemer—a Messiah—who will establish Heaven on Earth and create the holy city of Zion.

In terms of practices, Judaism makes observance of the Sabbath prominent. It is a day of great spiritual significance and rejoicing—a day of bodily rest. In addition are ceremonial observances, such as the Day of Atonement, the Festival of Passover, the Feast of Tabernacles, and Shavuoth (or Pentecost). Many festivals and holy days celebrate joy as well as suffering. Every ritual is a reminder to the Jews of God's place in their lives. A Jew is required to pray, and prayer at the synagogue encourages praying as a community. Some Jews observe certain dietary laws, but not all Jews follow them. In Judaism, each congregation governs itself. Rabbis are not priests but individuals who teach the people and clarify the laws. Today, Orthodox Judaism attempts to be faithful to the ancient traditions; Conservative Judaism promotes a reinterpretation of the Torah; and Reform Judaism attempts to adapt Judaism to modern life.

Today, Judaism is identified frequently with the nation of Israel, which was founded in 1948, but more Jewish people live outside Israel than in it. It is in Israel, however, where the ancient words come to life for many believers: "Israel chose Yahweh to be their God, and Yahweh chose Israel to be his people." Judaism is a religion that strongly values learning, and many Jewish people have obtained great distinction in art, business, and science.

Christianity

Christianity is based primarily on the life and teachings of Jesus Christ. The dominant Christian groups today are Roman Catholics, Protestants, and Eastern Orthodox. Christianity began as a Jewish sect, organized and centered in Jerusalem around a small group of followers proclaiming Jesus of Nazareth as the Messiah. Jesus is reputed to have been born during the reign of King Herod around 6 B.C. (This date conflicts with the beginning of the Christian calendar, which is based on a miscalculation of Herod's death by medieval monks.) The career of Jesus as a preacher and a teacher began with his baptism by John the Baptist. Afterward, he gathered his own disciples who accepted him as *Christ,* the chosen one, sent to fulfill God's promise. Jesus was said to have performed miracles and forgiven sins.

According to the New Testament, Jesus was born in Bethlehem of a virgin mother and was crucified by Pontius Pilate, the Roman procurator of Judea, in A.D. 30. After suffering death, he arose from the dead on the third day and ascended into heaven. The words and deeds of Jesus form the basis for the New Testament, which is said to be the word of God. At the time of Jesus's death, he had no more than a few hundred followers, and this new faith met such hostility in Jerusalem that its members withdrew to Samaria, Damascus, and Antioch. The Christians showed enormous zeal, and Saul of Tarsus (Saint Paul) spent more than 30 years establishing churches in Asia Minor and Greece. Christianity appealed to the poor and the oppressed, and by A.D. 150, many churches were established throughout Asia Minor. Christians continued to suffer persecution for three centuries, particularly in Rome under Nero, Domitian, and Diocletian. After Constantine I came into power, he established Christianity as the quasi-official state religion of the Roman Empire in 324. Rome became the center of Christianity under the Roman Catholic Church.

Christian philosophy dominated Europe after the decline and fall of the Roman Empire, through the period known as the Dark Ages, and into the Middle Ages, perhaps reaching its pinnacle of social control in the thirteenth century. According to Gibbon and other historians, Christianity was one factor that caused the fall of the Roman Empire.

Although Christianity is based largely on the works and life of Christ as recorded in the New Testament by Matthew, Mark, Luke, and John, it was later given a more philosophical background through various other writings. Christianity incorporated from Judaism its beliefs of divine creation and providence but placed greater emphasis on the fatherhood of God and in God's concern for humanity. Belief in Jesus as a divinity always has been the crucial difference between Judaism and Christianity, and the New Testament represents a distinctly more loving and caring God than the Old Testament does.

Thinkers like Augustine and Aquinas gave Christianity its Western philosophical bedrock. Drawing on philosophers such as Plato and Aristotle, they provided a core of beliefs that became central to Roman Catholic philosophy. As the Old and New Testaments of Christianity became more plentiful in Europe because of the development of printing, more people had access to them and new interpretations arose. This sparked the Protestant Reformation, which was spearheaded by Martin Luther (1483 to 1546).

Luther, a German Augustinian monk, was a professor of Biblical theology at Wittenberg University. He was appalled at the laxity of the Roman Catholic Church, and particularly with the selling of indulgences whereby one could buy salvation and escape the punishment of hell. He set out to rebuild the church in accordance with his conception of the Gospel and translated the Bible into German to make it easier for people to read. He believed that people should read the Bible and interpret it for themselves, what is called "the priesthood of all believes'." Luther strongly championed education, and he sponsored an educational movement that opened Lutheran schools to be under the authority of the princes rather than the church. However, Luther's belief in an individual interpretation of the Bible led to many independent positions and schisms in Christianity under such leaders as John Calvin, John Knox, and Huldreich Zwingli. In the United States today, more than 300 different Christian sects use the teachings of Christ as their basic orientation.

After Luther's reformation, a counterreformation was spearheaded by Ignatius Loyola. Loyola founded the Jesuit order known as The Society of Jesus in 1534. This movement had widespread influence and devoted much attention to education. The Jesuits believed that the right kind of education could provide leaders who would help stem the influence of Protestant theology.

Judeo-Christian thought continues to be an important religious and philosophical force in the world today. Most ethical and social mores, as well as laws, found in Western society today are based on Judeo-Christian principles.

Islam

Muhammad (571 to 632) was born in Mecca. His parents died when he was young, and he was brought up by a succession of relatives. He was employed by a wealthy widow to look after her camels while she was trading in Damascus. He first became her steward and then her husband.

Muhammad entered into an ascetic phase during which he would spend many hours in a cave on Mount Hira, a hill near Mecca. He would endure long fasts and vigils, praying and meditating. When Muhammad was in his fortieth year, Allah spoke to him through Gabriel, the Angel of Revelation. The angel commanded that Muhammad call on all the people to worship Allah, the one true God. Gabriel appeared to Muhammad again and told him that his mission was to restore to the Arabs the pure faith of their father Abraham and to free them from bondage and idolatry. Muhammad told his people that they had to give up the worship of many gods and goddesses and follow the will of Allah, the one true God.

Muhammad's revelations were not well received by the local populace, and in 622, to avoid persecution, he was forced to depart from Mecca to Yathrib, now known as Medina. Muhammad became successful in Medina and ruled as a Prince-Prophet for 10 years. He acquired several wives and claimed divine origin. This movement of the Muslims to Medina has since been called the *Hegira*, and Muslims date their calendars from this year. In this new community, Muhammad exercised great authority and power.

Eight years after he left Mecca, Muhammad returned and conquered the city with his armies. He stripped all idols from the Ka'aba, and Mecca became the holy city of Islam. He then sought to unify the Arab tribes and bring them together in one nation governed by the will of Allah. After the death of Muhammad, Abu-Bakr began to collect the recitations he received from Allah into a book entitled the *Koran* (*Qur'an*), which means "The Reading." To the Muslim, every word in the Koran is the word of God as revealed by the angel Gabriel. It is written in classical Arabic, and most Muslims believe that it should not be translated into other languages.

The growth of Islam can be attributed in part to the ideas of the Koran, which speaks to the hopeless, the poor, and the outcast, regardless of race, color, or nationality. The Koran also did away with intermediaries between God and humans. Any person, no matter how sinful, can bring a plea before God. One does not even have to go to a mosque to speak with Allah. The Koran denounces usury, games of chance, and the consumption of pork or alcohol. It also forbids lying, stealing, adultery, and murder. The *mosque* is the Muslim place of worship, but this religion has no organized priesthood.

Muhammad taught that Allah is a purposeful God who created things to reach certain desired goals. The Koran tells the Muslim that each person will be tried in the Last Judgment, when Allah will judge all souls. Those who have followed the will of Allah will be rewarded eternally in paradise, an oasis of flowing waters, pleasant drinks, food, and sensual delights. Those who have not followed the will of Allah will be condemned to eternal suffering in fire and heat.

The basic beliefs of the orthodox Islamic religion consist of the following:

1. One God.
2. Sacred ground (all the earth belongs to Allah, so wherever one prays is holy ground).
3. Equality before God.
4. A life hereafter.
5. A prohibition on intoxicating drink.
6. Truthfulness.
7. The sinfulness of adultery.
8. Charity.
9. Duty to animals (treat animals with kindness and compassion).
10. Limited polygamy (a Muslim man is allowed to marry four wives, provided he can take care of them).

The religious duties of Muslims are stated in the Five Pillars of Islam:

1. *Belief:* Muslims profess faith as "I bear witness that there is no God but Allah, and Muhammad is the prophet of Allah."
2. *Prayer:* Muhammad required formal prayer five times a day—sunrise, noon, midafternoon, sunset, and nightfall.
3. *Almsgiving:* One is encouraged to share goods and money with the poor and to support Muslim schools and mosques.

4. *Fasting:* A fast during the month of Ramadan is required for all. During this time, one cannot take food or drink between sunrise and sunset.
5. *Pilgrimage:* Muhammad urged his followers to travel each year to the sacred city of Mecca. At the least, one should do this once during his lifetime.

Like other religions, Islam also has experienced great reform. Two major changes have been the reform of Islamic higher education and putting Islamic doctrines into acceptable terms for the modern world. The seeming conflict between scientific and religious authority has been minimized, and secular education has grown. H. A. R. Gibb said that the orthodox positions in Islam resemble eighteenth-century positions in relation to Christian doctrine, and that during the past 100 years, the extension of secular education has exposed Muslims to the same global influences that revolutionized Western cultures: print media, movies, television, and computers.

EASTERN THOUGHT AND PHILOSOPHY OF EDUCATION

Much in Eastern philosophy speaks to a concern for education. All too often today, Western education is seen primarily as a way of acquiring a job or for social advancement. Many Westerners are so immersed in their material concerns that they see little value in lofty speculation, mysticism, or anything that takes much time. Our educational institutions emphasize order, regularity, science, and the importance of facts. It is true that much of the secularism and neutrality of Western thought developed as a reaction to speculative thought, particularly the religious speculations of the Middle Ages, but Western philosophy might have lost something of importance in its quest for objectivity.

Eastern thinking spawned many of the ideas that have found their way into Western philosophy, and Eastern philosophy still serves as a useful antithesis to current beliefs. The concept of progress, for example, when looked at by Eastern and Western thinkers, is quite different. For the Western thinker, progress can be measured in terms of better bridges and more practical and efficient social and political systems. For the Eastern thinker, progress might mean nonattachment and the development of one's inner being.

One thing is clear, however: Eastern thinkers always have concerned themselves with education. They have seen education as a way of achieving wisdom, maintaining the family structure, establishing the law, and providing for social and economic concerns. Eastern philosophy extols education, especially the role of the teacher, because many of the great Eastern thinkers were teachers as well as theorists. They saw the importance of the teacher in acquainting people with new doctrines and in providing instruction in the things one must do to achieve the good life. Eastern philosophers also see education as necessary not only for this life but also for achieving a good life in the hereafter.

Aims of Education

Certainly, Eastern philosophy has no one goal of education. The aim of the earliest writers was to provide information about the forces of nature so that one could best deal with them. These forces were often capricious and demanding. The authors of the Vedic writings made the forces more understandable in their anthropomorphic guise and thus acceptable to village people who believed that nature, like humankind, was not to be trusted. These writings also suggested ways one could cope with or propitiate these forces to mitigate or assuage their fury.

Later writings of Indian and Chinese philosophers became more sophisticated, and increasingly less attention was focused on gods and ceremonies than on ways to live. A feeling developed that the way one lives is the important thing, and the way one lives can change things. Eastern philosophers have paid much attention to the sufferings of life, and in humans' narrow framework of thinking today, people might be like the Buddha, who did not see suffering in the beginning but sees it now. Today, a terrible automobile accident is cleared away so quickly that few see the blood and the pain. Old people are shunted out of sight to die, and asylums and prisons incarcerate those who might be a nuisance or cause physical harm to others. Thus, people are shielded from much of the suffering of humankind.

In Eastern philosophy, suffering is to be accepted as a way of life. Suffering has its causes, and these causes can be external, internal, or both. Those who lived a dissolute existence in a previous life might now be paying for their misdeeds. Perhaps, too, we need to see suffering as being beneficial to our development if it helps us gain wisdom. Some philosophers think that we can mitigate suffering, but it might require following a way, a path—something that is difficult and long.

Eastern philosophy has not been as singular in its development as Western philosophy. One has to take it system by system, culture by culture, and school by school. Often, these schools, such as Confucianism, lasted long periods of time and influenced large numbers of people, including emperors. Sometimes, these schools vied with each other for influence, and some served as stepping stones to new and different ideas. The fact that so many of them still exist and have such large followings attests to their continued vitality. Unlike the Western approach, most Eastern philosophies begin with sense experience and carry it backward to consciousness. In the Western view, the belief is that one should steadily increase the number of sensory experiences one has in order to amass a mountain of facts and data. The Eastern approach often seeks to diminish sense experience, or at least to downplay its role in the achievement of wisdom (or enlightenment) as distinct from knowledge.

Eastern educational philosophy also tends to place a greater emphasis on the teacher-student relationship and to see great change coming from this relationship. The student is changed as a result of contact with the guru, the master, the prophet, or the spiritual leader. Change is important because most Eastern philosophies emphasize that one cannot live a good life without thought that brings change. Education also might be necessary for salvation, and thus it takes on a spiritual quality. The emphasis is on transformation because the individual must be transformed to be able to face life or suffering with equanimity. Attitude shaping is also important, and Eastern philosophers emphasize that the attitude one holds toward life is often the deciding factor. If one has an attitude that encourages the accumulation of material things, Buddhists point out that one never will achieve happiness.

The aim of social change underlies most Eastern philosophies, but this larger social change often begins with individual change. The individual seeks and is changed, and as many individuals are changed, so too will society be changed. Eastern philosophers believe that people are weak, that they seek pleasure and materiality, but they can be changed so that they do not seek these things. Failure occurs, but it is individual failure, and one can overcome this through meditation, giving, living close to nature, fasting, and prayer.

One recurring educational aim of Eastern philosophy is to put humanity in tune with nature. Great emphasis is placed on observing nature and learning through wanderings and pilgrimages. The art of the East tends to reflect a deep longing and even spiritual consideration of nature. A study of nature should promote introspection and emphasize the inner life. The importance of achieving wisdom, satori, enlightenment, or nirvana is supreme in Eastern philosophy. All paths must lead to this, and from wisdom springs virtue, right living, and correct social and political behavior.

Methods and Curriculum

Eastern philosophy uses many educational methods as diverse as oral traditions and today's modern methods of communication. In comparison with Western philosophy, Eastern philosophy probably has provided a greater variety of approaches in education for the purpose of living well, alleviating suffering, achieving enlightenment, or reaching nirvana. Hinduism, for example, emphasizes oral traditions and the reading of sacred literature; the *Upanishads* represent its spiritual and philosophical basis. In Hinduism, beliefs grew through a succession of stages and as a result of certain leaders who gathered together the thoughts of the day in the form of *Sutras,* which often required some commentary to make them intelligible. At each stage, one had to develop one's views, challenge criticisms, and provide answers to new problems.

When one thinks of a primary method connected with Indian philosophy (Hinduism), it is yoga, although this is certainly only one method. In Patanjali yoga, the mind enters a trance in which it is emptied of all content, unaware of subject or object, and absorbed into the ultimate, where it becomes one with the One. Through yoga, the mind is liberated from the body and achieves an inner freedom that transcends the material world of the senses. Chinese philosophy also emphasizes yoga (Buddhism), as well as attention to the teaching of rules of right conduct (Confucianism) and to attitude shaping (Taoism). It also emphasizes the here and now more than the supernatural views found in Hindu philosophy.

The Chinese were never so preoccupied with supernatural views or with preparing for the next world, and many observers believe that this is why communism, with its materialist philosophy, was able to make easy inroads into Chinese life. Chinese philosophy has been characterized by a sense of proportion, with people suitably arranging their attitudes and actions in sequence with proper priorities. One of these priorities traditionally has been the family and one's ancestors, who are to be remembered and honored. In connection with this, a great emphasis has been placed on rules of order and rules of right conduct within the family and society.

Role of the Teacher

Although one can pursue the search for nirvana on one's own, many sects promote the importance of a guru, or teacher, who already has obtained knowledge and can lead the student along the true path. Some aspirants to the role of the guru might prepare themselves for several decades. The potential guru is to be selected carefully and, through a variety of techniques, properly educated. The guru occupies a central place in the student's life and is revered for the wisdom he provides. In some cases, the guru might encourage students to do things that seem meaningless and absurd to them but that lead to enlightenment. Thus, students must be able to place much confidence in their teacher.

Japanese thought places even greater emphasis on being in harmony with nature than does Chinese thought, but both claim a great reverence for the teacher. Zen Buddhism, as one example, places the teacher in a position of great prominence. There is, through the teacher, the possibility of sudden enlightenment by the use of the *koan*, which consists of cryptic questions and sudden blows intended to shock the student. Often, students wander about seeking the perfect Zen master from whom they can obtain enlightenment. In addition to the koan, an emphasis is placed on tranquility from meditation and the absence of thought. Zen also has influenced such arts as archery. Eugen Herrigel's *Zen in the Art of Archery* shows that a study of archery can lead to knowledge of self and the meaning of existence.

The role of the teacher in Christian thought is equally important. Although the teacher may only point, as Augustine says, he is an important part of the learning process. Aquinas believed that the right kind of teacher also might help the student learn much about the physical world, but in a way that promotes spiritual knowledge, as well. Most religions see education as a way of teaching fundamental beliefs and converting others to their ideas.

Eastern philosophies tend to extol sacred literature, and Judaism, Islam, and Christianity all have their sacred books. In most cases, these writings demand explanation or clarification, and a class of priests, rabbis, or prophets is necessary to explain these writings to the people. Sacred rites, prayers, and sacrifices also can be made at certain observed times and under rather specific conditions. As modern-day beliefs, these religions are challenged often by changing social and political events in a fast-paced world. Unlike Western philosophies, however, which seem to change with every social upheaval, Eastern philosophies have remained more intact. The role of the school in Western societies, for example, has often focused on learning facts, rather than on exploring alternatives in a changing world. Eastern education has tended to remain largely apart from Western educational traditions, which many Easterners believe do not promote desirable philosophical and religious ideals.

CRITIQUE OF EASTERN PHILOSOPHY IN EDUCATION

One good reason to study Eastern philosophy is that it represents a vantage point from which to examine contemporary views on Western education. It encourages humans to question seriously their most basic commitments to science, materialism, nature, religious traditions, and education, as well as the meaning of progress and the good life. This is not to say that various Eastern philosophies do not deal with these things, but they generally do not view them in the same ways.

Western beliefs also differ from Eastern beliefs in their emphasis on upward social mobility. Getting to the top is the most important thing for many Westerners, and they promote the view that anyone can do it. They are taught that they should get to the top even if this alienates or separates them from family, friends, or community life. Priorities, rules of order, and decorum often are ignored or ridiculed if they block achievement of the desired material end. In Eastern philosophy, order, regularity, and patience are generally prized, and the order is proportional and in harmony with the law of nature.

Eastern philosophy has much to be criticized, such as its emphasis on an unyielding supernaturalism as in Hindu philosophy, and some Western philosophers see the danger of dogmatism in the close relationship between Eastern religion and philosophy, as well as between religion and government. Unlike Western philosophies, Eastern views often are characterized by a sense of vagueness, splits between various factions, and an individualistic attitude toward salvation. In many cases, they also seem to promote a callous disregard for human life through such devices as the caste system. Western philosophies have tended increasingly to extol freedom and a democratic approach to government, whereas many Eastern philosophies still promote a loyalty to rulers and a belief in one's fixed and ordered place in the universe.

Another aspect of Eastern philosophy that bothers Western philosophers, particularly contemporary ones, is the great reliance placed on codes, rules, and prescriptive ways of life, such as Buddhism with its eightfold path, the Jains with their five vows, the "correct principles" of Confucianism, and the commandments of Judaism and Christianity. People may need help and direction in their lives, but these lists of rules often strike thinkers as too contrived to be of any real use in modern life. The older philosophies indicate the need for a permanent structure, which might have been important in an emerging civilization but does not fit today's world, with its complex social and moral dilemmas. One also faces difficulty in interpretation regarding rules, such as whether to kill germs (Jain) or whether to kill an attacker (Christian). Codes that seem simple on the surface often are difficult to apply in real situations. It is not surprising, therefore, that many modern philosophies have promoted a situational or contextual approach to problems, rather than a reliance on such seemingly strict and narrow rules.

With regard to education, one finds a great respect and concern for it throughout Eastern cultures. Teachers have occupied an important and central role in the development of thought, and the great religious and philosophical leaders were, above all else, teachers. The emphasis in Eastern philosophy is on not only knowing but also teaching this knowledge to others. The Buddha was a teacher, as were Confucius, Jesus, and Muhammad.

Although Westerners are critical of approaches to learning that are primarily theoretical, Eastern ideas are a contrast to the view that education should be concerned primarily with social and vocational skills. Undue emphasis also seems to be placed, in the minds of many Western educators, on the role of the teacher in the learning process versus the role of students in learning on their own. The emphasis on perfection also seems misplaced to many Western thinkers, who believe that the important thing is not to achieve perfection but to improve one's current state in terms of livelihood, material gain, or happiness.

Although many millions of people still abide by Eastern beliefs, it is unlikely that those beliefs will change the course of Western development greatly. Indeed, it seems likely to be the other way around as the West enlarges its spheres of influence, power, and communications. Every indication is that this has been happening for some time as Western philosophies challenge traditional views. Japan, in particular, and China and India are fast becoming great industrial and banking centers, and this is changing the character of their beliefs, as well as the character of their socioeconomic institutions.

For some Westerners, the appeal of Eastern philosophy is more romantic than real. Many have turned to Eastern philosophy as an escape from a hectic, constantly changing, and highly industrialized society. Jack Kerouac, for example, spoke of fasting and solitary excursions in the mountains in his book *Dharma Bums*. Today, Eastern philosophy already has found a place in religion, psychoanalysis, and rock music; it often has provided us with a refreshing and original look at these fields. Despite the criticisms leveled against it, Eastern philosophy remains a fascinating study that emphasizes a wide variety of views. It is an important study not only because of its historical significance and large following but also because it forces people to reexamine in a new way the meaning and purpose of life.

BHAGAVAD-GITA

The Bhagavad-Gita, or Gita, was written sometime between the fourth and third centuries B.C., and it is one of the best-known and loved of Indian writings. Its title means "Song of the Lord" or "Song Celestial," and it still is chanted in Hindu temples today. The Gita is basically a dialogue between Arjuna, the great warrior, and Krishna, the Lord, who is an embodiment of the Supreme. Arjuna is asking Krishna about responsibility and mastery of oneself in the face of life's challenges. The dialogue between Arjuna and Krishna shows some of the distinctive ethical ideals to come out of Indian philosophy.

Sanjaya:
Him, filled with such compassion and such grief,
With eyes tear-dimmed, despondent, in stern words
The Driver, Madhusudan, thus addressed:

Krishna:
How hath this weakness taken thee? Whence springs
The inglorious trouble, shameful to the brave,

Barring the path of virtue? Nay, Arjun!
Forbid thyself to feebleness! it mars
Thy warrior-name! cast off the coward-fit!
Wake! Be thyself! Arise, Scourge of thy Foes!

Arjuna:
How can I, in the battle, shoot with shafts
On Bhishma, or on Drona—O thou Chief!—

Both worshipful, both honourable men?
   Better to live on beggar's bread
     With those we love alive,
Than taste their blood in rich feasts spread,
     And guiltily survive!
Ah! were it worse—who knows?—to be
     Victor or vanquished here,
When those confront us angrily
     Whose death leaves living drear?
In pity lost, by doubtings tossed,
     My thoughts—distracted—turn
To Thee, the Guide I reverence most,
     That I may counsel learn:
I know not what would heal the grief
     Burned into soul and sense,
If I were earth's unchallenged chief—
     A god—and these gone thence!

Sanjaya:

So spake Arjuna to the Lord of Hearts,
And sighing, "I will not fight!" held silence then.
To whom, with tender smile, (O Bharata!)
While the Prince wept despairing 'twixt those hosts,
Krishna made answer in divinest verse:

Krishna:

Thou grievest where no grief should be! Thou
   speak'st
Words lacking wisdom! for the wise in heart
Mourn not for those that live, nor those that die.
Nor I, nor thou, nor any one of these,
Ever was not, nor ever will not be,
For ever and for ever afterwards.
All, that doth live, lives always! To man's frame
As there come infancy and youth and age,
So come there raisings-up and layings-down
Of other and of other life-abodes,
Which the wise know, and fear not. This that irks—
Thy sense-life, thrilling to the elements—
Bringing thee heat and cold, sorrows and joys,
'Tis brief and mutable! Bear with it, Prince!
As the wise bear. The soul which is not moved,
The soul that with a strong and constant calm
Takes sorrow and takes joy indifferently,
Lives in the life undying! That which is
Can never cease to be; that which is not
Will not exist. To see this truth of both
Is theirs who part essence from accident,

Substance from shadow. Indestructible,
Learn thou! the Life is, spreading life through all;
It cannot anywhere, by any means,
Be anywise diminished, stayed, or changed.
But for these fleeting frames which it informs
With spirit deathless, endless, infinite,
They perish. Let them perish, Prince! and fight!
He who shall say, "Lo! I have slain a man!"
He who shall think, "Lo! I am slain!" those both
Know naught! Life cannot slay. Life is not slain!
Never the spirit was born; the spirit shall cease to be
   never;

Never was time it was not; End and Beginning
   are dreams!
Birthless and deathless and changeless re-
   maineth the spirit for ever;
Death hath not touched it at all, dead though the
   house of it seems!
   Who knoweth it exhaustless, self-sustained,
   Immortal, indestructible,—shall such
     Say, "I have killed a man, or caused to kill?"
       Nay, but as when one layeth
         His worn-out robes away,
       And, taking new ones, sayeth,
         "These will I wear to-day!"
       So putteth by the spirit
         Lightly its garb of flesh,
       And passeth to inherit
         A residence afresh.
I say to thee weapons reach not the Life;
Flame burns it not, waters cannot o'erwhelm,
Nor dry winds wither it. Impenetrable,
Unentered, unassailed, unharmed, untouched,
Immortal, all-arriving, stable, sure,
Invisible, ineffable, by word
And thought uncompassed, ever all itself,
Thus is the Soul declared! How wilt thou, then,—
Knowing it so,—grieve when thou shouldst not
   grieve?
How, if thou hearest that the man new-dead
Is, like the man new-born, still living man—
One same, existent Spirit—wilt thou weep?
The end of birth is death; the end of death
Is birth: this is ordained! and mournest thou,
Chief of the stalwart arm! for what befalls
Which could not otherwise befall? The birth
Of living things comes unperceived; the death

Comes unperceived; between them, beings
  perceive:
What is there sorrowful herein, dear Prince?
    Wonderful, wistful, to contemplate!
      Difficult, doubtful, to speak upon!
    Strange and great for tongue to relate,
      Mystical hearing for every one!
    Nor wotteth man this, what a marvel it is,
      When seeing, and saying, and hearing are done!
    This Life within all living things, my Prince!
Hides beyond harm; scorn thou to suffer, then,
For that which cannot suffer. Do thy part!
Be mindful of thy name, and tremble not!
Nought better can betide a martial soul
Than lawful war; happy the warrior
To whom comes joy of battle—comes, as now,
Glorious and fair, unsought; opening for him
A gateway unto Heav'n. But, if thou shunn'st
This honourable field—a Kshattriya—
If, knowing thy duty and thy task, thou bidd'st
Duty and task go by—that shall be sin!
And those to come shall speak thee infamy
From age to age; but infamy is worse
For men of noble blood to bear than death!
The chiefs upon their battle-chariots
Will deem 'twas fear that drove thee from the fray.
Of those who held thee mighty-souled the scorn
Thou must abide, while all thine enemies
Will scatter bitter speech of thee, to mock
The valour which thou hadst; what fate could fall
More grievously than this? Either—being killed—
Thou wilt win Swarga's safety, or—alive
And victor—thou wilt reign an earthly king.
Therefore, arise, thou Son of Kunti! brace
Thine arm for conflict, nerve thy heart to meet—
As things alike to thee—pleasure or pain,
Profit or ruin, victory or defeat:
So minded, gird thee to the fight, for so
Thou shalt not sin!

    Thus far I speak to thee
As from the "Sânkhya"—unspiritually—
Hear now the deeper teaching of the Yôg,
Which holding, understanding, thou shalt burst
Thy Karmabandh, the bondage of wrought deeds.
Here shall no end be hindered, no hope marred,
No loss be feared: faith—yea, a little faith—
Shall save thee from the anguish of thy dread.
Here, Glory of the Kurus! shines one rule—

One steadfast rule—while shifting souls have laws
Many and hard. Specious, but wrongful deem
The speech of those ill-taught ones who extol
The letter of their Vedas, saying, "This
Is all we have, or need;" being weak at heart
With wants, seekers of Heaven: which comes—
  they say—
As "fruit of good deeds done;" promising men
Much profit in new births for works of faith;
In various rites abounding; following whereon
Large merit shall accrue towards wealth and
  power;
Albeit, who wealth and power do most desire
Least fixity of soul have such, least hold
On heavenly meditation. Much these teach,
From Veds, concerning the "three qualities;"
But thou, be free of the "three qualities,"
Free of the "pairs of opposites," and free
From that sad righteousness which calculates;
Self-ruled, Arjuna! simple, satisfied!
Look! like as when a tank pours water forth
To suit all needs, so do these Brahmans draw
Texts for all wants from tank of Holy Writ.
But thou, want not! ask not! Find full reward
Of doing right in right! Let right deeds be
Thy motive, not the fruit which comes from them.
And live in action! Labour! Make thine acts
Thy piety, casting all self aside,
Contemning gain and merit; equable
In good or evil: equability
Is Yôg, is piety!

    Yet, the right act
Is less, far less, than the right-thinking mind.
Seek refuge in thy soul; have there thy heaven!
Scorn them that follow virtue for her gifts!
The mind of pure devotion—even here—
Casts equally aside good deeds and bad,
Passing above them. Unto pure devotion
Devote thyself: with perfect meditation
Comes perfect act, and the right-hearted rise—
More certainly because they seek no gain—
Forth from the bands of body, step by step,
To highest seats of bliss. When thy firm soul
Hath shaken off those tangled oracles
Which ignorantly guide, then shall it soar
To high neglect of what's denied or said,
This way or that way, in doctrinal writ.
Troubled no longer by the priestly lore,

Safe shall it live, and sure; steadfastly bent
On meditation. This is Yôg—and Peace!

Arjuna:

What is his mark who hath that steadfast heart,
Confirmed in holy meditation? How
Know we his speech, Keśava? Sits he, moves he
Like other men?

Krishna:

When one, O Prithâ's Son!—
Abandoning desires which shake the mind—
Finds in his soul full comfort for his soul,
He hath attained the Yôg—that man is such!
In sorrows not dejected, and in joys
Not overjoyed; dwelling outside the stress
Of passion, fear, and anger; fixed in calms
Of lofty contemplation;—such an one
Is Muni, is the Sage, the true Recluse!
He who to none and nowhere overbound
By ties of flesh, takes evil things and good
Neither desponding nor exulting, such
Bears wisdom's plainest mark! He who shall draw
As the wise tortoise draws its four feet safe
Under its shield, his five frail senses back
Under the spirit's buckler from the world
Which else assails them, such an one, my Prince!
Hath wisdom's mark! Things that solicit sense
Hold off from the self-governed; nay, it comes,
The appetites of him who lives beyond
Depart,—aroused no more. Yet may it chance,
O Son of Kunti! that a governed mind
Shall some time feel the sense-storms sweep,
    and wrest
Strong self-control by the roots. Let him regain
His kingdom! let him conquer this, and sit
On Me intent. That man alone is wise
Who keeps the mastery of himself! If one
Ponders on objects of the sense, there springs
Attraction; from attraction grows desire
Desire flames to fierce passion, passion breeds
Recklessness; then the memory—all betrayed—
Lets noble purpose go, and saps the mind,
Till purpose, mind, and man are all undone.
But, if one deals with objects of the sense

Not loving and not hating, making them
Serve his free soul, which rests serenely lord,
Lo! such a man comes to tranquillity;
And out of that tranquillity shall rise
The end and healing of his earthly pains,
Since the will governed sets the soul at peace.
The soul of the ungoverned is not his,
Nor hath he knowledge of himself; which lacked,
How grows serenity? and, wanting that,
Whence shall he hope for happiness?
        The mind
That gives itself to follow shows of sense
Seeth its helm of wisdom rent away,
And, like a ship in waves of whirlwind, drives
To wreck and death. Only with him, great Prince!
Whose senses are not swayed by things of
    sense—
Only with him who holds his mastery,
Shows wisdom perfect. What is midnight-gloom
To unenlightened souls shines wakeful day
To his clear gaze; what seems as wakeful day
Is known for night, thick night of ignorance,
To his true-seeing eyes. Such is the Saint!

And like the ocean, day by day receiving
    Floods from all lands, which never overflows;
Its boundary-line not leaping, and not leaving,
    Fed by the rivers, but unswelled by those;—
So is the perfect one! to his soul's ocean
    The world of sense pours streams of witchery;
They leave him as they find, without commotion,
    Taking their tribute, but remaining sea.

Yea! whoso, shaking off the yoke of flesh
Lives lord, not servant, of his lusts; set free
From pride, from passion, from the sin of "Self,"
Toucheth tranquillity! O Prithâ's Son!
That is the state of Brahm! There rests no dread
When that last step is reached! Live where he will,
Die when he may, such passeth from all 'plaining,
To blest Nirvâna, with the Gods, attaining.

Source: The *Bhagavadgita*, translated by Edwin Arnold.
London: Kegan-Paul, Trench, Traubner, and Co., Ltd., 1899,
pp. 9–24.

SUZUKI

ZEN MIND, BEGINNER'S MIND

In the 1920s, Daisetz Suzuki popularized Zen for Western audiences. Now, another Suzuki, Shunryu Suzuki, continues this tradition. Suzuki was a Zen master in Japan and came to America in 1959, when he was 55 years of age. He decided to stay in America and founded several Zen centers in the United States. The term "beginner's mind" was often used by Suzuki because he believed that we need to look at life in a straightforward, simple way, as if we were a beginner. Suzuki discusses the role of the teacher in the educational process, whereby both the teacher's mind and the student's mind become Buddha minds. There is also a great emphasis placed upon zazen as a true and tranquil form of meditation, which unifies mind and body, and helps us to transcend thinking.

My master died when I was thirty-one. Although I wanted to devote myself just to Zen practice at Eiheiji monastery, I had to succeed my master at his temple. I became quite busy, and being so young I had many difficulties. These difficulties gave me some experience, but it meant nothing compared with the true, calm, serene way of life.

It is necessary for us to keep the constant way. Zen is not some kind of excitement, but concentration on our usual everyday routine. If you become too busy and too excited, your mind becomes rough and ragged. This is not good. If possible, try to be always calm and joyful and keep yourself from excitement. Usually, we become busier and busier, day by day, year by year, especially in our modern world. If we revisit old, familiar places after a long time, we are astonished by the changes. It cannot be helped. But if we become interested in some excitement, or in our own change, we will become completely involved in our busy life, and we will be lost. But if your mind is calm and constant, you can keep yourself away from the noisy world even though you are in the midst of it. In the midst of noise and change, your mind will be quiet and stable.

Zen is not something to get excited about. Some people start to practice Zen just out of curiosity, and they only make themselves busier. If your practice makes you worse, it is ridiculous. I think that if you try to do *zazen* once a week, that will make you busy enough. Do not be too interested in Zen. When young people get excited about Zen they often give up schooling and go to some mountain or forest in order to sit. That kind of interest is not true interest.

Just continue in your calm, ordinary practice and your character will be built up. If your mind is always busy, there will be no time to build, and you will not be successful, particularly if you work too hard on it. Building character is like making bread—you have to mix it little by little, step by step, and moderate temperature is needed. You know yourself quite well, and you know how much temperature you need. But if you get too excited, you will forget how much temperature is good for you, and you will lose your way. This is very dangerous.

Buddha said the same thing about the good ox driver. The driver knows how much load the ox can carry, and he keeps the ox from being overloaded. You know your way and your state of mind. Do not carry too much! Buddha also said that building character is like building a dam. You should be very careful in making the bank. If you try to do it all at once, water will leak from it. Make the bank carefully and you will end up with a fine dam for the reservoir.

Our unexciting way of practice may appear to be very negative. This is not so. It is a wise and effective way to work on ourselves. It is just very plain. I find this point very difficult for people, especially young people, to understand. On the other hand it may seem as if I am speaking about gradual attainment. This is not so either. In fact, this is the sudden way, because when your practice is calm and ordinary, everyday life itself is enlightenment . . .

The most important point in our practice is to have right or perfect effort. Right effort directed in the right direction is necessary. If your effort is headed in the wrong direction, especially if you are not aware of this, it is deluded effort. Our effort in our practice should be directed from achievement to non-achievement.

Usually when you do something, you want to achieve something, you attach to some result. From achievement to non-achievement means to be rid of the unnecessary and bad results of effort. If you do something in the spirit of non-achievement, there is a good quality in it. So just to do something without any particular effort is enough. When you make some special effort to achieve something, some excessive quality, some extra element is involved in it. You should get rid of excessive things. If your practice is good, without being aware of it you will become proud of your practice. That pride is extra. This point is very, very important, but usually we are not subtle enough to realize it, and we go in the wrong direction.

Because all of us are doing the same thing, making the same mistake, we do not realize it. So without realizing it, we are making many mistakes. And we create problems among us. This kind of bad effort is called being "Dharma-ridden," or "practice-ridden." You are involved in some idea of practice or attainment, and you cannot get out of it. When you are involved in some dualistic idea, it means your practice is not pure. By purity we do not mean to polish something, trying to make some impure things pure. By purity we just mean things as they are. When something is added, that is impure. When something becomes dualistic, that is not pure. If you think you will get something from practicing *zazen*, already you are involved in impure practice. It is all right to say there is practice, and there is enlightenment, but we should not be caught by the statement. You should not be tainted by it. When you practice *zazen*, just practice *zazen*. If enlightenment comes, it just comes. We should not attach to the attainment. The true quality of *zazen* is always there, even if you are not aware of it, so forget all about what you think you may have gained from it. Just do it. The quality of *zazen* will express itself; then you will have it.

People ask what it means to practice *zazen* with no gaining idea, what kind of effort is necessary for that kind of practice. The answer is: effort to get rid of something extra from our practice. If some extra idea comes, you should try to stop it; you should remain in pure practice. That is the point towards which our effort is directed.

We say, "To hear the sound of one hand clapping." Usually the sound of clapping is made with two hands, and we think that clapping with one hand makes no sound at all. But actually, one hand IS sound. Even though you do not hear it, there is sound. But if sound did not already exist before you clapped, you could not make the sound. Before you make it there is sound. Because there is sound, you can make it, and you can hear it. Sound is everywhere. If you just practice it, there is sound. Do not try to listen to it. If you do not listen to it, the sound is all over. Because you try to hear it, sometimes there is sound, and sometimes there is no sound. Do you understand? Even though you do not do anything, you have the quality of *zazen* always. But if you try to find it, if you try to see the quality, you have no quality.

You are living in this world as one individual, but before you take the form of a human being, you are already there, always there. We are always here. Do you understand? You think before you were born you were not here. But how is it possible for you to appear in this world, when there is no you? Because you are already there, you can appear in the world. Also, it is not possible for something to vanish which does not exist. Because something is there, something can vanish. You may think that when you die, you disappear, you no longer exist. But even though you vanish, something which is existent cannot be non-existent. That is the magic. We ourselves cannot put any magic spells on this world. The world is its own magic. If we are looking at something, it can vanish from our sight, but if we do not try to see it, that something cannot vanish. Because you are watching it, it can disappear, but if no one is watching, how is it possible for anything to disappear? If someone is watching you, you can escape from him, but if no one is watching, you cannot escape from yourself.

So try not to see something in particular; try not to achieve anything special. You already have everything in your own pure quality. If you understand this ultimate fact, there is no fear. There may be some difficulty, of course, but there is no fear. If people have difficulty without being aware of the difficulty, that is true difficulty. They may appear very confident, they may think they are making a big effort in the right direction, but without knowing it, what they do comes out of fear. Something may vanish for them. But if your effort is in the right direction, then there is no fear of losing anything. Even if it is in the wrong direction, if you are aware of that, you will not be deluded. There is nothing to lose. There is only the constant pure quality of right practice....

The purpose of studying Buddhism is not to study Buddhism, but to study ourselves. It is impossible to study ourselves without some teaching. If you want to know what water is you need science, and the scientist needs a laboratory. In the laboratory there are various ways in which to study what water is. Thus it is possible to know what kind of elements water has, the various forms it takes, and its nature. But it is impossible thereby to know water in itself. It is the same thing with us. We need some teaching, but just by studying the teaching alone, it is impossible to know what "I" in myself am. Through the teaching we may understand our human nature. But the teaching is not we ourselves; it is some explanation of ourselves. So if you are attached to the teaching, or to the teacher, that is a big mistake. The moment you meet a teacher, you should leave the teacher, and you should be independent. You need a teacher so that you can become independent. If you are not attached to him, the teacher will show you the way to yourself. You have a teacher for yourself, not for the teacher.

Rinzai, an early Chinese Zen master, analyzed how to teach his disciples in four ways. Sometimes he talked about the disciple himself; sometimes he talked about the teaching itself; sometimes he gave an interpretation of the disciple or the teaching; and finally, sometimes he did not give any instruction at all to his disciples. He knew that even without being given any instruction, a student is a student. Strictly speaking, there is no need to teach the student, because the student himself is Buddha, even though he may not be aware of it. And even though he is aware of his true nature, if he is attached to this awareness, that is already wrong. When he is not aware of it, he has everything, but when he becomes aware of it he thinks that what he is aware of is himself, which is a big mistake.

When you do not hear anything from the teacher, but just sit, this is called teaching without teaching. But sometimes this is not sufficient, so we listen to lectures and have discussions. But we should remember that the purpose of practice in a particular place is to study ourselves. To be independent, we study. Like the scientist, we have to have some means by which to study. We need a teacher because it is impossible to study ourselves by ourselves. But you should not make a mistake. You should not take what you have learned with a teacher for you yourself. The study you make with your teacher is a part of your everyday life, a part of your incessant activity. In this sense there is no difference between the practice and the activity you have in everyday life. So to find the meaning of your life in the zendo is to find the meaning of your everyday activity. To be aware of the meaning of your life, you practice *zazen*.

When I was at Eiheiji monastery in Japan, everyone was just doing what he should do. That is all. It is the same as waking up in the morning; we have to get up. At Eiheiji monastery, when we had to sit, we sat; when we had to bow to Buddha, we bowed to Buddha. That is all. And when we were practicing, we did not feel anything special. We did not even feel that we were leading a monastic life. For us, the monastic life was the usual life, and the people who came from the city were unusual people. When we saw them we felt, "Oh, some unusual people have come!"

But once I had left Eiheiji and had been away for some time, coming back was different. I heard the various sounds of practice—the bells and the monks reciting the sutra—and I had a deep feeling. There were tears flowing out of my eyes, nose, and mouth! It is the people who are outside of the monastery who feel its atmosphere. Those who are practicing actually do not feel anything. I think this is true for everything. When we hear the sound of the pine trees on a windy day, perhaps the wind is just blowing, and the pine tree is just standing in the wind. That is all that they are doing. But the people who listen to the wind in the tree will write a poem, or will feel something unusual. That is, I think, the way everything is.

So to feel something about Buddhism is not the main point. Whether that feeling is good or bad is out of the question. We do not mind, whatever it is. Buddhism is not good or bad. We are doing what we should do. That is Buddhism. Of course some encouragement is necessary, but that encouragement is just encouragement. It is not the true purpose of practice. It is just medicine. When we become discouraged we want some medicine. When we are in good spirits we do not need any medicine. You should not take medicine for food. Sometimes medicine is necessary, but it should not become our food.

So, of Rinzai's four ways of practice, the perfect one is not to give a student any interpretation of himself, nor to give him any encouragement. If we think of ourselves as our bodies, the teaching then may be our clothing. Sometimes we talk about our clothing; sometimes we talk about our body. But neither body nor clothing is actually we ourselves. We ourselves are the big activity. We are just expressing the smallest particle of the big activity, that is all. So it is all right to talk about ourselves, but actually there is no need to do so. Before we open our mouths, we are already expressing the big existence, including ourselves. So the purpose of talking about ourselves is to correct the misunderstanding we have when we are attached to any particular temporal form or color of the big activity. It is necessary to talk about what our body is and what our activity is so that we may not make any mistake about them. So to talk about ourselves is actually to forget about ourselves.

Dogen-zenji said, "To study Buddhism is to study ourselves." When you become attached to a temporal expression of your true nature, it is necessary to talk about Buddhism, or else you will think the temporal expression is it. But this particular expression of it is not it. And yet at the same time it is it! For a while this is it; for the smallest particle of time, this is it. But it is not always so: the very next instant it is not so, thus this is not it. So that you will realize this fact, it is necessary to study Buddhism. But the purpose of studying Buddhism is to study ourselves and to forget ourselves. When we forget ourselves, we actually are the true activity of the big existence, or reality itself. When we realize this fact, there is no problem whatsoever in this world, and we can enjoy our life without feeling any difficulties. The purpose of our practice is to be aware of this fact….

If you want to understand Buddhism it is necessary for you to forget all about your preconceived ideas. To begin with, you must give up the idea of substantiality or existence. The usual view of life is firmly rooted in the idea of existence. For most people everything exists; they think whatever they see and whatever they hear exists. Of course the bird we see and hear exists. It exists, but what I mean by that may not be exactly what you mean. The Buddhist understanding of life includes both existence and nonexistence. The bird both exists and does not exist at the same time. We say that a view of life based on existence alone is heretical. If you take things too seriously, as if they existed substantially or permanently, you are called a heretic. Most people may be heretics.

We say true existence comes from emptiness and goes back again into emptiness. What appears from emptiness is true existence. We have to go through the gate of emptiness. This idea of existence is very difficult to explain. Many people these days have begun to feel, at least intellectually, the emptiness of the modern world, or the self-contradiction of their culture. In the past, for instance, the Japanese people had a firm confidence in the permanent existence of their culture and their traditional way of life, but since they lost the war, they have become very skeptical. Some people think this skeptical attitude is awful, but actually it is better than the old attitude.

As long as we have some definite idea about or some hope in the future, we cannot really be serious with the moment that exists right now. You may say, "I can do it tomorrow, or next year," believing that something that exists today will exist tomorrow. Even though you are not trying so hard, you expect that some promising thing will come, as long as you follow a certain way. But there is no certain way that exists permanently. There is no way set up for us. Moment after moment we have to find our own way. Some idea of perfection, or some perfect way which is set up by someone else, is not the true way for us.

Each one of us must make his own true way, and when we do, that way will express the universal way. This is the mystery. When you understand one thing through and through, you understand everything. When you try to understand everything, you will not understand anything. The best way is to understand yourself, and then you will understand everything. So when you try hard to make your own way, you will help others, and you will be helped by others. Before you make your own way you cannot help anyone, and no one can help you. To be independent in this true sense, we have to forget everything which we have in our mind and discover something quite new and different moment after moment. This is how we live in this world.

Source: Shunryu Suzuki, *Zen Mind, Beginner's Mind*. New York: Weatherhill, 1999, pp. 57–59, 59–61, 76–79, 110–111.

SELECTED READINGS

Bahm, Archie J. *Comparative Philosophy: Western, Indian, and Chinese Philosophies Compared.* Revised edition. Albuquerque, NM: World Book, 1995. An examination of standards for comparing Eastern and Western philosophies and a comparative treatment of Western, Indian, and Chinese philosophies.

Götz, Ignacio L. "Education and the Self: Cross-Cultural Perspectives," *Educational Theory*, 45(4), 1995. *www.ed.uluc.edu/EPS/Educational-Theory/Contents/45_4_Gotz.html* (accessed April 5, 2002). Explores the differences in the concept of self between Western and Eastern cultures by examining the identity crisis Arjuna faces in the *Bhagavad-Gita* and what lessons can be learned from it for multicultural education.

Hoff, Benjamin. *The Tao of Pooh.* New York: Penguin Books, 1982. An interesting and insightful approach that analyzes the relationship between the Pooh stories by A. A. Milne and the concept of the Tao.

Rosen, Jonathan. *The Talmud and the Internet.* New York: Farrar, Straus and Giroux, 2000. Compares and analyzes connections between the Talmud and the Internet, showing unforeseen similarities and resemblances.

Schumacher, Stephen, and Woerner, Gert, eds. *The Encyclopedia of Eastern Philosophy and Religion: Buddhism, Hinduism, Taoism, and Zen.* Translated by Michael H. Kohn, Karen Ready, and Werner Wunsche. Boston: Shambhala Publications, Inc., 1994. A comprehensive treatment of four leading Eastern philosophies and religions and of persons, places, and concepts related to each.

www.easternreligions.com/ (accessed April 5, 2002). Provides historical background and selected textual material on Buddhism, Confucianism, Taoism, Hinduism, and Zen, including philosophical and religious views. Links to other sites also are provided.

Companion Website

ONLINE RESEARCH

Utilizing some of the Web sites included in this book, as well as Topics 2 and 3 of the Prentice Hall Foundations Web site found at *www.prenhall.com/ozmon*, answer the following question with a short essay: What are some of the major methods of instruction that have been utilized in eastern philosophies of education? You can write and submit your essay response to your instructor by using the "Electronic Bluebook" section found in any of the topics of the Prentice Hall Foundations Web site.

4

Pragmatism and Education

The root of the word *pragmatism* is a Greek word meaning "work." Pragmatism is a philosophy that encourages us to seek out the processes and do the things that work best to help us achieve desirable ends. Because this idea is so sensible, one might wonder why people insist on doing things and using processes that do not work. This is true for any number of reasons: the weight of custom and tradition, as well as fear and apathy. Some habitual ways of thinking and doing might have worked well in the past but have lost value for today's world. Pragmatism examines traditional ways of thinking and doing and, where possible, seeks to incorporate them into everyday life, but it also supports creating new ideas to deal with the changing world in which people live.

Although pragmatism is viewed primarily as a contemporary American philosophy, its roots can be traced back to British, European, and ancient Greek philosophical traditions. One important element of this tradition is the developing worldview brought about by the scientific revolution. The questioning attitudes fostered by the Enlightenment and the development of a more naturalistic humanism also have been outgrowths of this movement. The background of pragmatism can be found in the works of such figures as Francis Bacon, John Locke, Jean-Jacques Rousseau, and Charles Darwin. However, the philosophical elements that give pragmatism a consistency and system as a philosophy in its own right are primarily the contributions of Charles Sanders Peirce, William James, and John Dewey.

ROOTS OF THE PRAGMATIST WORLDVIEW

The antecedents of the philosophy of pragmatism are many and varied, but some basic elements are vitally important. These are induction, the importance of human experience, and the relationship between science and culture.

Induction: A New Way of Thinking

Francis Bacon (1561–1626)

Francis Bacon's ideas put a premium on human experience of and within the world of everyday life. His influence on pragmatism has been significant. The inductive method he suggested has served as the basis for the scientific method, which in turn has been of fundamental importance to pragmatism. Whereas Bacon thought that science should be concerned primarily with material things, pragmatists extended its range to include problems in economics, politics, psychology, art, education, and even ethics. For instance, in *How We Think*, John Dewey set forth the process of scientific thinking as central to the method of education. Indeed, according to Dewey, when people think in an orderly and coherent fashion, they are thinking along the lines of scientific method although they may not be conscious of it as such. However, when Dewey used the term *Science*, he did not mean test tubes and statistics; rather, he meant orderly thinking and an experimental approach to the problems of life designed to bring about a better life for all. If the nature of the thinking process were made conscious—if we all were educated in it—then human thinking more likely would be characterized by orderliness, coherence, and desirable consequences.

The general thrust of pragmatism is toward a heightened sensitivity to consequences as the final test for thought, but it is by no means insensitive to principles. Hence, pragmatist results might not always be practical in the ordinary sense. First, pragmatists hold that means and ends cannot be artificially separated; that is, the means used always dictate to some degree the actual ends achieved. In this case, sensitivity to consequences calls for an increased vigilance over the means used. Second, the consequences of thinking are not always practical in the ordinary sense because the consequences can be aesthetic, or moral and ethical. Pragmatists, although enthusiastic advocates of scientific ways of thinking, are no recluses in sterile laboratories; rather, they wish to apply their version of scientific method to the problems of humanity to secure a more democratic and humane way of life.

The inductive approach that is so characteristic of pragmatism is illustrated by the thought of George Herbert Mead. Mead applied induction to social and psychological behavior in a more thoroughgoing manner than had been accomplished previously. His view of the self as a *social* self particularly influenced Dewey and other pragmatist thinkers in education. Mead thought that if the child is viewed inductively, then it will be seen that children do not learn to be social; rather, they have to be social in order to learn. In other words, for Mead, the self is by nature social and not some mental inner thing hidden from view.

William James applied inductive method to moral and religious questions. For him, the consequences that follow the application of a moral belief determine the truth or falsity, the rightness or wrongness, of that belief. This view shows James extending the inductive method far beyond previous attempts because to him, the inductive method was capable of extension to human experiences not included in ordinary empiricism. James was inductive to the extent that he rejected old assumptions about the nature of things and built his ideas on the basis of experience. In matters of religion, he held that religious beliefs had value if they provided suitable consequences. Belief in God, for example, might not be rejected if that belief provided personal meaning and value.

Thus, some pragmatists did not narrowly construe the meaning of induction so as to restrict it to only physical and material studies. Mead applied it to social and psychological areas; James used it in explaining religious and moral beliefs; and Dewey, learning from his predecessors, applied it to education and democratic society in broad terms.

Centrality of Experience

Human experience is an important ingredient of pragmatist philosophy. This ingredient and the central emphasis it receives have helped give pragmatism a decidedly environmental orientation. The emphasis on experience, however, had its precedent in British and European philosophical traditions.

John Locke (1632–1704)

John Locke investigated the ways human beings experience and come to know things, and his examination led him to the view that the individual's mind at birth is blank, a *tabula rasa*. Ideas are not innate, as Plato maintained; rather, they come from experience—that is, sensation and reflection. As people are exposed to experiences, these experiences are impressed on their minds; thus, a baby soon understands the idea of milk acquired through the sense of taste, perfume through the sense of smell, velvet through the sense of touch, and green through the sense of sight. These experiences are all imprinted on the mind through one or more of the five senses. Once in the mind, they can be related in various ways through reflection. Therefore, one can create the idea of green milk or perfumed velvet.

Locke believed that as people have more experiences, they have more ideas imprinted on the mind and more with which to relate. He argued, however, that one could have false ideas as well as true ones. A person can have a true idea of an apple or of a horse, but one also can create the idea of a mermaid by erroneously relating the ideas of a woman and a fish, both obtained from the sensory world. The only way people can be sure their ideas are correct is by verifying them in the world of experience. Physical proof can be found for a horse or an apple but not for a mermaid.

One might think of the human mind as a kind of computer: Until something is programmed in, one can get nothing out. Consequently, Locke emphasized the idea of placing children in the most desirable environment for their education, and he pointed to the importance of environment in making people what they are. In his book *Some Thoughts Concerning Education*, Locke describes the ideal education of a gentleman, who is to be exposed to many varied experiences, including extensive travel among people of different cultures. Locke's heightened sensitivity to the importance of experience and its relation to thought processes and personal development stimulated many thinkers who came after him.

Locke's notion of experience, however, contained internal flaws and caused difficulties. His insistence that mind is a *tabula rasa* established mind as a passive, malleable instrument buffeted by a weltering conflict of impressions received through the senses. When carried to its logical conclusion, Locke's notion leads to the separation of mind from body, with the result that one can know only ideas. This lay at the base of George Berkeley's conclusion that "to be is to be perceived" (the existence of anything is dependent on mind). David Hume took Locke's view and developed it to the point of skepticism regarding the existence and meaning of ideas and material objects. Thus, one arrives at the philosophical problems generated by the notion of a passive mind and uncertainty regarding the nature of reality.

According to John Dewey, Charles Sanders Peirce opened the road leading out of the impasse generated by Locke. Ideas are to be perceived not only as isolated impressions on a blank tablet but also as interrelated parts of experience. Dewey took this to mean that ideas have to be defined functionally in reference to a particular problem, rather than as mere mental constructs. Locke's view of mind was too passive for Dewey because it meant that one's ideas are formed primarily by external sources.

Dewey, like Kant, pointed to the importance of mind as an active agent in the formulation of ideas, as well as an instrument to effect changes in the environment that in turn might affect anyone. Dewey constantly stressed the transactional nature of the relations between the organism and the environment. Empirically, people experience things as beautiful, ugly, and so forth, but they do not experience such things as projections of a subjective mind on objective reality; rather, the ways we experience things result from the connection and continuity of experience and nature.

Dewey rejected not only Lockean epistemology but also Locke's social theories, which contributed to the philosophy of classic liberalism. Locke's notion of *freedom* was the power to act in accordance with choice. This view of freedom, combined with his concern for economic factors, led to a *laissez-faire* theory of property, industry, and trade that encouraged limited government and police functions, but it gave a free hand to economic exploiters. As Dewey saw it, Locke's *laissez-faire* views helped generate so-called popular philosophies of self-expression in which the self-expression of a few impeded the self-expression of the many. Classic Lockean liberals believed that individuals were endowed with ready-made capacities that, if unobstructed, would lead to freedom. Dewey maintained, however, that such a liberalism assisted the emancipation of those having a privileged antecedent status, but it provided no general liberation for the majority of people.

Dewey also challenged the notion (advanced by Baruch Spinoza) that real freedom can be achieved only when each individual gains power by acting in accord with the whole, "being reinforced by its structure and momentum." This idea of the individual acting in accordance with the whole leads to a kind of Hegelian subservience of individuals to the state or other such external agencies. Dewey argued, however, that we should act intelligently in terms of the practical world in which we find ourselves because we cannot act in isolation from other people, from nature, or from human institutions.

Because of Dewey's cognizance of such social forces, many interpreters believe that this gives support to a social-adjustment or "life-adjustment" view of education (that one should be taught to adjust to the way things are). Dewey did promote an awareness of contemporary conditions as well as interaction with them, but this did not preclude people from working constantly to improve existing institutions or to abolish them and establish new ones. Indeed, rather than advocating the kind of conservatism identified with Spinoza, Locke, and classical liberals, Dewey's views reflect an underlying reformist activism with regard to the individual and social action.

Jean-Jacques Rousseau (1712–1778)

Another figure whose philosophical views influenced pragmatism was Jean-Jacques Rousseau. Along with Locke, Rousseau wrote extensively about the relationship of education and politics. His *On the Social Contract* and *Émile*, both of which appeared in 1762, antagonized so many of those in power that Rousseau had to leave Paris and seek refuge in Bern, Switzerland.

Although he was born in Geneva, Switzerland, Rousseau lived most of his life in France. His first philosophical work was a prize-winning essay on a subject proposed by the Academy of Dijon in 1749: Has the Restoration of the Sciences and the Arts Contributed to Purify Morals? Rousseau's answer was an emphatic "No" because he followed Locke's insistence on the importance of environment in shaping human experience and thought. He maintained that civilization in its present form (that is, art and science) was harmful because it had led us away from nature.

Rousseau thought that individuals are basically good but have been corrupted by civilization. He did not believe that people should give up all of their artistic and technological developments, but he did think that these should be controlled, particularly where they prevented people from being natural. Simply put, Rousseau argued for only those aspects of civilization that are not corrupting to a natural life. He chose Daniel Defoe's story of Robinson Crusoe to represent the kind of "Noble Savage" he envisioned, and he used it as the basis for his most important book on education, *Émile.* In Defoe's story, Robinson Crusoe is shipwrecked on a deserted island, and he visits his shipwrecked vessel many times to remove civilized implements that he needs for survival. Yet, these things do not interfere with his natural life: He builds his own house, grows his own food, and devises his own means of transportation. Other similar Noble Savage types from literature include the Swiss Family Robinson, Natty Bumppo in the James Fenimore Cooper stories, and Thoreau at Walden Pond.

Similarly, in *Émile*, Rousseau describes a child taken out of civilization and brought up in the country. Once in the country, Émile has a private tutor who sees to it that he lives naturally, and the tutor tries to arrange things so that Émile learns from nature. Rousseau did not think highly of books, which he thought only reinforced the artificial nature of civilization. In *Émile,* he does not suggest book learning until Émile reaches age 12. Generally speaking, Rousseau gives little attention to the education of girls, but the book does have portions concerned with Sophy, who is Émile's counterpart. Sophy is to be Émile's helpmate, and she should have the kind of education that will complement Émile's.

Rousseau's major contribution to pragmatism was not his "Noble Savage" romanticism but the educational connection he made between nature and experience. Certainly, his connection of nature and experience influenced many educational theorists, including Johann H. Pestalozzi, Friedrich Froebel, Francis W. Parker, G. Stanley Hall, and John Dewey. Rousseau's emphasis on the place of naturalism in education affected the way pragmatist thinkers viewed the child. Children no longer were seen as miniature adults but as natural organisms going through various stages of development. This conception of the child as a developing person particularly influenced such psychologists as Hall, who was a pioneer in child psychology. Rousseau's views helped educators pose questions concerning what is natural for children. In other words, it is unnatural for children to sit still for long periods of time, to concentrate on abstractions, to remain quiet, or to exhibit refined muscle control. Rousseau helped educators become more sensitive to the physiological, psychological, and social stages of child development. His attention to the physiological aspects of learning directly influenced the theories of such people as Maria Montessori.

Rousseau's attention to the nature of child development and his belief in the inherent goodness of people set the stage for child-centered education. Although this theme is found in the educational theory and practice of some pragmatists, others object to the sentimental romanticism that has grown up around Rousseau's works—a romanticism that often has been identified as uninhibited permissiveness. Although this sentiment has been attributed to Rousseau, not even Rousseau believed in the kind of license that some present-day permissiveness suggests. One hears the charge of license leveled against the educational theories of pragmatists, but the charge is unfounded when one carefully examines the writings of leading thinkers.

One hallmark of Rousseau's philosophy is that the child's interests should guide education. An interest is not the same thing as a whim, however, for by *interest* Rousseau meant children's native tendencies to find out about the world in which they live. He believed in the child's autonomy but regarded it as a natural autonomy in which children have to suffer the natural consequences of their behavior. Rousseau's impact on pragmatism is his sensitivity to the part of nature in education and the natural developmental process involved in one's learning experiences.

Science and Society

Modern science has changed people's views of human destiny dramatically. That a scientific revolution has occurred is undeniable, for old metaphysical views, religious views, and social and political philosophies have been challenged. The advance of science has affected not only theoretical views of society but also the practical area of social structures and social relations, as well. The social problems resulting from this scientific advance have been of central concern to pragmatism. In this regard, such persons as Bacon, Locke, and Descartes have influenced pragmatism. Although science and technology have contributed to many contemporary social problems such as air disasters and environmental pollution, pragmatists believe that science also can help alleviate these problems.

Auguste Comte (1798–1857)

One of the most intensive philosophical efforts to apply science to society was by Auguste Comte. Although not a pragmatist, Comte, like Bacon, influenced the early development of pragmatism by helping thinkers become sensitive to the possibilities of using science to help solve social problems. For example, Dewey told how he was attracted to Comte's notion that Western civilization is disorganized because of a rampant individualism in which only a few are truly individuals while the many are submerged. From Comte, he drew the idea that science can be a regulative method in social life.

Comte's dream was to reform society by the application of science. Today, one might say that Comte was overly optimistic, for people have discovered that scientific and positivistic thought often produces results that threaten to destroy society. Comte did help establish the application of science more directly to society rather than only to physical matter. Indeed, Comte was one of the founders of modern sociology. His willingness to view social structures and relationships as capable of systematic study and control helped usher in elements of social theory that influenced pragmatism.

Charles Darwin (1809–1882)

Perhaps the most important influence on pragmatism from the standpoint of science was the work of Charles Darwin. Darwin first studied medicine at the University of Edinburgh and then studied divinity at Cambridge. Afterward, he was given the opportunity to go on a scientific expedition to the Southern Hemisphere. He spent 5 years aboard the *Beagle* and returned home in 1838. Thereafter, he devoted his life to developing his scientific theories, which were based largely on the data he collected during the voyage.

His major work, *On the Origin of Species by Means of Natural Selection* (or simply *The Origin of Species*, 1859), rocked the intellectual and religious communities of the Western world. Religionists attacked Darwin's theory because it challenged Biblical creation. Intellectuals were stunned because it challenged old cosmological beliefs. The underlying cosmology that Darwin used was that nature operates by a process of development without predetermined directions or ends. Predecessors such as Aristotle had expressed elements of Darwin's theory, but it was Darwin who gathered quantities of evidence and who painstakingly put it together in a most revealing way. Although his research was highly scientific, he wrote his findings in such a way that practically any literate person could understand them. He argued that species arise naturally through what he called a universal struggle for existence. This "descent with modification" occurs in an interplay between organism and environment. Food supply, geographic conditions, and presence or absence of predators set the stage for natural selection to occur. Favorable characteristics persist, and unfavorable characteristics die out. Through this process, some species arise and then disappear as conditions change; this selection process operates over a considerable time span.

Darwin's theory caught the popular imagination because he enunciated something every livestock farmer who practices selective breeding knows. It is not a high-blown, philosophical utopia but something connected with ordinary experience. These conditions helped foster an examination of many areas of intellectual inquiry, and the cosmology of development, spurred by Darwin's efforts, has become more widely applied in fields than even Darwin ever envisioned.

In philosophy, the cosmology of development directly attacked the Platonic notion of essences and universals. This supported philosophical views that the universe itself is in the process of development: Reality is not to be found in Being, but in Becoming. Gradually, such ideas led to the rejection of a "block" universe, fixed and eternal, capable of being entirely comprehended by intellect alone. For pragmatists, Darwin's views on natural selection and an evolving universe meant that reality is open ended in process, with no fixed end. These views of an open-ended process further encouraged the view in pragmatism that a person's education is tied directly to biological and social development. From this standpoint, pragmatists attempted to understand human experience as occurring within the natural order of things—a natural order that is itself subject to change and, perhaps to some small degree, to human control if it is approached intelligently.

AMERICAN PRAGMATISTS

It has been said that the philosophy of pragmatism is basically American, but pragmatism had its roots in European philosophical traditions. In addition, F. C. S. Schiller developed a British version of pragmatism. By and large, however, pragmatism received its fullest treatment from three Americans: Charles Sanders Peirce, William James, and John Dewey.

According to Louis Menand, the pragmatists were connected by one central thing: "an idea about ideas"—that ideas are not out there to be discovered as Plato claimed, but are tools, like hammers and microchips, that people devise to cope with the world. Furthermore, ideas are not solely individual creations but are generated by social groups. In other words, ideas are entirely dependent upon human beings and the environment.

Charles Sanders Peirce (1839–1914)

In many respects, Charles Sanders Peirce was never given the recognition in his own day that he deserved. Although he was a friend of such leading American intellectuals as William James, he never received a permanent post at any university, and his major ideas never won public acclaim. For most of his life, he was a lonely and reclusive man, and he died in straitened economic circumstances. It is interesting to note that Peirce's works have gained new attention in recent years.

His influence on later figures was Peirce's primary philosophical achievement. His works eventually were published posthumously, but probably his most influential work was in an article titled "How to Make Our Ideas Clear" (*Popular Science Monthly*, January 1878), in which he analyzed the dualism of mind and matter, or the subjective and the objective. He accepted the proposition that mind is different from material reality, but he also maintained that what is known about objective reality resides in the idea one has of any given object. The important thing, consequently, is to make sure that ideas are as clear and precise as possible. He argued that people always should remain extremely sensitive to the consequences of how they conceive of ideas. Peirce maintained that *the concept of practical effects makes up the whole of our concept of an object.* One might say that a mental grasp of any object is nothing more than the meaning we apply to that object in terms of consequences. As

Peirce put it, "Our idea of anything is our idea of its sensible effects." Thus, ideas or concepts cannot be separated from human conduct, for to have an idea is to be aware of its effects and consequences (or their probability) in the arena of human affairs.

Peirce concluded that true knowledge of anything depends on testing one's ideas in actual experience because, in and of themselves, ideas are little more than hypotheses until tried upon the anvil of experience. Although Peirce's complete thought system was complex—even going into speculations about the nature of God, immortality, and the self—his work on the nature of ideas and the necessity for testing them in experience profoundly influenced pragmatism.

William James (1842–1910)

The philosopher who brought the philosophy of pragmatism to a wider public audience was William James. The son of a prominent family, James rather leisurely tried his hand at several vocations, including medicine, but he made his mark in psychology and philosophy. His contribution to philosophy lay in the power of his ideas.

James took seriously Peirce's admonition about the practical consequences of ideas, an important part of James's theory of truth. For James, truth is not absolute and immutable, but is *made* in actual, real-life events. Truth does not belong to an idea as some property adhering to it, for it is found in *acting* on ideas—in the *consequences* of ideas. As James liked to say, "the proof is in the pudding", that is, before one can tell if the pudding (an idea) is any good (true), one has to taste (test) it.

Moreover, truth is not always objective, verifiable, or universal (Truth); it also is found in concrete individual experience that is unique (truth). For James, there is the "inexpugnable reality" of individual existence. In the life of an individual, experiences occur that have meaning and truth to that individual but that cannot necessarily be verified objectively to someone else. This view of truth—"workability" and inexpugnable reality—is what James called "radical empiricism." In effect, he held that truth is inseparable from *experience;* to get at truth, one must study experience itself, not some immutable, otherworldly Absolute, extraneous to experience.

Thus, for James, the primary datum is human experience. He concentrated on what he called the "stream" of experience—the sequential, serial course of events. *Experience,* he cautioned, is a "double-barreled" word because there is experienc*ing*—the actual lived, undergoing aspect—and there is the experienc*ed*—the things of experience or the experience itself. Thus, experience is the *primary datum* and is capable of being studied cross sectionally (the experiencing) and longitudinally (the experienced). James called on thinkers to concentrate on experience in lieu of essences, abstractions, and universals because, as his study of experience revealed to him, the universe is open-ended, pluralistic, and in process.

John Dewey (1859–1952)

James popularized pragmatism, and John Dewey "systematized" it and carried its leading ideas to far-reaching development. Dewey was born in 1859, the same year that Darwin's *The Origin of Species* was published, and Darwin's thought was to play an important part in Dewey's philosophy because the cosmology of development was

central to his beliefs. Like James, Dewey believed that no immutable absolutes or universals exist, and his primary datum was experience; like Peirce, he sought to clarify ideas in terms of their consequences in human experience. Although his ideas certainly had power and impact, as did James's, Dewey had the additional virtue of being able to pursue the most intricate problems doggedly and to search out their practical implications.

Dewey owed a great deal to Peirce and James, but he began his philosophical journey mainly in the Hegelian tradition. For Dewey, Hegel's primary influence was his study of historical development and his search for an emerging unity from contending historical forces—not that he arrived at Absolute Spirit. Dewey once remarked that "acquaintance with Hegel has left a permanent deposit in my thinking." If Dewey was taken with anything, it was the growing, developing, dynamic nature of life, not its speculative ultimates. He accepted James's notion of experience as a stream, and from this basis, Dewey was launched on a wide-ranging philosophical career that spanned from horse-and-buggy days through World War II and into the atomic age.

Nature and Experience.   For Dewey, experience is not just an isolated happenstance; it has depth and reaches into nature. Experience and nature are not two different things separated from each other; rather, experience itself is of nature. Experience could, in the reflective sense, be divided into the experiencing being and the experienced things, but in the primary sense of the word, experience is of nature. People do not experience "experience" but the world in which they live—a world of things, ideas, hopes, fears, and aspirations, all rooted in nature. What misled previous philosophy, Dewey believed, was the confusion over experience itself and our thoughts about it. Too many thinkers had concentrated on the reflective products of experience and had held these to be ultimate reality. Unfortunately, such philosophers settled on abstractions and not genuine experience.

The centrality of experience and the extent to which Dewey used it are revealed by the titles of some of his major books: *Essays in Experimental Logic, Experience and Nature, Art as Experience*, and *Experience and Education.* In these works, Dewey's investigations into experience are not just speculative adventures, because he directs his efforts primarily toward real-life problems. Dewey takes Peirce to heart and looks at the practical consequences of ideas. He holds that genuine thought begins with a "problematic situation," a block or hitch in the ongoing stream of experience. In encountering these blocks, consciousness is brought to focus and one is made more acutely aware of the situation. In dealing with these real-life problems, Dewey argued, creative intelligence is capable of development. Where traditional philosophies take "problematic situations" and attempt to fit them to a pre-existing set of abstractions, Dewey urged that each situation be viewed as unique and dealt with experimentally by investigating the probable consequences of acting in particular ways. This approach shows Dewey's position that the world—experience and nature—cannot be understood in a monolithic way. The consequences are that people must be sensitive to novelty and variation and they must seek to be creative in dealing with their problems. Dewey headed in the direction of developing an experimental methodology where method takes precedence over metaphysical claims.

According to Dewey, experience is *of* and *in* nature. Nature consists of stones, plants, diseases, social conditions, enjoyments, and sufferings. In short, one cannot separate experience and nature. Nature is what one experiences, and one must view this experience in terms of its natural connections. In this respect, nature is both precarious and stable, problematic and determinate; that is, some things change rapidly and make life precarious, whereas other things change slowly and provide a sense of stability. Some experiences are stable, whereas others are in fluctuating confusion. For example, natural changes in plant and animal species take place over long stretches of time, and it often takes centuries for the physical contours of landmasses to change. However, some forms of life, such as certain kinds of bacteria, are capable of fairly rapid evolution, and landmasses can be altered rapidly by volcanic action. Nature, therefore, has certain characteristics that are fairly stable and others that fluctuate, and the same can be said for human affairs, which Dewey considered to be a part of nature.

Some types of human behavior relating to family life seem to endure across the ages, whereas others change rapidly. One can speak of the so-called sexual revolution as an indication of change, but certain human needs relating to child rearing and family life seem to endure. By the same token, broad social and political upheavals, such as the Marxist Revolution in Russia in 1918, appear to be cataclysmic. However, closer examination reveals that the causes of such events often go back over time. Thus, Dewey believed that some things are fairly stable and some are subject to rapid change, whether we are speaking of biology, social institutions, or politics.

Dewey followed Rousseau's lead in seeing the importance of nature in education although he rejected Rousseau's romanticism. Rousseau established three sources of education: (1) *nature,* the spontaneous development of organs and capacities; (2) *human beings,* the social uses to which people put this development; and (3) *things,* the acquisition of personal experience from surrounding objects. Dewey thought that Rousseau regarded these three factors as separate operations, independent of the use to which they were put. Dewey's naturalism differs from Rousseau's in that he believed the three factors have to be viewed in terms of their interrelationships. Whereas Rousseau thought that a child should be removed and educated "naturally" in the formative years, Dewey maintained that the child should not be removed from a social environment conducive to proper education. Thus, for Dewey, nature includes not just physical entities but social relationships, as well.

Dewey argued that if one accepts the hypotheses of the open-ended universe and a pluralistic reality, it becomes less important to develop abstract explanations and more important to examine natural human processes. Acceptance of the open-ended nature of things does not necessarily lead to an overly optimistic view of life because some processes lead to human goods and some lead to human ills. People *can* control their own affairs, but not in an absolute sense. Dewey was not a wild-eyed optimist as some of his critics charge; he was fully sensitive to the tragic side of human affairs, but he steadfastly maintained that we have it within our power to work toward a more satisfying life. This can be done intelligently by using processes that have a chance of yielding more desirable results—processes that might help alleviate or even solve the problems of humankind. Scientific method and experimental thinking can, if used properly, help us achieve such desirable ends. In fact, thinking processes are of utmost importance because, Dewey believed, many if not most human difficulties result from faulty thinking. He was concerned mostly with connecting thinking processes with social processes; this is shown in his emphasis on social action and education.

Experimentalism and Instrumentalism. Dewey's attention to social action and education gave his philosophy a decidedly practical orientation. Instead of dealing only with unchanging theoretical constructs, he urged that philosophy should concern itself with human problems in a changing and uncertain world. He believed that most thinkers embarked on a "quest for certainty" in which they sought true and eternal ideas, when what is needed are practical solutions to practical problems. For Dewey, ideas are not immutable but are accepted on the basis of how well they solve a perplexing problem.

Dewey believed that people should use philosophy to help them be more "experimental" in their approach to social problems by testing ideas and proposals reflectively before acting on them, and by critical appraisal and reflective assessment of results after trying out the ideas and proposals in practice. In this sense, ideas are instruments in the solution of human problems, and those solutions should be tried on an experimental basis so that we can learn from our efforts and redirect them to better effect. Thus, he sometimes preferred the terms *experimentalism* and *instrumentalism* over *pragmatism*, but Dewey's philosophy is not a type of scientism, and he made no fetish of science. He was a philosopher first and foremost.

In *How We Think* (1910), Dewey showed how ideas could be used as instruments in the solution of real-life problems. He described his view in five stages:

1. *A felt difficulty* that occurs because of a conflict in one's experience or a hitch or block to ongoing experience.
2. *Its location and definition,* establishing the limits or characteristics of the problem in precise terms.
3. *Suggestions of possible solutions,* formulating a wide range of hypotheses.
4. *Development by reasoning of the bearings of the suggestions,* reflecting on the possible outcomes of acting on these suggestions—in short, mulling things over.
5. *Further observation and experiment leading to its acceptance or rejection,* testing hypotheses to see whether they yield the desired results.

In this regard, Dewey viewed *method,* rather than abstract answers, as a central concern. If the universe is open ended, if existence is precarious and uncertain, then people cannot expect to locate enduring solutions; instead, we have to take each human problem as it arises. This is not to say that answers are unimportant, but it does recognize that they must be couched in terms of real-life situations, no two of which are exactly alike. Consequently, one must view the place of ideas in an experimental and instrumental sense. Like Peirce, people understand something as true or false on the basis of what it does and what effects it has in human activity. Dewey's work at the Laboratory School at the University of Chicago demonstrated not only his concern for education but also his belief that ideas should be tested in the crucible of real-life experience.

The Individual and the Social.   One area of Dewey's philosophy around which controversy has swelled is his treatment of individuality in the social world. This controversy is somewhat surprising and lends credence to the observation that Dewey is much "cussed" and discussed but little read. On the one hand are those who claim that he exalted individuality at the expense of organized society. On the other hand, some critics charge that he submerged the individual under a stifling objectivity represented by scientific consciousness and centralized social institutions. The controversy is surprising because if one gives Dewey a fair reading, it is difficult to find that he maintains either position.

Rather than accepting the extremes of subjectivity or objectivity, Dewey tried to show that experience is first and primarily macroscopic and that distinctions of subjectivity (or individuality) and objectivity (or the social and physical environment) come out of experience. In short, one is not necessarily more real than the other because Dewey viewed subject and object or the individual and society in a precarious balance—a *transactional* relationship. Of course, individuality can be submerged or lost by rigid institutional restrictions, and sociality can be denied by a rampant individualism (such as the economic *laissez-faire* variety). What Dewey actually said is that individuality and sociality are interrelated: Both are possibilities and not guarantees. In other words, people have to work to see that better, more desirable kinds of individual and social life become actualities, not just theoretical propositions.

Dewey thought that modern industrial society had submerged individuality and sociality. Because of the confusion of modern society, he argued, the school should be an institution where the individual and the social capabilities of children can be nurtured. The way to achieve this is through democratic living. Individuality is important because it is the source of novelty and change in human affairs. Dewey defined *individuality* as the interplay of personal choice and freedom with objective conditions. To the extent that personal choice is intelligently made, then individuals can exercise greater control over their personal destinies and the objective world surrounding them; that is, they have more freedom.

Sociality refers to a milieu or medium conducive to individual development. In Dewey's mind, genuine individuality could not exist without humane, democratic, and educative social conditions; consequently, the category of the social is the *inclusive* philosophic idea because it is the means by which the distinctly human is achieved. Therefore, individuality and sociality cannot be divorced in Dewey's system; they are interdependent and interrelated.

In this respect, one can better understand Dewey's ideal for the school and his rejection of those philosophies that promote a separation of individuals from institutions. The school, through democratic education, must enhance the interplay of individuality and sociality, the one supporting and enlarging the other.

Religious Experience.   Pragmatist philosophy is attacked sometimes by the religious right for being a leading exponent of the so-called "secular humanist" influence in public education. However, the pragmatist philosophers themselves, such as James and Dewey, had an abiding concern for religious experience. One of James's leading works is *The Varieties of Religious Experience* (1902), which has been influential in philosophical and theological thought. Dewey's *A Common Faith* (1934) has not been as influential, but it is a concise statement of a position that underlies much of his thought on education and democratic theory. Neither James nor Dewey embraced supernaturalism or organized religion. Certainly, both were humanists in the long tradition of the Western humanities, as were many past thinkers on religion, such as Desiderius Erasmus.

Dewey's views on religious experience can be found succinctly stated in *A Common Faith*, published in 1934. He held that being "religious" did not require the acceptance of supernaturalism and thought that most organized religions have a negative effect because they tend to separate and classify people, which is an untenable practice in a democratic society. However, he rejected militant atheism and promoted instead a consideration of the human being in the realm of nature. He believed that religious ideas are rooted in humanity's natural needs. When human beings understand the connecting links between themselves and their social context and when they act to promote the desirable elements of this connection, they achieve a religious character. An unreligious attitude is that which attributes human purpose and achievement to the solitary individual in isolation from the physical and social environment.

Moral Development.   In *Human Nature and Conduct*, Dewey proposed a "broad sweep" of morals as these relate to all the social disciplines connected with the study of humankind. He thought that not only analyzing morals but also looking at them constructively was in the tradition of Hume's skepticism. Moral rules should be considered in light of particular situations and in terms of their consequences; hence, each action can be judged good or bad in terms of its moral outcomes. Essentially, this is an educative process because an understanding of consequences is to be arrived at only through careful and reflective thinking. Dewey rejected moral theory based on *a priori* reasoning or divine precept. Basically, he thought that moral traits are to be acquired by individual participation in the social context and its cultural heritage or by learning about morality through living and reflective inquiry.

A recent development that has stimulated much critical comment is the work of Lawrence Kohlberg, who claimed that his theory, at least in part, is an elaboration of Dewey's views on moral education. Kohlberg maintained that the key to understanding a person's moral character lies in understanding that person's moral philosophy. Every person is a moral philosopher, Kohlberg believed, and although variations occur from one individual to another, *universal* forms of moral thinking can be described as "cognitive developmental stages." Stage development occurs in an invariant sequence although the rate of development might vary and be hindered in some children at any stage. Stages consist of "structured wholes," or total ways of thinking, rather than mere attitudes toward particular situations.

Kohlberg's work has its critics. One point of contention has been how he interpreted Dewey's theory. Dewey thought that development occurs sequentially, or in stages. His view that the aim of education is *growth* is indicative of this sequential development, but he did not see development in terms of discreet, invariant stages along Kohlberg's lines. In schools, growth could be developed purposefully with the proper organization of curriculum, methods, and social life. In the final analysis, Kohlberg's approach to moral education owes more to Immanuel Kant than to John Dewey. Where Kohlberg's stage theory points toward a kind of fixed, ultimate end (justice), the closest thing to it in Dewey's philosophy is the concept of growth.

From Dewey's perspective, moral education should help students acquire vital ideas that become "motive forces in the guidance of conduct" or result in a "widening and deepening of conscious life." In *Democracy and Education* (1916), Dewey holds that "All education which develops power to share effectively in social life is moral"; in *Moral Principles in Education* (1909), he asserts that participation in social life is the school's chief moral end. For ideas to become motive forces in conduct, they must affect how an individual relates ethically with others. As Dewey put it, "Ultimate moral motives and forces are nothing more or less than social intelligence." For growth in social intelligence to occur, the school must be organized and arranged so that the education it provides relates to the personal experience of the students, enters into their personal lives, and helps shape their judgment—or what Dewey calls "social power" and "force of character." Individuals achieve this only to the extent that they are "continually exercised in forming and testing judgments." In short, *the* aim of education is growth in personal judgment and social intelligence.

Aesthetic Development.   According to Dewey, art is a marriage between form and matter; that is, artists attempt to incorporate their ideas into the object being created. Thus, they engage in their work until they achieve the desired end. The artist is not only the creator but also the perceiver. Dewey did not believe, however, that art and aesthetic experiences are to be left only to the realm of the professional artist. He thought that everyone can achieve and enjoy aesthetic experiences, provided creative intelligence is developed through education. Therefore, art need not be the possession of the few but can be available to everyone and can be applied to the ordinary activities of life. A truly aesthetic experience is one that is so engaging and fulfilling that no conscious distinction of self and object is made; the two are so fully integrated that such distinctions are not needed. In short, an aesthetic experience provides unity and completion; it is human experience at its highest point. Like the Greeks, Dewey thought that people should project art into all human activities, such as the *art* of education. For Dewey, education is an art rather than a science. Good education helps unify the mind and body, or thinking and doing, and when this is achieved, education becomes the supreme art form—the art of education.

Neopragmatism

Philosophical pragmatism never completely died out with the passing of John Dewey, but it suffered a decline, particularly in academic philosophy. More recently, however, it has experienced a resurgence as what could be called neopragmatism. According to William Caspary, the revival of interest in Dewey's philosophy, in particular, is largely a reaction against the analytic turn in philosophy, particularly among feminists, neoHegelians, and postmodernist thinkers. It also has been stimulated considerably by the works of American philosophers Richard Bernstein, Richard Rorty, and Cornel West. In Rorty's view, American and European philosophers who dismiss pragmatism are acting prematurely, for he maintains that James and Dewey wait at the ends of the dialectic roads being traveled by both analytic and postmodern philosophies. Caspary, reflecting some of Rorty's belief, finds Dewey's writings particularly pertinent today when so much conflict and clash of ideas occurs. Dewey's hopeful philosophy might help resolve some conflicts, but he also cautions that Dewey's answers are often fragmentary, and, like other great thinkers, he was not always consistent.

Richard Bernstein recognizes that Marxism, existentialism, pragmatism, and analytic philosophy all hold that philosophy should promote the ideal of free human activity. However, he concludes that pragmatism best promotes open and mutual criticism, rather than dogma, and it avoids the subjectivism and nihilism often found in some of the other philosophies. Bernstein also examines critical theory and postmodernism, both of which have questioned unity and elevated differences. Critical analysis must go on, but it also must include criticism for *reconciliation* as well, for however much people are committed to their own views, they should uphold the ideal of a *community* of inquirers. In Bernstein's view, pragmatism reflects a needed ethical sense of optimism and recognition of important common bonds of democracy.

Perhaps the most significant figure in the resurgence is Richard Rorty. Trained in the analytic mode of philosophy, Rorty found it restrictive and sought to break out of the mold. According to Rorty, people need an intellectual effort that is therapeutic and that attempts to "break the crust of tradition" so that people do not become stuck on singular vocabularies or particular philosophical modes of thought. Rorty criticizes the Cartesian and Kantian traditions and their impact on philosophy, which tends to see the mind as a great mirror, knowledge as accurate representations of objective reality, and philosophy as the tool to make the mirror get more accurate representations. His heroes are Ludwig Wittgenstein, Martin Heidegger, and John Dewey—whom Rorty calls the "great edifying, peripheral thinkers" who taught that when people think they have true beliefs about something, they might in fact have no more than "conformity to the norms of the day." They also taught that words and vocabularies acquire their meanings in human usage, rather than "their representative character" and "their transparency to the real."

As Rorty sees it, a healthy departure for philosophy is to cease trying to be the foundation of knowledge and to take up the view of philosophical activity as part of a "conversation of culture" in which knowing is not an essence described by scientists or philosophers, but a right to believe based on the best current standards. As Rorty maintains, people should understand knowledge as "alternative standards of justification," and changes in those standards are what makes up intellectual history. Rorty urges us to extend the best of our traditions, such as using democratic means to prevent the rich from cheating the poor, but also to recognize that humans are fallible and will make mistakes. These thrusts are clearly along lines followed by Dewey, who warned against the "quest for certainty."

Rorty argues that the philosophical search for objective knowledge has so permeated philosophical traditions that it has become normal discourse. What is needed, he believes, is "abnormal" discourse, meaning a criticism of comfortable assumptions to shake people loose and to develop new and more creative approaches to thought. Furthermore, Rorty's criticisms impact philosophy of education, because it is part of the Western philosophical tradition, as well.

From another angle, Cornel West proposes what he calls *prophetic pragmatism*. In *The American Evasion of Philosophy*, West sees pragmatism's origins in Ralph Waldo Emerson and its fullest developments in Peirce, James, and Dewey and more recently Bernstein and Rorty, but he also gives places to W. E. B. Du Bois, Reinhold Niebuhr, C. Wright Mills, and Lionel Trilling. West connects the African-American tradition of Christianity and liberation theology with pragmatism in ways that promise some new directions. He believes pragmatism offers hopeful ways of analyzing social and political life that avoid the traditional problems of philosophy. Pragmatists insist that social change should come through peaceful means, especially through education, public dialogue, and an experimental approach to social and political problems, which is what Dewey called the method of intelligence. This shows pragmatism's humane optimism, for rather than armed struggle and violence, pragmatists call for people to reason together, try things out, and evaluate them to gain new ends and a better, happier life for all. This does not mean that life has no tragic side; rather, a proper philosophical approach seeks to avoid the paralysis of despair that comes from being overwhelmed by the tragic.

Perhaps one can see the need for Bernstein's call for democratic optimism, Rorty's call for critical discourse, and West's hopeful "prophetic" approach. Today, the science of education uses a vocabulary of self-confident claims of the physical and behavioral sciences. Boasts are made about research-based education and how much people know about the educational process, but compelling evidence is lacking that much more is known about education now than in the past or that scientific analysis is a significant improvement over philosophical criticism. Perhaps some serious but helpful criticism is overdue.

Too many times in the past, the field of education has been awash with sweeping reform claims that could not be sustained, and would-be reformers were left high and dry. In the 1960s and 1970s, for example, calls were made for radical reform and revolution in education. Many practitioners in elementary and secondary schools simply ignored would-be reformers and went on about the more mundane business of traditional schooling. Still, talk about revolution and radicalism in educational theory helped make schools the recipients of angry public criticisms spearheaded by right-wing political interests, a loss of faith in educational institutions, and the recent imposition of reactionary reforms and accountability. If educators want to undertake a new criticism akin to what Rorty or West suggest, people must understand our educational traditions, learn the lessons of the present (about which conservative and radical educational theory can be informative), and proceed with a philosophical discourse that challenges entrenched ways of thinking about education in thoughtful and helpful ways.

Certainly, education must involve traditional knowledge because this includes not only the contemporary vocabulary of knowledge but also the intellectual traditions that helped establish such a vocabulary and that lie at the heart of the traditional curriculum. If pragmatism is taken seriously, those traditional and newer subjects in the curriculum—history, language, science, math, and cultural differences—should be explored with students in terms of current circumstances, and students should be prepared in ways that develop critical and creative intelligence to help them change the status quo and move toward a more humane, democratic society.

PRAGMATISM AS A PHILOSOPHY OF EDUCATION

The impact of pragmatism on American education has been considerable. Many schools have implemented elements of pragmatist ideas in one way or another, but this influence is not always connected consciously with the philosophy. One reason is that pragmatism in its most influential period often was identified with radical social reform, particularly progressive education. Many educators thought that this identification was a detriment to getting pragmatist ideas accepted into basically conservative and traditional schools; therefore, they were more interested in the practical use of pragmatist ideas than having those ideas identified with the philosophy of pragmatism or with progressivism. In a sense, therefore, elements of pragmatism came in through the back doors of schools, and this factor helps explain why pragmatist ideas and methods often are used (and misused) but are not always identified with the philosophy.

Although pragmatic philosophy greatly influenced progressivism, it would be a mistake to link progressivism too closely with pragmatism. Many progressives claimed to agree with the philosophy of John Dewey, but Dewey often was critical of the excesses of progressivism. His book *Experience and Education* (1938) was directed as much at progressive "child-centered" excesses as it was at tradition-bound, old-style American education. Dewey's name often was invoked but his works seldom studied, and many progressive zealots took his ideas out of context.

Progressive education as a movement began because many liberal thinkers in the late nineteenth and early twentieth centuries believed that American education did not reflect the ideas of justice and freedom found in democratic theory. Progressivism had its "hard" and "soft" wings. The soft wing identified with a romanticized view of the goodness of the child, and it sought a child-centered education that put few restraints on behavior or eschewed rigorous levels of academic performance. This led to charges of "permissiveness" being leveled against progressive theory and against Deweyan pragmatism too, because many progressives claimed Dewey as their philosophical leader. The hard wing of the movement believed that education should reflect advances made in the physical sciences, the social sciences, and technology. Some of these hard progressives, however, thought that scientific procedures should be used to measure, categorize, and separate children by ability and intelligence level to meet demands in the economy. This view led to grouping practices that aggravated social differences in school and society and resulted in Deweyan pragmatism being criticized as crassly materialistic and wedded to industrial capitalism, of which Dewey himself was critical.

Not all progressive ideas can be linked with pragmatism, however. Locke's view that no ideas are innate and that experience is the primary shaper of human existence found ready acceptance in the progressive movement. Some advocates came to believe that schooling was primarily a matter of encouraging children to experience a variety of things. Pragmatism, however, stresses the importance of seeing the child in relation to the variety of experiences encountered in the environment, not just school experiences. Pragmatists believe that children must be understood in terms of mental, physical, and emotional development and also in light of all other social and cultural factors that influence and shape their lives.

Rousseau influenced progressive thinking with his emphasis on nature, and some progressives took this to mean that "natural" education should be free from all societal restraints. Pragmatists maintain that education should be natural and related to the development of the human as a complex kind of animal. They have long championed schools where children can move about and where an open and stimulating environment brings the natural element into education. This is a far cry from Rousseau's romantic naturalism, however, which encouraged many soft progressives to develop educational theories that sentimentalized the natural goodness of the child and severely limited adult guidance and direction. Dewey did not champion either of the extremes on the soft or hard wings of progressivism, and so the identification of progressivism with Dewey and pragmatism should be made carefully.

Aims of Education

Dewey and the pragmatists believed that education is a necessity of life. It renews people so that they can face the problems encountered through their interaction with the environment. Cultures survive across time, Dewey pointed out, because education is the process by which a culture is transmitted across generations by the communication of habits, activities, thoughts, and feelings from adults to the young. Without this, social life cannot survive; therefore, education should not be viewed merely as schooling in academic subject matter, but as a part of life itself.

Dewey thought that the school should provide just this kind of environment. The school should be a place where the other environments that the child encounters—family, work, and others—are coordinated in meaningful ways for the child to study. In the pragmatist view, education should not be mere preparation for life, but an important part of life that children themselves live. Children's lives are as important to them as the lives of adults are to the adults. Thus, educators should be aware of the interests and motivations of children, as well as the environment from which they come. In "My Pedagogic Creed," Dewey set forth the belief that education has two fundamental sides: the psychological and the sociological. One should not be subordinate to the other because the child's own instincts and powers provide the material and starting point of all education, and the educator's knowledge of social conditions is necessary to interpret the child's powers. An educator does not know what these powers and instincts are until they can be translated into their social equivalents for students and projected into the future lives of students for insight into the consequences.

In sum, Dewey believed that individuals should be educated as social beings, capable of participating in and directing their own social affairs. This means a freer interaction among social groups, as well as attention given to developing all the potentialities an individual has for future growth. He looked on education as a way to free the individual to engage in continuous growth directed toward appropriate individual and social aims.

Whatever the specific aims of schooling and learning, pragmatists stress the importance of the way humans arrive at those aims. According to Dewey, aims (1) should grow out of existing conditions; (2) should be tentative, at least in the beginning, and maintain flexibility; and perhaps most importantly of all, (3) must always be directed toward a freeing of activities, an "end in view." This last suggestion is central to Dewey's idea of education. Properly speaking, Dewey thought that people (parents, students, and citizens) are the ones who have educational aims, not the process of education. Still, there is a sense of meaningfulness about the aims of education.

As stated in Dewey's *Democracy and Education*, the aim of education is growth: "Since growth is the characteristic of life, education is all one with growing; it has no end beyond itself." In this regard, Dewey was speaking of growth as an enlargement of the capacity to learn from experience and to direct future experience in a meaningful way. Here rests the importance of the third point, that education should free human activities and make people more capable of directing individual and social life because only in this way can proper growth in democratic living occur.

Sidney Hook, in *Education for Modern Man* (1963), maintained that education for growth goes together with education for a democratic society. In fact, the ideals of democracy establish the direction in which growth should occur, and the resulting growth should lead to a more democratic society. Intelligence is significant because it enables us to break the bonds of habit and makes it possible to devise alternatives that are more satisfying and desirable. Hook pointed out that growth, democracy, and intelligence are the inclusive and related aims of education.

According to Alven Neiman, premodern philosophers lived in a relatively stable world where views of the eternal prevailed and where all living things (like Aristotle's acorn) would become what they inherently were supposed to become. This was a philosophical Garden of Eden where God brought order out of chaos through creation and where true reality existed prior to human action. Modernism brought a fall from this garden because it rejected the view that nature unfolded according to some transcendent design; instead, nature worked only by natural selection, contingency, and brute force. Pragmatic philosophers looked on the new possibilities with cheerful hope, even though they were acutely aware of the chaotic aspects of the modern world. Dewey, for example, argued that because the old stability was gone, humans must now see themselves as the meaning-makers—the ones to bring order and meaning to the world. Humans might be no more than biological organisms, but they are organisms that must understand their own individual and collective experience, cope with the contingencies of life, and solve the problems of society. Dewey saw *growth* as the central educational aim because if humanity is left to its own devices, then it should grow to meet the challenge. As Rorty points out, however, it is not eternal Meaning but meaning contingent on an actual human context. In other words, humans need to go beyond a quest for *the* meaning of life and seek meaning in their present-day, actual-life circumstances.

However, Neiman argues, neopragmatists such as Rorty miss an important element of Dewey, and this is his faith in democracy and in the social intelligence that is unleashed when people learn to work together democratically. For Dewey, growth means not only understanding the natural world but also aesthetic appreciation of wholeness, harmony, and peace, which are outcomes that Dewey thought a democratic way of life promised.

William Heard Kilpatrick was an influential educator and one of Dewey's students and colleagues. He maintained that the overriding concern of each individual should be that all people have "the fullest and finest life possible." What has been accomplished and the possibility of future accomplishments are always uncertain; therefore, continued progress demands intelligent effort. Education becomes involved in teaching children how to live. The function of education, then, is to help people direct, control, and guide personal and social experience for a more democratic way of life.

Pragmatists argue that people need to be aware of the consequences of their actions so that they can guide their actions more intelligently, whether this action is at the personal or social level. In this way, individuals learn to direct and control their own actions and require less external support and direction. They learn to have a greater effect in the larger social context, even to the point of social change and reform. Educated people grow in this manner, and their growth depends on a good environment shared with others, as well as the natural flexibility inherent in the individual. Schools should foster habits of thought, invention, and initiative that will assist people in growing in the right direction—that is, toward democratic living.

According to pragmatists, education should be an experimental enterprise, as well as something that assists in social renewal. It should promote a humane spirit in people and the desire to find new answers to current economic, political, and social problems. Education should promote individual and social interests, which will diminish reliance on custom and encourage more reliance on intelligence and democracy. This does not mean that valuable traditions are to be disrespected or discarded; rather, it means that we must learn to solve pressing problems intelligently, rather than to rely mindlessly on traditions.

Dewey pointed out that a philosophy of education is not the application of ready-made ideas to every problem, but rather the formation of right mental and moral attitudes to use in attacking contemporary problems. When fundamental changes occur in social life, people should reconstruct their thinking *and* their educational programs to meet these challenges. Thus, human ideas will have a pragmatic function. Learning helps people adapt to environmental changes and affects their character as well. In this way, education has a moral influence and should play a vital part in helping us become the kind of moral persons who are interested in promoting growth, for others and for ourselves.

Methods of Education

Pragmatists prefer flexible education methods that can be used in various ways. They also prefer functional schools, with such things as movable, child-sized desks, large print in books for small children, and so forth, all of which came out of Dewey's experimental work at the Laboratory School in Chicago. Various methods are needed, because there is no single way to educate. In consequence, educators should be aware of many approaches, including the use of sources in the wider community.

Some pragmatists urge teachers and students to see that all knowledge is related. Reading, writing, and spelling can be combined as language arts. History, geography, government, economics, and multicultural studies can be put under social studies because of the relationships among these areas. Furthermore, relationships can be found between social studies and language arts and among other areas of the curriculum. This can be done by developing a cross-disciplinary approach to the curriculum so that students can understand how things are related. Then, students can select an area of concentration for a unit of study, such as "exploration," and all the subject areas would revolve around this. Language arts, for example, would deal with the literature of exploration, including the biographies of famous explorers past and present, historical accounts of the impact of exploration on people, science fiction about exploration themes, and student writings and research projects in which they explore personal inquiry into the theme of exploration.

In addition, they could integrate the study of mathematics in the theme of exploration, such as the practical mathematics needed in circumnavigating the globe and stories about mathematical explorations of the kind done from the time of Pythagoras to Albert Einstein and Stephen Hawking. One could hardly study exploration without becoming involved with scientific exploration. Students could inquire into the history and drama of scientific discoveries and their impacts on people. Indeed, the possibilities are numerous for integrating studies of various kinds on a single theme such as exploration, including art, drama, and music, all of which involve various kinds of exploratory aspects. These kinds of things do need to be done in ways that respect the developmental, experiential, and educational levels of the participating students. If approached in educationally sound ways, students would be involved with the fundamentals of knowledge in practical and applied ways so that the usefulness of knowledge would be more apparent. This approach demonstrates the relation of the various disciplines and shows students the interrelationships of knowledge.

Pragmatists are adherents of action-oriented education; therefore, they would suggest an activity-oriented approach so students would learn not only that they can relate various kinds of knowledge and use them to attack a problem but also that they can act on them. To understand exploration more fully, students might visit historical sites of exploration or contemporary sites, such as the Kennedy Space Center. At school, they could reconstruct past events and life situations to appreciate the difficulties involved in actual events and examine positive and negative effects that exploration has had. For example, the arrival of Europeans in the Americas had a profound impact on the Europeans and the Native Americans, with positive and negative outcomes that continue to have effects today. Reconstructing this part of human experience (questioning and studying this phase of human history) would help students gain a better understanding not only of the past but also of their world today. These reconstructions could involve readings, lectures or presentations, field trips, videos, and Internet connections; they also could take the form of student-constructed dramatizations, role playing, and model building.

Because pragmatists are concerned with teaching children how to solve problems, they believe that real-life situations encourage problem-solving ability in a practical setting. For example, the conservation and wise use of energy is a leading problem today. Suppose that in a particular science class, the students want to understand energy conservation. Someone suggests that they should plan an energy allocation system. This becomes the specific problem, and the students will need to look at the history of energy, how various sources of energy have been used for human needs, how the competition for energy aggravates world problems, what the science of energy offers for understanding, and what resources and plans are available.

The materials gathered must be appropriate for the age of the students, and the teacher must provide direction to keep the activities within reasonable limits. The motivation is in the students' interest, and the teacher serves as a resource person concerned with helping students get the maximum educational advantages out of the situation. Students do the work themselves, and they might encounter various problems about what kinds of allocation schemes to use, how to construct an equitable allocation basis, what social and economic issues must be considered, what possible alternative energy sources can be tapped, or how society could conserve energy better. In tackling such problems and trying to provide solutions, students come to appreciate actual hurdles to be overcome and to gain important understanding that will help them better control their own destinies.

Pragmatist educators advocate meeting the needs and interests of the child. This sometimes has been interpreted to mean letting children do anything they want, but "needs and interests" do not necessarily mean the dictates of whim. Suppose a child wants to build model airplanes. Pragmatists would point out that this child's interest could be used as a motivational basis by which basic areas of the curriculum could be related. For example, one could be taught mathematics and physics by examining the principles of the airfoil. One could do this by studying people's dreams to fly and the eventual realization of flight. Meeting the needs and interests of students does not always mean waiting for students to suggest a topic, because often they are unaware of their needs and interests. A properly prepared and motivated teacher will make suggestions and arouse student interests to help launch new learning projects. Indeed, the role of the teacher is to help students grow, and this means leading them into new areas of knowledge to help make their understandings, skills, and abilities become deeper, more complex, and more sophisticated. In Dewey's Laboratory School at Chicago, the principle followed was to start children in some activity that was of direct interest to them and then, and as they encountered practical problems in the activity, to involve them in gaining knowledge specific to the activity that, in turn, would lead to more general knowledge.

Pragmatists tend toward a broad education rather than a specialized one. They maintain that when one breaks knowledge down into discrete elements and does not put it back together, one faces the danger of losing perspective. With today's knowledge explosion, it is impossible for a person to know everything, but one can understand the general operating principles of nature and social conditions. Pragmatists do not oppose breaking knowledge down into its constituent elements, nor do they oppose specialization at the higher and professional levels of education, but they do encourage returning the elements of knowledge back into a reconstructed whole that gives new direction and insight.

The concept of experimentation is basic to pragmatism. The fact that Dewey called his school at Chicago the "Laboratory School" illustrates his view that education (and philosophy) should be experimental. Even though numerous guides, precepts, and maxims are related to education, pragmatists hold that in the final analysis, education is a process of experimentation because there are always new things to learn and different things to experience. Dewey gave the example of 7-year-old students who were cooking eggs and comparing them with vegetables and meats. If simply cooking eggs were the final goal, the students could have used a cookbook for directions. They even raised this point, but in cooking the eggs, asking questions, and seeking answers, they discovered that albumen is a characteristic feature of animal foods that corresponds to starches in vegetables. Thus, they learned an important lesson in nutrition. The teacher could have given them this information beforehand, but the lively manner of discovery clarified the knowledge in a much more profound way than mere telling ever could have accomplished. This type of learning is of twofold value: (1) An important piece of knowledge is learned, and (2) the skills of inquiry and self-sufficiency are developed, which will benefit individuals for years to come.

Another approach suggested by Kilpatrick is the "project approach" to learning. Projects should be chosen by students as much as possible through individual and group discussion, with the teacher as moderator and with student cooperation in pursuing the goals of the project. In some cases, the teacher has no definite idea what the outcome will be. Kilpatrick carefully pointed out that teachers can and should veto projects that are too ambitious or for which resources are lacking. He advocated that all of the elementary school years should be devoted to the project method and that it be extended into the secondary school but in diminishing amounts to make room for some specialization.

Although some variations can be found among pragmatists regarding methods, they all agree that the proper method of education is experiential, flexible, open ended, and oriented toward growth of the individual's capacity to think and to participate intelligently in social life.

Curriculum

Pragmatists reject separating knowledge from experience and fragmenting or compartmentalizing knowledge. When this happens, facts are torn away from experience. Compartmentalization focuses attention on subjects rather than the child's experiences with learning. For example, in specialized learning, students might be able to quote passages from Shakespeare, but without understanding how these can inform them about the world and their own lives. By the same token, those who ignore subject matter and make children the only starting point risk losing sight of the importance of organized knowledge.

According to Dewey, such cases have two major concerns: the logical and the psychological. The first emphasizes discipline; the second, interest. The error is to see a gap between a child's areas of interest and important subject matter because appropriate subject matter is not something fixed and ready-made outside a child's areas of interest. The difficulty resides in how subject matter is organized and presented to students. For example, history traditionally is taught as something students should study simply because it is good for them, yet it might be remote and alien to their everyday experiences. The study of history should enable children to connect their own experiences, customs, and institutions with those of the past. It should liberate and enrich personal life by furnishing it with context, background, and outlook. Dewey thought that the practice of divorcing history from the present is a grievous error because it robs historical study of the capacity to provide intelligent insight into the present. A divorced history loses its value for ethical instruction. It does not give understanding of the fabric of current life and may produce callous indifference to why things have become what they are.

When one views what a child learns as fixed and ready made, attention is directed too much on outcome and too little on process. Pragmatists want to focus at least some attention on process because ends should not be divorced from means. They assert that the means used to accomplish something dictate what the outcomes (or ends) are. For example, to say that the American school should produce democratic citizens and then establish the school in such a way that the students have almost no choice, judgment, or decision-making opportunity is, in actuality, to produce virtually anything but democratic citizens. The older generation then sits back and wonders why the young do not participate more in social and political activities. According to pragmatists, there is little doubt why such conditions exist.

Pragmatists believe in a diversified curriculum. This has resulted in an extension of American education into many areas not previously considered its domain. For example, pragmatists have advocated studies in occupations and hygiene and in such topics as the family and the economy. Consequently, many pragmatists advocate "problem-centered learning" as the proper approach to curriculum organization. Essentially, it starts with a central question or problem, and students are to attack the problem in diverse ways according to their interests and needs. Some might work independently, others in groups, and still others in various combinations and contexts. Information and ideas are drawn from books, periodicals, videos, travel, field trips, guest experts, and other resources. Materials are studied and evaluated, and students draw conclusions and construct suitable generalizations concerning the problem. Learning and growth are evaluated, and this sets the stage for the study. Traditional disciplines are not ignored but are used for knowledge background to accompany the problem and to aid student learning and growth.

Role of the Teacher

For Dewey, teaching and learning are essential for the continuation of human community and society. The process of continuity, of transmitting the things that make social life possible, is not a biological or genetic process but a social and communal one. A community exists because of what people hold in common (values, beliefs, language, etc.). Because these things are not transmitted biologically, they can be passed on to the younger generation only through social and educational processes. Otherwise, each succeeding generation would have to reinvent, not merely reinterpret, what previous generations knew and understood.

Because all social life is potentially educative, people learn most of what they know through informal processes instead of formal education; however, informal processes are not always accomplished with purpose and care. What makes formal education significant is that it is handled in a deliberate way to ensure that an orderly continuation of social life and community is possible. The danger is that formal education can become abstract and remote from students' actual life experiences, so constant attention must be given to appropriate linkages to life experience. This is where the teacher's role becomes crucial.

Education can be studied scientifically, but its effective practice is basically an art. Teachers express the highest concept of this art when they keep education from becoming routinized and lethargic. All living educates, but social living helps people extract the net meaning from their education. Dewey, like Plato, believed that society is a necessary part of people's learning experiences and that we must guard against schools treating subject matter as if it were a thing apart from social life itself.

Training is not the same thing as education. Children can be trained through behavioral conditioning to like or avoid things without understanding why they should do so. Most habits of animals are the result of training, but humans, unlike horses, have a wider range of understanding and can act on that understanding. Therefore, the educative process is fulfilled only when understanding and intelligent actions are promoted. Helping the child to think and act intelligently is *education* as opposed to training. Learning activities are used to convey ideas and help students develop understanding and skill, and educational settings are provided where students can act on and test their understandings and skills. This approach to education must be framed in an environment that has been regulated deliberately in order to achieve maximum educational effect.

Children are motivated to learn naturally, and the teacher should capture and use the motivation that already exists. Teachers must understand that all children are not at the same point, however, and cannot be educated in the same way. Although projects might motivate some students for group work, individual projects might have to be provided for others. Pragmatists believe that teachers should serve as knowledgeable guides and resources for students, not as taskmasters who just drill students in subject matter. Drill and recitation have occasional uses but are not the central function of teaching. In *Democracy and Education*, Dewey holds that the teacher's major role is to establish a proper learning environment to stimulate desired intellectual and emotional growth among students. A significant part of that environment is the subject matter to be studied, and the teacher must be knowledgeable of that subject matter in order to break it down into elements that students are able to connect with their own experience. This involves using students' present interests and life situations as starting points to show how knowledge has bearing on their lives. Teaching becomes a process of helping students identify problems and study organized knowledge in order to understand how social life developed from the past, what needs to be maintained, and what needs to be changed.

Dewey did not advocate ahistorical presentism; rather, he believed that learners are best motivated to study organized knowledge when they can see how it relates to the present. For example, Dewey had his students at the Laboratory School weave simple things on small hand looms—an activity they all enjoyed—to help launch them into studying the impact of textiles on human history. They learned to connect a current interest with a more remote but vital human interest. Using the hand looms helped make a point about how people in early cultures solved problems of survival. A variation of this approach can be applied to the more complex and abstract interests of mature students. For example, consider how virtually all high school students are interested in the adult world of responsibility in their futures. Continuing with the textile example, consider how textile manufacturing is a major point of dispute in today's global economy and how that dispute might affect the lives of high school students when they assume economic responsibilities in the adult world. This prospect involves not only job opportunities and providing for themselves and the families they might establish, but also their roles as responsible citizens and members of the larger community. Using their interest as a starting point, students will find that textiles are an enduring feature of human history. Making garments out of natural fibers was a major advance for prehistoric cultures; the silk trade was a point of contact and conflict between the Greco-Roman world and ancient China; wool and linen competition was an important stimulus in Europe's industrial revolution; cotton was central to the issue of slavery in the American Civil War; and natural and synthetic textile production are important to today's global economy. Such studies help students put their own lives in perspective historically and currently. A chief role of the teacher is to help learners identify problems, frame questions, and locate appropriate bodies of knowledge to better understand present issues and their histories.

Pragmatists put a premium on teaching that promotes an active role for students. Rather than teachers merely imparting knowledge and students passively receiving it, pragmatists want active teachers and students. The teacher's action involves arranging the learning environment, guiding student learning activities, and helping students locate knowledge and integrate it into their own experiences; the students' action involves questioning, seeking information and knowledge of the conditions that affect them, and growing in understanding and ability to manage their lives and to participate fruitfully in society.

The pragmatists' model of the teacher calls for an exceptionally competent person—one who possesses breadth and depth of knowledge, understands current conditions that affect the lives of students, knows how to organize and direct student investigations, understands psychological development and learning theory, provides a supportive environment in which students can learn, and possesses a refined understanding of school and community resources that are available for teaching and learning.

CRITIQUE OF PRAGMATISM IN EDUCATION

After the mid-twentieth century, few philosophers identified themselves as pragmatists; rather, analytic philosophy, existentialism, hermeneutics, and postmodernism became philosophically fashionable. Yet, a resurgence of pragmatism is occurring today, one reason being that because Dewey wrote so consistently and forcibly on the connection of democracy and education, his ideas continue to have an influence and following not only in education, but in other fields as well. Disagreement arises, however, on what Dewey meant. One camp accuses him of using education to shape a pluralistic society without due regard for unique cultural differences. Another sees him as downgrading individualism in his advocacy of cultural pluralism. Part of the difficulty resides in the fact that Dewey was an active philosopher for a long period of time, and the volume of his writings is extensive. Another problem is that Dewey did not always write in a way that ensured clarity. Yet, Dewey took positions on many important areas of thought, and his writings seem relevant to many contemporary issues.

Another measure of the continuing influence of Dewey and philosophical pragmatism is the work being accomplished at the Center for Dewey Studies at Southern Illinois University at Carbondale. The center houses Dewey's papers, correspondence, and other documents, as well as his publications. It has produced a widely acclaimed edition of his collected works, amounting to about 40 volumes of material. This material is contributing to a better, more systematic understanding of Dewey's philosophy, and it has helped raise the level of scholarship on Dewey's impact on education.

Debate continues, however, over what usefulness pragmatism has had or might continue to have on American education. Some critics lump progressivism and pragmatism together, overlooking the fact that the progressive movement was not a single thing, but rather a loosely joined movement encompassing several philosophic persuasions. Another criticism is that the pragmatist philosophy of education deprecates the acquisition of knowledge and waters down the curriculum by taking a piece of this and a bit of that discipline without ever fully exploring either in depth, catering to students' interests and slighting the basic disciplines they need. Some of this criticism has merit because past reforms were sometimes implemented too hastily and without adequate preparation of teaching staffs. In addition, some reformers did not completely grasp the essential ideas. The same kind of problem exists with regard to Dewey's views. Some educators have interpreted Dewey to mean that the intellectual and cognitive sides of education are unimportant. The fact is that Dewey placed intelligence and thinking in a central position in his philosophy. He thought that intelligence is developed in purposeful activity dealing with problems and arriving at solutions. He did not ignore books, subject matter, and the need for periodic drill. He simply rejected the assertion that these are the most important things in education. Dewey believed that every purposeful human activity has potential for intellectual, emotional, aesthetic, and moral growth.

Indeed, a wide gap exists between what Dewey urged and what often has transpired in his and other pragmatic philosophers' names. A case in point is the life adjustment movement. In the 1950s, some critics argued that pragmatists, and particularly Dewey, promoted an ethic of adjusting personal desires and interests to existing social and economic conditions. They said that such an outlook promoted monopolistic economics, *status quo* social divisions, and a general deadening effect. In fact, one former educational movement was called life adjustment, but there is no evidence that Dewey or any other leading pragmatist ever supported it. Dewey used the word *adjustment,* but he used it with regard to people adjusting objective conditions to themselves as much as the other way around. He pointed out that in order to reconstruct and reorient society, people first have to interact with existing conditions. In this sense, they have to adjust like any other organism, but they do it for the purpose of strengthening some conditions and changing others—*not* simply to conform to *status quo* authority and power relations.

Some critics attack pragmatism for its relative and situational approach to life problems. They maintain that pragmatism rejects traditional values in favor of values that are uncertain, changeable, and impermanent. Although these charges contain an element of truth, part of the criticism might relate to pragmatism's efforts to address social, cultural, and educational contexts rather than the metaphysical topics of traditional philosophy. Moreover, despite the critics' charges about relativism, pragmatists (such as Dewey) did not believe that traditional ideas and values should be rejected out-of-hand but should be important considerations. They do believe, however, that one cannot afford to rely only on hand-me-down values and should be seeking new ideas and values in every area of human activity. This problem is particularly apparent in the pragmatist's approach to education. It supports the idea that schools should maintain an experimental approach to learning. However, what such critics fail to realize, it seems, is that this does not mean that workable approaches, no matter how ancient in origin, are to be scrapped automatically. It is simply that for pragmatists, new ideas and approaches should be developed and implemented when they help solve perplexing human problems.

Several factors account for some of the difficulty found in the application of pragmatism to education: In addition to misinterpretation, an occasional lack of specificity in pragmatism makes it difficult to apply. In addition, zealous followers have attempted to apply broad ideas to specific educational problems and, hence, have oversimplified pragmatic positions. Sometimes a lack of energetic attention has been paid by educators to pragmatic philosophy itself in favor of secondhand interpretations. Some fault pragmatism for its shortcomings, but others see it as a major source of ideas.

William Paringer, in *John Dewey and the Paradox of Liberal Reform* (1990), takes a Marxist perspective that Dewey was not radical enough; he was too anchored in Enlightenment concepts and too lacking in ideological and political analysis. Thus, while Dewey examined power relations in classrooms, he failed to give adequate attention to power relations in the wider society that maintained racism, sexism, violence, and class division. In contrast, Sanford Reitman argues in *The Educational Messiah Complex* (1992) that American progressives and social reconstructionists who borrowed from Dewey were too radical. They came to view the school as an instrument of salvation from all the social ills that plague society and lost sight of Dewey's view that all social contexts have educational potential and that the educational task is to ensure that desirable educational results flow from those contexts. More recently, historian Dianne Ravitch claims, in *Left Back: A Century of Failed School Reform* (2000), that Dewey's progressive followers from child-centered progressives to social reconstructionists are the primary reason why schools seem to have lost sight of their appropriate academic mission today. The dispassionate reader might wonder how all of these criticisms can be true, and caring discernment is needed to avoid lumping too many historic influences and contemporary developments together. As for Dewey, he was definitely aware of class conflict and the need for remedies, but he opted for more gradual and less confrontational means than many leftist critics seem to prefer. Dewey also was concerned about the ways some of his followers interpreted his ideas, but he opted for polite criticism and persuasion rather than wholesale dismissal as some critics on the right seem to want. Finally, concerning the alleged failure of contemporary schools, one might wonder if it is so directly connected to Dewey, pragmatism, or even to the excesses of progressivism as many critics frequently maintain.

One criticism that could be made of Dewey's educational views is that the type of person needed to teach his way had to be exceptional, that is, extremely capable and highly educated in several disciplines. It is doubtful that a sufficient number of such persons could be prepared and retained today, particularly considering the level of financial outlay society seems willing to provide. It also does not to take into account the bureaucratic and politicized nature of American education, which often serves to stifle the more thoughtful and helpful kinds of reform.

The criticisms tend to show, however, that pragmatism and particularly Dewey's version of it continues to engage educational theorists. In some respects though, Dewey's philosophy of education has not had a truly systematic criticism because most critics have taken on only piecemeal aspects, have made polemical attacks rather than critical analyses, or have used particular aspects of pragmatism to support their own partisan views. Nevertheless, the philosophy of pragmatism has made important contributions to educational theory and practice and will continue to do so.

JAMES

TALKS TO TEACHERS

William James wrote little on education, but what he did produce reflected many of his central ideas. The following selection illustrates some of those ideas, notably the "stream of consciousness" and the child as a "behaving organism." Consciousness is complex and cannot be divided neatly into the intellectual and the practical, nor can it be divorced from the formation of habitual patterns of behavior. According to James, the process of education is the acquisition of important habits of behavior and the acquisition of ideas in ever higher and richer combinations.

The Stream of Consciousness

. . . The most general elements and workings of the mind are all that the teacher absolutely needs to be acquainted with for his purposes.

Now the immediate fact which psychology, the science of mind, has to study is also the most general fact. It is the fact that in each of us, when awake (and often when asleep), *some kind of consciousness is always going on.* There is a stream, a succession of states, or waves, or fields (or whatever you please to call them), of knowledge, of feeling, of desire, of deliberation, etc., that constantly pass and repass, and that constitute our inner life. The existence of this stream is the primal fact, the nature and origin of it form the essential problem, of our science. . . .

We have thus fields of consciousness,—that is the first general fact; and the second general fact is that the concrete fields are always complex. They contain sensations of our bodies and of the objects around us, memories of past experiences and thoughts of distant things, feelings of satisfaction and dissatisfaction, desires and aversions, and other emotional conditions, together with determinations of the will, in every variety of permutation and combination.

In most of our concrete states of consciousness all these different classes of ingredients are found simultaneously present to some degree, though the relative proportion they bear to one another is very shifting. One state will seem to be composed of hardly anything but sensations, another of hardly anything but memories, etc. But around the sensation, if one considers carefully, there will always be some fringe of thought or will, and around the memory some margin or penumbra of emotion or sensation. . . .

In the successive mutations of our fields of consciousness, the process by which one dissolves into another is often very gradual, and all sorts of inner rearrangements of contents occur. Sometimes the focus remains but little changed, while the margin alters rapidly. Sometimes the focus alters, and the margin stays. Sometimes focus and margin change places. Sometimes, again, abrupt alterations of the whole field occur. There can seldom be a sharp description. All we know is that, for the most part, each field has a sort of practical unity for its possessor, and that from this practical point of view we can class a field with other fields similar to it, by calling it a state of emotion, of perplexity, of sensation, of abstract thought, of volition, and the like. . . .

The Child as a Behaving Organism

I wish now to continue the description of the peculiarities of the stream of consciousness by asking whether we can in any intelligible way assign its *functions.*

It has two functions that are obvious: It leads to knowledge, and it leads to action.

Can we say which of these functions is the more essential?

An old historic divergence of opinion comes in here. Popular belief has always tended to estimate the worth of a man's mental processes by their effects upon his practical life. But philosophers have usually cherished a different view. "Man's supreme glory," they have said, "is to be a *rational* being, to know absolute and eternal and universal truth. The uses of his intellect for practical affairs are therefore subordinate matters. 'The theoretic life' is his soul's genuine concern." Nothing can be more different in its results for our personal attitude than to take sides with one or the other of these views, and emphasize the practical or the theoretical ideal. In the latter case, abstraction from the emotions and passions and withdrawal from the strife of human affairs would be not only pardonable, but praiseworthy; and all that makes for quiet and contemplation should be regarded as conducive to the highest human perfection. In the former, the man of contemplation would be treated as only half a human being, passion and practical resource would become once more glories of our race, a concrete victory over this earth's outward powers of darkness would appear an equivalent for any amount of passive spiritual culture, and conduct would remain as the test of every education worthy of the name.

It is impossible to disguise the fact that in the psychology of our own day the emphasis is transferred from the mind's purely rational function, where Plato and Aristotle, and what one may call the whole classic tradition in philosophy had placed it, to the so long neglected practical side. The theory of evolution is mainly responsible for this. Man, we now have reason to believe, has been evolved from infrahuman ancestors, in whom pure reason hardly existed, if at all, and whose mind, so far as it can have had any function, would appear to have been an organ for adapting their movements to the impressions received from the environment, so as to escape the better from destruction. Consciousness would thus seem in the first instance to be nothing but a sort of superadded biological perfection,—useless unless it prompted to useful conduct, and inexplicable apart from that consideration.

Deep in our own nature the biological foundations of our consciousness persist, undisguised and undiminished. Our sensations are here to attract us or to deter us, our memories to warn or encourage us, our feelings to impel, and our thoughts to restrain our behavior, so that on the whole we may prosper and our days be long in the land. . . .

No one believes more strongly than I do that what our senses know as 'this world' is only one portion of our mind's total environment and object. Yet, because it is the primal portion, it is the *sine qua non* of all the rest. If you grasp the facts about it firmly, you may proceed to higher regions undisturbed. As our time must be so short together, I prefer being elementary and fundamental to being complete, so I propose to you to hold fast to the ultra-simple point of view.

The reasons why I call it so fundamental can be easily told.

First, human and animal psychology thereby become less discontinuous. I know that to some of you this will hardly seem an attractive reason, but there are others whom it will affect.

Second, mental action is conditioned by brain action, and runs parallel therewith. But the brain, so far as we understand it, is given us for practical behavior. Every current that runs into it from skin or eye or ear runs out again into muscles, glands, or viscera, and helps to adapt the animal to the environment from which the current came. It therefore generalizes and simplifies our view to treat the brain life and the mental life as having one fundamental kind of purpose.

Third, those very functions of the mind that do not refer directly to this world's environment, the ethical utopias, aesthetic visions, insights into eternal truth, and fanciful logical combinations, could never be carried on at all by a human individual, unless the mind that produced them in him were also able to produce more practically useful products. The latter are thus the more essential, or at least the more primordial results.

Fourth, the inessential 'unpractical' activities are themselves far more connected with our behavior and our adaptation to the environment than at first sight might appear. No truth, however abstract, is ever perceived, that will not probably at some time in-

fluence our earthly action. You must remember that, when I talk of action here, I mean action in the widest sense. I mean speech, I mean writing, I mean yeses and noes, and tendencies 'from' things and tendencies 'toward' things, and emotional determinations; and I mean them in the future as well as in the immediate present. . . .

You should regard your professional task as if it consisted chiefly and essentially in *training the pupil to behavior;* taking behavior, not in the narrow sense of his manners, but in the very widest possible sense, as including every possible sort of fit reaction on the circumstances into which he may find himself brought by the vicissitudes of life.

Education and Behavior

. . . [Education] consists in the organizing of *resources* in the human being, of powers of conduct which shall fit him to his social and physical world. An 'uneducated' person is one who is nonplussed by all but the most habitual situations. On the contrary, one who is educated is able practically to extricate himself, by means of the examples with which his memory is stored and of the abstract conceptions which he has acquired, from circumstances in which he never was placed before. Education, in short, cannot be better described than by calling it the *organization of acquired habits of conduct and tendencies to behavior. . .*

. . . So it is with the impressions you will make . . . on your pupil. You should get into the habit of regarding them all as leading to the acquisition by him of capacities for behavior,—emotional, social, bodily, vocal, technical, or what not. And, this being the case, you ought to feel willing, in a general way, and without hair-splitting or further ado, to take up for the purposes of these lectures with the biological conception of the mind, as of something given us for practical use. That conception will certainly cover the greater part of your own educational work.

The Laws of Habit

It is very important that teachers should realize the importance of habit, and psychology helps us greatly at this point. We speak, it is true, of good habits and of bad habits; but when people use the word *habit*, in the majority of instances it is a bad habit which they have in mind. They talk of the smoking-habit and the swearing-habit and the drinking-habit, but not of the abstention-habit or the moderation-habit or the courage-habit. But the fact is that our virtues are habits as much as our vices. All our life, so far as it has definite form, is but a mass of habits,—practical, emotional, and intellectual,—systematically organized for our weal or woe, and bearing us irresistibly toward our destiny, whatever the latter may be. . . .

I believe that we are subject to the law of habit in consequence of the fact that we have bodies. The plasticity of the living matter of our nervous system, in short, is the reason why we do a thing with difficulty the first time, but soon do it more and more easily, and finally, with sufficient practice, do it semi-mechanically, or with hardly any consciousness at all. Our nervous systems have . . . *grown* to the way in which they have been exercised, just as a sheet of paper or a coat, once creased or folded, tends to fall forever afterward into the same identical folds.

Habit is thus a second nature. . . .

So far as we are thus mere bundles of habit, we are stereotyped creatures, imitators and copiers of our past selves. And since this, under any circumstances, is what we always tend to become, it follows first of all that the teacher's prime concern should be to ingrain into the pupil that assortment of habits that shall be most useful to him throughout life. Education is for behavior, and habits are the stuff of which behavior consists.

. . . The great thing in all education is to *make our nervous system our ally instead of our enemy.* It is to fund and capitalize our acquisitions, and live at ease upon the interest of the fund. *For this we must make automatic and habitual, as early as possible, as many useful actions as we can,* and as carefully guard against the growing into ways that are likely to be disadvantageous. The more of the details of our daily life we can hand over to the effortless custody of automatism, the more our higher powers of mind will be set free for their own proper work. There is no more miserable human being than one in whom nothing is habitual but indecision, and for whom the lighting of every cigar, the drinking of every cup, the time of rising and going to bed every day, and the beginning of every bit of work are subjects of express volitional deliberation. Full half the time of such a man goes to the deciding or regretting of matters which ought to be so ingrained in him as practically not to exist for his

consciousness at all. If there be such daily duties not yet ingrained in any one of my hearers, let him begin this very hour to set the matter right.

. . . Two great maxims emerge. . . . The first is that in the acquisition of a new habit, or the leaving off of an old one, we must take care to *launch ourselves with as strong and decided an initiative as possible.* Accumulate all the possible circumstances which shall reinforce the right motives; put yourself assiduously in conditions that encourage the new way; make engagements incompatible with the old; take a public pledge, if the case allows; in short, envelope your resolution with every aid you know. This will give your new beginning such a momentum that the temptation to break down will not occur as soon as it otherwise might; and every day during which a breakdown is postponed adds to the chances of its not occurring at all. . . .

The second maxim is, *Never suffer an exception to occur till the new habit is securely rooted in your life.* Each lapse is like the letting fall of a ball of string which one is carefully winding up: A single slip undoes more than a great many turns will wind again. Continuity of training is the great means of making the nervous system act infallibly right. . . .

We all intend when young to be all that may become a man, before the destroyer cuts us down. We wish and expect to enjoy poetry always, to grow more and more intelligent about pictures and music, to keep in touch with spiritual and religious ideas, and even not to let the greater philosophic thoughts of our time develop quite beyond our view. We mean all this in youth, I say; and yet in how many middle-aged men and women is such an honest and sanguine expectation fulfilled? Surely, in comparatively few; and the laws of habit show us why. Some interest in each of these things arises in everybody at the proper age; but, if not persistently fed with the appropriate matter, instead of growing into a powerful and necessary habit, it atrophies and dies, choked by the rival interests to which the daily food is given. . . . We forget that every good that is worth possessing must be paid for in strokes of daily effort. We postpone and postpone, until those smiling possibilities are dead.

I have been accused, when talking of the subject of habit, of making old habits appear so strong that the acquiring of new ones, and particularly anything like a sudden reform or conversion, would be made impossible by my doctrine. Of course, this would suffice to condemn the latter; for sudden conversions, however infrequent they may be, unquestionably do occur. But there is no incompatibility between the general laws I have laid down and the most startling sudden alterations in the way of character. New habits *can* be launched, I have expressly said, on condition of there being new stimuli and new excitements. Now life abounds in these, and sometimes they are such critical and revolutionary experiences that they change a man's whole scale of values and system of ideas. In such cases, the old order of his habits will be ruptured; and, if the new motives are lasting, new habits will be formed, and build up in him a new or regenerate 'nature.' . . .

The Association of Ideas

You remember that consciousness is an everflowing stream of objects, feelings, and impulsive tendencies. We saw already that its phases or pulses are like so many fields or waves, each field or wave having usually its central point of liveliest attention, in the shape of the most prominent object in our thought, while all around this lies a margin of other objects more dimly realized, together with the margin of emotional and active tendencies which the whole entails. Describing the mind thus in fluid terms, we cling as close as possible to nature. At first sight, it might seem as if, in the fluidity of these successive waves, everything is indeterminate. But inspection shows that each wave has a constitution which can be to some degree explained by the constitution of the waves just passed away. And this relation of the wave to its predecessors is expressed by the two fundamental 'laws of association,' so-called, of which the first is named the Law of Contiguity, the second that of Similarity.

The *Law of Contiguity* tells us that objects thought of in the coming wave are such as in some previous experience were *next to* the objects represented in the wave that is passing away. The vanishing objects were once formerly their neighbors in the mind. When you recite the alphabet or your prayers, or when the sight of an object reminds you of its name, or the name reminds you of the object, it is through the law of contiguity that the terms are suggested to the mind.

The *Law of Similarity* says that, when contiguity fails to describe what happens, the coming objects will prove to *resemble* the going objects, even though the two were never experienced together be-

fore. In our 'flights of fancy,' this is frequently the case. . . .

. . . [As] teachers, it is the *fact* of association that practically concerns you, let its grounds be spiritual or cerebral, or what they may, and let its laws be reducible, or non-reducible, to one. Your pupils, whatever else they are, are at any rate little pieces of associating machinery. Their education consists in the organizing within them of determinate tendencies to associate one thing with another,—impressions with consequences, these with reactions, those with results, and so on indefinitely. The more copious the associative systems, the more complete the individual's adaptations to the world.

The teacher can formulate his function to himself therefore in terms of 'association' as well as in terms of 'native and acquired reaction.' It is mainly that of *building up useful systems of association* in the pupil's mind. This description sounds wider than the one I began by giving. But, when one thinks that our trains of association, whatever they may be, normally issue in acquired reactions or behavior, one sees that in a general way the same mass of facts is covered by both formulas.

It is astonishing how many mental operations we can explain when we have once grasped the principles of association. . . .

To grasp these factors clearly gives one a solid and simple understanding of the psychological machinery. The 'nature,' the 'character,' of an individual means really nothing but the habitual form of his associations. To break up bad associations or wrong ones, to build others in, to guide the associative tendencies into the most fruitful channels, is the educator's principal task. But here, as with all other simple principles, the difficulty lies in the application. Psychology can state the laws: concrete tact and talent alone can work them to useful results. . . .

The Acquisition of Ideas

The images of our past experiences, of whatever nature they may be, visual or verbal, blurred and dim, vivid and distinct, abstract or concrete, need not be memory images, in the strict sense of the word. That is, they need not rise before the mind in a marginal fringe or context of concomitant circumstances, which mean for us their *date*. They may be mere conceptions, floating pictures of an object, or of its type or class. In this undated condition, we call them products of 'imagination' or 'conception.' *Imagination* is the term commonly used where the object represented is thought of as an individual thing. *Conception* is the term where we think of it as a type or class. For our present purpose the distinction is not important; and I will permit myself to use either the word *conception,* or the still vaguer word *idea,* to designate the inner objects of contemplation, whether these be individual things, like 'the sun' or 'Julius Caesar,' or classes of things, like 'animal kingdom,' or, finally, entirely abstract attributes, like 'rationality' or 'rectitude.'

The result of our education is to fill the mind little by little, as experiences accrete, with a stock of such ideas. . . . The sciences of grammar and of logic are little more than attempts methodically to classify all such acquired ideas and to trace certain laws of relationship among them. The forms of relation between them, becoming themselves in turn noticed by the mind, are treated as conceptions of a higher and more abstract order, as when we speak of a 'syllogistic relation' between propositions, or of four quantities making a 'proportion,' or of the 'inconsistency' of two conceptions, or the 'implication' of one in the other.

So you see that the process of education, taken in a large way, may be described as nothing but the process of acquiring ideas or conceptions, the best educated mind being the mind which has the largest stock of them, ready to meet the largest possible variety of the emergencies of life. The lack of education means only the failure to have acquired them, and the consequent liability to be 'floored' and 'rattled' in the vicissitudes of experience.

Source: William James, *Talks to Teachers on Psychology: And to Students on Some of Life's Ideals.* New York: Henry Holt and Co., 1916, pp. 15–19, 22–31, 64–69, 72–73, 76–84, 144–146.

DEWEY

DEMOCRACY AND EDUCATION

Perhaps the most important work that Dewey wrote on education was Democracy and Education, *published in 1916. His understanding of education was detailed and complex, and he struggled to express his ideas in a language that ordinary people could understand; however, he was not always successful because complex ideas are often difficult to express simply. The following selection is a lucid but general statement of Dewey's views. In it, he reflects on the social nature of education and how it is necessary for individuals to enter into social relations to become educated. Communication is central to the education of individuals in social contexts because communication enlarges experience and makes it meaningful. Education occurs in formal and informal settings, and philosophy's role is to help achieve a proper balance between the two.*

1. Renewal of Life by Transmission

The most notable distinction between living and inanimate beings is that the former maintain themselves by renewal. A stone when struck resists. If its resistance is greater than the force of the blow struck, it remains outwardly unchanged. Otherwise, it is shattered into smaller bits. Never does the stone attempt to react in such a way that it may maintain itself against the blow, much less so as to render the blow a contributing factor to its own continued action. While the living thing may easily be crushed by superior force, it none the less tries to turn the energies which act upon it into means of its own further existence. If it cannot do so, it does not just split into smaller pieces (at least in the higher forms of life), but loses its identity as a living thing.

As long as it endures, it struggles to use surrounding energies in its own behalf. It uses light, air, moisture, and the material of soil. To say that it uses them is to say that it turns them into means of its own conservation. As long as it is growing, the energy it expends in thus turning the environment to account is more than compensated for by the return it gets: It grows. Understanding the word *control* in this sense, it may be said that a living being is one that subjugates and controls for its own continued activity the energies that would otherwise use it up. Life is a self-renewing process through action upon the environment.

In all the higher forms this process cannot be kept up indefinitely. After a while they succumb; they die. The creature is not equal to the task of indefinite self-renewal. But continuity of the life process is not dependent upon the prolongation of the existence of any one individual. Reproduction of other forms of life goes on in continuous sequence. And though, as the geological record shows, not merely individuals but also species die out, the life process continues in increasingly complex forms. As some species die out, forms better adapted to utilize the obstacles against which they struggled in vain come into being. Continuity of life means continual readaptation of the environment to the needs of living organisms.

We have been speaking of life in its lowest terms—as a physical thing. But we use the word *life* to denote the whole range of experience, individual and racial. When we see a book called the *Life of Lincoln* we do not expect to find within its covers a treatise on physiology. We look for an account of social antecedents; a description of early surroundings, of the conditions and occupation of the family; of the chief episodes in the development of character; of signal struggles and achievements; of the individual's hopes, tastes, joys and sufferings. In precisely similar fashion we speak of the life of a savage tribe, of the Athenian people, of the American nation. "Life" covers customs, institutions, beliefs, victories and defeats, recreations and occupations.

We employ the word *experience* in the same pregnant sense. And to it, as well as to life in the bare physiological sense, the principle of continuity through renewal applies. With the renewal of physical existence goes, in the case of human beings, the re-creation of beliefs, ideals, hopes, happiness, misery, and practices. The continuity of any experience, through renewing of the social group, is a literal fact. "Education, in its broadest sense, is the means of this social continuity of life." Every one of the constituent elements of a social group, in a modern city as in a savage tribe, is born immature, helpless, without language, beliefs, ideas, or social standards. Each individual, each unit who is the carrier of the life-experience of his group, in time passes away. Yet the life of the group goes on.

The primary ineluctable facts of the birth and death of each one of the constituent members in a social group determine the necessity of education. On one hand, there is the contrast between the immaturity of the newborn members of the group—its future sole representatives—and the maturity of the adult members who possess the knowledge and customs of the group. On the other hand, there is the necessity that these immature members be not merely physically preserved in adequate numbers, but that they be initiated into the interests, purposes, information, skill, and practices of the mature members: Otherwise the group will cease its characteristic life. Even in a savage tribe, the achievements of adults are far beyond what the immature members would be capable of if left to themselves. With the growth of civilization, the gap between the original capacities of the immature and the standards and customs of the elders increases. Mere physical growing up, mere mastery of the bare necessities of subsistence will not suffice to reproduce the life of the group. Deliberate effort and the taking of thoughtful pains are required. Beings who are born not only unaware of, but quite indifferent to, the aims and habits of the social group have to be rendered cognizant of them and actively interested. Education, and education alone, spans the gap.

Society exists through a process of transmission quite as much as biological life. This transmission occurs by means of communication of habits of doing, thinking, and feeling from the older to the younger. Without this communication of ideals, hopes, expectations, standards, opinions, from those members of society who are passing out of the group life to those who are coming into it, social life could not survive. If the members who compose a society lived on continuously, they might educate the new-born members, but it would be a task directed by personal interest rather than social need. Now it is a work of necessity.

If a plague carried off the members of a society all at once, it is obvious that the group would be permanently done for. Yet the death of each of its constituent members is as certain as if an epidemic took them all at once. But the graded difference in age, the fact that some are born as some die, makes possible through transmission of ideas and practices the constant reweaving of the social fabric. Yet this renewal is not automatic. Unless pains are taken to see that genuine and thorough transmission takes place, the most civilized group will relapse into barbarism and then into savagery. In fact, the human young are so immature that if they were left to themselves without the guidance and succor of others, they could not even acquire the rudimentary abilities necessary for physical existence. The young of human beings compare so poorly in original efficiency with the young of many of the lower animals, that even the powers needed for physical sustenance have to be acquired under tuition. How much more, then, is this the case with respect to all the technological, artistic, scientific, and moral achievements of humanity!

2. Education and Communication

So obvious, indeed, is the necessity of teaching and learning for the continued existence of a society that we may seem to be dwelling unduly on a truism. But justification is found in the fact that such emphasis is a means of getting us away from an unduly scholastic and formal notion of education. Schools are, indeed, one important method of the transmission which forms the dispositions of the immature; but it is only one means, and, compared with other agencies, a relatively superficial means. Only as we have grasped the necessity of more fundamental and persistent modes of tuition can we make sure of placing the scholastic methods in their true context.

Society not only continues to exist by transmission, *by* communication, but it may fairly be said to exist *in* transmission, *in* communication. There is more than a verbal tie between the words *common, community,* and *communication.* Men live in a community in virtue of the things which they have in common; and communication is the way in which they come to possess things in common. What they must have in

common in order to form a community or society are aims, beliefs, aspirations, knowledge—a common understanding—like-mindedness as the sociologists say. Such things cannot be passed physically from one to another, like bricks; they cannot be shared as persons would share a pie by dividing it into physical pieces. The communication which insures participation in a common understanding is one which secures similar emotional and intellectual dispositions—like ways of responding to expectations and requirements.

Persons do not become a society by living in physical proximity, any more than a man ceases to be socially influenced by being so many feet or miles removed from others. A book or a letter may institute a more intimate association between human beings separated thousands of miles from each other than exists between dwellers under the same roof. Individuals do not even compose a social group because they all work for a common end. The parts of a machine work with a maximum of cöoperativeness for a common result, but they do not form a community. If, however, they were all cognizant of the common end and all interested in it so that they regulated their specific activity in view of it, then they would form a community. But this would involve communication. Each would have to know what the other was about and would have to have some way of keeping the other informed as to his own purpose and progress. Consensus demands communication.

We are thus compelled to recognize that within even the most social group there are many relations which are not as yet social. A large number of human relationships in any social group are still upon the machine-like plane. Individuals use one another so as to get desired results, without reference to the emotional and intellectual disposition and consent of those used. Such uses express physical superiority, or superiority of position, skill, technical ability, and command of tools, mechanical or fiscal. So far as the relations of parent and child, teacher and pupil, employer and employee, governor and governed, remain upon this level, they form no true social group, no matter how closely their respective activities touch one another. Giving and taking of orders modifies action and results, but does not of itself effect a sharing of purposes, a communication of interests.

Not only is social life identical with communication, but all communication (and hence all genuine social life) is educative. To be a recipient of a communication is to have an enlarged and changed experience. One shares in what another has thought and felt and in so far, meagerly or amply, has his own attitude modified. Nor is the one who communicates left unaffected. Try the experiment of communicating, with fullness and accuracy, some experience to another, especially if it be somewhat complicated, and you will find your own attitude toward your experience changing; otherwise you resort to expletives and ejaculations. The experience has to be formulated in order to be communicated. To formulate requires getting outside of it, seeing it as another would see it, considering what points of contact it has with the life of another so that it may be got into such form that he can appreciate its meaning. Except in dealing with commonplaces and catch phrases one has to assimilate, imaginatively, something of another's experience in order to tell him intelligently of one's own experience. All communication is like art. It may fairly be said, therefore, that any social arrangement that remains vitally social, or vitally shared, is educative to those who participate in it. Only when it becomes cast in a mold and runs in a routine way does it lose its educative power.

In final account, then, not only does social life demand teaching and learning for its own permanence, but the very process of living together educates. It enlarges and enlightens experience; it stimulates and enriches imagination; it creates responsibility for accuracy and vividness of statement and thought. A man really living alone (alone mentally as well as physically) would have little or no occasion to reflect upon his past experience to extract its net meaning. The inequality of achievement between the mature and the immature not only necessitates teaching the young, but the necessity of this teaching gives an immense stimulus to reducing experience to that order and form which will render it most easily communicable and hence most usable.

3. The Place of Formal Education

There is, accordingly, a marked difference between the education which every one gets from living with others, as long as he really lives instead of just continuing to subsist, and the deliberate educating of the young. In the former case the education is incidental; it is natural and important, but it is not the express reason of the association. While it may be said, without exaggeration, that the measure of the worth of any social institution, economic, domestic, political, legal, religious, is its effect in enlarging and improving experience; yet this effect is not a part of its original motive, which is limited and more immediately practical. Religious associations began, for example, in the desire to secure the favor of overruling powers and to ward off evil influences; family life in the desire to gratify appetites and secure family perpetuity; systematic labor, for the most part, because of enslavement to others, etc. Only gradually was the by-product of the institution, its effect upon the quality and extent of conscious life, noted, and only more gradually still was this effect considered as a directive factor in the conduct of the institution. Even today, in our industrial life, apart from certain values of industriousness and thrift, the intellectual and emotional reaction of the forms of human association under which the world's work is carried on receives little attention as compared with physical output.

But in dealing with the young, the fact of association itself as an immediate human fact, gains in importance. While it is easy to ignore in our contact with them the effect of our acts upon their disposition, or to subordinate that educative effect to some external and tangible result, it is not so easy as in dealing with adults. The need of training is too evident; the pressure to accomplish a change in their attitude and habits is too urgent to leave these consequences wholly out of account. Since our chief business with them is to enable them to share in a common life we cannot help considering whether or not we are forming the powers which will secure this ability. If humanity has made some headway in realizing that the ultimate value of every institution is its distinctively human effect—its effect upon conscious experience— we may well believe that this lesson has been learned largely through dealings with the young.

We are thus led to distinguish, within the broad educational process which we have been so far considering, a more formal kind of education— that of direct tuition or schooling. In undeveloped social groups, we find very little formal teaching and training. Savage groups mainly rely for instilling needed dispositions into the young upon the same sort of association which keeps adults loyal to their group. They have no special devices, material, or institutions for teaching save in connection with initiation ceremonies by which the youth are inducted into full social membership. For the most part, they depend upon children learning the customs of the adults, acquiring their emotional set and stock of ideas, by sharing in what the elders are doing. In part, this sharing is direct, taking part in the occupations of adults and thus serving an apprenticeship; in part, it is indirect, through the dramatic plays in which children reproduce the actions of grown-ups and thus learn to know what they are like. To savages it would seem preposterous to seek out a place where nothing but learning was going on in order that one might learn.

But as civilization advances, the gap between the capacities of the young and the concerns of adults widens. Learning by direct sharing in the pursuits of grown-ups becomes increasingly difficult except in the case of the less advanced occupations. Much of what adults do is so remote in space and in meaning that playful imitation is less and less adequate to reproduce its spirit. Ability to share effectively in adult activities thus depends upon a prior training given with this end in view. Intentional agencies—schools— and explicit material—studies—are devised. The task of teaching certain things is delegated to a special group of persons.

Without such formal education, it is not possible to transmit all the resources and achievements of a complex society. It also opens a way to a kind of experience which would not be accessible to the young, if they were left to pick up their training in informal association with others, since books and the symbols of knowledge are mastered.

But there are conspicuous dangers attendant upon the transition from indirect to formal education. Sharing in actual pursuit, whether directly or vicariously in play, is at least personal and vital. These qualities compensate, in some measure, for the narrowness of available opportunities. Formal instruction, on the contrary, easily becomes remote and dead— abstract and bookish, to use the ordinary words of depreciation. What accumulated knowledge exists in low grade societies is at least put into practice; it is transmuted into character; it exists with the depth of meaning that attaches to its coming within urgent daily interests.

But in an advanced culture much which has to be learned is stored in symbols. It is far from translation into familiar acts and objects. Such material is relatively technical and superficial. Taking the ordinary standard of reality as a measure, it is artificial. For this measure is connection with practical concerns. Such material exists in a world by itself, unassimilated to ordinary customs of thought and expression. There is the standing danger that the material of formal instruction will be merely the subject matter of schools, isolated from the subject matter of life-experience. The permanent social interests are likely to be lost from view. Those which have not been carried over into the structure of social life, but which remain largely matters of technical information expressed in symbols, are made conspicuous in schools. Thus we reach the ordinary notion of education: the notion which ignores its social necessity and its identity with all human association that affects conscious life, and which identifies it with imparting information about remote matters and the conveying of learning through verbal signs: the acquisition of literacy.

Hence one of the weightiest problems with which the philosophy of education has to cope is the method of keeping a proper balance between the informal and the formal, the incidental and the intentional, modes of education. When the acquiring of information and of technical intellectual skill do not influence the formation of a social disposition, ordinary vital experience fails to gain in meaning, while schooling, in so far, creates only "sharps" in learning—that is, egoistic specialists. To avoid a split between what men consciously know because they are aware of having learned it by a specific job of learning, and what they unconsciously know because they have absorbed it in the formation of their characters by intercourse with others, becomes an increasingly delicate task with every development of special schooling.

Source: John Dewey, *"Democracy and Education"*, pp. 1–9, in *The Collected Works of John Dewey, Middle Works, 1899–1924*, Vol. 9: 1916. Edited by Jo Ann Boydston. Carbondale: Southern Illinois University Press, 1980, pp. 4–13. Copyright 1980 by the Center for Dewey Studies, reprinted by permission of the publisher.

SELECTED READINGS

Dewey, John. *Experience and Education*. New York: Macmillan, 1938. Dewey's views on some excesses of the progressive movement and misinterpretations of his ideas in his larger work, *Democracy and Education*. He attacks either/or thinking as debilitating to educational theory and reiterates the view that a philosophy of experience must be central.

Garrison, James W., ed. *The New Scholarship on Dewey*. Boston: Kluwer Academic, 1995. A volume of 16 essays by authors from a cross section of disciplines and points of view. The essays explore ways the new scholarship on Dewey and neopragmatism have or could have an impact on philosophy of education and educational theory and practice.

Menand, Louis. *The Metaphysical Club*. New York: Farrar, Straus, and Giroux, 2001. An interesting history of pragmatism's development and impact on American life. Menand examines the major contributions of the founders of pragmatism, and he sees the reemergence of pragmatism as a consequence of the ending of the Cold War. He believes that in a time of competing belief systems, people need the tolerance of the pragmatists, but they also must build philosophy anew, just as they had to take new directions in their own day.

Rorty, Richard. *Philosophy and Social Hope*. New York: Penguin Books, 1999. A leading neopragmatist reaffirms pragmatism's hopeful approach toward solving human problems, including educational problems. Rorty maintains that today's philosophical task is not making people's ideas correspond to metaphysical views but generating the kind of trust and cooperation needed to deal with life's practical problems and creating a more democratic society.

www.pragmatism.org/ (accessed April 5, 2002). Site for the "Pragmatism Cybrary," a helpful source with features that include the history of pragmatism, the "Library of Living Pragmatists," the "Web Companion to Pragmatism," and numerous other major philosophical links to "nodes on the Web." An excellent source for material on pragmatism and its leading proponents, past and present.

www.cuip.uchicago.edu/jds/links.htm (accessed April 5, 2002). Homepage of the John Dewey Society. This site contains numerous Internet links concerning the works of Dewey and other philosophers, and on pragmatism, progressivism, and related topics.

Companion
Website

ONLINE RESEARCH

Utilizing some of the Web sites included in this book, as well as Topics 2, 3, and 4, of the Prentice Hall Foundations Web site found at *www.prenhall.com/ozmon*, answer the following question with a short essay: What was the progressive movement and how did it change American education? You can write and submit your essay response to your instructor by using the "Electronic Bluebook" section found in any of the topics of the Prentice Hall Foundations Web site.

Reconstructionism and Education

The philosophy of reconstructionism contains two major premises: (1) Society is in need of constant reconstruction or change, and (2) such social change involves a reconstruction of education and the use of education in reconstructing society. It is not unusual for people involved with change, particularly the kinds of immediate and necessary changes that every age seems to require, to turn to education as the most effective and efficient instrument for making such changes in an intelligent, democratic, and humane way. Reconstructionists advocate an attitude toward change that encourages individuals to try to make life better than it was or is. At the present time, particularly, reconstructionism could strike a responsive chord because people are faced with a bewildering number of problems regarding race, poverty, war, ecological destruction, and technological expansion—problems that seem to call for an immediate reconstruction of all existing religious and philosophical value systems.

Ideas and values that once seemed workable for religion, family life, and education no longer seem as viable as they once were. Individuals are bewildered not only by the changes that have taken place already but also by the prospect of future changes that must be made if humans are to cope adequately with these problems. Although persons of intelligence and vision who thought about and promoted social change have always existed, only in recent times has a systematic outlook developed called *reconstructionist philosophy.*

HISTORICAL BACKGROUND OF RECONSTRUCTIONISM

Reconstructionist ideas in one form or another have existed throughout history. Plato, in preparing his design for a future state *(The Republic)*, was a "reconstructionist" philosopher. He outlined a plan for a just state in which education would become the building material for a new and better society. Plato believed that his state would be eminently desirable. He proposed radical departures from the customs of his Greek contemporaries, such as sexual equality, communal child rearing, and rule by a philosopher-king. In the *Laws*, he envisioned a time when interest charges would be forbidden, profits would be limited, and human beings would live as friends.

The Stoic philosophers, particularly in their concern for a world state, promoted a reconstructionist ideal. Marcus Aurelius, a Roman emperor and philosopher, maintained that he was a citizen of the world, not of Rome. This concept is one that reconstructionists articulate today in their attempts to minimize nationalistic fervor and chauvinism.

Many of the Christian philosophers, such as Augustine, preached reconstructionist reforms to bring about an ideal Christian state. The kinds of reforms that Augustine asked for in *The City of God* were intended for the human soul rather than material being, but they had ramifications that carried over to the material world, as well. Theodore Brameld, a major twentieth-century reconstructionist, stated that Augustine raised several difficult questions that later utopian philosophers endeavored to answer, such as whether history encourages people to believe that their ideal goals can be reached. Thomas More, Thomas Campanella, Johann Valentin Andreae, Samuel Gott, and other Christian utopian writers also proposed things we might do to bring the state into better accord with Christian thinking.

The writings of eighteenth- and nineteenth-century utopian socialists, such as Comte de Saint-Simon, Charles Fourier, and François Noel Babeuf, advocated reconstructionist ideals through the development of various forms of socialism. Robert Owen and Edward Bellamy were influenced by the industrial revolution and saw the use of technology not for the production of wealth *per se,* but for improving the lot of humanity throughout the world. It was Karl Marx, decrying the harm done to workers by the dehumanization of the industrial system, who pictured a reconstructed world based on international communism.

Karl Marx received a doctorate in philosophy yet wrote extensively about economics and history. He deplored armchair philosophical thinking and, like reconstructionists, believed that education should not be an ivory-tower affair but a method of changing the world. In *Theses on Feuerbach*, Marx wrote: "Philosophers have only interpreted the world differently; the point, however, is to change it."

Marx had studied Hegel intensively, but where Hegel saw the dialectical movement of the universe in idealist terms, Marx saw it in terms of the clash of economic forces. These forces manifest themselves today by pitting the worker against the capitalist system. Education has been used as a way of maintaining the status quo because it has supported the interests of the ruling class, or *bourgeoisie*. Marx believed, however, that education also could be used to overthrow those interests and to place the proletariat in control. At such a time, Marx believed, the power of the state will begin to wither and eventually will be replaced by true rule of the people.

According to Marx, education has been an insidious device used to indoctrinate people into accepting and supporting the attitudes and outlooks of the moneyed interests. Although money is seemingly neutral, laborers are robbed of their freedom by exchanging work and production for money. Thus, workers are exploited by the system as their productive abilities are appropriated in exchange for the symbolic value of money.

Education, according to Marx, is a means to entrench this system by promoting the interests of the ruling class using the formal and the informal or "hidden" curriculum that encourages subservience and docility. Schools are controlled by elite governing authorities to accomplish this, and schools in turn control students through rules and regulations, discipline procedures, and the curriculum. Textbooks are censored when they challenge conventional views on economics and government, as well as sex, religion, and other touchy issues. Teachers, often without realizing it, promote conventional biases, attitudes, and practices in many subtle ways. Students also control each other through peer-group pressures that can be powerful and unconscious influences. As education can be used to enslave people, however, it also can be used, if properly understood, to free them. To do this would mean overthrowing the current economic system and instituting a new kind of education oriented toward raising the social consciousness of economic controls that would enable each person to be an end and not a means.

Although World Wars I and II turned people's thoughts away from optimistic pictures of future worlds and spawned such dystopias as Aldous Huxley's *Brave New World* and George Orwell's *1984*, reformers and optimists still existed, such as Bertrand Russell, whose *Principles of Social Reconstruction* listed steps that might be taken to avoid the holocaust of war. Today, various groups propose ways to change the world and to eliminate racism, poverty, and war. Some advocate the use of conditioning or "behavioral engineering" (as in B. F. Skinner's *Walden Two*) to make important and significant changes in everyday life through advancing technical skills. In *Beyond Freedom and Dignity*, Skinner maintains that people cannot afford freedom in the traditional sense and that they must resolutely engineer a new social order based on the technology of behavior.

When examining proposals from Plato to Skinner, one finds that many utopians recommend education as a primary instrument for social change. Plato, for example, thought of education as the *sine qua non* of the good society; Marx saw it as a way to help the proletariat develop a sense of social consciousness; Christian writers advocated the use of education as a means of inculcating religious faith and ideals; and modern technocrats see it as a way to promote technical change and to provide individuals with the necessary skills for living in an advanced technological society. In *Walden Two*, Skinner depicted a community of highly trained technicians, engineers, artists, and agronomists who are educated or conditioned to a high level of proficiency. This is certainly a far cry from the romantic heritage of Henry David Thoreau's *Walden* and Jean Jacques Rousseau's *Émile*, but even Rousseau saw his finished product (as did John Locke in *Some Thoughts Concerning Education*) as a person who would later guide society along newer and better paths. Locke's "gentleman" was to lead by virtue of his breeding and education, whereas Rousseau's Noble Savage would lead because of his purity and naturalness. They all looked for social change through education.

In the United States, some people have viewed education as a tool for social reform, such as Horace Mann and John Dewey. Dewey saw education as an instrument for changing individuals and society, and particularly during the 1920s and 1930s his philosophy became identified with radical social reform. Dewey's pragmatism was linked with a rejection of absolutes and an acceptance of relativism, and it rankled many who thought (and some who still do) that education was in the grip of forces destined to lead American society down the liberal path to eventual destruction. Although Dewey's philosophy is identified more readily today with moderate progressivism, at its peak it often was identified with radicalism.

Modern reconstructionism is basically pragmatic and owes a tremendous debt to Dewey. Reconstructionists promote such things as the scientific method, problem solving, naturalism, and humanism; however, reconstructionists diverge from pragmatists in how they believe the pragmatic method should be used. Although pragmatism advocates continuous change and a forward-looking approach to the problems of people and society, it has become (in the hands of many who call themselves progressivists) a tool for helping people adjust to society rather than change it. One can explain this attitude partly by reference to the immigrants coming to America in the early 1900s who needed to be adjusted to American language and customs to bring them more into the mainstream of American society. The need for education to adjust people to social and cultural values has existed and always will exist, but reconstructionists do not believe that this is the primary role education should undertake. Education, from the reconstructionist's point of view, is to serve as a tool for immediate and continuous change.

Although much has been written about Dewey's radicalism in politics, philosophy, education, and other areas, he also has been interpreted to view education as a way of making evolutionary, as opposed to revolutionary, progress toward social change. Dewey envisioned these changes occurring within an evolving democratic society rather than through the major revolutionary changes that many reconstructionists believe are necessary. Whereas some pragmatists support the idea of dealing with problems within the existing framework of society, many reconstructionists hold that although this might be a reasonable approach for some problems, it is often necessary to get outside the general bounds of the contemporary value system to look at problems from a fresh perspective without traditional restraints. Utopian writers have pointed out, and perhaps understood better than anyone else, that many of the great problems of society cannot be solved without changes in the structure of society itself. Many utopians and reconstructionists (and in all fairness, Dewey himself) believe that some things people consider evil are really part of the institutions to which they give allegiance, and we cannot hope to eradicate such evils without fundamental changes in these institutions.

Many people are perplexed when they hear that Socrates, the "gadfly of Athens," chose to face death rather than oppose the laws of Athens as they then existed. Some reconstructionists charge that pragmatists appear to have accepted the Socratic compromise: Pragmatists have championed change, but not at the price of alienating those who need to be persuaded gradually into accepting orderly and systematic movement through established democratic institutions. Dewey, for example, seemed to be somewhat reluctant to advance education much faster than society itself could be advanced. Reconstructionists maintain that modern individuals might not have the luxury of such delay. Thus, although reconstructionism has its roots in past philosophical systems and philosophers, it attempts to strike out in more radical directions than its predecessors.

PHILOSOPHY OF RECONSTRUCTIONISM

Reconstructionism is not a *philosophy* in the traditional meaning of the term; that is, it does not seek to make detailed epistemological or logical studies. As indicated, reconstructionism is more concerned with the broad social and cultural fabric in which humans exist. One might say that reconstructionism is almost a purely social philosophy. Its leading exponents are not so much professional philosophers as they are educational and social activists. They concentrate on social and cultural conditions and how these can be made more palatable for full human participation.

George S. Counts and Theodore Brameld exemplified this outlook more than anyone else. Brameld came closer to the more traditional role of the philosopher, writing in considerable depth about the philosophical nature of reconstructionism. Counts was the educational activist-scholar whose interests were wide ranging. Although not lacking in philosophical knowledge, his writings and professional activities were more broadly concerned with social activism.

George S. Counts (1889–1974)

George Counts came from a rural background and spent most of his adult life in some of America's major universities and intellectual circles. He engaged in extensive travel and study abroad, especially in Russia during the time of the Soviet Union. He was an acquaintance of John Dewey and was influenced greatly by that philosopher's social beliefs.

Counts's major work on reconstructionism is a small but widely read book, *Dare the Schools Build a New Social Order?* (1932). First delivered as three public lectures before a national group of educators, the central theme of *Dare the Schools* struck American educators with force. Counts had returned from the Soviet Union in 1930, where he had made a detailed study of that country's struggles. Seeing the United States bogged down in the social confusion of the Depression (a condition that Counts thought was inexcusable and needless), he sought to awaken educators to their strategic position in social and cultural reconstruction.

Counts's central message was that although education had been used historically as a means of introducing people to their cultural traditions, social and cultural conditions were so altered by modern science, technology, and industrialization that education now must be used as a positive force for establishing new cultural patterns and for eliminating social evils. He implied that educators must envision the prospects for radical social change and implement those prospects. Counts argued that educators should give up their comfortable role of being supporters of the status quo and take on the more difficult tasks of social reformers. Further, he expressed some dissatisfaction with the course of progressive education, charging that it had identified itself with the "liberal-minded upper middle class." He stated:

> If Progressive Education is to be genuinely progressive, it must emancipate itself
> from the influence of this class, face squarely and courageously every social issue,
> come to grips with life in all of its stark reality, establish an organic relationship
> with the community, develop a realistic and comprehensive theory of welfare,

fashion a compelling and challenging vision of human destiny, and become less frightened than it is today at bogies of imposition and indoctrination.

Counts's thesis that the school should take responsibility for social renewal met with heated opposition. He was criticized and condemned as a Soviet (or Communist) sympathizer. Critics pointed out that the school, a relatively weak institution, could not accomplish so great a task. However, Counts's view was not tied solely to the school, and his radicalism went much deeper. Indeed, he pointed out that the school should not promote any one reform, but rather it should "give our children a vision of the possibilities which lie ahead and endeavor to enlist their loyalties and enthusiasms in the realization of the vision." To him, all social institutions and practices should be scrutinized critically, and the school serves as a reasonable means whereby a rational scrutiny can be made. The actual reform, however, must be culture-wide and thorough.

Counts was the author of numerous books (several of them on Soviet culture and education) and hundreds of articles. He influenced many students, educators, and social reformers. His philosophical influence, though confined primarily to philosophy of education and within that to the philosophy of reconstructionism, was nevertheless considerable.

Theodore Brameld (1904–1987)

The person who was most influential in building reconstructionism into a more fully developed philosophy of education was Theodore Brameld. The author of many books, including *Toward a Reconstructed Philosophy of Education*, *Education as Power*, and *Patterns of Educational Philosophy,* Brameld taught philosophy and philosophy of education, lived and taught in Puerto Rico, and held posts in some of America's major universities.

Brameld viewed reconstructionism as a crisis philosophy, not only in terms of education but in terms of culture, as well. He saw humanity at the crossroads: One road leads to destruction, and the other to salvation only if people make the effort. Above all, he saw reconstructionism as a philosophy of values, ends, and purposes. Although he had definite ideas about which road we *should* take, he pointed out that he was by no means sure which road we *would* take.

According to Brameld, people are confronted with mass confusion and contradictions in modern culture. At their disposal is an immense capacity for good on the one hand, and a terrifying capacity for destruction on the other. Humans, he believed, must establish clear goals for survival. In broad terms, this calls for world unity. People must forego narrow nationalistic bias and embrace the community in a worldwide sense. This will involve world government and world civilization "in which peoples of all races, all nations, all colors, and all creeds join together in the common purpose of a peaceful world, united under the banner of international order." One major activity for philosophy would be an inquiry into the meanings of different conceptions of this central purpose of world unity. People need a democratic value orientation, an orientation in which "man believes in himself, in his capacity to direct himself and govern himself in relation to his fellows." It would involve, in terms of world government, majority policy making and provision for minority criticism. A basic means by which these goals can be achieved is education.

In *The Open Society and Its Enemies*, Karl Popper wrote about a piecemeal engineering approach versus the utopian approach to the problems of society. Popper was clearly in favor of the former, which fosters the view of an open society where many possibilities are explored. He opposed the utopian approach because he believed that long-range utopian goals could become fixed and unyielding. Brameld, however, saw value in both approaches—that is, utopian ends and piecemeal means. He recognized the need for piecemeal engineering on a daily basis but felt that this should be directed toward some goal even though goals can be changed from time to time. It is true, as Popper showed, that goals can become inflexible, but for Brameld, this did not have to be true and he was as opposed to absolutes in goal-setting as he was to absolutes in anything else. He was a dreamer as well as a worker, his proposals were more visceral than provable in any complete sense, and he had certain presuppositions about the continued perfectibility of individuals and society. Brameld was active in advancing proposals for consideration and implementation, and he saw the utopian concept as a technique for establishing useful goals and for orienting people toward an acceptance of change itself.

Reconstructionists tend to look at problems holistically. They understand that problems overlap and that in solving one problem, people might only create new ones; however, they maintain that if people can be encouraged to see problems in a broader perspective, the chances of eliminating the problems are greatly enhanced. Reconstructionists charge that the piecemeal engineers, for all their good intentions, often are only tinkering with problems rather than solving them, and perhaps unwittingly preparing the ground for other problems to come.

The argument often has been advanced that no empirical way exists to determine what the good society should be and that the reconstructionist operates on premises that are more a matter of wish fulfillment than anything else. Critics say that no one, including Brameld, can say definitively what the good society should be. Although Brameld was aware and appreciative of the empirical approach, he maintained that the results of scientific achievement should be used as broadly as possible for the benefit of humankind. He was critical, however, of the fact that science—no less than politics, education, and economics—often is dealt with too narrowly.

Scientific technology is involved in making societies more efficient but also more complex than ever before. It lends itself to misuse and destructive ends, as well. In this country, deaths through automobile and industrial accidents are another part of the price we pay for living in a highly mechanized society. Scientific technology also is used in making cigarettes and alcohol and in developing harmful chemicals used on food and crops. Technology often is used in industry in ways that belittle and dehumanize workers. Brameld certainly was not opposed to the advancement of science and technology, but he thought that their advancement should depend on humane use. He was aware that the determination of what is humane is difficult, but he maintained that through education, people can be encouraged to see human events in a much broader fashion.

Reconstructionists, such as Brameld, are future oriented and optimistic. This is not to state that it is certain that the future can be made better than the present or that underlying forces of class struggle or spirit, such as in the Marxian or Hegelian sense, are propelling us toward a higher point; rather, reconstructionists hold the belief that the future *can* be better *if* people adopt an attitude to work to make it better.

In addition to schools, individuals and organizations that push for ideas and reforms in accord with reconstructionist philosophy have always existed. Brameld maintained that although activist reformers, such as Saul Alinsky, hardly can be regarded as educators in the professional sense, they contribute far more richly to the education of grassroots Americans than any number of superintendents of schools and professors of education. For example, in Buffalo, New York, Alinsky taught poor people to unite against unemployment in favor of equal opportunity for every employable adult.

Many others also have served as change agents for society. Ralph Nader, who was a candidate for president of the United States in 1996 and in 2000, has long fought for consumer protection and has maintained that mass injustice can end only if enough private citizens become *public* citizens. Common Cause also has shown how people can work together to eliminate social injustices and to improve the political process. Buckminster Fuller was another person widely applauded for developing plans for future awareness and a humane control of technology. An engineer and inventor, Fuller pioneered the use of geodesic domes and wrote *Synergetics*, which is about the cooperation of nature and design. Lewis Mumford was another who dedicated a great deal of time to analyzing contemporary urban civilization and suggesting alternatives.

One of the earliest Americans to promote the reconstructionist ideal of challenging societal norms was Henry David Thoreau (1817–1862), who lived a solitary life for 2 years in the woods by Walden Pond near Concord village in Massachusetts. In *Walden,* he discussed the need for a reflective life and talked about "higher laws" that transcended obedience to social dictates. He championed opposition to taxes that were used to support slavery and war making, and he was willing to go to jail for his beliefs. He set many of these ideas forth in his essay "Civil Disobedience," which had a great influence on Gandhi in his campaign against British rule in India. Another American critic, one who attacked the evils of society through his writing, was Upton Sinclair (1878–1968). Sinclair wrote about abuses in the meatpacking industry in *The Jungle*; this led to passage of the first federal pure food laws. He also attacked religion in *The Profits of Religion*, and education in *The Goose Step* (1923).

A number of organizations agree with many reconstructionist ideas. For example, Greenpeace International engages in educational and activist enterprises, such as protecting whales and opposition to drilling for oil in fragile wilderness areas. The World Law Fund has developed models for world law, enlisting a variety of students in schools and colleges for their projects. The World Future Society consistently examines futuristic trends and develops models in government, family, science, and education as guides to human behavior. Basically, such organizations are concerned with alternative futures and engage in activities to meet those ends.

Reconstructionist philosophy on the whole is strongly inclined toward utopian or futuristic thinking. Reconstructionists have a penchant for utopian thinking, which manifests itself in their desire for an ideal world free of hunger, strife, and inhumanity. They believe that planning and thinking about the future is a good way of providing alternative societies for people to consider, and they believe that this kind of thinking should be promoted in schools, where teachers can encourage students to become future-oriented persons.

Alvin Toffler, who coined the term *future shock*, points out that people are suffering mental and physical breakdowns from too much change in too short a time. These breakdowns are revealed in the number of heart attacks, ulcers, nervous disorders, and similar ailments of modern people. To combat future shock, Toffler believes, "future studies" should be part of the curriculum on every level of schooling. Some forms this curriculum could take might include students preparing scenarios, engaging in roundtable discussions, role playing, computer programming of "futures games," and conducting futures fairs and clubs.

Toffler's *The Third Wave* is an appropriate sequel to *Future Shock.* In *The Third Wave*, Toffler describes three major changes, or "waves" that have affected human life greatly. The first wave was brought about by the development of agriculture, ending humans' nomadic existence. According to Toffler, this wave existed from 8000 B.C. to around A.D. 1650 to A.D. 1750. The second wave, the industrial revolution (or industrial wave), began after this time and lasted until about 1955. This wave not only brought industry and technology but also changed people's thinking accordingly. It encouraged schools to adopt routinized lockstep methods of instruction that paralleled factory life. Now, Toffler says, a third wave is occurring that emphasizes individuality, "hot relationships" in which people use technology at home to work together in joint projects, and a service economy. Toffler believes that homes are now "electronic cottages" with equipment that makes learning opportunities readily available to children and adults. Because of this, more and more learning is taking place within the home.

In *Learning for Tomorrow*, Toffler says:

> So long as the rate of technological change in such a community stays slow, so long as no wars, invasions, epidemics or other natural disasters upset the even rhythm of life, it is simple for the tribe to formulate a workable image of its own future, since tomorrow merely repeats today.

Today, the rate of change is rapid, but educational systems often deal with the world as a static system. The problem is reminiscent of that recounted in Abner Peddiwell's *The Saber-Tooth Curriculum,* in which the author shows that little or no change seems necessary in education until the encroaching glacier makes current practices out of date. Today, schools continue to teach theories and practices that no longer are useful in improving or maintaining the life of the tribe, and Toffler says that even now, "most schools, colleges and universities base their teaching on the usually tacit notion that tomorrow's world will be basically familiar: the present writ large." This is most unlikely. It is more probable that the future will be radically different from the world as people now know it. Still, schools continue to educate people, not for a future time, not even perhaps for a present time, but for a past time.

One contemporary approach in education is the application of business management theory to education. Some advocate the Japanese management technique extolled in a provocative book by Paul S. George entitled *The Theory Z School*. George designates the best of Japanese and American corporations as Type Z, and he believes that people should emulate successful business practices by applying them to schools. This involves setting forth a vital philosophy, curriculum alignment, classroom congruence, group involvement, and spirited leadership. One basic aspect of the Theory Z approach is that it treats workers as part of a family: Management listens to workers and pays attention to their concerns, fears, and motivations. Although George thinks that it might be difficult if not impossible to apply Japanese management theory to education *carte blanche*, many aspects of it could be used to make schools more effective, vital, and cooperative ventures than they now are.

James Herndon, in *How to Survive in Your Native Land*, noted that although his classes were engaged in new and creative activities, other classes in the same school slaved over lessons about ancient Egypt. One could compile a lengthy catalog of obsolete courses that should be replaced with those more germane to today's and tomorrow's needs. For example, some schools emphasize penmanship instead of keyboarding, sometimes forbid the use of calculators or computers in mathematics classes, teach spelling and the diagramming of sentences instead of creative writing, drill students in phonics instead of teaching speed reading, and so on. The inordinate attention they give to maintaining the status quo might represent the attitude of those who run schools—school boards and state legislatures. Frequently, such organizations promote a more conservative viewpoint and fail to see the need for change in education if it is to keep up with changes in society at large.

Reconstructionists, understandably enough, are critical of contemporary society. They point out the many contradictions and hypocrisies of modern life. Education, they think, should help students deal with these problems by trying to orient them toward becoming agents of change. Counts, for example, suggested that educators should enter areas, such as politics, where great change can be achieved. He also suggested that teachers run for political office or become active in organizations that promote change. Reconstructionists believe that students should think more about such things as world government; a world without schools; and approaches to ending war, bigotry, and hunger.

Although most educators have not heeded the philosophy advocated by reconstructionists seriously some have become aware of the great need for change. During the 1960s and 1970s, a rash of school programs was sparked by cries for relevance and innovation. Teachers were encouraged to innovate, although innovation was often of the most trivial kind, and relevance was interpreted to mean relevance to a system that was in decay. Few programs developed during this period changed education in any lasting way. Their lack of seriousness has today led to a reaction among parents and other laypeople calling for a return to basics and the kind of authoritarian school structure that existed in the past.

In many quarters, however, a more sober assessment is being made of the needs of education, not only for today but also for tomorrow. The World Future Society has sponsored numerous workshops for teachers in an effort to get them to think about the future. Such workshops have spawned some of the programs on the future currently found in elementary, middle, and secondary schools. Educators are becoming increasingly aware that classroom activities are not an end in themselves, and that years after their days in the classroom, students might face conditions for which they have not been specifically prepared. This concern led Dewey to point out that the facts children are taught today might be out of date by the time they graduate. Thus, he emphasized teaching a problem-solving method that he thought would be as useful in the future as it is in the present.

Many have speculated about where schools are headed and what direction they should follow in the years ahead. Some futurists have suggested such things as establishing longer hours for preschoolers, extending formal education from birth to death, increasing the use of computer technology to aid learning, and employing useful results from DNA research.

Many futurists think that people need to look even further, and long-range predictions usually start with things like reproductive technology. It is possible that future prospective parents will be able to predetermine the gender of their child and to program its intelligence, looks, and personality. *In vitro* fertilization will become commonplace, and embryo transfers will be widespread. Parents will be able to select twins or triplets. Children could be gestated in artificial wombs as in Huxley's *Brave New World*, and parents might one day purchase embryos in a "babytorium." Experiments with stem cell research and human cloning, for example, could have a profound effect on society and education and would necessitate changes in the way children are viewed. As children in the future grow up, they also might receive more of their education at home through various new media—not only traditional microchip technology but new ways not yet even envisioned. In addition, 24-hour daycare centers might be available where parents can leave children for extended periods, visiting them only when they choose.

From another perspective, schools themselves might be obsolete. In Cuernavaca, Mexico, Ivan Illich founded the Center for Intercultural Documentation (CIDOC), where he and other scholars studied and explored radical alternatives. A priest turned social reformer, Illich argues that no schools are needed at all as they presently exist. In *Deschooling Society*, he distinguishes between schooling and education, and believes that education should be spread throughout society rather than being conducted only in special buildings provided for that purpose. He thinks that people can be educated on the job, at home, and wherever else they might be during their day-to-day activities. Illich also has proposed the use of "learning webs" through which people can pool information and talents with others. Some critics point out that society once went through a period in history without schools or with few schools. Others see Illich's idea as having great implications for the future; they contend that special buildings set aside for elementary, secondary, and higher education may be *passé*.

Illich's wide-ranging interests include education, transportation, medicine, politics, and economic conditions in the Third World. In the last few years, he has not written a great deal on education, but much attention has been given to the ideas expressed in *Deschooling Society*, that "smart, silly book," as Sidney Hook called it. It has encouraged some educators, particularly educators concerned with social inequalities, to reassess the role that the school plays in a society—that is, that the school is not always a positive benefit.

Some critics say that what Illich is doing is assessing the role of education in a just society—the kind of medieval ideal that stressed the cooperative ties among the individual, the social community, and nature. Education, from Illich's viewpoint, should be a "convivial" activity in which institutions should treat people with concern and as individuals. A more recent work is *Medical Nemesis*, in which Illich points out that the human ability to cope with pain and death has been appropriated by the medical profession, which serves the needs not of the individual, but of the corporate industrial society.

Educators, such as Neil Postman, speak of an "Ivan Illich Problem" that has caused them to reassess how conservative they are and to reconsider the question of intellectual cowardice or, even worse, obtuseness. Illich raises the crucial issue of how effective schools are in seeing the complete student, as well as the needs of humanity; in so doing, he asks one to ponder how well schools serve the cause of a just and moral universe.

Ideas proposed by thinkers such as Ivan Illich might help educators approach the teaching of the future in new ways. To get students to think about the future, some courses raise such questions as these: What will your life circumstances be in 10 years? What will families be like in the future? What major changes will occur in the years ahead? In some schools, students even play a game called "What If?" in which they are asked such questions as "What if your eyes were closed and you opened them in the future? What would be the first thing you would see?" or "What if there were no schools and everyone had to find their own education? Where would you begin?"

In experiments in some schools, students work on projects that examine their possible life on Mars. Questions are posed about what laws they would enact. How would they manage limited food and air supplies? What activities might they engage in on Mars? Students can be asked to develop an ideal society, focusing on such areas as economics, politics, social patterns, and so forth. They might even prepare a wheel showing how all of these various activities would interrelate to develop an efficient and harmonious society. At one school, students were asked to write their own obituaries, stating the cause of death, the year they died, and major activities performed during their lifetimes. (One creative student reported that his death was caused by a hammer dropped by a careless robot.)

Students can use various forecasting techniques in making short- and long-range forecasts. As part of this assignment, they could evaluate the forecasts of others. Students can be asked to write scenarios or science fiction stories. They might even be encouraged to think about the future in terms of such present-day facts as the following: (1) The United States has a relatively small proportion of the world's population but consumes a major portion of the world's energy output; (2) a minority of the world's population is white, and the overwhelming majority is nonwhite; and (3) the average length of time people of the United States spend in any large city is less than 5 years. These and other facts might encourage interest in the future and serve as the basis for report writing and discussion. Students also might use these facts as springboards for dramatizations and role playing. Many students seem to have a natural interest in the future, and teachers can use this interest for motivation in the study of mathematics, science, and art. Some students who are not "turned on" by traditional approaches might be motivated by the novel and direct appeal of future concerns.

One unlikely futurist was Teilhard de Chardin, who was a Jesuit priest and a scientist. Teilhard's primary interest was in finding a way to unify science and religion. He believed the answer lay in technology, which was an advanced view in his time, antedating the wide use of television and computers. In *The Phenomenon of Man*, he stated that he believed God was creating a "compressive convergence" and that technology would help bring about this convergence, or what he called the "noösphere." Many of Teilhard's ideas were continued by Marshall McLuhan, whose concept of a "global village" resembles Teilhard's noösphere.

One novel approach to thinking is the so-called "chaos theory." This approach was developed from mathematical theories, particularly the work of Jules Henri Poincare. Chaos theory gained momentum through quantum mechanics in the field of physics—in particular, the work of Werner Heisenberg and his theory of indeterminacy, or the accidental, contingent, or indeterminate behavior of physical processes. Recent approaches have adopted the name "nonlinear dynamical systems" theory (NDS) or "complex systems" theory (CS). Basically, these theories point to the fact that no straight lines or perfect symmetry is found in nature, yet humans operate on the assumption of symmetry and predictability in their daily lives. People are not machines, but the "mechanical model of reality" is often used in measuring or describing human behavior. It is assumed, for example, that human behavior can be described with the precision of numbers in psychological testing or that social behavior can be measured with precision in sociological research. Stephen J. Guastello, in *Chaos, Catastrophe, and Human Affairs*, says that a great deal of knowledge about human social systems has been ignored by inattention to its nonlinear characteristics. It might be, as many philosophers have pointed out, that the order and regularity seen in nature and in social systems is what has been imposed on them through people's assumptions and thought processes. As Immanuel Kant put it, the very way our minds are structured affects the way we interpret things. Alvin Toffler says that research from the "Brussels school" of Ilya Prigogine and his associates indicates that instead of a well-ordered Newtonian or Laplacian model of the universe, the universe is seething with change, disorder, and process.

Chaos theorists see the world in terms of vitality, turbulence, and volatility. The idea of a fixed norm does not have a place in their theory. They reject conventional beliefs about finance, probability, and economics. Concepts such as the bell curve, regression to the mean, or other predictive models of behavior are simply human ideas imposed on nature to explain the order of things, and chaos theorists maintain that such models are weak and inaccurate representations of reality.

Proponents of chaos theory apply their thinking to a wide range of disciplines, such as ecology, biology, economics, and government. Paradoxically, some advocates maintain that many things heretofore considered chaotic are capable of being understood in a deterministic sense, leading to the phenomenon known as "deterministic chaos." This concept might prove useful in the social sciences and in education in many situations that must be interpreted from the standpoint of random chance or probability. It is well known in the social sciences that in measuring human behavior, all variables cannot be controlled. Although chaos theory has old roots, only in recent years has a concerted effort been made to apply this theory to natural events and social interactions.

Because the world of tomorrow will be run by the children of today, it is vital that young people be encouraged to be concerned about the future and have instilled in them the idea that they can help shape that future according to their own goals and aspirations. Rather than view it as something that just happens, people need to look at the future as something that they can, by their own efforts, make into a world of beauty and infinite promise.

Reconstructionism has influenced educators into thinking anew about the role of education. As a relatively recent philosophy of education, reconstructionism has been in the vanguard of those seeking to make education a more active social force. They have championed the role of the educator as a primary change agent and have sought to change schools in ways that would contribute to a new and better society. Because reconstructionism is a relatively new movement in education, it is difficult to assess its impact fully at this time.

RECONSTRUCTIONISM AS A PHILOSOPHY OF EDUCATION

Perhaps the most outstanding characteristics of reconstructionist educators are their views that modern society is facing a grave crisis of survival, that the educator must become a social activist, and that the school occupies a strategic position in meeting the crisis and in providing a necessary foundation for action.

Education and the Human Crisis

Numerous educators call themselves reconstructionists. The Society for Educational Reconstruction (SER) was established in 1969 to further reconstructionist ideals on a wider scale. A policy statement released by SER sets forth the two basic objectives of reconstructionism: (1) democratic control over the decisions that regulate human lives, and (2) a peaceful world community. SER members believe in assisting educators everywhere in presenting their deepest social concerns to their students with optimum effectiveness. They encourage leaders to apply reconstructionist values to experimental educational programs in schools and communities.

Members of SER believe that most approaches to educational and social reform are inadequate and outdated. From their perspective, people cannot wait for the kinds of gradual reform advocated by most philosophies, particularly when human survival might depend on the immediate steps needed to make society more humanistic and productive. Indeed, it appears that we are living in an age of crisis, and progressivism, which once promised so much, seems to them to be an outmoded way of dealing constructively with current issues. SER points out that humans now have the power to extinguish themselves and all living creatures from the face of the Earth, and that unless some way is found to integrate technological developments with the highest principles of human rights, all cogitations and discussions will become mere rhetoric. The schools have failed to take on this task. As one reconstructionist put it, "What academic concept will students be 'discovering' when the computers press the nuclear button?"

Reconstructionists see the primary struggle in society today as being between those who wish to preserve society as it is, or with little change, and those who believe that great changes are needed not only to ensure human survival as a species but also to make people's lives better. Such a struggle is not limited to the United States; it is a major international crisis that demands concerted and well-planned action. Central to this needed action, reconstructionists believe, is the crucial role of the educator and the school.

If the role of educators nationally and internationally is assessed in this time of crisis, one might conclude with reconstructionists that most educators are, at their worst, linked with the forces of reaction and, at their best, only liberalized. Many teachers come from the middle class, from families in which the parents seldom suffered loss of income from unemployment; they seldom had to worry about where the next meal was coming from, and their parents could afford to send them to college. Most of them attended schools that taught traditional genteel attitudes toward life and society. As a reward for their endeavors, some of them have obtained positions in which they have continued the teaching of preestablished materials in preestablished ways. Such teaching has failed to reach minority groups; to change racial attitudes; to create change-oriented individuals; to develop humane attitudes; or to solve the problems of poverty, repression, war, and greed. One might even argue that instead of solving such problems, education has helped perpetuate these problems. It has provided specialists for warfare and for Wall Street, and it has aided and abetted rampant consumerism. Reconstructionists maintain that people have indeed forgotten that education should create change, and they argue that, unfortunately, it is used to maintain the status quo.

For educators to make real changes in society, reconstructionists urge them to become involved in affairs outside their own classrooms and schools. Critics have challenged Counts's thesis of 1932 *(Dare the Schools Build a New Social Order?)* because educators are not located at those points in society where fundamental political and economic decisions are made. Although Counts suggested that teachers run for political office and engage in social issues outside the classroom, the number of teachers who have done so is pitiably small; those who have seem to have acted not for the purpose of advancing the cause of education or enacting great social reforms but for achieving personal gain or some other interest.

Some critics of reconstructionism think that teachers should not take part in social and political affairs because schools should be neutral places and teachers might lose objectivity by playing a partisan role. As the French philosopher Jean-Paul Sartre has pointed out, however, no neutral positions exist; not to act is to act by default. Teachers, by their deliberate nonaction, stand responsible for the absurdities all around us in the same sense that good Germans were responsible for Nazi atrocities. No neutral positions exist; even if they did, most reconstructionists would agree that "the hottest spot in hell is reserved for those who in times of moral crisis remain neutral."

Nobuo Shimahara, who challenged the neutrality in higher education after the student uprisings at Columbia University in the late 1960s, also explored this issue. Shimahara states that the appeal to neutrality as an attempt to resolve the dilemma was futile and obsolete. Why? Colleges and universities are politically influenced to a significant degree and occasionally adulterated by political and economic interests. Research in an advanced university, for example, is more or less determined by the structure of investments of private industries and the order of political priorities in government. University trustees and alumni are often high-ranking members in the corporate structure of the United States and greatly influence local and national political and economic power. They also strongly influence the basic policies of higher education in ways that reflect business attitudes and the economic interests of the business sector.

Reconstructionist educators tend to think of themselves as radical educational reformers rather than as reactionary conservatives, timid moderates, or weak-hearted liberals. In the past few decades, an increasing number of educators have called for radical changes in educational aims and methods; among them are Herbert Kohl, Kenneth Clark, Paul Goodman, A. S. Neill, Ivan Illich, and Neil Postman. Only a few, however, seem to have comprehended fully that radical changes in education cannot occur without radical changes in the structure of society. Some sociologists point out that educational reforms cannot be made apart from wider social reforms. It is generally true that educational reform follows social reform and rarely if ever precedes or causes it. For educators to engage in educational reform effectively, they must perform a dual role: educator and social activist. For the reconstructionist, the two roles should not be separated, for educators should be committed enough to act on those things they teach in the classroom. This is also what it means to be a *citizen* in the fullest sense of that term although this reference is to world citizenship rather than national citizenship. Acting as a citizen implies that one is not only a participating member of society but also a person who continually searches for better values and an end to degrading and harmful aspects of society. It also implies becoming willing to act in ways to bring society more in line with those better values.

The idea of an educator as an action agent, particularly as a social activist, disturbs some people. Reconstructionists explain that it is not necessary to separate knowledge and action. Knowledge should lead to action, and action should clarify, modify, and increase knowledge. This point is illustrated by a painting that hangs in the New York Public Library in New York City. It shows monks busily working on their Bible safe inside the monastery, while outside knights are burning down houses and cutting off the noses of the slower taxpayers. The monks apparently see no need to use their knowledge for the improvement of humanity in *this* world. Action without thought might lead to detrimental ends, but thought without action is no more defensible. Thus, educators, because of their nonintervention in the course of human affairs, have contributed to some extent to the problems facing humans worldwide. Actions are no more perfect than ideas, but placing an idea into action allows one, as Dewey argued, to reassess it in the world of human experience and, through subsequent thought, to make it a better idea. Reconstructionists would like to link thought with action, theory with practice, and intellect with activism.

Role of the School

Americans have asked a lot from their schools. When driver education needed to be taught, schools took it on, just as they have taken on sex education, home economics, drug education, and many other tasks. The belief that educators and schools are thus leading society in some better way, however, might be erroneous. The schools are fulfilling a need that by virtue of their organized and specialized structure, they can do better than any other institution. Yet, schools have remained basically the same, and the idea that society is being advanced by making education more relevant or accountable is only to say that it is being made more relevant to the needs of the status quo or more accountable to vested interests as they currently exist. To think that the changes recently undertaken to make school curricula more open or flexible also will result in necessary societal changes could be called wishful thinking. Such changes often do not succeed in altering the power structure as much as in maintaining or advancing it.

One great need in education today is to view the schools in a much wider perspective. Such a movement cannot simply be a movement in "life adjustment," "relevancy," "accountability," or "basic" education because these only prolong ideas and institutions that are in need of change. To be effective, this movement must be a more radical approach that seeks, through a variety of methods, to change existing social institutions, including the school, in ways that make them more responsive to human needs.

Such a movement must begin with the view that the school does not exist apart from society but within it and that the reconstruction of society will occur not through the school but with it. This movement requires educators who are willing to explore new possibilities through action. It requires teachers who can see alternatives and who have some conception of a better world. It demands a school institution freed from the traditional ideological framework so that it can project new goals and values. It needs individuals—teachers and students—who are moral in the sense that no conflict exists between the well-thought ideas and the well-planned actions they are willing to perform on a daily basis. This means insisting on the idea that people can change society through individual and collective effort, for not to be involved is to assist in the perpetuation of values and systems that are archaic, unworkable, and dehumanizing. Humans live in a world where nuclear destruction is possible, where the air and the water are polluted, where the population explosion grows more threatening every day—a world with worsening racial relations, international misunderstandings, and political ineptness on an international scale.

The United States embarked on a program of mass education unparalleled in human history. It has succeeded to the extent that a vast number of people who would have been denied schooling in many other countries have been educated. U.S. methods of teaching, though still far from ideal, have improved. Reconstructionists maintain, however, that the schools are still looking backward rather than forward.

In 1900, about 60 percent of our power rested on physical strength. Today, less than 6 percent is manual, as technology has become a bigger part of people's lives. Education was slow to cope with such changes. Efforts now must be redoubled to face the time ahead when even greater changes might occur. As difficult as the task might be, people need to be provided with education for a future that they do not know— one that most likely will be more complex than today's world.

The problem of goal setting in society and in schools is important because although many people are busily engaged in the affairs of life, much of what they do is harmful to themselves and others. People are turning out missiles, new methods of warfare, harmful products, unnecessary luxuries, and all the rest. They do not lack initiative, drive, and productivity. However, does all of this have any real purpose? The problem is a moral one. Reconstructionists view all our actions in a moral context because everything people do has consequences for the future. They believe that education in schools must be directed toward humane goals that result in better social consequences for all.

Ivan Illich struck a new radical note. He charged that modern societies, such as the United States, have become too dependent on established institutions, particularly with regard to education. Schools certify and license parasitical interests. They hold a monopoly over the social imagination, controlling standards for what is valuable through their degree-granting powers. It has come to the point that knowledge is suspect unless certified by schooling. The social and human results create psychological impotence and the inability to fend for oneself.

What must be done, Illich maintained, is detach learning from teaching and create a new style of education based on self-motivation and new linkages between learners and the world. Educational institutions have become too manipulative according to Illich; what is needed is a "convivial" system of education that promotes, rather than selectively controls, educational access by helping learners arrange for their own education. The results of this new system would be "learning networks" of information storage and retrieval systems, skill exchanges, and peer-matching capacities. It would provide learners with available resources at any time in their lives, and it would recognize those who want to share what they know and connect them with those who want to learn it. It also would provide opportunities for the open examination of public issues and provide for a wider dissemination of knowledge. Deschooling would liberate access to education, promote the sharing of knowledge and skills, liberate individual initiative, and free individuals from institutional domination. In some ways, Illich's learning networks anticipated the vast capabilities of computers using such avenues as the Internet and the World Wide Web. Although Illich's book did not bring forth a massive disestablishment of schools, it did help many people reevaluate their beliefs about education and schooling. The idea that many paths lead to education and that formal schooling is not the only or even the best way in every instance received a renewed emphasis.

A similar cry for reform was heard from Paulo Freire (1921–1997), the Brazilian philosopher and educator, who had to leave his native Brazil because of his political ideas, although he later returned. In *Pedagogy of the Oppressed*, Freire shows how education has been used to exploit poor people. Freire suggests that ideal teachers are friends of those they educate. Through proper techniques, a teacher can enable adult students to become cognizant of the forces that exploit them and to become aware of how they can use education and knowledge as a means to improve their lives. Freire criticizes the traditional concept of education in which people are not required to *know* anything; they just memorize information presented by the teacher. Instead, Freire wants education to be involved with the real and current everyday problems of people. According to Freire, if poor people need better health care, then education ought to help them comprehend or construct ways in which to secure it.

Aims of Education

Reconstructionism emphasizes the need for change. It is utopian in the idea of goals directed toward a world culture or civilization. Yet, it is also flexible because it holds that goals can be modified in process as problems and blocks occur along the way. Whatever the specific educational goals, one thing seems fairly certain to the reconstructionist: Social *change* and social *action* are needed.

The idea of promoting change is based on the notion that individuals and society can be made better. One may see in this idea a kind of evolutionary development or Hegelianism; that is, one can assist in the process of moving things from a less desirable to a more desirable state. Thus, reconstructionists would like to involve people more as change agents, to change themselves and the world around them. They are opposed to abstract or armchair philosophies in which the emphasis is more on knowing than on doing. Reconstructionists do not believe that any conflict exists between knowing and doing, for all actions should be well thought out in advance. Reconstructionists would like to see an end to the ivory tower mentality, with everyone involved in some way in social action. They believe that education includes individuals as well as society. The education that one generally receives in today's schools, based as it is on competition, tends to isolate and separate people. Reconstructionists do not think that school can be separated from the rest of society or individuals from each other. They strive for unity rather than fragmentation.

When Counts wrote *Dare the Schools Build a New Social Order?* he provided a rallying cry for reconstructionists. He criticized the direction that progressivism had taken in its life-adjustment phase and its failure to act on critical issues of the day. He argued for a new progressivism that would be more active and take the lead in social change. When looking at the situation today, one finds that schools and educators are still not leaders of change and often serve to prevent it. Even when society has moved ahead in accepting new social customs, the school often continues to preserve traditional ways. Counts urged educators to begin taking the lead in obtaining power and in exercising that power for the good of society. Educators should become more involved in social causes. In this way, they would be involved in improving their own education and would serve to educate others far more than in any classroom activity.

World community, brotherhood, and democracy are three ideals that reconstructionists believe in and desire to implement in schools and in society. Schools should foster these ideals through curricular, administrative, and instructional practices. Although schools cannot be expected to reconstruct society by themselves, they can serve as models for the rest of society by adopting these ideals.

Methods of Education

Reconstructionists are critical of most methods currently used in all levels of schooling. This is because the old methods reinforce traditional values and attitudes underlying the status quo. In such circumstances, the teacher becomes an unwitting agent of entrenched values and ideas. The "hidden curriculum" underlies the educational process, and students are shaped to fit preexisting models of living. To the extent that teachers are ignorant of this factor, they continue to nurture and sustain the system through the teaching techniques and processes they use. For example, school boards or states approve the textbooks that teachers must use in their classrooms, and teachers who accept and use these adopted materials without question become party to a devious kind of indoctrination. Often, such textbooks are approved because they are noncontroversial or contain distortions, such as subtle economic, racist, or sexist ideas popular in the dominant culture.

Instructional tools, such as texts and teaching techniques and processes, exert influences on learners. For example, where teachers are viewed as dispensers of knowledge and students as passive recipients, the way is paved for students to accept uncritically whatever is presented. Passivity on the part of students deprives them of any creative role in analyzing and constructing materials or in making judgments and decisions. Perhaps this kind of problem is seen most readily in the area of social studies, where objectivity and criticism often are not encouraged. What often passes as social studies is little more than nationalistic bias that reinforces chauvinistic tendencies. Prefabricated teaching materials with the questions and answers already established result in making students think alike about society, the economy, and the political structure. Social studies are designed to encourage good citizenship, but a built-in bias of what good citizenship is almost guarantees a narrow and provincial outlook among students.

It is regrettable that so few of the citizens of the United States bother to vote in national elections. Local elections are even more poorly attended, and some issues do not receive even a 15 percent turnout. Polls show that few citizens know who their representatives and senators are, and even fewer know the names of the members of the Supreme Court, the duties of the president, the branches of government, and so forth. Citizens, for the most part, take a passive attitude toward government. Although they might complain about high taxes, inefficient government, and the low quality of public officials, they do not often exercise their rights to change these things. Failure to vote is only an indication of a deeper problem, according to the reconstructionists. In addition to voting, citizens need to work for candidates they believe in or to run for office themselves. Reconstructionists want to see activism rather than the passivity that currently exists.

Education should be directed toward arousing interest in public activism. For example, one political science professor allowed his class to spend a semester working for the candidates of their choice. These students learned more about the political process through active participation than they could have by reading sterile books or by attending lectures. Reconstructionists would heartily endorse this kind of approach for at least a portion of a student's formal education. In *An Aristocracy of Everyone: The Politics of Education and the Future of America*, Benjamin Barber takes a similar line of reasoning. He believes that democracy and education are inextricably intertwined and that one cannot exist in its fullest sense without the other. He believes that education should be a leading national priority, and he has promoted what he calls "service learning" as an appropriate way to help get students involved in community service and gain firsthand knowledge and experience of community life. Not only would it build better citizens he believes, but it would strengthen democracy.

Curriculum

Reconstructionists favor students getting out as much as possible into society, where they can learn and apply learning. Brameld recommends that as much as half of a student's time be spent outside the traditional school structure, learning at some place other than a school. The traditional classroom setting might have some value, but the important thing is to get students to use what they learn, and traditional schools do not always encourage this.

One way of organizing curriculum is to modify the core plan advocated by progressivists into what Brameld calls "the wheel" curriculum. According to Brameld, the core can be viewed as the hub of the wheel—the central theme of the school program. The spokes represent related studies, such as discussion groups, field experiences, content and skill studies, and vocational studies. The hub and the spokes support each other, and the rim of the wheel serves in a synthesizing and unifying capacity. Although each school year would have its own wheel, continuity would be established from year to year, with each wheel flowing into and strengthening the other. Although each year would be different, it also would inherit the problems and solutions from previous years and would move on to new syntheses. Brameld thinks that the reconstructionist curriculum is a centripetal and a centrifugal force. It is centripetal because it draws the people of the community together in common studies and centrifugal because it extends from the school into the wider community. Thus, it has the capacity to help bring about cultural transformation because of the dynamic relationship between school and society.

In terms of curriculum, reconstructionists favor a "world" curriculum with an emphasis on truth, fellowship, and justice. They are opposed to narrow or parochial curricula that deal only with local or community ideas and ideals. They favor studies in world history, as well as explorations into the contemporary work of the United Nations and other world agencies. The curriculum should be action oriented by engaging students in such projects as participating in worthy community causes, informing citizens about social problems, and using petitions and protests. Students can learn from books, but they also can learn from such activities as voter registration drives, consumer research, and antipollution campaigns, in which they can make a genuine social contribution while they are learning.

One important development in recent years is how much attention schools are giving to the variety of cultures in American society. *Cultural pluralism* is the term generally used to describe this cultural diversity, and *multicultural education* is the term most often applied to educational programs designed to study it. The issue of multicultural education is so important that accrediting organizations, such as the National Council for Accreditation of Teacher Education, have encouraged it in studies for prospective teachers. These organizations have made multicultural education a necessary part of every accredited teacher education program. Their rationale is based on the historical and contemporary fact that American society is a conglomeration of many cultures and that this diversity needs to be recognized properly rather than ignored.

Originally, state systems of public schools had a cultural "melting pot" role in which schools were viewed as instruments to Americanize immigrant children by "melting" away cultural differences so that newcomers would fit into mainstream American society. More recently, however, awareness has been increasing that many cultural differences did not disappear, that these differences added strength to the American social fabric, and that such differences needed to be preserved. Thus, school curricula now include anthologies with stories about many cultural settings, and American history textbooks now include content on African-American history, the history of women, and Native Americans. Immigration to the United States has long been a fact of American life, and now attention has been given not only to the older immigrant groups from Europe and Asia but also to the newer groups, such as those from Latin American or Asian cultures.

Reconstructionists champion and welcome such developments. Recognition of the diversity of American origins is long overdue, and they look to this development as a fundamental way to promote peace and understanding among people. Indeed, they believe that multicultural education, if approached with proper care and understanding, should help change the ways Americans view themselves as individuals and as members of groups. Multicultural education should result in views that are in line with the facts of American historical and contemporary life.

One social problem that reconstructionists would like schools to address is the issue of nuclear war. Some educational organizations, such as the National Education Association, have prepared materials for teachers to use in classrooms in explaining the dangers and horrors of nuclear war. These materials have been strongly resisted by others who think that they scare children and may promote a defeatist attitude that encourages aggression from national enemies. Reconstructionists believe that nothing is to be gained by hiding one's head in the sand and that knowledge about the possibilities and dangers of nuclear war might be this nation's best hope for eliminating future conflicts. Many reconstructionists are in the forefront of those opposed to the further development and testing of nuclear weapons. Because of their belief in a "spaceship earth" mentality that points to the interconnectedness of all nations and all peoples, they would like to see people work together to end the destructive possibilities of nuclear energy.

Reconstructionists realize that it is all too easy to be enculturated so that people are not aware of the problems of other countries. They would encourage learning the language and the cultures of other peoples. They also would encourage reading the literature of other cultures, as well as newspapers and magazines that deal with issues on a worldwide basis. In some schools, considerable attention is given to other nations, with special activities designed to inform students about their cultures and customs. Sometimes students dress up in the costumes of other countries, serve their food, and engage in activities that provide a better understanding of cultural differences. Reconstructionists want teachers to be internationally oriented and humanitarian in their outlook. Teachers should be experts in engaging students in action projects of all kinds. When a student is involved in some social activity, that curriculum can produce far more learning than most classroom lectures.

Not only should students become oriented to other cultures, but they also should become future oriented and should study proposals for future development. They need to plan activities that lead to future goals. People must learn to confront the future; consequently, teachers should encourage students to construct plans for future societies, with some cognizance of problems regarding population, energy, transportation, and so on. They also could visit with various communal organizations where futuristic alternative lifestyles are being practiced.

Reconstructionists reason that if people are sincerely interested in society and education, then they will be at those pivotal places where decisions are made. They strongly urge community action and promote the kind of education needed to assist people in obtaining social and human rights.

Role of the Teacher

The kind of teacher that reconstructionists want is an educator who is also a social activist. They want a person who keeps up with things that are happening in the world, is deeply and personally concerned with important problems, and has the courage to do something about them. Basically, the reconstructionist teacher sees education as an important tool for solving the problems of society. First, the teacher can inform others about the nature and extent of the problem, perhaps about such actions as cutting down rain forests and dynamiting coral reefs. Second, the teacher can suggest what one can do about these problems, such as writing to elected officials or members of the United Nations, raising money through benefits, and even picketing or boycotting products. Reconstructionists believe that much of what goes on in school is too theoretical and that students need to become actively involved in solving problems not only worldwide but also in their local community, with cleanups, help for the homeless, and campaigning for desirable political candidates.

Some people would say that the role of the reconstructionist teacher is a precarious one. Many people, including educators, do not believe that the school is the place for social activism that might be partisan in nature. They believe that the role of the school is to teach people about things that have happened in the past, as well as about current events, but that the school should not be used as the place to challenge traditions. Reconstructionists point out that traditional beliefs and practices, such as the Declaration of Independence and the U.S. Constitution, were once radical ideas themselves but have now been accepted as mainstream thought. The improvement of society, reconstructionists believe, results from continuous thoughtful change, and the best change agent is the educational process.

Perhaps the reconstructionist teacher has a difficult role ahead in presenting ideas that many people are not yet ready to accept, but reconstructionists operate under a moral principle that states that education can and should be used to make the world a more humane place. Teachers need to be freed from passivity and fear of working for change. They need to focus on critical issues not generally found in textbooks or made a part of the school curriculum. They also need to make students more critical about the knowledge they receive. Neil Postman and Charles Weingartner suggest that teachers promote "crap detecting," whereby students are encouraged to examine critically the information they receive in schools, in the mass media, and from various social institutions such as church and government. Rather than being passive dispensers of knowledge, teachers would become facilitators for analysis and change.

It needs to be pointed out, however, that reconstructionists see all change occurring within a democratic framework. Therefore, although teachers might attempt to make students aware of problem areas and point out the pros and cons involved, students should be free to make their own decisions on the matter, as well as about the extent of their involvement with it. In fact, reconstructionists argue that democratic procedures should be at every level of schooling, with the student having an active say in the formulation and implementation of objectives, methods, and curriculum. The teacher can be a useful facilitator of learning, but decision making about schooling and about how it shall be used must also actively involve students, a point strongly emphasized by Theodore Brameld.

CRITIQUE OF RECONSTRUCTIONISM IN EDUCATION

Reconstructionists believe that their approach is a radical departure from pragmatism. This is true in terms of the positions that pragmatists have taken on social, economic, and political issues. It is misleading, however, to say that Dewey did not champion radical solutions. He argued that solutions to social problems must be thought out carefully and experimentally with an ever-watchful eye on possible consequences. The result of his approach might be that Dewey was a cautious radical and a reflective champion of social change. Critics often have attacked reconstructionism because it lacks Dewey's caution, charging that the reconstructionist analyses of social problems and the accompanying remedies suffer from shallowness and superficiality.

Often, in their strong desire for change, reconstructionists are precipitous in their recommendations for reform. The charge has been made that this precipitousness results in a great deal of talk and controversy concerning aims and methods in education but that it has little real effect. One can point to the actual effects that pragmatism has had on schools, but it is difficult to discern any concrete impact from reconstructionism. Perhaps this occurs because pragmatists' recommendations are easier to accept and less radical on the surface, but it also may be because of the depth and feasibility of their proposals. By the same token, reconstructionists' lack of impact might be attributable directly to their recommendations not being popular with the mass of people or with the majority of educators.

It seems that the recent attention to multicultural education represents a re-affirmation of reconstructionist ideas. Reconstructionists have long championed cultural pluralism (or what is now called multiculturalism), and any assessment of their impact must include multicultural education. It is also true, however, that ethnic groups promoting their own interests have been as responsible for the development of multi-cultural education as any organized reconstructionist effort. For example, Mexican Americans, rather than seeking radical change in American thought and institutions, have championed recognition of their cultural identity to gain acceptance in society as it exists. The same can be said of women, African-Americans, and Native Americans. What might be lost at the present time, however, is that philosophical reconstruction-ism had as part of its agenda many of the elements of multicultural education, even though this might not be nearly so obvious today as it is for, say, postmodernist thought. Perhaps a philosophical outlook is successful when its ideas become commonplace and its postulates are accepted by others without recognition of the source.

In many respects, reconstructionists have a romantic notion of what schools can do. Studies by such historians as Michael Katz and David Tyack and by such sociologists as James Coleman and Christopher Jencks show that expectations of what schools can do have far outstripped the benefits accrued. Indications are that schools cannot directly affect income, racial acceptance, and equality of opportunity. Counts believed that great social reforms could be achieved when educators banded together, but it is questionable whether teachers could ever obtain such power or use it any better than others.

Another charge leveled against reconstructionists is that their views of democracy and decision making are questionable. They start with the premise that change is needed, and often they state the goals before they start the journey. This is different from Dewey's conception of open-endedness and of the intimate relationship between means and ends. Reconstructionists advocate world law, but evidence suggests that people accept laws to the extent that the laws respect basic cultural patterns and are formulated by the people themselves or their representatives. Because of the diversity of world cultures, it is doubtful that a universal code to which every cultural group would pay allegiance could be constructed at this time. Not only does a world law code disregard cultural diversity, it also assumes that it is good to centralize the regulation of human behavior. Reasonable and intelligent objections to such centralization might be raised by people of different philosophical persuasions. There is the notion that change and novelty themselves come about because of individual variation and that any centralization on a world scale may have detrimental consequences for social change. Indeed, it could result in the destruction of cherished ideals in reconstructionism itself concerning change. People do not know whether world law is possible or desirable. The United Nations is perhaps humanity's most notable experiment in this regard, but its power to control war, international conflict, and economic injustice and hunger is weak. Reconstructionism's noticeable utopianism has some advantages, but it also might take our eyes off immediate problems to focus them on some ideal end.

Critics suggest that reconstructionists and other progressive reformers have been coopted by reforms of the forces they sought to overcome. They once fought vigorously for the social welfare programs of the early and mid-twentieth century. They argued for unemployment insurance, welfare, unionism, the graduated income tax, social security, and the extension of tax-supported education beyond public elementary and secondary schools to community colleges and state universities. They have accomplished these aims, and the programs are now part of the status quo; however, reconstructionists have failed to proffer new programs and goals to capture the imagination and verve of contemporary activists. In effect, organizations like the World Future Society and Greenpeace International have presented more alternative solutions to the world's problems in recent years than has reconstructionism. As a consequence, many of reconstructionism's thrusts now have the sound of a tired refrain, and its forcefulness has been dissipated.

Although reconstructionism has a less noticeable profile, its call for action remains. Despite liberal reform efforts of an earlier time, problems seem to endure and might even be more complex than they were. Today, people do not speak about crises, but about mega-crises that seem immune to the best-planned reforms. Many countries seem opposed to long-range planning, and they appear to muddle through with a crisis mentality that does not act until a problem is upon them.

Computer simulation of world trends shows humans moving toward a series of mounting crises as world population and runaway industrialization deplete natural resources and spoil the environment. The Club of Rome report is only one notable call to action about such problems. This group of 100 industrialists, scientists, economists, educators, and statespeople attempted to stimulate concerted and international political action in a rational and humane direction. They established graphic projections of impending disasters in population, food supply, economic collapse, and nonrenewable resources unless direct action was taken in the near future. *The Limits of Growth*, a book based on their initial work, predicted global catastrophe within the twenty-first century if such growth continued.

In their second report, *Mankind at the Turning Point*, the Club of Rome described two great gaps—one between human beings and nature and the other between the rich countries of the Northern Hemisphere and the poor countries of the Southern Hemisphere. These findings and conclusions stressed the need for the immediate and radical worldwide changes advocated by reconstructionists. The crises and impending disasters on the horizon have been anticipated by reconstructionists for many years and should not take people by surprise. Critics who have accused reconstructionists of being alarmists might need to reconsider. If anything, it appears that reconstructionists erred by failing to sound a stronger warning. Today, many people are unaware of the extent and depth of human problems, and reconstructionists can rightly claim that schools and educators have not been forthright in informing the public about the nature of the difficulties.

Reconstructionist philosophy has been an available antidote to the easy virtues of materialism, traditional cultural values, and social stability. Although reconstructionist theories are not always accepted, they can stimulate and provoke thinking about critical issues. They have provided visions of a more perfect world and have suggested means of attaining them. It is, perhaps, a shortcoming of some philosophies that they do not have future goals, either short range or long range. Concern for social values, humane justice, the human community, world peace, economic justice, equality of opportunity, freedom, and democracy—things in which the world is sadly lacking—are all significant goals for reconstructionism. If it is true that reconstructionists are impatient and precipitous in their desire to eliminate social evils, then it is understandable in a world still filled with hate, greed, bigotry, poverty, and war.

COUNTS

DARE THE SCHOOLS BUILD A NEW SOCIAL ORDER?

George S. Counts, many of whose ideas loom large in reconstructionism, was one of the most radical progressive educators. He thought that the aim of education should be social reform and urged teachers to throw off their "slave psychology" and to work for the good of the people. Counts was identified with the progressive movement in education but became disenchanted with its rhetoric for change and reluctance to act. In the following selection, written in 1932 in the depths of the Great Depression, Counts calls to educators to "reach for power" and initiate changes in society. The words still have a modern ring. [Education] . . . must . . . face squarely and courageously every social issue, come to grips with life in all of its stark reality, establish an organic relation with the community, develop a realistic and comprehensive theory of welfare, fashion a compelling and challenging vision of human destiny, and become less frightened than it is today at the bogies of imposition and indoctrination. . . .

This brings us to the most crucial issue in education—the question of the nature and extent of the influence which the school should exercise over the development of the child. The advocates of extreme freedom have been so successful in championing what they call the rights of the child that even the most skillful practitioners of the art of converting others to their opinions disclaim all intention of molding the learner. And when the word *indoctrination* is coupled with education there is scarcely one among us possessing the hardihood to refuse to be horrified. . . .

I believe firmly that a critical factor must play an important role in any adequate educational program, at least in any such program fashioned for the modern world. An education that does not strive to promote the fullest and most thorough understanding of the world is not worthy of the name. Also there must be no deliberate distortion or suppression of facts to support any theory or point of view. On the other hand, I am prepared to defend the thesis that all education contains a large element of imposition, that in the very nature of the case this is inevitable,

that the existence and evolution of society depend upon it, that it is consequently eminently desirable, and that the frank acceptance of this fact by the educator is a major professional obligation. I even contend that failure to do this involves the clothing of one's own deepest prejudices in the garb of universal truth and the introduction into the theory and practice of education of an element of obscurantism. . . .

There is the fallacy that the school should be impartial in its emphases, that no bias should be given instruction. We have already observed how the individual is inevitably molded by the culture into which he is born. In the case of the school a similar process operates and presumably is subject to a degree of conscious direction. My thesis is that complete impartiality is utterly impossible, that the school must shape attitudes, develop tastes, and even impose ideas. It is obvious that the whole of creation cannot be brought into the school. This means that some selection must be made of teachers, curricula, architecture, methods of teaching. And in the making of the selection the dice must always be weighted in favor of this or that. Here is a fundamental truth that cannot be brushed aside as irrelevant or unimportant; it constitutes the very essence of the matter under discussion. Nor can the reality be concealed beneath agreeable phrases. . . .

If we may now assume that the child will be imposed upon in some fashion by the various elements in his environment, the real question is not whether imposition will take place, but rather from what source it will come. If we were to answer this question in terms of the past, there could, I think, be but one answer: On all genuinely crucial matters the school follows the wishes of the groups or classes that actually rule society; on minor matters the school is sometimes allowed a certain measure of freedom. But the future may be unlike the past. Or perhaps I should say that teachers, if they could increase sufficiently their stock of courage, intelligence, and vision, might become a social force of some magnitude. About this eventuality I am not over sanguine, but a society lacking leadership as ours does, might even accept the guidance of teachers. Through powerful organizations they might at least reach the public conscience and come to exercise a larger measure of control over the schools than hitherto. They would then have to assume some responsibility for the more fundamental forms of imposition which, according to my argument, cannot be avoided.

That the teachers should deliberately reach for power and then make the most of their conquest is my firm conviction. To the extent that they are permitted to fashion the curriculum and the procedures of the school they will definitely and positively influence the social attitudes, ideals, and behavior of the coming generation. In doing this they should resort to no subterfuge or false modesty. They should say neither that they are merely teaching the truth nor that they are unwilling to wield power in their own right. The first position is false and the second is a confession of incompetence. It is my observation that the men and women who have affected the course of human events are those who have not hesitated to use the power that has come to them. Representing as they do, not the interests of the moment or of any special class, but rather the common and abiding interests of the people, teachers are under heavy social obligation to protect and further those interests. In this they occupy a relatively unique position in society. Also since the profession should embrace sci-

entists and scholars of the highest rank, as well as teachers working at all levels of the educational system, it has at its disposal, as no other group, the knowledge and wisdom of the ages. . . .

This brings us to the question of the kind of imposition in which teachers should engage, if they had the power. Our obligations, I think, grow out of the social situation. We live in troublous times; we live in an age of profound change; we live in an age of revolution. Indeed it is highly doubtful whether man ever lived in a more eventful period than the present. In order to match our epoch we would probably have to go back to the fall of the ancient empires or even to that unrecorded age when men first abandoned the natural arts of hunting and fishing and trapping and began to experiment with agriculture and the settled life. Today we are witnessing the rise of a civilization quite without precedent in human history—a civilization founded on science, technology, and machinery, possessing the most extraordinary power, and rapidly making of the entire world a single great society. Because of forces already released, whether in the field of economics, politics, morals, religion, or art, the old molds are being broken. And the peoples of the earth are everywhere seething with strange ideas and passions. If life were peaceful and quiet and undisturbed by great issues, we might with some show of wisdom center our attention on the nature of the child. But with the world as it is, we cannot afford for a single instant to remove our eyes from the social scene or shift our attention from the peculiar needs of the age. . . .

Consider the present condition of the nation. Who among us, if he had not been reared amid our institutions, could believe his eyes as he surveys the economic situation, or his ears as he listens to solemn disquisitions by our financial and political leaders on the cause and cure of the depression! Here is a society that manifests the most extraordinary contradictions: A mastery over the forces of nature, surpassing the wildest dreams of antiquity, is accompanied by extreme material insecurity; dire poverty walks hand in hand with the most extravagant living the world has ever known; an abundance of goods of all kinds is coupled with privation, misery, and even starvation; an excess of production is seriously offered as the underlying cause of severe physical suffering; breakfastless children march to school past bankrupt shops laden with rich foods gathered from the ends of the earth; strong men by the million walk the streets in a futile search for employment and with the exhaustion of hope enter the ranks of the damned; great captains of industry close factories without warning and dismiss the workmen by whose labors they have amassed huge fortunes through the years; automatic machinery increasingly displaces men and threatens society with a growing contingent of the permanently unemployed; racketeers and gangsters with the connivance of public officials fasten themselves on the channels of trade and exact toll at the end of the machine gun; economic parasitism, either within or without the law, is so prevalent that the tradition of honest labor is showing signs of decay; the wages paid to the workers are too meager to enable them to buy back the goods they produce; consumption is subordinated to production and a philosophy of deliberate waste is widely proclaimed as the highest economic wisdom; the science of psychology is employed to fan the flames of desire so that men may be enslaved by their wants and bound to the wheel of production; a government board advises the cotton-growers to plow under every third row of cotton in order to bolster up the market; both ethical and aesthetic considerations are commonly over-ridden by "hard-headed business men" bent on material gain; federal aid to the unemployed is opposed on the ground that it would pauperize the masses when the favored members of society have always lived on a dole; even responsible leaders resort to the practices of the witch doctor and vie with one another in predicting the return of prosperity; an ideal of rugged individualism, evolved in a simple pioneering and agrarian order at a time when free land existed in abundance, is used to justify a system which exploits pitilessly and without thought of the morrow the natural and human resources of the nation and of the world. One can only imagine what Jeremiah would say if he could step out of the pages of the Old Testament and cast his eyes over this vast spectacle so full of tragedy and of menace.

The point should be emphasized, however, that the present situation is also freighted with hope and promise. The age is pregnant with possibilities. There lies within our grasp the most humane, the most beautiful, the most majestic civilization ever fashioned by any people. This much at least we know

today. We shall probably know more tomorrow. At last men have achieved such a mastery over the forces of nature that wage slavery can follow chattel slavery and take its place among the relics of the past. No longer are there grounds for the contention that the finer fruits of human culture must be nurtured upon the toil and watered by the tears of the masses. The limits to achievement set by nature have been so extended that we are today bound merely by our ideals, by our power of self-discipline, by our ability to devise social arrangements suited to an industrial age. If we are to place any credence whatsoever in the word of our engineers, the full utilization of modern technology at its present level of development should enable us to produce several times as much goods as were ever produced at the very peak of prosperity, and with the working day, the working year, and the working life reduced by half. We hold within our hands the power to usher in an age of plenty, to make secure the lives of all, and to banish poverty forever from the land. The only cause for doubt or pessimism lies in the question of our ability to rise to the stature of the times in which we live.

Our generation has the good or the ill fortune to live in an age when great decisions must be made. The American people, like most of the other peoples of the Earth, have come to the parting of the ways; they can no longer trust entirely the inspiration which came to them when the Republic was young; they must decide afresh what they are to do with their talents. Favored above all other nations with the resources of nature and the material instrumentalities of civilization, they stand confused and irresolute before the future. They seem to lack the moral quality necessary to quicken, discipline, and give direction to their matchless energies. In a recent paper Professor Dewey has, in my judgment, correctly diagnosed our troubles: "The schools, like the nation," he says, "are in need of a central purpose which will create new enthusiasm and devotion, and which will unify and guide all intellectual plans."

Source: George S. Counts, Dare the Schools Build a New Social Order? New York: Arno Press and the New York Times, 1969, pp. 9–12, 19, 27–29, 31–37.

EDUCATING THE YOUNGEST FOR TOMORROW

Harold Shane and June Grant Shane are well known for their writings on the future. The following selection reflects the reconstructionist belief that the school should be on the "frontiers of social change." Education is viewed as perhaps the only sane way to prepare for the future and to bring about the major changes that are needed if humans are to achieve a civilized future. It also should be noted that this selection is taken from a book edited by Alvin Toffler, the author of the influential work Future Shock (1970). Reconstructionists/futurists, like the Shanes and Toffler, would like to see the future, as a topic of study, brought into schools at all levels of instruction. They promote efforts to change schools to promote more futuristic thinking.

Learning for Tomorrow: The Role of the Future in Education

From earliest times there have been divided opinions as to the purpose of schooling. In somewhat over-simplified terms, the major split has been between persons of conservative persuasion, those who are satisfied to support teaching that will reflect and preserve the status quo, and those who believe that the schools should be outposts on the frontiers of social change. Between these polar positions, of course, there are infinite nuances of opinion.

To accept the idea of a future-oriented education is to enter the ranks of those who believe that education must be an agent of cultural change. It is from this action viewpoint that we explore possible educational developments that promise better to school our children by teaching the future.

Any meaningful approach to conceptions of the future (when working with children of 12 or below) has at least two dimensions: (1) an image of the kind of world to be sought in the future, including the future-focused role-image with which the child identifies himself in this world, and (2) a perspective of the content and the educational conditions or "climate" which (hopefully) will create changes in the individual behavior of boys and girls—changes congruent with the self-image they have of themselves in the future.

Development of an image of a "good" future world implies a number of new teaching methods. Thus, it requires preparation without indoctrination, the extensive use of inquiry as a method of instruc-

tion, and the continuing development of the open-mindedness which is a prerequisite to inquiry. It also involves an understanding of the meaning of "duty" to one's society (as one of many world cultures of comparable respectability), instrumental skills that make one useful to himself and to his fellows, expressive skills that lend meaning to the individual human life, and the will to laugh (with kindness and compassion as needed) at and with a world in which individual humor—and even pleasant irony—have become diminished by the canned "overkill humor" or puerile farce poured out each season by mass media.

A "futurizing" education implies that the learner will begin to sense and to accept both the constraints and the advantages of freedom. Finally, future-directed teaching and learning should emphasize the ineluctable fact that education will increase rather than decrease inequality! To the degree that it personalizes, it will increase inequalities in the ability of different individuals to contribute to society, rather than suppress the differences and, in that way, create dull, egalitarian intellectual **bidonvilles**. (One important qualification must be voiced, however, with respect to education that "increases inequality." Such future-directed learning should **decrease** inequality in the ability of all persons to engage in effective, receptive, and expressive **communication** in their many forms, including the inaudible but eloquent languages of gesture and expression.)

These educational methods and targets are too important to postpone until students reach the secondary level, and, indeed, even to delay until the primary-school years. In an appropriate fashion they can be used with children under the age of three.

The Content of Learning

If one probes beneath the surface of a generalization such as "the school should make extensive use of inquiry as a method of instruction," what does such a phrase really mean when interpreted or applied with young learners? How shall we change the content (what is learned) and the climate (the spirit or tone) of the teaching-learning situations that we endeavor to develop?

Since most schooling up to the 1970s has tended to preserve the traditions of the past and to maintain much of the status quo, one might contend that the best future-oriented education could be based on a reversal of contemporary practice. Such a switch would create or accelerate curriculum trends and changes that carried us

From

Mass teaching

Single learnings

Passive answer-absorbing

Rigid daily programs

Training in formal skills and knowledge

Teacher initiative and direction

Isolated content

Memorized answers

Emphasis on textbooks

Passive mastery of information and so on

To

Personalized teaching

Multiple learnings

Active answer-seeking

Flexible schedules

Building desirable appreciations that stimulate a
    questing for knowledge

Child initiative and group planning

Interrelated content

Problem awareness

Use of many media in addition to texts

Active stimulation of intellect and so on

But to advocate or acquiesce in the mere reversal of present practices in elementary education is both simplistic and likely to build a false sense of success in teaching *for* and *of* the future. What is needed, in addition to many basic 180-degree turns, is a new conception of what constitutes fitting content and of the qualities of a suitable psychoemotional and social climate for learning.

We need a better understanding of the educational experiences that will implant, without numbing indoctrination, a wholesome future-focused self-image in the mind of the child. We also need to conceive of a desirable psychological field and an emotionally stabilizing matrix in which young learners become secure and self-directive in the acceptance and pursuit of a satisfying role-image.

The genuinely important content of instruction eventually resides in a body of skills, knowledge, attitudes, and convictions that govern the learner's behavior after he has forgotten many of the details of the input that he has absorbed through his schooling. What we propose is not a downgrading of such individual content-bred competencies but a closer linkage of the individual to the purposes of his experiencing, and to the acceptance of these purposes because he recognizes and accepts them as relevant to his personal future-focused role-image. . . .

We noted earlier that "teaching the future" was a twofold task. In addition to a reinterpreted approach to content which provides a more suitable role-image for the future with which a child can identify, there is the matter of maintaining a sound, affective milieu for learning: an emotionally wholesome climate that will mediate thinking and behaving in childhood in ways that are consistent with the objectives of education.

Competent teachers long have recognized that there is such a thing as a "good" or "right" setting and tone for learning experiences. Among familiar attributes of such a milieu are encouragement of inquiry, respect for the learner, an atmosphere of freedom, stimulating content, flexible teaching procedures, and so on. The climate of future-focused schooling is especially important because of the need to motivate children to make a sustained effort both to attain a better world of tomorrow and to create a realistic place for themselves in such a world.

This is not to imply that each child should be prepared for his slot in an Orwellian future. Rather, his learning experiences should free him to "create himself" in terms of a viable self-image of the finest, most contributive, joyful person he can become. Patently, a supportive environment that will help children accomplish this delicate task is tremendously important. But what are its characteristics? Here is a brief list of some of the important, often neglected, components of a psychological climate that promise to help free children for cumulative self-realization:

An Affective Approach Is Made to Cognitive Experiences

The learner should feel ready to learn. His attitude, his readiness, rather than a prescriptive curriculum guide or course of study, provide the clues as to the timing, the sequence, and the breadth of what is experienced.

Participation is encouraged. A suitable climate helps prepare the child of 12 and below for future effectiveness by ensuring that he is "in" on things, that his opinions are valued, and that they will govern decisions to whatever degree that they have merit. Confrontation, as a technique of forcing issues, thus becomes needless. Even very young children can develop this understanding. They also can begin to sense that genuine broad-based participation makes it unnecessary to support an elite to think for others in the years ahead.

Pressures for Uniform "Protestant Ethic" Behavior Are Sharply Reduced

At least some Americans have long been persuaded that unpleasant or hard school tasks had disciplinary value. They "helped make a man of you." Long, cold winter walks to school, penalties for being tardy, bell-regulated schedules, busywork that "kept idle hands from becoming the Devil's Workshop," and arduous, drill-type homework were some of the educational expressions of this Protestant Ethic.

Teaching for Maximum Self-Realization as Children Grow Older Will More Clearly Recognize That It Is Unwise to Attempt to Pour Human Individuality into an Eighteenth-Century New England Mold

The future requires flexibility and the power to adapt quickly, rather than an ability to respond to behavioral problems in terms of carefully transmitted, rigid conduct codes. This is not to suggest that elementary education will be without standards, but that the tone of teaching and learning will reflect an appreciation for a number of different values. Respect for human individuality—in recognition of the fact that children best do different things in different ways at different times—implies varied school entrance ages, perhaps different hours spent in learning, certainly a large number of personalized experiences, and new thinking as to the desirable limits of compulsory attendance at the secondary level.

Society Rather Than Child or School Is Held Accountable

Until recently children were held personally accountable for behavior and achievement in school. Punishment and report cards were the agents, respectively, for preserving order and for recording academic performance. In the late 1960s and 1970s there was much talk about the schools being held accountable, especially with respect to measurable academic skills. When teaching for the future, it probably will be desirable to do so in a classroom climate in which the child himself is not the fall guy who is blamed if he learns less than demanded for a "C" or better!

At the same time, there is considerable doubt in our minds as to whether the teacher of the school can be made accountable for formal discipline and uniform academic performance—particularly if an emotionally comfortable atmosphere is sought. Only in a comfortable atmosphere, free of unreasonable or premature academic pressure, can youngsters have experiences that will enable them to move into the future with a positive self-concept and a healthy future-focused role-image. Neither the teacher nor the learner can be held fully accountable. Society, itself, must once again accept some responsibility for the educative experiences of children.

When Tom Sawyer was a lad, virtually all of the adults in his riverfront town on the Mississippi felt responsible for *all* children's progress toward adult maturity. Recall how quickly someone took action or informed Aunt Polly when Tom strayed from the path of rectitude! In a broader, more dynamic sense, the community today needs once again to take on the responsible role it has played in most of mankind's history in being accountable for the next generation.

Source: Harold Shane and June Grant Shane, "Educating the Youngest for Tomorrow," in *Learning for Tomorrow: The Role of the Future in Education,* edited by Alvin Toffler. New York: Random House, 1974, pp. 183–186, 192–194. Reprinted by permission of Curtis Brown, Ltd.

SELECTED READINGS

Brameld, Theodore. *Toward a Reconstructed Philosophy of Education.* New York: Dryden, 1956. One of the most complete statements by a leading reconstructionist. This book explores the development and uses of reconstructionism as a philosophy of education.

Shimahara, Nobuo, ed. *Educational Reconstruction: Promise and Challenge.* Upper Saddle River, NJ: Merrill Publishing Co., 1973. A collection of reconstructionist writings. The book deals with significant educational and social problems and is one of the most complete statements of recent reconstructionist thought.

Stanley, William B. *Curriculum for Utopia: Social Reconstructionism and Critical Pedagogy in the Postmodern Era.* Albany, New York: State University of New York Press, 1992. An overview of the history of reconstructionism and a connection of that tradition with recent developments, including feminist scholarship, neopragmatism, poststructuralism, and critical theory.

Toffler, Alvin. *The Third Wave.* New York: William Morrow and Co., 1980. A leading treatise on futuristics that attempts to explain the dramatic changes that have affected human society. The author focuses on educational changes that he believes will come in the near future.

www.wfs.org (accessed April 5, 2002). Homepage for the World Future Society. Emphasizing social and technological developments that might shape the future, this site provides access to interviews, book reviews, Web forums, and other materials that students might find helpful.

Companion Website

ONLINE RESEARCH

Utilizing some of the Web sites included in this book, as well as Topics 2 and 3 of the Prentice Hall Foundations Web site found at *www.prenhall.com/ozmon,* answer the following questions with a short essay: What are some of the major differences between progressive education and reconstructionism? Why did reconstructionists deem these changes necessary? You can write and submit your essay response to your instructor by using the "Electronic Bluebook" section found in any of the topics of the Prentice Hall Foundations Web site.

6

Behaviorism and Education

Behaviorism generally is not considered a philosophy in the same sense that idealism, realism, pragmatism, and other such thought systems are. It most often is classified as a psychological theory, a more specialized and less comprehensive theory than a systematic philosophy. At the same time, behaviorism has been given increasing attention and acceptance in the field of education—so much so, that in many instances it has extended into areas ordinarily considered the domain of philosophy. These extensions include theoretical considerations dealing with the nature of the human being and society, values, the good life, and speculations or assumptions on the nature of reality.

Perhaps no theory, psychological or otherwise, can escape dealing with philosophical assumptions and implications. For a long time, psychology was thought to be a philosophical study; only in recent times have most psychologists come to think of themselves as scientists. Indeed, the leading proponents of behaviorism do consider themselves scientists, perhaps more justifiably laying claim to that title than proponents of some other schools of psychology. Be that as it may, most psychologists at some point in their endeavors encounter philosophical questions, and much psychological theory rests upon assumptions about human nature that have had a long career in the history of philosophy. Behaviorists, even though they lay claim to an objective scientific orientation, are no less involved with philosophical questions than are other psychological theorists.

This chapter shows some connections of behaviorism with past philosophical systems and how these systems have influenced modern behaviorist theory. It also explores philosophical themes in behaviorism, primarily as these are given in the works of B. F. Skinner. Finally, it considers the educational uses and implications of behaviorism—what might be more appropriately called *behavioral engineering.*

PHILOSOPHICAL BASES OF BEHAVIORISM

Behaviorism has roots in several philosophical traditions. It is related to realism, and the realists' thesis of independent reality resembles the behaviorists' belief that behavior is caused by environmental conditions. Behaviorism also is indebted to materialistic philosophy, such as that promoted by Thomas Hobbes, who held that reality is primarily matter and motion and that all behavioral phenomena can be explained in those terms.

Realism

Behaviorism's connection with realism is primarily with modern realism and its advocacy of science. It has some similarities to classical realism, however. For example, Aristotle thought that humans reached form or essence through the study of particulars, and behaviorists think that people can understand human behavior by a meticulous study of particular behaviors. Indeed, they expand this approach to the effect that human nature (if there be such) can be explained by what traditionally has been considered only a particular aspect of human nature—behavior. In addition, no "internal" reality is hidden from scientific discovery for behaviorists because what is real is external, factual, and observable behavior that can be known.

Thus, one realist element of behaviorism includes going from particular, observable facts (particular behaviors) to "forms," or the laws of behavior. Behaviorists think that the human traits of personality, character, integrity, and so forth are the results of behaving in certain ways. These traits are not internally determined by each individual, but come from behavior patterns developed through environmental conditioning. The emphasis on environment shows another realist leaning toward the importance of the discernible, factual, observable aspects of the universe. In other words, by understanding particular behaviors and how they are caused by environmental circumstances, one can detect the patterns and processes by which behavior comes about. Thus, it is possible, behaviorists maintain, to discern the laws of behavior and thereby come to exercise control over them.

These notions about behavior would be foreign to Aristotle, but it is possible to see similarities between him and behaviorists in at least the basic framework. The connection becomes even more apparent with more recent versions of realism, especially the realism that came about with the advent of modern science. For example, Francis Bacon, in his efforts to develop an inductive scientific method, held that people must reject indubitable dogmas in favor of an inquiry approach that seeks meaning in the facts as one finds them. Behaviorism holds that one should cease accentuating the mind, consciousness, or soul as the causal agents of behavior and look rather to the facts of behavior, or what is observable and capable of empirical verification. This consideration is not only Baconian but also representative of contemporary realism.

The idea of the "laws" of behavior, though having similarities to Aristotelian and Baconian realism, is akin to Alfred North Whitehead's contention that the philosopher should seek out the patterns of reality. Behaviorists do this by seeking the processes and patterns through which behavior is shaped. Once we have sufficient understanding of these, they maintain, it will be possible to engineer more effectively the kinds of people and social conditions society wants.

Materialism

Materialism has its roots in Greek philosophy, but as it exists today, it is essentially a theory developed along with modern science in the sixteenth and seventeenth centuries. *Materialism* is the theory that reality can be explained by the laws of matter and motion. Behaviorism is definitely a kind of materialism because most behaviorists view human beings in terms of their neurological, physiological, and biological contexts. Beliefs about mind, consciousness, and soul, they say, are relics of a prescientific age. Behaviorists seem to be saying that the body is material and that behavior is motion. Thus, humans can be known from the standpoints of matter and motion as Hobbes suggested.

Elements of behaviorism are akin to some aspects of mechanistic materialism. This philosophical perspective also dates back several centuries. For the materialist, human beings are not partially supernatural beings above nature (as some religious persons might hold); rather, they are a part of nature. Even though they are one of the more complex natural organisms, they can be studied and are governed by natural law like any other natural creature.

Thomas Hobbes (1588–1679)

Thomas Hobbes was an exponent of mechanistic materialism. He was acquainted personally with some of the greatest figures of his day, including Descartes, Galileo, and Kepler. He learned a great deal about philosophy and science from these men but was also a first-rate thinker in his own right. Hobbes was a thoroughgoing determinist, and he rejected the elements of self-determination and free will in the thought of Descartes. In most respects, he was more at home with the thinking of Galileo and Kepler. He applied some of their ideas about the physical universe to human beings and social institutions. Life is simply motion, Hobbes held; one can say that a machine has life, albeit artificial. By the same token, an organized society is like a machine: It has an artificial life that has to be maintained. Even biological natural life is mechanistic in the sense that it operates according to its own design.

For Hobbes, an individual's psychological makeup can be explained in mechanistic terms. People experience objects by their qualities (color, odor, texture, and so forth) through sensation. Sensation is physical, what is sensed is quality, and quality is motion. Even imagination, according to Hobbes, is motion. The same can be said for thinking. Therefore, all that truly exists is matter and motion, and all reality can be explained in terms of mathematical precision.

Behaviorism's close affinity with mechanistic materialism is evident in several areas. Materialists and behaviorists believe that people behave in certain ways according to their physical makeup. Bodily functions occur in certain objectively describable and predictable ways. Because of this physical makeup, people are capable of numerous motor responses, and organs and limbs operate according to known physiological processes. The brain, for instance, contains no soul but does contain physiological and neurological materials and processes because chemical and electrical processes make up a large part of the brain's functions. Body-in-situation is significant, however, because human behavior or motion is present. The significant thing to observe is the behavior (motion) of a body in an environment (supporting material conditions). Although this is not precisely what behaviorists say, the similarity to mechanistic materialism is obvious. For behaviorists, human behavior or motion is the significant datum and knowledge of matter is crucial because it helps one understand behavior itself.

Early Behaviorists

Ivan Pavlov (1849–1936)

Ivan Pavlov was an eminent experimental psychologist and physiologist in pre-Soviet Russia. He was noted for his studies of the reflex reaction in humans and animals and devised conditioning experiments. Pavlov found that when a bell is rung each time a dog is fed, the dog is conditioned to associate the sound of the bell with food. Consequently, when the bell is sounded, the dog physiologically anticipates food. Pavlov was the father of conditioning theory and was also a strong opponent, throughout his life, of the Freudian interpretation of neuroses.

Pavlov's conditioning studies show how realism and materialism are related. For a dog, bodily response is not based on something mental going on inside the dog; rather, the response is made on the basis of conditioning, and conditioning can be explained by external circumstances. This idea is at the heart of Pavlov's opposition to Freudianism. It could be argued that Sigmund Freud recognized conditioning by his extensive work on the influence of early childhood and family training. The difference, however, is that Freud claimed that this influence resides in a mentalistic unconscious, an "inner" thing. Pavlov wanted an explanation based on controllable external conditions that require no inner source of action. This search for external causation illustrates the realists' affinity for an independent reality and the materialists' claim that things can be explained in terms of matter and motion.

Contemporary behaviorists hold that Pavlov was headed in the right direction but that his explanations were too simplistic. Pavlov considered only conditioned reflex behavior, whereas contemporary behaviorists use operant conditioning that includes action on the part of the organism being conditioned. The organism can act to change its environment, and the resulting changes reinforce the behavior of the organism in some way. The contemporary view tends more toward a two-way flow, whereas Pavlov showed it only as one way. Nevertheless, his pioneering work was of crucial importance.

John B. Watson (1878–1958)

John Watson repudiated the introspective method in psychology as delusive and unscientific. He relied solely on an observational technique restricted to behavior. He believed that fears are conditioned responses to the environment. In experiments, he conditioned people to be fearful and then deconditioned them. He thought of the environment as the primary shaper of behavior and maintained that if he could control a child's environment, then he could engineer that child into any kind of person desired. Following his work with infants in the maternity ward of Johns Hopkins Hospital in Baltimore, he announced that as far as behaviorists believed, there was nothing within the organism to develop. If one started with a healthy body at birth, he continued, it would be possible through proper behavioral conditioning to make a person "a genius, a cultured gentleman, a rowdy, or a thug." Watson was influential, and the strong movement in American psychology toward behaviorism often is attributed directly to him.

Watson was even more materialistic than preceding behaviorists. He thought that the chief function of the nervous system is simply to coordinate senses with motor responses. Thus, the brain is only a part of the nervous system and not the seat of mind or consciousness or a self-active entity. He thought that the senses not only gain knowledge of the world but also are instruments in guiding activity. In rejecting mentalistic notions of mind and consciousness, Watson also rejected such concepts as purpose, feeling, satisfaction, and free will because they are not observable and therefore not capable of scientific treatment or measurement.

Behaviorism and Positivism

Watson's penchant for giving acceptance only to directly observable things set a pattern for those who came after him. E. L. Thorndike solidly followed Watson's viewpoint when he proclaimed that anything that exists, exists in some quantity capable of being measured. This kind of thinking has been influential in psychology and has parallels in philosophy. One movement that has given a philosophical basis to such positions as Watson's and Thorndike's is known as *positivism.*

Philosophical positivism was initiated by Auguste Comte, often referred to as the founder of modern sociology. His objective was to reform society, and he argued for a positive social science to achieve this end. He thought that by applying scientific principles to social conditions systematically, one would be able to recognize the laws constituting the social order, their evolution, and ways to apply them more systematically. This could be accomplished through discovering the real and exact knowledge of society, and the test of this knowledge would be the extent to which it helps people change the material world and society to more desirable conditions.

Comte divided history into three periods, each characterized by a particular way of thinking. The first is the *theological,* in which things are explained by reference to spirits and gods. The second period is the *metaphysical,* in which events are explained by causes, inner principles, and substances. The third, or *positive* period, is the highest stage, in which one does not attempt to go beyond observable and measurable fact.

Comte influenced subsequent thinkers to use science in devising social policy, and behaviorists follow this tradition. Contemporary behaviorists take seriously Watson's belief that through the use of scientific conditioning, virtually any kind of person can be produced from a reasonably healthy child. Thus, no longer is science simply a concern for scientists, but for social-policy makers, as well. In this view, *social* science is the key to a better society. In some quarters, psychology, sociology, anthropology, and similar disciplines no longer are referred to as the social sciences but as the *behavioral* sciences. This change in terms has occurred because *behavior* is the objective, observable human element susceptible to scientific manipulation.

Whereas earlier positivism was founded on the empirical science of the nineteenth century, contemporary positivists have been more interested in the logic and language of scientific concepts. This was exemplified most by the school of thought called *logical positivism*. Logical positivism dealt with areas familiar to behaviorists and the older positivists, but it is known primarily because of its emphasis on the logic of propositions and the principle of verification. The movement began in the early decades of the twentieth century and was identified with a group of European scholars known as the Vienna Circle. The Circle later dissolved, but one goal of logical positivists was to develop a consistent set of logical or linguistic phrasings and structures. This effort came about to rectify the language difficulties encountered in scientific investigation because investigation often can be sidetracked or misled by confusions caused by the words and statements used.

Suppose one is scientifically studying an educational problem and the problem is involved largely with self-concept or self-esteem. What if one cannot discover that such a thing as "self" exists in any measurable quantity? Then what one needs to do is examine what one means by the term *self*. This word is so colored by prescientific and metaphysical considerations that its usage is vague, much like the terms *mind*, *consciousness*, or the theological *soul*. To be truly scientific, an objective statement is needed of the problem in such terms that an objective resolution can be made. In other words, one must specify clearly what one is talking about.

The connection of this philosophical school of thought with behaviorism is that behaviorists seek a language framework that more accurately reflects the facts of behavior. Rather than use the word *self* to signify personal identity or the characteristics of an individual, behaviorists speak of "conditioned" or "reinforced behavior," "repertoire of behavioral responses," or perhaps "operant conditioning" in regard to the specific organism one might call Jane Jones. For behaviorists, self or self-concept is tied too much to mentalistic constructs, and the danger exists of being misled in the direction of imputing certain mysterious, internal, driving forces to Jane Jones to explain her behavior.

Logical positivists are sensitive to the fallacies that the wrong uses of language can foster. What one should do, they maintain, is make meaningful statements conveying information regarding the observable, verifiable facts of the situation. In the context of behaviorism and logical positivism, it is one thing to make a statement such as "There are matches in this box" and quite another thing to state, "There is a self-concept in Jane Jones." It is easy to verify whether matches are in the box by opening the box and examining it. Matches are either in there or they are not. However, one cannot open Jane Jones and find a self. It is possible, however, to observe Jane Jones's behavior to see what stimulates her to behave as she does.

The behaviorist maintains that because so little is known about behavior, people wrongly impute meaning to behavior by reference to an "inner being," a self, mind, consciousness, soul, or some such hidden entity that causes the behavior. Even the most meticulous and rigorous scientific experiments have not been able to locate this inner being. Behaviorists and logical positivists alike would agree with the British philosopher Gilbert Ryle that traditional meanings of mind really imply a "ghost in the machine" (or a mind in the body).

Coupled with their concern for more linguistic precision, logical positivists also have championed what is called the *principle of verifiability*. This principle means that no statement should be taken as truthful unless it can be verified empirically or at least until it is capable of being verified. For example, a statement about elves is not verifiable in any scientific way, nor can it be verified at some future date because of the nature of the statement itself. Even those who believe in elves do not maintain that elves can be verified by science. Such a statement as "Intelligent life exists in outer space," however, might not be amenable to verification immediately, but it is within our technical capacity to verify that statement in the future. Thus, logical positivists try to discourage nonsense statements and promote language and thought that are more controllable and rigorous. The behaviorist, mindful about careless linguistic and logical statements, also seeks to avoid such mistakes. Behaviorists maintain that observable, factual behavior and environmental conditions do exist, and they must be described in objective, logical, and accurate terms.

PHILOSOPHICAL ASPECTS OF BEHAVIORISM

B. F. Skinner (1904–1990)

Burrhus Frederic Skinner was born in Susquehanna, Pennsylvania. He studied at Hamilton College and Harvard University, and later taught at the University of Minnesota and at Indiana University before returning to Harvard as a professor of psychology. He sometimes is called the high priest of behaviorism. Others more sympathetically refer to him as one of the most important twentieth-century psychologists. Skinner's work and influence certainly have caught people's attention and comment, even though opinions have ranged from bitter criticism to disciple-like emulation.

Skinner himself often debunked philosophical approaches to psychology. He thought, on the one hand, that much error and misunderstanding have come about because philosophers have tried to deduce an understanding of human beings from *a priori* generalizations. (In other words, they have been "armchair scientists" content with introspection.) He claimed, on the other hand, to base his findings on observations and controlled scientific experiments. Yet, he often found it necessary to make statements about such traditional philosophical topics as human nature and the good society. In fact, Skinner was not the sterile scientist in the laboratory; he was also a dreamer and a utopian. Thus, it is possible to discern a strong element of social radicalism in his writing.

Human Nature. Traditionally, the study of human nature has been an important aspect of philosophical endeavor. It has been central to the metaphysics of many great philosophers and influential in the philosophical treatment of ethics. Skinner maintained that less philosophical speculation and more "realistic" observation of behavior are necessary, but he still posed the question "What is man?"

In *Beyond Freedom and Dignity*, Skinner attacked what he called traditional views of humanity. Those views have imputed all kinds of internal drives, forces, or otherwise mysterious actions to the "autonomous person"—such forces as aggression, industry, attention, knowing, and perceiving. Traditionally, such capacities were assumed to be there somewhere, hidden from direct scrutiny, and were said to make up (at least in part) the essence of human nature. Skinner, in contrast, maintained that aggression, for example, is not inherent in human nature in the sense that people will harm or damage others automatically. It makes more sense to say that people behave in an aggressive manner because that behavior is reinforced by particular environmental contingencies. For Skinner, the contingencies of reinforcement themselves explain the aggressive behavior apart from some assumed internal or genetic force within people.

As an example, in wartime, some persons commit acts that are called depraved. During the Vietnam War, some American soldiers indiscriminately killed noncombatant women and children. When one such event was made known in America, it raised outcries of disbelief and horror. In searching for explanations, some observers said that these actions indicated an inherent evil in human nature. A widely publicized court martial was held, and an officer was found guilty of having participated in the massacre. From a Skinnerian point of view, one could say that however deplorable the behavior, finding a guilty culprit and punishing him does not get at the real problem (what conditions caused the problem). Punishment might seem to extinguish such behavior, but it is usually ineffective and counterproductive in the long run because it does not attack the root of the problem.

Does a soldier under combat conditions kill others because he is basically evil? Or does it make more sense to observe his behavior in terms of the environmental contingencies and the reinforcement of particular aggressive behaviors under those conditions? Although not all soldiers kill noncombatant civilians, it also seems likely that civilians would not have been killed by soldiers if there had been no war, no warlike behaviors, and no existing environmental conditions that would make warlike behavior rewarding. The evil lies in making war, training people to kill, and maintaining and securing conditions that make such behavior rewarding—not in some innate evil within people.

Skinner said that the traditional view sees an autonomous individual who, in perceiving the world, reaches out or acts on that world to know it, to "take it in," and to "grasp it." The implication is that the action and the initiative come from the autonomous person, but Skinner maintained that the reverse is the case. Knowing is really a case of the environment acting on people. We perceive and know to the extent that they respond to stimuli from environmental contingencies. For instance, one might respond to heat, light, colors, and so forth according to the arrangement of contingencies. As Skinner put it, we move into or out of sunlight, depending on how hot or cold it is. Thus, one comes to know sunlight, heat, and cold. Sunlight also figures in how time is arranged, schedules are set, and certain activities are performed. Knowledge of the sun, heat, and light is expanded to the extent that people behave in relation to these environmental conditions and are reinforced by that behavior. Too often, people think that knowing is a cognitive process, but it is behavioral and environmental, neurological, and even physiological.

Some critics say that behaviorism cannot deal with individual consciousness—with an awareness of oneself. They insist on an "inner realm" that the behaviorist ignores. Perhaps Skinner's best-known critic on this issue was Carl Rogers, another psychologist who approached his work philosophically. Rogers maintained that the "inner realm" of individuals is real—a reality characterized by freedom. He agreed that humans are conditioned by outside factors and that they respond to external stimuli, but Rogers thought that Skinner did not explain how free and responsible choice can be exercised in the way a person responds to external conditions. An individual does not have to respond to a stimulus in a preestablished and set way but can examine the alternatives or even create new ones. In other words, an individual can choose a direction, be responsible in pursuing it, and give commitment to sustaining it. This, Rogers argued, shows that the person has freedom of choice and freedom of responsible commitment, and this freedom springs from the inside. Freedom is a subjective, inner thing. Skinner said that this charge is serious and cannot be lightly passed over. At stake, however, is what an individual knows when doing this self-analysis. For Skinner, what one knows in this respect is difficult to comprehend because it is largely a matter of responding to the natural contingencies of individual circumstances. People respond to their own internal stimuli (without much awareness), as in such behavior as walking, jumping, and running. To the extent that one *knows* these behaviors and their causes, one must do more than merely respond to them. This kind of knowing involves systematic study beyond a mere internal soliloquy and would include knowledge of bodily functions, environmental conditions, and contingencies.

Knowing one's desires, beliefs, and feelings—the things usually thought to be most private—is even more difficult because many people lack the necessary verbal tools to accomplish this. Without some form of verbalization, behavior is largely unconscious. Skinner maintained that consciousness in the verbal awareness sense is a social product and not within the range of a solitary individual. Really knowing this inner realm is difficult because people have not developed appropriate words for it. We are too prone to rest the case on our conviction of an inner or autonomous person. We have not effectively uncovered the contingencies of reinforcement to describe this personal awareness.

Skinner did not deny that some personal awareness might be involved in human efforts to know, but he did affirm that *what* people know would be essentially the objects and conditions of the external world. That is, the *what* or content of the knowledge will be that which is observable. In Skinnerian terminology, that content will be knowledge of behavior and contingencies of reinforcement, and not the old catchall of a mind, soul, consciousness, or an "inner man."

Skinner's reply to the charges of his critics that he was destroying or abolishing what is known as humanity was that a scientific analysis in no way destroys this because no theory destroys the objective conditions it attempts to describe. What can be truly destructive is actual human behavior, not a theory. Skinner put it this way: "What is being abolished is autonomous man—the inner man, the *homunculus*, the possessing demon, the man defended by the literature of freedom and dignity." What is left is the real, observable human organism who is biological and animal. Although Skinner maintained that humans are not machines in the classic sense, he held that we are machinelike in the sense that we are a complex system behaving in lawful, observable ways. Even if humans are simply animal and mechanical, Skinner was fascinated by our complexity, our uniqueness, and our intricacy.

Perhaps the most accurate description of Skinner's view is that we are both controller and controlled. In a real sense, we humans are our own makers. It is Skinner's position that people have developed through two processes of evolution; one is the biological process from which we evolved, and the other is the cultural process of evolution that people have largely created. This latter process was more important and intriguing for Skinner. He pointed out that the environment is largely contrived, not natural, and that it is a condition humans have wrought; the environment people live in contains the significant contingencies of reinforcement that make one human.

The Good Society Through Cultural Design.   Skinner was paradoxical. On the one hand, he appeared to be a hard-nosed scientist, dealing only with factual, observable behavior. On the other hand, he seemed to be a utopian dreamer. Perhaps the best statement of Skinner's utopian ideals is expressed in his work *Walden Two*, a fictional account of a futuristic social experiment. This book became the impetus for a community called Twin Oaks, which was founded in Louisa County, Virginia in 1967. At Twin Oaks, children are educated in a modified Skinnerian approach. Skinner visited Twin Oaks and was impressed with what members were doing to make *Walden Two* a reality. He also realized that they had to make modifications to his proposals in order to adapt to the necessities of everyday life.

In *Beyond Freedom and Dignity*, however, Skinner gave a nonfictional descriptive account of his views. Accordingly, the important thing is the social environment. It could even be said that for Skinner, social environment *is* culture. This position is in opposition to those who say that culture is essentially ideas or values apart from human behavior. For Skinner, behavior carries the ideas and values of a culture, and it transforms, alters, and changes a culture. In a large sense, cultural evolution is an evolution of behavioral practices that are established within a social milieu or a milieu of contingencies of reinforcement. So it could be said that in cultural evolution, what evolves are practices set in a social context.

Skinner makes a strong case for controlled cultural evolution. In the past, people had a confused sort of control—often as not, blind and accidental. The nature of the control or how it could be more effectively used was not fully understood. Skinner maintained that controls are needed to make us more sensitive to the consequences of their behavior. Reinforcement follows behavior; it does not precede it (even though most human behavior is conditioned by previous reinforcement). Behavior develops in directions that are positively reinforced; consequently, people should be controlling, devising, or using contingencies that reinforce desired behaviors. In short, control lies at the crux of sensitivity to the consequences of human behavior.

Skinner admitted that we do not know the *best way* to rear children, to educate effective citizens, or to build the good society; he did maintain that *better* ways than we now have could be developed. To change culture or individuals, behavior must be changed, and the way to change behavior is to change the contingencies of reinforcement (culture or social environment).

What are *contingencies of reinforcement*? Simply put, contingencies are the conditions in which behavior occurs; they reinforce it and influence the future direction and quality of behavior. For example, one cannot drive an automobile unless an automobile exists. The behavior of automobile driving is contingent upon an actual automobile. Furthermore, the way we drive is contingent upon numerous other conditions, such as the functions and capacities of that particular automobile, road and traffic conditions, and a host of other supporting conditions. Finally, driving an automobile does things for people. It gets them to a desired destination, helps them earn a living, and increases their range of mobility. What an automobile does is rewarding, so human behavior of driving automobiles is reinforced. Some of these conditions serve as particularly strong contingencies. Much of the trouble with the operation of motor vehicles, such as speeding, comes about because of a lack of understanding and control of the contingencies.

Skinner stated that contingencies of reinforcement are difficult to discern in many instances. For one thing, we are not used to viewing human situations in behavioral terms (or else we fail to recognize the behavioral point of view). For another, human understanding is at least hampered, if not misled, by holding to such notions as the autonomous individual. People have not developed sensitivity to the *conditions,* the contingencies, in and with which behavior occurs. However, Skinner maintained that contingencies are accessible (even if with difficulty), and as we progressively come to understand the relationship between behavior and environment, we will discover new ways of controlling behavior. It is possible, as further understanding is developed, to design and control not just isolated behaviors and their contingencies but a whole culture.

Skinner viewed the educational process as one chief way of designing a culture, and his attention also was directed at numerous other institutions. He believed that positive reinforcement could induce people to begin to alter and control schools and other institutions. Behavior is shaped in the direction of reward; that is, behavior is reinforced to the extent that its consequences are good or bad. Good consequences are positive reinforcement, and bad consequences are aversive reinforcement. A problem arises in that humanity is too often ignorant of long-range consequences. Immediate positive reinforcement might have negative effects later. It is important to examine cultural contingencies critically in light of likely consequences.

The critical analysis of culture is not to be taken lightly. It is easier to proceed piecemeal because planning and foresight of consequences are simplified. Thus, it is easier to change particular teaching practices than a whole educational establishment, and it is easier to change one institution than a whole culture. For Skinner, the greatest mistake is to stop trying.

The big questions, however, are "What is the good society?" "How do we get it?" "Who is to say what is good?" and "Who controls the good society?" Such questions have been stumbling blocks to social or cultural reconstruction throughout history. Recently, these questions have been considered to be outside the realm of science. As the claim goes, science deals with what is, whereas questions about a good society deal with what should or ought to be. Such questions involve value judgments and not matters of fact. This would seem to rule out any part for the behavioral scientist or other scientists.

On the contrary, Skinner rejected the claim that value judgments are more remote from scientists than from other human beings. He posed this question as a more suitable one: "If a scientific analysis can tell us how to change behavior, can it tell us what changes to make?" To Skinner, this is a question about the behavior of those who advocate and promote changes. In other words, people act to effect changes for reasons, and among these reasons are behavioral consequences. To say that we would like a culture in which making war is absent is to say that we would like to eradicate war-making behavior. Whatever the behavioral consequences considered in efforts to effect change, these consequences include things that people call *good* or valuable. Thus, one can see that for Skinner, the good society and values are within the domain of the behavioral scientist precisely because those goods and values are involved in behavior, even based in it and coming out of it.

As a behavioral scientist, Skinner might have been solidly involved with values and the good, but it makes just as much sense to say that he also was behaving like a philosopher and dealing with philosophical issues. Critics might quibble over what label should be applied to Skinner, but he did concern himself with values and the good, and these are woven intricately into his views of achieving a better culture or social environment.

What, then, is good and of value from the Skinnerian standpoint? Simply put, to classify something as "good" is to classify it as a positive reinforcer. Certain foods are good because they give positive reinforcement (they are pleasing, delicious, palatable, healthful, and so forth), and people tend to seek out and eat good food. By the same token, some foods are bad because they do not taste good, are unhealthful, and are undesirable, so people avoid them. However, tastes vary, and what is positively reinforcing to one might be aversive to another. This applies in many areas, such as things that feel good or bad, look good or bad, sound good or bad, and so on. Skinner called these goods "personal goods."

Other goods can be considered, those that Skinner called "goods of others," and they refer to more social-like behaviors even though they also might flow from personal goods. Most societies have found rampant dishonesty to be aversively reinforcing. Although some people find dishonest behavior to be rewarding, society has instituted measures to control behavior to the extent that certain kinds of dishonesty are met with punitive (or aversive) measures, whereas honesty is praised and rewarded. Even among criminals, honesty with one's colleagues might be highly prized, and dishonesty might be rewarded only when it is conducted against an outsider or enemy.

Skinner called another kind of good "the good of culture." This good induces the members of a culture to work for the survival and enhancement of that culture.

Generally, such goods might have dim cultural and genetic roots. It is not always clear why we work to support our culture or to change it for what is deemed a better state of affairs. As Skinner pointed out, people are faced with so many enormous problems today that immediate changes are needed just for survival. People are confronted with warfare, overpopulation, starvation, and environmental pollution, all of which, if allowed to run rampant, can mean disaster.

Change does not occur simply because of the passage of time but because of what *occurs* while time passes. Thus, we are thrown back to behavior. All change is not necessarily good and valuable, and neither is all behavior. However, directed and intended change depends on people's awareness of their behavior and its consequences. One could phrase the behavioral context of the goods of culture in this way: If people are reinforced by human survival, and if human survival depends on the cultural and physical environment in which people exist, then they will work for human survival by designing culture to that end. Skinner seems to say that there is little choice. We must act.

What, then, is good? Good is that which is positively reinforcing in terms of personal, social, and cultural survival contexts. What is of value? Value is that which has desired reinforcing effects. The good society is one that gives personal satisfaction, supports social interaction, and furthers our survival. The good society is valuable, and the way to achieve it is through the proper design of the culture—that is, through the proper arrangement and development of the contingencies of reinforcement.

Skinner maintained that people need a sophisticated science and technology of human behavior. Although such a development would be morally neutral and could be misused and abused, he believed that it has a definite survival value. The survival value will not ensure against abuse, but he thought that survival would go a long way in aiding desirable usage. When one surveys the plight of the modern world and the brink on which humans often totter, one might be strongly inclined to agree with Skinner.

BEHAVIORISM AS A PHILOSOPHY OF EDUCATION

The principles of behaviorism and the techniques of behavioral engineering go back at least to Pavlov and Watson, but Skinner pioneered their implementation in many fields of contemporary life. Skinner saw behaviorism extending into politics, economics, and other social organizations. He strongly championed it as an educational method that is more practical and produces greater results than any other.

Aims of Education

Although many people disapprove of the concept of behavioral engineering, it has increasingly become part of the educational process. One might even argue that conditioning has always gone on in education although it has not been labeled as such. Teachers have conditioned students to sit up straight and to be quiet through looks, grades, and physical punishment. When students are emotionally disturbed, conditioning is one way to develop a step-by-step program through rewards (or punishment) so that they are led to achieve complex patterns of behavior. At some institutions for people with emotional disabilities, students can earn tokens and use them to buy things: a drink, playtime, or even time away from the institution. Students might acquire tokens in diverse ways. They could obtain them for staying in their seats, for doing a certain amount of required work, or for approved social behavior. Critics often consider it undesirable for children to be rewarded extrinsically for every action, but Skinner responded by saying that extrinsic rewards are necessary when other methods do not work or do not work as well, and they should be replaced by more intrinsic rewards at a later date.

Behaviorists consider the child to be an organism who already is highly programmed before coming to school. This programming is accomplished by—among other influences—parents, peers, siblings, and television. Some programming might have been bad, but the child has been receptive to it and has absorbed a lot of it. Skinner believed that one reason why people have trouble making moral decisions is that the programming they have received on morality has been contradictory. Parents, for example, often say one thing and do another.

Skinner wanted to replace the erratic and haphazard conditioning that most people receive with something systematic and meaningful. To do this, some kind of agreement about what is meaningful and important (toward which children ought to be conditioned) must be reached. This point raises a storm of controversy because it indicates that some people will decide how other people will be conditioned. Skinner maintained that one obligation of adults, and particularly of educators, is to make educational decisions and then to use whatever methods are available (conditioning being the best) to achieve them. He believed that people should try to create a world of peace and justice, and if conditioning can help, then it should be used.

It is easy to see that the way children are being conditioned in school is unsatisfactory. Either the teacher does not condition systematically or reinforcement does not follow immediately. Skinner wanted teachers to see that what they are doing generally involves some kind of conditioning; hence, they should learn how to do it more effectively.

Many people see education and conditioning as two different things. Education presumably represents a free mind being exposed to ideas that one can look at critically and accept or not accept, whereas conditioning is seen to represent the implementation of certain specific ideas in the student's mind with or without the student's critical consent. Skinner, however, drew no distinction between education and conditioning. He did not believe that the mind is free to begin with. Whatever kinds of critical judgments or acceptance of ideas students make already are predicated on ideas with which they have been conditioned previously.

Because so much of today's education involves rote or memory learning, Skinner believed that computers also have a useful part to play. Usually, the programs prepared for computers have been structured in ways that provide for more systematic learning, and they provide the kinds of immediate reinforcement that Skinner believed is lacking in education. Computer programs can take different forms, but they all are based on the theory that the kinds of responses one wants should be rewarded and it should be done immediately.

Behavioral engineering, one might argue, has been based primarily on experiments with laboratory animals. Some claim that Skinner's experiments with animals are inapplicable to humans and to human education, but Skinner argued that the human being is an animal, though highly developed, and that the difference between humans and other animals is of degree and not of kind.

The primary aim of behaviorist techniques is to change behavior and point it in more desirable directions. The question of whether one should go in a special direction is raised immediately: Who decides what changes and what direction? Skinner replied that people already are controlled by environmental forces such as parental upbringing, schooling, peer groups, media, church, and society. He argued that the question of control is not a good one; that is, we might feel free and even be relatively free, but we always are controlled by something—although we might assist in the control that is exercised over us, such as accepting good habits of punctuality and cleanliness. Thus, Skinner does away with the concept of innate freedom by saying that people always have been controlled although we have not always been aware of the control and the direction in which it leads.

One thing primarily wrong with control is not that it always has existed but that it has been random and without any real direction. People have been controlled by politicians for their own ends and purposes and by business interests for their own profits, but such controls have been directed toward base ends and, unfortunately, in ways that adversely affected those on the receiving end of the controls. Skinner advocated what he believed were controls for good ends, and he thought that a new society can be shaped through control. This means that someone must be in charge to make sure the control is exercised efficiently toward the highest aims that can be established. Currently, many kinds of control are possible, but they are directed toward consumerism, superstition, and greed. Skinner pointed out that people have been talking for years about a world devoted to peace, kinship, and freedom, and that now, for the first time, people have in their hands a method for bringing about such things. Not to use control for such high purposes would be immoral.

Skinner was a strong advocate of education, although many critics argue that what he meant by education is not education but training. Skinner charged that much of what passes for education is not good education because it is not reinforcing, does not properly motivate students to progress, and does not deal with immediate reinforcement. When students take a spelling test, for example, they are interested in knowing what responses are right or wrong at the time of the test. When the test is returned to them a week later, they usually have lost interest. Skinner maintained that children should know immediately when they are right or wrong and that this is why he has championed such methods of immediate reinforcement as programmed learning.

Although many behaviorists use positive and negative methods of reinforcing behavior, Skinner advocated positive reinforcement. Aversive (or negative) reinforcement, though it might be effective, often has many bad side effects. The same results can be achieved through rewarding good behavior rather than punishing bad behavior. For example, in experiments to train pigeons to perform certain activities, the pigeons are rewarded with food when they peck the proper square. Such behavior can be discontinued simply by stopping the reward. The behavior may continue for a short time after it is no longer rewarded, but eventually it will cease. Some behaviorists would punish the pigeon with shocks or similar devices, but Skinner maintained that the most effective procedure is to withdraw reward. It could be argued that depriving the organism of reward for a particular task is punishment. In most situations, Skinner would disagree: It is simply a matter of ceasing to reward a specific behavior.

Many people argue that the aim of behavioral engineering is to turn out robots—people who are at the beck and call of others who control them. Skinner countered that this is not true; in looking around at the current world, one finds that most people are controlled by forces of which they are not conscious. He believed that people today live in a world where advanced technology in conditioning can be used to improve human life if used in the right way. *Walden Two* shows a world where technology is used to make people better, more humane, creative, and even more individualistic. Skinner did not believe that individuality could exist apart from social development. The title *Walden Two* is drawn from Henry David Thoreau's *Walden Pond*, which describes Thoreau's sojourn in the woods where he was "a majority of one" who lived a life entirely of his own choosing. Most people today would probably believe such Walden-like schemes to be rather romantic notions, and even may view Skinner's efforts in the same ways. A major difference, however, is that Skinner was attempting to show what technology can do when it is used wisely.

In *Walden Two*, the only unhappy person is Frazier, who is the conditioner of others. He is aware that he is in control, and whatever decisions he makes involve numerous conflicts. Skinner pointed out that one who is conditioned might not assent to or be aware of being conditioned. Humans are all conditioned anyway, consciously or unconsciously, and could even assist in their own conditioning. People do this when they reward themselves for doing something right and punish themselves for doing something wrong. The development of personal habits depends largely on conditioning techniques that people themselves use.

Methods and Curriculum

According to the behaviorist, teachers have many rewards or reinforcers at their disposal, including praise, a smile, a touch, stars, or candies. In some schools, paper money or tokens are used as reinforcing mechanisms. Many people have questioned the use of such extrinsic rewards, but behaviorists claim that they are only to be used in place of intrinsic ones that should be encouraged later. Studies indicate that rewards need not be given every time, for they also can be effective on an intermittent basis. One example is a situation in which a child would be called on three successive times to spell words but then would not be called upon again. The child will raise a hand to answer the first question and answer it correctly. This is repeated for the second spelling word and the third. She is not to be called on again, however. The child might continue to raise her hand several more times without being called on, but if she is not called on again, the hand-raising gradually will diminish. If the same child were called on only occasionally, one probably could get as strong a response as if she were called on every time, because Skinner thought that intermittent reward is as strong or stronger than continual successive rewards. Skinner believed that this is why gamblers, or perhaps people who fish, are so ardent in their activities (because they receive intermittent reinforcement).

One might describe briefly a procedure for behavior modification in the ordinary classroom as follows: (1) Specify the desired outcome, what needs to be changed, and how it will be evaluated; (2) establish a favorable environment by removing unfavorable stimuli that might complicate learning; (3) choose the proper reinforcers for desired behavioral manifestations; (4) begin shaping desired behavior by using immediate reinforcers for desired behavior; (5) once a pattern of desired behaviors has begun, slacken the number of times reinforcers are given; and (6) evaluate results and reassess for future development.

Suppose, for example, that a student runs in the hallways, endangering other students and himself. For safety, the teacher wants to modify the behavior so that running ceases; the objective will be achieved when the student stops running. Investigation shows that the student runs partly because he must go all the way to the other end of the building for his next class and fears that the time for class change is too short. Also, he seems to like to run. The teacher works to get the student's class time shortened so that he can be excused earlier. The teacher begins to compliment the student when he does not run, and the student's classmates are less hostile toward him because he is not bumping and jostling them constantly in the hall. Because the student gets more positive reinforcement from his peers, the teacher finds it less necessary to compliment him. In addition, the student finds that he can make it to class on time if he does not dawdle, even without extra time. Finally, because he now finds walking more rewarding than running, extrinsic reinforcers no longer are needed or can be reduced.

Evaluation by the teacher shows that the desired behavior has been fairly well achieved and that it eventually may be possible to stop all external reinforcers. This does not mean that the teacher loses interest in the problem; he should check periodically to see whether the student's desired behavior is being continued. One also might observe that this approach has reinforced the teacher's behavior. The positive success reinforces the teacher to use this technique in similar instances.

Skinner thought that one of the most effective kinds of instruction might be accomplished through the use of what he called teaching machines (or in today's terms, personal computers). He often is referred to as the "father of the teaching machine" and did significant research in this area. One type of program might ask, "Who was the first president of the United States?" Students type in their answer in the proper space, and their answer appears on the screen when they click a button. If they answer correctly, they are rewarded by the program, which reinforces them to remember the answer.

The questions in such a program are interrelated and usually arranged in sequences of increasing complexity. Skinner thought that learning should take place in small steps and that succeeding questions should have some relationship to the preceding ones. He preferred that students have nothing but success. They should simply go on if they miss a question or two. If they miss too many questions, then they probably do not belong on that particular program. Some early teaching machines rewarded the children with candy or spoke to them, but recent studies indicate that getting the right answer is often reward enough.

Other more sophisticated programs are designed primarily for adults. One program might have extensive material that the student can read. After reading, the student is asked to choose one of several possible answers. If the correct answer is chosen, the student goes on to the next screen. If the wrong answer is chosen, however, two contrasting views exist about what should happen. Skinner thought that to make the student repeat the material is too much punishment and that if one misses the answer, the program still should go on to the next screen. Other behaviorists, such as S. J. Pressey, maintain that repeating the material is not too aversive and that the student should get the right answer before moving to the next screen. Some programs make this process as painless as possible, and if the student clicks the wrong button, then the program will go to a screen that tells why the answer was wrong and then refer back to the material to be reread.

Some early teaching machines were also "branching" machines; that is, they contained programs for average, slow, and bright students. A student who completed exercises one through ten without making a mistake might be able to skip the next ten lessons because they were repetitious. A student who made a single mistake would have to do the next ten, and one who made two mistakes would be referred to a remedial program before beginning at Lesson 1 again.

According to behaviorists, the advantages of programmed learning are many: Immediate reinforcement is given, the programmed material is written by competent people, and the learning takes place in many small steps so that the student can avoid making mistakes. One major objection to programmed learning is that although it might be good in teaching factual material, it cannot teach material of a more conceptual or creative nature. Skinner disputed this and claimed that programs can be developed to teach complicated ideas as well as programs that provide reinforcement every time a child gives what is considered a more creative answer.

For behaviorists, the curriculum should be organized into small, discrete units that can be managed easily and for which simple and straightforward learning objectives can be readily devised and assessed. For example, history should be taught not as some grand and encompassing story, but in small, easily managed units. The same would be true for the sciences, wherein small units are constructed and subject matter is arranged so that it can be learned successfully without complicating side issues coming into the picture. The "big picture" should emerge after successful completion of these small units. One thing stands out in the behaviorist curriculum: Objectives must be stated in behavioral terms, and not only for the subject matter to be learned. In other words, whatever the subject being studied, the objective outcomes of learning will be observable or measurable behavior, either as behavioral change or as reinforced behavior that is deemed desirable. Behaviorists believe that their view of curriculum is a more scientific one: It is highly structured, it is based on tested evidence, and its results can be measured and verified. In this regard, behaviorists reflect some leading characteristics of realism and positivism.

Behavioral engineering has many implications for modern education but raises many troubling philosophical questions regarding control and democratic procedures.

Its application and apparent effectiveness make it an important concern in the educational process. Nothing seems to bring out more ire among educators than a discussion of behavioral engineering as applied to education. Skinner was always interested in education, wrote about it, spoke to educational groups, and did pioneering work in the field.

Skinner's views about education must be seen as an integral part of his overall views concerning the individual and society. He believed that education must be seen not simply as giving people information but as a controlling influence over people's lives. Many have related Skinner's ideas to those of Aldous Huxley *(Brave New World)*, George Orwell *(1984)*, and Anthony Burgess *(Clockwork Orange)*. Although Skinner maintained that his ideas about conditioning are different and more humanitarian, he did not deny that the forces for control (as discussed by Huxley, Orwell, and Burgess) could exist.

Today, wide varieties of behavioral techniques are already in use. All of these methods rest essentially on a particular theory: People first determine the kind of behavior they want, and then they get it repeated by reinforcing it through various rewards. Some educators seriously question the use of rewards, but behavioral engineers argue that rewards are to be used sparingly and only to the point where students learn to reward themselves without outside tangible rewards. Tangible rewards are used often with students in special education, for example, who are rewarded for desired behavior and work. Carl Bereiter and Siegfried Engelmann used behavioral techniques with students who had poor learning abilities. Other psychologists have used such techniques for purposes as diverse as toilet training and piloting aircraft. The essential thing about any of these techniques, however, is that whatever reward is used should be systematic and immediate. Skinner and others believe that a primary problem with most education at present is a lack of immediate reinforcement.

In recent years, a shift has occurred away from mechanistic, passive models of behavior modification toward ones that emphasize self-management and the active role of participants in shaping their own behavior. Earlier Watsonian or Skinnerian models used a "person as machine" approach in which manipulation of the environment was the critical factor. Today, many behaviorists are concentrating on the environment–organism interplay in which organisms contribute to their own learning. This can be done, in part, by helping people become better problem solvers and analysts of their own condition.

What this shift points to is that many behaviorists now concentrate on "processes in the head"—that is, people's belief systems, thinking, and self-control. Individuals can be induced to study their own behavior, detect elements of danger, and take appropriate steps to prevent negative actions from taking place or at least to mitigate their effects. This approach might well remind one of Kant's notion of the mind as an active agent in the transformation of ideas. Thus, many behaviorists now study the philosophical question of how people think and how thinking in turn shapes behavior.

Today, some people promote a behavioral approach toward changing individual personality through shaping behavior with biofeedback. Biofeedback techniques can be used to change such behaviors as smoking and to relieve such physical ailments as headaches, insomnia, and high blood pressure. This approach uses medical monitoring devices along with meditation and exercise. The primary purpose of biofeedback is to put the body back into harmony with the environment.

This more recent approach to behavior modification is characterized by an emphasis on the inner person. *Cognitive theory* stresses the human qualities in people and says that people can change their lives through their own thinking, creativity, and willpower. Many destructive and upsetting emotions and behaviors are caused by what people believe about themselves. A mentally healthy person is one who has an accurate perception of things and who can act intelligently on the basis of such perceptions.

Those who promote a cognitive approach insist that it is a more humanistic method because it looks at the individual, not as a passive mechanism to be manipulated by the environment, but as a consciously aware being. Individual existence can be shaped by the power of one's own thinking and thus not be controlled solely by external forces or unconscious drives. Individuals can shape their own destinies and improve and create themselves through their own power using behavioral techniques. In using this power, behaviorists believe people best express what it is to be human.

Role of the Teacher

All teachers use behavioral techniques of one kind or another in their classrooms. This is true even if they are not aware of this fact. Teachers condition students through grades, their attitudes toward them, gestures, and in a thousand other ways. Such conditioning is often unconscious and unreflective; however, behaviorists see this kind of conditioning as too random and counterproductive because one kind of conditioning may wipe out another. For example, a teacher might reward a particular behavior on Monday but because of other outside variables, fail to reward it on Tuesday or Wednesday. Also, the teacher may fail to reward an appropriate behavior in a timely manner. This often happens in a school where one teacher might reward a particular behavior but another teacher might not.

Skinner and other behaviorists would like to see some consensus among educators as to the kinds of behavior they would like to see reinforced and then use proven methods of conditioning to achieve such behaviors. This means that teachers must work together and agree on goals and methodology. It also means that teachers not only will reward good behavior uniformly but also will not reward undesirable behavior uniformly. Although this technique sounds authoritarian in nature, it is probably true that most teachers already agree on the kinds of behavior they would like to see repeated: students studying more, doing their homework, being on time for class, and so forth. Skinner believed that if teachers adopted such goals and used appropriate methods, then such things could be realized in a relatively short period of time.

One of the most important things a teacher can do is learn the theory and the techniques of the conditioning process. Although all teachers affect the behavior of their students, they do not all affect behavior in ways that behaviorists would approve. Teachers must not only learn the techniques of conditioning but also use them effectively. Critics say that the school cannot compete with outside influences such as the peer group, television, home, and the Internet, but behaviorists argue that teachers can make a difference if they act cooperatively and intelligently.

CRITIQUE OF BEHAVIORISM IN EDUCATION

Interest in the use of behavioral engineering has been increasing steadily in many walks of life. Businesses, religious organizations, the military, and schools use it, and it is becoming more prevalent for such institutions to assess their own growth by their success with behavioral techniques.

Probably the most outstanding feature of this approach for many advocates is that it is scientific and research based, and researchers can point to measurable success with this method. It has been used in education since the 1960s, and many educators are zealous supporters of the behavioral techniques they currently are using in their classrooms. In such areas as special education, teachers find the concept of immediate reinforcement particularly useful in controlling and directing children with motor and mental disabilities. Even within the ordinary classroom, one sometimes hears about a token economy with positive and negative reinforcements as effective aids in the educational process.

The popularity of behaviorism arose because the techniques seem to work when so many other approaches fail. Furthermore, the approach used by many behavioral engineers—Skinner in particular—tries to avoid any aversive methods of education, and this fact appeals to many contemporary educators. Children also respond well to a method that provides incentives and rewards for their achievements. Educational computer programs provide immediate reinforcement and are popular with teachers and students. They are effective and efficient ways of imparting knowledge, with the range increasing with new software and more powerful computers.

Behavioral engineers suggest the use of their methods not only in education but in social life, as well. Skinner, for example, took the possibilities of his theories into the area of social and cultural reform. He thought that behavioral engineering would be applicable on a global scale, maintaining that it is possible to solve problems of hunger, warfare, and economic upheaval through a technology of behavior.

Many people scoff at Skinner's recommendations and launch vitriolic attacks on his theories, particularly where he held that the individual has no inherent freedom and dignity. They say that if his suggestions are followed, then Orwell's *1984* with "Big Brother" in charge will be a certainty. Skinner replied that his theory is perhaps the only hope for survival in this technologically complex age. He believed that people have come to the point where they no longer can afford the old luxuries of self-centeredness, violence as a way of life, the wealth of a few at the expense of the many, and the old philosophical and theological notions about the human being's inner makeup that support these old luxuries. Freedom and dignity in the old sense are emotive ideas that generate strong support, but Skinner maintained that these ideas are used too often for hiding a multitude of sins. Aggressiveness, for example, often is said to be a part of the human being's inner makeup or is connected with Original Sin, and nothing can be done about it because we cannot change human nature. Skinner considered such easy escapes and superficial assumptions regrettable. The net result is to give up before one begins because aggressiveness and greed are learned behaviors and can be unlearned or extinguished if one takes an intelligent approach in controlling them.

Some critics charge that Skinner's theories belittle and limit humanity, but a strong argument can be made that his views are optimistic, holding the promise that humans can become practically anything through proper behavioral engineering. From the Skinnerian standpoint, little in people's inner makeup limits development in a variety of creative ways. For these reasons, the Skinnerians maintain that it is possible to build the good society with good people in the foreseeable future if people have the fortitude to plan and cooperate in this venture. The controls will be on the environment—on the contingencies of reinforcement—and in this way, individuals are controlled indirectly. Some critics, however, see Skinner's *Walden Two* as the kind of dystopian *Brave New World* Huxley wrote about.

Behavioral techniques might be successful in the laboratory, but legitimate questions also can be raised about their applicability to human society, where so many variables and unknowns exist. In the laboratory, rigorous control can be maintained, but control is difficult in the rough-and-tumble, out-of-doors world. Behaviorists are probably on soundest grounds when they are dealing with the step-by-step procedures of learning. It is certainly possible to construct a theory that ignores or discounts inner human nature and it might work beautifully, but this still does not mean that no innate human capacities or characteristics exist. Skinner said that "no theory destroys what it is a theory about," and this idea cuts both ways. To say that the individual has no inner freedom and dignity does not destroy such inner freedom and dignity if they do exist.

In many respects, this controversy is a continuation of the old nature versus nurture debate, or the argument over whether human development is fixed genetically (by nature) or can be affected by upbringing and other educational influences (by nurture). Perhaps one of the most glaring weaknesses in the nature–nurture debate is that proponents of each side seem unwilling to accept that human development might be a combination of both influences. Indeed, Skinner was adamant that virtually all human behavior is controlled by environmental influences of some kind or another whether or not people are aware of it. Skinner once told the Philosophy of Education Society that he was there as a speaker because all of the nurturing influences in his life—where he lived, schools he attended, and other things—had led him to that point. Those who accept a nature or biological point of view, however, seem unwilling to admit such impact from environmental influences. Nature advocates say that such things as schizophrenia are genetic in origin and need to be treated medically. Nurture advocates say that such dysfunctional behavior is likely caused by environmental factors and can be treated through behavior-modification techniques.

An interesting development in the nature–nurture debate has been advanced by Edward O. Wilson, and it comes not from philosophy but from science. In *Sociobiology: The New Synthesis,* Wilson argues that the mind is not a blank tablet, a *tabula rasa* as Locke termed it, but rather a negative waiting to be developed. Wilson has given new impetus to Darwinism, and he believes that the influence of genes is absolute. Free will, the soul, mind, self—all are illusions. However, environmental conditions might influence genetic structures, a view that has been advanced by Richard Dawkins in *The Selfish Gene*, who talks about the existence of "memes." Memes are ideas, slogans, and beliefs passed on to the brain and that operate like genes. His point is that learned experiences might influence genetic structures, a view that is controversial. However, Wilson believes that when the Human Genome Project is completed and all the thousands of genes are correctly identified, then all knowledge will be capable of being explained in biological terms. Similar ideas about naturally determined human characteristics have long impacted educational theory, perhaps most recently in such books as *The Bell Curve* by Charles Murray and Richard Hernstein. They promote the view that intellectual ability is not endowed equally among people and that natural and inherent differences exist in intelligence (or I.Q.) among individuals and even among groups of people.

Perhaps the real truth of the matter is somewhere in between: People are predisposed toward certain behaviors through genetic factors, but these influences can be modified or even changed through nurturing conditions. A significant challenge to behaviorism today, as well as to realism and its impact on education, comes from a psychological theory called constructivism. This theory holds that students are not passive recipients of information, but actively connect it with previously assimilated knowledge and make it their own. Like behaviorism, it too has philosophical precursors. As Maxine Greene points out, constructivism's numerous philosophical roots include pragmatism, existentialism, phenomenology, hermeneutics, and some modes of idealism, all philosophies that have for a considerable time attacked objectivity, overweening rationality, and disembodied abstract meaning. They affirm—as constructivism does—that truth is made (or constructed), not discovered or uncovered.

As a psychological theory, constructivism draws heavily from Jean Piaget (1896–1980) and Lev Vygotsky (1896–1934). According to Catherine Fosnot, constructivism is nonpositivistic and stakes out new ground in opposition to behaviorism and biological stage theory. Rather than maturation or behavioral conditioning, the goal of constructivism is the growth of active learners through the construction and reorganization of cognitive structures. As Fosnot traces it, constructivism leans heavily on Piaget's interest in equilibration, which includes assimilation and accommodation. The drive for equilibration is a dynamic process of growth and change.

According to Fosnot, Vygotsky contributed his work on social interaction to constructivism. He studied "spontaneous" concepts developed by the child in everyday experience, and "formal" concepts learned or imposed in structured activity as in a classroom or learning environment. Spontaneous concepts provide the vitality of the child's experiential learning, whereas formal concepts provide disciplined structures for a more mature consciousness and application, "scaffolding" for the growth of the child's conceptual understanding. The child gets important cognitive structure from the outer world but also provides individualized cognitive structure from personal experience. The point, Fosnot claims, is that constructivism adds a new voice to the idea that humans are constantly making and remaking their versions of reality, and in the process humans transform themselves and the world.

Advocates of behaviorism do not deny that children have spontaneous learning moments or that they can assimilate, relate, internalize, and construct ideas. They still maintain, however, that learning is controlled and reinforced by environmental conditions, not some mysterious inner force.

Critics claim that behaviorists not only make questionable assumptions about human beings, they also make them about the nature of the universe. One assumption undergirding much of their thinking is that the universe operates mechanistically. They view the scheme of things as orderly, regular, predictable, and thus controllable. Serious questions have been raised about whether the universe operates this way or whether behaviorists impose this notion of order on the inscrutable face of the universe. This penchant for order and regularity is most noticeable in behaviorists' efforts to develop a technology of behavior. They are trying to make an exacting approach out of something based on highly questionable assumptions. This drive for exactness seems to be modeled after the physical sciences, but some physical scientists maintain that exactness is much overrated even within their disciplines. In other words, behaviorists might be constructing their theory on the shifting sands of the quest for certainty.

One of the most glaring weaknesses that critics point to is the social policy recommendations of behaviorists such as Skinner. Behaviorists may be on solid ground when they are describing how learning takes place or how behavior is altered in the laboratory or classroom, but they make a quantum leap from the laboratory to broad social, political, and economic conditions. In *Walden Two*, Skinner recommends a group of planners and controllers for the reshaping of Walden society, but the controllers sound much like the psychologist in the laboratory. Again, the laboratory is different from society at large. History is replete with examples of individuals and groups who thought that they and only they could lead society in the proper direction. History also shows the disastrous effects of such thinking. In so many respects, there seems to be little difference in deriving the powers of government from divine authority, the laws of dialectical materialism, or the laws of behavior.

One recurring concern is who controls the controllers. Skinner maintained that the controlled exert influence over the controllers, just as the behavior of schoolchildren affects the teacher's behavior. In other words, the directions of the behavior of the controlled set the conditions to which the controllers react. This argument seems weak because the initiative is loaded in favor of the controllers, who have social, political, intellectual, and economic power concentrated in their hands. It seems predictable that the powerless of the Skinnerian society will be just as manipulated (even if for their own good) as the powerless in any other authoritarian structure.

In Alfie Kohn's *Punished by Rewards*, the basic assumptions of behaviorism are criticized as intrinsically objectionable and counterproductive. One problem is that behaviorism stems largely from animal research on pigeons and rats. Kohn argues that human behavior is not the same as rat or pigeon behavior. Furthermore, he finds that behaviorism has become pervasive in modern life. For example, children are bribed from birth with rewards, such as sweets and allowances, to manipulate their behavior. As adults, they are rewarded with such devices as merit pay, hierarchical promotions, and special titles. It has even been proposed to pay children to read books and do their homework. Kohn believes that intrinsic motivation is being destroyed. Children do not have to be rewarded to learn because learning has its own value and reward. The moral issue is whether a person has to be rewarded to do what should be done. Kohn fears that the influence of behaviorist theory is destroying the notion of the self, individual responsibility, and self-reliance.

Although Skinner and other behaviorists strongly maintain that their aims and methods do not belittle people or eclipse inner feelings and purposes, the charge that their programs result in a robotization of humanity has some basis. Some critics believe that behaviorists ignore what is truly human in favor of a new, more mechanistic view of human nature. Frazier, in *Walden Two*, says that he is the only unhappy one in the controlled society because he is the only one who was not reared there. Given the option of being Frazier, with all his frustrations, hopes, and fears, or the new-engineered individual of *Walden Two*, who is in blissful ignorance of the controls exerted on him, many people would choose the former.

HOBBES

THE LEVIATHAN

Thomas Hobbes, the seventeenth-century English philosopher, was not a behaviorist, but his materialist philosophy contains many ideas central to behaviorism. The following selection is from Leviathan, or the Matter, Form, and Power of a Commonwealth Ecclesiastical and Civil, *first published in 1651. Hobbes thought that the human mind connects with environmental objects (the behaviorist's "stimuli") by way of the senses. Motion (or behavior) is vital (inborn or genetic) and acquired (learned). His notions of "appetite" and "aversion" have close affinity with positive and negative reinforcement. Hobbes's belief that science and reason could be used to build the good society is akin to behavioral engineering. Finally, like such behaviorists as Skinner, Hobbes saw liberty or freedom as depending on external conditions.*

The Introduction

Nature, the art whereby God has made and governs the world, is by the *art* of man, as in many other things, so in this also imitated—that it can make an artificial animal. For seeing life is but a motion of limbs, the beginning whereof is in some principal part within, why may we not say that all *automata* (engines that move themselves by springs and wheels as does a watch) have an artificial life? For what is the *heart* but a *spring,* and the *nerves* but so many *strings,* and the joints but so many *wheels* giving motion to the whole body such as was intended by the artificer? *Art* goes yet further, imitat-

ing that rational and most excellent work of nature, *man.* For by art is created that great LEVIATHAN called a COMMONWEALTH or STATE—in Latin, *Civitas*—which is but an artificial man, though of greater stature and strength than the natural, for whose protection and defense it was intended. . . .

Of Sense

Concerning the thoughts of man, I will consider them first singly and afterwards in train or dependence upon one another. Singly, they are every one a *representation* or *appearance* of some quality or other accident of a body without us which is commonly called an *object*. Which object works on the eyes, ears, and other parts of a man's body, and by diversity of working produces diversity of appearances.

The original of them all is that which we call sense, for there is no conception in a man's mind which has not at first, totally or by parts, been begotten upon the organs of sense. The rest are derived from that original. . . .

The cause of sense is the external body or object which presses the organ proper to each sense, either immediately as in the taste and touch, or mediately as in seeing, hearing, and smelling; which pressure, by the mediation of the nerves and other strings and membranes of the body continued inward to the brain and heart, causes there a resistance or counter-pressure or endeavor of the heart to deliver itself, which endeavor, because *outward,* seems to be some matter without. And this *seeming or fancy* is that which men call *sense,* and consists, as to the eye, in a *light* or *color figured;* to the ear, in a *sound;* to the nostril, in an *odor;* to the tongue and palate, in a *savor*; and to the rest of the body, in *heat, cold, hardness, softness,* and such other qualities as we discern by *feeling.* All which qualities, called *sensible,* are in the object that causes them but so many several motions of the matter by which it presses our organs diversely. Neither in us that are pressed are they anything else but divers motions, for motion produces nothing but motion. But their appearance to us is fancy, the same waking that dreaming. And as pressing, rubbing or striking the eye makes us fancy a light, and pressing the ear produces a din, so do the bodies also we see or hear produce the same by their strong, though unobserved, action. For if those colors and sounds were in the bodies or objects that cause them, they could not be severed from them as by glasses, and in echoes by reflection, we see they are, where we know the thing we see is in one place, the appearance in another. And though at some certain distance the real and very object seem invested with the fancy it begets in us, yet still the object is one thing, the image or fancy is another. So that sense, in all cases, is nothing else but original fancy, caused, as I have said, by the pressure—that is, by the motion—of external things upon our eyes, ears, and other organs thereunto ordained. . . .

Of Reason and Science

. . . [It] appears that reason is not, as sense and memory, born with us, nor gotten by experience only, as prudence is, but attained by industry: first in apt imposing of names, and secondly by getting a good and orderly method in proceeding from the elements, which are names, to assertions made by connection of one of them to another, and so to syllogisms, which are the connections of one assertion to another, till we come to a knowledge of all the consequences of names appertaining to the subject in hand; and that is it men call Science. And whereas sense and memory are but knowledge of fact, which is a thing past and irrevocable, science is the knowledge of consequences and dependence of one fact upon another, by which[,] out of that [which] we can presently do[,] we know how to do something else when we will, or the like another time; because when we see how anything comes about, upon what causes and by what manner, when the like causes come into our power we see how to make it produce the like effects. . . .

To conclude, the light of human minds is perspicuous words, but by exact definitions first snuffed and purged from ambiguity; reason is the pace; increase of science, the way; and the benefit of mankind, the end. . . .

Of the Interior Beginnings of Voluntary Motions Commonly Called the Passions . . .

There be in animals two sorts of *motions* peculiar to them: one called *vital,* begun in generation and continued without interruption through their whole life—such as are the *course* of the *blood,* the *pulse,* the *breathing,* the *concoction, nutrition, excretion,* etc.—to which motions there needs no help of imagination; the other is *animal motion,* otherwise called *voluntary motion*—as to *go,* to *speak,* to *move* any of our limbs in such manner as is first fancied in our minds. That sense is motion in the organs and interior parts of man's body caused by the action of the things we see, hear, etc., and that fancy is but the relics of the same motion remaining after sense, has been already said in the first and second chapters. And because *going, speaking,* and the like voluntary motions depend always upon a precedent thought of *whither, which way,* and *what,* it is evident that the imagination is the first internal beginning of all voluntary motion. And although unstudied men do not conceive any motion at all to be there where the thing moved is invisible or the space it is moved in is, for the shortness of it, insensible, yet that does not hinder but that such motions are. For let a space be never so little, that which is moved over a greater space, whereof that little one is part, must first be moved over that. These small beginnings of motion within the body of man, before they appear in walking, speaking, striking, and other visible actions, are commonly called endeavor.

This endeavor, when it is toward something which causes it, is called appetite or desire, the latter being the general name and the other oftentimes restrained to signify the desire of food, namely *hunger* and *thirst*. And when the endeavor is fromward something, it is generally called AVERSION. These words, *appetite* and *aversion,* we have from the Latins; and they both of them signify the motions, one of approaching, the other of retiring. . . . For nature itself does often press upon men those truths which afterwards, when they look for somewhat beyond nature, they stumble at. . . .

That which men desire they are also said to LOVE, and to HATE those things for which they have aversion. So that desire and love are the same thing, save that by desire we always signify the absence of the object, by love most commonly the presence of the same. So also by aversion we signify the absence, and by hate the presence of the object.

Of appetites and aversions, some are born with men, as appetite of food, appetite of excretion, and exoneration, which may also and more properly be called aversions from somewhat they feel in their bodies; and some other appetites, not many. The rest, which are appetites of particular things, proceed from experience and trial of their effects upon themselves or other men. For of things we know not at all, or believe not to be, we can have no further desire than to taste and try. But aversion we have for things, not only which we know have hurt us, but also that we do not know whether they will hurt us or not.

Those things which we neither desire nor hate we are said to *contemn,* CONTEMPT being nothing else but an immobility or contumacy of the heart in resisting the action of certain things; and proceeding from that the heart is already moved otherwise by other more potent objects or from want of experience of them.

And because the constitution of a man's body is in continual mutation, it is impossible that all the same things should always cause in him the same appetites and aversions; much less can all men consent in the desire of almost any one and the same object.

But whatsoever is the object of any man's appetite or desire, that is it which he for his part calls *good;* and the object of his hate and aversion, *evil;* and of his contempt, *vile* and *inconsiderable*. For these words of good, evil, and contemptible are ever used with relation to the person that uses them, there being nothing simply and absolutely so, nor any common rule of good and evil to be taken from the nature of the objects themselves—but from the person of the man, where there is no commonwealth, or, in a commonwealth, from the person that represents it, or from an arbitrator or judge whom men disagreeing shall by consent set up and make his sentence the rule thereof.

As in sense that which is really within us is, as I have said before, only motion caused by the action of external objects, but in appearance to the sight light and color, to the ear sound, to the nostril odor, etc., so when the action of the same object is continued from the eyes, ears, and other organs to the heart, the real effect there is nothing but motion or endeavor, which consists in appetite or aversion to or from the object moving. But the appearance or sense of that motion is that we either call *delight or* trouble of mind.

This motion, which is called appetite, and for the appearance of it *delight* and *pleasure,* seems to be a corroboration of vital motion and a help thereunto; and therefore such things as caused delight were not improperly called *jucunda, à juvando,* from helping or fortifying, and the contrary, *molesta, offensive,* from hindering and troubling the motion vital.

Pleasure, therefore, or *delight* is the appearance or sense of good; and *molestation* or *displeasure* the appearance or sense of evil. And consequently all appetite, desire, and love is accompanied with some delight more or less, and all hatred and aversion with more or less displeasure and offense.

Of pleasures or delights, some arise from the sense of an object present, and those may be called *pleasures of sense*—the word *sensual,* as it is used by those only that condemn them, having no place till there be laws. Of this kind are all onerations and exonerations of the body, as also all that is pleasant in the *sight, hearing, smell, taste,* or *touch.* Others arise from the expectation that proceeds from foresight of the end or consequence of things, whether those things in the sense please or displease. And these are *pleasures of the mind* of him that draws those consequences, and are generally called JOY. In the like manner, displeasures are some in the sense, and called PAIN; others in the expectation of consequences, and are called GRIEF.

These simple passions called *appetite, desire, love, aversion, hate, joy,* and *grief* have their names for [diverse] considerations diversified. As first, when they one succeed another, they are diversely called from the opinion men have of the likelihood of attaining what they desire. Secondly, from the object loved or hated. Thirdly, from the consideration of many of them together. Fourthly, from the alteration or succession itself.

Of the Virtues Commonly Called Intellectual . . .

Virtue generally, in all sorts of subjects, is somewhat that is valued for eminence, and consists in comparison. For if all things were equal in all men, nothing would be prized. And by *virtues intellectual* are always understood such abilities of the mind as men praise, value, and desire should be in themselves and go commonly under the name of a *good wit,* though the same word *wit* be used also to distinguish one certain ability from the rest.

These *virtues* are of two sorts: *natural* and *acquired.* By natural, I mean not that which a man has from his birth for that is nothing else but sense, wherein men differ so little one from another and from brute beasts as it is not to be reckoned among virtues. But I mean that *wit* which is gotten by use only and experience, without method, culture, or instruction. This NATURAL WIT consists principally in two things: *celerity of imagining—that is, swift succession of one thought to another—and steady direction* to some approved end. On the contrary, a slow imagination makes that defect or fault of the mind which is commonly called DULLNESS, *stupidity,* and sometimes by other names that signify slowness of motion or difficulty to be moved.

And this difference of quickness is caused by the difference of men's passions that love and dislike, some one thing, some another; and therefore some men's thoughts run one way, some another, and are held to and observe differently the things that pass through their imagination. And . . . in this succession of men's thoughts there is nothing to observe in the things they think on but either in what they be *like one another* or in what they be *unlike,* or *what they serve for* or *how they serve to such a purpose. . . .*

As for *acquired wit*—I mean acquired by method and instruction—there is none but reason, which is grounded on the right use of speech and produces the sciences. . . .

The causes of this difference of wits are in the passions, and the difference of passions proceeds partly from the different constitution of the body and partly from different education. For if the difference proceeded from the temper of the brain and the organs of sense, either exterior or interior, there would be no less difference of men in their sight, hearing, or other senses than in their fancies and discretions. It proceeds, therefore, from the passions, which are different not only from the difference of men's complexions, but also from their difference of customs and education.

The passions that most of all cause the difference of wit are principally the more or less desire of power, of riches, of knowledge, and of honor. All which may be reduced to the first—that is, desire of power. For riches, knowledge, and honor are but several sorts of power.

And therefore a man who has no great passion for any of these things but is, as men term it, indifferent, though he may be so far a good man as to be free from giving offense, yet he cannot possibly have either a great fancy or much judgment. For the thoughts are to the desires as scouts and spies, to range abroad and find the way to the things desired, all steadiness of the mind's motion, and all quickness of the same, proceeding from thence; for as to have no desire is to be dead, so to have weak passions is dullness. . . .

Of the First and Second Natural Laws . . .

The RIGHT OF NATURE, which writers commonly call *jus naturale,* is the liberty each man has to use his own power, as he will himself, for the preservation of his own nature—that is to say, of his own life—and consequently of doing anything which, in his own judgment and reason, he shall conceive to be the aptest means thereunto.

By LIBERTY is understood, according to the proper signification of the word, the absence of external impediments; which impediments may oft take away part of a man's power to do what he would, but cannot hinder him from using the power left him according as his judgment and reason shall dictate to him.

A LAW OF NATURE, *lex naturalis*, is a precept or general rule, found out by reason, by which a man is forbidden to do that which is destructive of his life or takes away the means of preserving the same and to omit that by which he thinks it may be best preserved. For though they that speak of this subject use to confound *jus* and *lex, right* and *law,* yet they ought to be distinguished; because RIGHT consists in liberty to do or to forbear, whereas law determines and binds to one of them; so that law and right differ as much as obligation and liberty, which in one and the same matter are inconsistent. . . . Consequently it is a precept or general rule of reason *that every man ought to endeavor peace, as far as he has hope of obtaining it; and when he cannot obtain it, that he may seek and use all helps and advantages of war.* The first branch of which rule contains the first and fundamental law of nature, which is *to seek peace and follow it.* The second, the sum of the right of nature, which is, *by all means we can to defend ourselves.*

From this fundamental law of nature, by which men are commanded to endeavor peace, is derived this second law: *that a man be willing, when others are so too, as far forth as for peace and defense of himself he shall think it necessary, to lay down this right to all things, and be contended with so much liberty against other men as he would allow other men against himself.* For as long as every man holds this right of doing anything he likes, so long are all men in the condition of war. But if other men will not lay down their right as well as he, then there is no reason for anyone to divest himself of his, for that were to expose himself to prey, which no man is bound to, rather than to dispose himself to peace. This is that law of the gospel: *whatsoever you require that others should do to you, that do ye to them.*

Source: Thomas Hobbes, *Leviathan, Parts I and II*, edited by Herbert W. Schneider, by permission of the Bobbs-Merrill Company. Copyright 1958, The Liberal Arts Press, pp. 23, 25–26, 49, 50–55, 64, 68, 109–110.

SKINNER

BEYOND FREEDOM AND DIGNITY

Of all the behaviorists, Skinner probably has been the most important. Following the leads of Pavlov and Watson, he constructed a science of behavior based on operant conditioning. Although much of his work was based on laboratory experiments, he took considerable pains to discuss the social and political consequences of his theory. In the following selection, Skinner argues against traditional notions of the freedom and dignity of the human being, views that are often supported by various philosophies. His claim is that such notions can be socially harmful, particularly the notions of permissiveness championed by some philosophical and educational schools of thought. At the same time, his rejection of permissiveness does not imply a resort to punishment; instead, he argues for control based on the principles of a technology of behavior.

Those who champion freedom and dignity do not, of course, confine themselves to punitive measures, but they turn to alternatives with diffidence and timidity. Their concern for autonomous man commits them to only ineffective measures, several of which we may now examine. . . .

A method of modifying behavior without appearing to exert control is represented by Socrates's metaphor of the midwife: One person helps another give birth to behavior. Since the midwife plays no part in conception and only a small part in parturition, the person who gives birth to the behavior may take full credit for it. Socrates demonstrated the art of midwifery, or maieutics, in education. He pretended to show how an uneducated slave boy could be led to prove Pythagoras's theorem for doubling the square. The boy assented to the steps in the proof, and Socrates claimed that he did so without being told—in other words, that he "knew" the theorem in some sense all along. Socrates contended that even ordinary knowledge could be drawn out in the same way since the soul knew the truth and needed only to be shown that it knew it. The episode is often cited as if it were relevant to modern educational practice. . . .

Intellectual, therapeutic, and moral midwifery is scarcely easier than punitive control, because it demands rather subtle skills and concentrated attention, but it has its advantages. It seems to confer a strange power on the practitioner. Like the cabalistic use of hints and allusions, it achieves results seemingly out of proportion to the measures employed. The apparent contribution of the individual is not reduced, however. He is given full credit for knowing before he learns, for having within him the seeds of good mental health, and for being able to enter into direct communication with God. An important advantage is that the practitioner avoids responsibility. Just as it is not the midwife's fault if the baby is stillborn or deformed, so the teacher is exonerated when the student fails, the psychotherapist when the patient does not solve his problem, and the mystical religious leader when his disciples behave badly.

Maieutic practices have their place. Just how much help the teacher should give the student as he acquires new forms of behavior is a delicate question. The teacher should wait for the student to respond rather than rush to tell him what he is to do or say. As Comenius put it, the more the teacher teaches, the less the student learns. The student gains in other ways. In general, we do not like to be told either what we already know or what we are unlikely ever to know well or to good effect. We do not read books if we are already thoroughly familiar with the material or if it is so completely unfamiliar that it is likely to remain so. We read books which help us say things we are on the verge of saying anyway but cannot quite say without help. We understand the author, although we could not have formulated what we understand before he put it into words. There are similar advantages for the patient in psychotherapy. Maieutic practices are helpful, too, because they exert more control than is usually acknowledged and some of it may be valuable.

These advantages, however, are far short of the claims made. Socrates' slave boy learned nothing; there was no evidence whatever that he could have gone through the theorem by himself afterward. And it is as true of maieutics as of permissiveness that positive results must be credited to unacknowledged controls of other sorts. If the patient finds a solution without the help of his therapist, it is because he has been exposed to a helpful environment elsewhere.

Another metaphor associated with weak practices is horticultural. The behavior to which a person has given birth grows, and it may be guided or trained, as a growing plant is trained. Behavior may be "cultivated."

The metaphor is particularly at home in education. A school for small children is a child-garden, or kindergarten. The behavior of the child "develops" until he reaches "maturity." A teacher may accelerate the process or turn it in slightly different directions, but—in the classical phrase—he cannot teach, he can only help the student learn. The metaphor of guidance is also common in psychotherapy. Freud argued that a person must pass through several developmental stages, and that if the patient has become "fixated" at a given stage, the therapist must help him break loose and move forward. Governments engage in guidance—for example, when they encourage the "development" of industry through tax exemptions or provide a "climate" that is favorable to the improvement of race relations.

Guidance is not as easy as permissiveness, but it is usually easier than midwifery, and it has some of the same advantages. One who merely guides a natural development cannot easily be accused of trying to control it. Growth remains an achievement of the individual, testifying to his freedom and worth, his "hidden propensities," and as the gardener is not responsible for the ultimate form of what he grows, so one who merely guides is exonerated when things go wrong.

Guidance is effective, however, only to the extent that control is exerted. To guide is either to open new opportunities or to block growth in particular directions. To arrange an opportunity is not a very positive act, but it is nevertheless a form of control if it increases the likelihood that behavior will be emitted. The teacher who merely selects the material the student is to study or the therapist who merely suggests a different job or change of scene has exerted control, though it may be hard to detect.

Control is more obvious when growth or development is *prevented*. Censorship blocks access to material needed for development in a given direction; it closes opportunities. De Tocqueville saw this in the America of his day: "The will of man is not shattered, but softened, bent, and guided. Men are seldom forced . . . to act, but they are constantly restrained from acting." As Ralph Barton Perry put it, "Whoever determines what alternatives shall be made known to man controls what that man shall choose *from*. He is deprived of freedom in proportion as he is denied access to *any* ideas, or is confined to any range of ideas short of the totality of relevant possibilities." For "deprived of freedom" read "controlled."

It is no doubt valuable to create an environment in which a person acquires effective behavior rapidly and continues to behave effectively. In constructing such an environment we may eliminate distractions and open opportunities, and these are key points in the metaphor of guidance or growth or development; but it is the contingencies we arrange, rather than the unfolding of some predetermined pattern, which are responsible for the changes observed.

Jean-Jacques Rousseau was alert to the dangers of social control, and he thought it might be possible to avoid them by making a person dependent not on people but on things. In *Émile* he showed how a child could learn about things from the things themselves rather than from books. The practices he described are still common, largely because of John Dewey's emphasis on real life in the classroom.

One of the advantages in being dependent on things rather than on other people is that the time and energy of other people are saved. The child who must be reminded that it is time to go to school is dependent upon his parents, but the child who has learned to respond to clocks and other temporal properties of the world around him (not to a "sense of time") is dependent upon things, and he makes fewer demands on his parents. . . .

Another important advantage of being dependent on things is that the contingencies which involve things are more precise and shape more useful behavior than contingencies arranged by other people. The temporal properties of the environment are more pervasive and more subtle than any series of reminders. A person whose behavior in driving a car is shaped by the response of the car behaves more skillfully than one who is following instructions. . . .

But things do not easily take control. The procedures Rousseau described were not simple, and they do not often work. The complex contingencies involving things (including people who are behaving "unintentionally") can, unaided, have very little effect on an individual in his lifetime—a fact of great importance for reasons we shall note later. We must also remember that the control exercised by things may be destructive. The world of things can be tyrannical. Natural contingencies induce people to behave superstitiously, to risk greater and greater dangers, to work uselessly to exhaustion, and so on. Only the counter control exerted by a social environment offers any protection against these consequences.

Dependence on things is not independence. The child who does not need to be told that it is time to go to school has come under the control of more subtle, and more useful, stimuli. The child who has learned what to say and how to behave in getting along with other people is under the control of social contingencies. People who get along together well under the mild contingencies of approval and disapproval are controlled as effectively as (and in many ways more effectively than) the citizens of a police state. Orthodoxy controls through the establishment of rules, but the mystic is no freer because the contingencies which have shaped his behavior are more personal or idiosyncratic. Those who work productively because of the reinforcing value of what they produce are under the sensitive and powerful control of the products. Those who learn in the natural environment are under a form of control as powerful as any control exerted by a teacher.

A person never becomes truly self-reliant. Even though he deals effectively with things, he is necessarily dependent upon those who have taught him to do so. They have selected the things he is dependent upon and determined the kinds and degrees of dependencies. (They cannot, therefore, disclaim responsibility for the results.)

It is a surprising fact that those who object most violently to the manipulation of behavior nevertheless make the most vigorous efforts to manipulate minds. Evidently freedom and dignity are threatened only when behavior is changed by physically changing the environment. There appears to be no threat when the states of mind said to be responsible for behavior are changed, presumably because autonomous man possesses miraculous powers which enable him to yield or resist. . . .

Beliefs, preferences, perceptions, needs, purposes, and opinions are other possessions of autonomous man which are said to change when we change minds. What is changed in each case is a probability of action. A person's belief that a floor will hold him as he walks across it depends upon his past experience. If he has walked across it without incident many times, he will do so again readily, and his behavior will not create any of the aversive stimuli felt as anxiety. He may report that he has "faith" in the solidity of the floor or "confidence" that it will hold him, but the kinds of things which are felt as faith or confidence are not states of mind; they are at best by-products of the behavior in its relation to antecedent events, and they do not explain why a person walks as he does.

We build "belief" when we increase the probability of action by reinforcing behavior. When we build a person's confidence that a floor will hold him by inducing him to walk on it, we might not be said to be changing a belief, but we do so in the traditional sense when we give him verbal assurances that the floor is solid, demonstrate its solidity by walking on it ourselves, or describe its structure or state. The only difference is in the conspicuousness of the measures. The change which occurs as a person "learns to trust a floor" by walking on it is the characteristic effect of reinforcement; the change which occurs when he is told that the floor is solid, when he sees someone else walking on it, or when he is "convinced" by assurances that the floor will hold him depends upon past experiences which no longer make a conspicuous contribution. For example, a person who walks on surfaces which are likely to vary in their solidity (for example, a frozen lake) quickly forms a discrimination between surfaces on which others are walking and surfaces on which no one is walking, or between surfaces called safe and surfaces called dangerous. He learns to walk confidently on the first and cautiously on the second. The sight of someone walking on a surface or an assurance that it is safe converts it from the second class into the first. The history during which the discrimination was formed may be forgotten, and the effect then seems to involve that inner event called a change of mind.

Changes in preference, perceptions, needs, purposes, attitudes, opinions, and other attributes of mind may be analyzed in the same way. We change the way a person looks at something, as well as what he sees when he looks, by changing the contingencies; we do not change something called perception. We change the relative strengths of responses by differential reinforcement of alternative courses of action; we do not change something called a preference. We change the probability of an act by changing a condition of deprivation or aversive stimulation; we do not change a need. We reinforce behavior in particular ways; we do not give a person a purpose or an intention. We change behavior toward something, not an attitude toward it. We sample and change verbal behavior, not opinions.

Another way to change a mind is to point to reasons why a person should behave in a given way, and the reasons are almost always consequences which are likely to be contingent on behavior. Let us say that a child is using a knife in a dangerous way. We may avoid trouble by making the environment safer—by taking the knife away or giving him a safer kind—but that will not prepare him for a world with unsafe knives. Left alone, he may learn to use the knife properly by cutting himself whenever he uses it improperly. We may help by substituting a less dangerous form of punishment—spanking him, for example, or perhaps merely shaming him when we find him using a knife in a dangerous way. We may tell him that some uses are bad and others good if "Bad!" and "Good!" have already been conditioned as positive and negative reinforcers. Suppose, however, that all these methods have unwanted by-products, such as a change in his relation to us, and that we therefore decide to appeal to "reason." (This is possible, of course, only if he has reached the "age of reason.") We explain the contingencies, demonstrating what happens when one uses a knife in one way and not another. We may show him how rules may be extracted from the contingencies ("You should never cut *toward yourself*"). As a result we may induce the child to use the knife properly and will be likely to say that we have imparted a knowledge of its proper use. But we have had to take advantage of a great deal of prior conditioning with respect to instructions, directions, and other verbal stimuli, which are easily overlooked, and their contribution may then be attributed to autonomous man. A still more complex form of argument has to do with deriving new reasons from old, the process of deduction which depends upon a much longer verbal history and is particularly likely to be called changing a mind.

Ways of changing behavior by changing minds are seldom condoned when they are clearly effective, even though it is still a mind which is apparently being changed. We do not condone the changing of minds when the contestants are unevenly matched; that is "undue influence." Nor do we condone changing minds surreptitiously. If a person cannot see what the would-be changer of minds is doing, he cannot escape or counterattack; he is being exposed to "propaganda." "Brainwashing" is proscribed by those who otherwise condone the changing of minds simply because the control is obvious. A common technique is to build up a strong aversive condition, such as hunger or lack of sleep and, by alleviating it, to reinforce any behavior which "shows a positive attitude" toward a political or religious system. A favorable "opinion" is built up simply by reinforcing favorable statements. The procedure may not be obvious to those upon whom it is used, but it is too obvious to others to be accepted as an allowable way of changing minds.

The illusion that freedom and dignity are respected when control seems incomplete arises in part from the probabilistic nature of operant behavior. Seldom does any environmental condition "elicit" behavior in the all-or-nothing fashion of a reflex; it simply makes a bit of behavior more likely to occur. A hint will not itself suffice to evoke a response, but it adds strength to a weak response which may then appear. The hint is conspicuous, but the other events responsible for the appearance of the response are not.

Like permissiveness, maieutics, guidance, and building a dependence on things, changing a mind is condoned by the defenders of freedom and dignity because it is an ineffective way of changing behavior, and the changer of minds can therefore escape from the charge that he is controlling people. He is also exonerated when things go wrong. Autonomous man survives to be credited with his achievements and blamed for his mistakes. . . .

The freedom and dignity of autonomous man seem to be preserved when only weak forms of nonaversive control are used. Those who use them seem to defend themselves against the charge that they are attempting to control behavior, and they are exonerated when things go wrong. Permissiveness is the absence of control, and if it appears to lead to desirable results, it is only because of other contingencies. Maieutics, or the art of midwifery, seems to leave behavior to be credited to those who give birth to it, and the guidance of development to those who develop. Human intervention seems to be minimized when a person is made dependent upon things rather than upon other people. Various ways of changing behavior by changing minds are not only condoned but vigorously practiced by the defenders of freedom and dignity. There is a good deal to be said for minimizing current control by other people, but other measures still operate. A person who responds in acceptable ways to weak forms of control may have been changed by contingencies which are no longer operative. By refusing to recognize them the defenders of freedom and dignity encourage the misuse of controlling practices and block progress toward a more effective technology of behavior.

Source: From *Beyond Freedom and Dignity* by B. F. Skinner. Copyright © 1971 by B. F. Skinner. Reprinted 2002 by Hackett Publishing Company, Inc., through special arrangement with B. F. Foundation. All rights reserved.

SELECTED READINGS

Kohn, Alfie. *Punished by Rewards: The Trouble with Gold Stars, Incentive Plans, A's, Praise, and Other Bribes.* Boston: Houghton Mifflin, 1993. A critique of behaviorism that examines how behavior-shaping rewards are used and abused in education. Kohn believes that behavioral techniques as currently used are more damaging than beneficial.

Meichenbaum, Donald. *Cognitive-Behavior Modification.* New York: Plenum Press, 1977. A look at conditioning techniques that takes into account more than simple environmental factors. Cognitive-behavioral modification includes not only organism-environment relations but also the ways an organism modifies and changes the environment through its belief system.

Pavlov, I. P. *Conditioned Reflexes.* London: Oxford University Press, 1927. A classic study of conditioning. Pavlov's work has had great influence on the historical development of behaviorism.

Skinner, B. F. *Walden Two.* New York: Macmillan, 1948. A fictional treatise that has attracted a wide audience of readers from scientists to utopian-minded thinkers. Skinner presents a picture of what behavioral engineering might be like in communal form.

www.bfskinner.org (accessed April 5, 2002). Homepage of the B. F. Skinner Foundation. General information about the foundation, with brief documents concerning operant conditioning and other topics.

plato.stanford.edu/entries/behaviorism/ (accessed April 5, 2002). An example of a specific entry in the *Stanford Encyclopedia of Philosophy.* This particular page is devoted to the philosophical roots of behaviorism.

Companion Website

ONLINE RESEARCH

Utilizing some of the Web sites included in this book, as well as Topics 2 and 3 of the Prentice Hall Foundations Web site found at *www.prenhall.com/ozmon,* answer the following question with a short essay: What are the essential components of behaviorism and how is it utilized in educational practices? You can write and submit your essay response to your instructor by using the "Electronic Bluebook" section found in any of the topics of the Prentice Hall Foundations Web site.

Existentialism, Phenomenology, and Education

The roots of existentialism can be traced as far back as the Sophists, but as a distinct philosophy it began with the works of Søren Kierkegaard and, to a degree, by Friedrich Wilhelm Nietzsche in the nineteenth century. In the twentieth century, it was further developed by such figures as Martin Buber, Karl Jaspers, and Jean-Paul Sartre. Phenomenology, which is closely allied with existentialism, deals primarily with the phenomena of consciousness and usually is attributed to Edmund Husserl in the early twentieth century, and greatly extended by such figures as Martin Heidegger and Maurice Merleau-Ponty.

Although differences are found between existentialism and phenomenology, the two have much in common. Sartre as much as anyone was identified with existentialism, yet he also wrote as a phenomenologist. Heidegger, who rejected the existentialist label, wrote philosophy that many existentialists have found compatible with their views. As these philosophies have been used in philosophy of education, they have been so closely allied that some advocates refer to their work as existentialist phenomenology of education.

Although traditional philosophers consider questions about the nature of knowledge, truth, and meaning, existentialists are concerned with how these questions are educationally significant within the lived experience of individuals. Phenomenologists see their inquiry more specifically focused on the phenomena of consciousness, the significance of education in perception, and the development of meaning in concrete individual experience.

EXISTENTIALIST PHILOSOPHERS AND THEIR THOUGHT

Existentialism offers an array of interpretations because it is spread across so many different cultures. Its seemingly tortured and mixed varieties could be a result of the nature of the existentialist credo—the lonely, estranged, and alienated individual caught up in a meaningless and absurd world.

In some respects, the nature of individualism studied by existentialists was influenced by the works of Friedrich Wilhelm Nietzsche (1844–1900), a German philosopher. Nietzsche attempted to establish a morality that went beyond traditional Judeo-Christian morality because he believed that traditional morality had tamed people too much, making them weak. In *Thus Spake Zarathustra*, he explored the individual transcending conventional social values and becoming a "superman," a being beyond the confines of the conventional. This theme was expanded in *Beyond Good and Evil* and *Toward a Genealogy of Morals*. In *The Will to Power*, he explored the political ramifications of his ideas and favored a leadership of exceptional people who would create and define values for others, a position that Nazi Germany usurped for propaganda purposes.

The difference between Nietzsche and most other existentialists, however, is the existentialists' deep sense of moral reservation, even moral uncertainty, about individual existence. Rather than a drive to be a Nietzschean overlord, the individualism of existentialists is characterized by anxiety, a lack of definition, and paradox. To understand what existentialists themselves are attempting to say, one can examine the particular thought systems of four representative philosophers: Kierkegaard, Buber, Heidegger, and Sartre.

Søren Kierkegaard (1813–1855)

Søren Kierkegaard's childhood was spent in close association with his father, who demanded that his children excel in intellectual matters. Under the eye of his father, young Kierkegaard learned to act out the plots of literary works, became proficient in Latin and Greek, and developed the habit of pursuing ideas for intellectual satisfaction. As a young man, he studied Hegel but revolted against his systematization and adherence to a society-oriented outlook. Kierkegaard chose instead to search out individual truths by which he could live and die.

Kierkegaard was a devout Christian who attacked conventional Christianity with a vengeance, producing biting literary works, such as his *Attack Upon "Christendom."* He believed that Christianity had become warped by modern times, for conventional Christianity seemed to perpetuate many modern absurdities. These views did not endear him to the religious establishment. He called for a "leap of faith" in which the modern individual would accept the Christian deity even though there is no proof that God exists and no rational way to know Him. Only through the leap of faith can one begin to restructure one's life and truly live out the principles of Christianity.

Kierkegaard's category of philosophical study was the lonely individual against an objective and science-oriented world. He was biting in his criticism of science and what it has wrought, and he believed that the scientific penchant for objectivity has largely driven modern society away from a viable Christian belief. People have embraced objectification, and this has led them to become group centered or, in the words of some contemporary American sociologists, "other directed." Instead, Kierkegaard argued for the subjective individual who makes personal choices, eschewing the scientific demand for objective proof. This unfounded subjectivity means that one must abandon reason and accept groundless belief.

Kierkegaard was not concerned with "being" in general but with individual human existence. He believed that people need to come to an understanding of souls, destiny, and the reality of God. He attacked Hegelian philosophy and other abstract speculation for depersonalizing individuals by emphasizing the thought rather than the thinker. He believed that individuals are confronted with choices in life that they alone can make and for which they must accept complete responsibility. Kierkegaard described three stages on "life's road." The first is the *aesthetic* stage, where one lives in sensuous enjoyment and where emotions are dominant. The second, the *ethical* stage, occurs when one arrives at the "universal human" and achieves an understanding of one's place and function in life. The third is the *religious* stage, which for Kierkegaard was the highest, where one stands alone before God.

Kierkegaard held that there was an unbridgeable gulf between God and the world that we must somehow cross through faith. This takes passion, and passion is sorely lacking in modern life. We achieve such passion, not through reflection, but through understanding ourselves as creatures of God. Kierkegaard thought that education should be subjective and religious, devoted to developing individuality and the individual's relationship with God. He opposed vocational and technical studies because they are directed primarily toward the secular world of objectivity.

Although Kierkegaard was largely ignored in his own time, his writings and thoughts were revived in the twentieth century because it was then that Kierkegaard's fears of an unchecked and raging objectification and technological revolution seem to have become largely realized. World wars, with their ever-increasing engines of death and destruction, characterized the twentieth century, and the rise of totalitarianism and the loss of individuality seem to go along with this objectification. Thus, Kierkegaard's thought appeared to many European and American intellectuals to point the finger most aptly at the true condition of the modern individual. Through the efforts of such thinkers, the word *existentialism* gained familiarity with increasing numbers of people.

Martin Buber (1878–1965)

Martin Buber, a philosopher–theologian, was one who took Kierkegaard seriously and began to develop his own system of thought. Although born and educated in Europe, Buber immigrated to Palestine (now Israel) to join in the attempt of the Jewish people to reclaim their homeland. Perhaps this struggle epitomized the human predicament for Buber, because his writings reflect the need for mutual respect and dignity among all humans. Buber's best-known book is *I and Thou*, a work that seeks to get at the heart of human relations.

In *I and Thou*, Buber describes how the individual is capable of relating to and identifying with the outside world. An objective relationship is characterized as "I–It." In this relationship, one views something outside oneself in a purely objective manner, as a thing to be used and manipulated for selfish ends. One needs to look on one's fellow human beings in terms of the I–Thou relationship; that is, one must recognize that each individual has an intense, personal world of meaning. To the extent that this personal or subjective reality of each individual is discounted or ignored, human beings will continue to suffer from the absurdities in which they are caught. It is from

EXISTENTIALISM, PHENOMENOLOGY, AND EDUCATION

the standpoint of I–It that inhumanity, death, and destruction are foisted upon one person by another.

Buber found that people are treated as objects (Its) in business, religion, science, government, and education. Many students today believe that they are seen only as numbers stored in a computer. In college classes of 200 or more, it is not surprising that this concern becomes reinforced when the teacher cannot remember a student's name or perhaps not even remember who is enrolled in the class. The teacher assigns material, marks papers, and gives grades, but student and teacher each go their separate ways. When the students leave that class, they are replaced by other equally anonymous people. Buber did not believe that things have to be this way. In a proper relationship between teacher and student, a mutual sensibility of feeling exists: There is empathy. This is not a subject-to-object relationship as in an I–It relationship, but rather a subject-to-subject relationship—one with a sharing of knowledge, feelings, and aspirations. It is a relationship in which each person involved is both teacher and learner, sharing in a personal way with the other. Buber believed that this kind of relationship should pervade the educational process at all levels, as well as society at large.

Buber thought that a series of I–Thou relationships constitute a continuum with humanity at one end and God at the other. The divine and the human are related, and through one's communication with fellow human beings, one experiences a reciprocal subjectivity that makes life more spiritual. The existence of mutuality between God and humanity cannot be proved, just as God's existence cannot be proved. Yet, one's faith in God and in one's fellow human beings is witness to one's devotion to a higher end.

Buber's humanism has had a profound impact on many thinkers, not only in philosophy and theology but also in psychology, psychiatry, literature, and education. In fact, Buber was one of the few existentialists who wrote specifically about education, especially the nature of the relationship between teacher and student. He was careful to point out that education, like many other areas, also could consist of an I–It relationship in which the student is treated as an object. What Buber wanted was the kind of education in which the teacher and student, though differing in kinds and amounts of knowledge, were on an equal footing at least in terms of their humanity.

Martin Heidegger (1889–1976)

Martin Heidegger was born in Messkirch, Germany, and was reared in the Catholic faith. He attended the University of Freiburg, where he was influenced by Kantian philosophy and later by the teachings of philosopher Edmund Husserl, who developed a philosophical method known as phenomenology. Heidegger adopted this methodology and extended its usage with *hermeneutics*, or the interpretation of lived experience. In his mature years, he became famous as a professor of philosophy at the University of Freiburg, where he taught many young philosophers, including Sartre, who probably was his most renowned student. His teachings and works, particularly his major work, *Sein und Zeit* (Being and Time), published in 1927, have influenced many philosophers.

On several occasions, Heidegger took pains to state that his major category of investigation was Being, and not the lonely, estranged individual. Be that as it may,

Heidegger's starting point was what he called "being-in-the-world," or lived experience at the individual–environment (world) level. The individual existent is *dasein,* and Heidegger devotes considerable space to an analysis of *dasein.* Thus, although Heidegger's intent and purpose are to investigate Being, his analysis largely rests on the individual interpreting and constructing a personal world of meaning.

Individual existence, or being-in-the-world, consists of three basic aspects. The first aspect is the individual experiencing the world as a surrounding environment *(Umwelt).* *Umwelt* is not just the physical environment in the objective sense; rather, it is the environment as experienced by the individual. Thus, it is not strictly an objective experience. The second aspect is the experience of others, or fellow individuals *(Mitwelt).* This is the complicated ground of social relations; not only does the individual experience others subjectively, but others are also subjectivities with their own personal viewpoints. The third aspect is the individual becoming aware of himself as a distinct and subjective existence *(eigenwelt).* This is the intensely personal level encountered when one poses such a question as "Who am I?" In encountering such a fundamental question, the individual comes face to face with existential anguish and anxiety because the question has no apparent answer at the level of lived experience. No laws, guidelines, or objective reality automatically give the answer. People must answer the question for themselves.

This brief exposition of Heidegger's *dasein* analysis in no way does justice to his complex philosophy. In fact, he found it extremely difficult to find adequate words to describe the intricacies of Being from the standpoint of the individual existent, and he has been criticized for the terminology and style in which he wrote. The weighty and intricate particular meanings he had to attach to such words as *dasein* and *eigenwelt* complicate any understanding of his thought. This complexity is heightened further for those who must read him in English translation; one will encounter many words, such as *dasein,* that have no accurate English equivalent.

Although Heidegger did not write specifically about education, educators might better understand the intense personal side of existence after studying his thoughts. The question "Who am I?" is a profound and troubling one that most people face more or less with consternation while growing up and one that probably is never answered fully. It could be said that this condition lies at the heart of the identity crisis that each person encounters at various times in life.

Jean-Paul Sartre (1905–1980)

Of all the leading existentialist philosophers, probably the best known is Jean-Paul Sartre. Born in France, he was brought up in a home where he was encouraged to develop his intellectual talents. At an early age, he began to write, emphasizing the predicaments of the human condition. Influenced a great deal by his grandfather, who was a language teacher, Sartre aspired to become a teacher of philosophy. He was an excellent student, and after completing his education in France, he went to Germany where he studied with Heidegger in the 1930s. He later settled in Paris, where he became a professor of philosophy.

At the same time, he pursued his literary ambitions, writing several novels and plays that became best sellers. However, Sartre, like so many others, was caught up in the destructive web of World War II. He joined the French Army and was captured by the Germans early in the war. After the fall of France, he was allowed to return to Paris on parole, and there he joined the French Resistance. The Nazis were brutal and swift in their punishment of captured Resistance fighters: Men and women in the Resistance were faced constantly with instant death, and this kind of situation sharpened Sartre's thinking on the absurdity and meaninglessness of individual existence.

Even in the face of the Nazi death machine, Sartre was able to write and publish a major philosophical work in 1943, *L'Être et le néant (Being and Nothingness)*. It stands as one of the original philosophical treatises of the twentieth century, and it is Sartre's most thorough philosophical statement. It investigates consciousness (being-for-itself) and the objects of consciousness (being-in-itself). *Consciousness,* or being-for-itself, is the reflection and negation of the objective world. It is as if human consciousness tries to be its objects, as in the case of the self-conscious person who, in playing a role, literally tries to be the other person, or the dedicated teacher who tries to be the essence of all teachers. Such attempts are always failures; consciousness, or individuality, cannot be what it is not. Being-for-itself always transcends, negates, or goes beyond being-in-itself. This means that human consciousness or individuality is free. In a sense, it could be said that consciousness deals with the meaning of things and not with raw objectivity or things-in-themselves.

In his philosophical works, Sartre viewed the human predicament in terms of the lonely individual in an absurd world. He viewed human existence as primarily meaningless because people are thrown into the world totally without meaning, and any meaning that is encountered in the world must be constructed by oneself. The development of meaning is an individual matter, and because the world and the individual are without meaning, no justification is found for existing. There is no God to give existence meaning (Sartre was an atheist), nor does any realm of ideas or independent physical reality exist with its own independent and immutable meaning. Humanity, individually and collectively, exists without any meaning or justification except what people make themselves.

Sartre's point of view is austere, at least when compared with, say, idealism or realism, and it is pessimistic when compared with pragmatism. Yet, it would be an error to take this notion too far. Sartre stated that "existence precedes essence" and meant that if we are indeed without meaning when we are born, then we can fashion our own meaning in the world in any way we see fit. According to Sartre, if there is no God (no First Cause), then there is nothing to prevent us from becoming whatever we desire because there is no predetermined self or essence.

The same can be said for physical reality and science because Sartre saw science as a human creation, no better and no worse in and of itself than any other creation. Thus, when people step back and view themselves as they really are, they see that nothing determines them to do anything; all the absolutes, rules, and restrictions are simply the puny and absurd creations of humans. If no primal restrictions exist, then there is no determinism. Everything is possible. Humanity is absolutely free; as Sartre put it in his characteristic terminology, "Man is condemned to be free."

Human freedom is awesome, for if we are totally free, we are also totally responsible for our choices and actions. In other words, we cannot do something and then claim that it was God's will or caused by the laws of science or that society made us do it. We are free; therefore, we are totally responsible. We have no excuse, as Sartre tried to show in his play *No Exit.*

If one thinks seriously about this existentialist proposition, one might come to understand that human existence is a sword that cuts two ways. Existence today might be characterized by war, disease, hunger, or starvation on the part of many, and conspicuous consumption on the part of a few. Ignorance, racial strife, and a host of the most severe and depressing conditions make up the human predicament, but who is responsible? Is it God? The law of supply and demand? National honor? No. People themselves are responsible. If people can create war, then they also can create peace. If people can, through absurd economics, create conditions of starvation by allowing a few individuals to control the wealth of a country, then people also can likewise redistribute the wealth so that no one need starve. In other words, if humans are the creators of their ills, then they also can create a better and more humane way of living. It is up to us. All people have to do is make choices and act accordingly. These choices and actions are not easy, however, for in an attempt to change such conditions, those who benefit from the current conditions will resist. Sartre did not disregard existing society and customs; he was well aware that many individuals do not see anything wrong with war, the surplus controlled by a few, or even starvation.

We may argue that although all of this is true, we do have to contend with nature and scientific law. Sartre would answer by pointing out that "nature," "law," and "science" are themselves meanings created by humans. We may then object that although this is true for science and scientific laws, surely we cannot ignore nature, our oldest enemy that thwarts us at every turn. However, that which we call nature is itself meaningless and without justification, and people give it meaning as nature. Witness how the laws of nature have changed through the ages: Once it was accepted that the world was flat, but this has changed. No one would want to stake his or her life on the proposition that people will view the world 1000 years from now in the same way they do now. This argument points out that even nature itself is endowed with meaning by human beings. Through this endowment, we come to control nature, however limited this control might be. We say that people cannot control nature because they do not understand it, but it makes just as much sense to say that people do not control nature because they have not given it sufficient meaning. Scientific investigation is, after all, nothing more than striving to endow the natural world with meaning so that people can control their own lives better. Again, humans are even responsible for the meaning of nature.

Lest one begins to think that Sartre makes the human being into God, it should be pointed out that this is just the opposite of his view. Instead, he says that people try to be God, but because God does not exist, this is only further evidence of human absurdity. In fact, Sartre calls humans a "useless passion" when they try to set themselves up as God.

Much of the foregoing might sound strange. We are used to thinking differently about existence, if we bother to think about it at all. We may tend to view life as a "bowl of cherries," or we may go the other way and become cynical pessimists who bemoan our fate. Sartre is trying to call our attention to what is obvious: We *can* make a difference, but not without choosing our goals and working toward them. It could be said that every advance that humans have made, every humane act committed, has happened because some individual or group of individuals chose to make it happen and then struggled to achieve that choice. Few if any of the things we achieve come about by accident. Even those events that occur by accident show Sartre's insight because they are *accidents,* meaningless in and of themselves. They depend on humans to experience them, suffer, undergo, endure, or enjoy them. *Humanity* gives them their meaning *for* humanity.

Critics have pointed out that existentialism in general, and Sartre's philosophy in particular, lacks an adequate social theory to deal with complex institutions such as schools, and that this factor has hampered a more thorough application of existentialist thought to the problems of education. Sartre, who was perhaps the most individualistic of all the existentialist philosophers, eventually came to align himself with Marxist theory although he did not adopt a doctrinaire Marxist position and preferred to think of himself as an independent thinker. This happened primarily because (as Sartre put it) his theory could not stand alone: It needed Marxism for completion, and Marxism needed the humanizing influence of the existentialist perspective. Apparently, Sartre came to agree that individuals might find value in participation in the social and political process as long as the individual defines that participation.

EXISTENTIALISM IN MODERN LIFE

Existentialism has affected many areas of thought. It has been influential in the realm of theology, particularly the writings of Rheinhold Niebuhr, Gabriel Marcel, and Paul Tillich. It also has made inroads into the fields of psychology and psychiatry and has been championed by such advocates as Carl Rogers and Abraham Maslow.

Carl Rogers, for example, believed that teachers should risk themselves for their students in classroom experimentation. The teacher should look for the "potentiality and wisdom of the person" and work for self-directed change on the part of the learner. This risk involves not only the individual teacher's sense of self but also his or her willingness to trust the learner. This means that the teacher must become a "facilitator of learning" to help release a student's potential. Rogers was against the concept of teaching as showing, guiding, or directing; rather, the teacher should "prize" the learner and make the learner feel worthwhile. This can be accomplished through prizing the feelings and opinions of the student, and it involves the development of what Rogers called "empathic understanding." The result of successful education and living should be a "fully functioning person."

Maslow talked about a hierarchy of needs and differentiated between basic needs and "metaneeds." *Basic needs* are primary: the need for air, food, protection from danger, and a familiarity with the environment. *Metaneeds* transcend these basic needs and involve a personal reaching or growing to realize one's potential. Metaneeds include such things as belongingness, esteem, and aesthetic needs. They are necessary, in Maslow's view, to help people become "self-actualized" persons who are realistically oriented, autonomous, and creative. Maslow also differentiated between pseudo-self-actualization and authentic self-actualization. *Pseudo-self-actualization* is the undisciplined release of impulses in which, for example, someone behaves like a spoiled child. An authentic self-actualized person says, "I've considered my feelings and yours, too." The central idea is that people should be encouraged to make their own decisions, respect themselves, and treat others with compassion. Life is full of paradox and contradiction, and no single lifestyle is necessarily the true one. To recognize the existentialist frame of reference is to recognize individual differences and variation.

The intensity of modern life has brought on increasing tension and anxiety. The nature of individual choice, individual action, and commitment is such that anxiety is real and present in all human beings regardless of their station in life or their ideology. This feature of modern life is of great concern to existentialists and has been treated extensively in their works. Some critics have castigated existentialists for an inordinate amount of attention to anxiety, charging that they dwell too much on the tragic, the perverse, and the morbid side of life and exclude more hopeful and optimistic themes. Existentialists reply that too many people wrongly emphasize the optimistic, the good, and the beautiful—all of which create a false impression of existence. For example, if friends from out of town visit, the host usually takes them to the beautiful spots—the parks, the museums and art galleries, and the best restaurants. One does not take a guest to the slums, the depressing areas of poverty, and places where extensive suffering is evident. Without experiencing these other things, visitors get a one-sided picture of the city. Existentialists believe that it is time to balance the scales, but even more fundamentally, they think that the tragic side of life more nearly illustrates human existence, and the individual must face up to this condition. Humans have no recourse but themselves. Humans' very existence is one of anxiety.

Strange as it might sound, Christian theologians have found existentialism to give new meaning to the Christian experience. At first glance, it might seem that existentialism is against religion. It was Nietzsche, who had an important influence on existentialism, who proclaimed that God is dead. Although Christianity traditionally has had a strong streak of optimism in its promise of eternal salvation, atheistic existentialists agree with Karl Marx that religion is the opiate of the masses, pointing toward some supposed heaven and keeping attention diverted from the real problems of the world. The result is that the masses are brutally exploited by the few. Recall, however, that another founder of existentialism—Kierkegaard—found Christian belief to be characterized by anxiety, anguish, and doubt. Christian existentialist theology has embraced these themes, holding out to the believer the proposition that anxiety and doubt are real and necessary experiences to be encountered in living the Christian life.

Marcel, a French religious existentialist, wrote about the Christian experience of the "subjectivity" or "presence" of others. This presence should not be treated as a mere object of experience but as a fellow human in line with perhaps the theme of the Golden Rule. The idea of "presence" has similarities to Buber's I–Thou concept. It also resembles Sartre's being-for-itself (subjectivity) and being-in-itself (objectivity), but Marcel was more attuned to the characteristics and necessities of social relationships than was Sartre. Marcel recognized anxiety and "baseless" choice and held that although a person's belief is always subject to doubt and questioning, one is not totally isolated from all other existence and needs to be open to the "presence" of others.

Other Christian thinkers, such as Tillich, examined human nature in all its ambiguity. Tillich questioned how people should define themselves in modern times, an "age of anxiety." His answer was that we must have "the courage to be" despite fate, death, meaninglessness, and despair. The "courage to be" is based on a belief in God when God has "disappeared," and it involves a faith undermined by resulting doubt, akin to Kierkegaard's "leap of faith." Thus, courage becomes a necessary characteristic of the believer in order to sustain belief. The impact of existentialism on modern Christianity has been notable. It has thrown new light on the mystical aspects of religion and reduced the emphasis on the material side of life. It also has helped make religion more a matter of personal commitment and inner conviction.

Some critics have even questioned whether existentialism should be considered a philosophy. Certainly, it is not systematic in the traditional pattern, but it still has a strong claim as a philosophy in the tradition of Socrates. Just as Socrates was the "gadfly" of Athens, pricking the consciences and shells of decency of the Athenians, so also do existentialists call people to examine their personal lives and to break away from superficial beliefs and uncommitted action.

PHENOMENOLOGICAL PHILOSOPHERS AND THEIR THOUGHT

Edmund Husserl (1859–1938)

Edmund Husserl was born in Czechoslovakian Moravia and was educated in schools and universities in Austria and Germany. Although he received a doctorate in mathematics, he was drawn to philosophy after studying under Franz Brentano. He taught philosophy at several universities, including Göttingen and Freiburg. The term *phenomenology* was used earlier by Kant and Hegel. The use of this term today to designate a particular philosophical method, however, generally is attributed to Husserl.

Husserl was influenced by Kant and Hegel, but he saw his work as a radical departure from theirs, similar to René Descartes's call for philosophy to be grounded on insight beyond the possibility of doubt. In *Ideas*, Husserl's main work, his aim was to use phenomenology to help make philosophy into a rigorous science, but a science different from the physical and behavioral sciences. The latter take what Husserl called "the thesis of the natural standpoint"; that is, the thinker's perception is attuned wholly toward things of the environment or of overt behavior. Traditional science, then, assumes an autonomous world outside human thought. Husserl, in contrast, wanted to study the *original intuition* of the things outside; that is, he wanted to study people's original conscious grasp of things before they begin to impute meaning or interpretation to them. His field of investigation was the preconceptual level of awareness, the original and immediate data of consciousness. The phenomenologist, then, seeks to understand "original experience," or the primordial phenomena of consciousness, prior to the time when one brings previous learning or prejudices to bear on the perception of subsequent meanings. Husserl's call to go "back to the things themselves" means to return to these original, immediate data of consciousness.

Husserl thought that if the phenomenological method were applied and executed rigorously, then it would make philosophy scientific but different from the traditional sciences. Traditional scientific realism teaches that the objects of experience—the sticks, stones, and events of life—are just what they are, independent of conscious perception. This reality is outside consciousness and can be understood or brought to consciousness by the exacting descriptions of scientific method. Husserl argued, however, that scientific descriptions are abstractions filtered from scientific methodology, that they are not the stuff of primordial conscious perception. Consequently, if one wants to understand primordial conscious experience, then one has to perform a "phenomenological reduction"; that is, one must strip away or "bracket" the assumptions and presuppositions of culture (of which traditional science is but one part) and get back to the immediate or original consciousness.

In many respects, Husserl's philosophy is a form of transcendental idealism. On the one hand, he took Descartes's notion of the *cogito,* an idealistic view of subjective thought, and transformed it into a transcendental ego—that is, a consciousness that transcends natural conditions and confronts pure Being. This is seen in his belief that the bracketing of the cultural world was possible. On the other hand, his thought also contains a sense of realism; his phenomenology can be seen as a form of empiricism—of trying to arrive at meaning through conscious experience.

Heidegger and Phenomenology

Martin Heidegger served for a time as Husserl's assistant, and he accepted the notion of phenomenology as a method and as a science of the phenomena of consciousness. An analysis of the term *phenomenology* provides a better idea of Heidegger's conception: *Phenomenon* is that which shows or presents itself, and *logos* is rational discourse about phenomena. For Heidegger, the task was not, however, simply an effort to describe phenomena, but rather to get at what lies behind them—their *being*. Thus, for Heidegger, phenomenology was the science of Being—ontology.

To get to the being of phenomena, Heidegger concentrated his analysis on *dasein,* which signifies a human *being* in the sense of "being there," situated within a historical context. This helps show why Heidegger resisted being lumped with existentialism; *dasein* is not the isolated ego that many existentialists write about. The human being is indelibly historical, he argued, and history is the indelible determinant of human nature. Individual *dasein* has a past and is oriented toward a future, and although phenomenology looks at the immediate present, this historical background colors any given situation of *dasein*, for *dasein* is always arriving out of a past and anticipating a future. Thus, Heidegger changed Husserl's notion of bracketing in any absolute sense because to understand immediate *dasein*, it is necessary to consider its history. With Heidegger, this meant that historical background needs to be interpreted, and this steered him toward hermeneutics, or historical interpretation. His focus was on concrete history, however, not history writ large as Hegel or Marx would view it.

Two developments by Heidegger would help steer phenomenology away from Husserl's transcendentalism: the importance of language (after the *logos,* or discourse, aspect of phenomenology) and hermeneutics (which interprets lived experience). Heidegger's major work was *Being and Time* (1927, English translation 1996), which concentrated on *dasein* analysis. In *The Basic Problems of Phenomenology* (1975, English translation 1982), a work published shortly before his death, one can see certain directional changes in his thought. The study of the philosophic concept of time becomes more important than *dasein* analysis alone, and this gives added importance to hermeneutics and the need for interpretation.

Maurice Merleau-Ponty (1908–1961)

Where Husserl looked for a complete bracketing of the world through phenomenological reduction, Maurice Merleau-Ponty maintained that there could be no denial of the world and hence no complete bracketing. Where Heidegger sought to understand Being, Merleau-Ponty concentrated on the primacy of perception. Where Sartre saw a radical dichotomy between consciousness and the world, Merleau-Ponty saw perception as always a part of the world. For Merleau-Ponty, perception is in and of the world. Because reflection is carried out in the temporal flux of the world, the only way to view it with any accuracy is to accept this worldly base in philosophical study. He saw the roots of the mind in the body and the world and maintained that perception is not simply the result of the action of external things on people, for no pure interiority or exteriority exists.

Merleau-Ponty was attempting to devise a philosophical program that would enable him to lay down a new base for research on imagination, language, culture, ethics, and politics. Unfortunately, his untimely death in 1961 prevented him from carrying out this objective, and only hints remain of what his plans might have produced. His major work was *Phenomenology of Perception* (1945), and several of his more important papers and articles were published posthumously as *Primacy of Perception* (1962). It has been said that he used the fundamental concepts of phenomenology but interpreted them in his own unique way.

For Merleau-Ponty, our "facticity," our worldly existence, cannot be escaped. We must recognize that human consciousness itself is a project of the world, a world that it neither possesses nor embraces but without which it cannot exist. Consciousness is directed perpetually toward the world of things, ideas, events, persons, or experience. Perception is not a purely intellectual synthesis; rather, perception is experienced bodily and in the world at the prereflective level. Reflection comes after perception and helps solidify or clarify perception, for a perception that is not followed by thought is soon lost. Reflection involves language, and this puts us even farther away from immediacy. As Merleau-Ponty put it, to use language, to name a thing or describe it with language, is to tear oneself away from a thing's individual and unique characteristics and to see it as representative of an essence or category. It is to go from the concrete to the categorical, where words establish meaning.

Nevertheless, for Merleau-Ponty, perception is primary. He believed that previous philosophy had erred in viewing a person's primary relationship to the world as that of a thinker to an object of thought. Thinking, thought, and the objects of thought are not concrete but abstract. Perception occurs in a concrete, temporal world of flux, and what one thinks about it later might not hold for similar future perceptions. In other words, perception is immediate and prereflective, and "every perception takes place within a particular horizon. . . . We experience a perception and its horizon 'in action' rather than by 'posing' them or explicitly 'knowing' them." The significance of this realization, which inserts a note of skepticism into Merleau-Ponty's philosophy, is that one cannot view perceptions as pure, unified abstractions or theorems; no transcendent Cartesian *cogito* grasps truths, nor is truth immanent in perception. These things come secondarily, not primarily. Certainty might be had in reflection, but it is a certainty that is abstract, categorical, and secondary. In other words, abstract truth is not self-evident in perception, but perception has within it the potential for arriving at truth in a more suitable fashion as it is sensed or experienced, rather than as it is filtered through the philosophical dogmatisms and assumptions of the past.

Phenomenology and Hermeneutics

Whereas phenomenology seeks an ordered description of the objects of consciousness, hermeneutics concentrates on the interpretation and meaning of conscious experience over time. Language is central to hermeneutics because it is through language that fruitful interpretation and meaning are secured. What Heidegger was striving for in his analyses of *dasein* and time was a rational understanding of human existence or human *being*, and this could not be secured without attention to language. As he put it in *The Basic Problems of Phenomenology*, "In speaking about something, the dasein speaks itself out, expresses itself, as existent being-in-the-world, dwelling with and occupying itself with beings." In effect, when people contemplate or mull over something, they are projecting themselves into a future understanding of themselves and the world. To project oneself into some new understanding is, so to speak, to redefine oneself and to strike out in new directions. This is how the self (or *dasein*) grows and evolves; it was just this history, this concept of time, that Heidegger was attempting to understand. Furthermore, understanding (and thought itself) is carried on through some form of language or symbolization. To gain clarity or rational understanding, one must be attentive to language and engage in hermeneutics.

Two philosophers who have been prominent in developing hermeneutics are Hans-Georg Gadamer (1900–2002) and Paul Ricoeur (1913–). Gadamer has taken the position that Heidegger's later philosophy was not concerned with just the being of *dasein*, but rather the being of *dasein* that understands itself, or self-understanding. This is shown in Heidegger's concentration on historicity and time. In effect, consciousness and selfhood, in and of themselves, are banished in favor of self-understanding in the historical sense and establish the essential unity of self-understanding. This is not, however, the same as focusing one's gaze inward. Rather, it is a self-understanding that comes from trying to understand oneself and the world, from trying to be as rational as possible about the things around us. Hence, hermeneutical phenomenology does not embrace the radical (and perhaps self-centered) individualism on which some existentialists dwell.

Hermeneutics does, however, focus on the "internal" process of using language; as Gadamer puts it, "hermeneutics is primarily of use where making clear to others and making clear to oneself has become blocked." In Gadamer's view, a chief value of hermeneutical philosophy is the educational value of self-formation (or *Bildung*). It is his belief that this self-formation is a more important goal for philosophical study than traditional epistemology.

Paul Ricoeur, in some respects like Gadamer, shifts the point of departure of phenomenology from the perceptualist mode to the linguistic mode. He maintains the concrete subject as the focus of inquiry but does not believe that one can know oneself directly or introspectively. The only course is to seek understanding indirectly, and this explains his concentration on language. His linguistic and phenomenological hermeneutics is based on the notion that through language, one expresses one's self-understanding. Through words, through language, people bring into the open whatever understanding they have of themselves. His phenomenology, then, focuses on a description of the phenomena of consciousness indirectly, as these phenomena are revealed through language, and hermeneutic interpretation is brought to bear on the question of how the comprehension of signs (language) relates to the comprehension of self.

EXISTENTIALISM AND PHENOMENOLOGY IN PHILOSOPHY OF EDUCATION

Because existentialism is a protest type of philosophy, many of its adherents have not been overly concerned with methodology and systematic exposition. Some philosophers, however, have seen phenomenology as providing a rigorous methodology for describing lived experience, and hermeneutics as providing an interpretive approach to individual experience.

Aims of Education

Existentialists believe that most philosophies of the past have asked people to think deeply about abstractions that had little or no relationship to life. Scholastic philosophy, in which thinkers debated such questions as how many angels could sit on the head of a pin, might be a case in point. The answers to such questions provided nothing except perhaps some psychological satisfaction at winning a debate through argumentation. Even then, the answers were unprovable. Existentialists reject this approach to ideas. They believe that in their philosophy, the individual is drawn in as a participant. People explore their own feelings and relate ideas to their own lives. Consequently, in an existentialist education, the emphasis is not on scholarly debate but on creation; that is, one can create ideas relevant to one's existence.

Existentialists, such as Sartre, believe that "existence precedes essence." First comes the individual and then the ideas the individual creates. Ideas about heaven, hell, and God are all human inventions. Even theistic existentialists admit that ideas about God are unprovable although they might parallel something in existence. Thus, the individual can be given credit for the creation of concepts like peace, truth, and justice but blamed for things like bigotry, war, and greed. Because people are the creators of all ideas, this focuses as much attention on humans as on the ideas themselves; if it is true that people have created ideas that are harmful in practice, then they also can create new ideas to replace them.

Because the individual human is so important as the creator of ideas, existentialists maintain that education should focus on individual human reality. It should deal with the individual as a unique being in the world—not only as a creator of ideas, but also as a living, feeling being. Most philosophies and religions, existentialists charge, tend to focus on the individual only as a cognitive being. The individual is this but is also a feeling, aware person, and existentialists think this side deserves attention.

Existentialists assert that a good education would encourage individuals to ask such questions as "Who am I?" "Where is my life headed?" and "Why do I exist?" In dealing with these questions, people would have to recognize that the individual is an emotional and irrational creature as much or more than an unemotional and rational one. The individual is always in transition, so the moment people believe they know themselves is probably the moment to begin the examination all over again.

Most educational philosophies up to this point have emphasized the concept of a person as a rational being in a rational world. Much of this stems from the Aristotelian notion that we can understand our place in the universe and that this understanding is primarily a result of sharpening our powers of intellect through reason and observation. Even through the Age of Enlightenment, some held a strong conviction that we could steadily increase our knowledge and power over the universe. Yet, with this rise of rationality, we continued to be plagued by wars, inhumanity, and irrationality—often perpetrated by those who believed that they had attained a mastery of logic and philosophy.

For the modern existentialists, World War II was a watershed in such irrationality and inhumanity, and existentialists, particularly in France and Germany, began to take a new look at human nature. They reexamined such things as death, courage, and reason. Reason, often used to justify the death and destruction inflicted by war, was particularly scrutinized. Existentialists found that reason was used to justify cruelty and aggression to the extent that millions of Jews were sent to the gas chambers through what some Nazis thought were rational motives. Reason was used to defend these actions, so people could say they were only following orders, it was not their decision, or it was done for purposes of the state.

Existentialists believe that a good education emphasizes individuality. It attempts to assist each of us in seeing ourselves with our fears, frustrations, and hopes, as well as the ways we use reason for good and ill. The first step in any education, then, is to understand ourselves.

Existentialists maintain that the "absurd" side of life needs serious exploration. Perhaps what people take to be a rational explanation of the universe is their own application of what they think is rational. It is difficult to see things as they are, objectively, as if one is from another planet. Yet, if people did so, how strange many things would seem that are taken for granted, such as women walking on little stilts that they call shoes, and men wearing flashy-colored nooses that they call ties. Further areas of absurdity might be explored, such as the pierced ear from which to dangle bright, shiny objects, or the efforts of one who hates blacks but wants to change his skin coloring to dark tan in the summer. Are these rational acts, or do people use their reason to say that they are rational?

One area of drama is known as *theater of the absurd.* Eugene Ionesco, Samuel Beckett, Edward Albee, and others wrote plays in this genre. Theater of the absurd is about life, magnifying and emphasizing certain aspects of it to show its irrationality and absurdity. In the play *Who's Afraid of Virginia Woolf?* a married couple spends a great deal of time attacking each other to the extent that each has become skillful at it through practice. Seemingly, such people remain together for the purpose of developing greater ways of hurting each other. Books like *Games People Play*, by Eric Berne, also show how people use others to achieve their own narrow ends.

People are not encouraged through most education to see the absurdities of life; rather, the good side is emphasized. For example, most reading books for children focus on the uniformity and reliability of existence. They show children in settings with no marital conflict, war, hunger, or death. Existentialists believe that a vital part of one's education is to examine the perverted and ugly side of life, the irrational as well as the good side. Yet, in education we are always covering up. Apparently, adults do not believe that a child should be exposed to such human realities as death, and so the children are told that their dead grandmother went on a long trip or that she is away. Adults lie to children about birth, sex, money, and a host of other things. Existentialists believe in a truthful kind of education, where children learn about many facets of life, whether good or bad, rational or irrational.

Existentialists believe that education should foster an understanding of anxiety. Many people certainly are frustrated by life, but this frustration often is caused by a kind of education that did not prepare them for a world of conflict. What existentialists mean by anxiety is an awareness of the tension of existence. When people are involved in life, when they are acting persons, they are bound to feel some tension through involvement. Existentialists point out that no tension exists after death and that some people are trying to make their lives like death by avoiding conflict at all cost. The opposite of death is life, and life for the existentialist requires some degree of tension. Although Marx talked of religion as the opium of the people, Christian existentialists say that Christians are people in conflict, people who must wonder constantly whether what they believe is true and if they are acting enough in support of those beliefs.

One distinguishing feature of existentialist phenomenology in philosophy of education is the emphasis on *possibility* as a goal of education. It could be said that the emphasis on human *being* is an emphasis on *becoming* because human consciousness never can be static. This is reminiscent of Sartre's argument that human consciousness (being-for-itself) never can become a substance, an objective *thing* (being-in-itself). Hence, when one speaks of the aims of education from an existentialist phenomenological perspective, possibility takes on central importance.

As Gordon Chamberlin puts it in *The Educating Act*, "The life-world out of which we interpret what happens to us has been constituted through our interpretations of what has happened to us in the past." This life-world interpretation can be characterized by adequacy or inadequacy, but each person reacts to a new experience in terms of this interpreted background. This life-world "history" is the history that Heidegger wanted to understand in his hermeneutics. It is what Gadamer was seeking to understand in his notion of education as *Bildung,* or edification. In short, each new experience adds to the funded meaning of experience that each of us has and sets the stage for present and future possibilities. Educators, then, must be cognizant of their own and their students' life-worlds. Indeed, it could be said that the chief goal of the educator is to help learners construct the best life-worlds possible. The emphasis is not simply on the past, however, but on the present and the future, on *possibility.* As Chamberlin points out, "Education always leads to action. Education always follows action. Indeed, education is an activity."

The point is illustrated further by Paulo Freire in *Pedagogy of the Oppressed.* Freire asserts that often people are oppressed because they serve as "hosts" for the oppressors. An oppressor is whoever or whatever serves as an overriding influence that is uncritically accepted or chosen by the oppressed. In Freire's view, oppression will be present wherever one's consciousness is characterized by the condition "in which *to be* is *to be like,* and *to be like* is *to be like the oppressor.*" Oppression thus forces passivity, and passivity provides a degree of security because nothing is risked. For Freire, however, an education that liberates is painful because, similar to childbirth, it brings a new person into the world. It is an education that cannot be achieved in idealistic terms or simply by talking about it; rather, it is something to be achieved through purposeful action.

From the phenomenological standpoint, liberating education initially results in the perception that the world of oppression is not a closed world from which one cannot escape; instead, oppression is a limiting situation that can be transformed. This perception is tentative, however, because it must result in action that seeks to change existing conditions. The phenomenological import of this educational view resides in how people perceive conditions or in how conditions present themselves to consciousness. On the one hand, the oppressive perception is fatalistic, believing that the given cannot be changed. On the other hand, liberated perception does not accept the given as inevitable, but rather looks to *possibilities,* to a world to be born through *praxis* or purposeful action.

Maxine Greene's expression for education as possibility is *wide-awakeness.* The aim is to enable learners to become attentive, perceptive, or wide-awake to possibilities. Many things in contemporary life hinder wakefulness. Many people live in societies that are characterized by stifling bureaucracies and mindless consumerism. Others suffer from grinding poverty and ignorance. These and other forces almost guarantee passivity in conditions of domination and powerlessness. Greene forcefully suggests, however, that such feelings can largely be overcome through the conscious effort of individuals to keep themselves alert, to think about their worldly condition, to inquire into the forces that seem to dominate them, and to interpret their daily experiences. Education can help tremendously in achieving this wide-awakeness, but it must be conceived and conducted in the right way. For the educator, it means not accepting dominating administrative hierarchies as inevitable. It means becoming aware that hierarchies are made by human beings and are not a part of the inevitable order of the universe. It means developing awareness about such things as state-adopted classroom material, mandated testing programs, or curriculum censorship instigated by politically powerful interest groups. It means becoming aware of the moral issues involved in such things as mandated testing programs that unfairly discriminate or any host of institutionalized practices that interfere in free educational activity. Finally, it means that the educator should develop phenomenological and hermeneutical competence to demystify such conditions and help learners develop similar competence. People must learn to evaluate comfortable conventions and pressure to go along with the crowd against carefully chosen moral principles. They must become attuned to possibility, to being wide-awake.

Despite the seeming fascination of existentialists with the irrational, they rarely if ever have advocated irrationality as a goal. To the contrary, their effort has been to confront irrationality as an aspect of the human condition and to put it in proper perspective. Many existentialists have talked about the "tragic side of life," and a large part of that tragedy is the result of irrationality. Phenomenology helps put the irrational in proper perspective because the thrust of phenomenology is toward rational description. As phenomenology has been applied to education, emphasis has been put on helping learners understand and comprehend lived experience. As Donald Vandenberg put it, education involves becoming as reasonable a person as humanly possible. Thus, reasonableness should be added as one goal of an existentialist phenomenological philosophy of education.

Greene makes the point that one problem of the contemporary world is the polarization of those who embrace an authority of science and those who embrace an authority of affective behavior. On the one hand are those who extol scientific knowledge as the objective and final answer to fundamental questions; on the other hand are those who extol the subjective and private inner world as the only source of answers. Although educators may not accept either side of the argument, they cannot remain unaffected by this kind of polarization, or what has been called "the crisis of culture." Buffeted by such polarizations, young people may throw up their hands in discouragement from sorting out the conflicting claims of life. They might try to fit into the mold and be accepted by their peers. What often results from the frustration of such culture conflict is anti-intellectualism, but the educator must help enable the young to conceptualize and develop a rational perspective of their worlds.

The rational understanding sought by the phenomenologist is not that of an older rational empiricism that looked solely on the impact of the outer world; instead, the phenomenologist looks toward a rationality that proceeds from primal consciousness, which thrusts toward the outer world and engages with it. From Greene's point of view, phenomenology does not glorify inwardness and introspection. It concerns itself with how the individual touches the outer world through perceiving, judging, believing, remembering, and imagining. What composes the inner "stream of experience" has to do with the outer world and involves what phenomenologists call intentionality.

This notion should be explored further because it lies at the heart of any phenomenological concept of education. Much of human conscious life occurs without people being explicitly conscious of being conscious; that is, consciousness is absorbed with everyday events, and we take for granted the commonsense reality of things. Occasionally, however, we become explicitly aware of things on the horizon of consciousness that become suddenly questionable and throw barriers before the flow of everyday events (similar to the Jamesian-Deweyan "hitch" or "block" to the flow of conscious experience). As a consequence, people must try to sort things out through existentialist critique, phenomenological description, and hermeneutical interpretation. People must try to be as reasonable as possible, not in the sense of objective and removed rationalism, but a reasonableness that is ever cognizant of the human condition. If we are going to be open to possibility and wide-awake, we also must be reasonable.

Methods of Education

The first thing that most existentialists want is a change in attitude about education. Instead of seeing it as something a student is filled with, measured against, or fitted into, the existentialist suggests that students first be looked at as individuals and that they be allowed to take a positive role in the shaping of their own education and life. Every student brings to school a background of experiences that will influence personal decisions, but by and large, existentialists urge that schools and other institutions be free places where students are encouraged to do things because they want to do them. Some writers, such as Van Cleve Morris, look at A.S. Neill's *Summerhill* as a sketch of the kind of education that existentialists prefer. Neill's book, first published in 1960 and in several editions since, gave Summerhill School an international reputation for emphasizing student freedom, spontaneous play, open expression of feelings, and student participation in the democratic control over community life in the school. While these themes often strike a responsive chord among educators with existentialist leanings, the school does not identify itself with existentialism but calls itself a "progressive" school. It is an environment where students are encouraged to make their own choices and are free to do so. Summerhill has its rules and regulations, some made by the students and some made by the administration, but basically it is a free institution as compared with most other schools.

For the existentialist, no two children are alike. They differ in the information, personal traits, interests, and desires they have acquired. It is ridiculous to think that they should have the same kind of education. Yet, too often children not only are lumped together but also taught the same things that are supposedly appropriate to their grade level. People have expressed much concern over "mass society," "the lonely crowd," and "a nation of sheep," but today's educational institutions still foster conformity and obedience.

Many existentialists are disturbed by the emphasis that some educators put on education for adjustment. Although John Dewey believed that education should be in the forefront of change, he also recognized the need to prepare the child for existing society while working for change. Some "progressive" educators, however, under the guise of pragmatic philosophy, made "life adjustment" the primary focus of education and promoted education that stifled individuality and social change.

Existentialists would like to see an end to the manipulation of the student, with teachers controlling students along predetermined behavioral paths. Existentialists would like the children to choose their own paths from the options available to them. Schools often contain uniform materials, curricula, and teaching, and although educators have talked quite a bit about promoting individuality in education, most programs and teaching methods have tended to become more alike. Existentialists argue for diversity in education—not only in curriculum but also in the ways things are taught. Some students, they point out, learn well through one approach and others through another. Many options for learning should be open to them.

Existentialists are concerned with the role of the teacher or educator in the learning process. They believe that every teacher should be a student and every student a teacher. Buber discussed this in detail in his description of the I–Thou and I–It concepts. In the I–It relation, a teacher treats a student as someone to direct and fill up with knowledge; the student is an object to be manipulated. Followers of Buber support an I–Thou approach in which student and teacher learn from each other and the relationship is more one of mutual respect.

Vandenberg, in *Being and Education*, gives a phenomenological description of traditional pedagogic methods as characterized by dominance/submission and commanding/obeying relations. The teacher dominates and commands, and it is the role of the student to submit and obey. In such relations, teachers and students are moved away from what could be a more satisfying educational relationship into playing roles that defeat education. In other words, the teacher is pulled into spending time controlling students, and students are drawn into defeating teacher control. Educational method is not used to help students be open to possibilities for growth by understanding their "being-in-the-world" (their individual histories and ways of responding), nor is it used to help them secure a better understanding of their own potentials on which to engage in educational activity. As a result, they are alienated from the teacher. What phenomenologist-educators must seek, then, is to construct educational methods that provide an openness to the world for themselves and their students. This does not imply a laissez-faire role for teachers; rather, because of the greater experience, knowledge, and phenomenological understanding of teachers, it is their responsibility to develop an educational environment that promotes awareness of the past and present and of future possibilities. This awareness is also sensitive to phenomenological time—that is, to the past-present-future nature of conscious life. Proper educational method, then, brings the possibilities of the world before teacher and student—to the teacher in rediscovering the excitement of learning and to the student in opening up a whole new world of possibility.

In practical terms, this involves, for example, methodology that helps a student gain greater command of a language and realize more effective ways to communicate— ways that make the student more articulate and capable of comprehension and self-expression. Another example is an openness to human history and the development of a greater understanding of why human culture has developed as it has. Students become educated into a better understanding of the human adventure and their own circumstances within it. They become more sensitive to human possibility and understand that they themselves are not necessarily and fully determined by the past.

Every present is conditioned by the past, but every present is also pregnant with future possibility for change and new direction. To accomplish this kind of educational approach and outcome, the teacher must understand that the chief requirement is to help students explore the world and to open up the possibilities of the world for them.

In a sense, the phenomenologist seeks a method that helps students internalize the world and make it their own, but it is always more than a mere internalizing. Chamberlin describes the educational experience as "the meeting of two complex streams of experience"— the stream of the teacher and the stream of the learner. Although the teacher's experience might be greater than the learner's simply because of maturity and extent, both are complex; the educational process essentially brings these streams together. The student is dependent because of immaturity, lack of understanding, or other factors, but this does not mean that all the initiative is on the side of the teacher. The teacher's role is that of an enabler who helps the student appropriate, internalize, and make over. The teacher takes a cue from the responses of the learner, whether these responses are active or passive, and the learner can initiate new directions by posing questions and expressing a desire to learn.

As Chamberlin sees it, the teacher can make authority claims over the learner, but that authority derives from an understanding of the educational process and the phenomenological world of the learner. The learner also has authority—the authority to interpret the teacher's intent and the authority to interpret how learning is appropriated and meaning imputed within the learner's own life-world.

The convergence of the two streams of experience of teacher and learner, then, depends to some degree on the antecedents that each brings to an educational encounter. It also depends on the present and on the interpretation that each makes of ongoing activity. Finally, the convergence depends on ensuing action—that is, on how the teacher becomes more effective and how the learner grows and is more capable of managing personal affairs and the affairs of the world.

In *Teacher as Stranger*, Greene set forth the kinds of questions an educator must ask in confronting the phenomenological conditions of human relationships between a teacher and a student. The teacher must ask not only the existentialist question "Who am I?" but also "How am I to conceive *the other* as a fellow human being?" It is simply not enough to know the scientific characteristics of a fellow being, such as biological and psychological characteristics; one also must know the phenomenological conditions. Teachers must confront phenomenologically what they understand (and feel and imagine) as significant fact, as useful knowledge, or as serious belief. Contemporary life is a time of uncertainty and confusion, and this is even more reason for the educator to seek rational understanding and comprehension—not from some all-encompassing, objective platform removed from living experience but from a phenomenological standpoint that attempts to understand the primary world of consciousness that each person brings to the educational situation. Consequently, the educator will not view the educational process as simply something to be imposed from the outside onto impressionable students but will strive to understand how each of us approaches learning from a unique background.

This is not to say that structured knowledge will not be presented by the teacher and by learning materials or that students will not have to struggle with difficult ideas. As Greene sees it, educators must be capable of "tough mindedness" and "tender mindedness"; that is, they must be able to comprehend the educational process from the standpoint of subject matter to be learned and from the lived experience perspective of the learner. Of course, no educator ever can climb into the consciousness of the learner and see the world as it is presented to and experienced by the learner; however, each of us is a learner, and each of us is presented with situations that are difficult to embrace and understand. Educators, by trying to understand rationally their own experience and the learning difficulties presented by so many experiences of life, also will have a better understanding of the proper methods of education by understanding the difficulties, mysteries, uncertainties, and joys experienced by the learner.

The phenomenologist's concern with educational method is not so much with specific techniques, although these are important, but with clearing the way for a pedagogical encounter. In the words of Vandenberg, the concern is "to lay the groundwork so that being can clear a space for itself within the teacher–pupil relation."

Curriculum

It is interesting that most existentialist and phenomenological philosophers have had lengthy and rigorous educations. Most of them taught at one time or another, usually in a university setting. They were concerned primarily with the humanities and have written extensively in that genre. Through the humanities, existentialists have tried to awaken modern individuals to the dangers of being swallowed up by the megalopolis and runaway technology. This seems to have taken place because the humanities contain greater potential for introspection and the development of self-meaning than other studies.

The humanities loom large in an existentialist curriculum because they deal with the essential aspects of human existence, such as the relationships among people, the tragic as well as the happy side of human life, and the absurdities as well as the meaningful aspects of life. In short, existentialists want to see humankind in its totality—the perverted as well as the exalted, the mundane as well as the glorious, the despairing as well as the hopeful—and they believe that the humanities and the arts do this better than the sciences. Existentialists do not have any definite rules about what the curriculum should comprise, however. They believe that the student-in-situation making a choice should be the deciding factor.

Although phenomenologists have been more interested in understanding the lived experience of the learner than in the specific content of things to be learned, some of them have given attention to curriculum organization and content. The tendency, however, is to view curriculum from the standpoint of the learner rather than as a collection of discrete subjects. Vandenberg suggests that an appropriate way to conceive of the tasks involved in curriculum decision making is to see the learner in terms of "landscape" and "geography." "Landscape" is the correlate of the learner's prereflective consciousness. It is disorganized, even chaotic, and education should proceed to expand continually the horizons of this landscape within the limits of the learner's own finitude. "Geography" involves bringing order and logic to this landscape and providing the learner with a structured education as represented by the organized curriculum. Landscape is the original setting of one's being-in-the-world, and geography is the world of fact and universal concept, a world of abstraction. Authentic existence is in neither one nor the other but, in a sense, has a foot in each or resides in between. To ignore landscape is to court alienation of the learner. To ignore geography is to court a disorganized and chaotic conscious life. The educator, then, must deal with what Vandenberg calls the "pedagogic paradox." The educator must seek a context in which students can unite their originality, their landscape, with the geography of organized curriculum so that originality gains power and direction.

Greene makes a similar point although in a different manner. She has spoken more explicitly about specific subject matter because she is a steadfast advocate of the humanities and the arts and also has given attention to the basics. Greene believes that the disciplines constituting the curriculum should be presented as opportunities for individual "sense making." It is difficult in many circumstances to arouse student interest in traditional curriculum because so many youths exist in conditions of dominance and alienation. If the teacher attempts to introduce students to dogmatic "truth" and if students are cut off from using the curriculum to make meaning in their own lives, then the possibility exists that students will only become more alienated from organized educational activity. This is a difficult path for the teacher, who is obligated at some point to take the student out of the familiar into the realm of more remote subject matter. In some cases, this is not all that difficult because the subject matter lends itself, with appropriate interpretation, to the lived experience of learners.

Greene illustrates many ways in which literature, for example, can be used to help students interpret the moral dilemmas humans face as a society and as individuals. In addition to literature, other art forms express meanings that can be interpreted fruitfully for the lives of learners. Some subject areas, such as linear algebra or chemistry, do not lend themselves readily to such application and might seem remote to many students, but they also have the capacity to help students gain meaning. Whatever the subject and whatever the nature of the students with whom the teacher works, it is necessary for the teacher to confront the task of education and to balance as well as humanly possible the tension between the demands of individual learners and their need to understand a variety of subjects.

Certainly, one responsibility of the teacher is the transmission of cherished values and ideals, and another is the communication of the skills and concepts needed to survive and thrive. Students, however, might not appreciate abstract justifications for education and, in fact, may resist them. Furthermore, little social consensus exists about what education should be, and so the wider society offers no clear support for what should be in the curriculum. This further complicates the teacher's task, but Greene maintains that the task is not impossible. She recommends that a dialogue be initiated to involve the community in conversation and shared activity regarding education. Although there is no absence of public talk about education, it is as if one group speaks past another. For example, some advocates of the basics seem to want to go back to an idealized earlier time. Some debate the merits of computers in the classroom, vocational education, or the humanities. In Greene's view, the need is to build community understanding of the complexities of curriculum issues; their importance is too great simply to be settled by professional educators.

In the meantime, the teacher must decide what to include and how to approach it within the restrictions of requirements, time, and circumstance. This means the educator must be knowledgeable about students' needs and students' perceptions of the world. The teacher must study and wrestle with the moral choices involved in curriculum selection and arrangement and the difference those choices might make in the lives of students. It is not an easy task, but an existentialist phenomenological understanding of education is an invaluable source of insight. One insight is that students need considerable freedom in order to merge their own perceived possibilities with those of the organized curriculum and to synthesize their own courses of action with the best of communal life.

Role of the Teacher

Existentialists have many role models for the ideal teacher, including philosophers like Socrates and Sartre. Even though Socrates was not an existentialist by name, his lifestyle embodied many things that existentialists admire, particularly his refusal to change his ways even at the price of his life. Sartre, too, stood firm in the face of tyranny (from the Nazis in World War II) and challenged many conventional beliefs, even when it was dangerous to do so.

Existentialists extol the knowledgeable person who is not simply an ivory-tower type of philosopher. They believe in knowledge and wisdom, to be sure, but they believe that these ideas need to be tested in the crucible of everyday existence. Thus, knowledge needs to be put to work, and if you are not willing to back up ideas in terms of your own actions, then you do not really believe these ideas. They are only lip service to real positions.

Sartre evidenced his commitment to his ideas in terms of his support of the French underground during World War II, with his fervent support of Algerian independence, with his condemnation of the Vietnam War, and with his defense of a free press. Sartre pointed out that not acting is still a form of action, because by our non-actions evil things are allowed to happen. Sartre's views about commitment and action influenced many young people in the late 1960s and early 1970s to protest the Vietnam War and the growing mechanization of life. His views also led to a variety of movements supporting individual freedom, and he constantly preached that we are "condemned to be free." Because we are existentially free, even in the face of tyranny and bureaucratization, we can take stands and oppose actions with which we disagree. Truly moral persons act in accordance with their beliefs.

Many educational theorists who embrace existentialist ideas urge that teachers should have strong beliefs and commitments of their own but that they should not expect students to accept these beliefs unless the students have thought them out for themselves. The teacher can and should present ideas, but the positions and actions that students take should be their own choices. At Summerhill, for example, an environment was created that supported and encouraged individual choice. The students themselves made the curriculum, the tests, and even the rules of behavior. In

Summerhill, Neill pointed out that he had a vote equal to any student and that he often was out-voted for good reasons.

Some existentialist educators believe that today's schools are too bureaucratic and have too many rules, rules not made by the students themselves, but imposed on them. They believe that schools should promote "inner-directedness," whereby students are encouraged to act in accordance with their own convictions even if this means challenging the status quo. Buber urged that teachers should treat students with a sense of equality and mutual respect.

The role of existentialist teachers is not an easy one because although they may struggle against the absurdities around them in everyday life, including what happens in schools and in the teaching profession, others may not agree and may even oppose them. This is where the notion of courage arises, and existentialists believe that teachers, like Socrates, must act with courage to fulfill the notion of true individuality.

The phenomenologist gives much attention to the student's conscious acquisition of knowledge. Phenomenologists believe that students act in a conscious way on the things that confront them and that people need to be aware of how this consciousness works. Indeed, this places the teacher in the role of a psychologist, but instead of believing that knowledge is fostered on a passive mind as in behavioristic techniques, phenomenologists believe that meaningful learning occurs only when the student actively faces the world and interacts with it. The problem with this approach is that although people face or accept knowledge in many similar ways, many individual differences still exist, and one needs to understand such differences. Phenomenologists believe that students can and should discover knowledge through their own efforts and that the role of the teacher is to act as a guide or facilitator in this learning process. Although pragmatists also believe in the teacher as a guide or facilitator, the phenomenologist is much more individualistic in the process and the outcome of such learning, and does not believe that it has to relate to either democratic or social development. Greene, who uses many existentialist-phenomenologist themes in her writing, says that to be in touch with our "landscapes," our personal/social life circumstances and environments, is to be conscious of our evolving experiences, and to be aware of the ways we encounter the world and the ways we can change the world. Students need to be encouraged to be "self-reflective," "wide-awake," and engaged in creating their own particular landscapes.

CRITIQUE OF EXISTENTIALISM AND PHENOMENOLOGY IN EDUCATION

Existentialist philosophy has been hailed as a helpful antidote in American education, especially where that education has become dominated by an organizational mentality and the continuing bureaucratization of the American school. Existentialism's challenge that people must not be beguiled by the technological society has been heeded by many members of society, such as the counterculture described by

Theodore Roszak. This challenge has awakened us to the tragedy and absurdity of life and to the lonely, baseless existence of the modern individual. It has been a needed medicine for contemporary Americans who never have experienced the direct effects of widespread hunger, devastating war, or wide-scale genocide. Most American philosophies have an optimistic tone, and existentialism has served the purpose of sounding a sobering note—sobering but not hopeless.

If it is sobering, then it also calls people to reexamine American culture in terms of its rampant materialism, robotization of the worker, anti-intellectualism, and devastating effect on individuality. Probably no modern philosophy devotes as much concern to individuality in political, social, and economic life as existentialism. It speaks in terms that belong distinctly to the modern age and the enduring human predicament. It encourages self-examination in a world that tends to force one outward to nonpersonal concerns.

People are bombarded constantly by advertisements that induce us to be something other than what we are. Individuals are manipulated by religion, school, family, business, industry, government, and other institutional forces. Existentialism points to the possibility that these enticements and seductions *can* be refused, that we are *free* to choose ourselves if we will but exhibit the courage. We do not have to be pawns buffeted about like helpless victims without succor. Even though efforts to resist might be puny and end in death, the individual human being is forged in the struggle to overcome such forces. Albert Camus wrote *The Myth of Sisyphus* to describe the struggles that people must undergo to create change and to survive in a hostile and difficult world.

With regard to education, existentialists and phenomenologists have been among the most severe critics. They have condemned the school as a dehumanizing force that indoctrinates the individual and steals personal initiative. It is as if the school's main function is to process human beings as a canning factory processes tuna. Everyone comes out alike. Although this analogy might exaggerate the case with schools, the existentialist criticism calls attention to a definite problem of magnitude. Teachers and students are victims of such conditions, and modern society cannot hope to find itself if its educational institutions are aligned against individual identity, personality, and well-being. Rather than uplift individuality, schools all too often seem to submerge it.

These conditions helped give rise to a popularization of existentialist thought, mainly because it vigorously protested against such conditions. However, popularization also has had its drawbacks, perhaps best shown by the glorification of the individual (meaning, in this case, an abstract individual). The individual is glorified to the exclusion of the real-life needs of particular, concrete, live children. Some educators have rejected all order, discipline, and study in the guise of promoting true individuality. They have preached an individualism that is often harmful to real individuals because it promotes selfishness, egoism, and disregard for others. "Spoiled brats" have sometimes been the result. Existentialists have called on us to become aware of our existence as authentic beings, but this has been corrupted by the "do-your-own-thing" ethic. These corrupters seem to be ignorant of

Sartre's reminder that although an individual can do anything, personal actions are a message to others that they can do likewise. If one is totally free, Sartre cautioned, one is also totally responsible, and this is an awesome responsibility for any individual.

Repeated criticisms of the individualistic and nihilistic character of existentialist thought have led some adherents to strike off in new directions. Phenomenology has been used as a more adequate method to investigate educational problems from an existentialist perspective. Vandenberg, a leading figure in this methodological movement, advocates analyzing problems from the standpoint of the lived experience of the child—that is, the child's world, existence, and experiences. Proponents of the phenomenological method try to understand and develop a more adequate theory of what Vandenberg calls "the chronological development of inwardness and outwardness"—that is, understanding how people's consciousness is developed or educated from their own perspective. This method investigates phenomena related to the expansion, development, and integration of conscious existence through learning. *Learning,* in this case, means "coming to know things" and "being aware of something of which one was not previously aware." Thus, educational phenomena are those things that generate awareness of conscious existence. The emphasis is still on the lived world of the child, but the focus is not so much on doctrinaire notions of a nihilistic lifestyle as on methodological steps toward understanding how individuals come to be whatever they are in the modern world.

Despite its promise of more methodological rigor for existentialist educational theory, the phenomenological movement presents some persistent problems. One of these is the difficulty that many people have with phenomenological terminology. Its reliance on hard-to-translate German terms and its penchant for hyphenated expressions create comprehension problems for many readers. Critics argue that these devices obfuscate our thinking, and that a theory is useful only to the extent that it clarifies rather than confuses. Supporters reply that although phenomenological theory is complex, this is because the nature of the human condition it seeks to clarify is complex. Furthermore, the ideas uncovered by phenomenology seem strange to people who are enamored with "objective" scientific terminology, and more familiarity with phenomenological philosophy might help solve many comprehension difficulties. Finally, supporters maintain, the difficulties of comprehension are a small price to pay for the greater understanding that phenomenology can bring to human education and the lived experience of the learner.

Existentialist and phenomenologist ideas of education do not mean that individuals cannot learn from others, cannot profit from discipline, or cannot gain from formal study in school. They insist, however, that these are not the only ways people can create new avenues and identities. Although existentialism and phenomenology have helped foster the movement known as alternative education, proponents sometimes forget that formal study—even the three R's—is an alternative open to consideration. Existentialist and phenomenological philosophers seek to open our eyes to human possibility and not necessarily to make narrow, doctrinaire ideologues out of us. Such an outcome would be anathema to the letter and spirit of existentialism and phenomenology.

SARTRE

EXISTENTIALISM AND HUMANISM

Jean-Paul Sartre was a prolific writer and produced major works in many different genres, including novels, plays, and formal philosophical treatises. In the following selection, he offers a defense of some of his ideas and, in the course of this defense, presents some central themes of his philosophical views. He claims that existentialism is indeed humanistic and provides insight into human freedom and human responsibility. Although Sartre did not write directly about education, his views have been applied to learning, curriculum, and the ethical aspects of education.

My purpose here is to offer a defense of existentialism against several reproaches that have been laid against it.

First, it has been reproached as an invitation to people to dwell in quietism of despair. For if every way to a solution is barred, one would have to regard any action in this world as entirely ineffective, and one would arrive finally at a contemplative philosophy. Moreover, since contemplation is a luxury, this would be only another bourgeois philosophy. This is, especially, the reproach made by the Communists.

From another quarter we are reproached for having underlined all that is ignominious in the human situation, for depicting what is mean, sordid or base to the neglect of certain things that possess charm and beauty and belong to the brighter side of human nature: For example, according to the Catholic critic, Mlle. Mercier, we forget how an infant smiles. Both from this side and from the other we are also reproached for leaving out of account the solidarity of mankind and considering man in isolation. And this, say the Communists, is because we base our doctrine upon pure subjectivity—upon the Cartesian "I think": which is the moment in which solitary man attains to himself; a position from which it is impossible to regain solidarity with other men who exist outside of the self. The ego cannot reach them through the cogito.

From the Christian side, we are reproached as people who deny the reality and seriousness of human affairs. For since we ignore the commandments of God and all values prescribed as eternal, nothing remains but what is strictly voluntary. Everyone can do what he likes, and will be incapable, from such a point of view, of condemning either the point of view or the action of anyone else.

It is to these various reproaches that I shall endeavour to reply today; that is why I have entitled this brief exposition "Existentialism and Humanism." Many may be surprised at the mention of humanism in this connection, but we shall try to see in what sense we understand it. In any case, we can begin by saying that existentialism, in our sense of the word, is a doctrine that does render human life possible; a doctrine, also, which affirms that every truth and every action imply both an environment and a human subjectivity. The essential charge laid against us is, of course, that of over-emphasis upon the evil side of human life. I have lately been told of a lady who, whenever she lets slip a vulgar expression in a moment of nervousness, excuses herself by exclaiming, "I believe I am becoming an existentialist." So it appears that ugliness is being identified with existentialism. That is why some people say we are "naturalistic," and if we are, it is strange to see how much we scandalise and horrify them, for no one seems to be much frightened or humiliated nowadays by what is properly called naturalism. Those who can quite well keep down a novel by Zola such as *La Terre* are sickened as soon as they read an existentialist novel. Those who appeal to the wisdom of the people—which is a sad wisdom—find ours sadder still. And yet, what could be more disillusioned than such sayings as "Charity begins at home" or "Promote a rogue and he'll sue you for damage, knock him down and he'll do you homage"? We all know how many common sayings can be quoted to this effect, and they all mean much the same—that you must not oppose the powers-that-be; that you must not fight against superior force; must not meddle in matters that are above your station. Or that any action not in accordance with some tradition is mere romanticism; or that any undertaking which has not the support of proven experience is foredoomed to frustration; and that since experience has shown men to be invariably inclined to evil, there must be firm rules to restrain them, otherwise we shall have anarchy. It is, however, the people who are forever mouthing these dismal proverbs and, whenever they are told of some more or less repulsive action, say "How like human nature!"—it is these very people, always harping upon realism, who complain that existentialism is too gloomy a view of things. Indeed their excessive protests make me suspect that what is annoying them is not so much our pessimism, but, much more likely, our optimism. For at bottom, what is alarming in the doctrine that I am about to try to explain to you is— is it not?—that it confronts man with a possibility of choice. To verify this, let us review the whole question upon the strictly philosophic level. What, then, is this that we call existentialism?

Most of those who are making use of this word would be highly confused if required to explain its meaning. For since it has become fashionable, people cheerfully declare that this musician or that painter is "existentialist." A columnist in *Clartés* signs himself "The Existentialist," and, indeed, the word is now so loosely applied to so many things that it no longer means anything at all. It would appear that, for the lack of any novel doctrine such as that of surrealism, all those who are eager to join in the latest scandal or movement now seize upon this philosophy in which, however, they can find nothing to their purpose. For in truth this is of all teachings the least scandalous and the most austere: It is intended strictly for technicians and philosophers. All the same, it can easily be defined.

The question is only complicated because there are two kinds of existentialists. There are, on the one hand, the Christians, amongst whom I shall name Jaspers and Gabriel Marcel, both professed Catholics; and on the other the existential atheists, amongst whom we must place Heidegger as well as the French existentialists and myself. What they have in common is simply the fact that they believe that existence comes before essence—or, if you will, that we must begin from the subjective. What exactly do we mean by that?

If one considers an article of manufacture— as, for example, a book or a paper-knife—one sees that it has been made by an artisan who had a conception of it: And he has paid attention, equally, to the conception of a paper-knife and to the pre-existent technique of production which is a part of that conception and is, at bottom, a formula. Thus the paper-knife is at the same time an article producible in a certain manner and one which, on the other hand, serves a definite purpose, for one cannot suppose that a man would produce a paper-knife without knowing what it was for. Let us say, then, of the paper-knife that its essence—that is to say the sum of the formulae and the qualities which made its production and its definition possible—precedes its existence. The presence of such-and-such a paper-knife or book is thus determined before my eyes. Here, then, we are viewing the world from a technical standpoint, and we can say that production precedes existence.

When we think of God as the creator, we are thinking of him, most of the time, as a supernal artisan. Whatever doctrine we may be considering, whether it be a doctrine like that of Descartes, or of Leibnitz himself, we always imply that the will follows, more or less, from the understanding or at least accompanies it, so that when God creates he knows precisely what he is creating. Thus, the conception of man in the mind of God is comparable to that of the paper-knife in the mind of the artisan: God makes man according to a procedure and a conception, exactly as the artisan manufactures a paper-knife, following a definition and a formula. Thus each individual man is the realization of a certain conception which dwells in the divine understanding. In the philosophic atheism of the eighteenth century, the notion of God is suppressed, but not for all that, the idea that essence is prior to existence; something of that idea we still find everywhere, in Diderot, in Voltaire and even in Kant. Man possesses a human nature; that "human nature," which is the conception of human being, is found in every man; which means that each man is a particular example of a universal conception, the conception of Man. In Kant, this universality goes so far that the wild man of the woods, man in the state of nature and the bourgeois are all contained in the same definition and have the same fundamental qualities. Here again, the essence of man precedes that historic existence which we confront in experience.

Atheistic existentialism, of which I am a representative, declares with greater consistency that if God does not exist there is at least one being whose existence comes before its essence, a being which exists before it can be defined by any conception of it. That being is man or, as Heidegger has it, the human reality. What do we mean by saying that existence precedes essence? We mean that man first of all exists, encounters himself, surges up in the world—and defines himself afterwards. If man as the existentialist sees him is not definable, it is because to begin with he is nothing. He will not be anything until later, and then he will be what he makes of himself. Thus, there is no human nature, because there is no God to have a conception of it. Man simply is. Not that he is simply what he conceives himself to be, but he is what he wills, and as he conceives himself after already existing— as he wills to be after that leap towards existence. Man is nothing else but that which he makes of himself. That is the first principle of existentialism. And this is what people call its "subjectivity," using the word as a reproach against us. But what do we mean to say by this, but that man is of a greater dignity than a stone or a table? For we mean to say that man primarily exists—that man is, before all else, something which propels itself towards a future and is aware that it is doing so. Man is, indeed, a project which possesses a subjective life, instead of being a kind of moss, or a fungus or a cauliflower. Before that projection of the self nothing exists; not even in the heaven of intelligence: man will only attain existence when he is what he purposes to be. Not, however, what he may wish to be. For what we usually understand by wishing or willing is a conscious decision taken—much more often than not—after we have made ourselves what we are. I may wish to join a party, to write a book or to marry—but in such a case what is usually called my will is probably a manifestation of a prior and more spontaneous decision. If, however, it is true that existence is prior to essence, man is responsible for what he is. Thus, the first effect of existentialism is that it puts every man in possession of himself as he is, and places the entire responsibility for his existence squarely upon his own shoulders. And, when we say that man is responsible for himself, we do not mean that he is responsible only for his own individuality, but that he is responsible for all men. The word *subjectivism* is to be understood in two senses, and our adversaries play upon only one of them. Subjectivism means, on the one hand, the freedom of the individual subject and, on the other, that man cannot pass beyond human subjectivity. It is the latter which is the deeper meaning of existentialism. When we say that man chooses himself, we do mean that every one of us must choose himself; but by that we also mean that in choosing for himself he chooses for all men. For in effect, of all the actions a man may take in order to create himself as he wills to be, there is not one which is not creative, at the same time, of an image of man such as he believes he ought to be. To choose between this or that is at the same time to affirm the value of that which is chosen; for we are unable ever to choose the worse. What we choose is always the better; and nothing can be better for us unless it is better for all. If, moreover, existence precedes essence and we will to exist at the same time as we fashion our image, that image is valid for all and for the entire epoch in which we find ourselves. Our responsibility is thus much greater than we had supposed, for it concerns mankind as a whole. If I am a worker, for instance, I may choose to join a Christian rather than a Communist trade union. And if, by that membership, I choose to signify that resignation is, after all, the attitude that best becomes a man, that man's kingdom is not upon this earth, I do not commit myself alone to that view. Resignation is my will for everyone, and my action is, in consequence, a commitment on behalf of all mankind. Or if, to take a more personal case, I decide to marry and to have children, even though this decision proceeds simply from my situation, from my passion or my desire, I am thereby committing not only myself, but humanity as a whole, to the practice of monogamy. I am thus responsible for myself and for all men, and I am creating a certain image of man as I would have him to be. In fashioning myself I fashion man.

Source: Jean-Paul Sartre, *Existentialism and Human Emotions.* New York: Philosophical Library, 1957, pp. 9–18. Reprinted by permission of Philosophical Library, Inc.

LANDSCAPES OF LEARNING

Maxine Greene has been an important contributor to an existentialist phenomenology of education. She has urged educators to use the creative products of human struggle to help youngsters come to grips with their own lives. To be "wide-awake" is to be open to the possibilities of human existence, but it is also to be aware of the need for meaning. In this selection, Greene sketches ways the arts and humanities can be used to help students become more acutely conscious of their existential situation. Literature is Greene's special concern, and she proposes to use it to help students gain personal meaning through a phenomenological interpretation of human predicaments as portrayed in literature.

In an ironic account of how he "became an author," Søren Kierkegaard describes himself sitting in the Frederiksberg Garden one Sunday afternoon asking himself what he was going to do with his life. Wherever he looked, he thought, practical men were preoccupied with making life easier for people. Those considered the "benefactors of the age" knew how to make things better "by making life easier and easier, some by railways, others by omnibuses and steamboats, others by telegraph, others by easily apprehended compendiums and short recitals of everything worth knowing, and finally the true benefactors of the age . . . (making) spiritual existence systematically easier and easier. . . ." He decided, he says, "with the same humanitarian enthusiasm as the others," to make things harder, "to create difficulties everywhere."

Writing that way in 1846, Kierkegaard was anticipating what certain contemporary thinkers speak of as a "civilization malaise" reflecting "the inability of a civilization directed to material improvement—higher incomes, better diets, miracles of medicine, triumphs of applied physics and chemistry—to satisfy the human spirit." He saw the individual subsumed under abstractions like "the Public," lost in the anonymity of "the Crowd." Like others responding to the industrial and then the technological age, he was concerned about depersonalization, automatization, and the bland routinization of life. For him, human reality—the *lived* reality—could only be understood as a difficult, indeed a dreadful freedom. To make things harder for people meant awakening them to their freedom. It meant communicating to them in such a way that they would become aware of their "personal mode of existence," their responsibility as individuals in a changing and problematic world.

Henry David Thoreau was living at Walden Pond in 1846, and, when he wrote about his experience there, he also talked (in the first person) of arousing people from somnolence and ease. *Walden* also has to do with making life harder, with moving individuals to discover what they lived for. Early in the book, Thoreau writes passionately about throwing off sleep. He talks about how few people are awake enough "for a poetic or divine life." And he asserts that "To be awake is to be alive." He speaks personally, eloquently, about what strikes him to be the requirements of the truly moral life. But he never prescribes; he never imposes his own ethical point of view. The *point* of his kind of writing was not simply to describe a particular experiment with living in the woods; it was to move others to elevate their lives by a "conscious endeavor," to arouse others to discover—each in his or her own terms—what it would mean to "live deliberately."

The theme has been developed through the years as technology has expanded, fragmentation has increased, and more and more people have felt themselves impinged upon by forces they have been unable to understand. As time has gone on, various writers and artists have articulated experiences of being conditioned and controlled. Contemporaneous with the advance of scientific and positivistic thinking, therefore, an alternative tradition has taken shape, a tradition generated by perceptions of passivity, acquiescence, and what Thoreau called "quiet desperation." It is what may now be called the humanist tradition, if the human being is understood to be someone always in search of himself or herself, choosing himself or herself in the situations of a problematic life. There are works of art, there are certain works in history, philosophy, and psychology, that were deliberately created to move people to critical awareness, to a sense of moral agency, and to a conscious engagement with the world. As I see it, they ought—under the rubric of the "arts and humanities"—to be central to any curriculum that is constructed today.

My argument, as has been suggested, has to do with wide-awakeness, not with the glowing abstractions—the True, the Beautiful, and the Good. Like Nick Henry in Ernest Hemingway's *Farewell to Arms,* I am embarrassed by, "Abstract words such as *glory, honour, courage,* or *hallow.* . . ." Wide-awakeness has a concreteness; it is related, as the philosopher Alfred Schutz suggests, to being in the world:

> By the term *wide-awakeness* we want to denote a plane of consciousness of highest tension originating in an attitude of full attention to life and its requirements. Only the performing and especially the working self is fully interested in life and, hence, wide-awake. It lives within its acts and its attention is exclusively directed to carrying its project into effect, to executing its plan. This attention is an active, not a passive one. Passive attention is the opposite to full awareness.

This goes beyond ordinary notions of "relevance" where education is concerned. Schutz is pointing out that heightened consciousness and reflectiveness are meaningful only with respect to human projects, human undertakings, not in a withdrawal from the intersubjective world. He is also pointing out that human beings define themselves by means of their projects and that wide-awakeness contributes to the creation of the self. If it is indeed the case, as I believe it is, that involvement with the arts and humanities has the potential for provoking precisely this sort of reflectiveness, we need to devise ways of integrating them into what we teach at all levels of the educational enterprise; we need to do so consciously, with a clear perception of what it means to enable people to pay, from their own distinctive vantage points, "full attention to life."

It is, at least on one level, evident that works of art—*Moby Dick,* for instance, a Hudson River landscape painting, Charles Ives' *Concord Sonata*—must be directly addressed by existing and situated persons, equipped to attend to the qualities of what presents itself to them, to make sense of it in the light of their own lived worlds. Works of art are, visibly and palpably, human achievements, renderings of the ways in which aspects of reality have impinged upon human consciousness. What distinguishes one art form from another (music from poetry, say, the dance from painting) is the *mode* of rendering, the medium used, and the qualities explored. But all art forms must be encountered as achievements that can only be brought to significant life when human beings engage with them imaginatively.

For all the distinctiveness of the arts, there is a characteristic they share with certain kinds of history. I have in mind, as an example, Edward Hallet Carr's conception of history as dialogue. Carr talks about the historian's provisional interpretations of provisionally selected facts and about the subtle changes that take place through the "reciprocal action" of interpretation and the ordering of those facts:

> And this reciprocal action also involves reciprocity between present and past, since the historian is part of the present and the facts belong to the past. The historian and the facts of history are necessary to each other. The historian without his facts is rootless and futile; the facts without their historians are dead and meaningless. My first answer therefore to the question, What is history?, is that it is a continuous process of interaction between the historian and his facts, an unending dialogue between the present and the past.

What is striking here is the emphasis on selecting, shaping, and interpreting, the ordering of raw materials according to distinctive norms. The process itself is not unlike the process of art-making. The crucial difference is that the historian is in quest of truth, in some degree verifiable, while the artist strives for coherence, clarity, enlargement, or intensity.

Even more important: In the aesthetic experience, the mundane world or the empirical world must be bracketed out or in some sense distanced, so that the reader, listener, or beholder can enter the aesthetic space in which the work of art exists. Captain Ahab's manic search for the white whale cannot be checked in any history of the whaling industry; its plausibility and impact have little to do with a testable truth. Thomas Cole's painting, "The Ox-Bow," may look in some way like the river, but, if it is not encountered as a drama of color, receding planes, and light, it will not be experienced as a work of art. A historical work—Thucydides' *The Peloponnesian War*, John B. Bury's *The Idea of Progress*, or Richard Hofstadter's *The Age of Reform*—refers beyond itself to events in time past, to the changing situations in humankind's ongoing experience, to whatever are conceived to be the "facts."

Most significant of all, however, is the possibility that these histories, like Carr's own history, can involve their readers in dialogue. Reading any one of them, readers or students cannot but be cognizant of a distinctive individual behind the inquiry. They cannot but gain a sense of a living human being posing questions to the past from his own standpoint and the standpoints of those he chooses to be his fellow-historians, working at different moments in time. Students may well come upon the insight Jacob Burckhardt describes when he speaks of history as "the break with nature caused by the awakening of consciousness." They may begin, from their own vantage points to confer significance on moments in the past, to push back the horizons of the meaningful world, to expand the scope of lived experiences. Maurice Merleau-Ponty, speaking of what this kind of awareness can mean, writes, "My life must have a significance which I do not constitute; there must be strictly speaking an intersubjectivity. . . ." Engaging with the kind of history I have been describing, individual human beings can locate themselves in an intersubjective reality reaching backwards and forwards in time.

These are the reasons why I would include certain works of history in an arts and humanities program—works that provoke wide-awakeness and an awareness of the quest for meaning, which has so much to do with feeling alive in the world. I would exclude from the program (although not from the total curriculum) mathematicized or computerized history, exemplified by, say, *Time on the Cross.*

I would approach my choices in philosophy, criticism, and psychology in the same fashion: those works that engage people in posing questions with respect to their own projects, their own life situations. William James, John Dewey, George Herbert Mead, George Santayana, Alfred North Whitehead, Jean-Paul Sartre, Maurice Merleau-Ponty: These, among the modern philosophers, are likely to move readers to think about their own thinking, to risk examination of what is presupposed or taken for granted, to clarify what is vague or mystifying or obscure. To "do" philosophy in this fashion is to respond to actual problems and real interests, to the requirements of sense-making in a confusing world. It may also involve identification of lacks and insufficiencies in that world—and some conscious effort to repair those lacks, to choose what *ought* to be. Some of the humanistic or existential psychologies may function similarly as they engage students in dialogue about what it is to be human, to grow, to *be*.

If the humanities are indeed oriented to wide-awakeness, if dialogue and encounter are encouraged at every point, it might be possible to break through the artificial separations that make interdisciplinary study so difficult to achieve. If students (and their teachers as well) are enabled to pose questions relevant to their life plans and their being in the world, they might well seek out answers in free involvement with a range of disciplines. Once this occurs, new perspectives will open up—perspectives on the past, on cumulative meanings, on future possibilities.

The important thing is for these perspectives to be sought consciously and critically and for meanings to be perceived from the vantage points of persons awake to their freedom. The arts are of focal significance in this regard, because perceptive encounters with works of art can bring human beings in touch with themselves. Jean-Paul Sartre writes that literature addresses itself to the reader's freedom:

> For, since the one who writes recognizes, by the very fact that he takes the trouble to write, the freedom of his readers, and since the one who reads, by the mere fact of his opening the book, recognizes the freedom of the writer, the work of art, from whichever side you approach it, is an act of confidence in the freedom of men.

I believe this may be said, in essence, about all the arts. Liberating those who come attentively to them, they permit confrontations with the world as individuals are conscious of it, *personally* conscious, apart from "the Crowd."

I would want to see one or another art form taught in all pedagogical contexts, because of the way in which aesthetic experiences provide a ground for the questioning that launches sense-making and the understanding of what it is to exist in a world. If the arts are given such a central place, and if the disciplines that compose the humanities are at the core of the curriculum, all kinds of reaching out are likely. The situated person, conscious of his or her freedom, can move outwards to empirical study, analytic study, or quantitative study of all kinds. Be-

ing grounded, he or she will be far less likely to confuse abstraction with concreteness, formalized and schematized reality with what is "real." Made aware of the multiplicity of possible perspectives, made aware of incompleteness and of a human reality to be pursued, the individual may reach "a plane of consciousness of highest tension." Difficulties will be created everywhere, and the arts and humanities will come into their own.

Source: Reprinted by permission of the publisher from Greene, Maxine, *Landscapes of Learning,* (New York: Teachers College Press, © 1978 by Teachers College, Columbia University. All rights reserved.), pp. 161–166.

SELECTED READINGS

Gallagher, Shaun. *Hermeneutics and Education.* Albany, New York: State University of New York Press, 1992. A comprehensive exploration of the varieties of hermeneutics—conservative, moderate, critical, and radical—and how each can inform educational theory. Although hermeneutics has relevance for educational theory, the analysis of educational experience also might help develop hermeneutical theory.

Morris, Van Cleve. *Existentialism in Education.* New York: Harper and Row, 1966. A comprehensive overview of existentialism as a philosophy of education. This work tries to provide some insight into possible uses of existentialist thought. Like Kneller, Morris has been vigorously criticized for treating existentialist thought as another "ism."

Troutner, Lee. "Making Sense Out of 'Existential Thought and Education': A Search for the Interface," in *Philosophy of Education,* 1975. Proceedings of the 31st Annual Meeting of the Philosophy of Education Society. San Jose, CA: Philosophy of Education Society, 1975, pp. 185–199. Explores the contributions of existentialist thought to education. The author sketches possible future contributions existentialism can make.

Vandenberg, Donald. *Being and Education: An Essay in Existential Phenomenology.* Upper Saddle River, NJ: Prentice Hall, 1971. A different work in that it does not present existentialist thought as another "ism." Instead, it attempts to apply phenomenological method to selected problems in education.

www.knowdeep.org/existentialism (accessed April 5, 2002). Provides approximately 50 connections to papers, articles, and other sources on existentialism.

www.spep.org/resource.html (accessed April 5, 2002). Homepage of the Society for Phenomenology and Existential Philosophy, a professional organization devoted to supporting philosophy inspired by Continental European traditions. SPEP also promotes such traditions as critical theory, existentialism, feminism, German idealism, hermeneutics, and post-structuralism.

ONLINE RESEARCH

Companion Website

Utilizing some of the Web sites included in this book, as well as Topics 2 and 3 of the Prentice Hall Foundations Web site found at *www.prenhall.com/ozmon,* answer the following question with a short essay: What are some of the essential ideas of existentialist philosophy, and how have these ideas influenced educational theory and practice? You can write and submit your essay response to your instructor by using the "Electronic Bluebook" section found in any of the topics of the Prentice Hall Foundations Web site.

8

Analytic Philosophy and Education

Analytic philosophy is not a systematic philosophy like idealism, realism, or pragmatism. Indeed, most analytic philosophers take pains to repudiate identity with a systematic philosophy because they say that the systems approach in philosophy has brought more problems than solutions to human understanding. For the most part, analytic philosophers seek to clarify the language, concepts, and methods used in such fields as science, politics, and education.

Clarification is the one simple unifying theme in analytic philosophy. The underlying assumption of the analysts is that most philosophical problems of the past were not problems concerning ultimate reality or truth, goodness, and beauty, but problems with confused language, warped or unclear meanings, and conceptual confusion. Genuine knowledge, most analysts claim, is the business of science, not philosophy. Thus, the true role of philosophy is critical clarification.

Several kinds of approaches can be taken within the general movement of analytic philosophy, and the movement itself has undergone a somewhat puzzling historical evolution. Basically, philosophical analysis has always taken place; Socrates was analyzing when he investigated the meaning of justice. However, the modern movement of analytic philosophy has its more immediate roots in several recent philosophical developments.

The first part of this chapter shows the evolution of analytic philosophy from the late nineteenth and early twentieth centuries to the present, and the second part concerns the way philosophical analysis has been applied to educational theory and philosophy of education.

ANALYTIC MOVEMENT IN PHILOSOPHY

The analytic movement has undergone an evolution stemming in part from the influence of contemporary realism as it was being shaped at the turn of the century by G. E. Moore and Bertrand Russell. Furthermore, analytic philosophy has been developed largely in the Anglo-American cultural context although several of its exponents, primarily of Germanic-Austrian origin, came from Continental Europe. This latter aspect, however, was to have its impact mainly in Britain and the United States because the Germanic-Austrian figures came to these two countries as they found Nazism repulsive and Continental social conditions restrictive. One important aspect of the influence that came from the Continent and finally merged for the most part with the Anglo-American analytic movement was *logical positivism*. This was a philosophical school originally identified with a group of philosophers known as the Vienna Circle.

More recently, the analytic movement (including many persons formerly associated with logical positivism) often has been identified with the name "linguistic analysis," and most of its advocates were greatly influenced by Ludwig Wittgenstein. Overall, these developments are referred to sometimes as "the linguistic turn" in philosophy, a turn away from traditional philosophy (such as concern with absolute knowledge and truth) toward examining the way people discuss and describe their conceptions of things and ideas.

Realism and the Early Analytic Movement

Realism is not the sole parent of the analytic movement, but the family resemblance is strong. Moore and Russell did not found the analytic movement, because some of their contemporaries were more directly involved, but Moore and Russell are perhaps most representative of the realist backgrounds.

George Edward Moore (1873–1958)

G. E. Moore was instrumental in the development of twentieth-century realism and one of its outgrowths, philosophical analysis. He influenced Bertrand Russell and is often credited with heading Russell toward a realist orientation when Russell had become infatuated with Hegelian idealism. Moore and Russell became good friends and philosophical colleagues, but gradually a difference emerged. Moore's realism went toward commonsense philosophy and ordinary language, whereas Russell's went toward science, mathematics, and formal language.

A Defense of Common Sense is one of Moore's better-known works. Primarily, he was interested in the things people say in ordinary life. He believed that most commonsense things are true and that we know what people are talking about in their ordinary, commonsense language. Many philosophers, in contrast, had made a career out of disputing ordinary common sense. In ordinary language and philosophy, however, one can find many statements that can neither be proved nor disproved, and Moore saw as his task not the discovery of the truth or falsity of the propositions of ordinary language and philosophy, but an analysis of the meaning of propositions. He thought that analysis would clear the way toward a better understanding of the truth and propriety of what people say and write.

Moore's investigations went primarily into ordinary language because he thought there were better reasons for accepting it than philosophical propositions. For one thing, ordinary language deals with the commonsense, everyday world. Its statements and propositions are about commonly encountered matters of fact and real-life experiences. Ordinary language and common sense deal with the real and have done so over the centuries, withstanding the test of time. Moore sought to analyze commonly used terms, such as *good, know,* and *real.* Everyone knows what these words mean when they are used in ordinary language. Moore believed that people have a concept of *good* already in mind before they use the term and that knowing the meaning (or having the concept) and analyzing the meaning are two different things. An analysis of the meaning would help clarify the propriety of the meaning—or, its "goodness of fit."

How often do all kinds of difficulties and troubles arise because of confusion over meaning? Many if not most problems of the modern world are a result of misunderstanding and confusion over ideological positions, political beliefs, and so forth, all of which depend heavily on key word meanings and concepts. Moore sought to analyze the meanings of key words so as to shed light on the nature of the confusion. Consequently, he became much involved in ethical meanings of language. In *Principia Ethica,* he analyzed the various meanings that people have in mind when they use the word *good.*

This can be explored further in light of ideological and political confusion. It is probably safe to assume that most serious-minded political theories incorporate notions or concepts about what is good. What one theory holds to be good is often different from what another theory holds. Think about economic considerations in political theories as an example. Marxist theory holds that collective ownership of the means of production results in certain desirable ends or goods. Other political theories, such as capitalism, maintain that private ownership is one of the supreme goods. In other instances, a political theory might contain internal inconsistencies and even contradictions about what is good. Perhaps a great deal of human strife results from such confusion over the various meanings of the word *good.*

From Moore's standpoint, philosophers were also guilty of adding to the confusion because they attempted to wrest meaning from common sense and ordinary language and to make that meaning remote and abstract—for example, by using words like *good* in abstract ways. Moore believed that common sense knows "where the shoe pinches" and that abstract theories do not. He accused philosophers of abusing language when they took it away from common, ordinary usage and meaning. However, it was not just meaning that Moore was after; he was after the *analysis* of meaning. His characteristic approach was to analyze a given concept (or meaning) in light of similar concepts and to distinguish one from another in precise ways.

Moore's influence diminished because of the development of Russell's more formalistic analytic approach and the appearance of logical positivism. Some philosophers, however, are reexamining Moore's ideas.

Bertrand Russell (1872–1970)

Whereas Moore regarded analytic philosophy as the analysis of meanings in ordinary language and common sense, Bertrand Russell developed a more formal logical analysis akin to the exact sciences. In *Principia Mathematica,* by Russell and Alfred North Whitehead, mathematics is reduced to a logical language. Russell held that mathematics gives a clarity and a logic that are not found in the general uses of language. Because language is such an important part of life, people must try to make it more precise and clear.

Aristotle's syllogistic logic was a logic of classes. Russell's logic, however, dealt with the relationship of propositions to each other: "If it is raining, then the streets are wet." The clauses "it is raining" and "the streets are wet" express propositions that have a certain relationship, or what Russell called *implication*. In *Principia Mathematica*, he attempted to demonstrate that mathematics is, in fact, a part of logic and that language has a basic logical structure similar to that of mathematics. Thus, he hoped that mathematical logic could be used to provide philosophy with an instrument for precisely clarifying the meaning of language.

Russell distinguished between what he called *atomic* sentences and *molecular* sentences. An atomic sentence has no parts that can stand alone as sentences. Thus, "Megan is human" is an atomic sentence. "Megan and Bonita are going shopping" is a molecular sentence because it is a complex sentence containing two parts, each of which is itself a sentence: "Megan is going shopping" and "Bonita is going shopping." Molecular sentences are created out of atomic sentences by connective words, such as *and, or,* and *if*. Russell thought that any molecular sentence could be analyzed into a set of atomic sentences with the logical connectives. Thus, the meaning of a molecular sentence could be explained by breaking it down into its constituent atomic sentences. This often is referred to as Russell's *logical atomism*.

Accordingly, when an atomic sentence is true, the subject denotes an individual thing or object and the predicate refers to some characteristic of this thing or object. In showing that atomic sentences refer to such objects and characteristics, one is informed that the world is made up of facts and that all facts are atomic and can be described by atomic sentences. Russell believed that no molecular facts exist in nature because the connectives *and, or,* and *if . . . then* are only linguistic devices used to combine atomic sentences in various ways. Atomic sentences are syntactic only. No generalized facts exist either, such as "All humans are mortal," because this can be reduced to the atomic sentences "Megan is mortal," "Bonita is mortal," and so on for every individual.

Russell dealt with what he called the *theory of descriptions*, in which he attempted to show that philosophers, through a faulty analysis of language, had been led by specious arguments into believing that the sorts of things ordinary people regard as fiction, or nonexistent, in some sense actually do exist. For example, we seem to be making a true statement when we say "Captain Ahab pursued the white whale." This is true in a sense even though no Captain Ahab or white whale actually existed except in a work of fiction. Russell put it this way: "How is it possible for there to be such a sentence as 'The present king of France is wise,' when there is no king of France?" Russell dealt with this kind of problem by distinguishing between the "grammatical form" of a sentence and its "logical form." Thus, the grammatical structure leads one to believe that the phrase "the present king of France" is logically the subject term and "is wise" is the predicate term and that this is an atomic sentence. However, this sentence is not "logically" of the subject–predicate form. When analyzed, one finds the following three sentences:

1. Something is the current monarch of France.
2. Not more than one thing is the current monarch of France.
3. Whatever is the current monarch of France is wise.

Each of these three sentences is a general sentence, not an atomic one. No proper names are used; instead, such generalities as "something," "whatever," and so forth are used. Thus, "the present king of France" is not logically a proper name although it might function to form a grammatical point of view. In pointing out that "the present king of France" is logically a "general" sentence and not an atomic one, Russell showed that such a phrase has no relationship to any object in the world and thus has no meaning on its own. If a sentence is translated into logical language, its meaning becomes clear. If it turns out not to be of the subject–predicate form, then its grammatical subject refers to nothing directly because, in a perfect language, every subject term denotes an actual object in the world and every predicate term denotes an actual characteristic of that subject.

Russell's efforts to construct a logical language, or a more perfect language that is objective and oriented to the facts of science, show the difference between Moore and Russell. Russell wanted a formal, logical language and called his approach *logical analysis*.

The term *analytic* takes on special meaning for Russell. Much of the philosophy of the past had been *synthetic;* that is, it had tried to take disparate parts or issues and synthesize them into a "great answer" or a "block system." Russell argued that philosophers already had their great answers in hand and that they erroneously tried to make the disparate parts fit into the answers. He believed that the way out of trouble is to discard block universe conceptions in favor of taking on issues one at a time. By reducing each issue or problem to its smallest parts (its "atoms," so to speak), clarity and precision of meaning could be gained.

This is Russell's analytic approach—to whittle each problem down to its constituent parts and then to examine each part in detail to pick out its essential features. Thus, rather than arriving at great answers or syntheses, one has small but significant and well-worked analyses. Science does this, according to Russell, and philosophy should do it, too. Russell's analytic approach is *reductive:* It reduces propositions to their smallest, bare-bones significance. It is also *empirical* because the bare-bones significance of a proposition must square with reality or with the facts of the case. This is demonstrated by the example about the king of France. It is useless to talk about the king of France if there is, in fact, no king. If no king exists, this nonexistent king cannot possibly be wise. This, in effect, illustrates Russell's condemnation of the synthetic, "grand manner" philosophy of the past. He believed that too much talk and system building has gone on around nonexistent, nonwise "kings" or great answers.

In fact, this aversion to a "systems" or "grand manner" approach to philosophy fairly well characterizes the analytic movement as a whole. Analysts oppose categorization of ideas into philosophical systems, preferring to view ideas as overlapping and not belonging to any single viewpoint. Thus, they believe that a systems or "ism" approach defeats the purpose of the kind of thinking philosophy should promote. They prefer to analyze language meaning and to clarify ideas rather than to categorize them.

Although Russell helped develop philosophical analysis, his interest in analysis was primarily methodological, and his orientation was based strongly in realism.

Russell's emphasis on fact, his insistence on going to the atomic as opposed to molecular and general propositions, shows his acceptance of the realist's thesis of independence. It should be pointed out that a figure of Russell's stature is difficult to pin into any school. He willingly gave up positions and renounced views when he discovered what to him were errors, and he seemed to lose faith in the analytic approach as the essence of philosophy. At the end of his life, he still was making the philosophical quest, still searching for wisdom wherever that search led and whatever sacred ox was gored. That his influence has extended in many directions is testimony of his virtue as a thinker.

Moore and Russell showed the strong roots that analysis has in realism: Moore for his insistence on anchoring analysis in the ordinary world of facts and sense experience, and Russell for his insistence on the scientific model of a logical, orderly, and systematic treatment of particulars. The analytic movement still has much of this realist orientation, although most modern analysts reject identity with any philosophical system.

Logical Positivism and Analysis

Logical positivism originated with a group of European philosophers, scientists, and mathematicians. In 1929, they formally designated themselves the "Vienna Circle" and began publishing a journal, *Erkenntnis*. Members included Moritz Schlick, Rudolph Carnap, Herbert Feigl, Felix Kaufmann, and A. J. Ayer. The works of Bertrand Russell, especially the *Principia Mathematica*, exerted some influence on this group, as did the earlier works of Ludwig Wittgenstein, especially his *Tractatus Logico-Philosophicus*. Perhaps the most notable feature of the members of the group was their fascination with the progress of modern scientific method (especially the theory of relativity) and what has been called the *principle of verification;* that is, no proposition can be accepted as meaningful unless it can be verified on formal grounds (through logic and mathematics) or verified on empirical or sense-data grounds. The former shows their indebtedness to modern mathematics and logic, and the latter their indebtedness to modern empirical science.

After several years, however, they encountered difficulties with the principle of verification because, in their zeal, they had given it a narrow and rigorous application that ruled out any consideration of unverifiable propositions. It was found that some fundamental assumptions of science itself are unverifiable in the rigorous application the logical positivists used. The important weight given to empirical sense data presented problems too; such data depend on human beings observing some phenomenon, and this lets in the subjective element of perception. One encounters the *observation* of the object or phenomenon and not the objective reality of the thing itself, as Immanuel Kant maintained with *das Ding an sich*. Thus, this probable error of subjectivism always exists, and this particularly sticky problem led to various splinterings among logical positivists.

For this reason, few people have subsequently identified themselves with logical positivism; its assumptions have proved to be perhaps too simple and its methodology too rigid. Nonetheless, its influence should not be discounted even though its career as a dominant philosophical position was short lived.

Two leading figures important in the analytic movement, but with roots in logical positivism, were Ludwig Wittgenstein and A. J. Ayer.

Ludwig Wittgenstein (1889–1951)

Ludwig Wittgenstein's connection with logical positivism stems from his earlier works, primarily *Tractatus Logico-Philosophicus*. In this book, he argues that the natural sciences are the primary source of true propositions and the primary means of finding new facts. Philosophy should not be seen as the discovery of truth, but rather as an activity to solve dilemmas, elucidate problems, and clarify ideas obtained from other sources. A true proposition might be referred to as an atomic proposition" that reveals the particular structure and arrangement of objects and facts. Philosophers should not concern themselves with the *truth* of the data, but rather should deal with the *language* and *statements made about it.* Thus, we need to specify what we can and cannot say—that is, the limits of language.

Wittgenstein was born in Austria and raised by rather rigid parents who expected only excellence from their children. His father wanted Ludwig to become an engineer, so he studied engineering first in Berlin and later in Manchester, England. He specialized in aircraft propulsion and consequently developed a deep interest in pure mathematics as an outgrowth of his work.

While in England, he was introduced to the mathematical logic of Russell. He soon went to Cambridge and became a student and personal friend of Russell, but World War I interrupted his studies and philosophical research. He returned to Austria, served in the Austrian Army, and was captured on the Italian front. He completed most of the work on *Tractatus Logico-Philosophicus* while serving in the army. Also during this time, he apparently had some sort of mystical experience, because after the war, he returned home, gave away his considerable wealth, and became an elementary school teacher.

Wittgenstein's views in the *Tractatus* revealed that he was an even more rigorous empiricist than Russell, which might account for his appeal to logical positivists. He thought that the only significant use of language was to picture the facts or to state tautologies; beyond this, he thought language was nonsensical. During the 1920s, he again came into contact with Cambridge intellectual circles, and in 1929 he moved to Britain and became a British subject. He began revising his philosophy, and by the mid-1930s, arrived at an altered position that was to have profound effects on Anglo-American philosophy.

Although in his later works Wittgenstein repudiated or revised some of his ideas, the members of the Vienna Circle understood his early views to mean that philosophy should be primarily an activity that tries to clarify concepts. They, too, believed that philosophy should not produce propositions—that it merely should clarify the meaning of statements, showing some to be scientific, some mathematical, and some nonsensical. Thus, every significant statement is either a statement of formal logic (which includes mathematical statements) or a statement of science. Other statements may be partial, emotive, pictorial, or motivational but are not cognitive. Philosophy, then, should show the limits of language, try to make propositions intelligible, and provide clarity. The insistence of this is not on the development of truth, but on the meaning of propositions as they currently exist.

The principle of verification was adopted by the Vienna Circle and stands as one of its chief methods. The members believed that all propositions must be verifiable by either logic or sense perception statements. An example of a logical statement is "Mothers are females"—a logically true statement based on the terms employed. "Mothers are workers," however, is not necessarily true or meaningful. This kind of proposition is meaningful only if it can be verified empirically by sense experience. Proponents of logical positivism distinguished between what they called "analytic" and "synthetic" sentences. Sentences whose truth logically follows from their meaning, such as the statement "All bald-headed men have no hair," are called *analytic*. Sentences that have some sort of empirical investigation for their confirmation are called *synthetic,* such as the statement "John has brown hair." Kant made this distinction between analytic and synthetic in his *Prolegomena to Any Future Metaphysics* and insisted that synthetic *a priori* statements are permissible only in mathematics.

Positivists believed that all analytic sentences are in the realm of formal logic—they are true because of their structure—and all synthetic statements belong to science, requiring empirical investigation for their validity. It should be pointed out that analytic sentences do not refer to the world the way synthetic sentences do. We cannot, for example, infer that the items mentioned by the terms of an analytic sentence actually exist. Thus, from the analytic statement "Mermaids are women," one cannot infer that any actual mermaids exist. However, the statement "This cat is white" can be verified by checking the facts of the situation. Logical positivists thought that analytic sentences are "trivial" but that synthetic ones are "informative." Analytic statements are true only by definition, whereas synthetic statements make claims about reality that can be verified as true or false.

Care should be taken here with the terms *analytic* and *synthetic*. Positivists were not using the term *synthetic* in the older meaning. They, too, were as suspicious as Russell had been of the old "philosophy in the grand manner" that sought to construct "great answers" and elaborate systems out of a synthesis of conflicting ideas. To Wittgenstein and the logical positivists, the old manner of synthesis was too metaphysical and nonsensical. The only *sayable* propositions are the propositions of natural science. Logical positivists took Wittgenstein's position to mean that true propositions must be capable of empirical verification. Wittgenstein, however, was also interested in the limits of language or what is sayable, and he did not anchor his position on empirical verification. Apparently, logical positivists understood his statement about natural science to mean "the empirically discoverable" or "what can be verified by the senses." At any rate, they arrived at the "principle of verification" and gave a rather exalted position to "synthetic," "informative" statements because these can be verified empirically.

Alfred Jules Ayer (1910–1989)

A. J. Ayer was another who seriously sought to combine logical positivism with analytic approaches. He was educated at Eton and Oxford, taught for several years at the University of London, and became a professor at Oxford in 1959. He was a prominent member of the Vienna Circle and sought to interpret logical positivism for the English-speaking world not only through teaching and writing but also through radio and television.

Ayer attempted to reconcile and order the principal doctrines of analysis from the works of Russell, Wittgenstein, and the Vienna Circle. He thought that the task of philosophy is to classify language, distinguish genuine propositions from others, and explain the meaning and justification of propositions by their reductive analysis into basic statements about immediate experience. Ayer used the principle of verification to show that religious, evaluative, and metaphysical utterances are not propositions.

In *Language, Truth and Logic*, Ayer uses the verifiability criterion of meaning. Accordingly, a sentence can be factually significant to a given person if and only if that person knows how to verify the propositions that it purports to express—that is, if the person knows what observation would lead them, under certain conditions, to accept the proposition as being true or to reject it as being false. Thus, it must be possible to describe what sorts of observations would have to be made to determine whether a sentence is true or false. If some observations can be made that will be relevant in determining the truth or falsity of a sentence, then the sentence is significant; if not, then it is meaningless. For example, no *observation* can occur to confirm or deny the proposition "Angels have silver wings," and thus it is meaningless. This is different from a statement such as "Intelligent beings live on another planet"; although this statement is not verifiable at present, it could possibly be verified at some point in the future.

Ayer thought that philosophers would do well to abandon the metaphysical grand manner approach, especially where that approach starts with first principles and then constructs a deductive system from them as a complete picture of reality. The problem with this approach is that first principles are taken to be logically certain. What makes more sense, according to Ayer, is the inductive approach, in which any derived generalizations are viewed only as probable and hypothetical. More to the point, the most valuable thing that philosophy can do is to reveal the criteria used in showing whether a proposition is true or false. The truth or falsity of any proposition must be determined by empirical verification, not philosophical clarification.

Ayer softened somewhat on the finality of the verification principle because of the criticism directed at the rigorous application he and the logical positivists used. Consequently, he ceased to identify himself with any definable school of thought, but he did retain some elements of the empirical approach of logical positivism. It has been suggested that Ayer most aptly could be called an analytically minded empiricist.

Linguistic Analysis

Linguistic analysis is the name many observers prefer to use when discussing analytic philosophy. This is because of the general trend away from trying to construct an ideal language as precise as the scientific model of mathematics or trying to construct too rigid a set of rules for ordinary language. Perhaps tacking the word *linguistic* in front of *analysis* is still a far-from-accurate way to describe this philosophy. Indeed, many kinds of analysis are occurring, but the term *linguistic* is still accurate. The task is as much linguistic as it is a matter of formal logic or some brand of positivism. The trend just noted can be credited to the later works of Wittgenstein as much as to any one figure, for in his mature stage, his viewpoint opened considerably to recognize many uses of language. Hence, *linguistic* becomes an apt term to signify this approach to philosophy.

Wittgenstein's Later Works

Wittgenstein was mentioned earlier, yet his ideas deserve additional attention because of the complexities of his career and thought, as well as the historical development of philosophical analysis. Wittgenstein's later ideas set new directions in philosophy, and these new directions had a profound impact on linguistic analysis.

These views first came to light in written form as mimeographed notes on lectures he had delivered to students in the early 1930s. They were called the *Blue Book* and the *Brown Book* and were not published until after his death. The basic ideas of these works appear in a much expanded and revised form as *Philosophical Investigations,* also published posthumously. Of all his writings, perhaps the easiest to read is the *Blue Book*.

Wittgenstein's revised philosophy no longer took the narrow view of language but saw language consisting of indefinite possibilities of usage. In effect, he was saying that people need to understand the *context* of language usage, and in order to understand the meaning of that language usage, we may construct "language games." He thought that most philosophical problems are not problems at all but puzzlements brought about by linguistic confusions. The proper issue is these puzzlements and how most people, early in life, get locked into certain language uses from which they cannot escape readily. Humans are, in Wittgenstein's view, like flies in a bottle, haphazardly flitting about and banging against the walls in their confusion. The role of philosophy, then, should not be to construct explanations about reality and so forth but to solve the puzzles of linguistic confusion. Philosophy should be viewed as a method of investigation (although no specified, singular method) that results in pure description, and language should be seen as having no necessary or ideal form.

Historically, philosophy has posed such questions as "What is real?" and "What is meaning?" Wittgenstein thought that these kinds of questions only lead to mental cramp. It is better to ask "What is an explanation of meaning?" than to ask "What is meaning?" Thus, he focused on the explanation of meaning, or the meaning of meaning. According to Wittgenstein, problems occur when, upon hearing a word, people immediately begin to look for its meaning in some corresponding object. He believed that what people ought to do is look at the word itself, the sign, and the statement, and examine the context of its usage. Usage depends on the meaning of signs (names or words) in relation to other signs within a system of signs—in short, within a language. According to Wittgenstein, understanding a sentence involves understanding a language. (By *language,* he did not mean English, French, or German, for any of these can have many languages within them in terms of usage and context.)

For example, consider a word over which philosophers have long argued: *thinking.* According to Wittgenstein, the meaning of *thinking* varies. When confronted with the word, most people associate it with mind and mental activity. What happens, however, when we begin to explain what one means by the sign *thinking*? Is it hidden away inside the cranium? If we could open people's heads while they were thinking, could one see it? Likely, one would see physiological structures (brain matter, blood vessels, etc.). What, then, is happening when thinking is going on? Some suggestions might come easily to mind: writing, reading, and speaking. Is thinking done by the mouth and larynx? Why does one say *mind* is doing the thinking? Where is its locus, its seat? Thinking can be explained only by signifying such agents as the brain, hand, and larynx.

Wittgenstein did not question that thinking also occurred in the brain, but he did maintain that when we try to describe thinking in words and statements, they signify agents of thinking and we draw *analogies* from them. People try to summarize all of these into a general term such as *mind* and then relate this to a thing or object. For centuries, philosophers have argued about mind, mental, and thinking and have tried to locate and delineate them. Wittgenstein suggested that the puzzle is linguistic. People became fascinated with a linguistic form when they thought they had a problem with a thing.

Part of this difficulty, Wittgenstein maintained, is that people have come to crave generality, a concept linked to many philosophical puzzlements. Philosophers have taught that we should look for commonality in all things that can be brought under a general term. The tendency to generalize is rooted in forms of expression. Words have come to possess the meaning of a general image of things associated with, or corresponding to, the words. The result is a confusion of the things named with the names themselves—the words. We have come to confuse, as in the case of *thinking,* mental processes and mechanisms with states of consciousness or awareness. Part of this is a result, Wittgenstein thought, of human preoccupation with the method of science, which seeks to reduce the explanations of natural phenomena to the smallest possible number of natural "laws" or principles—or, if you will, scientific generalizations. He stated that this preoccupation is the source of metaphysics in philosophy. For Wittgenstein, it is not the proper business of philosophy to reduce anything, to produce generalizations, or to offer grand explanations. Philosophy's business is to be purely descriptive.

Wittgenstein believed that the problem with modern philosophy is the "contemptuous attitude towards the particular case." For example, the word *kind* is used a great deal. This shows the human penchant for generalization because people quickly want to subsume something under a larger heading. When confronted with strange words about something, a quick reaction is to ask, "What kind of thing is it?" as if it has to be subsumed under some heading of animal, vegetable, or mineral before the meaning of the word can be understood properly. Think again about the philosopher's plight with the word *thinking.* The desire is to locate it, and in the analysis several cases of thinking are described. Something is still lacking, though, because it is virtually impossible to define *thinking* in a manner to cover all cases so that the word truly designates a general class. In actual usage, the word has no sharp boundary. To Wittgenstein, the idea that one must find a common element in all applications of a word or statement is a hindrance to philosophical investigation. It has led philosophers to the grievous error of dismissing the concrete particular.

Furthermore, Wittgenstein held that the explanation of the meaning of a word depends on the actual context of usage and the language structure being used. In attempting to construct generalizations, people are thrown into the pit of drawing analogies from one context to another, relying on conventions rather than specifics of behavior; devising criteria and symptoms of usage; and then arbitrarily picking one convention, criterion, or symptom as more important than another. In effect, one is reduced to constructing arbitrary and abstract rules and procedures that get away from the concrete usage and meaning in context. We come to view language according to the mathematical rules of calculus. Language, however, is rarely like calculus. The craving for generality leads to abstract exactness that gives rise to philosophical puzzlements and linguistic confusion.

Wittgenstein believed that in actuality, words have no true meaning given to them by some independent power. They have the meanings *people* give them. Thus, one cannot scientifically investigate what a word *really* means, and one cannot tabulate strict rules of usage. It is also fruitless to construct an ideal language to replace ordinary language: Rather, an ideal language should remove the trouble of thinking that one had gotten the exact usage of an ordinary word. Thus, Wittgenstein rejected any *necessary* form of language.

In actual usage, people construct and play language games, or "systems" of communication. The understanding of language is as varied as the games. What makes anything a language, anyway? Commonality or generality is necessarily involved, but it is a commonality like a family resemblance and not the complete picture of the family. Wittgenstein thought that people could invent their own language games to help them understand actual usage by showing the similarities and differences of a language. These constructed games would be used to examine actual and possible uses of language in various contexts.

Wittgenstein had no systematic doctrine, no rules of procedure, and no lockstep grand manner approach to philosophizing. This makes his philosophy difficult to comprehend because people are accustomed to seeing answers put forth and explanations offered for the world's origin and destiny. Wittgenstein would have none of this and asserted that philosophy needs to be purely descriptive. One could say that his view recommends uncorking the bottle and letting the fly out to see where it will go.

Gilbert Ryle (1900–1976)

Gilbert Ryle was born, reared, and educated in England. Early in his philosophical career, he was attracted to certain aspects of Continental philosophy, especially Husserl's work, but by the age of 31, Ryle had become well versed in philosophical analysis. He viewed analysis as a matter of finding the sources of linguistic confusion by examining some of the continually perplexing problems in philosophy, such as the mind–body dualism. His work on the use of the words *mind, mental, thinking, knowing,* and related words made him one of the most influential and widely read contemporary British philosophers. His best-known work is *The Concept of Mind,* which is one of the more famous books in twentieth-century philosophy.

In *The Concept of Mind,* Ryle attacks the Cartesian doctrine of splitting off body and mind. This doctrine holds that the body is in the realm of matter, susceptible to and subject to the laws of matter. It can be studied objectively, and its behavior can be observed and measured publicly. In contrast with this, the mind is hidden from view—a private, secret realm. It is subjective, and although one may have access to one's own mental operations, one cannot read another's mind objectively. Thus, although the material body can be studied scientifically, mind is not available to science but is amenable to a special subjective method of investigation called *intro-spection*. Ryle disputed these contentions, calling this theory "the dogma of the Ghost in the Machine." It is false in principle, he maintained, because it is a "category mistake," and he referred to the dogma as "the philosopher's myth."

According to Ryle, a category mistake occurs when one allocates concepts to logical types to which they do not belong. He gave the example of the visitor who came to Oxford and was shown the various colleges, laboratories, libraries, offices, and so forth. The visitor then asked, "But where is the university?" This is a category mistake; the visitor was allocating the concept of university to the same logical type as its constituent colleges. In the case of Oxford, *university* is a collective logical type and *college* is a "constituent element" logical type. A similar kind of category mistake can be made with the word *institution*. One speaks of marriage as an institution and of Harvard University as an institution, but there is a world of difference between the logical meanings of the term *institution* in these cases.

How did the mind–body confusion come about? According to Ryle, the science developed by Galileo and others maintained that certain mechanical laws of matter governed every object occupying space. René Descartes, being concerned with science, could accept such laws, but as a philosopher, he could not accept a mechanistic theory for the human mind. Mental was not the same as mechanical, but its exact opposite. This is a category mistake because it puts body and mind under the same logical type in the manner of exact opposites. Both are things, but things of entirely different natures. If body is a machine, then mind is a nonmachine. The belief that mind and body (or mind and matter) are at polar positions came about because of the belief that they are both of the same logical type, although opposites. Ryle was not trying to absorb the one into the other by saying that it is either all material or all mental. He held that although the dogma is absurd, making distinctions between physical activity and mental activity is justifiable. It all hinges on the *sense* in which one is speaking.

Perhaps most of the problem belongs to the confusion engendered by such words as *mind, mental, thinking,* and similar mentalistic terms. Certainly, Ryle maintained, it is legitimate to describe doing long division or thinking things over as mental activity. It is an error, however, to ascribe any sense of place to mental activity. People picture "in the head" when they say "mental activity." This is what Ryle called the "intellectualist legend," that intelligence is some internal operation. Yet, it is justifiable to speak of mental activity "in the head" if we understand that we are speaking metaphorically. One does not necessarily do arithmetic in the head; it can be done just as well (if not better) by speaking it aloud or by writing it on paper. The same can be said of imagined noise. People can hear music in their heads. Who has not heard a tune over and over in their mind? If someone else placed an ear against the head of the subject, the tune would not be heard; if the subject were speaking or singing aloud though, it could be heard by means of cranial bone vibrations. The tune that people metaphorically say is in their minds is not really in their heads. A great deal of confusion over the mind–body problem results from mixing the literal sense with a metaphorical one.

A related problem is associated with the term *knowing*. Knowing and knowledge have long been of concern to philosophers, and epistemology (theory of knowledge) traditionally has been a main discipline of philosophy. Yet, all sorts of problems have been encountered with understanding *knowing* because of confusion with the term. Ryle maintained that people have confused "knowing that" and "knowing how." "Knowing how" is having the capacity to perform, being able to do, and so forth. However, Ryle pointed out, knowing that something is the case does not mean that we necessarily know how to do it. In the same way, to be able to perform or do does not necessarily mean that the purposes and reasons for doing are understood. Too often, it is assumed that knowing and knowledge are too much on the side of "knowing that." This has resulted in an ignorant approach to formal education whereby it is assumed that after students' heads are crammed with facts and "knowledge," they will be able to go out into the world and perform successfully. A healthier concept of knowing and knowledge would be that to know in the best sense is to "know that" *and* "know how."

Many problems go back to the mind–body dualism. These can be traced all the way back to Plato, who extolled the mental over the material; to the churchmen who extolled soul (mind) over body; and to Descartes, who devised the *cogito*. Ryle pointed out that the fault was not so much that of Descartes as it was of a long philosophical and theological tradition. Furthermore, he thought that such myths as the mind–body dualism have their uses. The creation of myths helps people get around many difficulties. It often has been observed that modern science would never have been accepted in Christendom if the Cartesian myth had not been developed, for it helped reconcile scientific findings with theological dogmas.

Perhaps new myths will be needed to get around science's dogmas. New methods of investigation will need to be devised to replace current ones. At any rate, Ryle's analysis is instructive in helping people wend their way through the linguistic confusions in which they find themselves.

PHILOSOPHICAL ANALYSIS AND PHILOSOPHY OF EDUCATION

Although philosophical analysis generally is considered a relatively new development, all philosophies deal with the logical analysis of concepts, meanings, and problems to some extent. One can certainly see a great concern for analysis in the writings of Plato, Aristotle, Kant, Descartes, and Nietzsche. The dialectic, for example, is not only a method for arriving at truth but also a method for eliminating contradictions that stand in the way of truth. Francis Bacon talked about the Idol of the Marketplace being the most troublesome of all; as he put it, "Men believe that their reason governs words, but it is also true that words react on the understanding, and this it is that has rendered philosophy and the sciences sophistical and inactive."

The argument has been made many times that human thinking is governed in whole or in part by language and the meanings of words. It is difficult to conceive of thoughts without language, and what thinking is done can be expressed only in some kind of language. Some people believe that without language symbols (whether mathematical, verbal, written, pictured, or gestured), there would be no means of communication and hence no mind. Many analysts say that because thinking is so dependent on language, thinking problems are also language problems resulting from faulty usage and lack of clarity.

The use of analytic philosophy in education has some direct bearing on students, but perhaps it is most useful for educators in helping them clarify what they propose to teach students. The consequence of this use of analytic philosophy is not to develop some new educational "ism" or ideology but to help people understand better the meanings of ideologies. The benefits accrue to students as a result of a clarified and more meaningful approach to the educational process.

An illustrative example is the educator's confusion with the word *knowing,* an example given by Ryle. "Knowing that" has been confused with the complete picture of knowing; consequently, once having "filled students' heads" with all kinds of data, teachers assume that their task is finished. Ryle pointed out, however, that knowing also includes "knowing how," or being able to do and perform. In one sense, this involves the old problem of the separation of theory ("knowing") from practice ("doing"), a problem to which John Dewey devoted much discussion. Dewey spoke of the philosophical dichotomy between knowledge and action, or knowing and doing. In other words, he maintained that knowing and doing have been separated artificially. The knowing side is similar to "knowing that," and the doing side is similar to "knowing how." Dewey thought that these two should go together as much as possible, particularly with regard to the education of the young. The "learning by doing" slogan so often voiced by progressive educators has at least some of its roots in Dewey's thought. Knowledge is learned or gained by becoming actively or physically involved with significant tasks. In fact, it could be said that this idea goes back to the ancient Greeks, who talked about the merging of *areté* and *téchne* (virtue and skill).

Take, for example, learning how to ride a bicycle. Prospective riders need to know that the machine is steered by turning the handlebars in the desired direction and by shifting body weight to maintain balance. They also must know that the bicycle's momentum has to be maintained at a particular minimum speed for the machine to remain upright. So far though, prospective riders know only that certain things must be done to ride successfully. In other words, they know that bicycle riding has certain specific "principles." They have, so to speak, the "theory" of bicycle riding. All cyclists realize, however, that they also must know how to ride a bicycle; they must have a practical knowledge of cycling, and this involves the actual, out-of-doors "doing" of riding a bicycle. Educators have stopped too often with the "knowing that" aspect of knowing. Students get the theory but not the practice.

A more complex example is the objective of producing democratic citizens—an objective that is dear to the hearts of many Americans. American schools have largely accomplished this task by informing students of something called democracy and by stating that in the United States, this usually is associated with government, American history, and such things as the right to vote. As a general rule, however, few students ever get to be democratic by doing things democratically. They are required to have hall passes, they need permission to speak, and they must abide by restrictive rules they usually have had no voice in constructing. They know of something called democracy, but they do not know how to be democratic. It is readily apparent why so little democracy is practiced in American life: Most people have not had the opportunity to know how. In education, usage of the term *knowing* has had a narrow meaning. People are confused about knowing because its meaning has been too arbitrarily restricted to exclude considerations about knowing that extend far beyond a mere cognitive or intellectual thing.

Thus, many analysts maintain that analytic philosophy has an important role to play in education because so much of education deals with logic and language. Teachers and students constantly deal in generalizations and value judgments about educational materials that need to be examined critically.

The analyst emphasizes that the role of language is learning and that it is necessary to apply criteria for evaluating and clarifying the statements people make, a need that goes beyond the traditional studies of grammar. Some educators believe that language analysis should be the primary role with which philosophy of education is concerned. Their thesis is based on the idea that deliberate education should become more precise and scientific and that analysis offers one way to do this. They are quick to point out that other philosophies of education usually are based on highly questionable metaphysical assumptions and too often result in prescriptions that are more emotive than anything else. Analytic philosophers of education believe that students should study the language that the students themselves use to describe and justify the meanings they apply in life.

Language is certainly important. It is doubtful that people could even think without language; thinking usually parallels language concepts, and bad thinking could be, in many cases, a poor use of language. Some educators protest that language analysis should be only a small part of philosophy, but philosophical analysts point out that the problems of language are so numerous, diffuse, and complex that the desired analytic study is a major undertaking of great significance. They contend that many educational problems are largely language problems and that if the language problems can be solved, people can, in effect, better solve the educational problems.

Language as an educational problem goes far beyond the confines of the school or classroom into practically all facets of life. Not only is language a prime concern for students in terms of curriculum, textbooks, and other conveyances of knowledge, but it is also an integral part of their everyday life. Perhaps a special need today is for students to have a greater sensitivity to the place of language. The language they encounter heavily influences their behavior, because language stimulates a variety of behaviors. For example, Hitler came to power partly because of his ability to manipulate language, and many contemporary totalitarian regimes maintain their power largely through a careful control of the language media because they fear the consequences of an unfettered language.

George Orwell, in his novel *1984*, writes about the creation of "Newspeak," a language developed so that linguistic techniques could be used to control behavior. The Newspeak word *doublethink* means "the ability to believe two contradictory ideas at the same time"; for example, "War is peace" and "Love is hate." He also writes about "crimestop," whereby people can be so conditioned by linguistic control that they are mentally incapable of entertaining any idea hostile to the state or "Big Brother." One can find many examples of governments using such techniques to cover up problems by using language (or corrupted versions of language) to protect their power and vested interests.

It is easy to sympathize with the position of the philosophical analyst when one thinks of the barrage of advertising, sloganeering, and cliché thinking that people are exposed to daily. Because most people have had little training in logical thought, they are easy victims for the misuse of language to make them buy something, vote a certain way, or support a particular position. People are exposed constantly to many nefarious language devices, and some are effective in influencing their thinking. Individuals representing vested interests have learned the techniques of language manipulation and have found them so effective that they have used them to persuade people to behave in ways they want them to behave. Books such as Vance Packard's *The Hidden Persuaders* show how easily people can be manipulated and influenced by advertisers and politicians and how the methods used are often subtle and ingenious. Theodore White's *The Making of the President* points out how a variety of techniques, including the manipulation of language, can be used to help a particular candidate win an election.

A further example is the term *the law*. Many people say that one should or should not do certain things because it is the law. But what is the law? Laws change from time to time or differ from one country or state to another. Further, they are subject to interpretation, and thus a law as determined by one court might be overturned by another. In effect, it could be said that the law is an abstraction developed for a mythical person. Critics charge that lawyers prefer that laws remain vague and abstract, because this gives them something to interpret and manipulate for clients and thus leads to large incomes and an abundance of lengthy court cases. Therefore, for practical and philosophical reasons, analysts argue that people should be sensitive to language problems and attempt to make language more precise and clear. This is a laudable goal but also difficult to achieve; words have as many meanings as users intend them to have.

Language usage affects students and teachers. Teachers often become unwilling tools of other interests as they use language in the educational process. The teacher teaches primarily with language, and because of its many possibilities, can use it in a variety of ways to influence the thinking of children. Teachers express ideas and information through language (including gestures), and the way they use it has a profound effect, often unrecognized and unintended. Marxists have charged that teachers in capitalist societies are so caught up in the system in which they are teaching that they cannot see they are indoctrinating their students with the values inherent in a particular economic system.

By the time children reach adolescence, they are conditioned to the "language games" of education and can use language in similar ways to manipulate others. Language is employed in textbooks, computer programs, videos, and other media where the choice of words, the size of letters, and the kinds of grammatical constructions all contribute to certain effects on a child's mental development. For example, many social studies texts omit critical discussions of various political, social, and economic policies because they might offend some pressure group or vested interest. The textbooks that children use in schools are not written in a vacuum and reflect many biases.

Educators themselves are victims of language devices contrived to get them to think or vote in certain ways and also to develop particular attitudes about education, children, and society. Teachers seem as susceptible to specious language concerning social issues as anyone else, and an enormous amount of sloganeering and jargon is generated within the education profession. One hears talk about "the teachable moment" and "school choice" and the use of many other slogans. Some critics have asked: What is a teachable moment? Shouldn't the education system be working to achieve teachable minutes, periods, and hours? Some talk about "school choice" as if everyone is going to be able to choose the best schools for their children. It is clear that everyone cannot possibly go to the best schools, if for no other reasons than geographical distance, overcrowding, and prohibitive costs of transportation. Critics see "school choice" as an example of political sloganeering to make people think something that is not truly intended and is impossible to grant. People talk about the "democratic process" in instances where little or no democracy exists, about "individuality" when it is seldom allowed, and about "freedom" only within narrowly prescribed limits. Often, the case is similar to the sense of *1984*: We say "peace" when we mean war, "truth" when we mean falsehood, and "justice" when we mean injustice.

Aims of Education

Philosophical analysts are interested in improving the educator's concepts about education and the ways these concepts are used. One of the first steps is to become acutely aware of language and its potential. Once this is done, the chances are better that people will have a greater concern for the sensitive use of language in the educational process. The analytic philosopher is after clarification. It must be clear what educators propose to do in education in a philosophically adequate manner, and philosophical analysis is a major tool in accomplishing this task of clarification.

Analysts believe that educators should be attuned to the logical complexities of language. Language is a complex cultural development, and words have a variety of meanings and usages. What do words such as *knowing, mind, freedom,* and *education* mean? Although most analysts do not believe that words have inherent meanings, they do insist that words can be used in more precise ways to reflect accurately what is intended. Many concepts have an emotive effect that must be taken into consideration. Such words as *justice, patriotism, honor*, and *virtue* may give a "halo" or "hurrah" effect to statements about the aims of education.

Some analysts, such as R. S. Peters, insist that one cannot speak legitimately about the aims of education because if education is initiation into worthwhile activities, then it already has all the aims it needs. Making statements about what education *should* do is to make prescriptions—an activity that most analysts reject as outside the realm of analytic philosophy. Peters has questioned the use of the concept of "education" in general and has attempted to show how confusing the usage of the word has been. Ryle attempted to show that the meaning of the term *knowing* could be more inclusive than the way it is used ordinarily by educators. Wittgenstein stated that words do not necessarily have an inherent, objective meaning; rather, they mean whatever the user intends them to mean. Peters, Ryle, and Wittgenstein caution people to examine the context and precision of their word usage. In short, the analysts do not attempt to prescribe any particular kind of education as much as they seek to clarify the linguistic devices employed by the educator, the processes of using them, their underlying presuppositions, and the purposes involved.

It seems that the use-value of words determines their meanings as much as any dictionary definition. In fact, dictionary definitions are altered periodically by practical use. Language itself is always changing and evolving; one can neither define a word forever nor prescribe its meaning for everyone else. The educational consequence of this, the analysts claim, is that one must see concepts, word meanings, and statements about education in their practical context as opposed to a theoretical, prescriptive construction.

Teachers constantly call for practical solutions to educational problems. However, this concern with practicality is itself open to analytic inquiry: Just what does *practical* mean in this instance? Often, the "practical" teacher wants a technique or a gimmick to apply to and solve a problem. It is reasonable, however, to observe that such practical solutions are often theoretical in the worst sense. Techniques sometimes are used indiscriminately. They are applied generally and universally in situations for which they were not designed; however, they are deemed practical because their mechanics are known and they can be acted upon.

"Achievement" is a talisman by which many educators swear, and the worth of any educational activity is judged on students' achievement scores. Achievement in such instances usually is understood to be a practical outcome of education, but such emphasis might serve to retard one's education if the meaning of the term *achievement* is vague and unclear. Suppose one wants to learn how to play the piano, and the educator says that the practical approach is to proceed by achievement in learning to play scales. Such a method might result in the student learning to play scales but not in developing an ability to play the piano or in sustaining interest. The question can be posed: How practical is this approach?

People's use of words is intimately connected with the presuppositions underlying their use. In the case about learning to play the piano, what was believed to be practical was not practical at all. The proposition that one learns to play the piano by achievement in playing scales is itself theoretical and not always supported by factual circumstances (although playing the scales might *help* achieve that goal). Similar conditions exist with regard to numerous other educational prescriptions.

Thus, rather than prescribing aims to be achieved in the educational process, the analyst prefers to look at what is meant by education and what advantages may accrue from a clarified concept of education. Peters spoke about the "justification" of education rather than mere aims. He pointed to at least four considerations that help people situate the meaning of education to arrive at better educational aims:

1. Education is more than mere specialized skills because it includes developing one's capacity to reason, justifying beliefs and conduct, knowing the *why* as well as the *what* of things, and organizing experience in terms of systematic conceptions.
2. Education is more than mere specialized knowledge and includes developing one's cognitive perspective, expanding moral understandings, and developing aesthetic appreciations.
3. Education includes doing and knowing things for their own sake, for the joy of doing and knowing.
4. Education is the process by which people are initiated into their particular lifestyles.

Thus, in speaking about education, one must never forget that *means* figure in the meaning as well as *aims*. Peters aptly illustrated the problem of speaking about the aims of education when the meanings of education are so diverse. To be intelligent and reasonable in establishing aims in education, people need to clear the ground to arrive at what is meant by education before they can construct particular aims reasonably. It might be that aims belong to particular teaching strategies and not to some esoteric word with confused meanings, such as *education.*

Dewey once said that "aim" was akin to a target and implied a definite goal or outcome. Peters agreed and pointed out that if "aim" refers to specific outcomes, then it is ridiculous to speak of the aims of education as if these were universally agreed-up-on norms. It is more the case that in any given historical period, the meanings of education have particular norms built into them by practical use. Thus, when people ask for the aims of education, they are requesting clarification and specification of their particular contemporary norms. Any number of aims of education is possible, depending on the kinds of life people think are most important at any given time in history. Today, for instance, Peters says that some aims are worthwhile overall, such as growth and the self-realization of the individual. However, aims of this sort have their roots within a cultural system that supports individualistic thought patterns. They point to autonomy and self-actualization as important, whereas those living in another cultural epoch or historical period might view these as minor or not even recognize them at all.

Such analysts as Peters believe that the process of formulating aims in education must be separated from the general question "What is *the* aim of education?" This question is not apt because its answer must be either conceptually true or persuasive. It falls into timeworn rubrics, such as "good citizenship is the proper aim of education" or "one cardinal aim of education is worthy home membership." The analyst thinks that such statements only confuse the issue, for then one is pushed to define "good citizenship" or "worthy home membership." As Wittgenstein pointed out, no sooner is something uttered than people begin searching for its assumed objective or existing equivalent.

Israel Scheffler critically analyzed how the word *relevance* is misused or overused so as to complicate rather than clear up educational issues. Practically everybody would agree that education ought to be relevant. Being for relevance is like being for mother love and apple pie. But what is relevant? Scheffler maintains that the primary task of education is not relevance so much as supporting and ensuring a society dedicated to the ideals of free inquiry and rationality. Thus, it is not *the* aim of education that people must seek but an understanding of what kinds of desirable aims may be developed, what the possibilities are of achieving them, and what kinds of consequences can be expected from acting on them. These latter considerations are not within the province of the philosopher of education as much as they are within the province of sociologists, psychologists, scientists, political leaders, and ordinary citizens. The analytic philosopher's role is simply to clarify and criticize the meanings involved.

Methods of Education

Analysts are concerned that both methods and materials of contemporary education undergo a serious analytic study. Although most analysts avoid prescribing what should or should not go on in the educational process, they are interested in seeing that the educator and the student critically examine the curriculum from the standpoint of materials, methods, policies, and procedures.

Analysts are aware that methods and media of all kinds educate the child in many ways. Although educators should understand that words and concepts are value-laden, they do not always operate with an awareness of this fact. When the McGuffey readers were used in the early 1900s, for example, they taught not only reading skills but also particular values concerning religion, patriotism, and family. Books of the Dick-and-Jane type that came later supposedly attempted to provide a more neutral kind of material that was value-free. Neutrality was not achieved, however, for these readers contained assumptions about gender roles, children's rights and their relationship to society, and dominant social class themes, such as the work ethic and respect for authority.

Analysts do not attempt to say what kinds of books children should read; rather, they examine the meaning of the claims made regarding the merits of such activities. Instead of saying what a child *should* read, think, study, or learn, the analyst examines what is meant by the words *think, read,* or *learn* and the statements people make regarding these words. Some analysts avoid not only prescriptive statements about what students ought or ought not do but also statements of value about the importance of such activities.

Some analysts advocate devising *paradigms*—that is, constructing models of logic that help clarify and order concepts. This resembles Wittgenstein's idea of language games in some respects but differs in that a paradigm has a rather specific use. It is tailored to particular kinds of problems. Gordon Eastwood once described an appropriate analytic paradigm as one that has "a syntactically and semantically appropriate language system" that should be prescriptive only to the extent that it "enable[s] the formation of hypotheses to guide research for facts not now known."

In this regard, paradigms are useful for looking at educational problems in an objective, nonpartisan, and unemotive way.

Eastwood even suggested that large-scale paradigms could be used, and he criticized many analytic philosophers of education who direct their attention to small (or insignificant) problems. Instead, philosophy of education must be concerned with theory, and we need appropriate large-scale paradigms to help us approach the task adequately.

Jerome Popp notes that one can choose different paradigms for different purposes and that it is unnecessary to choose global or universal paradigms. At the same time, however, consistency seems preferable to wild eclecticism. The search for large-scale paradigms involves, to some extent, worldview outlooks that are close to old grand manner philosophy. It could be argued, for example, that the paradigm approach contains the seeds of destruction for the analytic approach to philosophy. It eschews the large-scale point of view but needs the larger picture to give coherence and meaning to its task.

Jonas Soltis has observed that in the late 1950s and early 1960s, a shift occurred from a "pragmatic paradigm" to an "analytic paradigm" that students of philosophy believed to be more in line with the concerns of the day. Analysis is now apparently coming to suffer from similar shortcomings, however, and perhaps it should shift its focus from small-scale problems to larger, more encompassing ones.

One area with which analysts have spent much time is the activity of teaching. Paul Hirst has shown the need for empirical research on the effectiveness of various teaching methods. Most methods, he claims, are based on little more than hunches and personal prejudices. Teachers need to be clear about the nature of the central activity in which they are involved professionally. How, for example, does one distinguish teaching from other activities? Are teachers teaching when they sharpen a few pencils and break up squabbles among the children? In Hirst's opinion, teaching is a "polymorphous" activity that can take many different forms. To know that teaching is going on, the aims and intentions must be clarified so that each activity is seen in a clear relationship to those aims.

Successful teaching seems to be teaching that brings about desired learning. Yet, this desired learning could result from conditioning or indoctrination. In order to study the difference between conditioning and indoctrinating, one should postulate a perfect case of each in its most literal and ordinary use. Then one can understand the differences in the meaning of each term—that is, conditioning or indoctrinating. Even though differences will arise, there also will be similarities of meanings for each term with which everyone will agree, thus clarifying the meaning of each term. The clarified, agreed-upon meanings become the different modes of teaching by which actual cases are compared. Thus, teaching methodologies, based on teaching modes that serve as benchmarks or standards of minimal performance, are established. If one were to ask "How would you teach X to someone?" then reference could be made to the appropriate mode. Of course, disagreements as to proper modes could continue, so there might be several other models on how to teach.

Analysis is an ongoing activity. Conclusions are not arrived at full-blown and axiomatic. They do not precede investigation but flow from it. The major thrust of analytic philosophy is to try to arrive at clarified principles, agreements, and conclusions, rather than to start with them. In this sense, philosophical analysis follows in the footsteps of the Socratic view of philosophy as the search for wisdom.

Curriculum

Richard Pring points out that such curricular terms as *integrated studies, integrated curriculum, unified knowledge, broad fields of experience,* and *problem solving* are confusing and misleading. Such phrases as "the seamless coat of learning" and "the unity of all knowledge" lack clarity of meaning and have no inherent value. Conversely, such terms as *traditional, subject matter,* and *compartmentalization* are not necessarily bad in and of themselves, but these slogans and phrases dealing with curricula have been used to set up straw men polarized along conceptions of good and bad.

Curriculum used to be viewed as something established to achieve certain ends, but it seems that today the ends flow from the curriculum itself. Hugh Sockett maintains that the literature on curriculum contains much talk about taking means to ends and conceiving of the relationship between means and ends as contingent. Sockett argues that what must be maintained as central to any account of curriculum, aims, and objectives is human intentionality—one's conception of what we are doing. Therefore, conceptions must be clear.

Philosophical analysts are concerned about the way educational plans are made. Curriculum planning is often superficial and badly done, and cultural bias is almost the only rationale that one can discover in many curriculum plans. Little planning seems to be systematic or careful. Often, this is not the fault of the persons involved so much as it is the faulty language, confused meanings, and unclear purposes that are used. People need to examine current curricula in terms of these problems, as well as to promote an ongoing critical attitude toward curriculum restructuring in which meanings and purposes are clarified.

Pring says that the foremost philosophical problems in curriculum and curriculum integration are what meanings are involved, what assumptions are made about knowledge, what the forms of knowledge are, what the interrelationship among these forms is, and what the structural unity of language is. Thus, any concern with curriculum goes far beyond the idea of plugging subject areas into a switchboard of school programs. Unfortunately, however, many people see curriculum reform narrowly and give little attention to the deeper questions involved. Analysts believe that greater attention must be given to the philosophical aspects, and they have encouraged greater work in this area.

Role of the Teacher

Linguistic analysts are concerned that teachers have a good understanding of the language used in their classrooms. Language can be in spoken or written form, and through this medium ideas are conveyed. Analysts point out, however, that language is not always used well and that it does not always convey ideas clearly. Because language is such an important part of education, teachers more than any other professionals need to be aware of the possibilities and the limitations of language. Further, they need to make their students aware of these possibilities and limitations.

Many people have a casual attitude toward the language they use, and this casualness leads to linguistic confusion and fuzzy thinking. Language is a powerful tool for conveying ideas when it is used carefully, but when it is used poorly, it makes good thinking difficult. An example of this can be found in the political arena when diplomats from various nations meet to discuss their differences. They have not only the primary problem of conveying positions in their own language but also the secondary problem of seeing that through translation, others understand their ideas as intended. Often, diplomatic procedures are fraught with confusion because some words lose much of their meaning in translation and convey inexact meanings from one culture to another. Words like *freedom, democracy,* or *justice* might mean different things in different cultures. As formidable as the task is, however, people do manage to generate treaties and other agreements by coming to terms with the problems of language. In the classroom, the problem is no different, and teachers need to use language in ways that make their meanings clear.

Much language is value-laden and emotive in nature. Not only are the words themselves capable of carrying hidden meanings, but the way the teacher uses words, the inflections and emphases, often convey a variety of unconscious and perhaps unintended meanings. These meanings may include religious and philosophical attitudes, economic beliefs, or even racial and class biases. Some cultural attitudes and biases are so built into the structure of a language that it requires considerable effort to eradicate them. It might seem offensive to use words like *mankind* when referring to both men and women, *Indians* when referring to Native Americans, or even B.C. and A.D. as reflecting a Christian bias in designating historical periods of time. It is often difficult to change such things because they are a part of historical usage and literature, and not everyone is sensitive to such expressions.

Analysts would like teachers to understand the logic of language. This might entail taking courses in logic to understand the various rules of good word usage. Also, teachers need to be skilled in the ability to analyze language and to point out the improper use of language in whatever form it appears: newspaper editorials, textbooks, advertisements, television newscasts, and so on. Teachers need to share this knowledge with students to help them develop the ability to analyze language so that they, too, will become adept at uncovering fallacious usage. Analysts believe that if students develop this ability, then they will become better readers, better consumers, and also better citizens.

CRITIQUE OF ANALYTIC PHILOSOPHY IN EDUCATION

Analysis has been an indispensable part of philosophy since its inception, and every serious philosopher has been engaged in analyzing ideas. Much in the writings of philosophers from Plato to the present points to the need to use language carefully and to avoid inconsistent and illogical thinking. It is undoubtedly true that a major problem in life is the confusion in understanding brought about by unclear or careless language, and it is easy to document the misuse of many words and concepts, such as *liberal, conservative,* and *God*. History is replete with instances of how the misuse of words and the misunderstandings of meanings have led to internal strife, religious differences, and even full-scale wars. Some analysts maintain that because language is so important to thinking, it is almost inconceivable that humans could think at all without it. They further observe that confused thinking may well result from the poor use of words in the thinking process.

One function of philosophy is to develop a critical attitude toward language and meaning, and this is certainly something that analysts have fostered. Rather than accept ready-made answers, clichés, and slogans as solutions for educational and social problems, they have supported an approach that insists that all ideas and issues be examined every step along the way. Analysts are wary of "the grand manner of philosophizing," which entails a cry for synthesis and simple solutions to complicated problems. They are skeptical of a utopian attitude toward problems in which emotive or predetermined ends might lead people's thinking awry. They are also fearful of the emotional factors that could overshadow clear and dispassionate thinking. This is not to imply that analysts are cold and unemotional, but they are well aware of the dangers of emotive and fuzzy thinking.

Critics of analytic philosophy of education have pointed out that although analysis has helped educators clarify and define some educational problems better, this might be too limited a view of philosophy to meet the demands of a changing, complex world. Shying away from prescription has helped make philosophers of education more wary of grandiose statements; at the same time, however, some critics note that although philosophers have ceased to prescribe, many other people, such as psychologists, sociologists, and even politicians, continue to make grand prescriptions for education. Scant evidence supports the idea that these latter sources for contemporary educational prescriptions are necessarily superior to the philosophical sources. Indeed, some critics say that they are worse.

One thing that frustrates critics of philosophical analysis is the difficulty of ascertaining what analysts want in terms of education. In fairness to philosophical analysts, it should be emphasized that they have seldom claimed to introduce any prescriptive maxims for educational practice itself. Yet, although analysts say their only wish is to clarify concepts and language, it is extremely difficult for many critics to see that their work has achieved any great clarification. Analysts have uncovered ambiguities and misconceptions in education, but where does the educational system go from there?

Suppose a nicely clarified and precise language were developed with regard to education. The purely descriptive and analytic approach might be able to give positive clarity about what is being done in education; however, if the wrong things are being done to begin with, the wrongness is not necessarily corrected simply by language clarification. To maintain that language clarification itself will reveal inhumane and wrong educational practice is, it seems, to express a mystical belief in the power of language at the expense of action. Clarification does not necessarily rule out prescriptions and recommendations about the problems of life, and indeed, it should help people arrive at better formulated and constructed recommendations for action.

Perhaps part of the critic's frustration lies in the efforts of some philosophical analysts to say that true philosophy can only be analytic or that analysis inevitably leads to the "death" of traditional philosophy. However, as Harry Broudy asked, "Where will our visions come from?" Surely, philosophy is not the only historical source for social renewal, and many philosophical recommendations and utopian schemes are unworkable. It seems just as certain, however, that philosophy has as great a role to play in formulating social and educational policy as any other intellectual pursuit. According to Broudy, people have a need for speculation and dreams, and if philosophers fail to provide it, then people will seek it elsewhere. Dewey, in his quaint way, remarked that "while saints introspect, burly sinners rule the world."

Analytic philosophers seem content to quarrel over the meanings of terms, phrases, and statements while the world around them pays respect to their efforts by simply ignoring them. It could be said that philosophical analysis is little more than a new form of scholasticism, where instead of arguing about how many angels can stand on the head of a pin, analysts debate about how the words *should* and *ought* can be used. One disgruntled critic charged that when someone points a finger at a problem, the analytic philosophers study the finger rather than the problem.

Although analysts claim to eschew prescriptive and a priori assumptions, it seems that, in general, philosophical analysis has its own underlying assumptions or prescriptions. The penchant for paradigmatic models of analysis betrays a hidden assumption that there are clear, certain, and specifiable ways of doing things, what Richard Rorty has criticized as the "mirror of nature" view of philosophy. This seems close to the philosophical realists' belief in a reality with its own inherent and universal principles. For example, Hirst has stated that people need to know about the effectiveness of different teaching methods but that "without the clearest concept of what teaching is, it is impossible to find appropriate behavioral criteria whereby to assess what goes on in the classroom." This assumes that a *clear* concept of teaching can be uncovered. It also assumes that teaching can be assessed on the basis of appropriate behavioral criteria. The assumptions are these: (1) Teaching has a clear form; (2) there are appropriate teaching behaviors; and (3) these things have an existence that can be studied, described, classified, and objectively duplicated.

This universalizing tendency in analytic philosophy has been a bone of contention for many postmodern thinkers, who attack all efforts to define the philosophical enterprise into a single universal approach. Although postmodernists are sympathetic to analytic philosophy's sensitivities to language, they maintain that the chief value to come out of the tradition lies with Wittgenstein's approach—that is, to a fuller appreciation of the variety of usages that language can have and to the interplay of meanings that are possible. On other points, however, postmodernists find analytic philosophy too constraining and too defining.

No doubt, teaching models can be constructed that can be taught and duplicated. This fact is no proof that such models are ethically desirable. Because something *can* be done is no grounds logically, morally, or socially for *doing* it. Clarity and logic do not equal rightness, perfection, or moral certainty; human problems, including the problems of education, seem contingent on many fluctuating variables. No sooner do people think they have arrived at a solution than intervening events push them off on another troublesome tangent.

The analysts have attacked pragmatists, existentialists, reconstructionists, and others because they recommend certain changes and make substantive judgments about social and educational policy. Pragmatism, for example, tried to make us sensitive to the means–ends continuum in achieving a more democratic society; that is, the actual ends achieved in social and educational endeavors are continuous with, and contingent on, the means used. Analytic approaches also might help people clarify intended and actual means and ends, but their aversion to using philosophy in actively pursuing broad social and educational changes seems to some critics to be a classic case of the philosophical "failure of nerve" to meet the challenges we face today.

Analysts have attempted to redefine the work of philosophy by refuting the old grand manner or systems approach. This effort has had some healthy effects because it helps people stop thinking in terms of ultimate answers and sweeping conclusions, and it has helped philosophers develop and implement more refined linguistic and logical tools. The problem with analytic philosophy is, critics charge, that the tools seem to have become ends in themselves apart from the ethical and political uses to which they may be put.

MARTIN

ON THE REDUCTION OF "KNOWING THAT" TO "KNOWING HOW"

In this selection, Jane R. Martin, a contemporary American educator, further attempts to clarify Gilbert Ryle's distinction between "knowing that" and "knowing how." Martin demonstrates how the techniques of analytic philosophy can be used to examine crucial philosophical concepts in terms of education. She distinguishes between several kinds of knowing and suggests how they might enter into the teaching process. Without proposing what should be taught or who should teach it, Martin maintains that there are several kinds of "knowing that" and "knowing how," and she examines the further implications of Ryle's distinction for theory and practice.

The distinction between "knowing how" and "knowing that," which Gilbert Ryle makes in Chapter 2 of *The Concept of Mind*, is the point of departure for this paper. Ryle's object in writing *The Concept of Mind* was to discredit once and for all Cartesian dualism, or what he calls "the Myth of the Ghost in the Machine." The particular aim of Chapter 2 is to show that there are many activities which directly display qualities of mind, yet are neither themselves intellectual operations nor yet effects of intellectual operations. When we describe such activities, we are not referring to a "second set of shadowy operations." According to Ryle, intelligent practice, that is, "knowing how," is not a "step-child of theory." On the contrary, theorizing, that is, "knowing that," is "one practice amongst others and is itself intelligently or stupidly conducted." In distinguishing between "knowing how" and "knowing that" Ryle hopes to correct the intellectualist doctrine which tended to view all knowing as "knowing that." He strongly opposed the view that intelligent performance must be preceded by an intellectual acknowledgment of rules or criteria, that a person must "preach to himself before he can practice."

Ryle's distinction is clearly relevant to the problems of teaching and learning. For example, the learning of skills need not be preceded by knowledge of rules: Men knew how to reason correctly before the rules of correct reasoning were formulated by Aristotle. Knowledge of rules is not sufficient for the performance of a skill: We do not say that a boy knows how to play chess if he can recite the rules but cannot make the required moves. In judging a performance we must look "beyond," not "behind," the performance. This does not mean we seek an occult cause for a skillful performance, but rather that a single sample of behavior is not sufficient to attribute "knowledge how" to an actor; we must take account of past record and subsequent performance as well.

Because of its simplicity and apparent obviousness, the distinction between "knowing how" and "knowing that" has great appeal, but like any dichotomy it gives rise to much controversy and perplexity. Hartland-Swann has argued that "knowing that" can be reduced to "knowing how." Let us grant that his reduction holds if "knowing how" and "knowing that" are used to refer to a rather limited range of dispositions. Once "knowing that" is reduced to "knowing how," however, a distinction must be made between two types of dispositions subsumed under "knowing how."

It is of practical importance to analyze the various types of "knowing how" and "knowing that" sentences in ordinary speech and to make such differentiations as are necessary, even if the simplicity of Ryle's dichotomy or Hartland-Swann's reduction is thereby lost. Just as Ryle has drawn our attention to the dangers to education inherent in the reduction of "knowing how" to "knowing that," one may point out dangers inherent in a reduction of "knowing that" to "knowing how" if analysis is discontinued at that point. It would seem no more desirable to teach mathematical or historical facts as if they were skills like swimming than to teach swimming as if it were Latin or geometry. And an equally grave mistake would be to teach moral judgments and rules of conduct as if they were either Latin or swimming.

Ryle's Distinction

In order to formulate Ryle's distinction between "knowing how" and "knowing that" as clearly as possible, it is necessary to ascertain the meaning of the terms "knowing how" and "knowing that." Ryle calls "know" a capacity verb, and thus it is safe to conclude that he would call both "knowing how" and "knowing that" capacities also. (Ryle differentiates capacities from tendencies, although both are dispositions. A tendency implies not only that something could be the case, but that it would be the case regularly when the appropriate conditions are realized; a capacity implies the ability to do something under specified conditions but does not imply frequency or regularity.) At no time does he say exactly what he means by the two types of knowing. From the examples he adduces and several of his statements, however, it is possible to determine that "knowing how" refers to skills or operations, for example, knowing how to play chess, knowing how to theorize, knowing how to speak Russian; and that "knowing that" refers to one's "cognitive repertoire," that is, to knowledge of factual propositions, as for instance, knowing that Sussex is a county in England, knowing that *Messer* is the German word for knife.

It is essential to note that Ryle assimilates all "knowing how" to the model "knowing how to perform a task" and all "knowing that" to the model "knowing that such and such is the case," for we then realize that his distinction is of a more limited nature than we might at first have thought. In ordinary language the phrase "knowing how" is often used when performances are not involved, and the phrase "knowing that" is found in sentences which do not refer to knowing factual propositions. For example, we say, "Johnny knows how a motor works," "I know how Eisenhower felt on election night," and "Jones knows how the accident happened." We also say, "Smith knows that he ought to be honest," "The child knows that he should be quiet when someone is speaking," and "Johnny knows that stealing is bad." None of these examples fits Ryle's paradigms for "knowing how" or "knowing that."

To summarize, Ryle's distinction between "knowing how" and "knowing that" is really a distinction between "knowing how to perform skills" and "knowing propositions of a factual nature." When Hartland-Swann discusses the question of the reducibility of "knowing that" to "knowing how," he too, I believe, is viewing "knowing how" and "knowing that" in this way. Thus in discussing his reduction one must not assume that it holds for all "knowing that" sentences. In fact, I think we will find that such sentences as

"Johnny knows that he ought to be quiet" and "Jones knows that he should be honest" cannot be reduced to Ryle's and Hartland-Swann's "knowing how." First those sentences to which Hartland-Swann's reduction applies will be analyzed.

Two Kinds of "Knowing How"

Hartland-Swann maintains that Ryle's distinction between "knowing how" and "knowing that" proves to be unstable when subjected to analysis. Every case of "knowing that," he says, is a case of "knowing how." This follows from the fact that "know" is a dispositional term. If I understand him correctly, what he means is that if we call the statement "Johnny knows that Columbus discovered America" dispositional, then it must be translatable into some such form as "Johnny knows how to answer the question 'Who discovered America?' or 'What did Columbus discover?' correctly." The only alternative to this inclusion of "knowing that" in the "knowing how" category, Hartland-Swann feels, would be to give up the dispositional analysis of "know."

I think one must agree with Hartland-Swann that a dispositional analysis of "knowing that" entails a translation of a "knowing that" sentence into a "knowing how" sentence of the type illustrated above, that is, knowing how to answer a question or to state a fact. It would be a mistake, however, to end the analysis of "knowing" with this reduction, for granted that "knowing that" can be reduced to "knowing how," there is still a fundamental distinction to be made within Hartland-Swann's new, expanded "knowing how" category. The basis for this distinction lies in the fact that two very different sorts of dispositions are subsumed under "knowing how."

Let us consider for a moment the case of Jones who was witness to the murder of Y. Without doubt Jones knows that X murdered Y, and this, in turn, means he knows how to state that X murdered Y and knows how to answer the question "Who murdered Y?" Yet it seems intuitively obvious that there is an essential difference between his knowing how to answer the question "Who murdered Y?" and his knowing how to swim or speak French. That is to say, the difference between the capacity involved in knowing how to state that X murdered Y and the capacity involved in knowing how to swim is more basic than the differ-ence between the capacities involved in knowing how to swim and knowing how to do logic, or in knowing how to ice skate and knowing how to play the violin.

I would like to suggest that the feature which distinguishes these two kinds of capacities from each other is *practice*. That is, "knowing how to swim" is a capacity which implies having learned how to swim through practice; "knowing how to answer the question 'Who murdered Y'" is a capacity which does not imply having learned how to answer the question through practice. When Jones was a witness to the murder, he knew immediately that X murdered Y and did not need to practice stating facts or answering questions. Similarly, when Jones looks out his window and sees rain falling, he knows that it is raining without any sort of practice in saying "It is raining" or answering the question "What is the weather like right now?" To be sure, if he knows that it is raining, he is able to state certain facts and answer certain questions, but his capacity to do so does not imply that he has practiced doing so. On the other hand, Jones could not know how to swim or speak French unless he had at some time practiced swimming or tried to speak French. If Jones tells us he knows how to swim we are justified in asking him if he has ever tried to swim. If he answers "No" to our query, his assertion will be discredited. But if Jones tells us that he knows that X murdered Y, it surely would be nonsensical for us to ask him if he has practiced that assertion or tried to answer questions on the subject before.

If, as I propose, the difference between the two types of capacities subsumed under "knowing how" is based on the notion of practice, some interesting consequences follow. If knowing how to swim requires learning to swim through practice, then we usually would not consider the practice itself to be swimming. The practice may consist in kicking and arm waving and, if all goes well, these will gradually approach swimming. Although the point at which the practice in swimming becomes swimming is not for us to determine, it is interesting to consider the case of the individual who practices just up to the point where he actually swims and then gets out of the water. I think we could say of him that he knows how to swim even though he has not yet actualized this capacity by swimming.

Just as there may be cases of knowing how to swim which are not cases of swimming, so there may be cases of swimming which are not cases of knowing how to swim. For example, it is conceivable that Jones falls into the water one day and swims to shore although he has never practiced or tried to swim before. We cannot deny that he is swimming, but we might well wish to deny that he knows how to swim. In the case of swimming, of course, it is logically possible but in fact unlikely that there would be a performance of the skill which had not been preceded by practice. If, however, we think of a skill such as hitting the target, we realize that it is not too unusual for a novice to hit the bull's-eye without any previous practice. In such a situation we would maintain that although he hit his mark he does not "know how" to hit it. For we would expect someone who knows how to hit the target to hit it again. In other words, hitting a target is an occurrence which may be due to accident or luck; knowing how to hit a target is a capacity, and we would be right to look for a certain degree of consistency of behavior.

"Practice," of course, is a vague term. Although I do not think its limits need be set here, it is important to realize that many skills are related and that practice for one skill may thus serve as practice for another. Hence, on those occasions when it appears that we know how to do something without having practiced it, upon reflection we will discover that we have had practice in a related skill. It is possible, also, for the accidental or lucky occurrence to serve as prac-

tice for a skill. For example, if Jones swims to shore although he has never had practice in swimming, this very swimming may provide him with practice.

It is not denied here that we do exhibit some patterns of behavior with consistency although we have not practiced them. Yawning, crying, sneezing are examples. We call these reflexes, not skills, however, and do not speak of "knowing how" to yawn, cry, or sneeze. The exception is the case of the actor who is able to perform these behaviors at will. We might actually say of him that he "knows how" to yawn, cry, or sneeze, but it is clear that he has learned to do so through practice.

It appears, then, that although Hartland-Swann's reduction of "knowing that" to "knowing how" is legitimate for those "knowing that" sentences which are cases of knowing factual propositions, there is still a basic distinction between these sentences and the kinds of "knowing how" sentences which are cases of knowing how to perform an operation. Whether or not it is agreed that the basis for the distinction is practice, I do not think the distinction itself can be denied.

Source: Jane Roland Martin, "On the Reduction of 'Knowing That' to 'Knowing How,'" in *Language and Concepts in Education*, edited by B. O. Smith and R. H. Ennis. Chicago: Rand McNally Company, 1961, pp. 399–404. Reprinted by permission of the author.

BARROW

DOES THE QUESTION "WHAT IS EDUCATION?" MAKE SENSE?

Robin Barrow examines one important question to be asked about education: What is it? He looks at education's historical use, as well as its activity. This article points to the use of analysis as a tool in looking at the fundamental concepts of education and shows the penchant of the philosophical analyst for exploring significant yet often assumed or passed-over educational questions.

There are those who object to discussions about method and procedure in philosophy. Both Jim Gribble, for example, in his *Introduction to Philosophy of Ed-*

ucation, and more recently Janet Radcliffe Richards, in *The Sceptical Feminist*, have suggested that one should get on with philosophizing rather than begin with an account of what it involves. But since philosophy, unlike most other subjects, is defined in terms of its procedures and methods rather than its content, since doing philosophy is engaging in a process rather than examining a product, to have a fine appreciation of what the activity involves is to be more than halfway along the road to philosophizing. Furthermore, it seems clear to me that we have a particular need to get clear about the nature of philosophical analysis at the present time, since its lack of impact arises partly out of it being confused with other studies, such as that of semantics, and since different philosophers evidently see themselves as engaged in somewhat different tasks. The issue has been well highlighted in a recent exchange between John Wilson and Philip Snelders in the *Journal of Philosophy of Education*, where the former appears, as it were, from stage right with a barely modified Platonic theory of forms, and the latter comes to meet him from stage left with a handful of Protean concepts of no fixed shape. My own view, broadly, is that Wilson has the right of it in that we take too many silly alleged conceptual doubts seriously (the structure of British Trade Unions just isn't democratic; influencing people or teaching them the mathematics tables is not indoctrination), but on the other hand Snelders has the right of it in seeing that nonetheless questions such as, "Is an educated man necessarily committed to the value of X and Y?" and "Does indoctrination necessarily presuppose intention?" cannot simply be dismissed on the grounds that education just *is* this, indoctrination just *is* that, and all sensible people know it.

So what is going on when one asks the question "What is education?" Does it make sense, or should it rather be rephrased in some other form, such as "What do you think education is?" "How is the word used in this society?" or "What do the professional educators mean by 'education'?" Is there an essence to education that cannot be ignored, or is one's conception just a matter of ideological perspective? In answering the central question I hope also to answer three others: "Can a concept be incorrect?", "Can a concept be invalid?" and "Does the claim that two conceptions of X are equally valid, imply that everything depends on your point of view?"

Let us start, unashamedly, with basics. A concept is a unifying principle. It is not to be identified with a mental image nor with a word. One has the concept of X when one appreciates what is common to all instances of X. How concepts are initially acquired is not my present concern, but it is evident that they are not all acquired in exactly the same way. Some, such as color and shape concepts, may arise through direct perception; others, such as the concept of house or philosopher, require understanding of function before they can be grasped. But still to have a concept of triangularity is to recognize particular triangles as such, just as to have a concept of house is to recognize cognitively that various seemingly dissimilar buildings perform the same particular set of functions, and to have a concept of happiness is to see the common factor between outwardly very different people contentedly at one or enmeshed with their situation.

As already noted, words and concepts are not the same thing. The same word may refer to more than one concept; one concept may be referred to by a number of synonymous words; things can be said about words that do not make sense in reference to concepts, and vice versa; in each of the above examples one might have the concept without having the word. Concepts, even when they refer to what we term concrete nouns, are by definition abstract and general. It is simply bad English to use the word concept in reference to particular instances, as in "my concept of Mrs. Thatcher" or "my concept of this desk."

So much is obvious. However, because as a matter of fact we use words to identify concepts and we can seldom, if ever, communicate except through words, there is both a temptation and a justification for trying to get at concepts by examining words. And this of course is what we are advised to do by a variety of linguistic philosophers. And they have a point. If we want to examine the concept of education, then surely we must start with the word "education," and surely it is significant in respect of understanding the concept that it appears to make little sense to say, for example, "His education improves every time he eats a chocolate pudding." On the other hand there are four serious problems with this procedure. First, if we are concerned with the use of the word either we must engage in the empirical task of finding out about and studying *all* uses of the word (which would make philosophy and linguistics indistinguishable), or we must judge some uses to be more central, more ordinary, or in some other way more acceptable than others, in which case we need criteria for making such judgments, which we do not in fact have. Secondly, although it may be of some interest to know about the use of a particular word, it is not at all clear what significance or importance it is supposed to have. What hangs, for example, on the fact that the Greek word *areté* is used in very different ways from the English word "virtue" by which it is conventionally translated? What is such scrutiny telling us about virtue, which is to say the notion itself, as opposed to what the Greeks and we variously think about it? Or is this the crunch point: do we conclude here and now that there is nothing more to be considered than what various groups happen to think? Thirdly, if we do assume that the concept of virtue is to be identified with the use of the word "virtue" (whether this be a matter of definitional logic or practical necessity), it becomes logically impossible to have a revolutionary or original thought about a concept. Imagine that we live in a society that finds it inconceivable that non-human animals should be happy. Their conception of happiness, their use of the word "happy," in other words, makes it impossible for me to say correctly, "That dog is happy." But this makes it impossible for us to extend the application of our concepts. Moore traded, unknowingly, on just this muddle when he used the open question argument to show that good cannot be identified with anything since it is always possible to say, "I know this is X, but is it good?" Of course it is always possible to *say* that, because what we think it makes sense to say necessarily reflects our current views. But suppose we are just wrong? Suppose X and good *are* to be identified, and it doesn't make sense to say "I know this is X, but is it good?" All Moore's argument does is confirm our prejudices. (Indeed one might suggest that change in language presupposes a clear distinction between concepts and words. Words change their meanings, because people have original ideas that initially make ordinary language use inadequate or even wrong.) Fourthly, and most important of all, we have to remember that this link between words and concepts is only contingent. One can have a concept of beauty without the word "beauty" or any other word open to public scrutiny. And the truth is that many of us when we ask, "What is reality?" "What is free-will?" or "What is justice?" are manifestly not asking, "How do other people use the words 'real,' 'free will' and 'justice'?" which would at best tell us something about how other people would answer the questions, but are seeking to grapple with certain complex notions on which we have a tenuous hold.

The solution to the problem is very simple, although it has certain consequences which some seem unable to come to grips with. We should start with the word, allow usage to guide us to one or a set of target areas, and from that point on refuse to be bound by usage. For example, we may start with the word "education," make such observations as that it is a commendatory term, is sometimes used in somewhat unexpected contexts ("the educated left-jab of the boxer"), is generally presumed to imply something about knowledge and understanding, and so on. In doing that we are gaining something useful, for we are getting some hints and clues about what people in general think about what we call education. But we should remember (1) that this is only information about the use of the word and what people may therefore be presumed to think, and (2) that consequently we may get some contradictory or even incoherent hints and clues.

What will happen with many words is that a number of clearly distinguishable uses will emerge. In that case one settles on one such use (this is one of the target areas) and tries to gain a more complete and refined understanding of that use, that sense of the word, that idea or conception, if necessary making a positive contribution to knock shape into or shed light on it. At this stage no appeal is made to use, for we are trying to explicate in greater detail an idea that is already in our mind in response to a particular use of the word. The whole operation can be illustrated quite neatly by reference to creativity. Johnny, aged two, splashing paint about at will, is said by some to be creative. Fred, an adult, converting his attic into a habitable room, is regarded by his neighbors as creative. Beethoven glowering over the manuscript of the Ninth Symphony is once again in creative mood. Now these are distinct cases. There may very well be points of contact between the examples, and some individuals might even want to call them all "creative" because they want to highlight some common denominator. Nonetheless the cases, as a whole, are indubitably distinct. Unless therefore someone does explicitly offer a lowest common denominator account of creativity, one may presume we are dealing with different, if related, uses of the word. They are different conceptions of creativity. To arrive at or note such different uses, to comment on the emotive meaning of the term in each case, to consider etymological origins, even to trace common denominators, are activities that belong to verbal analysis. But to concentrate on one use and to try to explicate the idea it refers to more precisely and clearly is to analyze a concept. Philosophical analysis no doubt should include both, but it seems to me that we have spent a disproportionate amount of time on verbal analysis and failed to appreciate that conceptual analysis soars away from usage. What I am trying to get at when I examine the notion of Beethoven as a creative artist should owe no more to how the word is used: I am alone with the notion seeking to giving an account of it that makes explicit what otherwise may remain a hazy accolade.

There are some immediate consequences of this view. The first is that conceptual analysis is a personal matter at rock bottom. You clear your mind. You are trying to clarify this idea of Beethoven being creative; you are trying to lay out a coherent account of what the idea involves for you. Of course the task does not have to be engaged in privately. We can have seminars and discussions and we can share conceptions. Very often we will, because, as has nowhere been denied, a lot of our concepts are initially acquired through a common language. But the fact that we are all brought up to use the word "democracy" with the same rough denotation, so that we are all contemplating the same target area, does not mean that any of us can give a decent explication of that concept. A second consequence of this view is that the phrase "*the* concept of X" needs explanation. Superficially it doesn't make sense, since there is no such thing as a unitary concept except contingently. Rather there are conceptions of democracy, education or whatever. However, the phrase can be taken as meaningful, if we interpret it to mean something such as "the conception dominant in Western culture" or "the conception in this circle."

A third consequence, as I have argued before, is that much philosophy of education is not engaging in *bona fide* conceptual analysis, and is as a partial result rather stultifying, besides providing a vulnerable point of attack for those who seek to dismiss philosophy altogether. Kevin Harris's book *Education and Knowledge*, for example, bases its entire attack on philosophy of education, on a misunderstanding of what conceptual analysis is for some of us, but in that he has been helped by the fact that some of what passes for conceptual analysis is in fact merely verbal analysis. Too many people seem to assume that when there's a word there's a paper to be written. But not all words refer to problematic or interesting concepts. In an otherwise most generous review of my *The Philosophy of Schooling*, I was recently taken to task by D. Bob Gowin for having failed to include a chapter on learning, which he suggests is one of the central concepts in the educational enterprise. I agree with him entirely about its centrality; I disagree with his view that it requires analysis. Learning, like play, teaching, and schooling itself, seems to me to be unproblematic as a concept. That is to say I know what learning is, even if I don't know various non-philosophical things such as how to facilitate it, in a way that I do not really know what my conception of free will amounts to, even though I quite often make claims about it. Naturally there is room for judgment over what concepts are problematic, and indeed it follows from the thesis I am arguing, that some concepts may be more problematic for one person than another. The important point here is the general one: we surely want to confine our attempts to explicate X to those cases where X, though often referred to, is really rather hazy, incoherent or ill-articulated in our minds. We want papers on moral personhood rather than homo sapiens, on education rather than schooling.

I will not dwell here at any length on a point that I have made in the book just mentioned: given that conceptual analysis is a personal matter the criteria of success are essentially internal to the activity. Good conceptual analysis results in explications that are clear, coherent, internally consistent and implying nothing that the agent finds himself logically unable to accept at the same time as something else to which he is committed. (One cannot, for example, both hold that education and indoctrination are incompatible, and explicate the latter concept in terms that render it compatible with the former.) But I will add that it is, of course, a consequence of my view that conceptions of coherence and consistency might also vary. However, this does not seem to me to be problematic. As a matter of fact, because of our common linguistic background and because they happen to be relatively simple concepts, most of us share the same conceptions of coherence and consistency. But if someone were not to do so, if someone, for instance, regarded internal contradiction as quite compatible with coherence and consistency, I should merely have to clarify the issue by stating that the kind of conceptual analysis that I am advocating would be concerned with consistency in my sense of the word.

We are now in a position to answer the questions that I outlined at the beginning of this paper. It is clear that a person cannot in any ordinary sense of the word be said to be "wrong" when he offers his account of a concept, whatever he says. He may be criticized for attaching a word to an unusual concept (as, if he uses "refute" when he means reject) for having muddled or hazy concepts, for preoccupying himself with trivial concepts, or for having an idiosyncratic conception, but provided he can give a clear, coherent, consistent and compatible account of concept X, whatever name he gives to it, it is meaningless to say that his conception, as opposed to his use of language, is incorrect. The only way to retain the sentence "That is an incorrect conception" to any purpose, would be to interpret it to mean either "That is not my/our conception" or "That is an incoherent conception." Much the same has to be said in reply to the question "Can a concept be invalid?" Indeed I only include reference to this since misuses of the words "valid" and "invalid" seem to be on the increase, and it is not usually clear what precisely is meant. Validity is, strictly speaking, something that belongs exclusively to arguments. All we can say therefore is that if the claim that a concept is invalid is taken to mean that the concept is incoherent, unclear, inconsistent or incompatible, then obviously it may be invalid. If it is taken to mean that the wrong label is being attached to a concept, then it may be invalid. (In this sense the concept of validity here is invalid.) If it is taken to mean that the concept in question is morally repugnant to one, then it may be invalid. If it is taken to mean that the concept is not much entertained these days or is out of vogue, as one might say is the case with chivalry, then it may be invalid. Naturally if the invalidity of a concept is taken to be the same thing as its incorrectness, then we must conclude that the claim that a concept is invalid makes no sense.

Given that there are senses in which two concepts of X might be equally valid, acceptable or admissible, though different, does it follow that everything depends upon your point of view? The real question is what might be being suggested here. Suppose, for example, we have a conception of education that is bound up with breadth of understanding, and another that doesn't make reference to understanding at all. What can we say? At the verbal level we can say that the latter use of the label "education" is odd, possibly even incorrect in terms of standard English. At the conceptual level we might wish to criticize either conception for being insufficiently explicated. We are also at liberty to say that either one is more attractive as a concept to us, more morally acceptable perhaps, or more in line with our other goals. So the answer to the question is (1) the fact that no conception can be dismissed as wrong certainly doesn't necessarily imply that *everything* depends upon your point of view, and that you cannot be in any way brought into a public arena; rather, it just *entails* that your conception of X *is* your point of view on this matter, but (2) while you may entertain any idea you like, you may still be criticized on grounds of coherence, morality, practicality and wisdom.

Does the question "What is education?" make sense then? Not if it is taken to imply that there is an unalterable, imperishable idea that is always to answer to the name (or at any rate the English name) of "education." But certainly it makes sense provided that we interpret it either as a verbal question, requesting information about the use of the word amongst a given group, or as a way of asking one's interlocutor "What is *your* conception of education?"

Source: Robin Barrow, "Does the Question 'What Is Education?' Make Sense?" *Educational Theory*: 191–195, Summer–Fall 1983. Reprinted by permission of the publisher.

SELECTED READINGS

Peters, R. S. *Ethics and Education.* London: Allen and Unwin, 1965. An analytic exploration of such concepts as freedom, authority, equality, and democracy. It sets forth an ethical position with a point of view regarding moral theory.

————, ed. *The Philosophy of Education.* New York: Oxford University Press, 1973. A collection that brings together writings of such figures as Paul Hirst, Israel Scheffler, and D. W. Hamlyn. The various contributors analyze and attempt to clarify such important concepts as the aims of education, curriculum planning, and educational relevance.

Scheffler, Israel. *The Language of Education.* Springfield, IL: Charles C. Thomas, 1960. A major statement by a leading analytic philosopher in the field of education. He examines the uses of language in education and the meanings of various educational concepts.

Soltis, Jonas F. *An Introduction to the Analysis of Educational Concepts*, 2d ed. Reading, MA: Addison-Wesley, 1977. A brief but well-written introduction to analytic philosophy in education. This book is more restricted in scope than some introductory works in the field. It is recommended as an excellent beginning treatise on the uses of analysis.

analytic.ontologically.com/ (accessed April 5, 2002). A Web site providing numerous options and links to sources on analytic philosophy, including persons and works. Its "links" option provides access to electronic journals and texts in the field.

ONLINE RESEARCH

Companion
Website

Utilizing some of the Web sites included in this book, as well as Topics 2 and 3 of the Prentice Hall Foundations Web site found at *www.prenhall.com/ozmon,* answer the following question with a short essay: What is analytic philosophy and what suggestions does it make for how we should teach? You can write and submit your essay response to your instructor by using the "Electronic Bluebook" section found in any of the topics of the Prentice Hall Foundations Web site.

Marxism and Education

Of all the philosophies considered in this text, perhaps none has been more controversial than Marxism. The reasons for this are several. First, Karl Marx's ideas helped launch some of the most far-reaching social and political revolutions in the twentieth century. Second, Marxism played a significant role in the global competition called the Cold War, especially the contest between the United States and the former Soviet Union. Third, there is the historical Marx, whose numerous works have influenced many thinkers.

Marx's writings sometimes are divided into an earlier humanist period and a later revolutionary period. His later works energized communist revolutionaries, but his early, more humanistic works were mostly unpublished until the middle decades of the twentieth century. As a consequence, philosophical disputes have arisen over which is the "real" Marx—the humanistic social critic or the communist revolutionary.

A further complication is the confusing assortment of neo-Marxist doctrines that have since developed, such as structural Marxism, phenomenological Marxism, feminist Marxism, critical Marxism, and numerous other varieties. Despite this diversity, some basic divisions of Marxist thought provide a variety of insights into Marxist educational ideas. These insights rest on the original works of Marx, the theory of Marxism–Leninism, and "Western" or neo-Marxism.

ORIGINS OF MARXISM

Materialism

One distinguishing feature of Marxism is the importance of materialist ideas. Two materialist traditions (British and French) lie at the foundation of Marxism.

British Materialism

One chief architect of British materialism was Francis Bacon (1561–1626). He maintained that science is a tool for creating new knowledge that can be used to advance human well-being and progress. Marx drew considerably from Bacon's work because he believed that Bacon had emancipated science from theology. Bacon taught that the senses are infallible and the source of all knowledge *if* they are guided by scientific method. Because of Bacon's work, Marx stated, "Matter smiled at man with poetical seasons of brightness."

Thomas Hobbes (1589–1679) systematized Bacon's materialism but made it more abstract. According to Hobbes, science is the process of discovering and studying the laws of motion and their effects on material bodies. He viewed moral philosophy as the science of the motion of human minds and rejected the spiritual dimension, holding that matter permeates the universe. His influence on Marx was not in terms of the universal law of motion (an idea Marx rejected), but rather in the idea that materialism should be used in arranging the practical affairs of humanity and civil society.

John Locke (1632–1704) also influenced Marx's thought, and his empiricism was one of its key ingredients. He held that human nature is malleable. The French took this view and made it into a "philosophy of progress"; if human nature can be shaped, they reasoned, then it is possible to shape and direct human society and institutions. This idea had a profound impact on Marx.

French Materialism

According to Marx, French materialism humanized British materialism by placing it more squarely within a social context. French materialism was influenced by René Descartes (1596–1650), who separated his physics from his highly idealistic metaphysics. From the standpoint of physics, he viewed motion as the driving force of matter and matter as the only basis of being and knowledge—a view that French materialists found supportive. The two most influential French materialists undergirding Marx's thought, however, were Étienne Condillac (1715–1780) and Claude Adrien Helvétius (1715–1771).

Condillac used Locke's sense empiricism to oppose traditional ideas about a static human nature and an invariant human social order. In his "doctrine of sensationalism," Condillac maintained that human activities and thinking processes are matters of experience and habit, and therefore the whole development of humanity depends on education and environment. Helvétius pushed this idea even further by proclaiming that education could be used to bring about human perfection. He and Condillac argued that an individual's social class is simply a result of education and circumstance. For Helvétius, even individual differences in intelligence could be attributed to these factors. Human nature, he held, is neither good nor bad; circumstances, particularly education, make the individual, and the desired course is to arrange circumstances and education to produce human progress and a more satisfying life for all.

Marx drew from materialist philosophies some important ingredients. One was the view that science should be used to transform human circumstances. Allied to this was the view that human perception and knowledge are based on the sense experience of the material world. Finally, the notions of human perfectibility and the possibility of social progress through changes in the material world were used by Marx.

Socialism

The word *socialism* first came into use in the late 1820s and was associated with the theories of such people as Henri Saint-Simon (1760–1825), Charles Fourier (1772–1837), and Robert Owen (1771–1858). Henri Saint-Simon embraced industrialization and pushed for the scientific study of industry to serve the needs of society. He viewed industrial labor as *the* essential form of labor and held that industrialists rather than "idle aristocrats" should govern society. He called his theory the "industrial doctrine" and advocated progress in terms of society-wide improvement rather than simply individual improvement, a focus of great importance for Marx.

Charles Fourier believed in human perfectibility and called for new forms of social organization based on his theory of "perfection by association," a notion derived from Isaac Newton's law of gravitation. He believed that progress would occur through proper human association, the basic unit of association being anchored in a community of interest. Marx adopted many of Fourier's criticisms of capitalism's lack of social responsibility and its selfish absorption in the accumulation of wealth.

The leading socialist for Marx, however, was Robert Owen, who started as a child laborer in Manchester, England, and eventually became a wealthy and important industrialist. In the textile mills of New Lanark, Scotland, he was instrumental in establishing shorter working hours, schools for child laborers, infant schools for the small children of working mothers, and improved housing and health conditions for all employees. Despite the initial fears of other mill owners, Owen's reforms increased the earnings of the mills. However, when Owen tried to spread his ideas among other industrialists, he had limited success. He eventually came to believe that radical social change was needed and that human progress would come about only through widespread fundamental changes in social and environmental conditions. Marx said that English communism began with Owen, for Owen took the lead in sowing the seeds of a cooperative social system.

Political Economy

The discipline of political economy is distinguished by the study of sociological, political, historical, and philosophical thought and using them to analyze the political and economic forces of society. One chief architect of this approach was Adam Smith (1723–1790), a Scottish philosopher whose major treatise, *The Wealth of Nations*, published in 1776, greatly influenced subsequent economic thought—particularly the theory of capitalism and the point of view that promotes minimum government regulation of economic life. Smith used the metaphor of the "invisible hand" to describe the way the economy is supposed to regulate itself if left to private individual initiative and market competition.

Another leading political economist was David Ricardo (1772–1823). Smith and Ricardo recognized productive labor as one prime base of wealth, but Ricardo refined the definition of *wages* as the labor time it takes to produce a commodity. Marx thought that Smith and Ricardo had provided a valuable service in formulating new economic laws that advanced the production of wealth, but most of the policy implications he drew from them were the opposite of their intent. Marx used their ideas on labor as a basis of wealth, but he also added the notion of "surplus value"; that is, a worker produces more than his wage or the cost of production, and it is this surplus value from which profits are gained and by which workers are exploited.

THE PHILOSOPHY OF KARL MARX

Karl Marx (1818–1883)

Karl Heinrich Marx was born into comfortable middle-class circumstances in Trier, in the German Rhineland. His father was a lawyer, and both parents were Jewish. The family converted to Christianity shortly before Marx's birth, at least in part because otherwise Jews could not enter the professions legally at that time. Although his father encouraged Marx's interest in philosophy, he wanted him to become a lawyer. Marx entered the University of Bonn to study law but soon transferred to the University of Berlin, where he studied history and philosophy.

Hegel, Feuerbach, and Materialism

When Marx arrived at the University of Berlin, the faculty and students were mostly followers of Georg Hegel. Marx caught the enthusiasm of these "Young Hegelians," and although he later broke from it, Hegelianism made a lasting impression. Of the ideas that Marx gained from Hegelianism, at least two stand out: the concept of alienation and the process of the dialectic. Hegel thought that alienation came from people's failure to recognize that truth is connected intimately with human thought. He rejected the realist position that truth is independent of the human mind and argued that alienation is the result of Spirit externalizing itself. This alienation will cease, Hegel believed, when people become self-conscious and realize that they are thinking beings and that truth is a facet of this self-consciousness. Humanity will realize that "objective" reality, such as culture and the human environment, is an emanation of Spirit.

Hegel maintained that reality could be comprehended through the dialectic, a system of logic with its triadic thesis, antithesis, and synthesis—in which contradictions could be dispelled and agreement eventually achieved in the synthesis of Absolute Idea (or Spirit). If a person thinks of a category, such as nature, he is forced to think of its opposite—history. In studying the development of the tension between nature and history in any given period, one is led to the next era. Natural conditions shape what occurs in history, and the human activities that make up history have a way of transforming or altering natural conditions. The synthesis of ideas about nature and history in any given era is the creation of the beginning of a new era.

Marx rejected Hegel's idealism but kept the concept of alienation and a dialectical version of history. Some say that Marx stood Hegel on his head because he retained the Hegelian conceptual apparatus but changed it from an idealist to a materialist philosophical base. Instead of humans being alienated from Spirit objectifying itself, Marx maintained, people become alienated from their own creations, such as society and the means of production. Rather than a dialectic occurring between ideas, Marx adopted the notion of a dialectic between economic conditions and human action, or what has been called "the materialist conception of history."

A second major influence on young Marx's philosophical development came from Ludwig Feuerbach (1804–1872). Where Hegel had maintained that human thought and action are determined by Spirit as it develops to any point in history, Feuerbach argued that the "spirit" of an era is nothing more than the totality of events and material conditions occurring during that era, for history is determined by the material influences on the thoughts and actions of real persons existing in a world of material conditions. This view greatly appealed to Marx, and although he later broke with Feuerbach by adhering to the position that human action *does* affect the course of history (how else could he advocate revolution?), he did maintain that material conditions exert the primary influence on humanity and its institutions.

Feuerbach also held that all ideologies, including religion, are usually an effort to construct an ideal world as a form of escape from the miseries of the material world. Marx, in turn, came to interpret religion as the fantasy of the alienated individual. In an oft-quoted statement, Marx called religion "the opium of the people," for, like Feuerbach, Marx believed that religion diverts people's attention from the necessity for reform and revolution in the here and now.

In his *Theses on Feuerbach,* however, Marx asserts that the older materialist theories had erred in viewing human beings as passive, because they failed to account for human action. For Marx, then, circumstances are changed only by human thought and practical action and not by passive contemplation. This position is somewhat similar to the pragmatist view of the unity of thought and action. For Marx, however, the human action to be valued is "practical-critical" or revolutionary action *(praxis)*—even violent revolutionary action.

The "Real" Marx

In his early years, as he was struggling with Hegelianism and developing his own views on socialism and reform, Marx wrote with a decidedly humanistic tendency. As he matured, he moved to revolutionary communism, particularly after he began collaborating with Friedrich Engels. He emerged as a severe critic of bourgeois capitalistic society and became a leading advocate of sweeping change.

The debate within philosophical circles over the "real" Marx has occurred, at least in part, because important early works were published only after such figures as Vladimir Ilich Lenin, the leader of the Russian Revolution, already had formed views based on Marx's later works. Lenin's approach has been compared unfavorably with the early humanist writings of Marx. A rule of thumb for dividing the early period from the later period is the year 1848, when Marx and Engels' *The Communist Manifesto* was published. Some critics have wondered whether Lenin's interpretation of Marx would have been so influential had the early works been widely available. Others, attracted to the power of revolutionary Marxism but repelled by the authoritarian and statist behavior of Marxist regimes, have sought to humanize Marxism. Jean-Paul Sartre attempted to do this by attaching his view of existentialism to a Marxist base. Adam Schaff, however, a Polish philosopher, held that Marx maintained his humanism throughout and that, to understand Marx's thought, one must view it from both early and later perspectives.

Part of the debate also relates to the nature of Marx's writing. Much of his work is difficult to understand because he was not always consistent in his use of terms and meanings. Some of his writing was directed at specific issues of his day, and so it lacks any precise bearing on the present. But more importantly, much of Marx's work was in unfinished drafts, examples being the *Economic and Philosophical Manuscripts of 1844* (published in 1932), *The German Ideology 1844* (written in 1845 and published in 1932), and *Grundrisse 1844* (written in 1857–1858 and published in 1941). Even his most important work, *Das Kapital* (in English, *Capital*, first published in 1867), was envisioned as only the first part of a six-part work, but the other parts were never completed. The *Grundrisse* is a sketch of what this massive work might have entailed.

In the "Preface to *A Critique of Political Economy*," written in 1859, Marx comments on his intellectual development. He calls the "guiding thread" of his studies the conception that to understand the nature of society, one has to go not to Hegel's view of mind and spirit but to the material conditions of life. It is in how people produce necessities and create institutions that they become enmeshed in forces beyond their conscious wills. To understand how these forms of control come about, one must examine the way people produce material things. The sum of the material forces of production—agriculture, handicrafts, industry, and so forth—is the material *base*. All social relations—the class structure, institutions, legal and political authority, and so forth—are the societal *superstructure*. The material base is the foundation on which the superstructure of society is built; hence, rather than look first at the superstructure to understand society, one must go to the foundation, the material base. The ways of producing *material things* set the stage for social, political, and intellectual life. As Marx states in the "Preface," this means "It is not the consciousness of men that determines their lives, but, on the contrary, their social being that determines their consciousness."

According to Marx, at critical junctures in history, the material forces of production come into conflict with the social, political, and intellectual forces because material forces outpace institutional frameworks. Marx thought that the leading example of his own day was the way industrial development had outpaced social development. Industrial technology had grown tremendously, but society still was immersed in private property and monopolistic control of the many by the propertied few. Workers were enslaved in a system of subsistence wages, existing as little more than appendages to machines that produced wealth controlled and consumed by the few. The workers, the proletariat, would not accept such conditions indefinitely, and when the conflict between the forces of production and the outmoded superstructure of social institutions became severe enough, rapid social change would be almost inevitable. Marx thought, however, that no superstructure ever changed until all the material forces of production underlying it had developed and that these material forces contained within themselves the bases for a new order. Industrial capitalism was therefore a necessary condition on which to build because it provided the material base on which a new era of more expansive wealth could be realized.

Alienation

One of the best illustrations of Marx's humanism is the *Economic and Philosophical Manuscripts of 1844*, in which he describes and analyzes the alienation of industrial workers. Under competitive capitalism, according to Marx, workers become reduced to little more than commodities, for they must sell their labor on the market like any other commodity at the lowest price to those who own the means of production. The owners, in turn, are forced to compete in finding markets and in selling products at the lowest price. Owners must squeeze out the greatest amount of surplus value, and this means paying the lowest wages possible. In this system, the weak and poor are overcome by the strong and rich, and the result is the accumulation of wealth in the hands of the few and the reduction of the many to servile dependence. Society becomes divided into two great classes—the property owners and the propertyless, or the "haves" and the "have-nots."

As Marx viewed it, labor becomes "objectified"; that is, both the workers' labor and the products they make belong to someone else. The workers come to view the products, which could give creative satisfaction, as alien objects that belong to another. Personal labor, which could give the workers a sense of power, is now only a means of securing a bare subsistence. The result is alienated labor and alienated people because the workers become "strangers," not at home with themselves or their labor. As a consequence, they feel free only in their animal activities—eating, drinking, and procreating. These functions are essential to human life, but when they become divorced from creative production and participation in the more fulfilling aspects of cultural life, they become merely animal activities.

In this state of affairs, workers become separated from their humanity, or what Marx called their "species being." In their species being, people relate to themselves as members of a universal and free humanity and hence can relate to such ideas as "all men are created equal." Human beings are like all animals in that they are dependent on nature for food, shelter, and other material necessities of life; however, unlike other animals, they can create things beyond bare necessities and engage in art, science, and intellectual life—or what Marx called "conscious vital activity." These things, along with the raw materials of nature, are the objects of an individual's conscious existence and give human life its intellectual meanings. When workers' products (what they produce) are alien to them and when their creative force (their labor) is alien, then the workers are alienated from their species being. Their humanity, their species being, then becomes not a source of identity but just another object for survival. The worker is "objectified" and reduced to an animal-like existence.

According to Marx, private property is the cause of alienated labor. When the control of property, and hence the control of the means of productive life, is concentrated in the hands of a few, the result is alienated labor. If alienated labor robs people of their humanity, and if private property is the cause of alienated labor, then private property must be abolished. Marx believed that to emancipate society from private property, the worker must be emancipated, and to emancipate the worker is to emancipate humanity because the whole of human society is involved in the relationship of the worker to the product.

One can see from the foregoing how Marx's humanistic orientation led him to become more and more concerned about the impact of private property, which he thought was the key element in the superstructure of capitalism. His analysis of the problem incorporated not only philosophical criticism but also a philosophy of history that was central to his mature thought.

The Materialist Interpretation of History

Much has been made of the "dialectical materialism" of Marxism. It has been characterized as a deterministic movement of humankind through various historical epochs until the inevitable triumph of communism over capitalism in the dialectic of history. Marx believed that communism eventually would triumph, but he did not think that it was a mechanical inevitability of the dialectic of history. He was a dedicated revolutionary who believed that human resolve and action are necessary to bring about a new social order, but he did not see his view of history as any mechanical dialectic. Some of his philosophical descendants, however, have been more dogmatic, and *dialectical materialism* is a term they have employed frequently.

It has been suggested that perhaps the most appropriate way to describe Marx's view is "the materialist interpretation of history," wherein the dialectic is seen as an interpretive device rather than the deterministic structure and process of history itself. Marx thought that in producing the means of living, human beings make history. Roughly speaking, the stage of development of a people is seen in the level and type of its division of labor. Historically, this led first to the separation of industrial and commercial production from agricultural production and hence to the separation of town and country—with its resulting clash of interests. Next came the separation of industrial production from commercial production and the divisions of labor within these categories. Thus, human history can be traced through the ever-increasing divisions of labor; the more "developed" a society becomes, the more division or specialization it experiences. The various stages of development are, in effect, just so many different forms of ownership, for the resulting divisions of labor determine the relations of individuals to each other regarding the materials, instruments, and products of labor.

Marx believed that humanity had advanced through five great stages of historical development:

1. *Tribal ownership,* a kind of naive communism in which the tribe functioned as an extended family and members cooperated in producing the means of subsistence.
2. The *ancient city–state,* wherein several tribes joined together for mutual benefit, and slavery and private ownership became more pronounced.
3. *Feudal kingdoms and empires* resulting in the division of labor into enserfed peasants, a nobility of landed estates, a proletariat of town-dwelling craftsmen, a small but growing class of lesser merchant–capitalists, and a few great merchant–capitalists.

4. *Modern industrial "bourgeois" society,* the bourgeoisie or modern capitalists, akin to the city-dwelling merchant–capitalists (the "burghers" in the Middle Ages), who had their origins in the breakdown of the feudal order.

5. A future yet to come that will witness the rise of the proletariat, the industrial worker, in a new socialist era.

Marx thought that history could be interpreted as a history of class conflict, and he believed that his own time would see the advent of the socialist era. What characterizes the epoch of the bourgeoisie, however, is that bourgeois domination, in effect, simplifies class conflict. According to Marx, this occurs because society has become divided into two great classes of bourgeois capitalists (the "haves") and proletarian workers (the "have-nots"). Bourgeois society developed through a series of revolutions in the methods of production, culminating in modern capitalistic industrialism. In this respect, then, the bourgeoisie played a revolutionary role because it destroyed the old feudal order and instituted a simplified social order of haves and have-nots.

For the modern bourgeoisie to maintain its preeminence, however, it must constantly reinvigorate the means of production. Based as it is on competition, the bourgeoisie must expand its markets constantly, and in doing so, it drags reactionary societies into its fold and transforms them into modern producing and consuming societies. It transcends national boundaries and establishes international forms of communication, production, and commerce. It builds immense cities, creates new forms of urban living, and transforms peasant populations into industrial and urban populations. According to Marx, to accomplish all this, the bourgeoisie must exploit labor and wring from it all the profits it can; however, such a society contains within itself the means of its own destruction, for bourgeois society is too narrow to encompass all the forces of production that it has erected. It has created an immense new class of alienated labor that it cannot accommodate to its own internal structures, and this class will rise and overthrow it.

The triumph of the workers is not, however, a guaranteed result. The workers form an incoherent mass, divided among themselves by competition. Some small form of cohesion can be gained through such devices as trade unions, but this is not enough. The workers have to see that their strength lies in solidarity. Indeed, this was the end toward which Marx aimed in the publication of *The Communist Manifesto,* and this was behind the closing lines of that document where he and Engels proclaimed: "Let the ruling classes tremble at a communist revolution. The proletarians have nothing to lose but their chains. They have a world to win. Working men of all countries, unite!"

Interpretations of Marx

As is the case with most seminal thinkers, Marx attracted disciples, some of whom took his thought in directions that, had he lived to see them, he might have rejected vigorously. Even in his own lifetime, Marx is said to have declared that whatever else he might be, he was certainly not a Marxist. One reason for the variety of "Marxisms" lies with Marx himself. He was ambiguous on many key points, and conditions changed sufficiently so that over the years, his followers found it necessary to revise some of his basic conceptions.

Marxism–Leninism

Friedrich Engels (1820–1895), the son of a wealthy textile manufacturer, was born in Germany. After receiving a classical education, he moved to Manchester, England, to work in one of his father's mills. Influenced by the works of Owen and other reformers, he became convinced that radical social reforms were needed. He met Marx in 1844 and began a collaboration that lasted 40 years. Because of his association with Marx and his interpretation of Marxist ideas after Marx's death, Engels gained an eminent position within socialist circles that enabled him to exercise great influence.

Engels was one of those who helped popularize "dialectical materialism." In Engels's view, history is determined by a dialectical process, and material conditions are the deciding factor; therefore, the course of wisdom is for people to attune themselves to this historical process so that they are not at odds with it. As Engels viewed it, when science forsook the study of *things* and embraced the study of natural *processes*, it came nearer to discovering the universal laws of motion. Although he knew that human actions and social institutions are different from nature, where blind unconscious processes work on one another, Engels nonetheless held that history, too, has its own inner general laws. Human designs and individual actions often conflict, and so history works much like nature in effect—for many blind and unconscious human processes act against each other; consequently, as in the case of nature, history can be understood by discovering its inner general laws through dialectical materialism.

Engels gave history a deterministic twist that Marx never intended. As early as 1877, Engels was espousing determinism in *Anti-Dühring*, where he began formulating his idea of "scientific socialism." Although Marx had referred to his own view as "materialistic and thus scientific method," Engels, it has been charged, converted Marx's method into a *deterministic philosophy*. In short, Marx's "historical materialism" became, in Engels's hands, a variant of Hegelian philosophy where, in *The Dialectics of Nature*, "matter" is substituted for "Spirit" as the ontological or metaphysical foundation.

If Marx and Engels were men of theory, Vladimir Ilich Lenin (1870–1924) was a man of theory and action. The son of a college professor, he was born with the surname of Ulyanov but took the name Lenin after joining the socialist movement. Lenin welded his own ideas to those of Marx and Engels so that the orthodox philosophy of the Soviet Union and several other countries was called "Marxism–Leninism." Lenin's view of materialism, following Engels, resulted in a type of naive realism, a "mirror-image" epistemology that influenced subsequent views on education in the Soviet Union. As he expressed it in *Materialism and Empirio-Criticism*: "Our sensation, our consciousness is only an image of the external world, and it is obvious that an image cannot exist without the thing imaged, and the latter exists independently of that which images it." He rejected the Kantian dilemma about knowing the thing-in-itself and held that the only difference between the noumenon and the phenomenon is what is known and what is not yet known.

This penchant for cut-and-dried clarity (his critics would call it narrow dog-matism) is one hallmark of Lenin's interpretation of Marx. In his conception of the state, Lenin followed Engels on the inevitability of dialectical materialism—that the state will eventually "wither away" after the establishment of the dictatorship of the proletariat. In *The State and Revolution,* Lenin interpreted Marx to mean that violent revolution to overthrow bourgeois forms of the state, including represen-tative democracy, is part of this inevitability. This is clearly not Marx's view; al-though Marx did not shrink from violence, he maintained that in some of the more advanced industrial and democratic countries, such as England, Holland, and the United States, the proletariat could achieve its ends through peaceful means. As late as 1880, in a letter to the English socialist Henry Hyndman, Marx wrote: "If the unavoidable evolution turns into a revolution, it would not only be the fault of the ruling classes, but also of the working class." Lenin, however, argued that the dicta-torship of the proletariat, "in accordance with the general rule, can only be brought about by violent revolution."

Lenin's view was no doubt influenced by the autocratic conditions in Russia at the time, and this might have compelled him to take what his critics allege to be a nar-row view. These same critics maintain that following the Russian Revolution, Lenin's ideas on the nature of the state and the need for a dictatorship controlled by a small, disciplined party apparatus led only to the establishment of a dictatorship by the of-ficial Communist Party. This party showed little sign of "withering away" until reforms led by Mikhail Gorbachev resulted in the dissolution of the Soviet Union. Today, Marxism–Leninism apparently has been rejected in favor of market economies in most former republics of the old Soviet Union, notably Russia during the administrations of Boris Yeltsin and Vladimir Putin. Whereas the old Soviet Union prided itself on achiev-ing universal literacy and making education widely available to everyone, by the be-ginning of the twenty-first century, Russia was bogged down in political and economic problems, and education seemed to take a back seat to other concerns.

WESTERN MARXISM AND THE ORIGINS OF "CRITICAL THEORY"

After Engels's death in 1893, the mantle of Marxist leadership was passed to the Ger-man Social Democratic Party, which became the leading organization of Marxist thought in the West. Western Marxism lost its revolutionary edge, however, after changes in capitalist societies during which workers' wages improved and "corpo-rate" capitalism displaced older forms of capitalism. Many Marxists concluded that the Western proletariat had lost the will for revolutionary *praxis*. In the East, Lenin and his followers launched the revolution that was to focus attention on Marxism–Leninism as the orthodox standard-bearer of Marxism. In the West, however, Georg Lukács (1885–1971) and Antonio Gramsci (1891–1937) developed Marxism further along lines that Marx had been associated with in his youth—the social criticism of the Young Hegelians. This theme was to be taken up by a group of philosophers and developed into a school of thought known as the Frankfurt School. Two distinguishing features of Western or neo-Marxism are its philosophical orientation and its efforts to move beyond material production and class conflict as the chief explanatory constructs of Marxist analysis and toward broad cultural explanations of power relations and conflict.

Marx was somewhat ambivalent about the role of philosophy. He thought that it was a remnant of bourgeois culture, but he continued to criticize existing society in philosophical critiques that he claimed were scientific. Georg Lukács, however, took the unorthodox view that philosophy still had a role to play in mediating between changing capitalistic forms and the development of workers' understanding of their condition. According to Lukács, the failure of workers to take matters in hand was the result of (1) *reification*—that is, taking prevailing capitalistic ideas about the nature of society as the way things must be; (2) the division of labor that keeps workers submerged; and (3) capitalist evolution and its accommodation to the less threatening demands of workers.

Italian philosopher Antonio Gramsci, building on Lukács's work, maintained that ideology as cultural *hegemony* (overriding cultural influence or authority) is an important aspect of power over society, even more than the modes of material production. Through the cultural hegemony of ideology, workers *reify* (accept an idea or assumption as true) capitalistic ideas and acquiesce to them. Consequently, ideology is a powerful tool of capitalism (as it is in any "ism"), and for those who struggle against capitalism, the proper course is to question hegemonic bourgeois culture and its control over the consciousness of the proletariat. The unorthodox views of Lukács and Gramsci challenged some basic tenets of historical materialism itself and helped forge a new role for philosophy within Western Marxism.

The Frankfurt School

The term *critical theory* probably was applied first to the work of the Frankfurt School. This group of leftist scholars gathered at the Institute for Social Research at the University of Frankfurt in 1923, but many later immigrated to other countries because of the threat of Hitler and the Nazis. The critical theory that they developed was influenced by the work of several thinkers, including Kant, Hegel, Nietzsche, Freud, and Marx—to name a few. Central to the Frankfurt School's critical approach, however, is Marx's method of examining ideologies and showing their shortcomings. Some leading figures in the Frankfurt School were Max Horkheimer (1895–1971), Theodor Adorno (1903–1969), and Herbert Marcuse (1898–1979). A prominent recent figure in the movement is Jurgen Habermas (1929–).

Max Horkheimer studied the transformation of Western society from old-style capitalism to contemporary corporate or state capitalism. He held that individuality had been debased by bourgeois capitalism and that the centralizing capacities of capitalism threatened to eradicate individuality through mass culture, fascism, and the fetishism of the technocratic consciousness. Horkheimer struck a decidedly pessimistic note, reflected in the titles of some of his works: *Eclipse of Reason* and *Dawn and Decline.* Horkheimer and Theodor Adorno coauthored *Dialectic of Enlightenment,* in which they expressed the belief that humane culture cannot prosper without reasoned thought; but because of centralization and authoritarianism in modern mass culture, theory and an elevation of technologism are feared. Consequently, Horkheimer and Adorno believed that centralized planning and the authoritarian state should be the foci of critical philosophy.

According to Adorno, the use of various art and communication forms (such as radio, motion pictures, modern advertising, and so forth) creates the preplanned, mass-produced social and cultural outlooks he called "mass culture." Such conditions overwhelm individual initiative and result in the "administered society," characterized by a "technological veil" behind which those in control hide facts and use them to dominate. The result is that people cannot think for themselves. Adorno distrusted the old Marxist notion of the "spontaneous power of the proletariat in the historical process," for he held that spontaneity is inadequate in the face of the domination that exists. Although he developed no single meaning for critical theory, in *Negative Dialectics* Adorno advocated dialectical thinking; that is, the thinker must try to envision the negation of things in order to create new alternatives.

Herbert Marcuse developed the Frankfurt School's themes about the eclipse of individuality into what he called "one-dimensional man." In a work by that title, he describes how technological consciousness and authoritarianism result in the paralysis of criticism and the inability to devise alternatives. "One dimensionality" results from the historical process by which the corporate, bureaucratic, scientific, and technological modes of organization have become so reified and entrenched that society as a whole mobilizes to protect them. The problem is that people apparently cannot move beyond this one dimension. For a time, Marcuse thought that the student radicalism of the 1960s would help bring about change because its "Great Refusal" showed the limits of the contemporary order. His work *An Essay on Liberation* was meant to further that movement toward a new socialism.

In some respects, Jurgen Habermas has taken neo-Marxist theory not only beyond more traditional Marxism but also beyond the Frankfurt School's approach. In *Communication and the Evolution of Society*, he attempts to develop an empirical philosophy of history with a practical (or political) intent, and he incorporates the developmental psychology of Jean Piaget and Lawrence Kohlberg into his theory, as well as elements of American pragmatism. His interest in communication theory also incorporates elements of language analysis. He emphasizes, however, the Frankfurt School's view that sociocultural conditions are more significant than mere material forces of production. Rather than historical evolution springing only from material modes of production, it springs from social processes and structures produced by societies to maintain and enhance themselves. From the standpoint of individuals, this occurs through individual learning capacities. In this sense, societies are dependent on individuals. Individuals, however, are dependent on the symbolic structures of the social world for their meanings and competence; that is, individuals need systems of language and behavioral expectations to communicate, organize, and resolve conflicts. For Habermas, then, material forces of production, though important, are not decisive for historical evolution. Forms of cooperation are just as decisive, and what is needed is not further clarification of the modes of production but more general principles of social organization and communication.

As can be seen, Western Marxism and critical theory have taken Marxism away from some basic tenets of both Marx and Marxism–Leninism. Although Marx resisted describing any specific vision of the future of socialism, he did envision a society characterized by free association and self-management. As Stanley Aronowitz points out in *The Crisis in Historical Materialism*, however, what actually developed was authoritarian state socialism. Free association and self-management are still utopian dreams, not actualities, and the impulse for creative social theory eventually has come from outside old-style Marxism itself in the form of feminism, the ecology movement, the drive for racial freedom, new nationalism, and even liberation theology. Yet, Aronowitz continues, Marx's thrust against domination, his dialectical theory of capitalist development, and his vision of social transformation still might serve as useful guideposts for those who seek to change the old order.

MARXISM AS A PHILOSOPHY OF EDUCATION

Although Marx did not write extensively about education, his educational ideas, coupled with his general theory, greatly influenced other Marxist philosophers and educators. Subsequent Marxist theory, however, has seen several divergent directions. For example, the Marxist-Leninist version was dominant in such countries as the former Soviet Union and the former East Germany, but Marxism–Leninism has had little direct influence in the West. Western Marxism, though exerting more influence on the theory of education in the West, has had more impact on educational policy and practice in such countries as the United States, although this has not been extensive. The point is that to understand Marxism's historic significance for philosophy of education, one must recognize not only Marx's original works but also divergent interpretations.

Aims of Education

The aims of Marxist education can be found in the Marxist conception of history and the critical analysis of existing conditions, for Marxist theory holds that human society must move from capitalism to socialism and eventually to communism. In those countries where Marxism–Leninism once held sway, educational aims were viewed primarily in terms of this dialectical movement, and the immediate goals were to mold a socialist consciousness and a socialist society. This effort was greatly enhanced by providing an education to develop a new socialist human being.

The Socialist Consciousness

Marx wanted to overcome human alienation, which he thought was the direct result of private property and the control of production by an elite. The aim was to free conscious, vital human activity by putting individuals back in control of their own labor. Marx thought that his particular task was to develop proper theoretical bases so that the working class would be aware of general directions to be taken. In this sense, it could be said that Marx saw his role as an educational one.

In the 1840s, Marx criticized the education allowed the working classes of England and Germany as a paternalistic device used by the ruling classes to produce docile and obedient subjects. Public education should result, he argued, in individual aims becoming public aims, natural independence becoming spiritual freedom, and raw drive becoming ethical drive. One bourgeois spokesman maintained that the neglected education of the working class resulted in their unrest because they failed to understand the "natural laws of commerce" that reduced them to pauperism. Marx had no patience for such attitudes; instead, he thought that the "brainlessness" of the bourgeoisie led them to be "embarrassed" by the unrest among the poverty-stricken working class.

Marx thought that the ruling classes would not provide a proper public education for working-class children because this would mean the eventual freeing of the proletariat and result in the abolition of pauperism and a subjugated proletariat. The bourgeois state, the organization of society by which the ruling classes maintained control, was based on the contradiction between public and private life. For the state to serve broad public needs and interests, the ruling classes would have to forego their advantage of private gain, and this they would not do. In short, the bourgeois state used education for ruling-class ends and not for the ends of children or a freer, more humane society.

Perhaps Marx's conception of education is represented best in summary form in *Theses on Feuerbach*, where, in the third thesis, he separates his view of materialism from the older, more mechanistic view. The materialist doctrine that people are the product of circumstances and education, he states, overlooks the fact that *people* change *circumstances* and that "educators must themselves be educated"; that is, before one can purposefully educate others, that person must first be educated through some purposeful human activity. In other words, for Marx, human action is necessary to change socioeconomic circumstances. Likewise, the changing of educational processes and circumstances for better effect can be understood rationally only from the standpoint of purposeful human activity, or *praxis*.

In *The Holy Family*, Marx relates how Locke, Condillac, and Helvétius taught that the whole development of humankind depends on education and environment. For Marx, this means that if people derive all knowledge and sensation from the world of sense experience, then it follows that the empirical world must be transformed and made suitable. If humans are by nature social beings, then they will develop their full humanity only in circumstances that are truly social. This further illustrates Marx's idea of revolutionary *praxis* and the part it would play in a new education as he envisioned it. This message is summarized in the eleventh thesis on Feuerbach: "The philosophers have only interpreted the world, in various ways; the point is to change it."

At least one approach to changing the world through the establishment of a socialist consciousness can be illustrated by going to the orthodox Marxist-Leninist approach as it was practiced in the former Soviet Union and the German Democratic Republic (East Germany). In 1957, George Counts quoted Lenin as follows: "The school must become a weapon of the dictatorship of the proletariat." Stalin was even more direct: "Education is a weapon whose effect depends on who holds it in his hands and who is struck with it." According to Counts, the Soviet approach was to eradicate from the consciousness of the people all traces of antisocialist mentality and to instill the ideology of Communism through an unremitting emphasis on Communist morality. The Communist Party's view was that for the educational program to operate with maximum efficiency, it was necessary to "protect" the people from all competing ideologies and to educate them in the one true way.

In the 1970s, Susan Jacoby maintained that although Communist political indoctrination was not so crude or abrasive as it formerly was, it was still "woven through every subject in the regular curriculum." It ranged from respect for Lenin to agreement with Marxist-Leninist economic principles. If the general values of identification with the group, muted individualism, and respect for authority were achieved, then educators thought they were successful. By 1982, Mervyn Matthews, in his study of Soviet education after Stalin, found that despite the moderate relaxation of Soviet dogma, the demands of Marxist-Leninist ideology still retained their preeminence. Efforts to build a socialist consciousness continued to be "exceptionally narrow and sectarian," with "hardly a trace of non-Marxist thought, or shift from long-standing anti-Western orientations." This emphasis continued until the dissolution of the Soviet Union in 1991, after which Russia and the other ten former Soviet republics created the Commonwealth of Independent States and embarked on dramatic social, political, and economic reforms. The change also impacted education, but what long-term effects this will make in education remain to be seen.

In her study of the former German Democratic Republic's educational system, Margrete Klein described how East German officialdom held Marxist-Leninist philosophy to be inherently correct and moral but that, in actuality, it led only to a lack of tolerance for other philosophical systems. Hence, in East Germany, as in the Soviet Union, the aim was to develop among the young a singular socialist consciousness characterized by dedication to such objectives as the communist cause, socialist patriotism, internationalism, conscientious labor, a high sense of public duty, and solidarity with the working class of all countries. Recent history indicates, however, that this aim (or at least the ways it was implemented) was hardly as successful as its adherents hoped, because when finally faced with strong internal opposition, those Marxist-Leninist regimes crumbled. Even before the former Soviet Union split into independent republics, East and West Germany were reunited in 1990 in alignment with the West.

Two Soviet educators who stood out in helping shape orthodox Marxist-Leninist education were Nadezhda Krupskaya (1869–1939), who was Lenin's wife, and Anton Makarenko (1888–1939). Both were important in developing an educational approach to help shape socialist consciousness. Nadezhda Krupskaya thought that this could best be achieved through an education that resulted in, among other things, "conscientious and organized communal instincts" and "a purposeful and well-thought-out world view." Anton Makarenko advocated education by means of the collective; that is, one should develop group loyalties and identify oneself within a group context. The school served as the most important collective, where each member must realize dependence and subordination of personal interests to the collective. This deemphasis of individualism and the emphasis on the collective were drawn from Marx's distrust of capitalistic individualism, which he thought was socially irresponsible and based only on self-interest.

Orthodox Marxist-Leninists embraced the materialist doctrine that human beings are the product of education and environment. They took to heart Marx's admonition against allowing any intrusion of bourgeois principles into socialist education. If bourgeois indoctrination was banished, however, socialist indoctrination was not. Part of the explanation comes from the philosophy of Marxism–Leninism itself, for it was sure of its principles and took dogmatic positions on all issues.

For a more complete view, however, it is necessary to examine Western Marxism from outside a Marxist-Leninist perspective. One such outsider was Paulo Freire (1921–1997), the Brazilian philosopher–educator, who incorporated themes from such sources as Western Marxism, liberation theology, and phenomenology into his philosophy of education. In *Pedagogy of the Oppressed*, he sets forth a view of education based on liberation and dialogue that is critical of traditional education, which he claims is based on the banking concept. By *the banking concept,* Freire means an approach to education in which the teacher chooses content and the student tries to absorb it. Knowledge is like a bank deposit placed in the care of students. It is not theirs to create, appropriate, make over, or shape; rather, students are under the power of the depositor (the teacher and the social system the teacher represents). Thus, students are induced to reify—view as necessary and inevitable—the outlooks and values of the status quo. In such a system, the students are dependent on the oppressor for knowledge, and Freire believed that this approach annuls learners' creative potential and deadens their critical faculties. In the banking concept, the effort is made by the oppressor to change the consciousness of the learners without changing the social, political, and economic conditions in which they exist. In this manner, the oppressor can maintain hegemony over the oppressed by controlling how individual consciousness is formed.

Freire proposed a "problem-posing method" (not unlike John Dewey's approach) that starts with the learner as an active rather than passive being. It takes its content from the actual experiences of learners or from learners' desires to expand their understanding. Thus, teachers and students work together in a dialogical relationship, learning about problems that begin within the domain of the student and then spread outward to the wider world. Freire believed that this approach helps create a critical consciousness because it helps learners see how they live and exist in the world and that the world is not static but in a process of becoming. Learners come to see themselves and the world as becoming, a dialectical relationship with the world through which the learner can exert some influence on surrounding conditions. As Freire maintained in *Education for a Critical Consciousness*, once an individual perceives a challenge and understands the possible responses, constructive action to change objective conditions is possible. In short, critical consciousness leads to critical action—to *praxis*.

The Socialist Society

If one aim of Marxist education is to build a socialist consciousness, then perhaps an even greater aim is to build a socialist society, for social conditions are an important part of the conditions that produce people with the desired consciousness. To repeat

Marx's view, "It is not the consciousness of men that determines their being, but, on the contrary, their social being that determines their consciousness." Contemporary scholars, such as Stanley Aronowitz and Henry Giroux, have taken pains to point out that this is much more complex than it appears, and they have cautioned against the kind of mechanical determinism that many Marxist advocates have championed.

Orthodox Marxist-Leninist theory, however, accepted such determinism. As Susan Jacoby notes, Lenin thought that mass exposure to a single mind-set had many advantages for a revolutionary government attempting to build a new society. Typical practice in the former Soviet Union began with political indoctrination as early as nursery school and kindergarten, where children were told stories about Dyadya Lenin (Uncle Lenin) and his efforts on behalf of the workers. Although in many respects this was not overly different from American practices concerning George Washington (the "Father of Our Country"), Jacoby maintains that the attention given to Lenin bordered on religious practice.

Joseph Zajda points out in his study of Soviet education that the emphasis on a strong national identity in Russian educational theory predated Lenin and the Revolution but that the stress on Communist morality in Soviet education was based on a Leninist interpretation of Marx's ethics and humanism. In this outlook, collectivism denotes Communist morality, and individualism denotes capitalist morality. In effect, in Marxist-Leninist educational theory, moral education and political socialization are inseparable, and the collective serves as the backbone for both. The collective might be one's military unit, workplace, athletic team, or school at the local level; in the Soviet Union, it extended upward to identity with the Communist Party on a national basis or the working class on an international basis. In theory, every Soviet citizen was supposed to identify strongly with some collective aspect of life. Thus, collectivism and Communist morality were the binding principles of Soviet society although Marx envisioned the new socialist individual as issue oriented and dedicated to rational principles rather than merely showing allegiance to persons or groups.

Western or neo-Marxist philosophy took a different theoretical approach, an example being the educational theory in *Schooling in Capitalistic America*, by Samuel Bowles and Herbert Gintis. They contend that liberal reform efforts in the United States have failed and that equalization of educational opportunity has not led to a noticeable economic equalization among individuals. This is because in capitalist societies, schools produce workers by reproducing the conditions of the workplace. The motivating force of the capitalist economy is profit, and because workers must satisfy their own economic needs, the capitalist system induces workers to enter the economic structure with their labor to earn wages and to produce profit (or surplus value) for capitalists. Under such conditions, the school has a dual function: (1) It provides skills and knowledge that make workers more economically valuable, and (2) it socializes people to existing economic structures by modeling the school after the workplace with its rules, lines of authority, bells (or beepers), and hierarchies. The educational experience gained in school, however, also produces at least a few who question the existing social order. This presents a contradiction between capitalist educational goals and the actual educational outcome of at least a few rebels and "misfits" who question capitalism's principles.

According to Bowles and Gintis, under progressive liberalism, education became a panacea for social ills at a time when capitalism was really the root cause of the problems. The schooling process turned to changing *people* rather than to changing the *economic system*. The resulting bureaucratic nature of schooling means that schools exert socializing pressure through requiring obedience to existing norms and values. Therefore, rather than liberation, schools promote conformity to a set of authority relationships existing in the capitalistic economic system.

Bowles and Gintis maintain that progressive educational theory has basic flaws, for its objectives of integration, equality, and development contradict the economic principles of capitalism. For example, they charge that Dewey erred in characterizing American society as democratic when, in fact, capitalism, because of its hierarchical organization and division of labor, is authoritarian. Further, they charge that Dewey looked to technological solutions when, in reality, the ills and their solutions are social and political. Perhaps they overlook the fact that Dewey certainly advocated social and political changes and urged greater efforts toward achieving a more democratic society, but Bowles and Gintis take the classic Marxist position that the economy "produces" people and that capitalists use education to produce a large pool of laborers, a kind of surplus value that capitalists can "invest" at their whim. Furthermore, because changes in the structure of production usually precede changes in the educational structure, a strong causal relationship exists between economic structure and educational structure. If the economy "produces" people (or people's consciousness or outlook), then schools participate in this people-production process. If the production of people results in inequality, then schools also participate in this, too. Changing schools will not necessarily change existing inequalities. At the most, it changes only people's perceptions or consciousness of conditions because the eradication of economic inequities is ultimately a *political* and not an educational question.

Bowles and Gintis argue that it follows from this that an equitable and liberating educational system can flow only from a broad-based transformation of economic life brought about by fundamental political changes, such as democratic control over production processes by working people. Their immediate goal for education is to continue the struggle for school reform as a contribution to the development of a democratic, revolutionary socialist movement. They agree with Marx that a peaceful socialist revolution might be achieved in the United States and that the strategy is to create a working-class consciousness. The initial phase of the revolution must occur by working through existing capitalistic institutions to enable people to remake oppressive institutions and to learn how to exercise power and make cooperative decisions. An egalitarian and liberating educational institution is an essential element of this process.

Methods and Curriculum

Marx did not look favorably on public education provided by the bourgeois capitalist nation–state, primarily because he distrusted the curriculum it would include and the way this curriculum would be taught. Although Marx came out in favor of compulsory education in 1869, he was opposed to any curriculum based on class distinctions.

Only such subjects as physical science and grammar were fit for schools, he believed, because the rules of grammar and the laws of physical science would be the same regardless of who taught them. He spoke out against a proposal that children should be taught "the laws that regulate the value of the produce of their labor," for he believed that this topic would only uphold bourgeois economic theories. He approved of nineteenth-century American public schools, whose school boards composed of citizens at the local community level controlled the hiring of teachers and the curriculum. The only form of state control that Marx favored was the idea of school inspectors to see that general school laws were obeyed. As late as 1875, he still found education by the state objectionable on the grounds that state control too often led to indoctrination in the interest of the bourgeoisie. Marx objected to education under a bourgeois state—not a state under "the dictatorship of the proletariat." The *Manifesto* set forth a brief sketch of what this latter kind of state might institute, and free public education for all children was one recommendation.

Marx advocated technical and industrial education, but not narrow vocationalism. In a lecture entitled "Wages," delivered before a German workingmen's association in 1847, he noted how modern industry at that time used children to tend machinery, a simplified labor requiring virtually no education. Intellectual education, if the child or worker had any, made no difference in wages, for the kind of education advocated by the bourgeoisie was a narrow industrial education that made workers reluctant to challenge bourgeois interests. Marx approved a three-part curricular organization: mental education, physical education, and technological training, the latter including not only practical training in the trades but also the general principles of production processes. This was meant to compensate for the deficiencies of apprentices, who learned only specific, task-oriented things. A thorough understanding of the whole production process was needed so that ignorance of the inner workings of the economic system would not be used as a way to hold the proletariat in industrial bondage.

Marx's views had a subsequent impact on education in Marxist-Leninist countries, particularly with regard to technological education. The attempt was to ensure the linkage of theory and practice and to avoid differentiations between intellectual and physical labor. In the early years after the Russian Revolution, Krupskaya advocated "polytechnical education" as a way of making people "masters of industry." As the word *polytechnical* indicates, the concept refers to a broad technical preparation in production processes. In Krupskaya's view, it should include theoretical and practical emphases, as well as Marxist-Leninist philosophy. Polytechnical education was an inclusive concept and was difficult if not impossible to implement.

Klein, in her study of education in the former German Democratic Republic (East Germany), found that those in power followed the epistemological doctrines of Engels and Lenin that what is perceived is a copy or mirror image of objective reality. Learning and the acquisition of knowledge were seen as the process by which mind is raised from a level of ignorance to one of knowledge, and this was regarded as a dialectical process. In other words, a dialectic of matter and motion must exist in which a person acts on his perception of material reality by seeking to alter or transform matter in terms of its own internal laws. According to Lenin, each piecemeal action in this regard results in *relative* knowledge, but the accumulation of these instances eventually will result in *absolute* knowledge revealed through practice.

This kind of certainty had some direct results for education under Marxist-Leninist systems of education. Lenin was certainly sympathetic to the plight of the proletariat, but he did not think that workers could launch and maintain a revolution without proper guidance. He believed that a small, disciplined party apparatus was needed to provide leadership for the proletariat. Lenin called this "democratic centralism," but the school curriculum that he advocated was not simply what any group might establish but what the vested authority of the party established. This resulted in an authoritarian view of knowledge and curriculum for schools. It ensured that political ideology was a central consideration even in those areas of the curriculum that one might suppose to be free from it.

Perhaps the most notorious example of the pervasiveness of political ideology was the case of the theories of Trofim Lysenko, an agronomist during the Stalinist era. Contrary to Mendelian genetics, Lysenko argued that *acquired* characteristics could be *genetically* transferred. Because Stalin liked this theory, it was given official sanction and was taught in biology courses in Soviet schools for many years. Lysenko's ideas—and Stalin's insistence on following them—had disastrous results on Soviet agriculture during this period, yet the top-down authoritarian nature of deciding agricultural issues and educational policy overcame all objections.

Despite the many drawbacks now so apparent in Marxist-Leninist educational theory, many scholars continue to find other variants of Marxist and neo-Marxist thought helpful in analyzing the problems of education in contemporary society. Several educational theorists have used elements of Western Marxist critical theory to analyze educational problems in capitalistic society and to make recommendations for new forms of critical pedagogy and policy. In addition to Samuel Bowles and Herbert Gintis are Martin Carnoy, Henry Levin, Basil Bernstein, Michael Apple, and Henry Giroux, to name a few. Giroux's work serves as a good example. In *Ideology, Culture, and the Process of Schooling*, Giroux develops the position that the curriculum embodies dominant forms of culture in the way it reproduces the modes of knowing, learning, speaking, style, and manners of the dominant social classes. Furthermore, this is done in the guise of objectivity, fairness, and merit. In fact, the knowledge conveyed by schools reflects the principles of the dominant group, particularly with regard to political principles and the technical knowledge needed to legitimate its power and to enhance its capital accumulation. What people learn sometimes helps transform their perceptions and enable them to resist hegemony more effectively.

Giroux does not accept a simple correspondence theory of the relation of social being and consciousness, but he argues a neo-Marxist position that recognizes many mediating influences between the two. In other words, the content of the curriculum and the way it is organized and learned can serve as mediating influences, and these influences may be unconsciously and passively received or purposefully organized for liberating effects.

The history–social studies curriculum serves as an example. In recent years, discussion has revolved around a crisis in historical consciousness, the "death of history," which has resulted in the development of an ahistorical outlook. People operate out of a set of assumptions that accepts (or as Lukács maintained, "reifies") conditions and ideas as they are received, without seeking explanations or an understanding of the origins of those conditions and ideas. Under such conditions, people suffer from a social amnesia and lose sight of the changing nature of social processes by which hegemony is maintained.

Contemporary cultural hegemony reproduces itself in many ways. As Adorno showed, the mass-produced objects and messages of the culture industry make for a common public outlook; the result is the one-dimensional technological consciousness that Marcuse described, a positivism that presents itself as the unalterable result of the gathering force of science and technology. Whereas at one time in American history, people looked on improvement as moral self-improvement and self-discipline, today improvement is seen in the one-dimensional terms of improving material possessions or technological growth. These outlooks are tied to the present, denying the importance of historical consciousness. According to Giroux, such developments have removed political decisions from public discourse by removing "fact" and "solution" from social and historical contexts and by making them simply technological concerns. This ahistorical consciousness has developed at the expense of the growth of independence of thought and a more rational mode of thinking among the public.

From Giroux's perspective, curriculum theory must become cognizant of the dialectic between sociocultural conditions and the active nature of human beings. Students must be seen as self-conscious agents who, with proper education resulting in heightened awareness of social and cultural realities, are able to move beyond an ahistorical consciousness and toward active participation and change.

Role of the Teacher

Because Marxist philosophy places little emphasis on the role of genetic inheritance in learning, the importance of the teacher and the environment in which one learns is paramount. Marxist educators who operated under the Soviet regime believed that children could be made into whatever the leadership chose to make them, provided that all aspects of learning were controlled. For this reason, children were placed early in life in state-controlled nursery schools and then moved up the ladder of learning in a systematic fashion. Students wore uniforms or other insignia representing the level they were on, and academic excellence was highly prized. Public education was free and available to all through high school. After that point, students who showed further promise were sent to a university, where they could specialize in a variety of areas. University students were paid stipends if they excelled in their studies. Primarily, students specialized in some technical field and then after graduation were placed in positions deemed suitable to their achievements.

Ideal teachers under the Soviet system would be accomplished in their areas of study and understand clearly the political aspects of their disciplines. This would mean that a teacher teaching literature, for example, would be able to show students how this study supported Soviet ideals. Not only did all studies at all levels have a political dimension, but learning was to be used to further the goals of the Soviet Union, not mere individual development. The Soviets rejected Western-style education that encouraged individualism and the criticism of government.

Most education that took place in the former Soviet Union was of an "essentialist" nature; that is, it dealt primarily with factual knowledge. Major emphasis was given to studies in science and mathematics, and these, too, had a political dimension, one that was to be explained by the teacher and not interpreted by the student. Speculation and a critical analysis of ideas were not strongly promoted, and students were expected to learn useful things.

Textbooks and other materials that a teacher used were standardized and approved by party officials. Teachers were not allowed to introduce other materials or ideas into a classroom setting unless previously approved. Soviet education, as it developed, became rigid, inflexible, and bureaucratic. Teachers were not encouraged or allowed to innovate or to change established educational policy. In the early period, however, an effort was made to include people formerly excluded under the old Czarist regime. Many students who entered the Soviet system came from backgrounds such as agricultural communities, where book learning was not highly valued and the belief that these students could become intelligent and productive was strong. Makarenko, a leading proponent of the new Soviet order, stated that he would consign to the fire any previous record of a child's development lest it prejudice him from seeing the full potentialities that existed in that person.

Since the fall of the former Soviet Union, education has been undergoing a transformation. Now education might allow more outside influences and might not be as rigid as it was formerly. In accord with this, teachers may also be changing the ways they view and practice education.

CRITIQUE OF MARXISM IN EDUCATION

Marxism has had a major impact on the world and its education, but this impact, like the philosophy itself, is subject to various interpretations. The most direct impact has been in those countries under a Marxist-Leninist system, but Marxism also has affected other countries. In the West, that impact was often negative in the sense that some countries attempted to construct educational policy to counteract what leaders saw as the threat of the Cold War and monolithic Marxist encroachment. Conversely, neo-Marxist adherents frequently found themselves in the position of having to "apologize" for the failure of existing Marxist regimes to match actions with Marxist humanistic rhetoric.

In recent years, neo-Marxist theory has exerted an influence different from the older Cold War attitudes. In the United States, elements of neo-Marxist theory have been used to analyze the nature of leading American educational policies and practices. This has not resulted yet in any local or state school systems adopting large-scale policy redirection or widespread new instructional methodologies, but it could show some results in the future. Certainly, neo-Marxist ideas have been used by theorists to help gain new perspectives on education.

One characteristic of orthodox Marxism, and one to which Marx himself contributed, was the relegation of philosophy to the "dust bin of history." Adorno vigorously criticized this view and argued that Marx's criticism of philosophers talking about the world rather than changing it, and his call for the unification of theory and practice, led subsequent followers to ignore mistakenly the place of philosophical theory in human affairs. This was why orthodox Marxism–Leninism, secure in its belief that dialectical materialism answered all the needs for philosophizing, became ossified. For Adorno, more adequate theory was needed, a position supported by the Frankfurt School.

This outlook has been important for some recent scholars in education who use Western Marxist or critical theory ideas in their work, but they are by no means of a single mind regarding the directions this should take. Their work is not generally within traditional philosophy; rather, they focus on a critical analysis of education from an interdisciplinary basis—using such disciplines as history, sociology, economics, and feminist studies but with philosophical emphases. For example, some scholars have used Marxist theory to help interpret the historical development of education, such as how business values influenced educational provisions in the United States or how many curriculum reforms are instituted for social control to protect power interests rather than humanitarian interests. Some studies suggest that any changes in basic core values of a society result in a fundamental shift in the economic system.

The impact of Marxism on educational theory can be seen in several ways. Madan Sarup has urged that sociology of education needs a Marxist framework to deal with the problems of alienation, division of labor, and class. Marxism helps give sociology a more encompassing view of the ensemble of social relations, and it gives a basis for action in its emphasis on *praxis.* Michael Apple has applied neo-Marxist ideas to curriculum theory and the ways schools reproduce knowledge to maintain existing social, economic, and political conditions. He holds that education not only functions as a way of reproducing social class and capital accumulation but also reproduces gender stratification, the privileges of culturally dominant groups, and the limitations imposed by the structure of the state. Carnoy and Levin are political economists who examine the traditional American justification of public education as the way to alleviate poverty and argue that the elimination of poverty and inequality, including racism, sexism, and unemployment, cannot progress far in a capitalist-dominated society. Rather than being independent of the ills of society, schools are an integral part of the capitalist system, and as such their potential for reform is severely limited. Only by reform of the economic and political system can schools help raise the condition of the dispossessed.

Yet, for all the analysis that has come out of the varieties of Marxist educational theory, it does not seem to have generated as yet a growing momentum among ordinary people to carry out the social and economic reforms the critics advocate. This is true not only in education but in the wider society, as well. In the advanced industrial societies, Marxist theories and policy recommendations seem to get an indifferent reception or even hostile reactions from rank-and-file members of society. This has been recognized by theorists such as Giroux, who notes that the failures of existing socialisms to elevate the working class to assume its envisioned role have dealt Marxism a fatal blow. What radical educators must do, he argues, is to see Marxism not as a system valid for all times, but as a "way of seeing" in which discourse is linked with the spirit of critical inquiry, a position clearly within the philosophical tradition of thought.

One strength of Marxism as a philosophy is that it provides a view of social transformation and promotes a view of purposeful human action to carry through on that transformation. It portrays a world where things are not fixed, and it strives for change. Because of these features, Marxism often appeals to those who see themselves as oppressed. In addition, Marxism emphasizes an ideal of social power for the lower classes. Thus, it has a strong appeal for those who live under regimes or in circumstances that show little regard for the dispossessed. Finally, Marxism offers a utopian vision of collective destiny.

Marxism also has the strength of its critical role—the potential to help societies look at themselves in ways they would not ordinarily pursue. For example, it has been said that Marx's works have provided more insight into capitalism than capitalist theory itself. Whether or not this is true, Western Marxist critical analysis has issued warnings about alienation, technologism, bureaucratic centralization, mass culture, and presentism that are timely for contemporary society. Its scholarly analysis of education from an interdisciplinary approach has offered alternative insights for education in capitalist societies.

Marxists have been major advocates of making resources available to everyone, and public education is one social good they have advocated. In its educational theory, Marxism claims to blend theory and practice and to bring before learners the crucial need for rational activity and a sense of social responsibility needed for a more humane existence. Where Marxists have gained political control (and this usually has occurred in societies that are not industrially and technologically advanced), leaders have put a high premium on providing formal education for the population where virtually no one was educated before except for the elite.

After the collapse of the Soviet Union, many pundits predicted the demise of Marxism on a worldwide basis. Yet China, the most populous nation in the world, continues to have a Marxist-oriented system, as does Cuba. One also could argue that many nations have been influenced by Marxist ideas to the point of instituting employment safeguards, national health care, and other "womb-to-tomb" social welfare programs. Marxist-oriented nations had or have, for whatever reasons one might ascribe, been greatly concerned with education. China claims that all of its students receive a minimum of 9 years of formal education, and Fidel Castro claims that illiteracy has been wiped out in Cuba, something the United States does not claim for itself. At any rate, Marxist-oriented systems suffered a setback in the late twentieth century but have not completely disappeared.

Critics of Marxism abound, however, and not simply for what they see as major philosophical or theoretical weaknesses but for practical reasons, as well. A glaring detraction of Marxism is the examples of Marxist regimes in action. In those countries where exponents of Marxism gained the upper hand, the model of education presented seldom demonstrated the theoretical humanistic ideals that Marxist theory espouses. Governments that have advocated Marxism have been characterized by an elite party structure, bureaucratic authoritarianism, rigid state control, and lack of personal freedom. Marxist-Leninist education in the former Soviet Union, for example, embraced rampant indoctrination, rigid curriculum control, and a disregard for intellectual freedom.

These drawbacks might be endemic to theoretical Marxism, whether of the orthodox or "neo-" varieties, and this has led many of the latter persuasion to attempt fundamental reconstructions of basic Marxist tenets in efforts to go beyond Marxism. Historically, the Marxist belief that no neutral education exists led orthodox proponents to indoctrinate single mindedly, whereas critical Western Marxists who drew back from indoctrination and violent revolution were left with only the role of critics on the fringes. Today, they decry the crisis in Marxist theory and cast about for new directions. For example, postmodern critical theorists, such as Aronowitz and Giroux, each have drawn considerably from the Marxist tradition but are also critical of some of its chief features. Aronowitz, in *The Crisis in Historical Materialism*, chronicled how Western Marxists of various hues became aware of the gap between Marx's intellectual vision and the blunt actualities of Marxist-based regimes.

Marxists also have been reluctant to push some issues to the extent they have pushed those of a political nature, and they would rather blame Marxism's difficulties on poor strategies of implementation rather than face the prospect that Marxism itself could have fundamental theoretical weaknesses. Giroux, in *Border Crossings*, notes that although Marxist analyses energized radical education in the late 1970s, he doubts that Marxism is the primary influence on radical education today. Giroux finds that Marxism also can be reductionist and one dimensional in its emphasis on class conflict. He argues that Marxism's flaws result in serious doubt about its appropriateness as a guiding theory but maintains that educators still should understand the Marxist tradition and its insight into the politicized nature of schools and how they reproduce the dominant social consciousness. In Giroux's opinion, the role Marxism plays today is more in terms of historical background or setting, not guiding vision.

Some contemporary observers argue that educators still have much fertile ground to explore in the Marxist way of viewing things. For example, Richard Brosio and Frank Margonis are among those who continue to find Marxist ideas valuable in analyzing contemporary education. Michael Apple has faulted postmodern critical theory persistently for its disillusionment with the Marxist concentration on structural tensions and material conditions. In *Official Knowledge: Democratic Education in a Conservative Age*, Apple draws attention to structures that promote domination and inequalities. He maintains that social class should not be dismissed too quickly and that attention still should be given to the material conditions that shape life chances. To back his contention, Apple cites what he sees as the growing dominance of official policy through tighter accountability and control of education, the privatization movement, and national curricula and assessment. He says that the issue comes down to a recurring conflict between property rights and personal rights, and so his basic argument runs counter to the postmodernist disillusionment with Marxist concepts.

More recently, Apple argues that the failure to be more class conscious is particularly regrettable in light of the self-confident market forces of capitalism today. Apple fears that if left unchallenged, these ideological influences will begin to change people's commonsense views of education. Apple argues that the time is ripe for greater attention to socioeconomic factors, reiterating some standard Marxist/ socialist arguments.

Marxism and its critical perspectives have played important roles in helping people see shortcomings and weaknesses in the social systems they have. However, as some observers note, adherents of the critical theory perspective often seem to have a Marxist agenda they want implemented in education—a movement toward a socialist society and a continuing strong distrust for any aspects of capitalism. These observers maintain that Marxists and neo-Marxists alike show a lack of sensitivity to the positive changes that nonsocialist industrial economies have undergone. They also note that *praxis* or purposeful human action might apply in nonsocialist theories and systems and that the dialectic of history—or historical evolution—might not be only a socialist or a materialist development.

MARX

ON EDUCATION

Karl Marx never wrote extended treatments of education, but his works are sprinkled with references to the importance of education. Marx thought that although modern industry had brought untold misery, it also could provide a new means for a better life for all; however, this possibility was thwarted by capitalist thinking that went to any lengths to make profit, including the vicious exploitation of children. The following selections provide examples of Marx's views on education. Notice how he differentiates between modern industry and capitalism and how his commentary interweaves concern for how children are exploited with his concern for children to be educated properly.

Circumstances Change Education

[From "Theses on Feuerbach," written in 1845, section 3.]

The materialist doctrine that men are the products of circumstances and education, hence changed men are the products of different circumstances and changed education, forgets that these circumstances are changed by men and that the educator himself must be educated. Necessarily, therefore, it divides society into two parts, of which one is superior to society (for example, Robert Owen).

The coincidence of the changing of circumstances and of human activity can be understood only as *revolutionary practice.*

Education and Environment

[From Marx and Engels, *The Holy Family* (1845), Chapter IV.]

Condillac, Locke's immediate follower and French translator, at once opposed Locke's sensualism in favor of seventeenth century metaphysics. . . .

In his *Essai sur l'Origine des Connaissances Humaines* [Amsterdam, 1746] he consummated Locke's ideas and proved that not only the soul but also the senses, not only the art of creating ideas but also the art of sensuous perception, are matters of *experience* and *habit*. Hence the whole development of man depends on *education* and *environment*. It was only by the *eclectic* philosophy that Condillac was supplanted in the French schools.

The difference between French and English materialism is the same as the difference between the two nations. The French endowed English materialism with wit, flesh, blood, and eloquence. They imparted to it the temperament and grace it had lacked. They *civilized* it.

In Helvétius, who likewise derives from Locke, materialism receives its proper French character. He conceived it primarily in connection with social life (Helvétius, *De l'Homme, de ses Facultés intellectuels et de son éducation* [London, 1775]). Sensuous qualities and self-love, enjoyment of understood personal interest, are the basis of all morality. The natural equality of human intelligence, the unity of the progress of reason and the progress of industry, the natural goodness of man, and the omnipotence of education are the main factors of his system. . . .

It requires no great acuteness to see from the teachings of materialism on such matters as the original goodness and equal intellectual endowment of men, the omnipotence of experience, habit, education, and the influence of environment on man, the great importance of industry, the justification of enjoyment, etc., that there is a necessary connection between materialism and communism and socialism. If man derives all knowledge, sensation, etc., from the world of the senses and sense experience, it follows that the empirical world must be so constructed that in it he experiences the truly human and becomes aware of himself as a man. If properly understood interest is the principle of all morality, it follows that the private interests of men coincide with the interests of humanity. If man is unfree in the material sense, that is, free, not through the negative power of avoiding this or that, but through the positive power of asserting his true individuality, it follows that crime must not be punished in the individual but that antisocial sources of crime must be destroyed and each man given the social scope for his essential life-expression. If man is by nature social, he will develop his true nature only in society, and the power of his nature must be measured not by the power of separate individuals but by the power of society.

Education for the Worker

[From "Wages," lectures delivered before the German Working Men's Association in Brussels, December 1847, and printed in the *Neue Rheinische Zeitung*, April 5, 6, 7, and 11, 1849.]

Another very favorite bourgeois proposal is *education*, especially many-sided *industrial education*.

We will not call attention to its trite contradiction, which lies in the fact that modern industry constantly replaces complicated work with more simple labor which requires no education. We will not call attention to the fact that it throws ever more children, from the age of 7 up, behind the machine and makes them sources of profit not only for the bourgeois class but also for their own proletarian parents. The factory system frustrates the school laws—for example in Prussia. We will not call attention to the fact that intellectual education, if the worker possesses it, has no direct effect at all on his wages, that education altogether depends on life conditions, that by moral education the bourgeois understands the drumming into the head of bourgeois principles, and that, finally, the bourgeois class has neither the means nor, assuming it had them, (even the desire to) apply them so as to offer the people a real education.

We confine ourselves merely to raising a purely economic point.

The actual meaning of education in the minds of philanthropic economists is this: Every worker should learn as many branches of labor as possible, so that if, either through the application of new machinery or through a changed division of labor, he is thrown out of one branch, he can easily be accommodated in another.

Education and Juvenile and Child Labor

[From "Instructions for the Delegates of the Provisional General Council (of the First International). The Different Questions." Written in English at the end of August 1866; published in the *International Courier*, February 20 and March 13, 1867.]

We consider the tendency of modern industry to make children and juvenile persons of both sexes cooperate in the great work of social production as a progressive, sound, and legitimate tendency, although under capital it was distorted into an abomination. In a rational state of society *every child whatever,* from the age of 9 years, ought to become a productive laborer in the same way that no able-bodied adult person ought to be exempted from the general law of nature, viz., to work in order to be able to eat, and work not only with the brain but with the hands too.

However, for the present, we have only to deal with the children and young persons of both sexes belonging to the working people. They ought to be divided into three *classes,* to be treated differently; the first class to range from 9 to 12; the second from 13 to 15 years; and the third to comprise of ages 16 and 17 years. We propose that the employment of the first class in any workshop or housework be legally restricted to *two;* that of the second, to *four;* and that of the third, to *six* hours. For the third class, there must be a break of at least one hour for meals and relaxation.

It may be desirable to begin elementary school instruction before the age of 9 years; but we deal here only with the most indispensable antidotes against the tendencies of a social system which degrades the workingman into a mere instrument for the accumulation of capital, and transforms parents by their necessities into slaveholders, sellers of their own children. The *right* of children and juvenile persons must be vindicated. They are unable to act for themselves. It is, therefore, the duty of society to act on their behalf.

If the middle and higher classes neglect their duties toward their children, it is their own fault. Sharing the privileges of these classes, the child is condemned to suffer from their prejudices.

The case of the working class stands quite different. The working man is no free agent. In too many cases he is even too ignorant to understand the true interest of his child, or the normal condition of human development. However, the more enlightened part of the working class fully understands that the future of its class, and, therefore, of mankind, altogether depends upon the formation of the rising working generation. They know that, before everything else, the children and juvenile workers must be saved from the crushing effects of the present system. This can only be effected by converting *social reason into social force,* and, under given circumstances, there exists no other method of doing so than through *general*

laws, enforced by the power of the state. In enforcing such laws the working class does not fortify governmental power. On the contrary, they transform that power, now used against them, into their own agency. They effect by a general act what they would vainly attempt by a multitude of isolated individual efforts.

Proceeding from this standpoint we say that no parent and no employer ought to be allowed to use juvenile labor except when combined with education.

By education we understand three things.

Firstly: *Mental education.*

Secondly: *Bodily education,* such as is given in schools of gymnastics, and by military training.

Thirdly: *Technological training,* which imparts the general principles of all processes of production, and, simultaneously, initiates the child and young person in the practical use and handling of the elementary instruments of all trades.

A gradual and progressive course of mental, gymnastic, and technological training ought to correspond to the classification of the juvenile laborers. The cost of the technological schools ought to be partly met by the sale of their products.

The combination of paid productive labor, mental education, bodily exercises, and polytechnic training will raise the working class far above the level of the higher and middle classes.

It is self-understood that the employment of all persons from 9 and to 17 years (inclusively) in night-work and all health-injuring trades must be strictly prohibited by law.

Elementary Education and Children in Factories

[From *Capital* (1887), Vol. 1, Chapter 15, Section 9.]

. . . From the factory system budded, as Robert Owen has shown us in detail, the germ of the education of the future, an education that will, in the case of every child over a given age, combine productive labor with instruction and gymnastics, not only as one of the methods of adding to the efficiency of production, but as the only method of producing fully developed human beings.

Modern Industry, as we have seen, sweeps away by technical means the manufacturing division of labor, under which each man is bound hand and foot to a single detail operation. At the same time, the capitalistic form of that industry reproduces this same division of labor in a still more monstrous shape; in the factory proper, by converting the workman into a living appendage of the machine; and everywhere outside the factory [in small-scale operations and cottage industries where machines are hand-driven rather than power-driven], partly by reestablishing the division of labor on a fresh basis by the general introduction of the labor of women and children, and of the cheap unskilled labor.

The antagonism between the manufacturing division of labor and the methods of Modern Industry makes itself forcibly felt. It manifests itself, amongst other ways, in the frightful fact that a great part of the children employed in modern factories and manufactures are from their earliest years riveted to the most simple manipulations and exploited for years without being taught a single sort of work that would afterwards make them of use, even in the same manufactory or factory. In the English letterpress printing trade, for example, there existed formerly a system, corresponding to that in the old manufactures and handicrafts, of advancing the apprentices from the easy to more and more difficult work. They went through a course of teaching till they were finished printers. To be able to read and write was for every one of them a requirement of their trade. All this was changed by the printing machine. It employs two sorts of laborers, one grown up, tenters, the other, boys mostly from 11 to 17 years of age whose sole business is either to spread the sheets of paper under the machine or to take from it the printed sheets. They perform this weary task, in London especially, for 14, 15, and 16 hours at a stretch, during several days in the week, and frequently for 36 hours, with only 2 hours' rest for meals and sleep. A great part of them cannot read, and they are, as a rule, utter savages and very extraordinary creatures. . . . As soon as they get too old for such child's work, that is about 17 at the latest, they are discharged from the printing establishment. They become recruits of crime. Several attempts to procure them employment elsewhere were rendered to no avail by their ignorance and brutality, and by their mental and bodily degradation.

As with the division of labor in the interior of the manufacturing workshops, so it is with the division of labor in the interior of society. So long as handicraft and manufacture form the general groundwork of social production, the subjection of the producer to one branch exclusively, the breaking up of the multi-

fariousness of his employment, is a necessary step in the development. On that groundwork each separate branch of production acquires empirically the form that is technically suited to it, slowly perfects it, and, as soon as a given degree of maturity has been reached, rapidly crystallizes that form. The only thing that here and there causes a change, besides new raw material supplied by commerce, is the gradual alteration of the instruments of labor. But their form, too, once definitely settled by experience, petrifies, as is proved by their being in many cases handed down in the same form by one generation to another during thousands of years. A characteristic feature is, that, even down into the eighteenth century, the different trades were called "mysteries" (mystères); into their secrets none but those duly initiated could penetrate. Modern Industry rent the veil that concealed from men their own social processes of production, and that turned the various spontaneously divided branches of production into so many riddles, not only to outsiders, but even to the initiated. The principle which is pursued, of resolving each process into its constituent movements, without any regard to their possible execution by the hand of man, created the new science of technology. The varied, apparently unconnected, and petrified forms of the industrial processes now resolved themselves into so many conscious and systematic applications of natural sciences to the attainment of given useful effects. Technology also discovered the few main fundamental forms of motion, which, despite the diversity of the instruments used, are necessarily taken by every productive action of the human body; just as the science of mechanics sees in the most complicated machinery nothing but the continual repetition of the simple mechanical powers.

Modern Industry never looks upon and treats the existing form of a process as final. The technical basis of that industry is therefore revolutionary, while all earlier modes of production were essentially conservative. By means of machinery, chemical processes and other methods, it is continually causing changes not only in the technical basis of production, but also in the functions of the laborer, and in the social combinations of the labor process. At the same time, it thereby also revolutionizes the division of labor within the society, and incessantly launches masses of capital and of workpeople from one branch of production to another. But if Modern Industry, by its very nature, therefore necessitates variation of labor, fluency of function, universal mobility of the laborer, on the other hand, in its capitalistic form, it reproduces the old division of labor with its ossified particularizations. We have seen how this absolute contradiction between the technical necessities of Modern Industry, and the social character inherent in its capitalistic form, dispels all fixity and security in the situation of the laborer; how it constantly threatens, by taking away the instruments of labor, to snatch from his hands his means of subsistence, and, by suppressing his detail function, to make him superfluous. We have seen, too, how this antagonism vents its rage in the creation of that monstrosity, an industrial reserve army [of the unemployed], kept in misery in order to be always at the disposal of capital; in the incessant human sacrifices from among the working class, in the most reckless squandering of labor power, and in the devastation caused by a social anarchy which turns every economic progress into a social calamity. This is the negative side. But if, on the one hand, variation of work at present imposes itself after the manner of an overpowering natural law, and with the blindly destructive action of a natural law that meets with resistance at all points, Modern Industry, on the other hand, through its catastrophes imposes the necessity of recognizing, as a fundamental law of production, variation of work, consequently fitness of the laborer for varied work, consequently the greatest possible development of his varied aptitudes. It becomes a question of life and death of this law. Modern Industry, indeed, compels society, under penalty of death, to replace the detail worker of today, crippled by lifelong repetition of one and the same trivial operation, and thus reduced to the mere fragment of a man, by the fully developed individual, fit for a variety of labors, ready to face any change of production, and to whom the different social functions he performs are but so many modes of giving free scope to his own natural and acquired powers.

One step already spontaneously taken toward effecting this revolution is the establishment of technical and agricultural schools, and of "écoles d'enseignement professionnel," in which the children of the workingmen receive some little instruction in technology and in the practical handling of the various implements of labor. Though the [English] Factory Act, that first and meager concession wrung from capital, is limited to combining elementary education with work in the factory, there can be no doubt that when the working class comes into power, as inevitably it must, technical instruction, both theoretical and practical, will take its proper place in the working-class schools. There is also no doubt that such revolutionary ferments, the final result of which is the abolition of the old division of labor, are diametrically opposed to the capitalistic form of production, and to the economic status of the laborer corresponding to that form. But the historical development of the antagonisms, immanent in a given form of production, is the only way in which that form of production can be dissolved and a new form established. . . . [H]andicraft wisdom became sheer nonsense from the moment the watchmaker Watt invented the steam engine, the barber Arkwright the throttle, and the working jeweller, Fulton, the steamship.

So long as Factory legislation is confined to regulating the labor in factories, manufactories, etc., it is regarded as a mere interference with the exploiting rights of capital. But when it comes to regulating the so-called "home labor," it is immediately viewed as a direct attack on the *patria potestas*, on parental authority. The tender-hearted English Parliament long affected to shrink from taking this step. The force of facts, however, compelled it at last to acknowledge that modern industry, in overturning the economic foundation on which was based the traditional family, and the family labor corresponding to it, had also unloosed all traditional family ties. The rights of the children had to be proclaimed. The final report of the Ch[ildren's] Empl[oyment] Comm[ission] of 1866, states: "It is, unhappily, to a painful degree apparent throughout the whole of the evidence, that against no persons do the children of both sexes so much require protection as against their parents." The system of unlimited exploitation of children's labor in general and the so-called home labor in particular is "maintained only because the parents are able, without check or control, to exercise this arbitrary and mischievous power over their young and tender offspring. . . . Parents must not possess the absolute power of making their children mere 'machines to earn so much weekly wage.' . . . . The children and young persons, therefore, in all such cases may justifiably claim from the legislature, as a natural right, that an exemption should be secured to them, from what destroys prematurely their physical strength, and lowers them in the scale of intellectual and moral beings." It was not, however, the misuse of parental authority that created the capitalistic exploitation, whether direct of indirect, of children's labor; but, on the contrary, it was the capitalistic mode of exploitation which, by sweeping away the economic basis of parental authority, made its exercise degenerate into a mischievous misuse of power. However terrible and disgusting the dissolution, under the capitalist system, of the old family ties may appear, nevertheless, modern industry, by assigning as it does an important part in the process of production, outside the domestic sphere, to women, to young persons, and to children of both sexes, creates a new economic foundation for a higher form of the family and of the relations between the sexes. It is, of course, just as absurd to hold the Teutonic-Christian form of the family to be absolute and final as it would be to apply that character to the ancient Roman, the ancient Greek, or the Eastern forms which, moreover, taken together form a series in historical development. Moreover, it is obvious that the fact of the collective working group being composed of individuals of both sexes and all ages must necessarily, under suitable conditions, become a source of humane development; although in its spontaneously developed, brutal, capitalistic form, where the laborer exists for the process of production, and not the process of production for the laborer, that fact is a pestiferous source of corruption and slavery.

Source: Karl Marx, *On Education, Women, and Children* (1975), Vol. 6 of The Karl Marx Library, edited by Saul K. Padover, pp. 20, 21–22, 25, 91–92, 112–113, and 114–118. Reproduced with permission of The McGraw-Hill Companies.

SELECTED READINGS

Bowles, Samuel, and Gintis, Herbert. *Schooling in Capitalist America: Educational Reform and the Contradictions of Economic Life.* New York: Basic Books, 1976. A leading example of the application of Marxist ideas to education in the United States. The authors articulate the point of view that schools serve capitalistic society by reproducing essential elements and values of the workplace.

Brosio, Richard A. *A Radical Democratic Critique of Capitalist Education.* Counterpoints: Studies in Postmodern Theory of Education, vol. 3. New York: Peter Lang Publishing, 1994. Assesses the conflict between capitalism and democracy and the problems this conflict presents for education. Brosio maintains that Marxism continues to be a relevant perspective for educational theory and practice.

Margonis, Frank. "Marxism, Liberalism, and Educational Theory," *Educational Theory* 43(4):449–465, Fall 1993. The author maintains that recent views that Marxism is dead are premature. Despite the theory's deficiencies in interpreting human differences and contemporary political movements, Marxism still has merit because people have not advanced beyond the conditions that spawned it.

Marx, Karl; Engels, Friedrich; and Lenin, V. I. *The Essential Left: Four Classic Texts on the Principles of Socialism.* New York: Barnes and Noble, 1965. Selections of some classic works of Marxist philosophy, including the *Manifesto of the Communist Party,* by Marx and Engels, and Lenin's *The State and Revolution.*

www.marxism.org (accessed April 5, 2002). A site devoted exclusively to the many varieties of Marxism. Contains a number of listings for other Marxist sites, including archives of Marx and Engels.

Companion
Website

ONLINE RESEARCH

Utilizing some of the Web sites included in this book, as well as Topics 2 and 3 of the Prentice Hall Foundations Web site found at *www.prenhall.com/ozmon*, answer the following question with a short essay: What are some of the essential components of Marxist philosophy and what kinds of education do they propose? You can write and submit your essay response to your instructor by using the "Electronic Blue-book" section found in any of the topics of the Prentice Hall Foundations Web site.

Philosophy, Education, and the Challenge of Postmodernism

At present, words with the prefix *post-* are heard frequently—*postindustrial, post-liberal, poststructural,* and even *postphilosophy*—but the most commonly heard term is *postmodern*. Proclamations about the postmodern fill the air, and the way the term is used often creates confusion: Is this a new historical epoch *after* the modern, something akin to the great epochs of past history? Does it merely mean a change in artistic and literary styles in the modern era itself, such as occurred with the rise of modern art and the modern novel? Or is postmodernism something else—an in-between period in which old ways of thinking are being questioned while a new era, hidden beyond the horizon, is yet to be born? In other words, reasonable questions can be raised about whether the modern era is dead or dying, whether postmodernism is truly an epochal watershed in human thought and culture, or whether the apparent change is merely a periodic fluctuation in, say, the artistic, literary, and theoretical tastes of intellectuals. Whatever the case, an intellectual upheaval is occurring, and it needs to be studied for what it portends.

POSTMODERN VARIETY

In virtually any scholarly journal devoted to literary or social criticism within the past few decades are writings about something called *the postmodern,* but the term itself is not easily defined or described. Frederic Jameson maintains that the reason postmodernism is a hotly contested concept lies in its parasitical relationship with modernism. Indeed, practically any characteristic of the postmodern can be attributed as easily to the modern, but Jameson argues that an important factor in the arrival of postmodernism was the upheavals of the 1960s, when the assumed truths of the time were brought into question and various experiments in "offensive" lifestyles and outlooks became prominent. For example, Third World countries threw off the yokes of colonialism, and minorities and people on the margins of dominant cultures took up new identities. Old-style Communism began its slide to oblivion under de-Stalinization, hopes were raised for a new left and new Communism, and opposition in the United States to the Vietnam War set a new generation on radical social and political paths.

Today, however, it is apparent that the promised liberation of the Third World was an oversimplification, that the new leftist movements retreated or died in the face of aggressive neoconservatism, that the Vietnam War opposition and its radical intensity are now but a memory, and that many of the offensive lifestyles so prominent in the abrasive 1960s—the art forms and modes of thought that served as a kind of high culture—have been brought down to the level of the mass production of commodities and ordinary aspects of daily life. In Jameson's view, then, what at first held so much promise had by the 1980s been co-opted, sidetracked, or made banal. Disillusionment and exhaustion followed.

Todd Gitlin claims that the search for unity that once characterized intellectual thought apparently has been abandoned, and a bewildering array of styles and interpretations are present. Concern about difference, diversity, and marginality juxtaposed against power and privilege are prominent, and traditional claims to universality are deconstructed and made to appear superfluous. If modernism is disintegrating now, postmodernism is fascinated with the residue.

Roger Mourad gives a more positive view: Postmodernism is still in its infancy but is nonetheless a significant influence on contemporary thought in the sciences, the visual and performing arts, literature, religious studies, cultural studies generally, and, of course, philosophy. Although its primary philosophical underpinnings come from French philosophers such as Michel Foucault, Jacques Derrida, Jean-François Lyotard, Jean Baudrillard, and Jacques Lacan, it has had its American contributors as well, such as Richard Rorty and Calvin Schrag. In no small part, postmodernism has come from a rejection of the Enlightenment and its concern with objective science and claims to universal values, morality, law, and art. In philosophy, scholarly debate breaks down into two camps: defenders of modernism who want to reform it, and postmodernists who want to displace it.

It should be noted that postmodernists resist being characterized as a school of thought. The postmodernists' dislike of encompassing narratives might be one reason for this, and philosophers who identify with postmodern views seek no consensus on an overriding philosophical doctrine. In general, the postmodern consciousness embraces the proposition that no single cultural tradition or mode of thought can serve as a *meta*narrative, a *universal* voice for all human experience. As Lyotard puts it in *The Postmodern Condition*, a simple definition of the postmodern is "incredulity toward metanarratives." One view that postmodernism has called into question most is modernism's Eurocentric metanarrative and its claims to universal rational structures by which to judge the good, the true, or the beautiful. In philosophy, this outlook is what Richard Rorty attacked in *Philosophy and the Mirror of Nature*, when he declared that philosophy simply could not serve as an objective "mirror" against which all knowledge claims are measured. In a similar vein, in *Paradigms Lost: Images of Man in the Mirror of Science*, John Casti critiques scientific rationalism for its claims of detached objectivity although scientific investigation relies to a considerable degree on hunches, intuition, and even aesthetic enjoyment rather than pure methodological procedures that yield universal "laws" of science.

Thus, postmodernism celebrates an iconoclastic outlook that breaks with modern claims of universality, and it rejects claims of objective certainty that seek to end discussion and debate. One result is that the defining boundaries of human thought that once seemed so clear now appear to be fading, including the knowledge boundaries between the academic disciplines. A case in point is how recent philosophical study has affected other disciplines and how those disciplines have affected philosophy. Such cross-fertilization has been perhaps most notable in the interchange between philosophy and the social sciences, history, language and literature, and also the theory of education.

For example, Stanley Aronowitz and Henry Giroux, in *Postmodern Education: Politics, Culture, and Social Criticism*, write that part of the difficulty in clarifying postmodernism is the ambivalence of postmodern conditions. They propose an "emancipatory" postmodern education that answers for its choices, however provisional those choices are. One feature that Aronowitz and Giroux offer is a radical approach to education and democracy to replace old-style master narratives found in the liberal arts, modern science, and philosophical positivism. Traditions of knowledge that see the curriculum grounded in traditional cultural canons, in scientific laws or first principles, are challenged as forms of continuing domination. The authors promote a curriculum that includes "marginal" knowledge and "discourses of difference" organized around such issues as gender, race, ethnicity, and class identities, elevating these marginal voices to equitable or even superior standing with traditional curriculum canons. Traditional knowledge is not ignored, but when it is studied, the effort should be to examine the content—to "deconstruct" the "text"—to see how it shapes one's notions of difference (race, gender, and so on) and contributes to elevating some segments of society to power and affluence but reduces others to subaltern status. This "rubs against the grain" of traditional-minded curriculum theorists.

POSTMODERNISM AND PHILOSOPHY

Postmodernism is not solely a brainchild of philosophers, but certainly philosophers have contributed a fair share to its genesis and development. Some postmodernists prefer the word *theory* to *philosophy* because they want to avoid traditional metanarratives and false separations between fields of knowledge, such as the boundary lines that keep traditional academic disciplines remote from each other. It is reasonable to speak of postmodern philosophy, however, if it is understood as not signifying an overriding agreement or unity of thought. If postmodernism, generally speaking, is parasitic on the modern, then this is no less true of postmodern philosophy, which seems fascinated with, even if highly critical of, what modern philosophy has wrought. So, a brief review sketch is in order to provide a context.

An earlier chapter examined the philosophy of pragmatism, which rejects metaphysical views of a block universe, recognizes that knowledge is provisional and uncertain, and involves a commitment to ameliorating or solving human problems, a commitment in which education takes a central role. Its chief proponents expressed optimistic hope for the future and the need for human action to solve problems. Pragmatism went into decline by the mid-twentieth century, but in its recent resurgence, neopragmatism identifies with certain postmodern themes in philosophy and education, such as a rejection of metanarratives and aversion to objective certainty, views that also were present in classic pragmatism's rejection of the "quest for certainty."

The postmodern consciousness responds negatively to behaviorism for its totalizing view of scientific objectivity and its reduction of human intentions and actions to a technology of behavior. Postmodernism also responds negatively to analytic philosophy because of its affinity with positivism and objectivism; however, postmodernism responds positively to analytic philosophy's sensitivities to language, particularly the later works of Ludwig Wittgenstein, who saw language as having a multiplicity of usages and meanings.

The influence of existentialism, phenomenology, and hermeneutics also was explored, including the perspectives of Friedrich Wilhelm Nietzsche, Martin Heidegger, and Jean-Paul Sartre. Nietzsche challenged conventional philosophy with his radical moral and political views. Heidegger promoted the examination of singularity and particularity, not history writ large, as Hegel or Marx would have it. Sartre developed the view that people must fashion their own meaning in the world, and his acceptance of Marxism was qualified by an insistence that no objective determinism could exist. Postmodernists find some support in these views, particularly the rejection of universal objectivity and the emphasis on particularity—themes that find sympathetic reception in postmodern philosophy and philosophy of education.

A previous chapter sketched a picture of Marx and how the mantle of Western Marxism eventually was passed to critical theory. A new outlook emerged that rejected class conflict as the central struggle and looked to structural changes in Western societies and conflicts among dominant and subordinate cultural groups. Theodor Adorno, Max Horkheimer, and Jurgen Habermas developed interdisciplinary studies of society and culture, and the term *critical theory* came to be applied. In turn, critical theory has been an important component of postmodern philosophical and educational theory.

For the most part, modern philosophy presents themes and ideas from which many postmodernists draw sustenance, although disagreement and repulsion exist, as well. With this background in mind, it is possible to understand better the context for postmodern philosophers because they criticize as well as adopt elements from their predecessors.

Postmodern Philosophy and Its European Backgrounds

Most generative postmodern ideas have come out of European philosophy, particularly from French thinkers. Although many philosophers have contributed important elements to the postmodern thrust, for purposes of illustration, the work of two leading French philosophers will be considered briefly: Foucault and Derrida. Although they rarely if ever referred to their own works as postmodern, their ideas have generated much commentary and stimulated philosophical thought that is characteristic of postmodernism.

Michel Foucault (1926–1984)

Michel Foucault is perhaps best known for writing philosophical histories on how notions about truth have their origins in historical conflict and struggle, and how these truth notions exercise power over institutions, social systems, and personal identities. For example, in *The Order of Things*, Foucault conducts an "archaeology of the human sciences" (psychology, sociology, and anthropology) to show how the modern view of man developed, not as a child of God or as a thinking being but as an object of study with predictable traits of behavior. This view did not appear until the concepts and methods of modern science were applied to the human sciences in the nineteenth century. In part, it was an outgrowth of the norms demanded by industrial society, but it was also a result of changing views of objective knowledge and truth. Foucault suggests that the modern concept of humanity may have run its course, because the human sciences that give it universality and objectivity mask all sorts of modern techniques of manipulation, domination, and power—techniques that control how people see themselves and discipline themselves to fit into various roles demanded by the existing political, social, and economic order.

In other studies, Foucault examines the truth/power connection in specific contexts, conducting what he calls a "genealogy" of how people use techniques of power and control to constitute themselves as subjects (selves) and objects of knowledge (things). His approach develops historical understandings from within specific historical events, or what he calls "eventalization." Rather than attempting to find uniform principles or objective anthropological traits to explain history as the way events necessarily had to occur, eventalization looks at breaches in the historical flow—singular historical events that become highly significant in how people define and organize themselves. For example, in *Madness and Civilization*, he examines how people came to define insanity and then built asylums to treat it; in *Discipline and Punish*, he does the same with criminality and prisons. His intent is to reveal how people developed institutions around particular notions of insanity and criminality when other ways of seeing these conditions might have been chosen at the time. In other words, Foucault attempts to understand how connections, strategies, meanings, and social forces and processes come together in historical events to send us in certain directions rather than in others.

By emphasizing singular events, Foucault is not looking simply for breaks in an otherwise-seamless weave of history; rather, specific historical events are made by multiple processes, including past practices, present variations, and social inventiveness. Rather than trying to find universal causal forces to explain history, the task is to look for *multiple* influences within historical events. For example, in his study of criminality and imprisonment, Foucault argues that people made the connection of imprisonment with schooling practices and military discipline. It is not that one of these influences caused the other (the existence of schools did not cause prisons to appear); rather, analysis of the processes internal to the historical development of prisons leads not to causes, but to a "polymorphism" of relations that induce people to conduct and govern themselves in particular ways at that historic moment. In other words, the ways people come to relate to each other in one social institution (such as how teachers and students relate to each other in school) establish patterns of relations that induce them to act in similar patterns in new institutional frameworks they might develop. These patterns, because they are familiar and appear to be the natural way of doing things, may not fit the new frameworks.

For example, prisons came about due to several factors. One was technology that resulted in new forms of architecture (such as buildings made of concrete and steel) that permitted secure forms of incarceration and surveillance of prisoners. Another was the development of strategies and tactics to control criminal behavior, without the public brandings, mutilations, and cruel executions that sometimes resulted in violent public disorder in the past. New theories also had impacts, such as ideas about humanitarian reform and the rehabilitation of criminals. All of these techniques, practices, and ideas were connected with reform ideas about schooling and military discipline, and they led to new ways to organize and operate prisons and to treat those incarcerated in prisons. Foucault maintains that the development of prisons did not come about by some external causal force; rather, prisons were rational and calculated measures connected to prevailing concepts of knowledge, truth, and the proper way to run institutions. The new institutions were meant to address perceived needs of the time, and existing ideas were reshaped into new narratives or discourses about the way to run institutions (or what counts as truth and knowledge in operating them). The result was a new "regime of truth" that exercised power and control over people and institutions. Power in this sense is not something people possess, nor is it imposed from without; it is found in the ways people conduct and govern themselves and how they perceive and define themselves and the society in which they live.

It could be argued that Foucault merely creates another narrative about human history and how historical events shape and are shaped by notions of truth and power, but the way he uncovers the subtleties of the relations of truth, knowledge, and power, and how individual and social identities are formed as a result, has provided new ways of viewing historical processes, ways not burdened by old metanarratives of unfolding causal forces such as Hegel or Marx envisioned. Indeed, for Foucault all disciplines are involved with power—political, economic, cultural, educational, and so forth. Postmodernists take Foucault to mean that the situations people face today, such as power regimes that pass themselves off as necessary and historically determined, are not the result of inevitable destiny but of human invention in specific historical contexts. If conditions are to be changed, then they must—once again—be changed by human invention, and this will involve what is considered at the time to be true knowledge and how people define and exercise power as a result. Great care must be taken in making changes, however, because people might carry over into the new situation unconscious or assumed "true" patterns of relations that may lie at the heart of their difficulties with the status quo. Moreover, even when people create truly *new* patterns to escape old conditions, they might only be creating new power relations that will control them in ways they are unable to predict.

Jacques Derrida (1930–)

Jacques Derrida has contributed significant philosophical critiques of the *logocentrism* of Western philosophy, and he has had an important influence on several fields, including literature and literary criticism. In *Of Grammatology*, Derrida holds that the philosophical quest of traditional metaphysics was to understand *logos* (from the Greek, meaning "speech, word, or reason," the central controlling rational principles of the universe). Philosophers have assumed at least since Aristotle that the human mind has a direct representational connection with the external world, and *logos* is the organizing rational principle of that world. Philosophers (or any speakers or writers, for that matter) use speech and writing to *represent* (or signify) something. Words and combinations of words are the *representations* (or signs) that stand for things, ideas, or any objects of thought. So, philosophers provide analyses, orderings, and descriptions of what they purport to be accurate *representations* of *logos;* that is, what appears to the mind or intellect is reported or described as representative of logos.

This metaphysical quest has resulted in contradictions and paradoxes. As Derrida sees it, this is because philosophers' representations do not belong to some external *logos* hidden from the rest of the people, but to the language people use— that is, to discourses, writings, or texts. To put it simply, language comes *before* knowledge, and word meanings are unstable and difficult to control with any certainty. Derrida sought to uncover and illuminate the instabilities and contradictions of language and tried to demystify them. Any universal meanings are withheld from us because of the vagaries of words and meanings, under which circumstances it is impossible to achieve exacting and universal clarity. In short, all people have is text, and nothing more. What is needed, then, is to "deconstruct" texts rather than try to make them reflect *logos* with exacting accuracy. The critic must work from inside a text, but not in order to get an objective view of *logos* or even of what the speaker/author/ philosopher really means; rather, the critic looks at how the vagaries of language confuse central meanings of texts. Part of the difficulty is that people never are fully in control of the language they use because words are representations with variable shades of meaning. When one defines a word, one recognizes that it could have several meanings and finds that it also relates to other words and their meanings. The author and the readers/listeners bring to a discourse their own shades of meanings shaped by experience, and the context in which the writing and reading occurs can further influence the understanding of readers/listeners. In other words, what people get when they encounter a text is not an objective account of *logos* or even what the author necessarily meant, but rather *their* current interpretation or understanding of that text. This understanding becomes, so to speak, their own "text" of the text.

A Derridian scenario can be stated this way: Consider a woman trying to shape an idea or understanding. As the woman seeks clarity and understanding, she tries to put the idea into words. As she struggles with the project, she is confronted with choosing exactly the right words to convey as precisely as possible just how she perceives the matter, but as soon as she chooses a word, she finds that it only implies or relates to other words. She might feel the need to talk with other people, to reflect aloud, and to receive criticism. In the process of discussion, she revises, discards, changes words and descriptions, and receives suggestions for additional changes. Next she might try to commit her thoughts to paper, and once again she confronts words and slippery meanings. If this thinker is like most thinkers, she probably will not be satisfied. She might put the paper aside and resolve to come back to it later;

but even then, the words she previously wrote might strike her with variant meanings, and so she revises more.

At each step her picture changes, but now it is composed of written statements. Chances are that when she stops, the results will convey something different from her original thoughts. As soon as she chooses words and composes sentences, they suggest other words and meanings, and the meaning of her project gets broadened, restricted, or redirected. Now suppose she publishes her work or orally delivers it before an audience. Will her audience grasp what she really meant? It is not likely, because her own intended meaning has changed and probably will change in the future; in addition, her readers/listeners each will bring their own sets of experiences and related meanings to the encounter. Her words will strike them in somewhat different ways than she intends, and they will impute their own shades of meaning and inference, perhaps discuss her remarks with their friends, and even be inventive and enlarge her remarks to suit their own contexts. As Derrida puts it in *Of Grammatology*, in this kind of situation the writing has become "enlarged and radicalized"; it "no longer issues from a *logos*." This thinker's assumed apprehension of *logos,* including her original thought and its later refinements, has been deconstructed of its original "truth."

Derrida coined a term for this kind of dilemma: *differance*. It is a combination of *difference* and *defer* to indicate how one's efforts at speech and writing always confront differences in interpretation and the relations of meanings. This exists not only in how one word implies other words, but also in how people understand or use words. People find themselves having to defer to the complexities and interplay of meanings encountered in any attempt to establish a central meaning. A system of signs and symbols—or language—simply cannot accomplish the task with absolute precision. Philosophers, in their efforts to find *logos* (central or universal principles and structures) have, in effect, merely played with words, substituting one version of *logos* for another. The result has been interminable disputes about nature and culture, mind and body, subject and object, being and becoming, and so on.

From Derrida's standpoint, philosophers have celebrated the *signifier* (reason, mind, consciousness) over the *signified* (words, signs, language), when it is the signified—the words and signs—that shape our thinking. In other words, philosophers have gotten it backwards, or at least out of kilter. Think of it this way: Philosophers have assumed a "metaphysics of presence" wherein the mind, the rational "organ," has a presence to *logos* such that it can apprehend it and "read" its intelligible features. Language is seen then as merely a tool, a medium by which to report philosophical findings about *logos*. The assumption is that mind precedes language (or words and signs), but as Derrida might ask, what would happen if we assumed that language precedes minds—that is, that we have minds because we have language? Another way to say this is that what we call *mind* comes from our cultural texts and how we read or interpret them. As Derrida puts it, all we have is text, and all we know is text.

Critics might say that Derrida merely elevates language over thought and that the "deconstruction" of cultural texts only reduces texts down to their "destruction." As some critics of postmodernism point out, the postmodern consciousness seems too prone to nihilism and relativism, too ready to say that because no central truth exists, everything is relative and any interpretation is legitimate; it leads to an ethical relativism where everything is permissible. However, this is not what Derrida argues, for he insists on a greater sensitivity to the dispersal and interplay of meanings throughout language, of how words refer to other words and meanings, and how each of us interprets meanings as a result. Furthermore, the thoughts that people have arise out of their historical context, their cultural epoch, their language and fund of meanings, and the uses to which they put these things. In short, what we think we know is unstable. This does not mean that we cannot develop understandings and take moral positions on issues we deem important; rather, our understandings and positions have no special privileged status over others'. It does not mean that we cannot communicate with each other, but it does mean that communication is problematic and inexact.

Criticisms of Postmodernism

In some respects, key postmodern themes are echoes of previous philosophical views. Postmodernists' disaffection with the status quo reflects elements of both Marxism and pragmatism. However, Marxism had a utopian vision of a new socialist society and pragmatism had a vision of a more democratic society, but postmodernism seems to have no comparable vision, at least where its Marxist and pragmatist critics are concerned.

In *Against Postmodernism*, Alex Callinicos uses a Marxist perspective to critique postmodernism's rejection of objectivity and its acceptance of a subjectivism composed of "incoherent sub- and trans-individual drives and desires." Contrary to its anti-realism claims, postmodernism embraces changes in the socioeconomic world that it interprets as moving away from industrial mass production toward a postindustrial system where theoretical research is "the engine of growth." Callinicos argues that this view is based on false assumptions because mass production and mass communications are still present, but he also sees how the view has an obvious appeal to the generation that came of age during the "revolutionary" 1960s. By the 1980s, many of its members were disillusioned that a socialist revolution would occur, but now occupying middle class professional, managerial, or administrative positions, and relatively comfortable with their material possessions, they became obsessed with consumerism, "discriminating" taste, and narcissistic preoccupation with "youthful" physique and appearance. Apocalyptic in tone, postmodernist intellectuals of this generation anticipated imminent collapse of the existing social order, but with their hope in a socialist revolution now gone, they seem unable to develop a positive belief in any future system. The "revolutionary resistance" of their youth now reduced to consumption and an attitude of ironic distance from the fate of the world, they find solace in philosophical pronouncements of apparent profundity but genuine obscurity, claiming nothing can be done. Callinicos dismisses such postmodern philosophers as akin to intellectuals who fiddle while Rome burns.

Neopragmatism projects a more optimistic countenance, however, and although it finds agreement with some postmodern themes, it also finds major points of disagreement. Richard Bernstein calls for finding common ground to meet the crucial "ethical-political" needs of the present day. Where postmodernists see ruptures in philosophical thought, Bernstein finds hope, not gloom, and he calls for contemporary philosophers to see themselves as fallible but engaged thinkers who are part of a community of inquirers. In a similar vein, Cornel West maintains that what is needed is a helpful response to contemporary issues, particularly cultural diversity and the need to include marginal groups in mainstream social life. Likewise, Richard Rorty argues that the lack of a great unifying theory does not mean that people should sink into negative despair but that they should seek solidarity with others to overcome cruelty in the world. These critics agree that philosophical arguments should be tested for how well they help solve problems in social life, not how well they represent the universal or find fault with claims about it.

Much criticism has been directed at the rather arcane and "transgressive" jargon postmodernists often use, a language as confusing to many philosophers as it is to the general public. Postmodernists' concern with fragmentation and overbearing rationalism might promote misleading "either-or" thinking, as can be seen in the call to escape the current nostalgia for wholeness and to "wage a war on totality," as if the only choice is *either* to yearn for wholeness *or* to war against totality. As Jurgen Habermas points out, the postmodern suspicion of totality is hardly new because classic pragmatists long ago warned against all-encompassing universals, opting for a fallibilistic consciousness rather than either absolute certainty or despairing nihilism. Rorty's postmodernist features are obvious, but he argues that postmodern leftists are so fearful of complicity with bourgeois liberalism that they have forgotten to fear political impotence, and they have abandoned *electoral* politics for *cultural* politics. Although their concern about class, race, and gender is admirable, their "politics of difference" and fear of liberalism lead them to avoid the mundane world of real politics where battles against "the strong depriving the weak" and "the rich ripping off the poor" must be fought. If postmodern leftists give up on democratic politics because they think the system is irredeemable, they risk becoming like the cynical critics who always knew democracy simply could not work.

POSTMODERN PHILOSOPHY AND EDUCATION

Variety is characteristic of postmodern philosophy of education, although its strongest element seems to be derived from the Western Marxist tradition of critical theory. Giroux is among the most prominent exponents of postmodern critical theory in philosophy of education. In addition, Peter McLaren developed an ethnographic approach closely aligned with Giroux, calling it "critical pedagogy." Others in the postmodern vein include Cleo Cherryholmes, who developed a poststructuralist critical pragmatism, and C. A. Bowers, who distances himself from critical theory and champions what he calls postliberalism. Numerous other contributors to postmodern education could be included, such as William Stanley, who joins postmodern critical pedagogy to the social reconstructionist tradition in education.

Critical theory contains strong elements of Marxism, but the postmodern suspicion of metanarratives also is directed at Marxist thought, so postmodern critical theory has made some adjustments. In *Border Crossings*, Henry Giroux credits

Samuel Bowles and Herbert Gintis for energizing radical education in the late 1970s with their Marxist interpretation of education as a form of social reproduction. Pierre Bourdieu provided a similar influence with his Gramscian perspective that schools reproduce "cultural capital" for those occupying positions of advantage. In Giroux's opinion, both views were too heavily influenced by Marxist theories of class conflict as the explanatory principle for domination, and they lacked a larger view of power along the lines of Foucault. Old-style Marxism has receded, but Giroux maintains it is still important to understand Marxist tradition in order to develop an effective criticism of modernism, even as it is also necessary to avoid the totalizing language of traditional Marxism. From Giroux's perspective, the philosophical task is to rethink the purpose and meaning of education as a convergence of modernism and postmodernism. On the one hand, he wants to retain the modernists' belief in human reasoning to overcome suffering (but without its pretensions to universality), and he values the modernists' emphasis on ethical, historical, and political discourse. On the other hand, he seeks social change and justice by emphasizing marginal discourses and the politics of difference to redefine relations between the margins and the center of society.

Critical theorist Michael Apple takes exception and maintains that class is more significant than postmodernists recognize, and that gender and race cannot be separated from class. He notes that a significant factor among people on the margins of American culture is the greater percentage of low incomes and unemployment among women and people of color. This shows that race and gender are not separate from class, and postmodernists err when they fail to recognize this. From Apple's more orthodox perspective, attention should be given to material conditions, class conflict, and the social structures that support them; educational theory that fails to do so is thereby weakened.

McLaren notes that although critical theorists have much in common, such as a Marxist background, they also show divergence—particularly the difference between the highly theoretical Aronowitz/Giroux approach and McLaren's ethnographic approach of "critical pedagogy." In *Life in Schools*, McLaren argues that critical pedagogy is not a singular set of ideas; rather, its common objective is to empower the powerless and to overcome inequities and injustices. Critical pedagogy challenges the way schools support dominant power elites and maintain existing inequities, and it envisions schools as agencies in which self- and social empowerment can be enhanced. Thus, critical pedagogy is "irrevocably committed to the side of the oppressed." It opposes positivistic, ahistorical, and depoliticized education and is particularly attuned to the politics of power relations found in schools that are part of the larger society. McLaren has increasingly called for greater unity among critical pedagogy advocates, and using elements of Marxist concern for socioeconomic conditions, he urges less cultural criticism and more social activism regarding educational and social transformations.

Cherryholmes prefers the term *poststructuralism* over *postmodernism,* primarily because he sees structuralism as the major obstacle to overcome in modern education, an argument he develops in *Power and Criticism: Poststructural Investigations in Education.* As Cherryholmes sees it, structuralism is a form of positivism with its roots in the Enlightenment tradition of rational control over human affairs. Structuralism presents the larger problem because it has been so intrusive in modern education, with its theory of rational linear progress and control. This is seen in the emphasis on a rigidly structured curriculum, the reliance on testing and sorting, and the extent of bureaucratic control. Simply described, structuralist theory defines social systems by the interconnections of the various parts with each other and with the whole, and it seeks to uncover the rational principles for the structural framework of social systems and schools. As such, structuralism is a metanarrative that says that structure is the key to *logos*.

Cherryholmes's version of poststructuralist thought, on the contrary, uses the work of Foucault and Derrida to analyze and deconstruct the assumptions of structuralism. The need is to go beyond mere negation, however, and Cherryholmes uses elements of Dewey and Rorty to develop what he calls "critical pragmatism" as a possible response to structuralist assumptions in education. He differentiates critical pragmatism from the vulgar pragmatism that uncritically accepts conventional discourses and uses education for functional and utilitarian purposes. Critical pragmatism emphasizes a sense of postmodern crisis and a thoroughgoing examination of standards of value and belief, how institutions are organized and conducted, and how people perceive and treat others.

Bowers takes a different stance from the other authors, and although he stands outside the tenor of the postmodern radical Left, he can be placed under the postmodern umbrella of variety. In *Elements of a Post-Liberal Theory of Education*, he examines the works of Carl Rogers, B. F. Skinner, Paulo Freire, and John Dewey, a divergent group of individuals that he believes represent various points within the liberal spectrum. Although he recognizes important contributions of liberalism, he claims that it stands as a "regime of truth," like those Foucault criticizes. Bowers's intent is to go beyond liberalism because he believes that its conceptual framework is too limiting and might contribute to the crisis in people's sense of social purpose and cultural authority. This gives his thought a postmodern thrust but one that includes cultural conservation, as well as negation. He attempts to update liberalism by using its "language of possibility" in contexts unknown to its founders, such as the ecological crisis.

Like the critical theorists, Bowers wants a "language of empowerment," but he distances himself from neo-Marxist critical theory because he believes that it is untested and inadequate to provide a basis for the radical empowerment needed today. He accepts Dewey's view of social intelligence and wants to preserve progressive liberal achievements in politics and education, but he believes that liberal individualism encourages the pursuit of self-interest, which accounts for such problems as the ecological crisis. What Bowers wants is a theory of education that conserves the "community of memory" of significant cultural achievements and that builds a reflective community that looks to the future. This includes a conception of individualism based on political participation and the common good.

Aims of Education

Giroux stresses that ethics must be a central concern to critical education, particularly the different ethical discourses that offer students a richer fund of meanings and help them relate to diversity in the wider society. This enables students to understand how an individual's experience is influenced by different ethical discourses and how ethical relations are formed between the self and others, including others of different background, origin, and perspective. The basic function of this process is to engage students in *social discourse* that helps them reject needless human suffering and exploitation, and the purpose is to develop a social sense of responsibility for others, including those considered "outsiders" on the margins of social life. Put another way, the aim is to develop student identities that enable them to struggle against inequality and to expand basic human rights. In this sense, then, the aim of education is emancipation from oppression.

Social discourse is a crucial consideration. In *Border Crossings*, Giroux maintains that postmodern critical theory views the production of meaning as more important than the production of labor in shaping the boundaries of human existence. The Marxist theory of inevitable class conflict between capital and labor fails to explain human circumstances, mainly because social conditions based on religion, gender, race, and ethnicity have dynamics that cannot be reduced simply to *class* conflict. How personal identities are influenced by language—by narratives and discourses—is more significant, so postmodernist critical theory concentrates on "the world of the discursive," in which signifying terms and practices affect how persons relate to themselves, to others, and to the surrounding physical and cultural environment. In this sense, then, the world of conscious life is a "textual" world—a "text" (or "discourse") that can be interpreted, analyzed, and reshaped or "reinvented." It is a text from which people develop their sense of self and their sense of social and cultural relations.

The discursive world is complex, not a simplistic world that can be explained neatly by binary oppositions such as class conflict or by rule-bound determinism found in the "laws" of science and economics. Recognition of the importance of signs and meanings does not imply ignoring political and economic forces; instead, it means giving the discursive an important place in understanding how personal and social identities and meanings are made and how they play powerful roles in shaping privilege, oppression, and conflict. In Giroux's perspective, the postmodernist aim of emancipation from oppression strives "to de-territorialize the map of dominant cultural understanding."

McLaren makes the point this way: Education should result in self- and social empowerment. He criticizes the American tradition in which schools attempt to develop a democratic and egalitarian society, with the traditional humanities curriculum informing students about humane values and ethical standards. As McLaren sees it, contemporary schools do precious little to promote even the Western humanist tradition, and the assumption that schooling produces social and economic mobility must be compared against an actual record of serving the interests of the affluent. This latter condition is seen in recent conservative reforms, where aims and curriculum are geared to the marketplace and international economic competition.

Dominant interests in control of education assume that existing educational arrangements are necessary, schools should serve the status quo, and all people—citizens, policy makers, and educators—should rely on scientific predictability and measurement to make educational decisions. They believe that students need to become educated in social and technical knowledge before they can become effective moral agents. McLaren, commenting negatively on some postmodern excessiveness in criticism of cultural texts, wants critical pedagogy, on the contrary, to assume that education for self- and social empowerment is *ethically prior* to accumulation of knowledge, although knowledge acquisition occurs along with empowerment. McLaren's point is that the primary aim of self- and social empowerment is to develop students' commitment to a social transformation that elevates marginalized groups, particularly the oppressed poor.

Cherryholmes also sees emancipation from oppression as an important aim of education, but in *Power and Criticism*, he highlights some notes of caution in the work of Foucault (who stressed that knowledge and truth claims are historically relative) and Derrida (who showed that meanings are dispersed and in constant play). Cherryholmes develops his argument along these lines: The prevailing discourse that supports existing educational arrangements as necessary are connected to the knowledge and truth claims of existing political power, and that particular discourse is simply unstable ideology, not timeless truth and knowledge. For Cherryholmes, then, an appropriate education would examine prevailing discourses to uncover the claims and instabilities of the dominant order and to recognize those discourses that oppress and those that can be built upon to liberate and expand human possibilities. He cautions, however, that combating oppression might involve other kinds of oppression and coercion, because people who hold power and status might not want to relinquish their privileges. Overcoming a discourse of power and its knowledge/truth claims might involve creating new discourses of power and privilege that themselves become oppressive regimes of truth, as Foucault stressed. Likewise, Derrida's conclusions about the instabilities of meanings and discourses should alert people that emancipation from an oppressive discourse could lead to a new one. Thus, Cherryholmes's critical pragmatism emphasizes helping students reflect on received as well as marginal knowledge and truth, and it is committed to helping students develop new discourses of emancipation. He also emphasizes Dewey's view of the experimental nature of education and of human fallibility; that is, the conclusions people draw and the choices they make *also* have political, moral, and ethical consequences. Those conclusions and choices must be subjected to frequent evaluation and readjustment or reconstruction.

Bowers advocates the restoration of community as the essential aim of education. He gives historic liberalism a culturally conservative analysis, but he also promotes a radical "bioregional" education that emphasizes building a culture in harmony with the natural environment. Important educational objectives include knowledge of worthwhile cultural traditions for a "community of memory"; understanding the self as a social being, including understanding historical forces that help constitute personal identity and social consciousness; and educating individuals for effective membership in a social and natural ecological community. He stresses the need to move beyond the liberal view of the autonomous individual to a view of the individual as a social-cultural being. In this view, language is the constituting ground of individual being and should be the starting point for education. People need to stop defining knowledge and learning in terms of traditional literacy; instead, oral communication should be included as an important feature of literacy, with emphasis on a shared language, how people use language and how it uses them, and communicative competence as preparation for membership in a political community.

Methods and Curriculum

Generally, postmodernists hold that the curriculum should not be viewed as discrete subjects and disciplines, but should include issues of power, history, personal and group identities, cultural politics, and social criticism leading to collective action. Rather than pretending that education has no connection with politics, postmodernists connect educational materials and processes (means) with the imperatives of a democratic community (ends). They envision a curriculum that is successful when it empowers people and transforms society, not when it maintains privileged economic and political interests. It is a curriculum that organizes itself from the inside out, so to speak—that is, from the concrete personal identities, histories, and ordinary experiences of students outward to the more abstract meanings of culture, history, and politics rather than the other way around. In this respect, postmodernists who follow this line of reasoning harken back to a central Deweyan concept of making the learner's experience the basic starting point.

Aronowitz and Giroux have treated extensively the debate about education among conservatives, liberals, and radicals in *Education Under Siege* and in *Postmodern Education*. They note an aggressive conservatism that has taken the initiative in education, redefining the curriculum by waging a cultural war in the schools against liberal and leftist ideas. Conservatives understand the school as a political site that can be used to help make their ideas dominant across the culture. For example, Allan Bloom, in *The Closing of the American Mind*, promotes the immersion of higher-education students in a curriculum that in his words is "universalistic" and "imperialistic" and whose main reason for existence is to preserve Western culture. In Giroux's opinion, works like Bloom's are unwittingly helpful to the radical Left because the neoconservative political agenda might help educators see schools as *active arenas of cultural politics* rather than simply as places where cultural domination and hegemony are reproduced.

The conservative ascendancy has led to school reforms that maintain traditional curricula, cut school budgets, and demand that schools cater to business needs. As a result, education as cultural politics has taken on added meaning for postmodern radical educators who question conservative reforms, just as they question the status of the scientific paradigm of thought in curriculum and evaluation. Postmodernists reject distinctions between high and low culture and maintain that the popular culture (such as the entertainment media, popular novels, and rock music) is deserving of study—not for emulation but as material to be analyzed and deconstructed to show how it helps or hurts.

Because postmodernists reject master narratives, they favor narratives from those who suffer marginalization because of race, gender, class, ethnic identity, or sexual orientation. They value the study of people who are on the margins for the specific histories and cultural contributions each can bring to the educational setting, curricular inclusions that help students understand the boundaries that often affect personal and social well-being. In addition, postmodernists spurn intellectual elites who set themselves above history and attempt to "get it right" for the rest of the people, so they promote a plurality of voices in the curriculum by including marginal narratives that in Giroux's words "represent the unrepresentable." Along with Foucault, they see reason and knowledge from within particular historical contexts of status and power, and students are encouraged to identify themselves in relation to the human struggles of those contexts. They want a variety of narratives to be included in the curriculum to help enlighten and liberate human possibilities.

An important aspect of curriculum for critical pedagogy is the inclusion of the ordinary, everyday experience of students as legitimate elements for study. This includes the competing identities, cultural traditions, and political outlooks that students bring with them, and it refuses to reduce the issues of power, justice, and equality to a single master discourse. Critical pedagogy recognizes that students' personal identities develop over time and are influenced by many factors, including personal experience. Thus, the everyday experience of students can be used (in addition to officially sanctioned knowledge) as serious objects of study. In critical education, the curriculum is developed as part of the ongoing engagement of students with a variety of narratives that can be reinterpreted and reformulated culturally and politically.

From a postmodernist critical perspective, then, the issue is not simply an argument for or against a curriculum composed of established canons of knowledge, but one that remakes the meaning and use of canons of knowledge. Generally, critical pedagogy emphasizes the need to break down traditional disciplinary boundaries in favor of interdisciplinary studies and a conception of knowledge that does not depend on traditional subject-matter disciplines. In some respects, this resembles what pragmatists recommended, especially the "problems" approach to the curriculum in which knowledge is drawn from many disciplines and integrated around a particular problem or issue. As Giroux puts it in *Border Crossings,* the curriculum must be "reclaimed as a cultural politics" and "a form of social memory." The traditional disciplines of history and literature, for example, with their various theories of history and interpretations of literary genres, always have served as forms of cultural politics and social memory. However, from Giroux's perspective, cultural politics involves understanding the production, creation, and interpretation of knowledge as part of a broader attempt to create public cultures. What is meant by "social memory" includes the everyday and the particular as a basis for learning, and from this one can proceed to traditional knowledge and popular culture as elements for study and critical evaluation to inform personal experience. An important consideration crucial to postmodernist critical theory is that such a curriculum must elevate the "silenced" narratives on the margins in order to avoid a totalizing outcome that maintains existing arrangements of power and privilege. A curriculum of this kind creates in students a social memory that is neither singular nor totalizing, but an enlarged understanding that includes voices ranging from the center of culture to the margins.

A major concern of postmodern pedagogy is to overcome the Enlightenment belief that the "universal laws of Nature" can, with the cold light of reason, be read from the face of an intelligible universe. According to Giroux, such a view of reason is not innocent because it promotes a "hidden curriculum" that, with its self-confident belief in the power of objective rationalism, exercises a totalizing form of power over thought and knowledge. Critical pedagogy urges educators to be skeptical of claims to "objective" and "universal" knowledge, because such claims put knowledge outside the history of human experience, timeless and untainted by ideology, beyond criticism and dialogue. Giroux argues that people must regain a sense of alternatives by combining a language of critique and possibility. Postmodern feminism, for example, exemplifies such an alternative in its critique of patriarchy that has opened many people's eyes to gender inequalities and to new forms of identity and social relations for women. Such critiques help extend human understanding of individual freedom and social responsibility, awakening people to new understandings of the oppression of individuals and groups on the basis of gender. Criticisms from the margins help promote useful utopian thought, not a distopianism that looks only backward and offers no viable options for how to extend human freedom and social responsibility in the present and future. Through a critical approach, the future is kept open with new possibilities, not frozen over by views that are ahistorical and closed.

Bowers combines elements of Freire and Dewey in a perspective that recognizes the danger of accepting received knowledge and existing conditions as inevitable. Unlike the radical perspective of the critical theorists, however, Bowers gives greater emphasis to cultural conservation. He recognizes that conservation must proceed with care and that education in critical awareness must accompany the emphasis on social responsibility. He faults Dewey and Freire for their emphasis on "living forward" at the expense of historical understanding and appreciation of what he calls "the community of memory." He argues that this continuous forward movement is a weakness of liberalism generally because it encourages individuals to escape community restraints and to make moral judgments merely a concern of relativistic individual interpretation.

According to postmodernists, liberalism promotes a view of individuality as self-interest that leads to the exploitation of other people and the environment. As a remedy, Bowers wants the authority of "the community of memory" (of important traditions and social norms) to be joined with critical reflection as an integral element in making moral and ethical judgments. This recognizes the relation of knowledge, truth, and power in Foucault's sense because individuals are always located in historical events or contexts. This differs from Giroux's notion of social memory because Bowers is not so intent on the radical liberation of self, and because Bowers wants the community of memory to provide the restraints of substantive traditional values. He differentiates his view of cultural *conservation* from *conservative extremism* because the community of memory, with its expansive fund of useful meanings, can liberate and empower the self.

Role of the Teacher

As Giroux states in *Border Crossings*, Gramsci helped pave the way for seeing the significance of hegemonic power in culture, and more recently such figures as Bourdieu have reintroduced it. Gramsci's theory showed how dominant interests depend less on overt force than on hegemonic leadership that wins the consent of subordinate groups to maintain the existing social order. This consent is organized in many ways, but in schools it is found in the ways curriculum and pedagogical processes are used to support the status quo. To counter this, teachers should use the issue of difference in an ethically challenging and politically transforming way. For example, personal-social differences can be incorporated into critical pedagogy to foster understanding of how personal identities are constructed in multiple and contradictory ways. This involves students exploring their own individual histories; using self-reflection on race, gender, and class; and studying how human experiences and identities are made in different historical and social conditions. Critical pedagogy focuses on how group identities are developed in social relations, how they are defined around differences, how these factors become significant, and how such differences affect a democratic society.

In *Teachers as Intellectuals*, Giroux calls for a critical pedagogy that views teachers as "cultural workers" who are "transformative intellectuals" occupying special political and social roles. Rather than define teachers in a technical language of professionalism, critical pedagogy wants to clarify the role of teachers as cultural workers who produce more appropriate social ideologies and practices. In this view, teachers are scholars and practitioners, and their role is not simply to teach a body of knowledge but to help students understand how curricular knowledge may serve ideological and political interests in various ways. It involves not only how knowledge can be used to totalize and objectify but also how it can be used to liberate students to become critical and responsible members of a democracy. For example, feminist scholars have made persuasive arguments that politics is local and personal, and this line of reasoning may be combined with politics in its more global aspects, not simply by collapsing the political into the personal or exploding it to the global sense, but by using a political focus to help students bridge gaps between the personal and the political and to understand themselves in relation to such forces as institutional forms of racism, sexism, and class exploitation in the wider society. Being a "transformative intellectual" means helping students develop a critical consciousness that connects schooling with the public spheres of culture, history, and politics.

From another perspective, Cherryholmes looks at classroom interaction between students and teachers as a crucial consideration in teaching. An asymmetry exists because teachers have authority by virtue of their official position and greater education and experience. These factors work to limit any symmetry in the teacher–student relationship. From a critical pragmatist perspective, however, greater symmetry can be had if students learn to express themselves and if they gain sufficient confidence to explore, experiment, and take responsibility for their personal and social actions. A primary condition for improving this symmetry is for teachers to be committed to critical discourse with and among students. This involves helping students move from dependence on positivistic knowledge to genuine experiment, critical reflection, and judgment. Teachers do not relinquish responsibility for management; rather, they discourage reification of authoritative knowledge and encourage students to analyze received arguments to help make their own arguments and judgments. Cherryholmes points to the need for good arguments and judgments based on the Deweyan view of helping students express responsible concern for the daily problems of the community. Making good arguments and judgments involves values—such as human dignity, liberty, equality, and concern for others—that are necessary standards for a democratic community.

The concern with teacher–student interaction is also important for Bowers, and he highlights the school's role in socialization. Historically, primary socialization of the young was conducted mostly in families, religious institutions, and occupational settings such as apprenticeships, in accordance with the traditions governing those settings. Today, schools carry a much larger burden in the socialization process, and Bowers sees this as an important opportunity for teachers to help students question prevailing assumptions, explore complex understandings, and shape perceptions. Success in this opportunity, however, depends to a large extent on teachers understanding their roles and the political nature of education. For example, teachers must be sensitive to their influence over the language process and how it shapes the way students think. Teaching and language have important political roles in what Bowers calls "communicative competence"; that is, students learning not only explicit knowledge and spoken and written language, but also body language and attitudinal expressions of approval and disapproval, all of which transmit culture and influence student socialization. The essential functions of teaching include helping students become competent communicators, conservers of meaningful traditions, and questioners of received knowledge. Education should make explicit the beliefs and practices that are socially and individually harmful, and it should help students think about social and cultural problems that make up the crises they face today.

CRITIQUE OF POSTMODERNISM IN EDUCATION

The confusing nature of postmodernism and its relative newness make assessment difficult. Critics might note that postmodern educational recommendations are largely untested as yet, but this judgment could be made against many theoretical perspectives in education. Despite its newness, the postmodern view has some obvious strengths. One is the attention given to moral and ethical education, such as the stance by Giroux and McLaren on the inclusion of difference and marginality and how "the other" (outcasts on the margins of culture) can add important dimensions to a learning community. The emphasis on social discourse adds a powerful moral dimension by including students from the center to the margins—not to indoctrinate in a single culture but to develop personal and social identities based on deeper understandings of cultural differences. The emphasis on diversity and social discourse has the additional virtue of promoting education for a pluralistic democratic community that can counteract the development of socially destructive self-interest. The sense of postmodern crisis applies not only to culture but to the environment as well, and sensitivity to the natural environment is an added dimension for developing social responsibility. Postmodern approaches to education promise to encourage a sense of personal, social, and ecological responsibility that is missing from many other educational perspectives.

The attention given to the political nature of education is another strength, but connections between education and politics have been recognized for a long time. Plato's *Republic* is an early example of the use of education for political ends, and Marxist theory has promoted a political view of education, as well. The postmodern emphasis on the politics of difference (race, class, and gender), however, is wedded to a view of the curriculum as a type of cultural politics. Attention given to the political nature of schooling and the relations of power within the schooling process provide some essential new insights. They shed light on how personal and social identities are formed by the subtle power narratives in the curriculum and the school structure. New understandings gained from these insights can help liberate students more adequately, just as they also might help educators become sensitive to the broader dimensions of their work.

The postmodern attention to language, to discourse and narrative that shape people's minds, calls for greater attention to how the curriculum and the teaching-learning process serves to liberate or oppress. Developing students' sense of membership in a political community, including a community that is dedicated to empowerment and freedom from cultural oppression, and one that understands and protects the bioregion, has strong potential for enhancing ethical and political growth. However, the reminder by Cherryholmes that discourses of difference might lead to new oppressive regimes is a healthy reminder for constant attention to the ethical and moral directions that discourses in education can take.

Finally, the crucial role of the teacher as a transformative intellectual whose role is to help students take personal and social responsibility for their futures is an important ingredient in the postmodern view of education. The tension between the radical views of Giroux and McLaren on social memory and the view of Bowers on conserving the community of memory illustrates postmodern variety, but in other respects, this brings attention to the crucial role that teachers play in helping students develop identity and a sense of historical place. The emphasis on transformation points to a key element of postmodern thought in education, and this is the need to go beyond the mere transmittal of received knowledge to an activist stance on possibility and future directions. Despite the variety, the postmodern emphasis on empowering students to understand their past and present circumstances and on preparing them with articulated goals for the future is clearly a strength.

Some weaknesses are also troubling. Postmodernists highlight the crisis in culture and promote student identity with those who are different, but their language of possibility is academic and, as critics frequently point out, difficult to decipher. One wonders how well people on the margins can identify with it, not to mention those in the mainstream culture who control policy and perhaps could be persuaded to the strengths of some postmodern arguments if those arguments were made in more palatable language. For postmodern philosophy of education to have an impact on the "real" world of education, attention must be given, as critics point out, to a *public* language that communicates and persuades.

In some respects, postmodernists are more conscious of what they oppose than what they promote; this is revealed in the lack of attention to the sometimes particularly negative tone of their delivery. Greater attention to the positive aspects of their message and to making that language more in tune with normal discourse could add to the attractiveness of their proposals for ordinary citizens. The "real" world of education is indeed a political world in which the power of persuasion is also a form of empowerment for those who advocate new directions. However, as critics point out, postmodernists seem so intent on "cultural" politics that they forget "real" politics, where policies and processes are hammered out. It is one thing to engage in academic arguments and another thing to inform public opinion, win elections, and change policies and directions.

Another troublesome feature is the desire of postmodern critical theorists to politicize schooling. Certainly, the existing forms of control over education represent entrenched political interests, but as Cherryholmes notes, if people have learned anything from Foucault and Derrida, it is that the creation of new truth regimes and power discourses might lead to unintended consequences. Postmodern critical theory seems to maintain a lingering Marxist tendency that claims that all views except its own are mere ideology. Thus, they critique other viewpoints as "totalizing theories" or "ideologies of power and control" and place themselves on the moral high ground. Perhaps this is an inevitable outcome of any sort of theory, but postmodernism could be strengthened by more attention to these kinds of problems.

Sensitivity to human differences and oppression is among postmodernism's strongest moral qualities; in celebrating human differences, though, postmodernists might fail to recognize important commonalities. Perhaps their fascination with ruptures and fragmentation blinds them to the characteristics that human beings hold in common. The rejection of totalizing metanarratives about universal human nature need not imply a rejection of commonalities that exist across the human spectrum. Certainly postmodernists, in rejecting universals and in recognizing human diversity, would not want to suggest that human differences imply species differences among humans, because the drumbeat emphasis on difference might serve to *anchor* fragmentation and separateness rather than promote a healthy recognition of common humanity. Moreover, the postmodern desire for empowerment and freedom from oppression seems to have a universal ring to it, as does its emphasis on "the world of the discursive."

It seems to be no stretch of reason to suggest that *all* people need a sense of personal and social worth nurtured in a democratic community; a reasonable sense of security regarding safety and health; and opportunities to fulfill basic needs for food, clothing, and shelter. Variations might occur from one part of a community to another (or from one part of the globe to another) on the best ways to meet these needs, but it is pointless to deny the great deal that humans share in common, and this commonality has a universal significance that postmodernism represses in its own discourses. Moreover, a discourse that minimizes or ignores the common bonds of humanity can become a form of totalizing narrative because it marginalizes or discounts the common, and therefore "universal," connections of humanity.

Finally, despite postmodernists' aversion to defining narratives and universal truths, their fascination with discourse and deconstruction shows an affinity for a tradition in philosophical idealism that says humans are removed from ultimate truth and are limited to their texts, words, languages, and representations—human ideas. This reflects Plato's view that the human knower never could grasp fully the ultimate or universal, but only poor representations filtered through the imperfections of the knower's material existence. Indeed, the better part of philosophical valor might be to reserve judgment on whether some universal truths, philosophical or scientific, exist. People would ignore them at their own peril if they were engaged in a headlong rush to deconstruct or discount every claim. In short, postmodern thought might betray a tendency for a negative idealism. What postmodernists project as their envisioned new society is sketchy, distinguished as much by what they oppose as by what they advocate. If they embrace a multicultural society, then they are short on the sociocultural glue that will hold it together. Of course, this also could be said of several reform-minded philosophies, such as the pragmatists' view of the social reconstruction role that education could play, but at least they wrote extensively about democracy as their end in view. The discordant voices in the postmodern pantheon seem unable to focus as well as, for example, Dewey. In addition, when postmodernist educators push the view that education for self- and social empowerment is *ethically prior* to accumulation of knowledge, they assume a chicken-or-egg style of argument, an argument pragmatists would counter by saying that the learner's ethical growth occurs *along with* a growth in knowledge and capacity to act. Generally, postmodernists spurn those intellectual elites who set themselves above history and attempt to "get it right" for the rest of us, but postmodernists appear to play a similar role when they use high-blown rhetoric and arcane jargon in their own discourses, when they insist that teachers must be "transformative intellectuals," when they assert that a plurality of voices rather than a common voice is the desired path education should cultivate, and when they elevate marginal narratives over others to "represent the unrepresentable" as the correct mode of curriculum development. Surely, their educational recommendations have brought a fresh ingredient into educational debate, but all of us—postmodernists included—need to avoid hubris.

GIROUX

BORDER PEDAGOGY AS POSTMODERN RESISTANCE

In the following selection, Henry A. Giroux provides a context in which postmodern thought can have an impact on education. Although he speaks specifically to the issue of racism, his comments also can be extended to additional forms of "Otherness," including gender and class identities. Notice his emphasis on how the totalizing nature of Eurocentric discourses freezes out other discourses and how inclusion of the voices of Others can enrich not only the lives of students but the lives of teachers and the larger society, as well.

Within the current historical conjuncture, the political and cultural boundaries that have long constituted the meaning of race and culture are beginning to shift. . . . First, the population of America's subordinate groups are [*sic*] changing the landscapes of our urban centers. . . . Second, while people of color are redrawing the cultural demographic boundaries of the urban centers, the boundaries of power appear to be solidifying in favor of rich, white, middle and upper classes. . . .

The dominant discourses of modernity have rarely been able to address race and ethnicity as an ethical, political, and cultural marker in order to understand or self-consciously examine the notions of justice inscribed in the modernist belief in change and the progressive unfolding of history. In fact, race and ethnicity have been generally reduced to a discourse of the Other, a discourse that regardless of its emancipatory or reactionary intent, often essentialized and reproduced the distance between the centers and margins of power. Within the discourse of modernity, the Other not only sometimes ceases to be a historical agent, but is often defined within totalizing and universalistic theories that create a transcendental rational white, male, Eurocentric subject that both occupies the centers of power while simultaneously appearing to exist outside time and space. Read against this Eurocentric transcendental subject, the Other is shown to lack any redeeming community traditions, collective voice, or historical weight—and is reduced to the imagery of the colonizer. . . .

If the construction of anti-racist pedagogy is to escape from a notion of difference that is silent about other social antagonisms and forms of struggle, it must be developed as part of a wider public disclosure that is simultaneously about the discourse of an engaged plurality and the formation of critical citizenship. This must be a discourse that breathes life into the notion of democracy by stressing a notion of lived community that is not at odds with the principals of justice, liberty, and equality. Such a discourse must be informed by a postmodern concern with establishing the material and ideological conditions that allow multiple, specific, and heterogeneous ways of life to come into play as part of a border pedagogy of postmodern resistance. This points to the need for educators to prepare students for a type of citizenship that does not separate abstract rights from the realm of the everyday, and does not define community as the legitimate and unifying practice of a one-dimensional historical and cultural narrative. Postmodernism radicalizes the emancipatory possibilities of teaching and learning as a part of a wider struggle for democratic public life and critical citizenship. It does this by refusing forms of knowledge and pedagogy wrapped in the legitimizing discourse of the sacred and the priestly; its rejecting universal reason as a foundation for human affairs; claiming that all narratives are partial; and performing a critical reading on all scientific, cultural, and social texts as historical and political constructions.

In this view, the broader parameters of an anti-racist pedagogy are informed by a political project that links the creation of critical citizens to the development of a radical democracy; that is, a political project that ties education to the broader struggle for a public life in which dialogue, vision, and compassion remain critically attentive to the rights and conditions that organize public space as a democratic social reform rather than a regime of terror and oppression. It is important to emphasize that difference and pluralism in this view do not mean reducing democracy to the equivalency of diverse interests; on the contrary, what is being argued for is a language in which different voices and traditions exist and flourish to the degree that they listen to the voices of others, engage in an ongoing attempt to eliminate forms of subjective and objective suffering, and maintain those conditions in which the act of communicating and living extends rather than restricts the creation of democratic public spheres. This is as much a political as it is a pedagogical project, one that demands that anti-racist pedagogical practices be developed within a discourse that combines a democratic public philosophy with a postmodern theory of resistance.

What is being called for here is a notion of border pedagogy that provides educators with the opportunity to rethink the relationship between the centers and the margins of power. That is, such a pedagogy must address the issue of racism as one that calls into question not only forms of subordination that create inequities among different groups as they live out their lives but, as I have mentioned previously, also challenges those institutional and ideological boundaries that have historically masked their own relations of power behind complex forms of distinction and privilege. What does this suggest for the way we develop the basic elements of an anti-racist pedagogy?

First, the notion of border pedagogy offers students the opportunity to engage the multiple references that constitute different cultural codes, experiences, and languages. This means providing the learning opportunities for students to become media literate in a world of changing representations. It means offering students the knowledge and social relations that enable them to read critically not only how cultural texts are regulated by various discursive codes, but also how such texts express and represent different ideological interests. In this case, border pedagogy establishes conditions of learning that define literacy inside the categories of power and authority. This suggests developing pedagogical practices that address texts as social and historical constructions; it also suggests developing pedagogical practices that allow students to analyze texts in terms of their presences and absences; and most important, such practices should provide students with the opportunity to read texts dialogically through a configuration of many voices, some of which offer up resistance, some of which provide support.

Border pedagogy also stresses the necessity for providing students with the opportunity to engage critically the strengths and limitations of the cultural and social codes that define their own histories and narratives. Partiality becomes, in this case, the basis for recognizing the limits built into all disclosures. At issue here is not merely the need for students to develop a healthy skepticism towards all discourses of authority, but also to recognize how authority and power can be transformed in the interest of creating a democratic society.

Within this disclosure, students engage knowledge as a border-crosser, as a person moving in and out of borders constructed around coordinates of difference and power. These are not only physical borders, they are cultural borders historically constructed and socially organized within maps of rules and regulations that serve to either limit or enable particular identities, individual capacities, and social forms. In this case, students cross over into borders of meaning, maps of knowledge, social relations, and values that are increasingly being negotiated and rewritten as the codes and regulations which organize then become destabilized and reshaped. Border pedagogy decenters as it remaps. The terrain of learning becomes inextricably linked to the shifting parameters of place, identity, history, and power. By reconstructing the traditional radical emphasis of

mapping domination to the politically strategic issue of engaging the ways in which knowledge can be remapped, reterritorialized, and decentered, in the wider interests of rewriting the borders and coordinates of an oppositional cultural politics, educators can redefine the teacher–student relationship in ways that allow students to draw upon their own personal experiences as real knowledge.

At one level this means giving students the opportunity to speak, to locate themselves in history, and to become subjects in the construction of their identities and the wider society. It also means defining voice not merely as an opportunity to speak, but to engage critically with the ideology and substance of speech, writing, and other forms of cultural production. In this case, "coming to voice" for students from both dominant and subordinate cultures means engaging in rigorous discussions of various cultural texts, drawing upon one's personal experience, and confronting the process through which ethnicity and power can be rethought as a political narrative that challenges racism as part of [a] broader struggle to democratize social, political, and economic life. In part, this means looking at the various ways in which race implicates relations of domination, resistance, suffering, and power within various social practices and how these are taken up in multiple ways by students who occupy different ethnic, social, and gender locations. In this way, race is never discussed outside broader articulations, nor is it merely about people of color.

Second, a border pedagogy of postmodern resistance needs to do more than educate students to perform ideological surgery on master-narratives based on white, patriarchal, and class-specific interests. If the master-narratives of domination are to be effectively deterritorialized, it is important for educators to understand how such narratives are taken up as part of an investment of feeling, pleasure, and desire. There is a need to rethink the syntax of learning and behavior outside the geography of rationality and reason. For example, this means that racism cannot be dealt with in a purely limited, analytical way. An anti-racist pedagogy must engage how and why students make particular ideological and affective investments and occupy particular subject positions in regard to issues concerning race and racism. This means attempting to understand the historical context and substance of the social and cultural forms that produce in diverse and multiple ways the often contradictory subject positions that give students a sense of meaning, purpose, and delight. As Stuart Hall argues, this means uncovering both for ourselves as teachers as well as for the students we are teaching "the deep structural factors which have a tendency persistently not only to generate racial practices and structures but to reproduce them through time and which therefore account for their extraordinarily immovable character." In addition to engaging racism within a politics of representation, ideology, and pleasure, it is also important to stress that any serious analyses of racism also has to be historical and structural. It has to chart out how racist practices develop, where they come from, how they are sustained, how they affect dominant and subordinate groups, and how they can be challenged. This is not a discourse about personal preferences or dominant tastes but a discourse about economics, culture, politics, and power.

Third, a border pedagogy offers the opportunity for students to air their feelings about race from the perspective of the subject positions they experience as constitutive of their own identities. Ideology in this sense is treated not merely as an abstraction but as part of the student's lived experience. This does not mean that teachers reduce their role to that of an intellectual voyeur or collapse his or her authority into a shabby form of relativism. Nor does it suggest that students merely express or assess their own experiences. Rather, it points to a particular form of teacher authority grounded in a respect for a radically decentered notion of democratic public life. This is a view of authority that rejects the notion that all forms of authority are expressions of unwarranted power and oppression. Instead, it argues for forms of authority that are rooted in democratic interests and emancipatory social relations, forms of authority that, in this case, begins [*sic*] from a standpoint from which to develop an educational project that reflects politics as aesthetics, that retains instead the significance of the knowledge/power relationship as a discourse of criticism and politics necessary for the achievement of equality, freedom, and struggle. This is not a form of authority based on an appeal to universal truths, it is a form of authority that recognizes its own partiality while simultaneously asserting a standpoint from which to engage the discourses and practices of democracy, freedom, and domination. Put another way, this is a notion of authority rooted in a political project that ties education to the broader struggle for public life in which dialogue, vision, and compassion remain critically attentive to the liberating and dominating relations that organize various aspects of everyday life.

This suggests that teachers use their authority to establish classroom conditions in which different views about race can be aired but not treated as simply an expression of individual views or feelings. . . . An anti-racist pedagogy must demonstrate that the views we hold about race have different historical and ideological weight, forged in asymmetrical relations of power, and that they always embody interests that shape social practices in particular ways. In other words, an anti-racist pedagogy cannot treat ideologies as simply individual expressions of feeling, but as historical, cultural, and social practices that serve to either undermine or reconstruct democratic public life. These views must be engaged without silencing students, but they must also be interrogated next to a public philosophy that names racism for what it is and calls racist ideologies and practices into account on political and ethical terms.

Fourth, educators need to understand how the experience of marginality at the level of everyday life lends itself to forms of oppositional and transformative consciousness. For those designated as Others need to both reclaim and remake their histories, voices, and visions as part of a wider struggle to change those material and social relations that deny radical pluralism as the basis of democratic political community. It is only through such an understanding that teachers can develop a border pedagogy which opens up the possibility for students to reclaim their voices as part of a process of empowerment and not merely what some have called an initiation into the culture of power. It is not enough for students to learn how the dominant culture works to exercise power, they must also understand how to resist power which is oppressive, which names them in a way that undermines their ability to govern rather than serve, and prevents them from struggling against forms of power that subjugate and exploit. . . . This is not to suggest that the authority of white dominant culture is all of one piece, nor is this meant to imply that it should not be the object of study. What is at stake here is forging a notion of power that does not collapse into a form of domination, but is critical and emancipatory, that allows students to both locate themselves in history and to critically, not slavishly, appropriate the cultural and political codes of their own and other traditions.

Moreover, students who have to disavow their own racial heritage in order to succeed are . . . being positioned to accept subject positions that are the source of power for a white, dominant culture. The ability of white, male, Eurocentric culture to normalize and universalize its own interests works so well . . . as a site of dominant narratives, [that it prevents] . . . black students from speaking through their own memories, histories, and experiences. . . . [We must illuminate] more clearly how power works in this society within the schools to secure and conceal various forms of racism and subjugation. Power is multifaceted and we need a better understanding of how it works not simply as a force for oppression but also a basis for resistance and self and social empowerment. Educators need to fashion a critical postmodern notion of authority, one that decenters essentialist claims to power while at the same time fighting for relations of authority and power that allow many voices to speak so as to initiate students into a culture that multiplies rather than restricts democratic practices and social relations as part of a wider struggle for democratic public life.

Fifth, educators need to analyze racism not only as a structural and ideological force, but also in the diverse and historically specific ways in which it emerges. This is particularly true of the most recent and newest expressions of racism developing in the United States and abroad among youth in popular culture, and in its resurgence in the highest reaches of the American government. This also suggests that any notion of an anti-racist pedagogy must arise out of specific settings and contexts. Such a pedagogy must allow its own character to be defined, in part, by the historically specific and contextual boundaries in which it emerges. At the same time, such a pedagogy must disavow all claims to scientific method or for that matter to any objective or transhistorical claims. As a political practice, an anti-racist pedagogy has to be constructed not on the basis of essentialist or universal claims but on the concreteness of its specific encounters, struggles, and engagements. . . .

Sixth, an anti-racist border pedagogy must redefine how the circuits of power move in a dialectical fashion among various sites of cultural production. We need a clearer understanding of how ideologies and other social practices which bear down on classroom relations emerge from and articulate with other spheres of social life. As educators, we need a clearer understanding of how the grounds for the production and organization of knowledge is [*sic*] related to forms of authority situated in political economy, the state, and other material practices. We also need to understand how circuits of power produce forms of textual authority that offer readers particular subject positions, that is, ideological references that provide but do not rigidly determine particular views of the world. In addition, educators need to explore how the reading of texts [is] linked to the forms of knowledge and social relations that students bring to the classroom. In other words, we need to understand in terms of function and substance those social and cultural forms outside the classroom that produce the multiple and often contradictory subject positions that students learn and express in their interaction with the dominant cultural capital of American schools.

Finally, central to the notion of border pedagogy are a number of important pedagogical issues regarding the role that teachers might take up in making a commitment to fighting racism in their classrooms, schools, communities, and the wider society. The concept of border pedagogy also helps to locate teachers within social, political, and cultural boundaries that define and mediate in complex ways how they function as intellectuals who exercise particular forms of moral and social regulation. Border pedagogy calls attention to both the ideological and the partial as central elements in the construction of teacher discourse and practice. In part, this suggests that to the degree that teachers make the construction of their own voices, histories, and ideologies problematic they become more attentive to Otherness as a deeply political and pedagogical issue. In other words, by deconstructing the underlying principles which inform their own lives and pedagogy, educators can begin to recognize the limits underlying the partiality of their own views. Such a recognition offers the promise of allowing teachers to restructure their pedagogical relations in order to engage in open and critical dialogue questions regarding the knowledge taught, how it relates to students' lives, how students can engage with such knowledge, and how such practices actually relate to empowering both teachers and students. Within dominant models of pedagogy, teachers are often silenced through a refusal or inability to make problematic with students the values that inform how they teach and engage the multifaceted relationship between knowledge and power. Without the benefit of dialogue, an understanding of the partiality of their own beliefs, they are cut off from any understanding of the effects their pedagogies have on students. In effect, their infatuation with certainty and control serves to limit the possibilities inherent in their own voices and visions. In this case, dominant pedagogy serves not only to disempower students, but teachers as well. In short, teachers need to take up a pedagogy that provides a more dialectical understanding of their own politics and values; they need to break down pedagogical boundaries that silence them in the name of methodological rigor or pedagogical absolutes; more important, they need to develop a power-sensitive discourse that allows them to open up their interactions with the discourses of various Others so that their classrooms can engage rather than block out the multiple positions and experiences that allow teachers and students to speak in and with many complex and different voices.

NUYEN

LYOTARD AS MORAL EDUCATOR

Contrary to many prevailing views on postmodernism, A. T. Nuyen insists that moral rules have a place in postmodern theory, even if the grand metanarratives of modernity fail to provide genuine universal guidance to moral choices. He maintains that Jean Francois Lyotard drew ideas from Wittgenstein and Kant that give direction to his ethical views. For Nuyen, Lyotard's view on "presenting the unpresentable" confronts contemporary injustice and helps people answer the question of why they should be moral at all.

The Ethical Question

. . . Admittedly, for many of Lyotard's critics, the phrase "Lyotard's postmodern ethics" is a kind of oxymoron, insofar as ethics is about the right and the just, the good and the obligatory, and insofar as Lyotard advocates a pluralism without universal rules, a postmodernism without "metanarratives." Against Lyotard's critics, it can be shown that there is a line of thought in Lyotard's postmodernism that is decidedly ethical, a line of thought consistent and robust enough to be called an ethics. As in any ethics, there is a clear identification of an ethical problem.

In *The Postmodern Condition,* Lyotard defines "postmodern as incredulity toward metanarratives" . . . . A metanarrative in turn is a "metadiscourse" which contains universal rules and principles to which we can appeal to resolve a dispute that may arise between the "small discourses," or "language games" (*petits récits*), in which different people are engaged. The history of philosophy is replete with metadiscourses "such as the dialectics of Spirit, the hermeneutics of meaning, the emancipation of the rational or working subject, or the creation of wealth". . . . The appeal to a metadiscourse is an attempt to legitimate one's own discourse. Legitimation, according to Lyotard, is characteristic of modernity. Indeed, he uses the term "*modern* to designate any science that legitimates itself with reference to a metadiscourse of this kind." Lyotard's main argument in *The Postmodern Condition* is that the modernist practice of legitimation ultimately fails. This is a familiar argument . . . that in the postmodern condition, metadiscourses have lost their authority, and it is no longer possible to appeal to rules and principles that

apply across discourses. In the postmodern condition, there are no universal rules and principles.
There are only language games, or small discourses,
each defined by its own set of rules.

In the absence of metadiscourses, a conflict
between language games cannot be resolved to the
satisfaction of all parties to the conflict. Without universal rules and principles, all that we have are rules
and principles internal to each game, or each small
discourse. To apply the rules internal to one discourse in the case of a conflict is not to resolve it: it is
to allow that discourse to dominate others that are in
conflict with it, or to allow it, as Lyotard puts it, to "totalize" the field. Thus, either a conflict remains unre-
solved, or it is dissolved into a totality dominated by
one of the discourses in conflict. Lyotard calls this
kind of conflict the differend, defining it as "a case of
conflict, between (at least) two parties, that cannot
be equitably resolved for lack of a rule of judgment
applicable to both arguments" (*The Differend*, 1988,
ix). If the postmodern condition means the death of
metanarratives, then the differend is its effect. . . .

. . . Lyotard's intention is clear: He wants to
stress the prevalence of wrongs in the postmodern
world *and* to make the normative claim that we have
to do something about these wrongs, that we cannot
let them go unnoticed. In giving us one example after
another and in returning again and again to the Holocaust, Lyotard wants to strengthen the normative
claim. To repeat, the normative claim is that "[e]very
wrong ought to be able to be put into phrases," that
"in the differend, something 'asks' to be put into
phrases, and suffers from the wrong of not being able
to be put into phrases right away." Given the ethical
demand that wrongs be put into phrases, the postmodern condition throws up an ethical problem: How
can wrongs be put into phrases? It is a problem because, as we have seen, the wrong arises in the first
place by virtue of the fact that the victim's rules of discourse are not valid, or not recognized, within the totalizing discourse. As Lyotard puts it, the victim's case
is *unpresentable* within the dominating discourse.
Thus, the ethical problem for postmodernity is how to
present the unpresentable, how to "bear witness to
differends" (13). Furthermore, Lyotard leaves the
reader in no doubt that we have to face this ethical problem with the utmost urgency, that what is
at stake is the question of life and death itself. For,
what happened to the Jews can happen again: "the

question 'Auschwitz' is also the question 'after
Auschwitz'?". . . .

Lyotard has been most consistent about the
ethical demand in the postmodern condition in the
various writings since the late seventies, even though
the contexts of the separate discussions do not always
make it clear that he has in mind the same ethical
problem. However, the link is clear enough to be seen,
and even the language remains more or less the same
throughout. Thus, toward the end of the essay "Answering the question: what is postmodernism?" Lyotard warns us that "we can hear the mutterings of the
desire for a return of terror," and urges that what must
be done is to "wage a war on totality" and to be "wit-
nesses to the unpresentable" (*The Postmodern Condition*, 82). In a recent book, *The Inhuman*, Lyotard
declares that the question of presenting the unpresentable is "the only one worthy of what is at stake in
life and thought in the coming century" (127). Lyotard has identified an ethical problem, an urgent one
"worthy of what is at stake in life and thought." In the
first half of *Just Gaming*, we find anticipated the arguments of *The Postmodern Condition* and *The Differend*. In a claim that is to become the theme of *The
Postmodern Condition*, Lyotard says that there is
"no metalanguage, and by metalanguage, I mean the
famous theoretical discourse that is supposed to
ground political and ethical decisions that will be
taken as the basis of its statements." Then, anticipating the argument in *The Differend*, Lyotard argues
that "language games are not translatable, because, if
they were, they would not be language games." Since
language games, or small discourses, are not translatable, "to import into a language game a question that
comes from another one and to impose it" amounts to
"oppression." Given the fact that there is a multiplicity of language games, the ethical problem is how to
avoid oppression. Failing to do so gives rise to the
problem of injustice, a problem that any ethical theory worth its salt must aim to solve, to resolve. Failing
to do so will perpetuate wrongs, such as the wrong
suffered by the Jewish people under Nazism, or the
wrong suffered by oppressed people everywhere.

What is the lesson from Lyotard? If Lyotard is
right, at the ethical core of all conflicts, ranging from
conflicts in the school yard leading to bullying to conflicts in the Balkans leading to ethnic cleansing, is the
problem of "presenting the unpresentable." When we
say that people are talking "at cross purposes," that

they are not "on the same wavelength," that they cannot "empathise" with each other and so on, we are in fact referring to the same ethical problem identified by Lyotard. The lesson we should learn from Lyotard is that the problem of presenting the unpresentable can have the greatest ethical consequences. This is an important lesson for moral educators in the postmodern condition.

Moral Pragmatics

Lyotard's postmodernism has many different kinds of educational implications. . . . We have seen that for Lyotard the moral question is the problem of presenting the unpresentable in the postmodern condition. But Lyotard does not just give us a diagnosis of the ethical problem in the postmodern condition. In various writings, he also suggests a response to the problem. This response consists of a political strategy and what might be called a reflective strategy. If I am right in thinking that Lyotard has offered us both a reflective strategy and a political strategy for dealing with the *wrongs* of differends, then it follows that to educate for such ethical problems is to educate in both of these aspects. To see Lyotard as a moral educator, we need to examine his political and reflective strategies for dealing with the ethical problem and to draw educational implications from them.

The political strategy can be found in *Just Gaming*. Here, Lyotard offers a strategy to avoid one discourse totalizing the others. The aim of the strategy is to "maximize as much as possible the multiplication of small narratives." Toward this aim, we ought to declare as an injustice the preventing of game playing, and to prohibit any activity that effectively restricts game playing. Lyotard writes: "Absolute injustice would occur if the pragmatics of obligation, that is, the possibility of continuing to play the game of the just, were excluded." What is advocated is similar to the libertarian strategy of prohibiting activities which cause harm to others. Indeed, Lyotard himself describes his position as "libertine or libertarian." Lyotard's conception of injustice allows us to declare unjust, for instance, terrorist activities such as hostage taking, kidnapping, blackmailing, and inflicting terror itself. Terrorism is unjust because it prevents others from playing their games: "The people whom [the terrorist] massacres will no longer be able to play the game of the just and the unjust." To demonstrate the practical power of his conception of injustice, Lyotard claims that we can use it to denounce the role of the Americans in Vietnam and that of the French in Algeria. For they "were doing something that prohibited that the whole of reasonable beings could continue to exist. In other words, the Vietnamese or the Algerians saw themselves being placed in a position where the pragmatics of obligation was forbidden them."

A question arises at this point, one that seems to have escaped Lyotard's notice. It is whether the negative rule about what is unjust, or the non-exclusion rule, is itself coherent. For, in applying it against terrorism, are we not excluding the terrorist from playing his or her terroristic game? Does the rule not preclude its own application? While Lyotard does not seem to be aware of this question, he inadvertently renders it inoperative by his answer to another question, namely: is it sufficient just to have a negative rule about what is unjust? Should such a rule not be based on, or grounded in, some positive conception of justice? Lyotard himself puts the question this way: "Can we have a politics without the Idea of justice?" Faced with this question, Lyotard admits that he hesitates between two positions: the "pagan position" of not grounding the negative rule, regarding it as something we have made up as we went along, and the "Kantian position" of regarding it as something grounded in a Kantian regulative Idea such as the Idea of justice as the proliferation of games, or the maximization of games. Taking the "pagan position" means that we regard the maximum "multiplication of small narratives" simply as a conventional rule. The problem with the "pagan position" is that there is nothing that prevents the society from making up different rules, for example, a rule that accepts rather than rules out terrorism: "A rule by convention would require that one accept . . . even Nazism. After all, since there was near unanimity upon it, from where could one judge that it is not just?" Thus, a politics that rules out terrorism is not possible without some Kantian Idea of justice.

With the Kantian position, we have a "regulator, that is a safekeeper of the pragmatics of obligation." However, how can we take the Kantian position without being committed to the Kantian metadiscourse? In the end, Lyotard settles for a modified Kantian position in which the Idea of justice (as the proliferation of games) is posited as merely a *regulative* idea rather than a determinate idea, that is, as an idea not itself grounded in any transcendental reality, any noumenality, or any

Kantian finality. . . . Rather, we act *as if* we are dealing with a community of rational beings who have come to accept the rationality of the idea of maximizing game playing. With this as a regulative idea, we have a solution to the question not noticed by Lyotard, namely how to apply the negative rule against terrorism without contradiction. We can say to the terrorist that his or her game is excluded because it minimizes rather than maximizes game playing. It is true that in applying the rule against terrorism, we exclude it, but there is no inconsistency because the rule is not applied for its own sake but rather for the sake of the regulative Idea of maximum game playing. Terrorism is ruled out because it is destructive of all other games; indeed, it is destructive of terrorism itself, as one terrorist group invariably tries to exclude other terrorist groups. By contrast, in excluding terrorism, the only thing we exclude is terrorism.

What we can learn from Lyotard's political strategy is that it must be part of the aim of education to instill in the learner the idea that we must accept certain restrictive rules and regulations as necessary for maximum game playing. What the strategy implies is that there is a need for those elements of education that strengthen the idea of citizenship and the idea of acceptable and unacceptable behavior. One problem frequently encountered here is the resistance to rule-following, which is typically seen as restrictive and undermining individuality and subjectivity. However, what we can also learn from Lyotard is that such rules and regulations do not necessarily undermine individuality and subjectivity, because they are regulative rather than determinant. Being regulative with the aim of ensuring maximum game playing, inventive individuals would be free to vary rules and regulations, thus inventing new games. Indeed, to take Lyotard seriously is to make it part of the aim of education to encourage inventiveness. One effective way to prevent one game totalizing the field is to have a proliferation of games.

In addition to the political strategy I have outlined, we can discern in Lyotard's writings what I call a reflective strategy. To guard against totalization, we need to reflect on what is not there in the games we play, what is not presented in the familiar discourses. Just because something is not there, not presented, does not mean that it does not exist, or has no right to exist. Silence does not mean absence or irrelevance. The failure to reflect in this way amounts to taking one's own discourses, or at best all the existing discourses, as

representing the totality of all there is. While this is not yet the terror of one totalizing grand narrative, it is what sets the course toward such terror. Thus, the war against totality is the struggle to raise and maintain the consciousness of what is not presented in the existing discourses; it is to present the unpresentable. The first crucial step is to develop the consciousness of the unpresentable. Since it cannot be put into phrases, we have to develop a *feeling* for it. This feeling can be generated if we *reflect* on our thinking. This feeling is a reflective judgment. "Reflective judgment" is a phrase used by Kant in the Third Critique to refer to an aesthetic judgment which is reflective, because it arises when thinking reflects on itself. It is not surprising that Lyotard turns to Kant for insights for a strategy to develop the consciousness of the unpresentable. . . .

From Lyotard's explorations of Kant's *The Critique of Judgment*, two lessons can be drawn. As Lyotard explains it in his *Lessons on the Analytic of the Sublime*, Kant's account of the sublime can be taken as an account of the presentation in thought of the unpresentable ideas of reason. Thus, in the feeling of the sublime, we have a solution to the problem of presenting the unpresentable. Learning from Lyotard, we can say that there is a need for inculcating in the learner the feeling for the sublime. . . . But the mind is able not only to present unpresentable (that is, undemonstrable) ideas of reason, but also to present unpresentable (that is, inexponible) aesthetic ideas. This is where the imagination comes to the foreground. . . . The role of the imagination has been widely recognized by educators . . . . In moral education in particular, the imagination has long been recognized as a vital ingredient in moral development. For instance, it would be hard to imagine a better way of teaching the Golden Rule, "Do unto others," and its negative form, "Do not do unto others," without asking the learner to use his or her imagination, thus imagining what it would be like to be in the other person's shoes. However, it is Lyotard who has drawn our attention to the fact that a great deal more is at stake, and hence to the urgency of developing the imaginative powers to their fullest possible extent.

The Normative Question

By "the normative question" I mean the age-old question "Why should I be moral?" To ask this question is to ask for a justification of morality's claims on us, or for a justification of the obligations of morality. . . . The frequency with which the normative question arises in the educational context is notorious. Teachers (and parents) cannot help but notice the persistence and stubbornness of the question "Why should I do that?" The ability to supply an answer to the question is the mark of a moral educator.

. . . Lyotard's view is that in the postmodern condition, we can no longer appeal to a metanarrative to justify universal rules, including moral rules. But it does not follow that there are no rules to follow, no obligations to be had. For instead of metanarratives we have the *petits récits,* the little games, the small discourses, each with its own rules. To play a game entails obeying the rules of the game. Indeed, it may be said that a game player is committed not just to the rules of the game but also to the kind of behavior that is beneficial to the game, or at least to the avoidance of behavior that is destructive of the game. . . . It is likely that any game whatsoever must include some rules that are moral in the traditional sense. For instance, the rule against cheating seems necessary for any game, for the simple reason that no game can meaningfully be played if cheating is rampant. Also, there are certain minimum obligations that a game player must take on, such as the obligation to respect any legitimate move made by another player of the game, or to respect other persons as players of the game. With this in mind, we can justify a whole host of rules traditionally seen as moral rules. . . .

The first step in answering the normative question, then, is to say that each game has its own rules and to play it we must obey its rules. Some of these rules are moral in the traditional sense of the word. The rules are binding but the real source of normativity, of the force of obligation, lies in the agent himself or herself who chooses to play a certain game, thus chooses to play by the very rules that define the game. One ought to do certain things because that is how the game is played, just as a member of a club ought to observe club rules. However, the moral skeptic is bound to ask: Why can't I choose not to play any game at all, thus choosing to follow no rules and to place myself under no obligations whatsoever? Unfortunately for the skeptic, not playing any game at all is not an intelligible option, indeed not really a choice. For simply to exist, to be, is to play some game or other. Ultimately, the skeptic's choice is the Shake-

spearean choice between to be or not to be, the choice between to exist or to commit suicide. One is here reminded of the Sartrean paradox that to exist is to be condemned to be free. To press home the point against the skeptic, we can remind him or her that simply to raise the normative question, to ask "Why should I be moral?" is already to be playing a game: the game of communication. As such, the skeptic is already committed to obeying certain rules, to accepting certain obligations. . . .

As we saw earlier, Lyotard's ethics has a rule against behavior that denies others the "pragmatics of obligation," or behavior that prevents others from playing their games, such as terroristic and murderous behavior. The question is how we can justify this rule. Again as we saw earlier, Lyotard is content to rest the case for such a rule on the regulative idea of maximum game playing. However, we still have to justify this regulative idea. For it is open to terrorists and murderers to claim that they do not see the desirability of maximum game playing, or the undesirability of preventing some people from playing their games. What Lyotard needs is an argument to show that the rule of just gaming is binding on all game players. I think a plausible one can be constructed. Notice that instead of relying on human reason and placing one's hope on its universal ability to lead us all into the [Kantian] Kingdom of Ends, postmodern ethics stresses the connection between game playing and observing the rules of a game. The source of normativity is not located in some mysterious and sacred place, such as autonomous human rationality. Rather, it is located right there in the very games that we are playing. Instead of the Kingdom of Ends, what we have is a community of game players. With this in mind, it is possible to show that the binding force of the rule of just gaming, its normativity, lies in the very idea of game playing itself, and that for there to be game playing at all, certain games must be ruled out and certain other games should be encouraged.

In arguing for the rules of just gaming, what we need is to establish the claim that the rules of just gaming are the *necessary* meta-rules of game playing itself. In other words, the rules of just gaming guarantee the conditions of possibility of game playing. Put this way, the claim establishes itself insofar as to play any game is to be committed to the possibility of game playing. A murderer, in playing the murderous game, is already committed to the possibility of game playing. The more terrorists and murderers insist on playing their games, the more they show their commitment to game playing. What is it to be committed to game playing? At the very least, it is to accept the conditions that make game playing itself possible, or in other words to accept the rules of just gaming. To put the matter differently, it can be said that to be a game player at all is to play the game, or meta-game, of game playing, the rules of which are none other than the rules of just gaming. A game player is committed to observing these rules by virtue of being a game player. If this is so then certain games must be ruled out because playing them breaks the rules of just gaming. Such games are impossible games in the context of game playing. What games break the rules of just gaming? Arguably they are, as Lyotard puts it in *Just Gaming*, the games that prohibit "that the whole of reasonable beings could continue to exist," games that place "the whole of reasonable beings . . . in a position where the pragmatics of obligation [is] forbidden them," in other words, games that prevent others from being game players, such as terroristic and murderous games. We have seen that a murderer cannot complain that the rules of just gaming are inconsistent because they prevent him or her from playing the murderous game. This is so because such rules do not prevent the murderer from being a game player as such, only from being a murderer, whereas by contrast the murderous game prevents others from being game players insofar as it prohibits that others "could continue to exist."

If it is accepted that to be a game player at all is to play the meta-game of game playing then it also follows that Lyotard's "presenting the unpresentable" is a postmodern moral imperative. This is so because not presenting the unpresentable, not bearing witness to it, just is to privilege one's own discourse, to accept that it alone has authority, that it constitutes the totality. It is to ignore the possibility of there being claims intelligible only in different rules of discourse, thus effectively preventing "reasonable beings" from being game players. It is worse than marginalizing them: it is placing them "in a position where the pragmatics of obligation [is] forbidden them." To be a game

player is to be committed to the rules of just gaming, and this means to have a pragmatic obligation to game playing generally. This obligation translates into the obligation to bear witness and to present the unpresentable, to wage a "war on totality." One could go further and say that there is an obligation to be a virtuous game player in making every effort to entrench the conditions of possibility of game playing, in strengthening one's commitment to the rules of just gaming. Deepening one's sensitivity to the unpresentable is one way of becoming a virtuous game player. Becoming less dogmatic about one's own discourses is another. If I am right in my reading of Lyotard, his postmodern ethics can be said to provide a plausible answer to the normative question. In summary, the answer goes something like this. If the skeptic who asks "Why should I be moral?" is *really* interested in the answer, then we can say that he or she is already a game player and as such should obey the rules of the game. He or she may be playing many other games and as such should obey the rules of such games. Some of the rules are moral in the traditional sense. Also, to be a game player is to be playing the game of game playing, hence to be committed to the rules of game playing, namely, the rules of just gaming. This is why one should not engage in certain acts, such as murderous and terroristic acts, and why one should cultivate certain virtues, such as being sensitive to the unpresentable. The alternative is not to be a game player at all, which is equivalent to not existing. As for those skeptics who are not really interested in our answer, who are like Pontius Pilate who asked "What is truth?" and then turned his back and walked away, our answer will not have any effect. But then, their question is not really a question at all.

I have argued that Lyotard has a coherent ethics. From his postmodern ethics, important moral lessons, as well as practical lessons for moral education, can be drawn. If I am right, Lyotard is a moral educator.

Source: A. T. Nuyen, "Lyotard as Moral Educator," *Lyotard: Just Education*, edited by Pradeep Dhillon and Paul Standish. New York: Routledge, 2000, pp. 97–109. By permission of the publisher.

SELECTED READINGS

Aronowitz, Stanley, and Giroux, Henry A. *Postmodern Education: Politics, Culture, and Social Criticism.* Minneapolis: University of Minnesota Press, 1991. One of the leading statements on postmodern educational theory. This work seeks to develop a radical discourse in opposition to the dominant narratives that tend to define the issues of the day, particularly current educational reform that is driven by market needs rather than focused on the needs of the community.

Dhillon, Pradeep, and Standish, Paul, eds. *Lyotard: Just Education.* Routledge International Studies in the Philosophy of Education. New York: Routledge, 2000. A collection of 13 articles written from various viewpoints assessing the value of Lyotard's thought for educational theory. An international cast of authors and a variety of viewpoints make this an informative collection of writings.

Hoeveller, David J., Jr. *The Postmodern Turn: American Thought and Culture in the 1970s.* New York: Twayne Publishers, 1996. A historical analysis of the origins of postmodern thought. The author highlights major developments in literature, art, political theory, and philosophy, and critiques the impacts these had on thought and culture.

Peters, Michael, ed. *Education and the Postmodern Condition,* with a Foreword by Jean-Francois Lyotard. Critical Studies in Education and Culture Series, Henry Giroux and Paulo Freire, eds. Westport, CN: Bergin and Garvey, 1995. A collection of interpretive and descriptive essays concerning the impact of postmodernism on education, particularly the thought of Lyotard but also other contemporary thinkers, as well. The emphasis is on the value of postmodern insights for educational theory, but analysis is included that helps provide critical perspectives on many postmodernist ideas.

carbon.cudenver.edu/~mryder/itc_data/postmodern.html (accessed April 5, 2002). A feature of the page for the School of Education at the University of Colorado at Denver. Their philosophy page is devoted to "Contemporary Philosophy, Critical Theory, and Postmodern Thought," with resources and readings on key ideas and people.

Companion
Website

ONLINE RESEARCH

Utilizing some of the Web sites included in this book, as well as Topics 2 and 3 of the Prentice Hall Foundations Web site found at *www.prenhall.com/ozmon,* answer the following question with a short essay: What is postmodernism and what do postmodernists find wrong in contemporary educational beliefs and practices? You can write and submit your essay response to your instructor by using the "Electronic Bluebook" section found in any of the topics of the Prentice Hall Foundations Web site.

Useful Web Sites
and Internet Links

Because electronic media and particularly computer access to the World Wide Web and the Internet are becoming such important tools of access to knowledge and information, students should become familiar with the technology and learn to use those resources that offer source materials fast and conveniently. In order to assist student access and learning, this comprehensive listing of some worthwhile sources is included. Many if not most of the sites listed and annotated will direct students to articles, analyses, and classic texts in philosophy and philosophy of education. In addition, students who use the sources effectively will locate many additional resources not listed here. The following site addresses are organized alphabetically after the *www* prefixes. Because Web sites are upgraded frequently and pages are moved sometimes to new addresses, please understand that the addresses were operative at the time this book went to press, but some might have changed by the time readers seek access to them.

www.american-philosophy.org (accessed 04/05/02). Homepage for the Society for the Advancement of American Philosophy. This site provides useful links to a number of Web sites students might find helpful.

analytic.ontologically.com (accessed 04/05/02). Home page of Analytic, a Web site providing numerous options and links to sources on analytic philosophy, including persons and works. Its "links" option provides access to electronic journals and texts in the field.

www.apa.udel.edu/apa/index.html (accessed 04/05/02). Homepage for the American Philosophical Association, a leading professional organization for philosophers. Provides access to some electronic books and journals, but students might need proxy authorization through their school's electronic library for access.

ask.elibrary.com/index.asp (accessed 04/05/02). eLibrary is a useful source of electronically available books and journals, providing material on a number of subjects, including philosophy and education. To receive its full benefits, students should access it through their college or university library, but the general public can access such services as eLibrary's Free Encyclopedia.

www.bfskinner.org (accessed 04/05/02). Homepage of the B. F. Skinner Foundation. General information about the foundation, with brief documents concerning operant conditioning and other topics.

www.Britannica.com (accessed 04/05/02). A general reference work that also contains considerable material on philosophy, ranging from entries on individual philosophers and schools to various other philosophical topics. Additional source materials can be accessed, such as magazine articles and links to other Web sites. Unless students are subscribers, however, they might need access through their college or university electronic library.

carbon.cudenver.edu/~mryder/itc_data/postmodern. html (accessed 04/05/02). A feature of the homepage for the School of Education at the University of Colorado at Denver. Their philosophy page is devoted to "Contemporary Philosophy, Critical Theory, and Postmodern Thought," with access to numerous materials and links to other sites, as well as additional pages featuring other theoretical fields.

www.cuip.uchicago.edu/jds/links.htm (accessed 04/05/02). Homepage of the John Dewey Society. This site contains numerous Internet links for material by and about John Dewey and other pragmatist philosophers, and on pragmatism, progressivism, and related topics.

ditext.com (accessed 04/05/02). Homepage of Digital Text International, it contains a variety of sites linking students to digital books available on the Internet. This provides access to works of and about certain individual philosophers as well as options such as the *Meta-Encyclopedia of Philosophy*. Also contains links to numerous other sources and search engines.

www.earlham.edu/%7Epeters/philinks.htm#jobs (accessed 04/05/02). Provides a helpful resource in Peter Suber's "Guide to Philosophy on the Internet" through the Hippias and Noesis search engines. This site offers many sources for researchers and students.

www.easternreligions.com/ (accessed 04/05/02). Provides historical background and selected textual material on Buddhism, Confucianism, Taoism, Hinduism, and Zen, including philosophical and religious views. Additional links also are provided.

www.ed.uiuc.edu/EPS/Educational-Theory/ (accessed 04/05/02). Site for accessing back issues of the journal *Educational Theory*. The most recent articles are available in abstracts, and older issues are provided in full text. An index of articles and authors is available to help students locate specific material.

www.ed.uiuc.edu/EPS/PES-yearbook/ (accessed 04/05/02). Site for the Philosophy of Education Society's Yearbooks, a source of presentations and responses at the society's annual meetings. This source provides valuable resource material, as well as an illustration of how ideas are debated and critiqued in the annual meetings.

www.encarta.msn.com (accessed 04/05/02). The Encarta Encyclopedia is a general reference work on the Internet that provides useful material on a number of subjects, including philosophy and philosophers.

www.epistemelinks.com/ (accessed 04/05/02). An important site for material on leading philosophers past and present, along with numerous philosophical issues, problems, and topics. This is a comprehensive site offering a large selection of resources for students and scholars.

www.greatbooks.org/index.html (accessed 04/05/02). Site for The Great Books foundation. Provides information on the foundation, its programs, and its publications.

www.hegel.org/ (accessed 04/05/02). Homepage of the Hegel Society of America. This site has a "Hegel links throughout the Internet" that students might find informative, including Hegelian influences on philosophy of education.

www.knowdeep.org/existentialism (accessed 04/05/02). Provides approximately 50 connections to papers, articles, lectures, and other sources on existentialism.

www.marxism.org/ (accessed 04/05/02). A site devoted to the many varieties of Marxism. Contains a number of listings for other Marxist sites, including archives of Marx and Engels.

naks.ucsd.edu/ (accessed 04/05/02). Homepage of the North American Kant Society. Provides links to relevant texts and electronic sources.

www.nd.edu/Departments/Maritain/ndjmc.htm (accessed 04/05/02). Web site of the Jacques Maritain Center at the University of Notre Dame. This site provides access to papers, articles, and readings by Maritain and others on Thomist and realist philosophy and philosophy of education.

pages.yahoo.com/nhp?h=entertainment___arts/ humanities/philosophy (accessed 04/05/02). A Yahoo-Geocities site with links to sources on major philosophies and leading philosophers. Topics range from Ancient Greek and Eastern philosophies to existentialism and philosophy of mind, as well as issues such as nihilism and objectivism.

www.paideia.org/ (accessed 04/05/02). Homesite of the National Paideia Center. This site promotes the educational philosophy of Mortimer Adler. It provides brief explanatory materials but also links to other sites that might support the Center's objectives.

www.philosophy-of-education.org (accessed 04/05/02). Homepage for the Philosophy of Education Society in Great Britain. It provides information about the Society but also contains a list of links to additional philosophy Web sites students might find helpful.

www.philosophyofeducation.org (accessed 04/05/02). Homepage of the Philosophy of Education Society, U.S.A. In addition to information on the Society, this site contains links to the journal *Educational Theory* and to the Philosophy of Education Society's *Yearbooks*, two important sources of electronically available material (see related site entries).

www.pragmatism.org/ (accessed 04/05/02). Site for the "Pragmatism Cybrary," a helpful source with features that include the history of pragmatism, the "Library of Living Pragmatists," the "Web Companion to

Pragmatism," and numerous links to philosophical "nodes on the Web."

www.radicalacademy.com/homepage.htm (accessed 04/05/02). Site with a traditional realist orientation but with many other materials as well. The Radical Academy supports and defends classical realism, but it also provides source materials on other philosophies in Western thought and history.

www.spep.org/resource.html (accessed 04/05/02). Homepage of the Society for Phenomenology and Existential Philosophy, a professional organization devoted to supporting philosophy inspired by Continental European traditions. SPEP also promotes such traditions as critical theory, feminism, German Idealism, hermeneutics, and post-structuralism.

plato.stanford.edu/contents.html (accessed 04/05/02). Site of the Stanford Encyclopedia of Philosophy. This source provides a large selection of materials and options on philosophy, philosophers, topics, and issues and problems.

plato.stanford.edu/entries/behaviorism/ (accessed 04/05/02). An example of a specific entry in the Stanford Encyclopedia of Philosophy. This particular page is devoted to the philosophical roots of behaviorism.

www.thoemmes.com/american/links.htm (accessed 04/05/02). Examines a wide selection of leading thinkers and influential developments in American philosophical thought. Provides access to articles, bibliographies, and numerous links to other Web sites.

www.utm.edu/research/iep/ (accessed 04/05/02). Site of the Internet Encyclopedia of Philosophy, a source of general information and descriptions of philosophy and philosophers. Contains good background material for beginning students, as well as helpful aid for the more experienced.

vig.prenhall.com/. Homepage for Prentice Hall, Incorporated, offering resources for students and faculty using this textbook. Readers are encouraged to browse the site for useful material. Of special interest for students is the page, "Resource Central, Higher Education Students" at *www.prenhall.com/resource_central/students/index.htm*, and instructors can use *www.prenhall.com/resource_central/professors/index.html.* These pages offer online tools and references, as well as links to other sites.

www.vlib.org/ (accessed 04/05/02). A Web catalog long recognized for its sources and services provided by a number of servers around the world. The Virtual Library provides links to many Web sites on philosophy from ancient times to the present, with access to leading works that are available electronically. Students may need to access this source through a subscribing college or university library.

www.wfs.org (accessed 04/05/02). Homepage for the World Future Society. This site emphasizes social and technological developments that could shape the future, and provides access to interviews, book reviews, and Web forums that students might find helpful.

www.xrefer.com (accessed 04/05/02). Home page for xrefer, a Web site containing encyclopedias, dictionaries, thesauri, and books of quotations from the world's leading publishers.

Selected Bibliography

Adler, Mortimer J. *Paideia Problems and Possibilities*. New York: Macmillan, 1982.

___. *The Paideia Proposal: An Educational Manifesto*. New York: Macmillan, 1982.

___, and Mayer, Milton. *The Revolution in Education*. Chicago: University of Chicago Press, 1958.

Adorno, Theodor W. *Negative Dialectics*, translated by E. B. Ashton. New York: Seabury Press, 1973.

Alcott, Amos Bronson. *Conversations with Children on the Gospels*. Boston: James Monroe and Co., 1836.

___. *Journals*. Boston: Little, Brown, 1938.

Alinsky, Saul. *Rules for Radicals*. New York: Random House, 1971.

Apple, Michael W. "Can Critical Pedagogies Interrupt Rightists Policies?" *Educational Theory*, 50 (2): 220–254, Spring 2000.

___, editor. *Cultural and Economic Reproduction in Education: Essays on Class, Ideology, and the State*. New York: Routledge and Kegan Paul, 1982.

___. "Education, Culture, and Class Power: Basil Bernstein and the Neo-Marxist Sociology of Education," *Educational Theory* 42(2):127–146, Spring 1992.

___. *Official Knowledge: Democratic Education in a Conservative Age*. New York: Routledge, 1993.

Aquinas, Thomas. *Basic Writings*. New York: Random House, 1905.

___. *Summa Theologica*, vols. 1–3, translated by Fathers of the English Dominican Province. New York: Benziger Brothers, 1947.

___. *The Teacher—The Mind*. Chicago: Henry Regnery, 1953.

Arato, Andrew, and Gebhardt, Eike, editors. *The Essential Frankfurt School Reader*. New York: Urizen Books, 1978.

Aristotle. *The Nicomachean Ethics of Aristotle*, translated by David Ross. New York: Oxford University Press, 1975.

___. *Politics*, translated by Benjamin Jowett. New York: Colonial Press, 1899.

Aronowitz, Stanley. *The Crisis in Historical Materialism: Class, Politics, and Culture in Marxist Theory*, 2d ed. Minneapolis: University of Minnesota Press, 1990.

___. *The Politics of Identity: Class, Culture, Social Movements*. New York: Routledge, 1992.

___, and Giroux, Henry A. *Education Under Siege: The Conservative, Liberal, and Radical Debate Over Schooling*. Westport, CT: Bergin and Garvey, 1985.

___, and Giroux, Henry A. *Postmodern Education: Politics, Culture, and Social Criticism*. Minneapolis: University of Minnesota Press, 1991.

Augustine. *The City of God*, translated by Marcus Dods with introduction by Thomas Merton. New York: Modern Library, 1950.

___. *Concerning the Teacher (De magistro) and on the Immortality of the Soul (De importalitate animae)*, translated from the Latin with the addition of a preface by George G. Lockie. New York: Appleton-Century-Crofts, c. 1938.

___. *Confessions*, translated by Edward B. Pusey. New York: Modern Library, 1949.

Aurelius, Marcus. *Meditations*, translated by Maxwell Staniforth. Baltimore: Penguin, 1964.

Ayer, Alfred Jules. *Language, Truth and Logic*. New York: Dover, 1952.

___. *Russell and Moore*. Cambridge, MA: Harvard University Press, 1971.

Bacon, Francis. *Advancement of Learning and Novum Organum*. New York: Colonial, 1889.

Bahm, Archie J. *Comparative Philosophy: Western, Indian, and Chinese Philosophies Compared*, rev. ed. Albuquerque, NM: World Book, 1995.

Banerjee, M. *Invitation to Hinduism*. New Delhi, India: Printsman, 1978.

Barber, Benjamin. *An Aristocracy of Everyone: The Politics of Education and the Future of America*. New York: Oxford University Press, 1994.

Bayles, Ernest. *Pragmatism and Education*. New York: Harper & Row, 1966.

Baynes, Kenneth, et al. *After Philosophy: End or Transformation?* Cambridge, MA: MIT Press, 1987.

Beck, Clive. *Educational Philosophy and Theory: An Introduction*. Boston: Little, Brown, 1974.

Bellah, Robert N., et al. *The Good Society*. New York: Alfred A. Knopf, 1991.

Bender, Frederic L., editor. *The Betrayal of Marx*. New York: Harper & Row, 1975.

Bereiter, Carl, and Engelmann, Siegfried. *Teaching Disadvantaged Children in the Pre-School*. Upper Saddle River, NJ: Prentice Hall, 1966.

Bergson, Henri. *Creative Evolution*, translated by Arthur Mitchell. New York: Modern Library, 1944.

Berkeley, George. *Principles of Human Knowledge*. New York: E. P. Dutton, 1910.

Berlin, Isaiah. *Karl Marx: His Life and Environment*. Home University Library of Modern Knowledge, No. 189, 3rd ed. London: Oxford University Press, 1963.

Bernstein, Richard J. *The New Constellation: The Ethical-Political Horizons of Modernity/Postmodernity*. Cambridge, MA: MIT Press, 1992.

___. *Philosophical Profiles*. Cambridge, UK: Polity Press, 1986.

___. *Praxis and Action: Contemporary Philosophies of Human Activity*. Philadelphia: University of Pennsylvania Press, 1971.

___. "The Resurgence of Pragmatism," *Social Research* 59(4):813–840, Winter 1992.

___. "Varieties of Pluralism," *American Journal of Education* 95(4):509–525, August 1987.

Berry, Thomas. *Religions of India: Hinduism, Yoga, Buddhism*. New York: Bruce Publishing Co., 1971.

Best, Steve, and Kellner, Douglas. *The Postmodern Turn*. New York: The Guilford Press, 1997.

Blake, Nigel; Smeyers, Paul; Smith, Richard; and Standish, Paul. *Education in an Age of Nihilism*. New York: Routledge/Falmer, 2000.

Bloland, Harland G., "Postmodernism and Higher Education," *Journal of Higher Education*, 66 (5):521–539 (September–October 1995).

Bloom, Allan. *The Closing of the American Mind*. New York: Simon and Schuster, 1987.

Bode, Boyd. *Progressive Education at the Crossroads*. New York: Newson, 1938.

Boisvert, Raymond D. *John Dewey: Rethinking Our Time*. Albany: State University of New York Press, 1998.

Bowers, C. A. *Elements of a Post-Liberal Theory of Education*. New York: Teachers College Press, 1987.

Bowes, Pratima. *Hindu Intellectual Tradition*. Columbia, MO: South Asia Books, 1977.

Bowker, John, editor. *Oxford Dictionary of World Religions*. New York: Oxford University Press, 1994.

Bowles, Samuel, and Gintis, Herbert. *Schooling in Capitalist America: Educational Reform and the Contradictions of Economic Life*. New York: Basic Books, 1977.

Brameld, Theodore. *Education as Power*. New York: Holt, Rinehart and Winston, 1965.

___. *Patterns of Educational Philosophy*. New York: Holt, Rinehart and Winston, 1971.

___. *Toward a Reconstructed Philosophy of Education*. New York: Dryden, 1956.

Brosio, Richard A. *A Radical Democratic Critique of Capitalist Education*. New York: Peter Lang, 1994.

Broudy, Harry S. *Building a Philosophy of Education*. Upper Saddle River, NJ: Prentice Hall, 1961.

___. "Philosophy of Education Between Yearbooks," *Teachers College Record* 81:130–144, 1979.

___. *The Real World of the Public Schools*. New York: Harcourt Brace Jovanovich, 1972.

Brubacher, John S. "The Challenge to Philosophize About Education," *Modern Philosophies and Education*. The Fifty-Fourth Yearbook of the National Society for the Study of Education, part I, chapter VII. Chicago: National Society for the Study of Education, 1942, pp. 289–322.

___. *Modern Philosophies of Education*. New York: McGraw-Hill, 1939.

Buber, Martin. *I and Thou*, translated by Ronald G. Smith. New York: Charles Scribner's, 1958.

Burnett, Joe E. "Some Observations on the Logical Implications of Philosophic Theory for Educational Theory and Practice," *Philosophy of Education, 1958.* Proceedings of the Fourteenth Annual Meeting of the Philosophy of Education Society. Edwardsville, IL: Philosophy of Education Society, 1958.

Burns, Hobart W. "The Logic of the 'Educational Implication,'" *Educational Theory* 12:53–63, 1962.

Butler, J. Donald. *Four Philosophies.* New York: Harper, 1951.

___. *Idealism in Education.* New York: Harper & Row, 1966.

Cahn, Steven M. *Classic and Contemporary Readings in the Philosophy of Education.* New York: McGraw Hill, 1997.

Callinicos, Alex. *Against Postmodernism: A Marxist Critique.* New York: St. Martin's Press, 1990.

Camus, Albert. *The Myth of Sisyphus*, translated by Justin O'Brien. New York: Alfred A. Knopf, 1955.

___. *The Rebel*, translated by Anthony Bower. New York: Alfred A. Knopf, 1978.

Carnoy, Martin, editor. *Schooling in a Corporate Society: The Political Economy of Education in America.* New York: David McKay Co., 1972.

___, and Levin, Henry M. *The Limits of Educational Reform.* New York: David McKay Co., 1976.

Caspary, William R. *Dewey on Democracy.* Ithaca: Cornell University Press, 2000.

Casti, John L. *Paradigms Lost: Images of Man in the Mirror of Science.* New York: William Morrow and Co., 1989.

Chai, Ch'u, and Chai, Winberg. *The Story of Chinese Philosophy.* New York: Washington Square Press, 1961.

Chamberlin, Gordon. *The Educating Act: A Phenomenological View.* Lanham, MD: University Press of America, 1981.

Chennakesavan, Sarasvati. *A Critical Study of Hinduism.* New York: Asia Publishing House, 1974.

Cherryholmes, Cleo. *Power and Criticism: Poststructural Investigations in Education.* New York: Teachers College Press, 1988.

Childs, John Lawrence. *American Pragmatism and Education.* New York: Holt, Rinehart and Winston, 1956.

___. *Education and the Philosophy of Experimentalism.* New York: Appleton-Century, 1931.

Chuang-tzu. *Chuang-tzu: Basic Writings*, translated by Durton Watson. New York: Columbia University Press, 1964.

Code, Lorraine. *Epistemic Responsibility.* Hanover, NH: University Press of New England, 1987.

College Entrance Examination Board. *Academic Preparation for College: What Students Need to Know and Be Able to Do.* New York: College Board, 1983.

Collins, Marva. *Ordinary Children, Extraordinary Teachers.* Norfolk, VA: Hampton Roads Publishing Co., 1992.

Comte, Auguste. *A General View of Positivism*, translated by J. H. Bridges. New York: R. Speller, 1957.

Conant, James Bryant. *Education and Liberty.* Cambridge, MA: Harvard University Press, 1953.

Confucius. *The Analects of Confucius: A Philosophical Translation*, translated, with an introduction, by Roger T. Ames and Henry Rosemont, Jr. New York: Ballantine Books, 1999.

Conze, Edward, editor. *Buddhist Texts Through the Ages.* Oxford, UK: One World, 1995.

___. *A Short History of Buddhism.* New York: George Allen & Unwin, 1980.

Copernicus, Nicolaus. *The Revolutions of the Heavenly Spheres*, translated by A. M. Duncan. New York: Barnes and Noble, 1976.

Corbin, Henry. *History of Islamic Philosophy.* New York: Kegan Paul International, 1993.

Counts, George S. *The Challenge of Soviet Education.* Westport, CT: McGraw-Hill, 1957.

___. *Dare the Schools Build a New Social Order?* New York: Arno Press, 1969.

Creel, Herrlee G. *What Is Taoism? (and Other Studies in Chinese Cultural History).* Chicago: University of Chicago Press, 1970.

Dahlstrand, Frederick C. *Amos Bronson Alcott: An Intellectual Biography.* Rutherford, NJ: Fairleigh Dickinson University Press, 1982.

Darwin, Charles R. *On the Origin of Species by Means of Natural Selection.* New York: Oxford University Press, 1958.

Das, Surya. *Awakening the Buddha Within: Eight Steps to Enlightenment.* New York: Broadway Books, 1997.

David-Neel, Alexandra. *Buddhism: Its Doctrines and Its Methods.* New York: St. Martin's Press, 1977.

Dawkins, Richard. *The Selfish Gene.* New York: Oxford University Press, 1989.

Dawson, Raymond Stanley. *Confucius.* Oxford, UK: Oxford University Press, 1981.

DeBary, Theodore, editor. *The Buddhist Tradition in India, China, and Japan.* New York: Modern Library, 1969.

Derrida, Jacques. *Of Grammatology*, translated by Gayatri Chakravorty Spivak. Baltimore: Johns Hopkins University Press, 1976.

Descartes, René. *A Discourse on Method and Meditations*, translated by Laurence J. Lofleur. Indianapolis: Bobbs-Merrill, 1960.

Dewey, John. *A Common Faith.* New Haven: Yale University Press, 1934.

___. *Art as Experience.* New York: Capricorn, 1959.

___. *The Child and the Curriculum and the School and Society.* Chicago: University of Chicago Press, 1990.

___. *Democracy and Education.* New York: Macmillan, 1916.

___. *Essays in Experimental Logic*. New York: Dover, 1953.

___. *Experience and Education*. New York: Macmillan, 1938.

___. *Experience and Nature*. LaSalle, IL: Open Court, 1929.

___. *How We Think*. Boston: D. C. Heath, 1933.

___. *Human Nature and Conduct*. Carbondale: Southern Illinois University Press, 1988.

___. *The Influence of Darwin on Philosophy and Other Essays in Contemporary Thought*. New York: Henry Holt, 1910.

___. *Moral Principles in Education*. Carbondale: Southern Illinois University Press, Arcturus Books Edition, 1975.

___. "My Pedagogic Creed," *School Journal* 54(3): 77–80, January 16, 1897.

___. *The Need for a Recovery in Philosophy*, in *On Experience, Nature, and Freedom: Representative Selections*, edited by Richard J. Bernstein. New York: Library of Liberal Arts, Bobbs-Merrill, 1960, pp. 16–69.

___. *The School and Society*. Chicago: University of Chicago Press, 1915.

___. *Theory of the Moral Life*. New York: Holt, Rinehart, and Winston, 1960.

Dhillon, Pradeep A., and Standish, Paul, editors. *Lyotard: Just Education*. New York: Routledge, 2000.

Durkheim, Émile. *Socialism and Saint-Simon*, edited by Alvin W. Gouldner and translated by Charlotte Satler. Yellow Springs, OH: Antioch Press, 1958.

Eastwood, Gordon. "Paradigms, Anomalies, and Analysis: Response to Jonas Soltis," *Philosophy of Education, 1971*. Proceedings of the Twenty-Seventh Annual Meeting of the Philosophy of Education Society. Edwardsville, IL: Philosophy of Education Society, 1971, pp. 47–54.

Edel, Abraham. "Analytic Philosophy of Education at the Crossroads," *Educational Theory* 22:131–153, 1972.

Emerson, Ralph Waldo. *Essays*. New York: Houghton Mifflin, 1883.

Engels, Friedrich. *Dialectics of Nature*, translated and edited by Clemens Dutt, with a preface and notes by J. B. S. Haldane. New York: International Publishers, 1940.

___. *Herr Eugen Duhring's Revolution in Science (Anti-Duhring)*, translated by Emile Burns and edited by C. P. Dutt. New York: International Publishers, 1966.

Erasmus, Desiderius. *The Education of a Christian Prince*, translated by Lester K. Born. New York: Columbia University Press, 1924.

Feibleman, James K. *Understanding Oriental Philosophy*. New York: Horizon Press, 1976.

Feng, Yu-Lan. *The Spirit of Chinese Philosophy*. Westport, CT: Greenwood Press, 1970.

Fischer, Ernst, and Marek, Franz, editors. *The Essential Lenin*, translated by Anna Bostock. New York: Herder and Herder, 1972.

Fosnot, Catherine Twomey. *"Constructivism: A Psychological Theory of Learning"* in *Constructivism: Theory, Perspectives, and Practice*, edited by Catherine Twomey Fosnot, editor. New York: Teachers College Press, 1996.

___, editor. *Constructivism: Theory, Perspectives, and Practice*. New York: Teachers College Press, 1996.

Foucault, Michel. *Discipline and Punish*. New York: Vantage Books, 1979.

___. *Madness and Civilization: A History of Insanity in the Age of Reason*. New York: Vintage Books, 1973.

___. *The Order of Things: An Archaeology of the Human Sciences*. New York: Vintage Books, 1973.

Frank, Daniel and Leaman, Oliver, editors. *History of Jewish Philosophy. Vol.2 of Routledge History of World Philosophies*. New York: Routledge, 1997.

Freire, Paulo. *Education for a Critical Consciousness*. New York: Seabury Press, 1973.

___. *Pedagogy of the Oppressed*, translated by Myra Bergman Ramos. New York: Seabury Press, 1970.

Freud, Sigmund. *Civilization and Its Discontents*, translated by James Strachey. New York: W. W. Norton, 1962.

Froebel, Friedrich. *The Education of Man*, translated by W. N. Hailman. New York: A. M. Kelley, 1974.

Garrison, James W., editor. *The New Scholarship on Dewey*. Boston: Kluwer Academic, 1995.

Gavin, William J., editor. *Context Over Foundation: Dewey and Marx*. Norwell, MA: Kluwer, 1988.

Gentile, G. *The Reform of Education*. New York: Harcourt, Brace, 1922.

George, Paul S. *The Theory Z School: Beyond Effectiveness*. Columbus, OH: National Middle School Association, 1983.

Geuss, Raymond. *The Idea of Critical Theory: Habermas and the Frankfurt School*. Modern European Philosophy Series. New York: Cambridge University Press, 1981.

Gilson, Etienne. *The Spirit of Medieval Philosophy*, translated by A. H. C. Downes. Notre Dame, IN: University of Notre Dame Press, 1991.

Giroux, Henry A. *Border Crossings: Cultural Workers and the Politics of Education*. New York: Routledge, 1992.

___. *Ideology, Culture, and the Process of Schooling*. Philadelphia: Temple University Press, 1981.

___. "Marxism and Schooling: The Limits of Radical Discourse". *Educational Theory* 34(2):113–136, Spring 1984.

___. *Teachers as Intellectuals: Toward a Critical Pedagogy of Learning*. New York: Bergin and Garvey, 1988.

Gitlin, Todd. "Postmodernism: Roots and Practices," *Dissent* 36:100–108, Winter 1989.

Goodlad, John I. *A Place Called School: Prospects for the Future*. New York: McGraw-Hill, 1984.

Gopalan, Subramania. *Outlines of Jainism*. New York: John Wiley & Sons, 1973.

Gramsci, Antonio. *Selections from the Prison Notebooks of Antonio Gramsci*, edited by Quintin Hoare and Geoffrey N. Smith. New York: International Publishers, 1971.

Greene, Maxine. "A Constructivist Perspective on Teaching and Learning in the Arts," in *Constructivism: Theory, Perspectives, and Practice*, edited by Catherine Twomey Fosnot. New York: Teachers College Press, 1996.

___. *Landscapes of Learning*. New York: Teachers College Press, 1978.

___. *Teacher as Stranger: Educational Philosophy for the Modern Age*. Belmont, CA: Wadsworth, 1973.

Gribble, James. *Introduction to Philosophy of Education*. Boston: Allyn and Bacon, 1969.

Guastello, Stephen J. *Chaos, Catastrophe, and Human Affairs*. Mahwah, NJ: Lawrence Earlbaum Associates, 1995.

Guillaume, Alfred. *The Tradition of Islam*. New York: Books for Libraries, 1980.

Gutek, Gerald L. *Historical and Philosophical Foundations of Education: A Biographical Introduction*, 2d ed. Upper Saddle River, NJ: Merrill/Prentice Hall, 1997.

___. *Philosophical and Ideological Perspectives on Education*. Boston: Allyn and Bacon, 1988.

Habermas, Jurgen. *Communication and the Evolution of Society*, translated and with an introduction by Thomas McCarthy. Boston: Beacon Press, 1979.

___. *On the Logic of the Social Sciences*, translated by Shierry Weber Nicholsen and Jerry A. Stark. Cambridge, MA: MIT Press, 1988.

___. *The Philosophical Discourse of Modernity*. Cambridge, MA: MIT Press, 1987.

___. *Theory and Practice*. Boston: Beacon Press, 1973.

Hackett, Stuart C. *Oriental Philosophy*. Madison, WI: University of Wisconsin Press, 1979.

Harris, William Torrey. "Moral Education in the Common Schools," in *Modern Philosophies of Education*, edited by John Paul Strain. New York: Random House, 1971.

Harshbarger, Luther H., and Mourant, John A. *Judaism and Christianity: Perspectives and Traditions*. Boston: Allyn and Bacon, 1968.

Hegel, Georg W. F. *The Logic of Hegel*, from the *Encyclopaedia of Philosophical Sciences*, translated by William Wallace. New York: Oxford University Press, 1892.

___. *The Phenomenology of Mind*, translated by J. B. Baillie. New York: Allen Unwin, 1949.

___. *Philosophy of Right*, translated by T. M. Knox. New York: Clarendon, 1957.

Heidegger, Martin. *The Basic Problems of Phenomenology*. Bloomington, IN: Indiana University Press, 1982.

___. *Being and Time: A Translation of* Sein und Zeit, translated by Joan Stambaugh. Albany: State University of New York Press, 1996.

Herndon, James. *How to Survive in Your Native Land*. New York: Bantam Books, 1971.

Herrigel, Eugen. *Zen and the Art of Archery*. New York: Pantheon Books, Inc., 1953.

Herrnstein, Richard J. and Murray, Charles. *The Bell Curve: Intelligence and Class Structure in American Life*. New York: Free Press, 1994.

Hinnells, J. R., and Sharpe, E. J. *Hinduism*. New Castle Upon Tyne, England: Oriel Press, 1972.

Hirsch, E. D. Jr. *Cultural Literacy: What Every American Needs to Know*. Boston: Houghton Mifflin, 1987.

Hobbes, Thomas. *Leviathan*, revised student edition. New York: Cambridge University Press, 1996.

___. *Selections*, edited by Frederick J. E. Woodbridge. New York: Charles Scribner's, 1930.

Hoff, Benjamin. *The Tao of Pooh*. New York: Penguin Books, 1982.

Hook, Sidney. *Education for Modern Man*. New York: Knopf, 1963.

Horkheimer, Max. *Dawn and Decline*. New York: Continuum, 1978.

___. *Eclipse of Reason*. New York: Continuum, 1973.

___, and Adorno, Theodor. *Dialectic of Enlightenment*, translated by John Cumming. New York: Herder and Herder, 1969.

Horne, Herman H. *The Democratic Philosophy of Education*. New York: Macmillan, 1935.

Hossein, Sayyed Nasr, and Leaman, Oliver, editors. *History of Islamic Philosophy*. Vol.1 of *Routledge History of World Philosophies*. New York: Routledge, 1996.

Howie, John, and Buford, Thomas O., eds. *Contemporary Studies in Philosophical Idealism*. Cape Cod, MA: Claude Stark and Company, 1975.

Hullfish, Henry Gordon, and Smith, Philip G. *Reflective Thinking: The Method of Education*. New York: Dodd, Mead, 1961.

Hume, David. *Treatise Upon Human Nature*. New York: Oxford University Press, 1941.

Husserl, Edmund. *Ideas*. New York: Macmillan, 1962.

Hutchins, Robert Maynard. *The Conflict in Education*. New York: Harper & Row, 1953.

___. *Great Books, The Foundations of a Liberal Education*. New York: Simon and Schuster, 1954.

Huxley, Aldous. *Brave New World*. New York: Bantam, 1932.

___. *Tomorrow and Tomorrow and Tomorrow*. New York: Harper, 1956.

Hyppolite, Jean. *Studies on Marx and Hegel*, translated with introduction, notes, and bibliography by John O'Neill. New York: Basic Books, 1969.

Illich, Ivan. *Deschooling Society*. New York: Harper & Row, 1970.

Jacoby, Susan. *Inside Soviet Schools*. New York: Hill and Wang, 1974.

Jaini, Padmanabh S. *The Jaina Path of Purification*. Berkeley, CA: University of California Press, 1979.

James, William. *Pragmatism, a New Name for Some Old Ways of Thinking*. New York: Longmans, Green, 1931.

___. *Talks to Teachers*. New York: Holt, Rinehart and Winston, 1899.

___. *The Varieties of Religious Experience*. New York: Longmans, Green, 1902.

Jameson, Frederic. *The Ideologies of Theory: Essays 1971–1986*. Two volumes. Volumes 48 and 49, *Theory and History of Literature*, edited by Wlad Godzich and Jochen Schulte-Sasse. Minneapolis: University of Minnesota Press, 1988.

Jaspers, Karl. *Philosophy of Existence*, translated by Richard F. Grabau. Philadelphia: University of Pennsylvania Press, 1971.

Jencks, Christopher. *Inequality: A Reassessment of the Effect of Family and Schooling in America*. New York: Basic Books, 1972.

Jervis, Kathe, and Montag, Carol, editors. *Progressive Education for the 1990s: Transforming Practice*. New York: Teachers College Press, 1991.

Kallen, Horace. *Culture and Democracy in the United States*. New York: Boni and Liveright, 1924.

Kant, Immanuel. *Critique of Practical Reason*, translated by Lewis White Beck. New York: Liberal Arts Press, 1956.

___. *Critique of Pure Reason*. Chicago: University of Chicago Press, 1949.

___. *Education*, translated by Annette Churton. Ann Arbor: University of Michigan Press, 1960.

Kellner, Douglas. *Critical Theory, Marxism, and Modernity*. Baltimore: Johns Hopkins University Press, 1989.

Kierkegaard, Søren Abye. *Kierkegaard's Attack Upon "Christendom,"* translated, with an introduction by Walter Lowrie. Princeton, NJ: Princeton University Press, 1968.

___. *Fear and Trembling, and the Sickness Unto Death*, translated by Walter Lowrie. Princeton, NJ: Princeton University Press, 1954.

Kilpatrick, William Heard. *Education for a Changing Civilization*. New York: Macmillan, 1927.

Klein, Margrete S. *The Challenge of Communist Education: A Look at the German Democratic Republic*. East European Monographs. New York: Columbia University Press, 1980.

Kneller, George F. *Existentialism and Education*. New York: John Wiley, 1958.

___. *Movements of Thought in Modern Education*. New York: John Wiley, 1984.

Kohlberg, Lawrence. "Moral Education Reappraised," *The Humanist* 38(6), November/December 1978.

___. "Stages of Moral Development as a Basis for Moral Education," in *Moral Education: Interdisciplinary Approaches*, edited by Clive M. Beck, et al. Toronto: University of Toronto Press, 1971.

Kohn, Alfie. *Punished by Rewards: The Trouble with Gold Stars, Incentive Plans, A's, Praise, and Other Bribes*. New York: Houghton Mifflin, 1993.

Koller, John M. *Oriental Philosophies*. New York: Charles Scribner's Sons, 1970.

Kuhn, Thomas. *The Structure of Scientific Revolutions*, 2d ed. Chicago: University of Chicago Press, 1970.

Lenin, Vladimir I. *Materialism and Empirio-Criticism*. New York: International Publishers Co., 1970.

Locke, John. *An Essay Concerning Human Understanding*. New York: E. P. Dutton, 1961.

___. *John Locke on Education*, edited by Peter Gay. New York: Teachers College Press, 1964.

___. *Some Thoughts Concerning Education*, edited by F. W. Goforth. New York: Barron's Educational Series, 1964.

Lyotard, Jean-François. *The Postmodern Condition: A Report on Knowledge*, translated from the French by Geoff Bennington and Brian Massumi, foreword by Frederic Jameson. Vol. 10 of *Theory and History of Literature*, Series. Minneapolis: University of Minnesota Press, 1984.

Marcel, Gabriel. *The Philosophy of Existentialism*, translated by Manya Harari. New York: Citadel Press, 1968.

Marcuse, Herbert. *An Essay on Liberation*. Boston: Beacon Press, 1969.

___. *One Dimensional Man*. Boston: Beacon Press, 1964.

___. *Reason and Revolution: Hegel and the Rise of Social Theory*. Boston: Beacon Press, 1960.

Margonis, Frank. "Theories of Conviction: The Return of Marxist Theorizing," *Educational Theory*, 47(4) 85–102, Fall 1997.

Maritain, Jacques. *Education at the Crossroads*. New Haven, CT: Yale University Press, 1943.

Marler, Charles D. *Philosophy and Schooling*. Boston: Allyn and Bacon, 1975.

Marx, Karl. *Capital: A Critique of Political Economy*. Vol. I. of *The Process of Capitalist Production*, edited by Friedrich Engels and translated from the third German edition by Samuel Moore and Edward Aveling. London: Lawrence and Wishart, 1965.

___. *The Communist Manifesto*, translated by Samuel Moore. London: Penguin, 1967.

___. *Economic and Philosophic Manuscripts of 1844*, edited and with an introduction by Dirk J. Struik, translated by Martin Milligan. New York: International Publishers, 1964.

___. *The Essential Writings*, edited by Frederic L. Bender. Boulder, CO: Westview Press, 1986.

___. *The Grundisse*, edited and translated by David McLellan. New York: Harper and Row, 1972.

___. *Karl Marx: Selected Writings*. London: Oxford University Press, 1977.

___. *Marx: Early Political Writings*, edited and translated by Joseph O'Malley with Richard A. Davis. New York: Cambridge University Press, 1994.

___. *Marx: Later Political Writings*, edited and translated by Terrell Carver. New York: Cambridge University Press, 1996.

___. *On Education, Women, and Children.* Vol. 6 of The Karl Marx Library, edited and arranged by Saul K. Padover. New York: McGraw-Hill, 1975.

___. *On Society and Social Change, with Selections by Friedrich Engels*, edited by Neil J. Smelder. Chicago: University of Chicago Press, 1973.

___. *The Portable Karl Marx*, selected, translated in part, and with an introduction by Eugene Kamenka. New York: The Viking Press, 1983.

___. *Writings of the Young Marx on Philosophy and Society*, translated and edited by Lloyd D. Easton and Kurt H. Guddat. Garden City, NY: Anchor Books, 1967.

___, and Engels, Friedrich. *The Communist Manifesto*, edited and with an introduction by David McLellan. New York: Oxford University Press, 1992.

___, and Engels, Friedrich. *The German Ideology: Part One, with Selections from Parts Two and Three, Together with Marx's "Introduction to a Critique of Political Economy,"* edited and with an introduction by C. J. Arthur. New York: International Publishers, 1970.

___, and Engels, Friedrich. *Karl Marx and Friedrich Engels: Selected Works, in One Volume*. New York: International Publishers, 1968.

___; Engels, Friedrich; and Lenin, V. I. *The Essential Left: Four Classic Texts on the Principles of Socialism*. New York: Barnes and Noble, 1965.

Maslow, Abraham H. *Motivation and Personality*. New York: Harper and Row, 1987.

Matthews, Mervyn. *Education in the Soviet Union: Policies and Institutions Since Stalin*. London: Allen and Unwin, 1982.

Mays, Wolfe. "Linguistic Analysis and the Philosophy of Education," *Educational Theory* 20:269–283, 1970.

McClellan, James E. "In Reply to Professor Soltis," in *Philosophy of Education, 1971.* Proceedings of the Twenty-Seventh Annual Meeting of the Philosophy of Education Society. Edwardsville, IL: Philosophy of Education Society, 1971, 55–59.

McLaren, Peter. *Life in Schools: An Introduction to Critical Pedagogy in the Foundations of Education*. New York: Longman, 1994.

___. "Revolutionary Pedagogy in Post-Revolutionary Times: Rethinking the Political Economy of Critical Education," *Educational Theory*, 48(4): 431–462, Fall 1998.

McLuhan, Marshall. *The Global Village*. New York: Oxford University Press, 1989.

Meadows, Donella H. *Beyond the Limits: Confronting Global Collapse, Envisioning a Sustainable Future*. Post Mills, VT: Chelsea Green Publishers, 1992.

___, et al. *The Limits of Growth*. New York: Universe Books, 1972.

Mehring, Franz. *Karl Marx: The Story of His Life*, translated by Edward Fitzgerald. Atlantic Highlands, NJ: Humanities Press, 1981.

Menand, Louis. *The Metaphysical Club*. New York: Farrar, Straus, and Giroux, 2001.

Merleau-Ponty, Maurice. *Phenomenology of Perception*, translated by Colin Smith. Atlantic Highlands, NJ: Humanities Press International, 1981.

___. *Primacy of Perception*, edited by James M. Edie and translated by William Cobb, et al. Evanston, IL: Northwestern University Press, 1964.

Mesarovic, Mihajlo D., and Pestel, Eduard. *Mankind at the Turning Point: The Second Report to the Club of Rome*. New York: Dutton, 1974.

Montessori, Maria. *The Secret of Childhood*, translated by Barbara Barclay Carter. New York: Longmans, Green, 1936.

Moore, George Edward. *Philosophical Papers*. New York: Allen and Unwin, 1959.

___. *Selected Writings*, edited by Thomas Baldwin. International Library of Philosophy. Series New York: Routledge, 1993.

Morris, Van Cleve. *Existentialism in Education*. New York: Harper & Row, 1966.

___, and Pai, Young. *Philosophy and the American School*, 2d ed. Boston: Houghton Mifflin, 1976.

Mourad, Roger P. Jr. *Postmodern Philosophical Critique and the Pursuit of Knowledge in Higher Education. Critical Studies in Education and Culture Series,* edited by Henry A. Giroux. Westport, CN: Bergin and Garvey, 1997.

Nakamura, Hajime. *Ways of Thinking of Eastern Peoples: India, China, Tibet, Japan*, rev. ed., edited by Philip P. Wiener. Honolulu, HA: Eastwest Center Press, 1964.

National Commission on Excellence in Education. *A Nation at Risk: The Imperative for Educational Reform*. Washington, DC: Government Printing Office, 1983.

National Society for the Study of Education. *Modern Philosophies of Education*. The Fifty-Fourth Yearbook of the National Society for the Study of Education, edited by Nelson B. Henry. Chicago: National Society for the Study of Education, 1955.

___. *Philosophies of Education*. The Forty-First Yearbook of the National Society for the Study of Education, edited by Nelson B. Henry. Chicago: National Society for the Study of Education, 1942.

___. *Philosophy and Education*: The Eightieth Yearbook of the National Society for the Study of Education, edited by Jonas Soltis. Chicago: National Society for the Study of Education, 1981.

Neill, Alexander Sutherland. *Summerhill: A Radical Approach to Child Rearing*. With a Foreword by Erich Fromm. New York: Hart Publishing Co., 1960.

Nietzsche, Friedrich Wilhelm. *Basic Writings of Nietzsche*, translated and edited and with commentaries by Walter Kaufmann. New York: Modern Library, 1968.

___. *Beyond Good and Evil*. New York: Viking Penguin, 1990.

___. *Beyond Good and Evil: Prelude to a Philosophy of the Future*, translated by Walter Kaufmann and R. J. Hillingdale. New York: Vintage Books, 1989.

___. *On the Genealogy of Morality*, edited by Keith Ansell Pearson and translated by Carol Diethe. New York: Cambridge University Press, 1994.

___. *Thus Spake Zarathustra*, translated by A. Tille. New York: E. P. Dutton, 1958.

___. *The Will to Power*, translated by Walter Kaufmann and R. J. Hollingdale. New York: Random House, 1967.

Olssen, Mark. *Michel Foucault: Materialism and Education*. Critical Studies in Education and Culture Series, edited by Henry Giroux. Westport, CT: Bergin and Garvey, 1999.

Oldenberg, Hermann. *Buddha: His Life, His Doctrine, His Order*. Delhi, India: Indologial Book House, 1971.

Organ, Troy Wilson. *Western Approaches to Eastern Philosophy*. Athens: Ohio University Press, 1975.

Orwell, George. *1984*. New York: Harcourt, Brace, 1949.

Oxtoby, Willard G., editor. *World Religions: Eastern Traditions*. New York: Oxford University Press, 1996.

___. *World Religions: Western Traditions*. New York: Oxford University Press, 1996.

Ozmon, Howard. *Contemporary Critics of Education*. Danville, IL: Interstate, 1970.

___. *Dialogue in Philosophy of Education*. Columbus, OH: Charles E. Merrill, 1972.

___. *Utopias and Education*. Minneapolis: Burgess, 1969.

Packard, Vance Oakley. *The Hidden Persuaders*. New York: Pocket Books, 1981.

Paringer, William Andrew. *John Dewey and the Paradox of Liberal Reform*. Albany, NY: State University of New York Press, 1990.

Pavlov, Ivan Petrovich. *Conditioned Reflexes*, translated by G. V. Anrap. New York: Dover Press, 1960.

Peddiwell, J. Abner [pseud.]. *The Saber-Tooth Curriculum*. New York: McGraw-Hill, 1939.

Peirce, Charles Sanders. *Philosophy and Human Nature*. New York: New York University Press, 1971.

Perkinson, Henry J. *The Possibilities of Error: An Approach to Education*. New York: David McKay, 1971.

___. *Teachers Without Goals, Students Without Knowledge*. New York: McGraw-Hill, 1993.

Pestalozzi, Johann H. *How Gertrude Teaches Her Children*, translated by Lucy E. Holland and Francis C. Turner. Syracuse, NY: George Allen and Unwin, 1894.

Peters, Michael, editor. *Education and the Postmodern Turn*, foreword by Jean-Francois Lyotard. Westport, CT: Bergin and Garvey, 1995.

___, editor. *Naming the Multiple: Poststructuralism and Education*. Critical Studies in Education and Culture Series, edited by Henry A. Giroux. Westport, CT: Bergin and Garvey, 1998.

Peters, R. S. *Ethics and Education*. London: Allen and Unwin, 1965.

___. *The Philosophy of Education*. London: Oxford University Press, 1973.

Plato. *The Laws*, vols. 1 and 2, translated by R. G. Bury. New York: G. P. Putnam's, 1926.

___. *The Meno of Plato*, edited by E. Seymer Thompson. New York: Macmillan, 1901.

___. *The Republic*, translated by B. Jowett. New York: Modern Library, 1941.

Plotinus. *The Enneads*, edited by John Dillon and translated by Stephen MacKenna. New York: Viking Penguin, 1991.

Popkewitz, Thomas S., and Brennan, Marie, editors. *Foucault's Challenge: Discourse, Knowledge, and Power in Education*. New York: Teachers College Press, 1998.

Popp, Jerome A. "Philosophy of Education and the Education of Teachers," *Philosophy of Education, 1972*. Proceedings of the Twenty-Eighth Annual Meeting of the Philosophy of Education Society. Edwardsville, IL: Philosophy of Education Society, 1972, pp. 222–229.

Popper, Karl. *The Open Society and Its Enemies*. Princeton, NJ: Princeton University Press, 1966.

Pratte, Richard. "Analytic Philosophy of Education: A Historical Perspective," *Teachers College Record* 81:145–165, 1979.

___. *Contemporary Theories of Education.* Scranton, PA: International Textbooks, 1971.

___. *Ideology and Education.* New York: David McKay, 1977.

Price, Ronald F. *Marx and Education in Late Capitalism.* London: Croom Helm, 1986.

___. *Marx and Education in Russia and China.* Totowa, NJ: Roman and Littlefield, 1977.

Prigogine, Ilya, and Stengers, Isabelle. *Order Out of Chaos.* New York: Bantam Books, Inc., 1984.

Putnam, Hilary. *The Many Faces of Realism.* The Paul Carus Lectures. LaSalle, IL: Open Court, 1987.

___. *Pragmatism.* Cambridge, MA: Blackwell Publishers, 1995.

___. *Realism with a Human Face.* Cambridge, MA: Harvard University Press, 1990.

___. *Reason, Truth, and History.* New York: Cambridge University Press, 1981.

___. *Renewing Philosophy.* Cambridge, MA: Harvard University Press, 1992.

___. *Representation and Reality.* Cambridge, MA: MIT Press, 1988.

___. *Words and Life.* Cambridge, MA: Harvard University Press, 1994.

Putnam, Hilary, and Putnam, Ruth Anna. "Education in a Multicultural Democracy: Two Deweyan Perspectives," *Educational Theory* 43(4):361–376, Fall 1993.

Rader, Melvin. *Marx's Interpretation of History.* New York: Oxford University Press, 1979.

Radhakrishnan, Sarvepalli, editor. *History of Philosophy—Eastern and Western*, vol. 1. London: Bradford and Dickens, Drayton House, 1952.

Rafferty, Max. *Suffer Little Children.* New York: New American Library, 1963.

___. *What Are They Doing to Your Children?* New York: New American Library, 1963.

Ravitch, Diane. *Left Back: A Century of Failed School Reform.* New York: Simon and Schuster, 2000.

Redl, Helen, editor and translator. *Soviet Educators on Soviet Education.* New York: Free Press, 1964.

Reese, William L. *Dictionary of Philosophy and Religion: Eastern and Western Thought*, enlarged edition. Atlantic Highlands, NJ: Humanities Press, 1996.

Reitman, Sanford W. *The Educational Messiah Complex: American Faith in the Culturally Redemptive Power of Schooling.* Sacramento, CA: Caddo Gap Press, 1992.

Richards, Janet Radcliffe. *The Sceptical Feminist: A Philosophical Enquiry.* Boston: Routledge & Kegan Paul, 1980.

Rickover, Hyman G. *Education and Freedom.* New York: New American Library, 1963.

Rogers, Carl. *Freedom to Learn*, 3rd ed., updated by Jerome Freiberg [Rogers & Freiberg]. Upper Saddle River, NJ: Merrill/Prentice Hall, 1994.

Rorty, Amélie Oksenberg. *Philosophers on Education: Historical Perspectives.* New York: Routledge, 1998.

Rorty, Richard. *Consequences of Pragmatism (Essays: 1972–1980).* Minneapolis: University of Minnesota Press, 1982.

___. *Contingency, Irony, and Solidarity.* New York: Cambridge University Press, 1989.

___. "Intellectuals in Politics: Too Far In? Too Far Out?" *Dissent* 38:483–490, Fall 1991.

___. *Philosophical Papers*, vols. 1 and 2. Cambridge: University of Cambridge Press, 1991.

___. *Philosophy and the Mirror of Nature.* Princeton, NJ: Princeton, University Press, 1979.

___. *Philosophy and Social Hope.* New York: Penguin Books, 1999.

___. "Two Cheers for the Cultural Left," *South Atlantic Quarterly* 89:227–234, Winter 1990.

Rosen, Jonathan. *The Talmud and the Internet.* New York: Farrar, Straus and Giroux, 2000.

Roshi, Eido Shimano. *Golden Wind*, edited by Janis Levine. Tokyo: Japan Publications, 1979.

Roszak, Theodore. *Making of a Counter Culture.* New York: Doubleday, 1969.

Rousseau, Jean-Jacques. *Émile*, translated by Alan Bloom. New York: Basic Books, 1979.

___. *On the Social Contract*, edited by Roger D. Masters and translated by Judith R. Masters. New York: St. Martin, 1978.

Royce, Josiah. *Lecture on Modern Idealism.* New Haven, CT: Yale University Press, 1964.

Russell, Bertrand. *Education and the Modern World.* New York: W. W. Norton, 1932.

___. *Education and the Social Order.* London: Allen and Unwin, 1932.

___. *Our Knowledge of the External World as a Field for Scientific Method in Philosophy.* London: Allen and Unwin, 1926.

___. *Principles of Social Reconstruction.* London: Allen and Unwin, 1916.

___. *Religion and Science.* New York: Oxford University Press, 1935.

Ryle, Gilbert. Collected Papers, vols. 1 and 2. New York: Barnes and Noble, 1971.

___. *The Concept of Mind.* New York: Barnes and Noble, 1949.

Saatkamp, Herman J. *Rorty and Pragmatism: The Philosopher Responds to His Critics.* Nashville, TN: Vanderbilt University Press, 1995.

Saksena, Shri Krishna. *Essays on Indian Philosophy.* Honolulu: University of Hawaii Press, 1970.

Sartre, Jean-Paul. *Being and Nothingness,* translated by Hazel Barnes. New York: Philosophical Library, 1956.

___. *Critique of Dialectical Reason,* translated by Alan Sheridan-Smith. New York: Schocken Books, 1976.

___. *Existentialism and Human Emotions,* translated by Hazel Barnes. New York: Philosophical Library, 1947.

___. *Search for a Method,* translated by Hazel Barnes. New York: Random House, 1968.

Sarup, Madan. *Marxism and Education.* New York: Routledge Kegan Paul, 1978.

___. *Marxism/Structuralism/Education: Theoretical Developments in the Sociology of Education.* London: Falmer Press, 1983.

Schaff, Adam. *Marxism and the Human Individual,* edited by Robert Cohen and translated by Olgierd Wojtasiewicz. New York: McGraw-Hill, 1970.

Scheffler, Israel. *Conditions of Knowledge: An Introduction to Epistemology and Education.* Chicago: University of Chicago Press, 1983.

___. *The Language of Education.* Springfield, IL: Charles C. Thomas, 1960.

Schubring, Walther. *The Doctrine of the Jainas,* translated by Wolfgang Buerlen. Delhi, India: Motilal Banarsidass, 1962.

Schumacher, Stephen, and Woerner, Gert, editors. *The Encyclopedia of Eastern Philosophy and Religion: Buddhism, Hinduism, Taoism, and Zen,* translated by Michael H. Kohn, Karen Ready, and Werner Wunsche. Boston: Shambhala Publications, Inc., 1994.

Searle, John R. *The Construction of Social Reality.* New York: Free Press, 1995.

___. "Is There a Crisis in American Higher Education?" *Partisan Review* 60(4):693–709, Fall 1993.

___. "Rationality and Realism: What Is at Stake?" *Daedalus* 122(4):55–83, Fall 1993.

___. *The Rediscovery of the Mind.* Cambridge, MA: MIT Press, 1992.

___. "The Storm Over the University," *New York Review of Books* 32:34–42, December 6, 1990.

Shimahara, Nobuo, editor. *Educational Reconstruction: Promise and Challenge.* Columbus, OH: Charles E. Merrill, 1973.

Shourie, Arun. *Hinduism: Essence and Consequence.* New Delhi, India: Vikas Publishing House, 1979.

Singh, Iqbal. *Guatama Buddha.* New York: Oxford University Press, 1994.

Skinner, B. F. *Beyond Freedom and Dignity.* New York: Hackett Publishing Company, 2002.

___. *Walden Two.* New York: Macmillan, 1976.

Smith, Adam. *An Inquiry Into the Nature and Causes of the Wealth of Nations,* selected and edited and with an introduction by Kathryn Sutherland. New York: Oxford University Press, 1993.

Smith, Terry L. *Behavior and Its Causes: Philosophical Foundations of Operant Psychology.* Boston: Kluwer Academic Publishers, 1994.

Soll, Ivan. "Hegel as a Philosopher of Education," *Educational Theory* 22:26–33, Winter 1973.

Soltis, Jonas F. "Analysis and Anomalies in Philosophy of Education," *Philosophy of Education, 1971.* Proceedings of the Twenty-Seventh Annual Meeting of the Philosophy of Education Society. Edwardsville, IL: Philosophy of Education Society, 1971, pp. 28–46.

___. *An Introduction to the Analysis of Educational Concepts,* 2d ed. Reading, MA: Addison-Wesley, 1977.

___. "Philosophy of Education for Educators: The Eightieth NSSE Yearbook," *Teachers College Record* 81: 225–247, 1979.

___. "Philosophy of Education: Retrospect and Prospect," *Philosophy of Education, 1975.* Proceedings of the Thirty-First Annual Meeting of the Philosophy of Education Society. San Jose, CA: Philosophy of Education Society, 1975, pp. 7–24.

___. "Philosophy of Education Since Mid-Century," *Teachers College Record* 81:127–129, 1979.

Spencer, Herbert. *Education: Intellectual, Moral, Spiritual.* Paterson, NJ: Littlefield, Adams, 1963.

___. *Herbert Spencer on Education,* edited and with an introduction by Andreas Kazamias. New York: Teachers College Press, 1966.

Stanley, William B. *Curriculum for Utopia: Social Reconstructionism and Critical Pedagogy in the Postmodern Era.* Albany: State University of New York Press, 1992.

Strain, John Paul. "Idealism: A Clarification of an Educational Philosophy," *Educational Theory* 25:263–271, 1975.

Suda, Jyoti Prsad. *Religions in India: A Study of Their Essential Unity.* New Delhi, India: Sterling Publishers Pvt., 1978.

Suzuki, Daisetz T. *The Awakening of Zen,* edited by Christmas Humphreys. Boulder, CO: Prajna Press, 1980.

___. *The Essentials of Zen Buddhism.* Westport, CT: Greenwood Press, 1962.

Ta Hui. *Swampland Flowers: The Letters and Lectures of Zen Master Ta Hui (Tsung-kao),* translated by Christopher Cleary. New York: Grove Press, 1977.

Task Force on Education for Economic Growth. *Action for Excellence: A Comprehensive Plan to Improve Our Nation's Schools.* Denver, CO: Education Commission of the States, 1983.

Task Force on Federal Elementary and Secondary Education Policy. *Making the Grade: Report of the Twentieth Century Fund Task Force on Federal Elementary and Secondary Education Policy,* with a background paper by Paul E. Peterson. New York: Twentieth Century Fund, 1983.

Taylor, Charles, et al. *Multiculturalism: Examining the Politics of Recognition*, edited, with an introduction by Amy Gutmann. Princeton, NJ: Princeton University Press, 1994.

Teilhard de Chardin, Pierre. *The Phenomenon of Man.* New York: Harper, 1959.

Thoreau, Henry David. *Walden and Civil Disobedience*. New York: Norton, 1966.

Thorensen, Carl E., editor. "Behavior Modification in Education," *The Seventy-Second Yearbook of the National Society for the Study of Education*, part I. Chicago: National Society for the Study of Education, 1973.

Tillich, Paul. *The Courage to Be.* New Haven, CT: Yale University Press, 1952.

Toffler, Alvin. *Future Shock.* New York: Random House, 1970.

___. *Learning for Tomorrow: The Role of the Future in Education*. New York: Vintage Books, 1974.

___. *The Third Wave.* New York: William Morrow and Co., 1980.

Troutner, Lee. "Making Sense Out of "Existential Thought and Education: A Search for the Interface," *Philosophy of Education, 1975.* Proceedings of the Thirty-First Annual Meeting of the Philosophy of Education Society. San Jose, CA: Philosophy of Education Society, 1975, pp. 185–199.

Tucker, Robert C. *Philosophy and Myth in Karl Marx.* New York: Cambridge University Press, 1961.

Usher, Robin, and Edwards, Richard. *Postmodernism and Education*. New York: Routledge, 1994.

Vandenberg, Donald. *Being and Education: An Essay in Existential Phenomenology*. Upper Saddle River, NJ: Prentice Hall, 1971.

___. "Existential and Phenomenological Influence in Education," *Teachers College Record* 81:166–191, 1979.

von Glaserfield, Ernst. "Introduction: Aspects of Constructivism," in *Constructivism: Theory, Perspectives, and Practice*, edited by Catherine Twomey Fosnot. New York: Teachers College Press, 1996.

Vygotsky, Lev S. *Mind in Society: The Development of Higher Psychological Processes*, edited by Michael Cole, et al. Cambridge, MA: Harvard University Press, 1978.

Watson, John Broadus. *Behaviorism.* Chicago: University of Chicago Press, 1957.

Weber, Max. *The Religion of India.* New York: Free Press, 1958.

Werner, Harold D. *Cognitive Therapy.* New York: Free Press, 1982.

West, Cornel. *The American Evasion of Philosophy: A Genealogy of Pragmatism*. Madison: University of Wisconsin Press, 1989.

White, Theodore Harold. *The Making of the President, 1972.* New York: Atheneum, 1973.

Whitehead, Alfred North. *The Aims of Education and Other Essays*. New York: Macmillan, 1929.

___. *Science and the Modern World*. New York: Macmillan, 1967.

___, and Russell, Bertrand. *Principia Mathematica.* New York: Cambridge University Press, 1968.

Wilson, Edwin O. *Sociobiology: The New Synthesis.* Cambridge, MA: Belknap Press of Harvard University Press, 1975.

Wittgenstein, Ludwig. *Preliminary Studies for the "Philosophical investigations," Generally Known as the Blue and Brown Books. 2nd ed.* New York: Barnes and Noble, 1969.

___, *Culture and Value*, edited by G. H. Von Right, translated by Peter Winch. Chicago: University of Chicago Press, 1980.

___. *Philosophical Investigations*, translated by G. E. M. Anscombe. New York: Macmillan, 1968.

___. *Tractatus Logico-Philosophicus*, translated by D. F. Pears and B. F. McGuinness. Atlantic Highlands, NJ: Humanities Press, 1961.

Yang, C. K. *Religion in Chinese Society*. Berkeley: University of California Press, 1961.

Yu, David C., and Thompson, Laurence G. *Guide to Chinese Religion*. Boston: G. K. Hall, 1985.

Zajda, Joseph. *Education in the USSR.* New York: Pergamon Press, 1980.

Zeldin, David. *The Educational Ideas of Charles Fourier.* New York: A. M. Kelley, 1969.

Index

About the Authors

Howard A. Ozmon is professor emeritus of education in the Division of Educational Studies at Virginia Commonwealth University. He received a bachelor of arts in philosophy from the University of Virginia and a doctorate from Teachers College, Columbia University. Dr. Ozmon has taught in elementary and secondary schools, as well as at several colleges and universities. He has published numerous books and articles dealing with philosophy and education.

Samuel M. Craver is a professor in the Division of Educational Studies at Virginia Commonwealth University. He received his doctorate from the University of North Carolina at Chapel Hill and has taught at the secondary and university levels. He is the author of numerous papers on historical and philosophical issues in education and currently teaches courses on the history of education, the philosophy of education, and professional ethics in education.